VALUES AND POLITICAL CHANGE
IN POSTCOMMUNIST EUROPE

Values and Political Change in Postcommunist Europe

William L. Miller
Edward Caird Professor of Politics
University of Glasgow

Stephen White
Professor of Politics
University of Glasgow

and

Paul Heywood
Professor of Politics
University of Nottingham

First published in Great Britain 1998 by
MACMILLAN PRESS LTD
Houndmills, Basingstoke, Hampshire RG21 6XS and London
Companies and representatives throughout the world

A catalogue record for this book is available from the British Library.

ISBN 0–333–64283–X

First published in the United States of America 1998 by
ST. MARTIN'S PRESS, INC.,
Scholarly and Reference Division,
175 Fifth Avenue, New York, N.Y. 10010

ISBN 0–312–21144–9

Library of Congress Cataloging-in-Publication Data
Miller, William Lockley, 1943–
Values and political change in postcommunist Europe / William L.
Miller, Stephen White, and Paul Heywood.
p. cm.
Includes bibliographical references (p.) and index.
ISBN 0–312–21144–9 (cloth)
1. Political culture—Europe, Eastern—Public opinion.
2. Political culture—Russia (Federation)—Public opinion.
3. Europe, Eastern—Politics and government—1989– —Public opinion.
4. Russia (Federation)—Politics and government—1991– —Public
opinion. 5. Post-communism—Europe, Eastern—Public opinion.
6. Post-communism—Russia (Federation)—Public opinion. 7. Public
opinion—Europe, Eastern. 8. Public opinion—Russia (Federation)
I. White, Stephen, 1945– . II. Heywood, Paul. III. Title.
JN96.A91M55 1997
306.2'094'091717—dc21   97–38376
                                                                        CIP

This book is printed on paper suitable for recycling and made from fully managed and
sustained forest sources.

10   9   8   7   6   5   4   3   2   1
07   06   05   04   03   02   01   00   99   98

Printed in Great Britain by
The Ipswich Book Company Ltd
Ipswich, Suffolk

Contents

Contents   vii

Acknowledgements

We must thank the British Economic and Social Research Council (ESRC) for the two grants which funded this research: a major grant to William L. Miller, Stephen White and Paul Heywood (R233538) which funded the main multinational study, and a small additional grant to William L. Miller and Elena Bashkirova (R221888) for the update survey of Russian opinion in 1996 on which chapter 19 is based.

The study would not have been possible without the enthusiastic involvement of our survey directors in Moscow, Kyiv, Budapest and Prague – Elena Bashkirova of ROMIR, Moscow; Tatyana Koshechkina of the Institute of Sociology, Ukraine Academy of Sciences, later of Socis-Gallup, and now of USM, Kyiv; Emoke Lengyel of MODUS, Budapest; and Ladislav Koppl of OPW Opinion Window, Prague. They not only carried out extensive surveys of MPs and the general public but advised us on political issues and public opinion in their respective countries. We should also thank Gordon Heald and Allan Hyde of Gallup, now with ORB, London, for bringing this international team together; and Nigel Swain, Mark Thompson, Gordon Wightman and Ase Grodeland for their helpful discussions and detailed advice. All remaining errors of fact and interpretation are our own, of course.

At Glasgow University we were extremely lucky to have the efficient research assistance of Matthew Wyman, now at the University of Keele. And not least, we should thank our speedy and enthusiastic secretaries Elspeth Shaw, Avril Johnstone and Jeanette Berrie for all their work on the manuscript.

William L. Miller
Stephen White
Paul Heywood
Universities of Glasgow and Nottingham

Note: We have usually transliterated Cyrillic according to the style employed by *Soviet* (now *Europe-Asia*) *Studies*, omitting diacriticals, and generally preferring familiar forms where these have become established in English. Reflecting quite rapidly changing English usage however, we have taken current Ukrainian names for all places in Ukraine including Kyiv, transliterated according to the Library of Congress scheme.

List of Tables

List of Figures

Political Values in Postcommunist Europe

This is a book about political values in five former communist countries: Russia, Ukraine, Hungary, Slovakia and the Czech Republic. Russia and Ukraine represent the core of the former Soviet Union ('the FSU' hereafter) and its predecessor, the Tsarist Empire. Hungary, Slovakia and the Czech Republic lie at the heart of east-central Europe ('ECE' hereafter) and all three share the experience both of communist rule after 1945 and of Hapsburg rule before the First World War.

Although we shall have something to say about sympathy and support for particular political parties, our focus is upon enduring political values rather than transient political preferences. Our investigation of these political values is based upon eleven surveys of public opinion in the FSU and ECE carried out between the end of 1993 and the beginning of 1996, involving interviews with 7,350 members of the public and with 504 members of parliament. Most of those were long and searching interviews that lasted for about an hour each, and together they provide a very detailed account of postcommunist political values. But we shall leave the detail to later chapters and, in this preface, provide a brief non-technical introduction to some of the broad outlines of our findings.

WHAT ARE POLITICAL VALUES?

Usually we distinguish between enduring political values and transient political preferences. Tracking the trends in values and preferences through the dramatic Russian election campaign of December 1993 highlights the stability of values at a time when political preferences were changing rapidly.[1] But that is not the essence of the distinction between values and preferences. Nor is it always the case that values endure while preferences change, though a change in values would certainly be more significant than a change in preferences. In their recent study of political values in western Europe, van Deth and Scarbrough note that a consensus on the definition of political values is hard to find but they eventually describe political values as 'conceptions of the desirable, used in moral discourse, with a political relevance for behaviour.'[2]

Let us be more concrete. We are concerned with FSU/ECE conceptions of the way politics and society should be organised. These conceptions are certainly about the 'desirable', and they are 'moral' in the sense that they describe the

1

way things 'should' or 'ought' to be, rather than the way that they are or have been. But they are also restricted to questions of broad political principle, avoiding questions of day to day politics. And they are more about procedure and process than about substance, more about systems of decision making than about decisions.

In the context of the postcommunist world, we have focused upon four kinds of broad political values: socialist, nationalist, liberal and democratic values. By *socialist values* we mean views about equality and about the proper role of the state in industry and welfare. By *nationalist values* we mean views about the integrity and uniformity of the state, and about the extent to which the state should be defined in ethno-linguistic terms. We have found it necessary, empirically, to distinguish three dimensions of nationalist values because they have very different patterns of support – *external nationalism* based on attitudes to the world beyond the state's borders; *centralist nationalism* based upon attitudes to regional autonomy and the territorial integrity of the state; and *cultural nationalism* based on attitudes towards imposing a uniform culture within the state (formerly a question of religious uniformity, now more a question of linguistic uniformity). By *liberal values* we mean attitudes towards individual freedom and its corollary, limited government. Liberal values concern freedom of information, freedom to publish, rights of assembly, organisation and protest, tolerance of diversity, respect for authority, and the need for government to be restricted and constrained by law. Finally, we are interested in *values of popular control* – the rights of citizens to have some say in how they are governed. Here again we have found it essential, for empirical as much as theoretical reasons, to distinguish two dimensions of such values because they have such different patterns of support: *populism* – which emphasises unmediated public opinion; and support for *representative democracy* – which emphasises such institutions as competitive elections and political parties.

To avoid any confusion, we should note at the outset that some writers limit their definition of *democratic values* to those that we have designated values of 'popular control'; while other writers, equally distinguished, define democracy and democratic values in terms of the fusion of liberal values with the values of popular control. The two kinds of values are obviously different in principle, but there are doubts about whether they can really be separated in practice. Citizens' ability to control and, on occasion, overthrow their government is a good, though not infallible way of ensuring that government does not tyrannise its citizens. Conversely, formal rights to control a government through elections may be rendered meaningless if there is no freedom of speech and information, no right to organise and protest. Liberal and popular control values may be conceptually distinct but they tend to reinforce and protect each other.

THE VALUE OF VALUES

Does it matter whether people have socialist, nationalist, liberal or democratic values? Sceptics assert that only military hardware matters. According to Mao Tse-tung 'Political power grows out of the barrel of a gun.'[3] Similarly, Stalin was alleged to have asked at the Potsdam Conference 'Mr Churchill, how many divisions did you say the Pope had?'[4] But the Papacy continues while, in different ways, the communism of Mao and Stalin has been abandoned by both the Soviet Union and China. Military might has proved an inadequate defence for their ideas.

Less heroically, political scientists have frequently asserted the need for a political system – especially a democratic political system – to be consistent with the political values of its people. Almond and Verba claim that 'a democratic form of participatory political system requires as well a political culture [i.e. a set of political values] consistent with it';[5] di Palma claims that the basic condition for the democratic consolidation of postcommunist societies is the 'contemporaneous formation of both valid democratic institutions and a democratic political culture';[6] Dahl's five preconditions for democracy to flourish include: 'among the people of a country, *particularly its active political stratum* [our emphasis] a political culture and a system of beliefs exists that is favourable to the idea of democracy';[7] Hahn claims that 'successful democratisation is unlikely to take place in the absence of a political culture which is supportive of democratic institutions';[8] White, Gill and Slider claim that 'democracy from above and the move to a law based state through legislative enactment cannot succeed without the development of an appropriate culture within the society as a whole';[9] Sorensen claims that 'the final phase of [democratic] consolidation is the process whereby democratic institutions and practices become ingrained in the political culture. ... *Not only political leaders* [our emphasis] but the vast majority of political actors and of the population come to see democratic practices as the right and natural order of things';[10] and Diamond claims that 'stable democracy requires a belief in the legitimacy of democracy'.[11]

If these political scientists are right, then it does matter, and matter a great deal, whether political values are supportive of the new postcommunist institutions or whether they are not. Of course dynasties and dictatorships have often persisted for a long time without any evidence that they were supported by a popular political culture. But the public have a unique role in a democracy. Perhaps it is sufficient for the stability of a dictatorship if the dictator alone believes in the values of dictatorship but, in a democracy, the public, at various levels of activism and involvement, must play the role of the dictator in a dictatorship. In a democracy, the people are the ultimate rulers and the ultimate guarantor of their democratic system.

Yet writing in 1993, Sorensen claimed that 'with few exceptions this stage [of widespread public support for democratic values] has not been reached in any of the transitions that have taken place in the last two decades';[12] while White, Gill and Slider noted that, at best, 'enlightened despotism [rather than a democratic political culture] has been the Russian way.'[13]

POLITICAL VALUES IN THE FSU/ECE

Based, in each case, on answers to many different individual questions we have constructed composite indicators of support for socialist, nationalist, liberal and democratic (or more strictly 'popular control') values.[14] We shall leave the technicalities to later chapters, but in essence the logic of these indicators is very simple: we categorise a person as being committed to socialist values if they take the socialist, rather than the anti-socialist, side in their answers to a majority of our questions about socialist values. And similarly with our indicators of other political values. Of course the categorisation depends upon the particular questions asked. We could choose some pathologically biased question on which everyone would take the socialist side, or the anti-socialist side. But we think our questions faithfully reflect the practical choices facing the public and that they categorise people reasonably. They certainly divide people into the *relatively* socialist and the *relatively* anti-socialist for example and thus provide a good foundation for comparative analysis. And they provide reasonable criteria for describing people as being socialist or anti-socialist, though that is admittedly more a matter of judgement rather than of certainty.

By our measures, we found that a large majority of the public in our five FSU/ECE countries were, on balance, committed to socialist values, and an almost equally large majority were committed to liberal values. Only a minority of 28 per cent took the nationalist side on questions of centralisation or cultural conformity within the state, but a larger minority, 40 per cent, took the nationalist side in their attitudes towards the lands beyond their borders. Almost two-thirds were committed to populist values and to the idea of competitive elections, though commitment to political parties was very weak (Fig. 0.1).

A RED–BROWN ALLIANCE

Much has been written about the existence of a 'red–brown alliance' between socialists and nationalists in postcommunist countries. For example, it is suggested that former communist leaders have tried to hang on to personal power by switching from a socialist to a nationalist rhetoric.

Our surveys show that there was some truth in this image of a 'red–brown alliance' but as much falsehood as truth. There was indeed a very strong

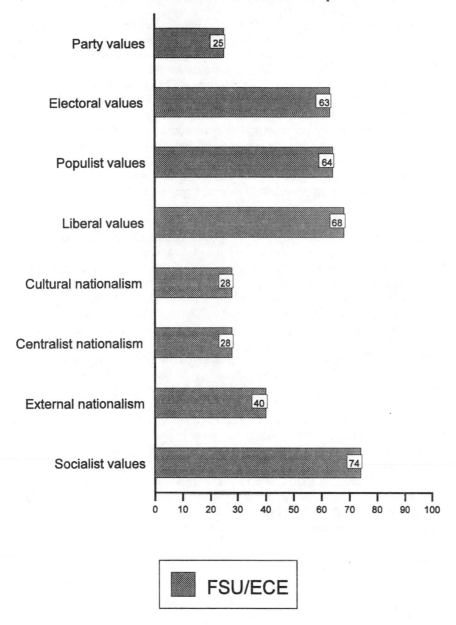

Figure 0.1   Political values in the FSU/ECE

correlation between support for socialist values and *external* nationalism in all five of our countries. But – and this is a most important qualification – the correlation between socialist values and *centralist* nationalism was weak; and between socialist values and *cultural* nationalism the correlation was close to zero or even negative (especially in Ukraine). That complex pattern actually fits well with the ideology of Soviet communism which demanded that its followers be patriotic and willing to defend their Soviet motherland but at the same time oppose national chauvinism and any manifestation of ethnic hatred, especially between the peoples of the Soviet commonwealth. It is not only communists who have said yes to patriotism, but no to jingoism; but, as inheritors of an empire they had originally reviled, Soviet communists said it loudly, often, and explicitly – for example in the 1986 Programme of the CPSU.

The correlation between support for socialist and nationalist parties was more variable than the correlation between support for socialist and nationalist ideas. Because the red–brown alliance of ideas linked socialist values to external nationalism but not to cultural nationalism we should expect that any red–brown alliance of party sympathy would vary from country to country depending upon the precise kind of nationalism that was advocated by the significant nationalist parties in different countries.

Whatever the degree of explicit rejection of parties as objects of loyalty, it was clear that people in every country used parties as reference points in their vision of politics. Their patterns of sympathy towards different parties were anything but random. As organisations or objects of positive commitment parties might be weak or insignificant; but as images and objects of sympathy and prejudice they were not. Sympathies and prejudices for different parties formed a coherent pattern in each of our five countries – though one which varied from country to country. In Russia and Slovakia we found a red–brown alliance of party sympathy and prejudice: people who were favourable towards the communists tended to be favourable towards nationalist parties as well. In Ukraine and Hungary however we found evidence of a 'right–brown alliance' of sympathy for both anti-communist right-wing[15] and nationalist parties (or prejudice against both). And in the Czech Republic there was a simple left/right pattern of party sympathy without a strong nationalist dimension.

LINES OF DIVISION

It is very tempting to draw lines on the map of Europe, dividing one zone of political culture and values from another and there are a great many lines that could be drawn. We have investigated six of them. Our fundamental question is always the same: to what extent, if at all, do those lines mark significant boundaries of political culture?

1 Between the FSU and ECE

To Dahrendorf, writing in 1990: 'Europe ends at the Soviet border, wherever that may be.'[16] To George Schopflin, writing in 1989, 'Soviet Russia...[is] unquestionably different. To measure Soviet Russia by European criteria becomes an attempt to impose those criteria on an alien world, something that we would seldom do with, say, China or Cambodia...[but] what I have argued about the Soviet Union is not to be taken as applicable to central and eastern Europe [which] is an organic part of Europe as a whole.'[17] Neglecting the ambiguity with which this statement treats Ukraine (included in the 'Soviet Union' but not in 'Soviet Russia'), this implies that Europe, European culture and European values stop at the old Soviet border.[18]

Others disagree: Richard Sakwa claims that public reactions to the August 1991 coup against Gorbachev 'demonstrably repudiated cultural theories that stressed Russian passivity and innate authoritarianism';[19] and Reisinger, Miller, Hesli and Maher claim that their data 'challenge those who rule out successful democratic consolidation because the Russian or Ukrainian people lack a political culture that is ready for it.'[20] So, do our own surveys indicate a difference in political values between the FSU and ECE? And, if so, how different? And in what way different?

Whatever the disputes about the definition of Europe, there can be no doubt that the historical experience of the FSU has been different from that of ECE. And our surveys reflect that. Almost twice as many people in the FSU as in ECE told us that they had once believed in communist ideals. Only half as many in the FSU as in ECE cited the oppression of human rights as the worst feature of the communist regime; and conversely twice as many in the FSU as in ECE cited an excess of bureaucracy as its worst feature. And in consequence, far less people in the FSU than in ECE told us that they wished to punish former officials of the communist regime. Different perspectives on the old regime also reinforced differences in their evaluation of the new regime. People in the FSU were far more critical of the change of regime than people in ECE. Compared to those who lived in ECE, people in the FSU were 23 per cent more critical of the effect of the change on defence, 27 per cent more critical of its effect on the economy, and 35 per cent more critical of its effect upon human rights!

People in the FSU clearly viewed the old regime, and the change of regime, very differently from those who lived in ECE. As well they might, since the old regimes in the FSU and ECE were different, largely indigenous in our two FSU countries but imposed from outside in ECE for example. But by itself that does not mean that the people themselves were different in the FSU and ECE. Interestingly, although twice as many in the FSU as in ECE told us they *had once believed* in communist ideals, they expressed no more (and actually slightly less) *current belief* in those ideals in the early 1990s.[21] The past was past. More generally, our surveys suggest that publics in the FSU and ECE did *not* differ greatly on broadly defined socialist, nationalist, liberal or democratic values. Overall, FSU/ECE differences were only about 10 per cent on socialist or popular control values and even less on nationalist or liberal values.

There were large FSU/ECE differences on some aspects of these values but only small differences or even compensating differences on others. On socialist values, for example, we found that people in the FSU were 24 per cent more committed to state control of industry but not very different, if at all, in their attitudes towards equality or state responsibility for social welfare. The sharp difference on attitudes to state enterprise is significant, and does reflect historical experience, but it is only one aspect of socialist values – and one which most European socialists no longer regard as fundamental.

Similarly, there was little FSU/ECE difference on the external aspect of nationalism but FSU publics were at once 12 per cent more nationalist in terms of centralism and 16 per cent less nationalist in terms of cultural conformism than those who lived in ECE. It is a reasonable combination: many of those who wish to preserve large multi-ethnic states such as Russia and Ukraine (still more those who regret the dissolution of the Soviet Union) may well feel that some concession to cultural diversity is a necessary price to pay for territorial integrity, though an extreme nationalist might not.

Again, there was little difference in overall liberal values between ECE and the FSU. FSU publics were 13 per cent less tolerant and 20 per cent more inclined to stress order and discipline, but hardly differed from ECE on support for citizens' rights to protest or on demands that government should only act within the constraints of the law and, on our measures, the people of the FSU (not, of course, their governments) were actually 20 per cent more willing than in ECE to support the principles of openness and freedom of information. So the FSU publics' illiberal support for more disciplined and constrained citizens was offset by their liberal support for more disciplined and constrained government.

Finally, FSU/ECE differences on the values of popular control were limited to those aspects of such values which focused on parties and elections. Compared to ECE, FSU publics were 11 per cent less committed to parties, 20 per cent less committed to the principle of multi-party elections, and 35 per cent more willing to ban parties towards which they felt 'very unfavourable',[22] yet actually more committed to the populist principle of responsive government bending to the dictates of public opinion. (Fig. 0.2).

In short, the traditional stereotypes of FSU/ECE value differences are true, but only half the truth, and we must pay as much attention to the boring similarities as to the exciting differences if we are to reach a balanced conclusion.

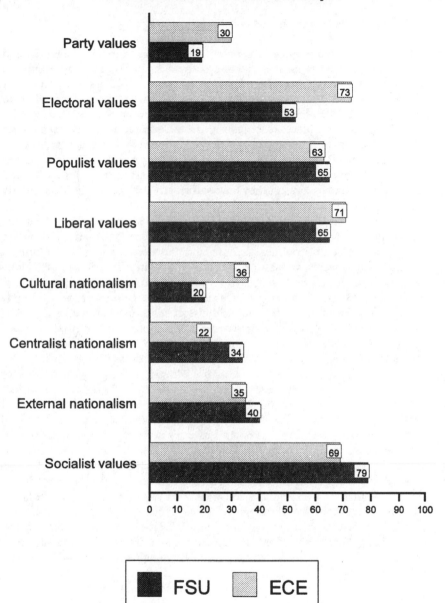

Figure 0.2 The FSU versus ECE

2   Between Catholic and Orthodox cultures

Another line runs close to the FSU border but deviates from it in the Baltics and within Ukraine: that is the line dividing Catholic and Orthodox cultures which is drawn, for example, by Huntington in his essay on 'the clash of civilizations'.[23] It is a line that has frequently been drawn by others: according to Krishan Kumar 'the idea of an east–west divide in Europe comes down fundamentally, in the first place, to religion... once Constantinople, in the eleventh century, rejected the supremacy of Rome.'[24] Indeed others assert that the significance of this line steadily increased after the Orthodox/Catholic schism since the 'Orthodox lands never experienced the Renaissance, Reformation and Enlightenment and as a result they have sufficiently different values particularly in relationship to the state.'[25]

But there are problems with this grand, perhaps overly grand, view of culture. Sorensen points out that 'it is difficult to demonstrate a systematic relationship between a democratic political culture and the larger system of culture in society.'[26] Moreover it seems to be an unstable relationship. It is not so long ago that Catholic culture was held to be inimical to democracy and democratic values which flourished mainly in areas of Protestant culture, yet while 'it may be that Catholicism did at one point in history work against democracy – the Catholic church also played an active role in the opposition toward authoritarian rule in the 1980s.'[27] And if Catholic culture can change its relationship to Protestant culture, then why should Orthodox culture not do the same?

Up to a point we can test this 'clash of civilizations' thesis by looking to see whether political values in western Ukraine – conventionally put on the western side of this Orthodox/Catholic cultural border – are more similar to values in the FSU or to those in ECE. But there is an epistemological problem: most of western Ukraine was ruled by Poland between the wars and by the Hapsburgs before that. So there is no way of knowing whether any distinctive values that we find in western Ukraine reflect the imprint of Catholic culture, or of Hapsburg rule before the Great War, or of Polish rule between the wars, or of the absence of Stalin's rule between the wars – or whether they result from the interplay of all these historical legacies.

Dividing Ukraine into east, mid and west Ukraine does little to support any of the grand theories of a clash of civilisations and, instead, focuses our attention on the more parochial question of Ukrainian nationalism. On several indicators, west Ukraine stood out not only from the rest of the FSU but from ECE as well. It was more distinctive as itself, or as the nationalist heartland of Ukraine than as part of either a greater Orthodox or Catholic culture.

The people of west Ukraine expressed far less belief in communist ideals than those who lived either in the rest of the FSU or in ECE – only about one third as much as anywhere else. They were three times as likely to declare that the communist regime had no good features as those who lived either in the rest of

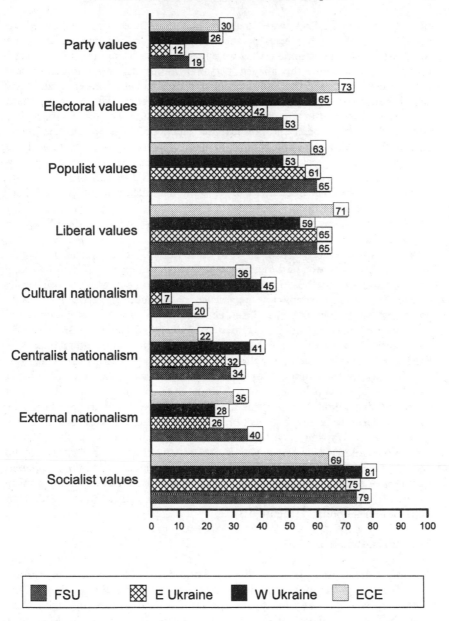

Figure 0.3 The clash of civilizations

the FSU or in ECE. They were far more likely than those who lived anywhere else to claim that they had been 'personally oppressed' by the communist regime but, under further questioning, they were far more likely than people who lived anywhere else to define this alleged 'personal oppression' in communal terms. They were even more likely than the people of ECE to want former communists sacked from their jobs in industry. And more than people who lived anywhere else they said that after the change of regime they now got more satisfaction from taking part in social and political life. The people of west Ukraine joined those in ECE citing the oppression of human rights as the worst feature of the old regime and in agreeing overwhelmingly that the change of regime had been good for human rights, but joined the rest of the FSU in agreeing even more overwhelmingly that it had been bad for economic management. Interestingly, they were even more likely than those in ECE to choose the present as the best time this century for their country – which very few others in the FSU were inclined to do.

Values in west Ukraine were closer to those in the FSU on socialism (reflecting its integration into the Soviet economy after the Second World War perhaps?), but closer to those in ECE on representative democracy (reflecting its limited but perhaps significant experience of democracy between the wars perhaps?). But nationalist, liberal and populist values in west Ukraine reflected distinctively Ukrainian concerns, not the concerns of Orthodox or Catholic, FSU or ECE cultures. Like the rest of Ukraine – but unlike either Russia or ECE – support for *external* nationalist values was unusually weak in west Ukraine. By contrast support for centralist nationalist values, and for cultural nationalist values, was higher in west Ukraine than anywhere else, while support for liberal and populist values was lower in west Ukraine than anywhere else. Those patterns were not a reflection of Catholic culture, still less of Polish culture, or of Hapsburg culture. Instead, they constituted an assertion of Ukrainian nationalism against Russia, against the Hapsburgs, against Poland and, if necessary, against less nationalistic Ukrainians. Even the apparent weakness of external nationalism in west Ukraine reflected a lack of antagonism towards the West (i.e. western Europe and America), rather than towards their immediate neighbours[28] (Figure 0.3).

3 Between Europe and Asia

Timothy Garton Ash dismisses 'the absurd exclusion of Russia from Europe' but admits that 'no one can quite agree where central Europe begins and ends...Germans naturally locate the centre of central Europe in Berlin; Austrians in Vienna.'[29] Using the criterion that Europe runs from the Atlantic to the Urals, Ukrainians locate it close to Lviv. The only thing they could all agree upon is that, contrary to the assertion of the then Prime Minister John Major, *Britain* is certainly not 'at the heart of Europe'.

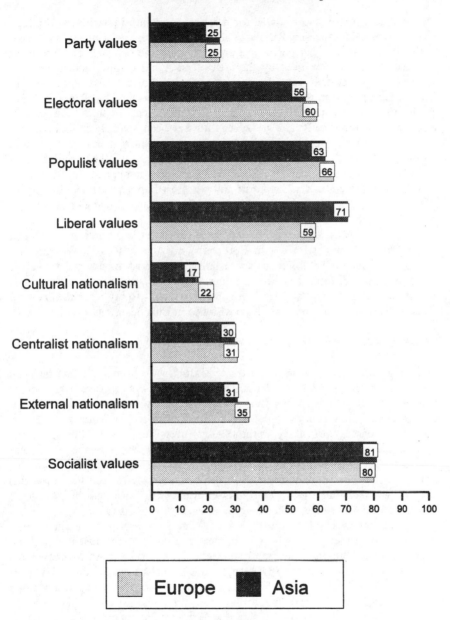

Figure 0.4   Europe versus Asia (within Russia)

Indeed it is instructive to dwell for a moment on the similarities and differences between Britain and Russia in their relationships to Europe and Asia. Both are undoubtedly peripheral to Europe; neither can plausibly claim to be at its heart. Both were seduced by the idea of an Asian empire, and during the nineteenth century they played out what was called the 'Great Game' not in Central Europe but in Central Asia. The main difference is that Russia's Asian empire was contiguous with the motherland and the part of that Asian empire which still remains in Russia today has always been sparsely inhabited. The populous parts were on the southern fringe and are now mainly independent states lying outside postcommunist Russia. Consequently the population of modern Asiatic Russia consists mainly of European immigrants or their descendants, whose culture is European and who just happened to live in what is geographically, but *only* geographically, Asia – more equivalent to British Australasia than to British India.

Dividing our Russian surveys at the Urals reveals little difference in political values between those who live in European and Asiatic Russia. We can find scarcely any detectable difference on socialist, nationalist, or democratic values and only a small difference on liberal values. Moreover, in our surveys, the people of Asiatic Russia appear slightly more liberal, which is to say more in tune with modern European culture, than those who live in European Russia (Figure 0.4).

4   Between former imperial powers and the rest

One geographic division that has attracted rather less comment, is that between the former imperial powers – Russia and Hungary – taken together, and the former 'subject nations'. It is a division that would have seemed more significant at the start of the century and yet it still corresponds to important value differences at the end of the century. In the 1990s we even found a small but significant minority in the former imperial powers – 12 per cent in Hungary and 17 per cent in Russia (rising to 22 per cent in Budapest and 37 per cent in Moscow and St. Petersburg[30]) who chose the pre-1914 days of empires as 'the best time this century' for their country; those figures contrast with 8 per cent in Ukraine, 3 per cent in the Czech Republic and only one per cent in Slovakia.

The two imperial powers hardly differed from the others on cultural nationalism or party values, and only by a modest amount on centralist nationalism, socialist values, liberal values or populist and electoral values. Moreover the differences amongst our rather heterogeneous set of subject nations – Ukraine, Slovakia and the Czech Republic – were sufficiently large as to cast doubt upon the significance of the imperial/non-imperial differences, such as they were, on these values. But *external nationalism* was different: the imperial powers were 21 per cent more committed to external anti-foreigner nationalism than the others, and the variation within each of the two sets of countries was relatively small (Fig. 0. 5).

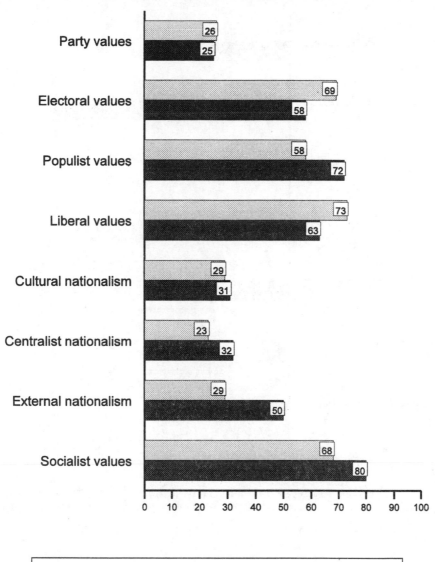

Figure 0.5 Former imperial powers

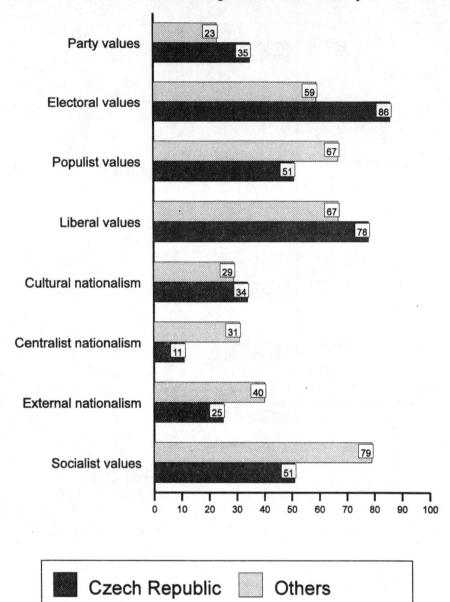

Figure 0.6 A successful economy (the Czech Republic)

Indeed if we go down to some of the original questions on which our scale of external nationalist values were based the effect of an imperial past becomes even more striking. We found that 60 per cent in Hungary and 71 per cent in Russia made irredentist claims on neighbouring territory, and 26 per cent in Russia (though only 3 per cent in Hungary) were willing to threaten the use of force to defend their ethnic kinfolk in neighbouring territories. These questions indisputably reveal the imprint of history, the sense of territory lost and, in Russia's case, the existence of a large diaspora in the 'near abroad'. In the non-imperial nations irredentist claims were less than half as strong: 32 per cent in Slovakia, 30 per cent in Ukraine and, interestingly, only 18 per cent in the Czech Republic less than a year after the break-up of Czechoslovakia.

5 Between successfully managed transitions and others

Of our five countries only the Czech Republic seemed to be making a swift and relatively successful transition to a market economy and to a political system that provided a clear left/right choice uncomplicated by nationalist divisions. Even the 'velvet divorce' from Slovakia could be considered a political success insofar as it was 'velvet' (peaceable) if not insofar as it was a 'divorce'. Political values seemed to reflect these economic and political successes. People in the Czech Republic were 28 per cent less committed to socialist values than in the other countries and also 27 per cent more committed to competitive elections (Fig. 0.6).

6 The iron curtain

Finally what was the significance of the old iron curtain line itself that had divided the communist controlled east from western Europe? In particular how different were values in the FSU/ECE from those in an old established democracy like Britain? Almond and Verba had assessed the prospects of democracy in the former fascist states of Germany and Italy by measuring their political cultures against that of Britain. Here our comparisons must be a little less formal since we did not apply our FSU/ECE questionnaire in western Europe. But our FSU/ECE questionnaire was inspired in part by our study of political culture in Britain and many of the questions we used in the FSU/ECE surveys were modified or simplified versions of ones we had used in Britain.

Comparison suggests that FSU/ECE publics were neither unusually socialist nor nationalist compared to Britain; but there was more fear of disorder, more support for strong government, and less tolerance of minorities and extremists, particularly in the FSU, which led to a rigid belief in the need for both citizens and public officials to stay within the law. Commitment to parties was also weaker in the FSU/ECE than in Britain, and particularly weak in the FSU. But elections in ECE won unusually high marks for being 'free and fair' and support for the key democratic principle that governments should alternate in power was as strong in the FSU as it was in Britain.

THE VANGUARD

Dahl had stressed the importance of political values 'particularly amongst [the] active political stratum.' Some people's values may matter more than other's in defining a country's political culture. Let us look at three important groups – the young, the highly educated, and members of parliament. MPs are certainly amongst the most politically active strata. The highly educated are influential either because they hold positions of power or because they contribute disproportionately towards setting the climate of opinion in which others act. Finally even if the young are not usually either active or influential in contemporary politics, and even if they are part of no contemporary 'elite', the future belongs to them. Together these three groups might be described as vanguard groups whose values are especially important for the consolidation of any new political and economic system.

Comparing those aged under 35 with those aged 55 and over, we found that the young were 23 per cent less committed to socialist values and 18 per cent more committed to liberal values. They were also somewhat less nationalist than their elders, though neither more nor less committed to any of the values associated with popular control (Fig. 0.7).

Graduates from higher education establishments were 31 per cent less committed to socialist values and 28 per cent more committed to liberal values than those with only an elementary education; though just 13 per cent less socialist and 8 per cent more liberal than those who had graduated from secondary and vocational schools. These differences should not be attributed to education as such. In the west, especially in America, education correlates with high income; in Soviet times, higher education correlated with being acceptable to the Soviet authorities and, in particular, with membership of the Communist Party; and in most countries, education correlates with youth – because university (and even secondary school) education has steadily expanded to take in an ever larger share of each age cohort as the century has progressed. But we are not greatly concerned here, with the reasons *why* the highly educated in the FSU/ECE countries had distinctive values: we are more concerned with the *consequences* that flow from the prevalence of those values amongst this influential group within society. And whatever the causes, the highly educated were less socialist, less nationalist, more liberal and more committed to the values of representative (though not populist) democracy than those with lower levels of education (Fig. 0.8).

In the short term, the values of politicians probably matter even more than those of the young or well educated. We interviewed 504 MPs in Russia, Ukraine, Hungary and the Czech Republic at the end of 1994 – after the

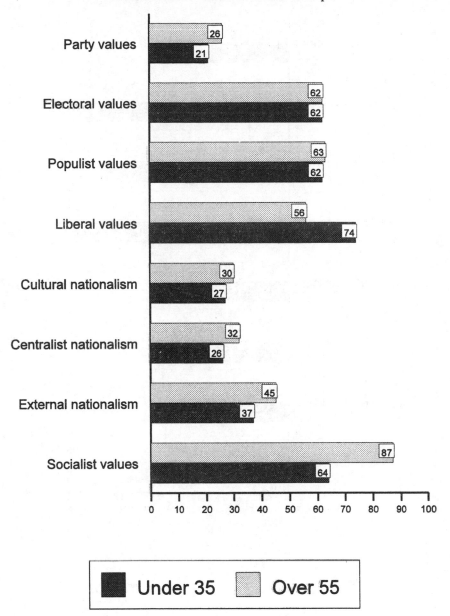

Figure 0.7 Young versus old

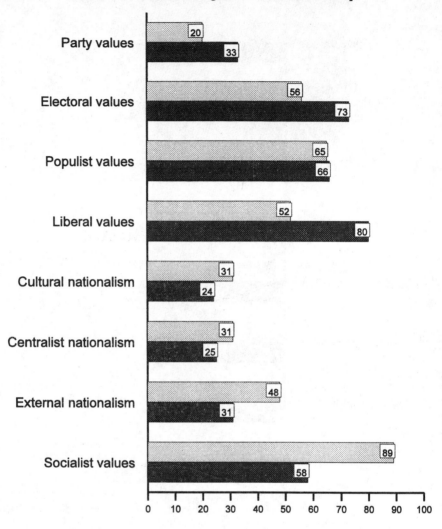

Figure 0.8   High versus low education

parliamentary elections of December 1993 in Russia, May 1994 in Hungary and March–April 1994 in Ukraine. Compared to their respective publics, MPs were 34 per cent less committed to socialist values – despite many having been former Communist Party members; and they were up to 17 per cent less committed to nationalist values (depending upon the aspect of nationalism in question), 27 per cent more committed to liberal values and 33 per cent more committed to competitive elections – though actually *less* committed than their publics to populist values. In short, MPs were remarkably committed to the values of the new regime, far more so than their publics, and far more so than a naive reading of their pasts would have indicated, since they were 42 per cent more likely than their publics to have been members of the Communist Party! (Fig. 0.9) So all three of our 'vanguard' groups displayed greater than average commitment to the values of the new regime – and by a considerable margin, though least amongst the young and most amongst MPs.

FSU/ECE MPs also revealed a pattern of values which we have called the 'governing perspective' in our study of the political culture of British politicians. Their unusually high level of support for the institutions of representative democracy (elections), combined with their unusually low level of support for populist values, is one aspect of this 'governing perspective'. A look at the components of our index of liberal values reveals other aspects of the MPs' 'governing perspective': although MPs were generally 27 per cent more liberal than their publics, they were on average 38 per cent more tolerant,[31] and 28 per cent more committed to law-based government – yet only 18 per cent more willing to defend citizens' rights of protest, and actually 13 per cent more inclined than their publics to emphasise order and the need to respect authority.

POTENTIAL COUNTER-REVOLUTIONARIES

Vanguard groups clearly supported the values of the new regime. But what of the veto groups? Amongst those groups which might be classed as veto groups or even as potential counter-revolutionaries we might consider former members of the Communist Party, those who had lost most economically under the new regime, those who were political losers under the new regime, and those who found themselves to be newly vulnerable ethnic minorities in the national states that replaced the less nationalist republics of the multi-national Soviet Union and its satellites.

Amongst the general public, former members of the Communist Party proved to have values that were no different from those of their fellow citizens on anything except commitment to parties – and on that they differed by only 13 per cent. (Fig. 0.10) Amongst MPs, former members of the Communist Party did prove to be 29 per cent more committed than other MPs towards socialist values – though that still left them less committed to socialism than their

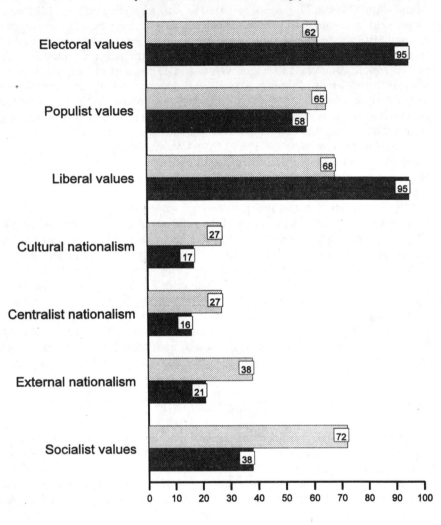

Figure 0.9   MPs versus the public

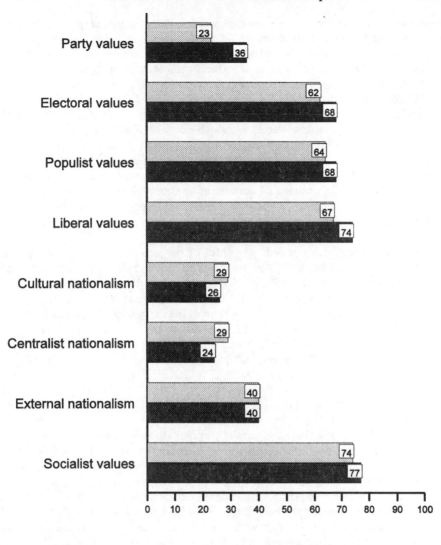

Figure 0.10 Former Communist Party members

publics. But MPs who were ex-Communist Party members proved just as committed to liberal and electoral values as other MPs, and just as opposed to nationalist values as other MPs. Taken as a whole, former Communist Party members, whether in parliament or in the public at large, were no threat to the values of the new regime.

Feelings of economic loss – whether they concerned respondents' families or their country – correlated quite strongly with support for socialist values and opposition to competitive elections though not with liberal values nor, in general, with nationalist values except for external nationalism. Contrasting the losers with the winners who thought things were at least staying the same or even getting better,[32] economic losers were 30 per cent more committed to socialist values than winners, 24 per cent more committed to external nationalist values, 23 per cent more to populist values and 35 per cent less committed to competitive elections. Economic pain turned people quite strongly against some of the key values of the new regime (Fig. 0.11).

Political losers also rejected the values of the new regime. Those who considered themselves (in 1993) as opponents of the incumbent governments (all anti-socialist at that time) were 17 per cent more committed to socialist values than government supporters, 31 per cent more populist and 34 per cent less committed to competitive elections – though the experience of opposition made them 14 per cent more committed to liberal values (Fig . 0.12). Amongst MPs government opponents differed from other MPs by even larger margins on socialist and nationalist values, but hardly differed at all on liberal values or support for representative democracy.

There were significant ethnic minority populations in Russia, Ukraine and Slovakia, though not in Hungary or the Czech Republic. In Russia their values scarcely differed from those of the majority except on the issue of cultural conformity, and even there the generally liberal attitude of the Russian majority on language questions prevented a large difference of values. In Ukraine there were larger differences but the ethno-linguistic Russian minority was distinguished most by its greater commitment to liberal values and its opposition to cultural conformity – both of which might be in its natural self-interest, yet both of which were more in the spirit of western liberal democracy than the values of the Ukrainian majority. In that sense the minority were, perforce, the ones who upheld the new democratic values most strongly. However, the Ukrainian majority itself took a generally liberal view on cultural conformity, which prevented a large difference in values. Ethnic differences were greater in Slovakia, where 39 per cent of the Slovak speakers but almost none of the Hungarian speakers supported the imposition of cultural conformity. That conflict affected other values in Slovakia: the Hungarian minority were not only 13 per cent more committed to liberal values, but 8 per cent less committed to competitive elections that they inevitably lost. Still, those value differences on everything except the language issue itself were remarkably small (Fig. 0.13).

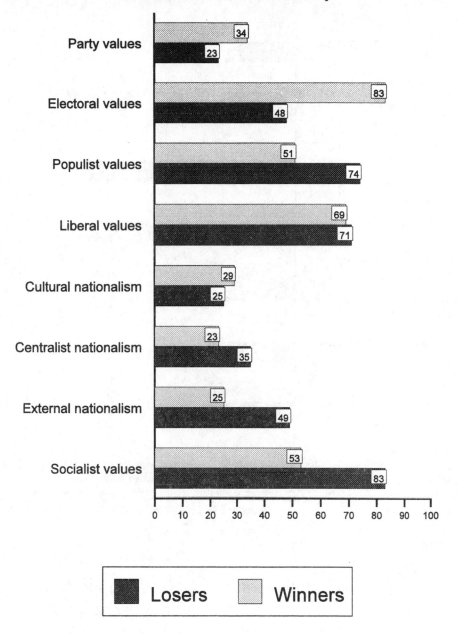

Figure 0.11 Economic losers

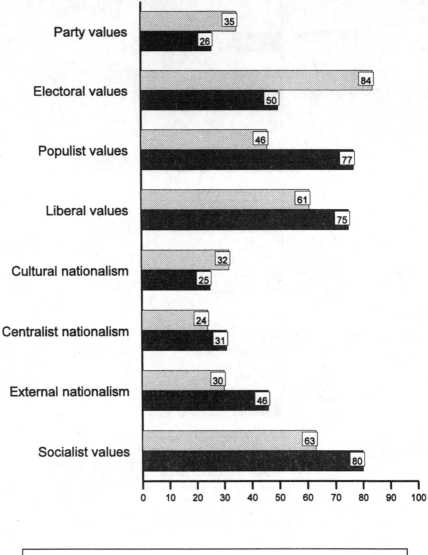

Figure 0.12 The political opposition

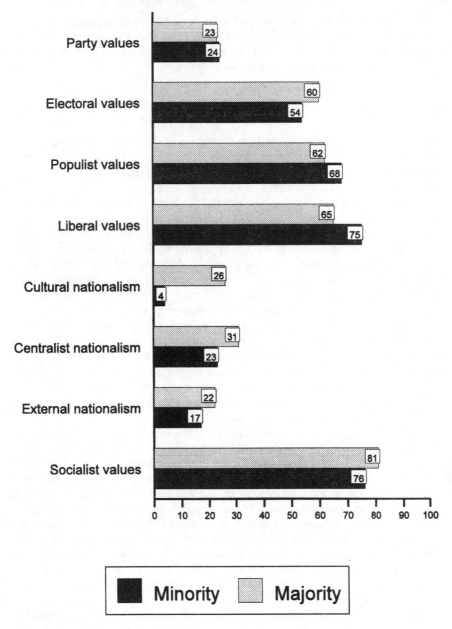

Figure 0.13   Linguistic minorities

Of the four bases for 'counter-revolutionary' values that we have considered, only economic and political losers seemed to have very distinctive values; the influence of ethnicity was limited in scope, while former membership of the Communist Party had no important influence at all.

CONCLUSION

Our overall conclusion is simply stated: in terms of democratic consolidation in the FSU/ECE, political values in the early 1990s were part of the solution, not part of the problem. There was no evidence that the people of the FSU/ECE were not yet ready for democracy.

Of course there were differences between the levels of commitment to socialist, nationalist, liberal and democratic values in different places and amongst different social and political strata. But the differences between political values in the FSU/ECE and an old established democracy like Britain were not that great. The socialist values of equality and welfare were popular in the FSU/ECE; and also popular in Britain – though there was some reluctance in both the FSU/ECE and Britain to pay the taxes necessary to put these principles into practice. Nationalist values won only minority support in the FSU/ECE especially when nationalism was directed inwards rather than outwards. And liberal and democratic values were supported by a large majority in the FSU/ECE, though there was somewhat more emphasis on strict legality and less tolerance of minorities and extremists than in Britain, especially in the FSU. In countries with a long history of arbitrary government moderated by corruption[33] however, an emphasis on strict legality is not necessarily inimical to democracy, though intolerance is harder to excuse.

Within the FSU/ECE, the lines of division that have excited so many theorists and historians seem remarkably faint in terms of contemporary political values. Large differences between the FSU and ECE on some aspects of socialist, nationalist, liberal or democratic values were moderated by smaller differences on other aspects of these values, or even offset by compensating differences. Large differences on state control of industry were moderated by smaller differences on other aspects of socialist values. Particularly strong illiberal tendencies in the FSU on some aspects of liberal values were moderated by FSU/ECE similarities on others and offset by liberal tendencies on some. Distinctive FSU antagonism to parties and elections was offset by strongly populist attitudes.

The 'clash of civilizations' line between Catholic and Orthodox Europe proved a complete irrelevance. The key area of west Ukraine – inside the FSU but outside the Orthodox area – did show quite distinctive political values, but these related to issues of Ukrainian nationalism not to Catholic or Orthodox culture. And the divide at the Urals, between Europe and Asia, revealed no significant value differences at all.

Two other geographic differences had a very strong influence upon political values but one that was, in each case, limited in scope. People in the former imperial countries of Russia and Hungary had much stronger external nationalist values than in Ukraine, Slovakia or the Czech Republic. And people in the Czech Republic – where, alone, there was a swift and relatively (not absolutely) successful switch to a market economy and an equally swift and successful resolution of the Slovak secession without an intense crisis and without bloodshed – were much less committed to socialist values and much more supportive of the institutions of representative democracy than people elsewhere.

Within countries, three vanguard groups – the young, the well educated, and members of parliament – were all more committed than average to the values of the new regime. In the case of MPs, the extent of their commitment to the new values, even after the electoral swing back to the left in elections to the Russian, Ukrainian and Hungarian parliaments, was remarkable.

On the other side two of the four potential counter-revolutionary groups – former members of the Communist Party and ethnic minorities – had values that differed little from the average. Opposition supporters were somewhat more committed to socialist values and much less committed to competitive elections, but many of those who supported the opposition in 1993 must have felt better about the principle of multi-party elections after the subsequent electoral success of their favoured parties.[34]

That leaves economic dislocation and despair, which we found committed people to socialist values – as it does within west European countries as well – but also turned them against the new system of competitive elections, though not against liberal values. It may be unwise to assume that economic mismanagement can go on for ever without damaging people's commitment to the political system of the new regime.

Which brings us back to our overall conclusion: political values in the FSU/ECE are part of the solution not part of the problem. The problem lies elsewhere. Democratic consolidation requires not only a supportive pattern of values amongst the public, but the development of democratic institutions. More important still, it requires the development of democratic precedents in government. Some progress has been made. Postcommunist Ukraine and Hungary (along with Lithuania, Poland and Bulgaria) now have an important precedent for the democratic replacement of one postcommunist government by another after an election defeat.[35] Russia, Slovakia and the Czech Republic do not, although electoral failures have cost governments their parliamentary majorities in these places. But too many of the precedents set by postcommunist governments and their officials – high and low – have not been democratic precedents. Destroying not one but two parliaments (in Moscow and Grozny) sets a poor precedent, reminiscent of Cromwell's dispersal of the English parliament in the seventeenth century, for a would-be democracy. Blatant corruption within government encourages and justifies corruption and massive tax evasion in business, industry and amongst the public.

Nonetheless, the political values of the people and their parliamentary representatives are more conducive to support for liberal democracy than many of the actions of their governments; and at the least they provide no excuse for especially illiberal or undemocratic behaviour by FSU/ECE governments, no excuse for them to be judged by special standards. Quite the opposite. The people are not the problem. If we may invert the warning that Wladyslaw Gomulka gave to the Polish people in January 1957[36]: the people's values pass the test, the question is whether the behaviour of political institutions and public officials, and the accumulating precedents set by them, will also pass the test.

I Introduction

1 Standing on the Ruins of Empire

Karl Marx told workers they 'had no country': in other words, that they had a common interest more important than the national loyalties that might otherwise have divided them. In 1917, the world's first socialist state was established in the USSR on the basis of his teachings. And for more than seventy years, latterly in association with a group of states in Eastern Europe, it was governed on the basis of Marx's belief that human labour was the only source of wealth, that productive resources should be owned by the people as a whole, and that the working class in capitalist as well as socialist countries would recognise their common interest in a form of shared ownership that would eventually extend across state boundaries. It was the longest attempt that has so far been made to place an 'ideology in power'.

THE LEADING ROLE OF THE COMMUNIST PARTY

In all the communist-ruled states factories, farms and other productive resources were owned by the state in the name of the people as a whole. Private ownership still existed: of personal effects, of savings, of housing, and – most notably in Poland and Yugoslavia – of agricultural land. Indeed there was more private housing in the USSR than in some Western countries such as Scotland. But it was a fundamental principle of communist rule that no-one could 'exploit' the labour of anyone else: and so there were no landlords or bankers, no private companies hiring workers off the street, no unemployed and no idle rich. As the Czech Constitution explained in a representative statement, a socialist economic system 'excluded any form of exploitation of man by man'; economic crises and unemployment had been ended, and liberated human labour had become the 'basic factor in the entire society'. The Soviet Constitution claimed similarly that the establishment of socialism had 'put an end once and for all to exploitation of man by man, antagonisms between classes, and strife between nationalities.'[1]

Not only was there public ownership: there was also public control through a system of central planning. The national plan, for instance, 'determined the economic life of the Hungarian People's Republic.' In Czechoslovakia the 'entire national economy' was based on central planning; and in the USSR the economy was a 'single complex' which was managed on the basis of state plans of economic and social development. There was scope for a wide range of economic activities outside the framework of the plan, including handicrafts

33

and even small businesses; but activities of this kind had to be 'useful', they could not involve the 'exploitation of other people's labour', and the state ensured that such activities served the 'interests of society' and took place 'within the limits of the socialist economic system.' This meant that there could be no private factories or farms, and no foreign investment; and apart from cooperatives, virtually all economic activity took place within a framework of state control and ownership.

By the 1980s, a distinctive form of government had developed in parallel to this system of economic and social management. It had several key elements. One of them was a single party: or at any rate, a dominant party, since several of the communist-ruled countries in Eastern Europe allowed other parties to exist although not to compete for power.

The Communist Party's dominant role was enshrined in the constitutions of these states, normally at the beginning. In the USSR, for instance, Article 6 of the 1977 Constitution made it clear that the Communist Party of the Soviet Union was 'the leading and guiding force of Soviet society and the nucleus of its political system, of all state bodies and public organisations.' There were similar provisions in Czechoslovakia (in Article 4) and in Hungary (in Article 3) as well as in the other communist-ruled countries.

The party itself was based upon the principle of democratic centralism, which was meant to ensure that office-holders were accountable and that there was the broadest possible discussion before decisions were taken, but then the discussion had to stop. In practice, this subordinated branches and members to the decisions of the leadership at each level. It was a part of the principle of democratic centralism that there could be no 'factions' or organised groups within party ranks that were opposed to its centrally determined policies. As the Czechoslovak party explained in its rules, the party was based on the 'ideological and organisational unity and cohesion of its ranks' and 'any manifestation of factionalism or group activity' was incompatible with membership.[2] The Communist Party of the Soviet Union, in another representative formulation, made it clear that any expression of factionalism or group activity was 'incompatible with Marxist–Leninist party loyalty and with remaining in the party.'[3] For one party amongst many in a competitive system, democratic centralism would not be unreasonable since the option of exit or breakaway would always be available to dissidents. But it took on a very different meaning in a system in which a single party had a political monopoly.

The party, moreover, played a 'leading role' in the wider society, which meant that it sought to control all forms of organised life, from elections and the administration of justice to creative writing and stamp collecting. Again, several key mechanisms were involved. One of them was the party's 'cadres policy', or in other words its control over all appointments to positions of influence. Another was its control over the flow of information, including a detailed censorship whose existence was itself subject to censorship. The operation of the censorship office in Poland became the best known in the communist countries when an official from Krakow defected to the West, bringing his instructions with him. All kinds of subjects – such as the Katyn massacre of 1940, when thousands of Polish officers were shot by Soviet forces – could not be mentioned at all; and there were bans on a whole range of other topics, including the potential dangers of chemical fertilisers and Polish meat exports to the USSR.[4] The party's leading role also meant that it sought to guide the activities of secondary associations of all kinds, including trade unions, women's movements, youth associations and sports clubs. There was, in effect, no 'private life' outside the circle of family and close friends.

THE STRUGGLE TO IMPOSE COMMUNIST VALUES

Our concern in this book is with political attitudes and values in the first five years after the fall of the communist system, particularly the attitudes and values of ordinary citizens but also those of MPs elected to the new postcommunist parliaments. In the communist period, values were a particular concern of the ruling party. In principle at least, the aim was to develop a productive, technologically advanced economy in which every reasonable need could be satisfied – this was what was understood by 'abundance'. But at the same time they were concerned to develop a communist way of life, including a commitment to Marxist values, a high level of political activism, and a 'scientific world outlook' (in other words, atheism). As these values developed, and as the economy matured, the whole society – it was assumed – would move closer to its ultimate goal of communism. For all their explicit materialism, communists laid as much stress on development of an appropriate set of values as any religious sect (party membership, indeed, was sometimes referred to as a 'priesthood').

One of the fullest statements of the value system that communist governments sought to impart was the 'moral code of the builder of communism', which was added to the Rules of the Soviet Communist Party in 1961 under Khrushchev's guidance. This committed party members to a comprehensive set of precepts:

devotion to the communist cause; love of the socialist motherland and of the other socialist countries;
conscientious labour for the good of society – he who does not work, neither shall he eat;
concern on the part of everyone for the preservation and growth of public wealth;
a high sense of public duty, intolerance of actions harmful to the public interest;
collectivism and comradely mutual assistance: one for all and all for one;

humane relations and mutual respect between individuals – man is to man a friend, comrade and brother;

honesty and truthfulness, moral purity, modesty, and unpretentiousness in social and private life;

mutual respect in the family, and concern for the upbringing of children;

an uncompromising attitude to injustice, parasitism, dishonesty, careerism and money-grubbing;

friendship and brotherhood among all peoples of the USSR, intolerance of national and racial hatred;

an uncompromising attitude towards the enemies of communism, peace, and the freedom of nations;

fraternal solidarity with the working people of all countries, and with all peoples.[5]

The same provisions were included in the Party Programme, a revised version of which was adopted at the same congress.[6]

An enormous effort was made to ensure that these values were extended to the whole society. The education system played a part, as the focus of political youth movements as well as the institution through which the new regime communicated its own view of history and other school subjects. A network of propagandists spread across the country, offering pep talks at the workplace as well as (for party members themselves) a more rigorous system of political instruction. Most important of all, the mass media were expected to *interpret* and not simply report the passage of events. Newspapers, for instance, were instructed on the themes they should prioritise and the people they should mention (or not mention). Television news began with economic achievements before passing on to the unemployment and social division of the capitalist world. And there was 'visual propaganda', including posters, statues of Marx and Lenin, graphs that pointed sharply upwards, and 'boards of honour' with pictures of outstanding workers.

For some, by the 1970s, it was already clear that this propaganda effort had 'succeeded' and that the Soviet Union had been a 'dramatically successful case' of planned change in a political culture.[7] The changes were partly behavioural. Elections, for instance, began to draw in larger numbers of voters, from 20–30 per cent in the 1920s to 80–90 per cent by the mid–1930s.[8] And there were substantial changes in political activity. Studies in the 1920s found that the average worker spent about 2.9 hours a month in activities of this kind; by the late 1960s, when follow-up studies were undertaken, the amount of time devoted to such activities had increased almost sevenfold.[9] The Soviet authorities themselves claimed, in the early 1970s, that a 'new historic community of peoples' had developed who shared a 'unity of economic, sociopolitical and cultural life, Marxist-Leninist ideology, and the interests and communist ideals of the working class.'[10] And there were claims, more generally, of a 'socialist way of life' that extended across the communist-ruled nations.[11]

But as communist rule entered the 1980s, their leaders had fewer grounds for optimism. For a start, there was increasing evidence that the campaign of mass persuasion had been less successful than they had hoped. Political lectures, it emerged, were attended unwillingly, they were doing little to raise levels of political knowledge, and they were attracting those who were already the best informed and most committed – 'informing the informed and agitating the agitated', as a Soviet party journal put it.[12] Relatively few, it appeared, gave any attention to the posters that decorated the street corners. Where they could, as in the Baltic or in East Germany, ordinary people turned to foreign radio or television, or to rumour and gossip, rather than the official media. And there was little sign, in daily life, that the communist society of the future was gradually forming. There were far more religious believers than party members, young people were discovering Western pop culture, there was a flourishing black market, and ordinary workers were more interested in the bottle than the fulfilment of the five year plan.

More fundamentally, there was increasing evidence that the communist economies had lost their growth dynamic – and that the tacit 'social contract' they had concluded with their populations was coming under increasing strain. Under the 'social contract', the mass populations of the communist-ruled nations had surrendered most of their civil and political rights – including freedom of speech and the right to elect a government of their choice – for a range of social and economic rights, including full employment, low and stable prices, cheap housing and free educational and medical services.[13] With high rates of growth in the 1950s and 1960s, communist governments were able to keep their side of this implicit bargain. But when growth rates began to fall in the 1970s and 1980s (see Table 1.1) it became difficult to resist moves towards a form of 'socialist market' with higher prices, income inequalities and overt unemployment. By the same token, it became difficult for communist governments to claim that they provided a form of comprehensive social welfare that was better than anything capitalism could offer.

Table 1.1: Average annual rates of growth, 1951–90 (net material product, percentages)

	1951–55	1956–60	1961–65	1966–70	1971–75	1976–80	1981–85	1986–90
Bulgaria	12.2	9.7	6.7	8.8	7.8	6.1	3.7	−0.2
Hungary	5.7	5.9	4.1	6.8	6.3	2.8	1.3	−0.4
GDR	13.1	7.1	3.5	5.2	5.4	4.1	4.5	−1.4
Poland	8.6	6.6	6.2	6.0	9.8	1.2	−0.8	−0.3
Romania	14.1	6.6	9.1	7.7	11.4	7.0	3.0	−3.3
Czechoslovakia	8.2	7.0	1.9	7.0	5.5	3.7	1.8	1.0
USSR	11.4	9.2	6.5	7.8	5.7	4.3	3.2	1.7

Source: Adapted from *Statisticheskii ezhegodnik stran-chlenov SEV 1990* (Moscow: Finansy i statistika, 1990), pp. 5–15, and *Economic Survey of Europe in 1990–91* (New York: Secretariat of the Economic Commission for Europe, 1991), p.41.

There was evidence of other kinds that the commitment to communist values was, in any case, a rather limited one. One sign of this was religious belief and behaviour. Only Albania, in its 1976 constitution, claimed to be a wholly atheist state; the other communist-ruled countries followed the Soviet model, in which church and state were formally separate and religious belief and observance were a matter for individual citizens. But all of these regimes were committed to the gradual elimination of religion and other 'superstitions', and it was generally illegal to give religious instruction to the young or to seek converts. In fact, as the experience of communist rule made clear, religious belief and observance were remarkably resilient – even in atheist Albania, where Muslim religious rituals continued to be observed on a *de facto* basis. In the USSR the Orthodox Church had an estimated 40–50 million adherents, three times the membership of the CPSU. And in Poland there was the closest accommodation of all, with Catholic groups in parliament, a Catholic press, Catholic chaplains in the armed forces, and a ruling party that was full of Catholic believers. The ratio of priests to people, in the 1980s, was the highest in Europe.[14]

Another stubborn remnant of the past was nationalism, within and between the states of the region. Most of the communist states, for instance, were members of the Warsaw Treaty Organisation, which had been established in 1955 and which provided for consultation and mutual assistance in the event of an armed attack upon any of its members. But Albania, one of the original signatories, took no part in WTO activities after 1962 and formally announced its withdrawal in 1968. Another member, Romania, did not allow WTO forces on its territory, took no part in the intervention in Czechoslovakia in 1968, and pursued an independent foreign policy – including friendly relations with China and Israel. A wider circle of states, including Cuba, Mongolia and Vietnam, were members of the Council for Mutual Economic Assistance, or Comecon. But there was strong resistance to full integration, and trade with the capitalist world expanded more quickly in all of these countries than it did with other CMEA members. Yugoslavia stood outside both organisations as a member of the non-aligned movement, and the wider communist movement was increasingly divided and losing the political influence it had once commanded.

RESISTANCE, REFORM AND REVOLT

More serious still were the revolts that took place against Soviet and communist rule. Communist rule in ECE, or even in the lands recovered by the USSR during and after the 1941–45 war, was never accepted for long without a struggle. The Ukrainian Insurgent Army and other partisans fought a bitter and extended campaign against communism in postwar Ukraine and the Baltic states that ran on in some places until the 1950s. Although they did well in the first postwar elections in Czechoslovakia, the communists later took total power there and in Hungary with the help of the Ministry of the Interior, which they controlled, and the backing of the Soviet Red Army. In both, the communist take-over was followed by a reign of terror which, in Hungary, was 'proportionately almost as severe as Stalin's purges of the 1930s . . . up to 40,000 people [in Hungary] were tortured and executed or given long terms of imprisonment, and far larger numbers were persecuted.'[15] In Soviet occupied Germany the communists sent 200,000 suspected opponents to the old concentration camps such as Buchenwald and Sachsenhausen in the years up to 1950.[16] But all of this failed to crush resistance.

The death of Stalin in March 1953 gave new hope to ECE. Three months later a revolt in East Berlin provoked the Soviet commandant into declaring martial law, following a decision to eliminate small traders and collectivise agriculture. Workers downed tools on Stalinallee in East Berlin and a wave of demonstrations spread throughout the city, demanding the resignation of the government as well as the withdrawal of the original decision. Several thousand demonstrators were involved and the protests spread to other East German cities; Soviet troops had to be called in to restore order.[17] Workers in Poznan erupted in July 1956; and in October 1956 a much broader crisis developed in Hungary following student demonstrations in support of political reform, free elections and the withdrawal of Soviet troops. A coalition government was formed under the reformist premiership of Imre Nagy, but Soviet troops were called in by party leader Janos Kadar and they had re-established control by early November. Three thousand Hungarians lost their lives in the conflict and thousands more were wounded; further executions followed; and Nagy and his colleagues were condemned to death and executed two years later.[18]

A more extended attempt at reform communism took place in Czechoslovakia in 1968, led by newly elected first secretary Alexander Dubcek. As summed up in the party's Action Programme, adopted in April 1968, the aim was to bring about a democratic socialism that would end the 'monopolistic concentration of power in the hands of party bodies' and give the party the rather different role of striving for the 'voluntary support of the majority of the people' through the persuasion and personal example of its members. Under the terms of the Programme censorship was to be abolished, citizens would be allowed to travel abroad, the victims of political trials would be compensated, and the secret police would 'no longer be used to resolve internal political questions and controversies.'[19] The reforms were immensely popular, and so were those who had introduced them. However, there was deepening concern among other communist governments about the way in which the Czech leadership was apparently losing its grip on national life, and on the media in particular; and in August 1968 the USSR led an invasion in which Dubcek was arrested and a hard-line administration installed in his place. Brezhnev, speaking to the Polish party congress later in the year, explained the intervention in terms of what became known as the 'Brezhnev doctrine': that any attempt by internal or external forces to restore capitalism would be regarded 'not just as a problem for that country, but as a problem and concern for the socialist countries as a whole.'[20]

The limits of reform were tested still further in Poland in 1970 after the price of foodstuffs had been increased, with lamentable timing, shortly before Christmas. The Baltic shipyards erupted, internal security troops had to be called in, and dozens of shipyard workers were shot when the troops opened fire at Gdynia and Szczecin. Continuing public pressure led to the resignation of first secretary Wladyslaw Gomulka and his replacement by Eduard Gierek, a miner from Silesia who promised a 'frank dialogue' with the working class. The price increases were suspended, economic growth began to accelerate, and real wages rose rapidly. But the government had borrowed abroad to finance its investment; the cost of its foreign debt rose as Western interest rates increased, and at the same time domestic subsidies ran out of control as wages rose rapidly but prices were held stable. Another attempt to increase prices was made in 1976, but it had to be withdrawn when workers took to the streets, party offices were seized and the main East-West railway line was blocked. The Polish prime minister appeared on television the same evening to announce that in view of the 'valuable amendments and contributions' put forward by the working class, the price rises would be withdrawn for further discussion.[21]

The gulf between regime and society deepened in the late 1970s as the party authorities turned to repressive means of enforcing their decisions while an alternative political culture began to form under the shelter of the Catholic church. The church had been enormously strengthened by the election of the Archbishop of Krakow, Cardinal Wojtyla, as Pope John Paul II in 1978, and by the massive audiences he was able to attract when he visited his native country the following year. The regime, for its part, became increasingly corrupt and authoritarian as its freedom of manoeuvre diminished. In August 1980 a work-in at the Lenin shipyard in Gdansk led by electrician Lech Walesa developed into a network of strike committees across the Baltic ports, and then into a popular movement called Solidarity which was able to force the regime to concede a range of objectives from pay and conditions to the broadcasting of the Catholic Mass and improvements in the health service and public housing. Solidarity, at its peak, involved more than nine million workers, the great majority of the labour force; and more than a third of the members of the Polish communist party had joined. A deepening polarisation between Solidarity and the party authorities was resolved in December 1981 when martial law was declared, apparently to forestall a Soviet invasion; Solidarity was suspended and then banned entirely, and its leading activists imprisoned.

By the 1980s, accordingly, there was little emphasis upon communist goals and rather more upon a negotiated relationship between a group of regimes that were prepared to concede a great deal if not their ultimate monopoly, and populations that had no means of replacing their governments but many ways of influencing their conduct. By the late 1980s, most strikingly in the USSR, the official media had begun to tolerate a variety of opinion, even antisocialist opinion. There was a choice of candidate at general elections, even if it was a largely nominal one, in Hungary from the 1960s, in Romania from the 1970s and in Poland and the USSR from the 1980s. The churches had resumed their place in public life. And a 'second economy' had developed to supplement the official economy that was managed by the state. This accommodation between regime and society was what the East German dissident, Rudolf Bahro, called 'actually existing socialism', and for reformers like Mikhail Gorbachev in the late 1980s it offered an opportunity to widen political choices still further on the basis of what they took to be a commitment to the socialist framework as a whole. In the end their reforms allowed the system as a whole to be challenged, not just the officials who were responsible for its administration.

THE LEGACY OF OLDER EMPIRES

As communist rule matured, it became increasingly differentiated. And it became increasingly clear that communist values had not superseded much older attachments and expectations, based in part upon the very different experiences of the communist-ruled nations before the establishment of single party government. Why, for instance, had the Prague Spring originated in Czechoslovakia? Almost certainly, because it had a long tradition of liberal freedoms and had been the only one of the East European democracies that survived throughout the interwar period. Why had Solidarity originated in Poland? Once again, it was hard to explain without reference to the traditional hostility of ordinary Poles towards both Russia and communist rule, and their commitment to the Catholic Church. Conversely it was difficult to explain the role of the Church without taking account of the part it had played in preserving a Polish national identity while the state itself had been divided up among its more powerful neighbours.

Historical experience was one of the factors that shaped the political culture of Eastern Europe: at the popular level, and also at the level of the political elites; and in the postcommunist years as well as those that preceded them. Political culture has been defined as the 'attitudinal and behavioural matrix within which the political system is located.'[22] It includes the values and beliefs that relate to government as well as foci of identification and loyalty, perceptions of history and politics, and political knowledge and expectations that originate in the 'specific historical experience of nations and groups';[23] and for the purposes of this study, it also includes patterns of political behaviour, in other words the political 'way of life' of the entire society.

A political culture is not shaped for all time by historical experience. Substantial changes have been demonstrated, for instance, in German attitudes towards government over the postwar years, including a growing commitment to 'democracy' as a political value.[24] But equally, a political culture is likely to be powerfully influenced by patterns of social and political development over very long periods. In Italy, for instance, the very different forms of politics that developed in the industrial north and the more traditional south have been traced back to patterns of republican self-government or autocratic rule that were established as early as the twelfth century. It was social patterns of this kind, formed in early medieval times, that were 'decisive' in explaining the effectiveness of government in various parts of the country in the late twentieth century; and they testified, at least in Italy, to the 'astonishing tensile strength of civic traditions.'[25] More generally, as Lipset and others have noted, cultural factors of this kind appear to be 'even more important than economic ones' in explaining the establishment and maintenance of democratic government.[26]

The Russian Empire, in this connection, stood apart among the other European nations in terms of the strongly authoritarian and centralised nature of its government. The modern state had developed from the principality of Moscow, rather than Novgorod and Pskov where assemblies of the heads of households had played some role in public decisionmaking. Moscow had no institutions of this kind, nor had Russia after Novgorod and Pskov were conquered at the end of the fifteenth century. And Moscow was expansionist, as it gradually extended its control by conquest or annexation into Siberia from the sixteenth century, into Ukraine and Belorussia in the eighteenth century, and into Central Asia and the Caucasus in the nineteenth. Writing at this time, Alexis de Tocqueville saw two great nations 'marked out by the will of Heaven to sway the destinies of half the globe'; but whereas America relied on the 'common sense of the people', in Russia all the authority of society was concentrated in a single person and the instrument of government was 'servitude'.[27] It was this principle that extended across Europe and Asia as the Russian Empire and then the Soviet Union widened their sphere of influence.

The position of the state in relation to Russian society was certainly a strong one. Trade unions and strikes were illegal until 1905, and thereafter severely restricted. Political parties were legalised at the same time, although their existence had to be approved by the authorities and no society body could be formed whose objectives were considered a threat to public morals or social order. It was difficult, moreover, to defend such civil liberties as did exist through courts of law. There were important reforms in the 1860s, including the introduction of trial by jury; but it was suspended in political cases after 1881 and a system of extraordinary courts was introduced at the same time, conferring virtually unlimited powers on governors-general to arrest any citizen, ban any meeting, and close any newspaper or journal.[28] Several European states had legislation on their statute books for dealing with crimes against the state, but none attached so much importance to them, or defined them as widely and loosely. In Russia, as Richard Pipes has noted, with just a short interlude between 1905 and 1917, it was a crime 'not only to seek changes in the existing system of government or administration, but even to raise questions about such issues', with politics 'declared by law a monopoly of those in power.'[29]

Tsarist rule did permit an element of consultation: there were elected local councils (*zemstva*) from the 1860s, and in 1905 a parliament – the State Duma – was eventually conceded, very late by the standards of the rest of Europe and North America (see Table 1.2). It met for the first time the following year. Formally speaking, the Duma had a considerable range of powers. It could enact and amend legislation; it could appoint and dismiss government officials; it had the right to consider national and departmental budgets; and it could address questions to the chairman of the newly-established Council of Ministers. Without the consent of the Duma, promised the Tsar's manifesto of October 1905, 'no law can come into force'. The Duma's real powers, as they were defined by subsequent legislation, were more modest. It had no right to make changes in expenditure connected with foreign loans, the army or navy, the imperial household, or the ministry of foreign affairs (about two-thirds of government spending was thus removed from its control). Ministers, moreover, were responsible to the Emperor, not to the Duma, and the Emperor alone had the right to appoint or dismiss them; he could reject the Duma's decisions if he wished to do so, and issue his own decrees which had the force of law.

Table 1.2: Constitutional development in selected countries

	Date of first constitutional regime	Date of first parliamentary regime	Date of universal suffrage
UK	1689	1741	1928
USA	1787	1789	1919
France	1789	1792	1944
Germany	1848	1918	1919
Italy	1848	1876	1946
Austria-Hungary	1848	1918	1919/1945
Russia	1905	1917	1917/1936

Notes: In Britain, many women got the vote in 1918, but not on equal terms with men until 1928. Hapsburg Austria-Hungary never introduced universal suffrage; post-Hapsburg Austria did so in 1919, post-Hapsburg Hungary only in 1945. Universal suffrage was introduced in post-Tsarist pre-communist Russia to elect a Constituent Assembly in November 1917; but the Assembly was forcibly dispersed in 1918 by the communists who also abolished universal suffrage and did not reintroduce it until the constitution of 1936.

Sources: Adapted from Allan Kornberg (ed.) *Legislatures in Comparative Perspective* (New York, NY: David McKay, 1973), pp. 100, 106; Thomas T. Mackie and Richard Rose, *The International Almanac of Electoral History*, 3rd ed. (London: Macmillan, 1991); David Butler, Howard Penniman and Austin Ranney *Democracy at the Polls* (Washington, DC: American Enterprise Institute, 1981); Chris Cook and John Paxton *European Political Facts 1918–84* (London: Macmillan, 1986); Georg Brunner 'Elections in the Soviet Union' in Robert K. Furtak (ed.) *Elections in Socialist States* (London: Harvester Wheatsheaf, 1990) pp. 20–52.

In practice, the powers of any Russian government were less impressive than they appeared on paper: distances were great, communications were imperfect, and the corruption of local officials moderated the effect of central directives. And yet there were differences from the rest of Europe that were very real to contemporaries. Russia, for instance, was the only European country apart from Turkey that required a passport from its European or North American visitors. And its customs inspections, Baedeker informed its readers in 1914, were 'exceptionally thorough'. Travellers were recommended to use unprinted paper for their packing so as to 'avoid any cause of suspicion', to 'avoid works of a political, social, or historical nature', and to be careful when photographing as the guardians of the law were 'over-vigilant'.[30] 'He must have sojourned in that solitude without repose, that prison without leisure, which is called Russia', wrote the Marquis de Custine in 1839, 'to feel all the liberty enjoyed in the other European countries, whatever form of government they may have adopted... Whoever has well examined that country will be content to live anywhere else.'[31]

What applied to Russia applied to Poland, after its limited autonomy had been extinguished in 1863, and to Ukraine, most of which had been absorbed by Russia as early as the 1660s. It applied less readily to Hungary and Czechoslovakia, which had experienced rather different practices within the Austro-Hungarian Empire. Czechoslovakia, in particular, emerged from the Versailles peace settlement as a model liberal democracy. In both of the successor states, Hungary and Czechoslovakia, men as well as women had been given the vote by 1920, and between a third and a half of all adults were participating in national elections in the 1920s and 1930s – levels of participation that were higher than in France, Italy and the United States, and as high as the USSR with its mobilised citizenry (Table 1.3). Two European countries, Portugal and Switzerland, did not introduce female suffrage until as late as the 1970s.

Table 1.3:   Electoral participation in selected countries (percentage of population voting in national elections)

	Before 1869	*1870–90*	*1891–1913*	*1918–30*	*1931–44*	*1945–59*
UK	5	12	12	48	47	57
USA	13	15	19	17	33	37
France	21	22	22	23	24	49
Germany	–	16	18	54	54	58
Italy	1	5	5	18	–	60
Austria-Hungary/ Austria	1	1	18	55	–	63
Russia/USSR	–	–	2	–	55	64
Hungary	4	4	4	32	27	66
Czechoslovakia	–	–	–	47	57	67

Source: Adapted from Dieter Nohlen, *Wahlsysteme der Welt* (Munich: Piper, 1978), pp. 37–8.

Czechoslovakia had a particular position as the only newly established democracy that did not succumb to authoritarian rule between the world wars. Czechs had enjoyed universal adult suffrage from as early as 1907. They had contested elections since the 1870s, and political life was sustained not just by a multiplicity of parties but by a network of voluntary associations of a cultural, religious or sporting kind. Indeed Czechoslovakia had 'strong claims to be regarded as by far the most democratic, libertarian and tolerant country within Central or Eastern Europe between the wars.'[32] It had an effective parliament and judiciary, and the rights of different nationalities were well protected; and all of this was sustained by the democratic and humanist philosophy of its first president, Tomas Masaryk. The Czech communist party was itself a part of this tradition: unlike most others, it was a mass party that incorporated most of its social democratic predecessor, and it was strongly parliamentary in its political orientation.[33] It was, indeed, a successful parliamentary party, winning 38 per cent of the vote – more than any other – in the first postwar elections in 1946; and it was perhaps because 'parliamentary illusions' were deepest that the purges that took place in the early 1950s were on a larger scale than in any of the other East European countries, and Stalinist forms of rule were sustained longer.

Hungarian self-government had begun in 1867 within the Austro-Hungarian Empire; the state itself emerged in 1918, stripped of much of its former territory and much of its population. A democratic government was replaced briefly by a communist administration under Bela Kun, and then by a fascist dictatorship under Admiral Horthy. Hungary fought on the side of the Axis powers during the war, and was conquered rather than liberated by the Red Army. The communists were a minority party in the coalition that emerged from the elections that were held in 1945, but had established a political monopoly by 1948–9. The communist period was dominated by the party leader Matyas Rakosi who had escaped the fate of Bela Kun in the Moscow purges of the thirties because he had been safely locked up in a Hungarian jail from 1924 to 1940. He was a dogmatic and authoritarian Stalinist in charge of a defeated land inhabited by clearly anti-communist people. There was however some continuity in the strategy that he and his associates pursued: the state had always been involved in large-scale programmes of economic and social change, and there was broadly based support for the goals of industrial development and social reform.[34]

There was much that united communist and then postcommunist Europe, but at least as much that divided it. All had shared in the experience of communist rule, with a single ruling party that was ultimately sustained by coercion; but communist rule had lasted for seventy years or more in Russia and Ukraine, and just forty in the Baltics and Eastern Europe. In some of these countries communist rule had some claim to be 'indigenous', in that the ruling party had come independently to power (Russia, Yugoslavia, Albania), but in the others it had been 'imposed' from outside by the Red Army. All these countries were predominantly Christian insofar as they were religious; the USSR had a substantial Muslim minority, Russia a much smaller one. Of those that were Christian, some adhered to Eastern Orthodoxy (like Russia and Ukraine); others (like the former Czechoslovakia and Hungary) were predominantly Catholic, though Hungary had a substantial Protestant minority. Most shared a Slavonic language and a common Slavic identity, though Hungary did not. And the former parts of the Hapsburg empire had a significantly more Western orientation than Russia or Ukraine – though not perhaps than other parts of the Tsarist empire such as Poland or the Baltic States. Some of the communist-ruled nations had ended the Second World War on the winning side (Czechoslovakia as well as Russia and Ukraine); while others (including Hungary and some Ukrainians) had fought with the Axis powers and gone down to defeat. And their levels of development were very different, with Czechoslovakia in particular among the most industrially advanced parts of the continent.

For all their diversity, there was perhaps one major 'fault line' that ran through the lands of Eastern Europe and the former USSR: the line between the countries that had been under Romanov rule and those that had been under the Hapsburgs (see Table 1.4). The Hapsburg world, from which the Czech Republic, Hungary and Slovakia emerged, had experienced feudalism and the slow development of a balance of obligations between ruling groups and their subjects. It was this balance that later developed into law, and it sustained parliamentary institutions as the means by which any differences that still remained could be peacefully resolved. It was a world that, even earlier, had experienced Roman law, with its framework of regulation based upon private property. It was a world that shared its Catholic faith with much of Western Europe. And later, it was a world in which political power was absolutist but constitutionally founded: governments were not accountable to parliament, still less to a mass electorate, but they ruled within defined parameters.

Table 1.4:   The Former Soviet Union and Eastern Europe: A cultural classification

Romanov rule	*Hapsburg rule*
'Eastern'	'Western'
Orthodox	Catholic (and minority Protestant)
'Frontier of Europe'	'Core of Europe'
USSR	Occupied after 1945
Countries	*Countries*
Russia	Czech Republic
Ukraine	Hungary
	Slovakia

The other countries with which we deal in this book fell within a rather different tradition. There had been no feudalism in Russia or Ukraine, at least in its Western form, and there had been a much more limited development of law and representative institutions. It was a world that had not experienced the Renaissance and Reformation, and which did not share to the same extent in a wider Catholic community. It had its own equally historic Christian faith, and, for some, a sense of a special mission that derived from its uniqueness. It was Asian as well as European, connections rivalled only by Britain's links with the Indian subcontinent. And it was a world in which government was much less constrained by parliament, or courts, or by the press. Indeed it was a world of straightforward autocracy: as the Basic Laws of the Russian Empire made clear as late as 1906, 'To the All-Russian Emperor belongs the Supreme Autocratic Power. To obey his power, not only by reason of wrath, but also for conscience's sake, is commanded by God himself.' To what extent these divergent experiences were obliterated by communist rule and to what extent they were succeeded by a common commitment to 'democratic values' is the subject of this book.

2 Communism and After

Communist rule still seemed viable in the 1970s and 1980s. Indeed it was expanding rapidly, particularly in the developing world. In Vietnam, following the conclusion of a long drawn-out war with France and then the United States, a socialist republic was established in 1976 after north and south had reunited. In Laos, the year before, a people's democratic republic had been formed after the king had abdicated and the monarchy had been abolished; and in Cambodia, the Khmer Rouge came to power after they had overthrown the pro-Western government of Lon Nol. There were at least sixteen communist governments of this kind by the mid–1980s; further afield, radical and Soviet-aligned regimes were established in many of the countries of Africa and Asia, including Afghanistan, Angola and Ethiopia. Nicaragua was ruled, after 1979, by the Sandinista National Liberation Front; and in Grenada the New Jewel Movement had established a People's Revolutionary Government. Leonid Brezhnev, addressing the 26th CPSU Congress in 1981, could reasonably claim that the 'revolutionary struggle of the peoples' had registered 'new victories'.[1]

The sixteen communist-ruled states constituted what the USSR and its allies defined as a 'world socialist system'; and at their core was a 'socialist community', consisting of those that were most closely associated in political or military terms. The USSR itself was the world's largest state and one of its two superpowers. Its military position rested on the Warsaw Treaty Organisation, which was renewed in April 1985 without amendment for a further twenty years. Of the leaders that took part in the signing ceremony, Mikhail Gorbachev had just taken up his post; but most of the other signatories had led their parties for the best part of two decades, Todor Zhivkov of the Bulgarian Communist Party for more than three. The treaty, Gorbachev told them, was one whose 'growing influence' had a 'positive influence on the general climate in the world.'[2] 'We can safely say', he wrote in his *Perestroika* two years later, 'that the socialist system has established itself in a large group of nations, that the socialist countries' economic potential has been steadily increasing, and that its cultural and spiritual values are profoundly moral and that they ennoble people.'[3]

Ten years later, none of these leaders was still in power; most of them (Nicolae Ceausescu, Janos Kadar, Gustav Husak and Erich Honecker) were dead, two (Zhivkov and the Polish leader Wojciech Jaruzelski) were in disgrace or awaiting trial, and only Gorbachev himself was still active in national politics. The Warsaw Pact itself had been dissolved. And yet in the mid–1980s not only the East European leaders but much of Western social science was convinced that the governments they headed were securely established, even 'legitimate'. The chances of democratisation in Eastern Europe, wrote Samuel Huntington in 1984, were 'virtually nil'.[4] Gorbachev in particular, wrote another Western scholar as late as 1991, would be 'very strong in the mid–1990s', with the CPSU well placed to become a 'dominant electoral party... for the rest of this century';[5] the American ambassador in Moscow, Jack Matlock, told his government in similar terms that Gorbachev was likely to remain in power 'for at least five (possibly ten) years'.[6] How did these regimes come to an end so suddenly and, for many, unexpectedly? What was the role of domestic and of international factors? And to what extent did the changes of government form a pattern, a single 'transition'?

POLITICAL CHANGE FROM BELOW

Political change in the communist world at the end of the 1980s took a variety of forms, but there was a relatively clear distinction between the regimes that were overthrown 'from below' by popular action, and those in which the regime itself initiated change 'from above' and, in some cases, retained power.[7] In Albania, for instance, the ruling Party of Labour introduced a number of modest reforms and won the general election that took place in March 1991, but continuing demonstrations and a general strike led to another election in March 1992 at which it was comprehensively defeated. A year later the collected works of Enver Hoxha, party leader until 1985, were being turned into cardboard boxes. In Yugoslavia the League of Communists renounced its political monopoly in January 1990, but a civil war began after Croatia and Slovenia had declared their independence in 1991 and the state itself began to disintegrate. In most cases the former communists lost power and the Yugoslav League of Communists itself collapsed, although in the largest of the republics, Serbia, a former communist was elected President and his Socialist Party won most of the seats at a general election in 1992 and again a year later on a programme of populist nationalism (here and elsewhere the organisational forms of Leninism were often popular long after communist policies had been abandoned).

Perhaps the clearest case of political change 'from below' was in Poland, where communist rule had always been strongly resisted because it was Russian and not just because it was Marxist, and where the experience of Solidarity in 1980–81 had convinced most Poles that, as Adam Michnik put it, there was no prospect of a 'socialism with a human face'; what remained was 'communism with its teeth knocked out'.[8] A number of attempts were made to establish a dialogue with society after Solidarity had been suspended and then banned: a national public opinion centre was established in 1982, martial law was lifted a year later, and the regime committed itself to a programme of 'socialist renewal' that in many ways anticipated the reforms that were conducted in the USSR under the Gorbachev leadership.[9] An attempt to secure popular endorsement in

November 1987, however, came badly unstuck when a referendum failed to secure the necessary majority of the electorate – although there was a majority of voters – for the government's proposals for economic and political change. A wave of strikes broke out in April 1988 and again in August, which were only brought to an end by the promise of negotiations between the authorities and representatives of Solidarity. Talks began – around a very large round table – in February 1989, and by April an agreement had been reached that included the legalisation of Solidarity and the holding of elections to a new two-chamber parliament.[10]

Under the terms of the agreement, Solidarity and other independent groups could propose candidates for 35 per cent of the seats in the Sejm, the lower house of parliament; the other seats were reserved for the Polish United Workers' Party and its allies. A new upper house, a Senate, would also be elected, with 100 seats all of which would be freely contested. In two rounds of voting in June 1989 Solidarity won all of the 161 seats they could contest in the Sejm, and 99 of the 100 seats in the Senate. The communist leader, General Jaruzelski, won the presidency when the new parliament assembled, but by a single vote. Attempts to form a communist-led government were less successful, and in August 1989 a new administration was formed under the leadership of Tadeusz Mazowiecki, a Catholic intellectual who had formerly edited Solidarity's weekly paper, with communist ministers left in charge of defence and internal security. Later in the year the Polish People's Republic became the Polish Republic, sovereignty was transferred from the 'working people of town and countryside' to 'the nation', and the reference to the leading role of the PUWP was removed from the constitution. The Soviet government, apparently unperturbed, congratulated Mazowiecki on his new responsibilities and noted that he intended to maintain Poland's international alliances;[11] it was nonetheless Eastern Europe's first non-communist government for more than forty years, and a clear breach in the power monopoly that had been established after the Second World War.

The process of political change 'from below' took still more dramatic forms in the German Democratic Republic, which was a special case in that it was a political construct rather than a nation state.[12] The transition began in July 1989 with an outflow of population through Hungary to West Germany, and developed into a widespread resistance movement led by the Lutheran Church and an oppositional coalition known as New Forum. Party leader Erich Honecker was forced to resign in October 1989, and later placed under house arrest; but the demonstrations continued, with up to half a million appearing weekly on the streets of Leipzig, and further concessions followed including the breaching of the Berlin Wall on 9 November 1989. In December the ruling Socialist Unity Party changed its name to the Party of Democratic Socialism, and elected a new leader; another reform-minded communist became prime minister. The new leadership announced that multi-party elections would take place the following year; at those elections, in March 1990, the conservative Christian

Democratic Union took the largest share of the vote and began to move rapidly towards union with the Federal Republic. A treaty of unification was signed on 31 August, and at midnight on 2 October 1990 the former German Democratic Republic became part of a larger German state under the Christian Democratic government of Helmut Kohl.

The most spectacular case of political change 'from below' was in Romania, although it was less clear that there had been a decisive break with communist rule – or at any rate, with the people and institutions that had ruled the country in the past.[13] Nicolae Ceausescu had been party leader and virtual dictator of Romania since 1965. The centre of a bizarre personality cult, he had been declared a 'genius of the Carpathians', a 'Danube of thought' and 'the Chosen One'; his home village became a place of pilgrimage (in 1976 the earliest traces of *homo sapiens* were 'discovered' nearby), and on his sixty-second anniversary in 1982 he was declared divine. His wife Elena was a first deputy prime minister and a member of the party leadership, his son was first secretary in Transylvania and a candidate member of the leadership, and other relatives were in key ministerial or diplomatic positions (this was sometimes described as 'socialism in a single family'). As late as November 1989 there was little obvious threat to Ceausescu at the Romanian Communist Party's 14th Congress, officially dubbed a 'Congress of the Great Socialist Victory'; the leader's own six-hour speech was interrupted by no fewer than 125 standing ovations (these owed something to a man in the control room who switched on pre-recorded applause at the appropriate moments), and the resolutions that were adopted showed little sign of compromise. The regime, in any case, could dispose of a security police, the Securitate, that operated wherever necessary outside the framework of the law and indeed beyond national boundaries.[14]

The fall of the regime in fact began shortly afterwards, with demonstrations in the largely Hungarian city of Timisoara, which were crushed with exceptional ferocity. The protest nonetheless spread to other towns and cities and to the capital Bucharest, where Ceausescu, addressing a public rally on 21 December, was ignominiously shouted down. The following day he fled the capital in a helicopter so overloaded that one of the crew had to sit on his lap, but he was captured shortly afterwards and brought to trial after further street fighting had claimed thousands of lives. On 25 December Ceausescu and his wife were put on trial, sentenced to death for 'genocide' and summarily executed; reports began to circulate at the same time of the extraordinary opulence in which the former dictator had lived, including a house crammed with art treasures and a nuclear bunker lined with marble. The functions of government were carried on, after Ceausescu's overthrow, by the National Salvation Council, a coalition within which former communists were in a commanding position. At the multiparty elections that took place in May 1990 the Front and its presidential candidate, Ion Iliescu, won convincing victories; Iliescu, a former Politburo member, won again in 1992. Arguably, the personal dictatorship of Ceausescu had ended but the regime itself had continued.

The process of change in Czechoslovakia was a more peaceful one, but it was also initiated from below against a regime that showed little sign of flexibility after the democratic and socialist objectives of the 'Prague Spring' had been suppressed by the country's Warsaw Pact allies.[15] Gustav Husak, appointed Dubcek's successor as party leader in April 1969, had not been involved in the call for intervention, but he accepted the Soviet view that socialism itself had been threatened by 'counter-revolutionary forces' and that their defeat required the 'restoration of Marxist-Leninist principles in the policy of the party and in the activities of the state.'[16] Reformers were purged from the communist party, which lost about a third of its membership, and from other positions of influence; Dubcek became a woodcutter, others became taxi drivers or night watchmen. Others still 'adapted', like the manager of the fruit and vegetable shop in an essay by Vaclav Havel who displayed the slogan 'Workers of the world, unite!' in his window but without necessarily experiencing an 'irrepressible urge to acquaint the public with his ideals.'[17] At the same time there were signs of intellectual dissent with the publication of a manifesto by Charter 77, a loose grouping of campaigners 'for the respect of civil and human rights in our own country and throughout the world';[18] and a Committee for the Defence of the Unjustly Persecuted was founded the following year.

The election of Mikhail Gorbachev as CPSU General Secretary confronted the Czech leaders with a serious dilemma. They had always quoted the USSR as their model; but they could hardly adopt the reforming policies its leadership was now pursuing without conceding that their own policies had been mistaken for nearly twenty years, and perhaps prejudicing their position. In the end they compromised. A more modest version of perestroika was approved in 1987, involving a greater degree of factory self-management and financial accountability; at the same time party and government leaders continued to repudiate the Prague Spring and to insist (as Husak put it) that they were 'looking for their own solutions' and not simply following the reforms that were taking place in the USSR, in which their own people were taking a close interest (Gorbachev himself had a very warm reception when he paid a visit in April 1987).[19] There was also some leadership change: Husak remained President, a post he had assumed in 1975, but the party first secretaryship went to Milos Jakes in December 1987. Jakes had been directly responsible for the purging of reformists from party ranks after 1968 and his appointment was a sign that the regime might be prepared to consider economic reform in response to falling growth rates, but that there would be no political liberalisation.

The following year saw a deepening disenchantment, set against a background of worsening shortages. There was public pressure for a greater degree of religious tolerance, particularly in Slovakia, and a petition in favour of religious freedom, initiated by the Archbishop of Prague, attracted almost

600,000 signatures. But there was still more substantial pressure for political reform. In August 1988, 10,000 demonstrated on the twentieth anniversary of the Warsaw Pact invasion. Several thousand rallied once again on 28 October, which was the seventieth anniversary of the foundation of the state, and thousands more on 10 December, the fortieth anniversary of the Universal Declaration of Human Rights. And then for several days in January 1989 thousands gathered at the spot in Prague's Wenceslas Square where student Jan Palach had set himself alight in 1969 to protest against the invasion the previous year; the police had to use batons, dogs and tear gas to disperse the demonstrators, and dozens were arrested. A national appeal, 'Just a few sentences', appeared in June calling for more far-reaching democratisation and the opening of a dialogue between the authorities and the society; within a month it had attracted ten thousand signatures, by September there were forty thousand.[20]

The eruption of demonstrations in November 1989 was nonetheless a surprise to most observers, as well as to the party leadership.[21] Inspired by the success of oppositionists in Poland and East Germany and by the evidence that the 'Brezhnev doctrine' was no longer valid, students in Prague took the opportunity of an officially-sponsored demonstration on 17 November, organised to honour student victims of the Nazis fifty years earlier, to demand more radical changes including 'genuine perestroika' and 'free elections'. As many as 15,000 took part, more than had been expected; and the brutality of the police response – at least 150 were injured – led to a widening public protest, initially among intellectuals in the main cities, and then among a wider public. An umbrella committee, the Civic Forum, was set up on 19 November to coordinate opposition protests, led by the playwright and founder of Charter 77 Vaclav Havel, and dedicated to the achievement of a 'legal, democratic state in the spirit of the traditions of Czech statehood and of the international principles expressed in the Universal Declaration of Human Rights and the International Covenant on Civil and Political Rights';[22] its Slovak counterpart was called Public against Violence. Faced with this mounting tide of popular dissatisfaction Jakes and the entire party leadership were obliged to resign at a stormy Central Committee meeting that took place on 24 and 25 November; and there were promises that there would be freedom of travel, a new press law and competitive elections.

Events, however, had acquired their own momentum. Three-quarters of a million demonstrated on Letna plain in Prague on 25 and 26 November, which was 5 per cent of the entire population, and there was a general strike the following day in which half the country was reported to have taken part. The Federal Assembly, meanwhile, voted to remove the leading role of the communist party from the constitution and withdrew its condemnation of the Prague Spring. A new coalition government was formed on 3 December with five noncommunist members, but it was unable to generate public confidence and resigned four days later. On 10 December President Husak swore in a 'government of national understanding' and himself resigned. The new government was headed by Marian Calfa, a Slovak reform communist, but it had a noncommunist majority; it was to hold office, in any event, only until new parliamentary elections could be held. On 28 December Alexander Dubcek, the hero of 1968, was elected speaker of parliament, and on 29 December Vaclav Havel, under arrest at the start of the year, was unanimously elected President. Their first task was to arrange for the elections, which took place in June 1990 and at which the Civic Forum took about half the vote in the Czech lands and Public against Violence about a third in Slovakia. It had been a quick but civilised change of regime and it became known as the 'velvet revolution'.

POLITICAL CHANGE FROM ABOVE

The end of communist rule was often the result of 'people power', as in the case of Czechoslovakia; but there were also changes 'from above', initiated by the regime itself. In Bulgaria it was party reformers that led the way, encouraged by the democratising changes that Gorbachev had been promoting in the USSR (the two countries, as Zhivkov once remarked, had a 'single circulatory system'). Party leader Todor Zhivkov, in power since 1954, set the process in motion with a speech in July 1987 that called for a shift from 'power in the name of the people to power by means of the people' and for a 'selfmanaging society'.[23] The changes became known as the 'July Concept'; later, in 1988, Zhivkov developed them into a Bulgarian version of perestroika.[24] The reforms, however, were implemented without conviction, and Zhivkov himself became increasingly arbitrary and corrupt: his speeches and writings appeared in large editions, prompting locals to remark that he was the 'only man who had ever written more books than he had read',[25] and his son was appointed to a senior position in the party apparatus. Dissidents, including a developing environmental movement, were treated harshly, many of the country's Turkish minority were forced to emigrate, and two potential rivals were forced out of office and expelled from the party in July 1988.

There were public demonstrations against the regime in October and again in early November 1989, which were the largest the country had experienced since the end of the Second World War. But Zhivkov's fall from power shortly afterwards was less the result of pressure of this kind than of the judgement of his party colleagues, in a close vote in the Politburo on 9 November, that he had become a threat to their collective survival. The new party leader was Petur Mladenov, who had been foreign minister since 1971 and apparently enjoyed Moscow's confidence. Under his guidance the party expelled Zhivkov and his son for 'serious violations of basic party and moral principles', and went on to condemn the 'dictatorship of a clan' that they had established.[26] A new party programme, adopted in February 1990, committed the party to 'democratic socialism' in Bulgaria, and to 'democratic and free elections' at the earliest opportunity; the party itself was renamed the Bulgarian Socialist Party, with a red rose rather than a hammer and sickle as its symbol.[27] Round-table talks meanwhile began with a newly formed Union of Democratic Forces; an agreement was reached at the end of March that provided for elections to a new parliament, which would approve a new constitution. At those elections, in June 1990, the former communists took a commanding 53 per cent of the vote; at further elections, in October 1991, they were forced into second place, but in December 1994 they returned to power with 44 per cent of the vote and an overall majority in the Bulgarian parliament.

In Hungary the suppression of the 1956 revolution had been followed by an attempt to develop a national consensus under party leader Janos Kadar, based upon his formula that 'whoever is not against us is with us.'[28] A cautious economic reform, the New Economic Mechanism, was launched in 1968, and the scope that was available for public debate and for private economic initiative steadily widened. By the 1980s, however, the economy had begun to falter, and there was increasingly open opposition from the cultural intelligentsia and from movements like the Democratic Forum, which was founded in 1987 as a framework for intellectual discussion. The construction of a new dam on the Danube, agreed with the Austrian government in late 1985, had given rise to particular concern among environmentalists. Meanwhile the regime itself began to experience pressure for change as reformers within its ranks extended the boundaries of permitted debate. Some used the columns of the party press to argue that parliament rather than the party leadership should be the locus of political authority; others were drawn into the preparation of statements that reflected the views of independent economists such as *Turnabout and Reform*, a call for more far-reaching reform that was circulated in late 1986. Another reform manifesto, 'A new social contract', appeared the following year, calling directly for political pluralism.[29]

The regime responded in a variety of ways, including personnel change. There was a new prime minister in 1987, Karoly Grocz; the following year Grosz took over the party leadership when Kadar and his supporters lost their positions and a young economist, Miklos Nemeth, became prime minister (Kadar himself died the following year). Action of some sort was clearly necessary if Hungary's rising foreign debt – the largest in the communist world – was to be contained, and it was agreed at a party conference in May 1988 that political as well as economic reform would be required, perhaps even a form of 'socialist pluralism'.[30] But there were divisions within the regime itself in the face of these pressures. Party reformers like Imre Pozsgay, a former minister of culture who was rumoured to be Gorbachev's candidate for the leadership, were willing to move towards a Western-style political pluralism with open elections and a choice of party; they were greatly encouraged by the Soviet leader's visit to Hungary in June 1986 and by his close interest in their experience of economic reform, and they were organised in a series of 'reform circles' that operated within party ranks. But others (including Grosz) stood for no more than a modified party ascendancy, although they were willing to accept publicly that the leadership had no 'monopoly of wisdom to solve Hungary's problems.' It would be 'decades', Grosz told *Le Monde* in November 1988, before Hungary could consider a move to multi-party democracy.[31]

The decisive change took place, as elsewhere, during 1989. In January, taking advantage of Grosz's temporary absence in Switzerland, Pozsgay used a radio interview to make public the conclusions of a Central Committee commission on the post-war history of Hungary, which described the events of 1956 as a 'popular uprising against an oligarchic system of power which had humiliated the nation' and went on to describe the 'socialist model' adopted in 1948–49 as 'wrong in its entirety'.[32] In February, following a Central Committee meeting, the party authorities announced that they would be introducing a new constitution in which the party would no longer have a guaranteed monopoly of power, and that they would be prepared to share power in a coalition government.[33] In May party reformers went further, drastically cutting back the nomenklatura system of control over appointments, dissolving the party militia and calling for a dialogue with other political forces.[34] In mid-September, after three months of round-table negotiations, the party leadership agreed to hold fresh presidential and parliamentary elections and also approved a new electoral law and depoliticisation of the armed forces.[35] In October, finally, a party congress was held at which a majority of delegates agreed to form a European-style Hungarian Socialist Party, committed to democratic socialism and a mixed economy;[36] a minority of hardliners, including Grosz, managed to preserve the formal existence of a Hungarian Socialist Workers' Party based on orthodox Marxist values. Hungary, meanwhile, became an 'republic' once again and not the 'people's republic' it had become in 1949.

Among the many new parties that emerged in these new circumstances, several were of particular significance.[37] One was the Hungarian Democratic Forum, which stood for an amalgam of populist, Christian and nationalist values and a uniquely Hungarian 'third way' that combined political pluralism, support for the traditional family and the defence of Hungarian interests, including Hungarian minorities abroad, tinged in some cases with anti-Semitism. An Alliance of Free Democrats was the successor to the intellectual opposition that had emerged in the 1970s; it stood for a more Western but also a more socially oriented form of liberal democracy than the nationalist HDF, and had more support in the towns than in the countryside. Both held their first national congresses in March 1989. An Alliance of Young Democrats (FIDESz), meanwhile, had been established a year earlier with a broadly social democratic orientation, and with a youthful membership (it was limited to those aged under thirty-five). Party reformers had hoped there would be a presidential election in early 1990, before the parliamentary election that was due later in the year and before oppositional parties could develop their strength; but this proposal was defeated by a narrow margin at a referendum in November 1989, which showed that the Socialists were not invincible. By the time the election was called in the spring of 1990 more than eighty other parties had come into existence, of which 48 were intending to nominate candidates.[38]

The election took place in two rounds, in March and April 1990. The Democratic Forum was the clear winner, with 42.5 per cent of the vote on a turnout of about 65 per cent. The Alliance of Free Democrats came second with 23.8 per cent and the Independent Smallholders, also anti-communist, were third with 11.4 per cent. The former communists, campaigning as the Hungarian Socialist Party, had to be content with fourth place and just 8.6 per cent of the vote.[39] A coalition government was formed under Jozsef Antall, a medical historian and leader of the Hungarian Democratic Forum whose father, a smallholder, had served in the post-war government. The presidency went to Arpad Goncz, a writer and Free Democrat who had spent six years in prison for his part in the 1956 revolution; and with some hesitation, the new government embarked upon the path of market and political reform that had been marked out elsewhere in Eastern Europe. There had been virtually no nationwide strikes or anti-government demonstrations, and no loss of life; instead of this a 'gigantic negotiating machinery' came into operation, involving at least a thousand meetings or discussions and at least as many that were less formally constituted. Not surprisingly, it became known as a 'negotiated revolution'.[40]

The most fundamental change of all took place in what used to be the USSR: fundamental in that it was the largest and most powerful of the communist-ruled countries, and in that it defined the parameters within which the East European states could operate. The USSR had used its military might to crush the Hungarian revolution of 1956, and led its Warsaw Treaty allies into Czechoslovakia to suppress the Prague Spring in 1968. But under Gorbachev, the Brezhnev doctrine was replaced by what his press spokesman jokingly labelled the 'Sinatra doctrine', under which the states of Eastern Europe were free to do it 'their way'. The Soviet leadership at this time, indeed, not simply permitted but sometimes instigated political reform in Eastern Europe of a kind that was greater than local leaderships were prepared to contemplate. The extent to which they directly intervened in the process of change is still unclear, but they certainly encouraged the opposition to Todor Zhivkov and Erich Honecker, and the student demonstrations that swept Jakes from power in Czechoslovakia.[41] Gorbachev's own view was that 'miscalculations by the ruling parties' had been the main reason for their difficulties, and he was clearly sympathetic to local party reformers who were more in line with his own approach to the kinds of issues they all confronted.[42]

There had been little indication that changes of this kind were likely in March 1985 when a stocky Politburo member from the south of Russia became general secretary of what was still a united and ruling party. Gorbachev, according to his wife at least, had not expected the nomination and spent some time deciding whether to accept it. All that was clear was (in a phrase that later became famous) 'we can't go on like this'.[43] Gorbachev told the Politburo meeting that agreed to nominate him that there was 'no need to change our policies',[44] and there was little public evidence of his objectives, or even of his personal background. He had not addressed a party congress, and had no published collection of writings to his name; and he had made only a couple of important visits abroad, to Canada and the United Kingdom, as head of a parliamentary delegation. Only a few important speeches – in particular an address to an ideology conference in December 1984 and an electoral address in February 1985, which mentioned *glasnost*, social justice and participation – gave some indication of his priorities.[45]

Of all the policies that were promoted by the Gorbachev leadership, *glasnost* was probably the most distinctive. *Glasnost*, usually translated as 'openness' or 'publicity', did not mean an unqualified freedom of the press or the right to information; nor was it original to Gorbachev. It did, however, reflect the new General Secretary's belief that without a greater awareness of the real state of affairs and of the considerations that had led to particular decisions there would be no willingness on the part of the Soviet people to commit themselves to his programme of reconstruction or perestroika. 'The better people are informed', Gorbachev told the Central Committee meeting that elected him, 'the more consciously they act, the more actively they support the party, its plans and programmatic objectives.'[46] This led to a more open treatment of social problems such as drugs, prostitution and crime; it also led to a more honest consideration of the Soviet past, including the 'wanton repressive measures' of the 1930s (as Gorbachev put it in a speech on the anniversary of the revolution in 1987), and to an attempt to root out the corruption that had become established during the Brezhnev years.

The 'democratisation' of Soviet political life, of which *glasnost* was a part, was also intended to release the political energies that, for Gorbachev, had been choked off by the bureaucratic centralisation that developed during the Stalin years. The political system established by the October revolution, he told the 19th Party Conference in 1988, had undergone 'serious deformations', leading to the development of a 'command-administrative system' that had extinguished the democratic potential of the elected soviets. The role of the bureaucratic apparatus had increased out of all proportion, with more than a hundred central ministries and eight hundred in the republics. And it was this 'ossified system of government, with its command-and-pressure mechanism', that had become the main obstacle to change.[47] The Party Conference duly adopted a resolution on 'radical reform' of the political system which provided for a choice of candidate in elections to the soviets, with secret and competitive elections to their executive committees for a maximum of two consecutive terms. There would also be a working parliament for the first time in Soviet history; and all of this would be sustained by a 'rule of law state', within which the rights of ordinary citizens would be securely protected.[48]

Together with these changes, for Gorbachev, there had to be a 'radical reform' of the Soviet economy and an attempt to reverse a decline in the rate of economic growth that had been worsening since the 1950s. In the late 1970s, in the view of Soviet as well as Western commentators, economic growth had probably fallen to zero. Indeed, as Gorbachev explained in early 1988, if the sale of alcoholic drink and of Soviet oil on world markets were excluded, there had been no real growth in the Soviet economy for at least the previous fifteen years.[49] Radical reform, as Gorbachev explained to the 27th Party Congress in 1986 and to a Central Committee meeting the following year, involved a set of related measures. One of the most important was a greater degree of independence for factory managers, allowing them to be guided much more by 'market' indicators than by directives from the central planners. Retail and wholesale prices would gradually be adjusted to reflect the cost of production, and enterprises that persistently failed to pay their way might be liquidated. Farming would increasingly be devolved to family units, there would be a greater diversity of forms of property, and there would be a closer relationship between the Soviet and the international economy, including a fully convertible ruble.

In the end, the search for a 'third way' that would combine these more democratic forms with a high degree of social equality proved impossible to realise. More open elections, in 1989 and 1990, led not to the return of committed reformers but to the success of nationalist movements in several of the republics, and to the triumph of Boris Yeltsin in the Russian presidential elections of 1991 (Gorbachev himself was elected President by the Soviet parliament in the spring of 1990 and never enjoyed the authority that a popular mandate would have conferred upon him). The opportunity to organise outside the framework of the CPSU led to 'informal' movements and then to political parties that were openly hostile to the CPSU and to socialism. There were demonstrations on an enormous scale, not in support of the 'humane and democratic socialism' to which the party was now committed but (in early 1990) for the removal of its political monopoly from the constitution. And writers and academics, taking advantage of the greater scope that glasnost made available to them, moved towards an explicit critique of Lenin as the founder of a 'totalitarian' system and on to a more general attack on revolutions as the progenitors of violence and repression.

Perhaps the most serious failure of all was in the economy, where the old structures of planning were dismantled but without any effective market mechanisms to replace them. Economic growth sustained itself for two or three years, but the economy contracted by 4 per cent in 1990 and then by a massive 15 per cent in 1991 as the state itself collapsed.[50] Greater autonomy for enterprises meant, at least in the short term, that they could put up prices more easily, reduce their workforces and eliminate less profitable forms of output.

One consequence was serious shortages, including soap and washing powder. 'What kind of a regime is it if we can't even get washed?', asked an indignant group of workers from the Vladimir region. A Moscow housewife threatened to send her washing directly to the ministry concerned: 'If they can't provide us with soap let them do the washing themselves', she reasoned.[51] Another consequence was a significant increase in poverty, as prices raced ahead of earnings and especially pensions; the budgetary deficit widened; and open unemployment emerged for the first time since the end of the 1920s. Gorbachev, his spokesman told the press, had won the Nobel Prize for Peace but not for Economics; anyone who read the plan results for these years would have understood why.

The decisive moment in the collapse of communist rule in the USSR was almost certainly the attempted coup that took place in August 1991. Gorbachev was placed under house arrest at his summer residence in the Crimea when he refused to declare a state of emergency, and in the early hours of 19 August a self-styled 'state emergency committee' announced that he was 'unwell' and that his powers as Soviet president were being assumed by vice-president Yanaev. The Soviet people, warned the conspirators, were in 'mortal danger'. The country had become 'ungovernable'. The economy was in crisis, with a 'chaotic, unregulated slide towards a market'. And crime and immorality were rampant.[52] But the coup was resisted from the outset by Boris Yeltsin, who made a dramatic appeal for resistance from a tank in front of the Russian parliament building. And the following night, an estimated 70,000 Muscovites surrounded the building in spite of a curfew and protected it against an expected attack. The next day the coup began to collapse – two of the leaders, it emerged, had been drunk for most of its duration – and by the day after the conspirators had been arrested and Gorbachev had been released.

The coup had not, in fact, been launched by the Communist Party, but the party leadership did little to resist it and the collapse of the attempted coup allowed Boris Yeltsin to order its dissolution. On 23 August, in the Russian parliament, he signed a decree suspending the CPSU throughout the Russian Federation; in November he ordered it banned entirely, and seized its property. The Soviet Union was a still greater casualty of the coup. Launched to block the signature of a treaty that would have reconstituted the USSR as a loose confederation, the coup led directly to a series of declarations of independence by the republics and to their assumption of full international sovereignty. The three Baltic republics left in September 1991. And after Ukraine had voted overwhelmingly for full independence in a referendum in early December, the three Slavic republics signed a declaration that established a new Commonwealth of Independent States, withdrawing at the same time from the treaty of union of 1922 that had established the USSR. Most of the other republics joined the CIS shortly afterwards, and Boris Yeltsin moved into Gorbachev's office in the Kremlin when the Soviet president resigned on 25 December. The post-Soviet era had begun.

It was still a little unclear why the world's first socialist state had collapsed so quickly and unexpectedly. Was it, for instance, the result of the falling rates of economic growth that had been experienced since 1990 and of the strain on the 'social contract' that they imposed? Perhaps; but national income fell much more sharply, by 15 to 20 per cent, in the early post-communist years without the same kind of consequences. Was it a repudiation of the CPSU and of its political legacy? To some extent; but there was no popular support for an anti-communist opposition of the kind that had swept across Eastern Europe, including the Baltic; and the party, when it was allowed to revive in 1993, was soon the largest in terms of a mass membership and it was the most successful of all the parties that contested the parliamentary elections in December 1995. Had people, then, rejected Marxism-Leninism? But the party, in the draft programme it adopted in July 1991, had already moved to a broadly social democratic position, and there was still strong support, if opinion polls were any guide, for state ownership and comprehensive social welfare. Even the USSR had hardly been repudiated: 76 per cent had supported the idea of a 'reformed federation' in a referendum in March 1991, and almost as many were prepared to support it long after it had disappeared. What had been rejected, and what had been retained, was still unclear years after the demise of the world's first socialist society.

The transition from communist rule, initiated in 1989, was still, in some senses, incomplete in the mid–1990s. In some cases former communists were winning back a share of power: in Poland, in the parliamentary elections that took place in 1993 and the presidential elections in 1995; in Bulgaria, as we have seen; and in Lithuania, in parliamentary elections in 1992 and presidential elections that took place in 1993. In other cases, like Romania, Serbia and Slovakia, the governments that were in office in the mid–1990s were heavily influenced by the personnel and policies of their predecessors. Further afield, former communists seemed to have established themselves as a parliamentary party in Mongolia, winning the elections that took place in 1990, though further elections in 1996 swept them from power. Meanwhile, communist power was still secure in China, with its 1.2 billion people, although it coexisted with an economy that had been turned over substantially to private enterprise. Communists had lost power in Cambodia, after internationally supervised elections in 1993; but in Cuba, in Laos, in North Korea and Vietnam there was no sign that their monopoly of power was about to be surrendered or seized by popular insurrection.

The ambiguity of change was clearly apparent in the countries with which this volume is primarily concerned. In Czechoslovakia, power had been taken 'from below'; but there was no mandate for the separation of the state itself into Czech and Slovak republics that took place at the end of 1992. In Hungary, political change had come about 'from above', but under the pressure of a deteriorating economy and an increasingly outspoken opposition. In the USSR political change had begun 'from above', with an ambitious plan for a democratic socialism for which there was assumed to be popular support; but once competitive elections had been introduced the initiative passed from the party to the wider society, and to nationalists and anti-communists. In some cases, the new rulers had formerly been political prisoners (like Havel); in others, they were former Communist officials (like Leonid Kravchuk in Ukraine and Boris Yeltsin in Russia). Just as there was no single 'transition', we may conclude, there was no single 'postcommunism' but rather a group of states that reflected the diverse past of the countries concerned as well as the variety of values that informed the choices their citizens were now free to exercise.

A WIDER PERSPECTIVE

There is now an extensive – and growing – literature on what has been termed 'transitology'.[53] The transition to some form of democracy in most of Eastern Europe and the former Soviet Union has generated enormous interest in the issue of whether there are common patterns, or even a model, which can help us to understand the determinants of successful transitions. The remarkable geographical range of the 'third wave' of democratisation (encompassing not just East-Central Europe and the former Soviet Union, but also Southern Europe and Latin America), as well as its seeming success, suggest that there may well be some explanatory key which unlocks the door to democracy. If the vital variables can be identified, then the continued spread of democracy might not only be accurately predicted, but also successfully encouraged and managed.

In practice, much of the literature on transitions to democracy which purports to develop explanatory frameworks – or models – instead provides taxonomies or typologies. Thus, there are abundant examples of different 'paths' to democratic transition identified in the literature, but few of these offer a genuinely explanatory framework.[54] We undoubtedly have a much more sophisticated understanding than used to be the case of the *ways* in which regimes democratise, and also of the central importance of various actors and institutions: élite accommodation, constitutional design, 'founding elections', electoral structure and party systems are all recognised as crucial factors in the success or failure of democratic transition.[55] Nevertheless, it can be argued that much recent research has primarily contributed to what might be termed 'deep description', providing ever more nuanced accounts of transitional processes. Sadly, descriptive detail is all too often purchased only at the expense of analytical insight.

This is in no sense to decry the search for general patterns in transitions to democracy: comparative analysis is essential to any attempt to isolate explanatory variables. Yet, for all that the recent research has refined our understanding of the complexity and variety of modes of regime transition, the central analytical debate effectively remains one over the respective role of 'agency' versus 'structure'. Sometimes referred to as 'genetic' and 'functionalist', these approaches revolve around the issue of whether transitions are 'determined' by structural developments which lie outside the direct control of individuals, or whether they can be brought about through the intentional design of autonomous agents, unconstrained by any such structural conditions. Attempts have certainly been made to reconcile the two positions – notably by Przeworski – but, ultimately, most such efforts end up privileging one position over the other. Indeed, it may not even be possible in epistemological terms to achieve a genuine compromise between the two approaches: arguably, the foundations upon which they are constructed must be seen as mutually exclusive. Our concern here, though, is not with the issue of structure versus agency, nor even with the broader question of investigating the process of *transition* in Russia, Ukraine, the Czech Republic, Slovakia and Hungary.

Our study starts instead from the contention that some form of democracy, however imperfect or immature, had been established in each of the countries in question prior to our surveys. The question of how and why these democracies came into being is naturally of immense importance, but lies outside the specific focus of our analysis. Nevertheless, the *context* within which democratic regimes were established in these countries is of considerable relevance for our study: values and attitudes are not simply 'givens', but instead are shaped and influenced by a host of factors. It is in terms of these contextual issues that a comparative dimension can perhaps be most useful, allowing consideration of whether there are common modalities in the development of democratic attitudes in newly-established democracies. As this study will make clear, there are distinct differences between countries in the FSU and ECE (and, to a lesser extent, within them) in terms of attitudes and values, even though broad support for democratic norms is evident throughout the countries that we consider.

Some analysts have argued that the Latin American experience of democracy punctuated by military intervention may be of particular relevance as a comparative example, pointing in particular to the instability generated by economic crisis and hyper-inflation. However, there is little evidence that the 'coup mentality' which has afflicted Latin America finds any direct parallel in the former communist regimes: the short-lived and unsuccessful coup of August 1991 in Russia represents the only serious military threat to democratisation in the countries that we examine – and a more appropriate comparison might be with the attempted coup of February 1981 in Spain, led by Lieutenant-Colonel Antonio Tejero. The so-called *Tejerazo* was a desperate effort by discontented sectors of the military to halt the process of democratisation; its failure restored the initiative firmly to the democratic political class. In general throughout the former communist regimes, the military-as-institution has not adopted the central *political* role familiar from the Latin American experience, even though several military figures, such as former General Alexander Lebed in Russia, have achieved political prominence through the democratic process.

Rather than Latin America, it may be more profitable to focus on other European examples of post-dictatorial transitions to democracy. The former communist regimes at least form part of the same land mass as the rest of Europe, and in the case of much of eastern Europe, share similar historical and cultural legacies; indeed, it was the former Soviet leader, Mikhail Gorbachev, who spoke of a 'common European home' stretching from Lisbon to Vladivostok. Within Europe, the obvious examples to consider are, on the one hand, the post-Second World War restorations of democracy in the former Axis powers of (West) Germany and Italy and, on the other, the Iberian transitions to democracy in the mid–1970s. The case of Spain, in particular, has often been seen as a 'model' transition, offering a paradigmatic example of how to move successfully from an authoritarian to a democratic regime.[56] However, there were crucial and immensely significant differences between all these earlier transitions to democracy and those which took place in the former communist regimes. These differences go beyond the obvious ones of temporal dimension and geographical location, and refer instead to the *nature* of regime transition. Of huge significance in the cases of Germany and Italy was the fact that their transitions were 'externally monitored' with the victorious Allies closely supervising the restoration of democracy. Indeed, democracy was not an option freely chosen by the citizens of Germany and Italy: no options were on offer.

In the Iberian case, again there were critical differences – not only between Iberia and the former communist regimes, but also between the Spanish and Portuguese experiences of transition. Although Spain has often been presented as an 'ideal type', the Portuguese case represents a closer parallel in terms of the process of transition. The dictatorship which had ruled Portugal since the 1920s first under Antonio Salazar, and then Marcello Caetano, was eventually overthrown in April 1974 through a popular uprising following a coup by discontented officers in the Armed Forces Movement (MFA). As would later occur in several of the former communist regimes, the groundswell of popular resistance to the dictatorship rapidly became an unstoppable torrent. Thus, to the extent that the dictatorship was abruptly ended by mass action, the Portuguese experience prefigured that of countries such as Czechoslovakia and Romania. Similarly, the political uncertainty and rapid changes of government which followed the overthrow of the Portuguese dictatorship would find a parallel in many of the former communist regimes. Where Portugal's experience differs from that of Russia and East-Central Europe is in its lack of ethnic division and conflict: the Portuguese nation is one of the most ethnically homogeneous in Europe. Equally, the initial process of transition in Portugal followed precisely the reverse pattern to that in the former communist regimes, with the Portuguese Communist Party under Alvaro Cunhal exercising major political influence and promoting mass-scale nationalisation of leading industries as well as land occupation. Indeed, the Portuguese Constitution of 1975 committed the country to socialism, a provision which was not removed until several years later.

In the case of Spain, the differences were even more marked. The Spanish transition came about not through any dramatic rupture with the Franco dictatorship, but through a peaceful process of negotiated settlement which took place entirely within the bounds of constitutional legality. The Franco regime was dismantled 'from within', not just 'from above', through negotiations led principally by Adolfo Suárez, a former Francoist *apparatchik*. Critically, those who framed and directed Spain's transition to democracy paid particular attention to accommodating those who had been leading protagonists in the Franco regime. There was no purge of personnel associated with the dictatorship, and special care was taken to avoid antagonising the army (resulting, for instance, in the highly sensitive legalisation of the Communist Party being left until just weeks before the 1977 elections). Consensus and elite accommodation were the keys to successful transition in Spain. However, that consensus cannot be divorced from Spain's specific historic experiences in the twentieth century: in particular, the Civil War of 1936–39 which culminated in establishment of the Franco dictatorship. The almost universal desire to avoid the kind of political polarisation that might lead to another civil war resulted in what has often been referred to as a *pacto del olvido*, a tacit agreement to engage in collective amnesia. It was this agreement not to rake over the past which allowed for the remarkable consensus that characterised the Spanish transition; and yet it was an agreement that depended upon the specific legacy of a given country, which was not necessarily exportable to others.

It is precisely the issue of legacies – cultural, historical and political – that has provided a focus of debate over the likely success or failure of democratic transition and consolidation. This is linked to the 'structure' versus 'agency' argument: at its most basic, do countries follow particular patterns of development which dispose them to a given form of political organisation, either more or less favourable to democracy? Such is the argument developed in the classic study by Barrington Moore, *Social Origins of Dictatorship and Democracy*.[57] Counter arguments take two basic forms. On the one hand, it is argued by some (for instance, Di Palma[58]) that the success or otherwise of democratic establishment is in no sense conditional upon historical legacies, since democracy relies on the active choice of citizens. On the other hand, a functionalist approach suggests that there is a necessary, if not yet precisely specified, link between a given country's level of socio-economic development and democratisation.[59] Once a certain level of development has been achieved, then democracy follows almost inevitably. More recent research has emphasised the significance of the relative distribution of income, rather than its absolute level.[60]

Whatever position one adopts on these issues, it remains the case that a democratic form does not guarantee its content. In other words, establishing the infrastructures of democracy – however that comes about – cannot ensure that democracy will function effectively, or even survive. Democracies require democrats. But more than this, they require a democratic culture that will encourage the development of system-supportive attitudes amongst the mass of the population. Tolerance, respect for the views of political opponents, belief in the rule of law and in political accountability – all of these are crucial to the survival prospects of any democratic regime. The extent to which they are able to develop, however, is inevitably conditioned by political and cultural legacies. Thus, where ethnic tensions are high, but have been held in check through some form of political repression – for instance, in the former Yugoslavia and in parts of Russia, such as Chechnya – it can be virtually impossible to develop more tolerant, pluralist norms once the source of that repression has been lifted. Hence the dramatic emergence of ethnically-based nationalist demands throughout much of the former Soviet Union. Even in countries where ethnic tension has stopped short of violence, such as in Czechoslovakia, it proved impossible to reach an accommodation that would have allowed the state to survive. The problem is not confined, of course, to newly democratising countries: well-established democracies – such as Belgium – can fall prey to creeping intolerance between ethnic groups, placing the continued survival of the current political structure under threat.

We may do best, in the end, to avoid placing the Russian and East-Central European experience too readily into categories that have been developed in other contexts. The East European countries, unlike those of Latin America and southern Europe, have been engaged in a dual process of transition, from public ownership to a form of capitalism as well as from the rule of a single party to a more pluralist form of government. Some, as in Latin America, were redemocratising after forty years of communist rule; others, like the former Soviet republics, were developing democracy more or less 'from scratch'.[61] Nor was it a process of change that moved in a single direction, any more than the first or second waves of democratisation had done in the years after the First and Second World Wars.[62] The former Soviet republics in central Asia, for instance, were moving in the 1990s towards new forms of authoritarian control that allowed less scope for public discussion and contestation than had been available in the later years of Soviet rule. And some of the democracies that emerged, most notably in Russia, were based on competitive elections and a wide range of formal liberties but with a very weak party system, widespread official corruption, an overly strong executive and a negligible parliament. In this book we focus on countries that can reasonably be described as 'postcommunist' but not necessarily as 'fully consolidated democracies'. They are interesting in themselves; they share elements of common experience and common problems; but they are not necessarily proceeding along a route already mapped out by other countries at other times and in other places.[63] So we shall try to respond to the concern some have expressed that 'scholars should stop writing about East Europe [in a comparative context] and begin to make the actual comparison.' We agree that 'It's time to get to work';[64] and we have sought to do so.

3 Methodology and Context

Since our findings and conclusions in later chapters are based upon intensive analysis of our surveys of public and parliamentary opinion in the FSU/ECE, we should begin by describing the design, content and political context of those surveys. Although our focus is on political values which are relatively slow changing aspects of political opinion, they may not be totally unaffected by political events. At the least, proper interpretation of even the most general of attitudes towards 'government' needs to take some account of who is in government at the time.

Our surveys focus on the state of public and parliamentary opinion between four and five years after the excitements of 1989, when the first flush of revolutionary enthusiasm had passed and the costs, as well as the benefits, of the transition from communism had become more visible. They provide possibilities for a wide range of comparative analyses and a solid baseline for the study of subsequent trends. We have also included an interim update survey which gives some indication of trends up to 1996 within Russia, but a more comprehensive study of trends will require a more extensive replication of our original surveys.

ELEVEN FSU/ECE SURVEYS

Altogether we carried out eleven different but closely related surveys, at two levels, in five countries, interviewing 7,350 members of the general public and 504 Members of Parliament. The design of this set of surveys allows a wide variety of different comparisons to be made. We began, at the end of 1993, with surveys of public opinion in the two principal countries of the FSU (Russia and Ukraine) and three countries of ECE (Hungary, Slovakia and the Czech Republic). That allows comparison between countries, or between blocs of countries such as the FSU versus ECE – as well as within-country analyses. Because a snap election had been declared in Russia for 12 December, we carried out two surveys in Russia, one just before that election, the other just after it. That allows comparison of opinion before, after, and even during an election campaign; and an investigation of very short term trends. A year later, at the end of 1994, we carried out surveys of MPs in Russia, Ukraine, Hungary and the Czech Republic[1] which allow us to compare the opinions of MPs with the opinions of their electorates. Finally we carried out an interim update survey of public opinion in Russia in January–February 1996 which allows some investigation of medium term trends.

All our surveys of public opinion used multi-stage clustered random samples of the population aged over 18 years, based on the normal methods of sampling in their respective countries, though the precise method varied from country to country according to national practices which, in turn, reflected the availability of data and the degree of cooperation afforded by government agencies. There were 118 sample points in the Czech Republic, 201 in Slovakia, 100 in Hungary, and 100 in Ukraine, with one interviewer at each sample point. Our Russian surveys used 185 interviewers at 128 sample points. Unlike some other surveys,[2] ours were all designed to be representative of the entire country including eastern as well as western Russia, and rural as well as urban areas. Refusal and non-completion rates were low; so that the overall response rate in the surveys of the general public was about 80 per cent.

After initial reluctance by party bureaucracies in some countries, MPs proved very cooperative, and they were sampled in proportion to the numbers in each parliamentary faction. They included some of the most senior political leaders in their countries. The size, dates and survey director of each survey is shown in the Table 3.1.[3]

Table 3.1: Five countries, two levels, eleven surveys: 1993–1996

	Surveys of public opinion		*Surveys of MPs' opinions*	
	Interview dates	*Number interviewed*	*Interview dates*	*Number interviewed*
Russia	25 Nov–9 Dec 1993	1095	4 Oct–8 Dec 1994	128
	12 Dec 1993–13 Jan 1994	1046		
	12 Jan–7 Feb 1996	1581		
Ukraine	3–15 Dec 1993	1000	15–18 Nov 1994	132
Hungary	20 Nov–6 Dec 1993	988	26 Oct–15 Dec 1994	110
Slovakia	2–12 Dec 1993	667	na	none
Czech Rep	23 Nov–10 Dec 1993	973	11 Oct–3 Nov 1994	134
TOTAL		7350		504

Note: Our FSU/ECE surveys were carried out under the direction of:
(in Russia) Elena Bashkirova of ROMIR, Moscow;
(in Ukraine) Tatyana Koshechkina of the Institute of Sociology, Ukraine Academy of Sciences and later Socis-Gallup, Kyiv;
(in Hungary) Emoke Lengyel of MODUS, Budapest;
(in Slovakia and the Czech Republic) Ladislav Koppl of OPW Opinion Window, Prague.

QUESTIONNAIRES

Precise comparison was aided by the fact that exactly the same questions were used, as far as possible, in the different surveys. All six of the original public opinion surveys used the same basic questionnaire modified only to take account of the different parties and political personalities in different countries and, in the case of Russia, some changes of tense between the wordings used before and after the election. Interviews in Russia were conducted in Russian; in Hungary in Hungarian; and in the Czech Republic in Czech. But in Ukraine respondents were interviewed in Ukrainian or Russian depending on their preference; and in Slovakia they were interviewed in Slovak or Hungarian again depending on their preference. To facilitate Hungarian language interviews with the relatively small linguistic minority in Slovakia, interviewers in Slovakia were equipped with a copy of the Hungarian translation. In Ukraine, which was divided much more evenly into Russian and Ukrainian speakers, two different versions of the questionnaire were used on an equal basis, and the Russian-language questionnaire for Ukraine was translated independently from the Russian-language questionnaire used in Russia in order to take proper account of Russian as spoken in Ukraine.

For MPs, the same questionnaire was used again, but with questions about political interest and participation removed because they would probably have irritated the MPs and/or produced obvious answers; with most social background questions removed to prevent individual MPs being identified and thereby maintain confidentiality; and with a few minor changes, mainly of tense, to take account of the different point in time – for example, in questions referring to the Hungarian election of spring 1994 which occurred after the survey of public opinion, but before the survey of MPs. For our interim update survey of Russian public opinion in 1996 we repeated only 13 of the many attitudinal questions used in the earlier surveys.

With the exception of that relatively short interim update survey, interviews with the public averaged out at just over an hour per interview, slightly less than average in Hungary but substantially longer than average in Slovakia. That length of interview allowed us to ask sufficient questions both to avoid over-reliance on the quirks of particular questions and to investigate some subtle shades of opinion towards, for example, different aspects of nationalism, or different elements of socialist values.

The questions were drafted (in English) at Glasgow University, then discussed and revised with our FSU/ECE partners. They were initially translated by our FSU/ECE partners, but the translations were then checked by language experts (including native speakers of Czech, Slovak and Hungarian) at Glasgow University and the translations discussed and revised in cooperation with our FSU/ECE partners. That was followed by a total of 113 pilot interviews (18 in the Czech Republic, 10 in Slovakia, 20 in Hungary, 20 in Ukraine and 45 in Russia) and, after a series of discussions with our FSU/ECE partners held in London, Prague, Budapest, Kyiv, Moscow and St Petersburg, a major revision of the questionnaire to take account of feedback from the pilot interviews.

In addition to these eleven FSU/ECE surveys we shall make limited use of a two level survey of public and politicians' attitudes towards somewhat similar questions in Britain – also carried out by Glasgow University at much the same time as our FSU/ECE surveys. That allows us to view FSU/ECE opinion in a western perspective, though the questions in the British survey were often somewhat differently worded and the comparison with the British survey cannot be so precise as the comparisons between different FSU/ECE surveys. Nonetheless it provides some useful insight.

WEIGHTING

Each sample of the general public was compared with official statistics on gender, age, education and rurality for the corresponding population. The unadjusted samples consistently under-represented males and, to a greater extent, the low-educated. Age and rural biases were smaller or less consistent. However, two rounds of rim-weighting by gender, age, education and rurality, brought the ECE samples within half a per cent of population parameters on all four variables, and the FSU samples within half a per cent on everything except education. Even after weighting, our FSU samples slightly under-represented the low-educated and over-represented the medium educated (those who had completed secondary education) though they were within one per cent of population parameters on the numbers with higher education (universities etc.). After weighting, these remaining inaccuracies – if indeed it was our samples rather than official statistics that were inaccurate, which is by no means certain – would have negligible effects on any analysis in this book.

Each sample of MPs was compared with the current breakdown of MPs into parliamentary factions at the time of the interviews – not always the same as the party labels under which they had been elected, especially in the FSU where many MPs were elected as independents and party loyalties were less rigid anyway. In all countries, the sampling procedure already guaranteed that the proportions of MPs in each faction within the sample closely matched that in the parliament as a whole, but weighting was applied to make the proportions in the sample exactly match those in the parliament.

SEARCHING FOR EVIDENCE OF CULTURAL LEGACIES.

We shall present our survey findings in a way that is sensitive to the possibility that imperial and communist cultural legacies might affect public opinion even in the 1990s. Obviously, we shall sometimes need to distinguish opinion in one or more of the particular countries where we carried out our surveys: Russia, Ukraine, Hungary, Slovakia and the Czech Republic. But we shall also routinely distinguish opinion in the former *Soviet Union* (FSU) from that in *east central Europe* (ECE), simply by averaging the entries for the appropriate countries.

We shall also routinely investigate the significance of other boundaries. We have divided our Ukraine survey into three parts: east Ukraine, close to the Russian border, including interviews in the oblasts of Kharkiv (first capital of the Ukrainian SSR which it remained until 1934[4]), Dnipropetrovsk, Donetsk and Zaporizhzhia; west Ukraine, including interviews in the oblasts of Volynia, Rivne and Lviv; and the remainder of our survey which comprised interviews in Kyiv city and the oblasts of Kyiv, Chernivtsi (in Romania between the wars), Vinnytsia, Kirovohrad, Kherson and Krym (Crimea).[5] A division of opinion between the FSU minus west Ukraine on the one side, against ECE plus west Ukraine on the other, would correspond to the line of cultural division, drawn by Huntington, between Catholic and Orthodox cultures.[6]

West Ukraine also differs from the rest of Ukraine in terms of more recent political experience as well as religious culture. Before the outbreak of the Great War in 1914, Volynia and Rivne, like much of modern Poland, had been ruled by the Romanov Tsar, while Lviv had been part of the Hapsburgs' Austro-Hungarian Empire. Clearly the possibilities for fractionating the territory of modern Ukraine in the search for cultural legacies are considerable. Any simple trichotomy is inevitably crude, and is less than entirely satisfactory. But between the wars, all three oblasts of Volynia, Rivne and Lviv were part of the Polish state – unlike other parts of west Ukraine which were under Romanian rule at that time. So the 'west Ukraine' which we have defined could be retitled, more exactly, as the 'inter-war Polish provinces' of modern Ukraine. Significantly that meant they were not ruled by Stalin between the wars and did not experience the oppression of communist dictatorship until the closing stages of the Second World War. Like Hungary, Slovakia and the Czech Republic, but unlike Russia and the rest of Ukraine, our 'west Ukraine' had only half a century of communist rule, and that rule was clearly imposed upon them from outside by force of arms. On the other hand many west Ukrainians regarded Polish rule as oppressive and their Catholicism was of a different kind (Greek Catholicism) from the Polish.

We have also divided east Ukraine from mid-Ukraine. The division between the oblasts bordering Russia and the rest of Ukraine hardly figures in the thinking of those with such a grand world-view as Huntington. Nonetheless it is potentially more important because it affects a much larger population. Ukraine without west Ukraine would still be Ukraine – as indeed it was between the wars. But Ukraine without east Ukraine would cease to be a viable state, or even a meaningful entity. Relatively quiet Russian feelings in the large population of east Ukraine could pose greater questions of national identity and state viability than the strident voices of the much smaller population of the former Polish provinces in west Ukraine. So we shall look to see how those in east

Ukraine differ, if at all, from those who live in the rest of Ukraine, and from those who live in Russia.

Within each empire or mega-cultural area (in Huntington's sense) the experience of individual countries has been very different. Both Russia and Ukraine were part of the Romanov Empire and the Soviet Union, but their roles within these empires were somewhat different. Tsarist and communist authority was centred in Russia, not in Ukraine, and Ukrainians were patronised as 'Little Russians' – a name which has unfortunately been immortalised by Tchaikovsky – or oppressed. The Stalin-induced Ukrainian famine of 1931–33 can be viewed as an example of national oppression as easily as an example of communist oppression. At the same time many individual Ukrainians did very well under both the Romanovs and the communists; and Ukrainians and Russians seemed almost indistinguishable when they took up residence in other Tsarist or communist provinces such as the Baltics or Central Asia. In short, Russia was clearly a master, but Ukraine was in some respects a subject nation while simultaneously being a master in others. Within ECE the historic situation of each country with respect to empire also differed. Hungary was one of the twin master-nations of the Hapsburg Empire while the Czechs and Slovaks were amongst the subjects. But after the Second World War Hungary was, and was treated as, a defeated rather than a liberated nation. So under the post-war communists, unlike the Hapsburgs, Hungary was also a subject nation. The course of Czech history ran in the opposite direction, at least for a short time. Czechoslovakia was not part of the Nazi alliance and it was clearly liberated rather than defeated in 1945. Moreover, the Czechoslovak communists did very well in the first free post-war elections. There was a strong indigenous element in Czechoslovakia's move towards communism, even though force and pressure was decisive in the final switch to a full communist dictatorship. So although Czechs had been a subject nation under the Hapsburgs, they were less obviously so under the immediate post-war communist system. After the suppression of the Prague spring in 1968 by Soviet-led Warsaw Pact forces however, the Czechs became unambiguously a subject nation once again. The Slovak tradition was that of a subject nation at all times, however: subject to the Hungarians under the Hapsburgs before 1918, subject to the Czechs in the new Czechoslovakia after 1918, and clearly subject to the Russians after 1968 if not quite so clearly before that.

Smoothing out the ups and downs of history, we shall find it useful to contrast Russia and Hungary as master nations with Ukraine, Slovakia and the Czech Republic as subject nations. This simplistic division of nations into masters and subjects must be offensive to some of our readers, as it is to us. If used normatively it has fascist overtones. But as a summary of historical experience this distinction – rough though it is – is a key factor in explaining some few but nonetheless important aspects of political values, particularly those that concern external and aggressive nationalism.

Whether all these differences of historical experience and long term socio-religious culture actually do produce significant differences in contemporary political culture remains to be seen. If history and culture were a prison from which there was no escape nothing could ever change anywhere and liberal democratic cultures would never have emerged anywhere. But it is equally unlikely that the experience of history leaves no imprint at all upon public opinion. We shall see.

THE POLITICAL CONTEXT OF THE SURVEYS

Proper interpretation also requires some attention to the precise timing of our surveys, and the events and conditions from 1993 to 1996 that surrounded them in each country – in particular, the elections and referenda that preceded, and in the case of Russia interrupted, our surveys; the governments and political leaders that were in place at the time of the surveys; and the elections that followed closely after them. Of course there were other events of great significance, especially in Russia: the suspension of parliament in September 1993, the subsequent shelling of the parliament building, and the 'invasion' of Chechnya. Although these events took place in Russia they were noted, with differing degrees of approval or alarm, in all the other countries but especially in neighbouring Ukraine. To a limited but significant extent, prior events can be seen as a potential influence upon political attitudes and values, subsequent events as a partial consequence.

Our first wave of interviews took place in November and December 1993, at the same time as Russians were electing their first postcommunist legislature. The election was intended to resolve a deepening stalemate between the Congress of People's Deputies, which had been elected on a largely competitive basis in the spring of 1990, and Boris Yeltsin, who had been elected in the first round of elections to a newly established Russian presidency in June 1991 (he took 57 per cent of the vote against five other competitors). A constitutional conference in the summer of 1993 had attempted to find a compromise with which both president and parliament would be satisfied, but without success. The issue was forced when President Yeltsin gave an address to the nation on the evening of 21 September in which he announced that there would be a 'gradual constitutional reform' involving the dissolution of parliament and a popular vote on a new constitution as well as new elections. The decree was resisted by parliamentarians, gathered in the 'White House' in central Moscow; but on 4 October, after a large-scale public demonstration of support by his opponents, Yeltsin ordered the parliament to be shelled in order to suppress what he described as a 'parliamentary insurrection'.[7]

The elections that took place on 12 December were unusual in many respects. In the first place, Yeltsin's main political opponents – his Vice-President,

Alexander Rutskoi, and parliamentary chairman Ruslan Khasbulatov – had been arrested for their part in 'organising mass disorder'. Several parties were banned, and so were a number of newspapers; others, including the Communist-inclined papers *Pravda* and *Sovetskaya Rossiya*, were ordered to change their titles and editors. There was a brief period of censorship, and the Constitutional Court – which had condemned Yeltsin's original broadcast – was ordered not to meet. The elections that took place in December were to an entirely new Federal Assembly, established under the constitution that was put to a popular vote on the same date. There was a new upper house, the Council of the Federation, which would represent Russia's 89 republics and regions, and a new lower house, the Duma, half of whose 450 seats were to be filled on a proportional basis by national party lists, the other half by votes in individual constituencies with the result determined by simple majority.

Table 3.2:   Elections to the Russian Duma, December 1993

Party	Party list vote %	seats	Constituency seats	Total seats
Russia's Choice	15.5	40	30	70
Liberal Democratic Party	22.9	59	5	64
Communist Party	12.4	32	16	48
Agrarian Party	8.0	21	12	33
Women of Russia	8.1	21	2	23
Yabloko	7.9	20	3	23
Party of Russian Unity and Concord	6.8	18	1	19
Democratic Party of Russia	5.5	14	1	15
Other parties	4.6	–	1	1
Against all/invalid votes	7.5			
Independents	–	–	141	141
Postponed	–	–	6	6
Total elected		225	225	450

    The outcome was a surprise for most observers, in that the largest share of the national party-list vote went to Vladimir Zhirinovsky's far-right Liberal Democratic Party (see Table 3.2). Russia's Choice, a pro-government grouping led by economist and former acting prime minister Yegor Gaidar, came second in the party-list vote, but did much better in the constituencies; the Communists were third, but they accounted for more than a fifth of the party-list vote in association with their allies in the Agrarian Party. Only eight groupings exceeded the 5 per cent threshold that was required to secure representation in the party-list section of the Duma, although four more won at least a single seat in the individual constituencies. More than half of the constituency seats, however, were won by independents, and they were by far the largest grouping in the new Duma with nearly a third of the total membership. The outcome was a parliament that was composed in almost equal parts of government supporters, opponents and the undecided; the larger outcome was a further strengthening of the presidency under the new constitution, which was approved by 58 per cent of those that voted if the official results were to be taken at face value.[8]

The new Duma was the one in which our MPs' survey was conducted, in late 1994; but it was elected for just two years, and in December 1995 Russians went to the polls again to choose another set of representatives. Our MPs were interviewed just before the start of the Chechen war, launched by President Yeltsin in December 1994 in an attempt to crush the independence that the small north Caucasian republic had claimed three years earlier, but at a time when relations with the Russian authorities were already deteriorating. Yeltsin, perhaps misled by his military advisers, expressed confidence in an early victory and promised that federal authority would be reasserted, here and indeed elsewhere. In the event the war dragged on until a ceasefire was concluded in late 1996 by the new head of the Security Council, Alexander Lebed. By this time the Chechen capital Grozny had been reduced to rubble, tens of thousands had been forced to flee their homes, and at least 30,000 had been killed in the first months of fighting.

The Chechen war was one of the factors that undermined the position of the President and the parties that supported him in the Duma after the December 1993 elections. Another was the steady fall in living standards, and another still was the rise in crime and in particular in organised, large-scale crime (Russians used the word *mafiya* for such activities). The Duma elections, when they took place in December 1995, saw these developments reflected in a shift towards the organised left, or (perhaps more precisely) towards Yeltsin's political opponents. This time the Communists took a commanding lead with 22.3 per cent of the party-list vote (and about a third of all seats), Zhirinovsky's Liberal Democrats came second with 11.2 per cent, and the movement organised by prime minister Viktor Chernomyrdin, Our Home is Russia, came third with 10.1 per cent.[9] It was in this context, one of hostility to the Yeltsin administration and to the policies with which it was associated, that our follow-up survey was conducted in early 1996; although Yeltsin and his supporters had managed to turn around this hostility by June and July 1996, when Yeltsin was able to defeat his Communist and other opponents in the two-round presidential election.

The largest of the other Soviet republics, Ukraine, held its own presidential election in December 1991. Leonid Kravchuk, a former member of the Ukrainian Politburo and parliamentary chairman, won a clear majority, and there was overwhelming support for independence in a referendum that was put to the vote at the same time. There were further elections in 1994 to a new Ukrainian parliament, and also to the presidency. The first round of elections to the

Supreme Rada (parliament), in March 1994, produced few clear results but marked a deepening division between the predominantly Russian-speaking east (where left-wing candidates were more successful) and the more traditional west (where nationalists were returned in some strength). The second round, in April, filled most of the 450 seats in the new parliament. Most successful candidates were unaffiliated, but among the recognised parties the Communists won the greatest number of seats. It was in this new parliament, with forty of the seats still vacant, that our interviews with MPs took place in November 1994 (see Table 3.3).[10]

Table 3.3:　Elections to the Ukrainian parliament, March–April 1994

Parties	Votes %	Seats No.
Left parties		
Communist Party	25.4	86
Peasant Party	5.3	18
Socialist Party	4.1	14
Communist Party of Crimea	1.5	5
Centrist parties		
Interregional Bloc for Reforms	4.4	15
Party of Democratic Renewal	1.2	4
Labour Party	1.2	4
Social Democratic Party	0.6	2
Civic Congress	0.6	2
National-democratic parties		
Rukh	7.4	25
Republican Party	3.3	11
Congress of Ukrainian Nationalists	2.1	7
Democratic Party	0.9	3
Christian Democratic Party	0.3	1
Nationalist parties		
Ukrainian National Assembly	0.9	3
Conservative Republican Party	0.6	2
Independents	40.2	136
Total elected		338

Note: Elections failed in 112 constituencies.

In the first round of the presidential election on 26 June 1994, Kravchuk won 38 per cent as against 31 per cent for the former prime minister and manager of the world's largest missile factory, Leonid Kuchma, with five other candidates sharing the remainder of the vote. In the run-off in July, however, Kuchma surged ahead to victory with 52 per cent as against Kravchuk's 45 per cent.[11] Kuchma had campaigned for more gradual economic reform, and for closer links with Russia (his own fluency in Ukrainian was uncertain though improving); but he took personal charge later in the year of a package of economic reforms that reflected the advice of the International Monetary Fund, including privatisation and price liberalisation.

There had been parliamentary elections in what was still Czechoslovakia in 1990, at which Civic Forum and its ally Public against Violence had secured by far the largest number of seats (see Chapter 2). There were further elections on 5–6 June 1992, both to the two houses of a new federal parliament and to subordinate legislatures in the Czech lands and Slovakia.[12] In the election that took place to the Slovak National Council, the Movement for Democratic Slovakia, which had separated from Public against Violence and was led by Vladimir Meciar, campaigned for a 'looser association' with the Czech lands and for a more gradual and limited economic reform. It was the most successful group, winning 37 per cent of the vote and 74 seats in the 150-member Slovak National Council. The MDS then formed a coalition with the Slovak National Party, which had won 15 seats and openly favoured the dissolution of the Czechoslovak state (opinion polls at this time suggested that most Czechs and Slovaks were in fact against a separation). Three other parties were represented in the new parliament: the ex-communist Party of the Democratic Left, the Christian Democratic Movement and a coalition of ethnic Hungarian parties.

Table 3.4:   Elections to the Slovak National Council, June 1992

	Votes %	Seats
Movement for a Democratic Slovakia	37.3	74
Party of the Democratic Left	14.7	29
Christian Democratic Movement	8.9	18
Slovak National Party	7.9	15
Hungarian Christian Democratic Movement and Coexistence	7.4	14
Other parties	23.8	0
Total		150

Following the election, the Slovak parliament adopted a declaration of sovereignty, and in September a constitution for an independent Slovakia was approved which was to come into force on 1 January 1993. The Federal Assembly voted the dissolution of the Czech and Slovak Federal Republic in November, after discussions had failed to resolve the wide differences between the two governments, and the two countries became independent at the end of year. At the time of our mass survey, in December 1993, Vladimir Meciar of the MDS was still prime minister, although he had lost his parliamentary majority; there were tensions within his party, differences over the pace of economic reform (there were three economics ministers in 1993 alone), and difficulties in relations with the President over nominations to government. National income fell by about 5 per cent during the year, and unemployment and inflation both rose rapidly. Meciar, nonetheless, was returned to office once again following elections in September and October 1994 at the head of another coalition government.[13]

Elections had also taken place to the Czech National Council in June 1992 at which the clear winner was Vaclav Klaus and his Civic Democratic Party, a right-wing grouping that had emerged from the Civic Forum. It took 76 seats in the 200-member Czech National Council; the Communist Party of Bohemia and Moravia came second with 35 seats, and six other parties were represented in the new parliament (see Table 3.5). The outcome was a right-wing coalition headed by Klaus and his CDP, including the Christian and Democratic Union, the Civil Democratic Alliance and the Christian Democratic Party. Klaus became prime minister, and Vaclav Havel was elected the first President of the Czech Republic by a parliamentary vote in January 1993. Klaus and his coalition were still in government at the time of our mass survey at the end of 1993, and our parliamentary survey late in 1994. Klaus continued in office after the parliamentary elections that took place in 1996, although his coalition's majority was sharply reduced. Despite this setback, the Czech Republic had one of the most successful of the postcommunist economies, with low levels of inflation and unemployment, and it was one of the most firmly committed of the postcommunist countries to membership of NATO and the European Union.

Table 3.5:   Elections to the Czech National Council, June 1992

	Votes %	Seats
Civic Democratic Party and Christian Democratic Party	29.7	76
Left Bloc	14.1	35
Czechoslovak Social Democratic Party	6.5	16
Liberal Social Union	6.5	16
Christian Democratic Union-Czechoslovak People's Party	6.3	15
Association for the Republic-Republican Party of Czechoslovakia	6.0	14
Civic Democratic Alliance	6.0	14
Movement for Self-governing Democracy-Society for Moravia and Silesia	5.9	14
Other parties	19.0	0
Total		200

In Hungary, finally, the government that was in power at the time of our mass survey was the administration that had been formed by the Hungarian

Democratic Forum, led by Jozef Antall, after the first competitive elections of March and April 1990 (see Chapter 2). Antall himself died in December 1993 after a long illness, and his government suffered a gradual loss of support both within the electorate, where its weakening position was highlighted by a series of by-election and local election losses, and within the Hungarian parliament, where it began to lose its former coalition partners. The HDF government found it difficult to devise and maintain a coherent economic policy, and divisions opened up within the Forum itself which led to the expulsion of a radical right-wing faction led by Istvan Csurka in early 1993. Survey evidence suggests that there was underlying support for social democratic values – the party system that operated during the 1990 elections had not mobilised it effectively;[14] and our own mass survey, at the end of 1993, predicted electoral success for the Socialists in the elections that were to take place in 1994. At those elections, in two rounds of voting in May, the Hungarian Socialist Party obtained an overall majority of votes and seats; they went on to form a coalition government with the Free Democrats, with the Socialist leader Gyula Horn as prime minister.[15] It was within this largely Socialist parliament, later the same year, that our interviews with MPs were conducted.

Table 3.6: Elections to the Hungarian Parliament, May 1994

	Votes %	Seats
Hungarian Socialist Party	53.9	209
Alliance of Free Democrats	18.1	70
Hungarian Democratic Forum	9.6	37
Independent Smallholders' Party	6.8	26
Christian Democratic Peoples' Party	5.8	22
Alliance of Young Democrats	5.3	20
Others	0.5	2
Total		386

II Perceptions

4 A Fond Farewell?

We might expect that public opinion would celebrate the end of dictatorship and the transfer of power to the people. But the normal trajectory of public opinion at a time of political change is a burst of intense excitement, hope and euphoria as the change takes place followed shortly afterwards by a combination of exhaustion, disillusionment and apathy. American Presidents seldom fulfil the hopes and expectations generated during their successful election campaigns. Even if they are judged favourably by history, they are likely to disappoint their contemporaries. Once newly elected governments have had time to make their own mistakes, or even become associated with contemporary disasters that are not of their own making, nostalgia for their predecessors is likely to grow. This cycle of public opinion is one of the fundamental dynamics of democracy that balances the government's power of propaganda and encourages alternation in office. So it would not be entirely surprising – nor even damaging to democracy – if, once the communist dictatorship had been dismantled, public opinion began to recall its good side as well as its bad. And, of course, the worse the performance of the postcommunist regime, the kinder people might be to the communist memory.

In this chapter we look at public perspectives on the communist past, as they had developed by the end of 1993–four years after ECE's revolutions of 1989, but just two years after the end of the Soviet Union itself.

BELIEF IN COMMUNIST IDEALS

We asked respondents in each country whether they had ever been a member of the Communist Party, whether they now 'believed in the *ideals* of communism even if, in practice, it was not perfect', and whether they had 'ever believed' in communist ideals.

By the end of 1993 at least, people were remarkably willing to answer such questions. Fewer than one per cent could not or would not answer the question about Party membership, 8 per cent the question of current belief in communist ideals, and only 5 per cent the question about past belief in those ideals. For clarity, we shall routinely exclude those who could not or would not answer questions when reporting our results, though we shall draw attention to questions which unusually large numbers could not or would not answer.

Overall, 12 per cent in the FSU and 16 per cent in ECE admitted they had once been party members. The highest level occurred in the Czech Republic where, despite its current right-wing politics, a full 21 per cent admitted past or present membership of the Communist Party. These figures for the FSU, for

83

Hungary, and for the former Czechoslovakia are each almost exactly twice as high as the reported level of Communist Party membership in the mid 1970s.[1] Since our figures refer to having 'ever' been a member they should be higher than the level of membership at any one time, but it is interesting that they are so much greater and that they follow the contours of varying membership levels in different states. It suggests our respondents were remarkably truthful about this aspect of their role in the old regime.

Yet according to our respondents, their belief in communist ideals had, in the past, been far greater in the FSU than in ECE. By our respondents' own accounts, the indigenous communist regime in the Soviet Union had succeeded in making over half its population believe in its ideals (however much they despised its practice) while the externally imposed regimes in ECE had been far less successful: in ECE fewer than a third had 'ever' believed even in the 'ideals' of communism.

By the early 1990s however, attitudes in the FSU had come into line with those in ECE. The decline in belief was precipitous in the FSU, over three times as great in the FSU as in ECE, bringing the level of current belief in communist ideals down to 18 per cent in the FSU compared to 20 per cent in ECE. This 2 per cent difference is so small that it could easily be attributed to sampling error, but it provides very strong evidence *against* any suggestion that belief in communist ideals in the early 1990s remained any *higher* in the FSU than elsewhere.

The bulk of Ukraine was not much different from Russia in terms of former Communist Party membership or belief in communist ideals, past or present. And even west Ukraine did not differ much from Russia in terms of former Party membership, whose levels were, of course, largely determined by central-ised Communist Party decisions. But the break point for belief in communist ideals was clearly not at the post-war FSU/ECE boundary: it was between west Ukraine and the rest of the FSU. In the past, the people of west Ukraine had never believed in communist ideals even as much as the people in ECE; but by the early 1990s they were uniquely antagonistic to communist ideals – only 6 per cent in west Ukraine, compared to 19 per cent in Russia, 21 per cent in east Ukraine, and 20 per cent in ECE declared a current belief in communist ideals.

In terms of declared past belief, west Ukraine looked like ECE rather than the FSU; though in terms of current belief it was quite deviantly anti-communist, indeed far more so than any of our three ECE countries.

GOOD AND BAD FEATURES OF THE COMMUNIST REGIME

Our questions about communist ideals emphasised the distinction between those ideals and the practice of communism. But we also asked about the practice. In particular we asked people to tell us what they thought had been the best and the worst features of the former communist regime. We offered a 'showcard'

Table 4.1:   The belief and practice of communism

	Were you ever a member of the Communist Party?	Did you ever believe in communist ideals?	Do you believe in communist ideals now?	Decline in belief
	%	%	%	%
Russia	12	60	19	−41
Ukraine	11	52	17	−35
East Uk	12	55	21	−34
Mid Uk	11	57	18	−39
West Uk	9	25	6	−19
Czech Rep	21	29	15	−14
Slovakia	16	36	23	−13
Hungary	12	29	21	−8
AVERAGE:				
FSU	12	56	18	−38
ECE	16	31	20	−11

Notes: 1. 'Don't Knows', 'Can't decide' etc. excluded from calculation of percentages.
2. There are many ways of dividing Ukraine. So many parts have had such different histories. Here we have defined east and west Ukraine very narrowly, as follows.
West Ukraine: the western and north western regions of Ukraine – interviews were carried out in the oblasts of Volynia, Rivne, and Lviv. This 'West Ukraine' might be called the 'inter-war Polish provinces'. Before 1914, Volynia and Rivne had been Tsarist territory, while Lviv had been part of the Hapsburg's Austro-Hungarian Empire, but all three were ruled by Poland between the wars. In our interviews, 89 per cent identified their 'nationality' as Ukrainian in the north western region, and 94 per cent in the western. We have excluded the south west region, where we conducted interviews in Chernivtsy, from our 'West Ukraine' here, because it has a different, less 'western' and more Ottoman history. Chernivtsy was ruled by Romania between the wars. Only 73 per cent in the south west region identified their 'nationality' as Ukrainian and a significant minority denied being either Ukrainian or Russian.
East Ukraine: the eastern and north eastern regions of Ukraine – interviews were carried out in the oblasts of Kharkiv (capital of Soviet Ukraine until 1934), Dnipropetrovsk, Donetsk and Zaporizhzhia. In our interviews, 34 per cent in the east region and 50 per cent in the north east described their 'nationality' as Russian; 65 per cent in the east region and 79 per cent in the north east spoke Russian at home. We have excluded the southern region and Krym (Crimea) although Russian identification was also strong there, because the southern region was further away from the heartland of Russia and, in Krym (Crimea), there was a significant minority who denied being Ukrainian or Russian.
Mid Ukraine: the rest of Ukraine – interviews were carried out in Kyiv city and oblast, and the oblasts of Chernivtsi, Vinnytsia, Kirovohrad, Kherson, and Krym (Crimea). With these definitions our Mid-Ukraine is something of a mixed bag of heterogeneous areas, but our West and East Ukraine are indisputably western and eastern both geographically and in terms of history and cultural links; and our analysis gains more from a homogeneous definition of east and west Ukraine than it loses through a heterogeneous definition of less theoretically interesting mid-Ukraine.
See Paul Robert Magosci *Ukraine: A Historical Atlas* (Toronto: University of Toronto Press, 1992), especially Maps 22 to 25.

listing five possibilities in each case. Each card also had the option of 'no good features' or 'no bad features' (respectively) on it, separated by a few blank lines from the five listed possibilities.

Obviously the value of such a question format depends critically upon the wisdom of our choices of proposed good and bad features. While we attempted to include the most frequently cited good and bad features of the communist regimes there is a small risk that respondents whose actual choice was not included on the card would be forced to opt for another that was included. But we deliberately avoided an 'open ended' question format, without a list of alternatives, because respondents' free-format answers would then be classified by research assistants, and our respondents would have no control over that classification. We preferred to leave things entirely in the hands of the respondents themselves.

Table 4.2:   The best feature of the communist regime?

	Job security	Economic stability	Peace between nationalities	More equality	Law and order	None
	%	%	%	%	%	%
Russia	29	22	24	7	12	7
Ukraine	24	32	20	8	8	8
East Uk	23	31	23	9	9	4
Mid Uk	22	35	20	8	8	7
West Uk	33	24	9	3	8	24
Czech Rep	59	5	12	5	7	12
Slovakia	61	10	8	9	7	5
Hungary	58	8	5	17	5	7
AVERAGE:						
FSU	27	27	22	8	10	8
ECE	59	8	8	10	6	8

Note: 'Don't Knows', 'Can't decide' etc. excluded from calculation of percentages.

Overwhelmingly, people in ECE chose 'job security' as the best feature of the communist regime. Within the FSU however, opinion was divided fairly evenly between 'job security', 'economic stability' – something very different from job security in command economies, and 'peace between nationalities'. Choices were fairly stable across the different countries of ECE, and within the FSU, though people in Ukraine emphasised 'economic stability' rather more even than those in Russia. Significantly, only an average of 8 per cent in both ECE and the FSU said that the communist regime had had no redeeming features.[2] Life was not all bad under the communists.

Once again, west Ukraine was deviant, different both from ECE and the bulk of the FSU. West Ukraine was similar to ECE and differed from the rest of the FSU in that so few quoted 'peace between nationalities' as a virtue of the communist regime; but it differed from both ECE and the rest of the FSU in that so many west Ukrainians – fully 24 per cent – could see no redeeming features in the old regime at all.

Table 4.3: The worst feature of the communist regime?

	Oppressed human rights	Too much bureaucracy	Corruption	Pollution	Economic stagnation	None
	%	%	%	%	%	%
Russia	17	32	15	12	11	13
Ukraine	22	30	17	11	6	14
East Uk	18	30	26	7	6	12
Mid Uk	18	34	13	15	5	17
West Uk	46	17	7	9	13	8
Czech Rep	46	11	6	20	15	3
Slovakia	35	18	13	16	14	5
Hungary	33	23	16	8	9	11
AVERAGE:						
FSU	20	31	16	12	9	14
ECE	38	17	12	15	13	6

Note: 'Don't Knows', 'Can't decide' etc. excluded from calculation of percentages.

While most people in ECE and the FSU could find something good to say about the communist regime, most could also find something to criticise: only 14 per cent in the FSU and a mere 6 per cent in ECE had no criticisms. Again there were striking differences between ECE and the FSU, but a degree of uniformity within each.

Only 20 per cent in the FSU, but almost twice as many in ECE (and even more in west Ukraine) cited the 'oppression of human rights' as the worst feature of the old regime. Within the FSU (except for west Ukraine) the chief criticism was that there had been 'too much bureaucracy' – that the system had been tediously inefficient rather than monstrously oppressive.

Within ECE, the Hungarians were the least likely to cite 'oppression' and the most likely to cite 'bureaucracy' but they were still much closer to the ECE norm than to the FSU on the balance of these criticisms. Corruption was cited relatively frequently in east Ukraine, pollution and economic stagnation most frequently in the Czech Republic.

PERSONAL EXPERIENCE OF OPPRESSION

We investigated allegations of oppression further, and at a more personal level, by asking 'in your daily life, did you yourself feel oppressed by the communist regime?' And, if so, 'in what way?' Complaints of personal oppression were least in Russia (11 per cent) and Hungary (17 per cent), greater in Slovakia (23 per cent) and greatest in the Czech Republic (29 per cent). Complaints in Ukraine as a whole were similar to those in ECE, but that concealed a very sharp east-west gradient within Ukraine itself: 36 per cent of those who lived in west Ukraine claimed personal experience of oppression but only 15 per cent in east Ukraine.

Table 4.4:   Did you yourself feel oppressed by
communist regime?

	%
Russia	11
Ukraine	21
East Uk	15
Mid Uk	20
West Uk	36
Czech Rep	29
Slovakia	23
Hungary	17
AVERAGE:	
FSU	16
ECE	23

Note: 'Don't Knows', 'Can't decide' etc. excluded
from calculation of percentages.

The supplementary question proved illuminating however. Overall about 27 per cent of those who complained, whether in the FSU or ECE, said their personal experience of communist oppression involved jobs – they had lost a job, failed to gain promotion or something similar. In Slovakia and the Czech Republic there were particular complaints about travel restrictions and blocked educational opportunities, while in the FSU the main focus of complaints, apart from jobs, was housing. But 22 per cent, both in ECE and the FSU, cited examples of personal oppression which our interviewers judged to be more about the general oppressiveness of the regime than about a purely personal experience – allegations of general corruption or oppression of human rights for example. And these wider criticisms were especially frequent in west Ukraine where they accounted for 43 per cent of all allegations of oppression. We are left with the impression that general feelings of national and communal oppression in west Ukraine spilled over into an inflated sense of personal oppression.

Table 4.5:   In what way were you personally oppressed ?

	Jobs	Travel	Housing	Education	Police	Other personal experience	Not purely personal experience
	%	%	%	%	%	%	%
Russia	31	5	26	2	6	11	19
Ukraine	24	7	14	4	6	21	25
East Uk	25	3	18	1	3	25	25
Mid Uk	25	9	16	3	8	23	16
West Uk	19	7	4	8	4	14	43
Czech Rep	27	21	2	12	7	15	15
Slovakia	25	17	2	19	3	13	21
Hungary	26	7	7	5	4	21	31
AVERAGE:							
FSU	28	6	20	3	6	16	22
ECE	26	15	4	12	5	16	22

Note: 'Don't Knows', 'Can't decide' etc. excluded from calculation of percentages.

Perhaps it is worth noting that relatively few in any country, and only about 5 or 6 per cent overall, cited experiences with the police or security services – such as being searched, interrogated or arrested. The bulk of the complaints about personal oppression that people recalled in the early 1990s concerned bureaucratic oppression that affected people's standard of living and sense of well-being rather than crude physical action by security forces.[3]

OUR COUNTRY'S BEST TIME THIS CENTURY

As a measure of people's overall attitude to the old regime we asked: 'taking *everything* into account, which of the times shown on this card do you feel was the best time for (country)?' The card varied from country to country but always included the pre–1914 empires at one end and the postcommunist present at the other. In the FSU the card also included 'under Stalin', 'under Brezhnev' and 'under Gorbachev'. In Slovakia and the Czech Republic it included 'under Masaryk', 'during the Prague spring of 1968', 'under Husak', and 'in the united democratic Czechoslovakia 1989–92'. Additionally, in Slovakia only, it included 'in the Slovak state 1939–45' – referring to the supposedly independent Slovakia set up by the Nazi occupiers. In Hungary, the card included 'under Admiral Horthy between the wars', 'under Kadar' and 'under the Reform-Communists before 1989'.

The present was not very popular in any country. In the FSU a massive 68 per cent plumped for Brezhnev's era of stagnation – somewhat less than that in

Russia, but even more than that in Ukraine.[4] Conversely, people in Russia opted much more strongly for the Tsar and Stalin (27 per cent between them) than those who lived in Ukraine (only 12 per cent). The Russian–Ukrainian distinction here reflects the crude master–subject nation distinction discussed in the preface. In west Ukraine, zero per cent opted for Stalin and, a remarkable 37 per cent for the present. Despite all the economic problems that afflicted postcommunist Ukraine, the people of west Ukraine were far more positive about the present than either the people of ECE or the rest of the FSU.

Table 4.6: Which was the best time this century for (country)?

	Pre–1914 Empires	Between wars	1939–45	Prague-spring 1968	Brez-hnev-time	Gorb-achev-time	Demo-cratic Czechos-lovakia	Since 1992 (1989 in Hungary)
	%	%	%	%	% .	%	%	%
	Tsar	Stalin	na	na	Brezh-nev	Gorba-chev	na	Since 1992
Russia	17	10	na	na	59	5	na	10
Ukraine	8	4	na	na	77	3	na	8
East Uk	6	7	na	na	83	2	na	2
Mid Uk	9	3	na	na	81	2	na	4
West UK	8	0	na	na	48	7	na	37
	Empire	Masaryk	1939–45	Spring '68	Husak	na	1989–92	Since 1992
Czech Rep	3	32	na	17	7	na	19	21
Slovakia	1	3	10	22	18	na	27	18
	Mona-rchy	Horthy	na	na	Kadar	Reform Cs	na	Since 1989
Hungary	12	8	na	na	51	16	na	14
AVERAGE:								
FSU	13	–	–	–	68	4	–	9
ECE	5	–	–	–	25	(H)16	(C+S) 23	18

Note: 'Don't Knows', 'Can't decide' etc. excluded from calculation of percentages.

About a fifth of those in Slovakia and the Czech Republic opted for the present but roughly as many – less in the Czech Republic, more in Slovakia – opted for the united democratic Czechoslovakia of 1989–92. But even taken together Czechoslovak support for a combination of the present and the recent past was not much greater than west Ukrainian support for the present. Around 19 per cent throughout the former Czechoslovakia opted for Dubcek's Prague spring of 1968.

Although 12 per cent in Hungary looked back to the pre-1914 Hapsburg empire, that figure sank to 3 per cent in the Czech Republic and a mere one per cent in Slovakia. So within ECE as well as within the FSU, the degree of nostalgia for pre-1914 empires correlated perfectly with the status of the nation as a master or a subject within those empires. Czechs and Slovaks differed sharply in their assessment of the Husak period, which was twice as popular in his native Slovakia; and they differed even more on attitudes towards the interwar period under Masaryk, which was the choice of 32 per cent in the Czech Republic but of only 3 per cent in Slovakia. Conversely 10 per cent in Slovakia opted for the supposedly independent puppet state set up under the Nazis during the war. Again, these patterns reflect the perceived master–subject nation distinction (wrong though that perception may have been) even within Masaryk's Czechoslovakia. Cultural legacies and historical memories focused on more than the communist experience, long and recent though it was.

In Hungary the Kadar period proved almost as popular as the Brezhnev period in Russia, and relatively few picked either the post-Kadar reform-communist period or the postcommunist present.

Our question had asked people to 'take *everything* into account' when choosing their country's 'best time' this century. We do not know how much weight they gave to nostalgia for an orderly economic life, for relative prosperity, for peace, order and discipline, or even for dictatorship and repression. Undoubtedly, different people would have weighted these factors differently. Nonetheless, the choice of periods gives some clue to the factors which people longed for most. Looking back over the century, relatively small numbers of people were nostalgic for the glory obsessed pre–1914 empires, or for the brutal dictatorship of Stalin. Throughout the FSU and in Hungary – though not in the former Czechoslovakia – the top choice was the period of late communism characterised, as it was, more by bureaucracy than brutality, by order and discipline without brutal repression, by relative if not absolute prosperity, and by modestly rising economic standards or even 'stagnation' but not sharp economic dislocation and decline.

Although opinion within the former Czechoslovakia was less consensual, it focused upon a variety of democratic periods of one kind or another: taking the interwar (Masaryk) and post–1989 periods together, these democratic periods were chosen by 48 per cent in Slovakia and 72 per cent in the Czech Republic, while around another 20 per cent in both countries opted for Dubcek's 'Prague Spring' which, in defeat and suppression, came to symbolise a more liberal and democratic regime than it had ever in fact achieved during its short existence.

FORGIVENESS

Whatever the virtues of the old regime – and we have seen that most people admitted it did have some redeeming features, most people agreed that the old regime had been too bureaucratic, oppressive, corrupt or all three. And many felt that the guilty should be exposed and punished, though their enthusiasm for this was inevitably tempered by their own personal compromises with the old regime. Pressure for revenge was greater in postcommunist Hungary and Czechoslovakia than elsewhere.[5] Despite the misgivings of President Havel, the post-communist Czechoslovak parliament amended a law threatening jail for anyone supporting a movement which promoted 'nationalist, racist or religious hate' to include 'class hate' and even 'communism' – and Havel signed it.[6] Similarly, despite initial resistance from President Goncz and Prime Minister Antall, the Hungarian parliament passed a law to allow prosecution of communist officials, and 'right wing deputies [wanted] not only trials and a purge, but also a cleanout of all communist *and liberal* sympathisers in the media.'[7] In the event, Welsh concludes that 'the past few years have been characterised by policies of moderation – not revenge seeking' but 'this has not happened from a desire for reconciliation but because prevailing power arrangements have prevented lustration.'[8] However, our concern here is with people's desire for vengeance rather than with the separate question of whether new laws fulfilled that desire.

Table 4.7: Forgiving and forgetting?

	Secret police files should be			Do mere to punish those responsible for the injustices of the communist regime	Dimiss factory managers who were members of the communist party
	made public	opened only to those named	kept secret or destroyed		
	%	%	%	%	%
Russia	37	50	13	55	31
Ukraine	49	39	12	54	28
East Uk	45	39	16	48	23
Mid Uk	48	41	12	51	25
West Uk	64	30	6	75	51
Czech Rep	52	18	30	81	42
Slovakia	50	12	38	75	39
Hungary	47	15	38	74	42
AVERAGE:					
FSU	43	44	13	55	30
ECE	50	15	35	77	41

Note: 'Don't Knows', 'Can't decide' etc. excluded from calculation of percentages.

We asked whether secret police files from the communist period should be 'made public for all to read, opened only to those named in them, kept secret, or destroyed?' Half of the public in ECE and Ukraine, though only 37 per cent in Russia, wanted secret police files made public. However there were sharp differences between attitudes in ECE and the FSU on whether these files should be kept entirely secret (or even destroyed) or should be released to those named in them: in the FSU there was much more support for releasing files to those named in them, while in ECE there was much more support for keeping them secret altogether or indeed, destroying them.

This probably related to the fact that the desire for vengeance was much stronger in ECE, where 77 per cent wanted 'more done to punish those people who were responsible for the injustices of the communist regime' while only 55 per cent thought that in the FSU. (Here also, west Ukraine lined up almost exactly with ECE rather than with the rest of the FSU.) However, there was much less support for a witch-hunt against those who had held office but could not be accused of specific injustices. Only 41 per cent in ECE and 30 per cent in the FSU agreed that 'factory managers who were members of the Communist Party should be dismissed.'[9] The highest and lowest levels of support for a witch-hunt both occurred within the borders of Ukraine, where it was supported by 51 per cent in west Ukraine – significantly more than in ECE – but only 24 per cent in the rest of Ukraine.

CONCLUSION

We have found that the old regime was widely criticised for its abuse of human rights, its bureaucracy and its corruption; and that there was considerable support for punishing those responsible. In the early 1990s only a fifth claimed to believe in the ideals of communism. Nonetheless over half in the FSU and almost a third in ECE admitted that they had believed in communist ideals at one time, and most people could see some redeeming features in the communist regime. Within the FSU a majority cited the Brezhnev period as the best this century for their country, and a majority in Hungary cited the corresponding time under Kadar.[10]

On most questions there was a sharp division between the people of ECE and the FSU, though west Ukrainians tended to side with opinion in ECE rather than the rest of the FSU. To a degree, Hungarian and Russian attitudes also reflected their former imperial dominance, while Slovak and Ukrainian atti-tudes reflected their reaction against Hungarian and Russian imperialism. Czech attitudes reflected their ambiguous history, distinguishing them from Hungarians and from Slovaks on different questions in easily interpretable ways. In the 1990s perspectives on the past revealed the imprint of several cross-cutting historical/cultural legacies from the Romanov and Hapsburg period of empire, and the non-communist inter-war period, as well as these countries' common but varied experience of communism.

One reason, amongst others, why people looked with some favour on the communist past was, of course, their disappointment with both the political and economic performance of their postcommunist regimes. We examine that dis-appointment in the next chapter.

5 A Brave New World?

In the last chapter we noted, in passing, that very few people in any country cited the postcommunist present as the best period this century for their country – around one fifth in Slovakia and the Czech Republic, 14 per cent in Hungary, 10 per cent in Russia and 8 per cent in Ukraine – although 37 per cent opted for the present in west Ukraine that was balanced by a mere 2 per cent in the much more populous east Ukraine.

ECONOMIC DECLINE

One obvious reason for this rejection of the postcommunist present – though not the only one – was the poor performance of the economy. Almost everyone outside the Czech Republic, and a majority inside it, said their country's

Table 5.1: Economic experiences and perceptions

	(Country's) economy has got worse over the last two years	Family's standard of living has got worse over the last two years	Family income is not enough to survive on	(Country's) economy will get worse over the next two years	Family's standard of living will get worse over the next two years	Govt action can improve or damage the economy – 'a great deal' or 'quite a lot'
	%	%	%	%	%	%
Russia	94	89	56	64	70	45
Ukraine	100	97	74	80	80	31
East Uk	100	97	73	81	80	30
Mid Uk	99	96	75	83	83	30
West Uk	100	99	72	63	67	38
Czech Rep	57	70	4	31	55	76
Slovakia	96	88	11	69	72	70
Hungary	96	92	25	71	79	46
AVERAGE:						
FSU	97	93	65	72	75	38
ECE	83	83	13	57	69	64

Note: 'Don't Knows', 'Can't decide' etc. excluded from calculation of percentages. Figures in the first, second, fourth and fifth columns of this table have been calculated as percentages of those who said 'better' or 'worse'; thus they also exclude those who said 'no change'; few were uncertain or undecided about the past, though more were about the future.

A Brave New World? 95

economy had worsened in the last two years. (See Table 5.1) Large majorities
everywhere outside the Czech Republic (and about one third within it) expected
that decline to continue. They were no more satisfied or optimistic about their
own family's living standards.[1] Indeed in the Czech Republic more people
reported a decline in their own living standards than in the economy's performance, and they were far less (24 per cent less) optimistic about their family's
prospects than about the future of their economy.

Nonetheless only 4 per cent in the Czech Republic and 11 per cent in Slovakia
reported that they had 'not enough income for their family to survive on'.[2] That
note of extreme despair rose to 25 per cent in Hungary, 56 per cent in Russia and
74 per cent in Ukraine. Luckily for governments everywhere, public perceptions
that government action could affect the economy varied inversely with the level
of despair. In Slovakia and the Czech Republic over 70 per cent attributed such
powers to government, but only 31 per cent in Ukraine. So where people felt
better off they held government responsible for their country's economic performance, and where they felt much worse off they largely absolved it from blame.

COMPARING REGIME PERFORMANCE

Present and even future economic problems can be blamed upon past governments if they are blamed upon government at all. We asked directly whether the
statement 'the economy is/was well run' was 'more true now, or more true of the
communist regime'. Close to half our respondents felt the communist and
postcommunist regimes were much the same on that score but, amongst those
who could decide, almost everyone in Ukraine and a very large majority in
every country except the Czech Republic said the economy was run better under
the communist regime; however, in the Czech Republic a very large majority
said exactly the opposite.

When we asked under which regime it was more true that 'the poor are/were
well cared for', an overwhelming majority of those who were willing to discriminate chose the communist regime. That was true in every country –
including the Czech Republic this time. Western critics have long argued that
the communist welfare systems were defective, and they might well have fared
badly in a comparison with those in western Europe, but people in the FSU/
ECE clearly thought they had been better than they were now under their
postcommunist regimes. In every country also, a majority thought that their
country had been more 'properly defended' under the communist regime,
though the majority varied considerably from a relatively narrow majority in
ECE to an overwhelming majority in the FSU. Moreover, a small majority (of
those who could discriminate) complained that their political leaders now had
more privileges than under the former communist regime. That was true in
every country except the Czech Republic.

Table 5.2:   Statements which are more true now than they were of the communist regime

	Political leaders have too many privileges	The poor are well cared for	The economy is well run	(Country) is properly defended	Human rights are respected by the government
	%	%	%	%	%
Russia	54	20	19	11	49
Ukraine	58	14	6	22	50
East Uk	63	12	4	14	39
Mid Uk	63	11	7	18	42
West Uk	37	31	6	58	85
Czech Rep	38	32	80	46	94
Slovakia	60	8	22	30	83
Hungary	57	17	18	43	78
AVERAGE:					
FSU	56	17	13	17	50
ECE	52	19	40	40	85

Note: 'Don't Knows', 'Can't decide' etc. excluded from calculation of percentages. The figures in this table are based only on those who said 'more true now' or 'more true of the communist regime'; so in this table they exclude very high numbers of people who said 'no difference'. As a result the figures highlight the direction of change very well, but perhaps dramatise the degree of change.

There was one exception to this wide-ranging criticism of the new regime: respect for human rights. A very large majority throughout ECE said human rights were better respected by the new postcommunist regime, though people in the FSU were evenly divided even on this.[3]

The Czechs were the most positive on every criterion. While perspectives on the past most frequently distinguished ECE as a whole from the FSU, perspectives on the postcommunist regime frequently divided the Czech Republic from everywhere else.

Once again, west Ukrainians stood out as much more positive about the change of regime than those who lived in the rest of the FSU. Indeed they were as positive towards the present as the people of ECE on the human rights criterion, and even more positive towards the present than the people of ECE on politicians' privileges, national defence, and treatment of the poor – though even west Ukrainians could not excuse the postcommunists' miserable record on running the economy.

PSYCHOLOGICAL PARTICIPATION

Around two-thirds to three-quarters in every country said they regularly followed politics on television, and around half – slightly over half in ECE and under half in the FSU – said they regularly followed politics in the press. Considerably fewer declared that they were at least 'quite interested' in politics or discussed it at least 'quite often'. Such psychological involvement in politics was highest in Slovakia and the Czech Republic and lower in the FSU, though lowest of all in Hungary.

Table 5.3:   Psychological participation

	Follow politics in the newspapers	Follow politics on television	'Very' or 'quite' interested in politics	Discuss politics 'very' or 'quite' often
	%	%	%	%
Russia	44	64	31	28
Ukraine	46	73	33	30
East Uk	44	75	36	33
Mid Uk	46	71	30	27
West Uk	52	71	38	33
Czech Rep	57	72	48	41
Slovakia	46	64	46	43
Hungary	59	77	26	20
AVERAGE:				
FSU	45	68	32	29
ECE	54	71	40	35

Note: 'Don't Knows', 'Can't decide' etc. excluded from calculation of percentages.

ACTIVE PARTICIPATION

Although substantial numbers said they 'spent time on' hobbies, sports or cultural activities, few 'took part in organisations' devoted to such matters. Few took part in religious organisations though more said they took part in trade union or professional organisations. And very few indeed, nearly always fewer than 7 per cent, said they had signed a petition, written to a newspaper, contacted an elected official, been on strike, or taken part in a protest march or demonstration during 'the last two years' – that is under the postcommunist regime.[4]

The only exceptions were that 10 per cent in west Ukraine had taken part in a protest, and 15 per cent had contacted an elected official; while around 15 per cent in Slovakia and the Czech Republic had signed a petition. Postcommunist societies did not have high levels of active participation.

THE DEVELOPMENT OR DECAY OF CIVIL SOCIETY

However, the absolute levels of involvement in society and politics were perhaps less significant than the change in these levels between the communist and postcommunist regimes. Naturally there had been an unusual burst of interest and activity during the crisis period from 1989 to 1991 but, since then, Plasser and Ulram noted an 'unmistakable de-mobilisation.'[5]

We asked people directly, whether they 'took more or less interest in politics now than under the communist regime?' and whether they now 'discussed

Table 5.4:   Active participation: In the last two years, have you...?

	signed a petition	written to a newspaper	contacted an elected official	been on strike	taken part in a demonstration, picket, march or protest meeting
	%	%	%	%	%
Russia	5	2	5	2	5
Ukraine	6	3	7	4	5
East Uk	4	2	5	5	4
Mid Uk	7	4	7	3	4
West Uk	6	5	15	5	10
Czech Rep	13	3	5	3	4
Slovakia	16	4	8	4	6
Hungary	7	2	6	3	4
AVERAGE:					
FSU	5	2	6	3	5
ECE	12	3	6	3	5

Note: 'Don't Knows', 'Can't decide' etc. excluded from calculation of percentages.

political questions more or less than under the communist regime?' Around three-quarters said they took more interest in politics than before, and four-fifths said they now discussed politics more than before. And this was true for both ECE and the FSU; indeed for every country. By these reports at least, purely psychological participation had increased since the days of the old communist regimes.

But we were particularly interested in the development of 'civil society', which means more active, but voluntary, involvement of citizens in social and political life – either as individuals or more especially as members of autonomous organisations.[6]

We asked whether people now 'took part in political life', and 'in non-political organisations', more or less than they had done under the communist regime. A majority everywhere except in west Ukraine said they now took *less* part in political life; and an even larger majority everywhere except west Ukraine (where, however, there was a small majority) said they now took *less* part in non-political organisations than before. Overall, about 63 per cent said they took less part in political life and 77 per cent said they took less part in non-political organisations than they had under the old communist regime. By these reports, active participation in civil society had gone down sharply since the days of the communist regime. And the decline could not be accounted for simply by the end of large official ruling parties since it extended to 'non-political organisations'.[7]

Table 5.5: The development or decay of civil society?

	take more interest in politics now	discuss politics more now	take less part in political life now	get less satisfaction from taking part in political life now	take less part in civil society now	get less satisfaction from taking part in civil society now
	%	%	%	%	%	%
Russia	79	84	59	65	79	76
Ukraine	74	81	67	76	78	79
East Uk	71	82	74	91	83	85
Mid Uk	72	80	72	80	81	83
West Uk	86	84	37	40	54	52
Czech Rep	80	81	64	49	76	59
Slovakia	74	84	65	62	78	70
Hungary	71	74	58	76	70	74
AVERAGE:						
FSU	76	83	63	70	79	77
ECE	75	80	62	62	75	68

Note: 'Don't Knows', 'Can't decide' etc. excluded from calculation of percentages. Since the figures in this table have been calculated as percentages of those who said 'more' or 'less', they also exclude very high numbers of people who said 'no difference'. Thus they highlight the direction of change very well, but perhaps dramatise the degree of change.

Of course, we are often reminded that participation under communism was not voluntary: it was encouraged, or even required, by the regime. It was a 'ritual of pseudo-participation',[8] 'regimented participation', 'organised enthusiasm, mobilising the population in support of policies determined by the leadership.'[9] In short, we are told that it was not Marx and Lenin's 'ideal of direct democracy' (soon abandoned by Lenin himself when in power) but 'false participation'. Even those who dispute the classic distinction between participation in democratic and totalitarian states, and claim the 'Soviet population was neither passive nor merely involved in mobilised rituals',[10] suggest that citizens' voluntary activity under communism was focused on the pursuit of their private interests against the state rather than on a more public, unambiguously political agenda. So we asked a pair of even more pointed questions: did people now get 'more or less *satisfaction* from taking part in political life', or 'from taking part in non-political organisations', than they had done under the communist regime? A large majority everywhere except in the Czech Republic reported that they now got *less satisfaction* from taking part in either political life or in non-political organisations than they had under the communist regime. And even in the Czech Republic, people were evenly divided on whether they now got more or less satisfaction from taking part in political life, and 59 per cent said they now got *less satisfaction* from taking part in non-political organisations than they had under the old regime.

There are all sorts of possible explanations for this. Even forced or at least 'encouraged' participation may have generated some satisfaction. Alternatively, the old regime provided plenty of leisure for such participation because it provided a modest but secure standard of living, while economic dislocation and growing inequalities under the postcommunist regime provided both the opportunities and the incentives to devote much more time and effort to earning – or perhaps just scraping – a living, rather than wasting time on non-essential activities. But whatever the cause, the consequence was that the switch from the communist to the postcommunist regime produced a *less participant* society throughout ECE and the FSU, and one which gained *less satisfaction* from participation – a more 'uncivil' rather than a more 'civil' society, which must have been a cruel disappointment to many of the reformers' hopes.

LACK OF TRUST IN THE INSTITUTIONS OF DEMOCRACY

This new postcommunist society was characterised by low levels of trust in the new political institutions of democracy.

Trust in 'most ordinary people that you meet in everyday life' was relatively high and hardly varied from country to country: 76 per cent in ECE and 78 per cent in the FSU trusted their fellow citizens – lower than in the West perhaps but high in absolute terms.[11] Their trust in their own more limited circle of family and friends is legendary, of course.[12] Trust in the institutions of civil society was somewhat lower, and more variable however. Radio and television were trusted by about 60 per cent in the FSU and around 70 per cent in ECE. The press was trusted by rather less than half in the FSU, though by rather more in ECE; but people had higher levels of trust in the 'newspaper they read most often' if not in the press in general. It is a familiar combination in Western societies also: in Britain, *Guardian* readers trust their own newspaper while despising much, or most, of the British press generally. Trade unions were trusted by rather less than 40 per cent in the FSU, though by rather more in ECE. Conversely, trust in churches was highest in the FSU (at 74 per cent), much lower in ECE and down at a dismally low 30 per cent in the Czech Republic – an intriguing pattern of national variation, but one that is corroborated by other questions about religion. Overall therefore, we could not say that trust in *ordinary people* or in the *institutions of civil society* was consistently higher either in ECE or in the FSU, and – with the exception of sharply varying levels of trust in the churches (over three times as high in West Ukraine as in the Czech Republic) – it did not differ greatly from country to country.

Table 5.6:   Trust in civil society: per cent who trust...

	Most ordinary people	Radio	Television	News-papers in general	The news-paper you read most often	Trade unions	Churches
	%	%	%	%	%	%	%
Russia	79	61	60	45	70	38	77
Ukraine	76	56	60	41	59	32	71
East Uk	77	50	55	34	53	33	58
Mid Uk	74	54	59	42	57	33	73
West Uk	80	78	77	55	81	28	92
Czech Rep	79	79	75	60	86	41	30
Slovakia	78	75	66	49	74	52	53
Hungary	72	64	54	52	74	38	61
AVERAGE:							
FSU	78	59	60	43	65	35	74
ECE	76	73	65	54	78	44	48

Note: 'Don't Knows', 'Can't decide' etc. excluded from calculation of percentages.

Table 5.7:   Trust organs of power?

	Army	Security services	Police	Judges and courts
	%	%	%	%
Russia	72	56	40	42
Ukraine	67	49	38	38
East Uk	64	48	37	35
Mid Uk	64	50	38	39
West Uk	84	48	41	42
Czech Rep	55	30	48	47
Slovakia	71	35	46	46
Hungary	76	70	72	75
AVERAGE:				
FSU	70	53	39	40
ECE	67	45	55	56

Note: 'Don't Knows', 'Can't decide' etc. excluded from calculation of percentages.

With the exception of the army, the general level of trust in *institutions of authority* was in line with the level of trust in the institutions of civil society.

Hungarians displayed high levels of trust – over 70 per cent of those who had an opinion – in their army, their police, their security services and their courts. But people in other countries displayed rather less trust in every one of these except the army. Compared to people in the FSU, Czechs and Slovaks were more suspicious of their security services, but trusted their police and courts rather more.

However, the supreme irony was that after the democratic revolutions of 1989–91, people everywhere had much lower levels of trust in their new *democratically elected* parliaments than in the old organs of power. It may not be surprising, but it is ironical. They also had low levels of trust in their new democratic governments, prime ministers or executive presidents in every country except the Czech Republic.[13]

Table 5.8:   Trust elected authorities?

	President	*Prime minister*	*The government*	*Parliament*
	%	%	%	%
Russia	39	37	36	(old) 24
				(new) 48
Ukraine	21	16	17	21
East Uk	17	16	15	21
Mid Uk	16	14	14	17
West Uk	49	28	36	38
Czech Rep	77	72	63	29
Slovakia	72	39	29	27
Hungary	71	35	24	29
AVERAGE:				
FSU	35	27	27	*29
ECE	73	49	39	28

Notes: 'Don't Knows', 'Can't decide' etc. excluded from calculation of percentages.
* The figure of 29 per cent for trust in FSU parliaments is based on averaging figures for the Ukraine parliament, and for the old and new parliaments in Russia. Excluding attitudes to the new Russian parliament, to which the old Tsarist term 'Duma' was applied to emphasise its lack of power, the figure for the FSU would be 23 per cent.

Since our surveys of public opinion took place at the end of 1993, shortly after Yeltsin had suspended, then dissolved the existing Russian parliament[14] and while elections were taking place for a new bicameral Russian parliament, we asked respondents in Russia about their level of trust in both their old and their new parliaments. Naturally the level of 'don't knows' was high when we asked about the newly elected parliament which had still to meet and show itself in action. So although an unusually high percentage, 48 per cent of those with a view, expected to trust the new parliament, 61 per cent of those interviewed before the election, and 44 per cent interviewed immediately after it, had no views at all on this matter. Excluding that peculiar case, trust in the postcommunist parliaments people had actually experienced, and about which most people did have views, was very low – about 22 per cent in the FSU and not much better, 28 per cent, in ECE. Even in the Czech Republic where people were relatively satisfied and optimistic about so many things, only 29 per cent of those with a view trusted rather than distrusted their parliament.

Both our FSU countries, Russia and Ukraine, were 'presidential republics', where the executive presidency played a leading role in day to day government and the levels of trust in president, prime minister and government were similar to each other and very low: in Ukraine they were certainly as low as trust in parliament, in Russia they were half way between the levels of trust in the old and new parliaments. By contrast, all three ECE countries were 'parliamentary' democracies whose presidents were supposed to stand outside day to day politics and, to a large extent, did so.[15] In these countries, levels of trust in prime minister and government were similar to each other, though prime ministers were always a little more trusted that their governments, but trust in both could be very different (and much less) than the level of trust in the non-executive figurehead president.[16] There was a very high level of trust in all three non-executive presidents, averaging 73 per cent, with little variation across ECE countries. However, there were sharply differing levels of trust in prime ministers and governments. In Slovakia and Hungary the level of trust in the 'government' was as low as the level of trust in parliament, and the prime minister scored only about 10 per cent better. But uniquely in the Czech Republic trust in both the government (63 per cent) and the prime minister (72 per cent) was high, far higher than the level of trust in parliament, and rivalled the level of trust in the president.

This finding suggests that high levels of trust in the organs of power, or what others have called 'traditional institutions' – the church, the courts, and especially the army – compared to low levels for new democratic institutions, may also reflect the fact that these traditional institutions were also seen as being above the fray of day to day politics under the postcommunist regime. In the Czech Republic, where the church was a particularly active player in the politics of restitution, it was heartily distrusted.[17]

Plasser and Ulram also contrasted low public confidence in democratic institutions with much higher public confidence in churches, courts and armies, and commented on the rapidly growing disaffection with democratic institutions in ECE 'mainly in the crisis year of 1993', just before our survey.[18] Similarly Rhodes contrasted the lack of public confidence in Russia's new democratic institutions with high levels of public confidence in 'such traditional pillars of the Russian state as the church and the armed forces.'[19] But commentators on the FSU and ECE might have been somewhat less concerned if they had noticed similar, though not so extreme, findings were appearing, at just the same time, for a model Western democracy. Anthony King noted that Gallup polls in Britain showed public confidence in parliament had dropped from 54 per cent to 30 per cent between 1983 and 1993, and confidence in the press to just 18 per cent, while confidence in the police stood at 70 per cent, and in the army at 84 per cent.[20] Similarly, Thomas Dye noted that NORC polls showed trust in American government fell from over 60 per cent in the 1960s to less than 30 per cent in the 1990s and that 'only the military had enjoyed an increase in confidence ... [making] the military the most highly regarded institutional leadership in American society.'[21] Both the US 'executive branch' and the US Congress scored badly in the early 1990s. Certainly, both King and Dye worried about the state of western democracy;[22] but at least their worries – and their evidence – put concerns about public confidence in FSU/ECE armies and democratic institutions into a proper perspective.

UNFAIR OFFICIALS

Trust was low not only in the arena of high politics but in that of low politics, in people's day to day dealings with state officials.[23] We asked people to 'suppose there were some problems you had to take to a government office – for example, a problem about tax or housing. Do you think you would be treated fairly by the officials in that office?' That was the complete extent of the question. By implication it invited a 'yes' or a 'no' by way of answer. But our interviewers were primed to note (without prompting in any way) answers which indicated that people expected fair treatment 'only by using connections or bribes.' We should stress that this phrase about 'connections or bribes' was seen only by the interviewer, and was not read out to the respondent. Such answers, if they occurred, were therefore spontaneous reactions to our apparently innocent question.

Only 14 per cent in the FSU gave an unqualified 'yes' to the question whether they expected fair treatment by officials. The figure was higher in ECE, progressively higher as we moved culturally (if not quite geographically) westwards: 43 per cent in Hungary, 53 per cent in Slovakia and 64 per cent in the Czech Republic.

With or without recourse to using connections and bribes, two-thirds of those in the FSU expected unfair treatment by officials of the new post-communist regime; half expected to be treated unfairly in Hungary; but just under one third in the former Czechoslovakia.[24]

Of course, the arbitrariness and corruption of officials under the old communist regime was legendary.[25] And despite changes in political leadership at the top, many junior officials stayed on under the new regime.[26] Indeed, reflecting on the governing style of Yeltsin (in Russia) or Meciar (in Slovakia) we would have to say that not only old personalities but also old instincts of government sometimes stayed on even at the very top in the new postcommunist regimes.

Table 5.9: Expect fair treatment by officials, for example in a tax or housing office?

	No	Only by using connections or bribes	Yes
	%	%	%
Russia	66	18	16
Ukraine	70	18	12
East Uk	66	20	13
Mid Uk	74	15	10
West Uk	64	21	15
Czech Rep	31	5	64
Slovakia	32	15	53
Hungary	50	7	43
AVERAGE:			
FSU	68	18	14
ECE	38	9	53

Notes: 'Don't Knows', 'Can't decide' etc. excluded from calculation of percentages.

Democratisation should mean greater popular control of officials if it is to mean anything at all. But the economic and administrative chaos of the transition to a new regime provided increased opportunities for officials to enrich themselves through acquiring state assets, indulging in unfair competition, and giving, selling or withholding favours to ordinary citizens – what became known as 'nomenklatura capitalism'.

Yet no matter whether this distrust of junior officials was inherited from the old regime or whether it gained anything during the chaos of transition, the fact remains that it was there, that it existed under the new postcommunist regime. So that while postcommunist parliaments were distrusted everywhere, the postcommunist bureaucracy was equally distrusted at a personal level in the FSU though to a significantly lesser degree in ECE.

CONCLUSION

Apart from the clear FSU/ECE division in attitudes to junior officials, one conclusion that emerges from this chapter is that the cultural division between the FSU and ECE applied somewhat less clearly to perspectives on the postcommunist present than to perspectives on the communist past. Instead, the Czech Republic was unique not only in its peoples' relative (though certainly not absolute) satisfaction with its economic progress, but also in the extent to which its people trusted their government, their prime minister, and their bureaucracy.

But a more general and more important conclusion is that public dissatisfaction with postcommunist regimes extended far beyond purely economic dissatisfaction. The new regimes were criticised for failing to defend their countries properly, for according too many privileges to political leaders, and for failing to look after the poor. People reported that they took less part in social and political life, and that they were also less satisfied by their participation in social and political life than they had been under the old communist regime. The new democratic parliaments were distrusted everywhere and – except for the Czech Republic – that distrust extended to governments and chief executives, if not to figurehead presidents. Junior officials were also heartily distrusted by the people they supposedly served in the FSU and regarded with very mixed feelings everywhere else – except, once again, in the Czech Republic.

It is a bleak picture with little to relieve the gloom. Even on respect for human rights, people in the FSU (except for west Ukraine) criticised the new regime for being worse than the old. No doubt they would have agreed that the postcommunist regime's performance on human rights was better than that of Stalin's regime, but not than Gorbachev's or perhaps even Brezhnev's.

Against that background we turn, in the next four chapters, to look at political values – the public's attachment to the principles of socialism, nationalism, liberalism and democracy.

III Values

6 Socialism after Communism

Socialism itself can be defined either in broad or in narrow terms, and the people who are socialists are usually something else as well. So in Britain, for example, a strong case can be made for the proposition that socialists are usually committed to principles of freedom and democracy as well as to principles of socialism.[1] But let us take a very narrow definition of socialism here; so that we can distinguish it from what may be its purely empirical, contingent, and culturally determined correlates. In later chapters we can then investigate whether those who were more committed to socialism (by this narrow definition) in ECE and the FSU were actually more or less committed to principles of democracy, or more or less committed to nationalism, than the average.

Purely for analytical clarity therefore, we shall focus in this chapter on a limited range of values associated with the degree of equality between citizens and the extent of the state's role in society. For present purposes, that will be our (narrow) definition of socialism.

SUPPORT FOR A MARKET ECONOMY

Support for the switch to 'a market economy' was a popular slogan of reformers in the 1980s and early 1990s, though many preferred to added their own personal adjectives to define what kind of market economy they had in mind – a 'free market economy', a 'social market economy', 'a socially oriented market economy' and so on.[2]

We avoided all such prejudicial adjectives and asked simply: 'Do you personally feel that the creation of a market economy is right or wrong for (country)?' About three-quarters in ECE and west Ukraine agreed, as did about two thirds in the rest of the FSU. In Russia, the same percentage (66 per cent) said they had supported 'the social and economic policies implemented since January 1992' in the referendum held by Yeltsin on that question in the spring of 1993.[3] Within ECE the level of support for an undefined 'market economy' increased steadily from 64 per cent in Hungary to 79 per cent in Slovakia and 88 per cent in the Czech Republic.

But support was neither unqualified nor enthusiastic. We also asked whether 'the idea of a market economy' was 'broadly satisfactory', or whether there was simply 'no real alternative'. Across both ECE and the FSU less than half (44 per cent) said they found the idea 'broadly satisfactory' while another 28 per cent reluctantly admitted they could see no real alternative.

There are varieties of market economy, of course. A majority in every country chose Sweden rather than the USA as the 'best model' for their country to follow.[4] That may have reflected attitudes to different kinds of market economy, though it was almost certainly influenced also by other factors including size and national pride: Sweden was a significantly more popular choice in the small countries of ECE than the large countries of the FSU and a particularly large number of respondents in Russia volunteered the reply, without being asked, that *neither* Sweden nor the USA was a good model for Russia. The 'third Rome'[5] should not seek models in the contemporary world.

Table 6.1: Qualified support for the principle of a market economy

	Attitude to the idea of a market economy:				Best model is Sweden rather than USA
	it is right for (country)	it is broadly satisfactory	there is no real alternative	there is a better alternative	
	%	%	%	%	%
Russia	65	48	22	31	60
Ukraine	63	39	33	28	58
East Uk	62	36	34	29	61
Mid Uk	60	39	33	28	59
West Uk	75	46	28	27	51
Czech Rep	88	58	21	22	74
Slovakia	79	33	36	41	75
Hungary	64	40	27	33	70
AVERAGE:					
FSU	64	44	27	29	59
ECE	77	44	28	32	73

Notes: 'Don't Knows', 'Can't decide' etc. excluded from calculation of percentages. On the 'best model' question: More than others, Russians tended to reject both Sweden and the USA as models; nonetheless, absolute support for the Swedish model was higher throughout ECE than in the FSU countries, while absolute support for the USA model was higher throughout the FSU than in the ECE countries.

THE ROLE OF THE STATE IN RUNNING INDUSTRY

We asked more direct questions, however, which tell us much more about the kind of market economy people wanted. First we asked whether each of the following 'should be run mainly by the state or mainly by private business?

- farming
- car factories
- computer manufacturers
- newspapers
- television programmes.'

Up to a quarter of respondents volunteered (without being explicitly offered the option) the reply that they should be run more or less equally by the state and private business. It is a reasonable response. But our interest is in the balance of opinion amongst the vast majority who did come down on one side or the other.

Car factories and computer manufacturers represented old and new industry. Attitudes towards them were almost identical however. Around three-quarters in the FSU – including west Ukraine – felt they should be run mainly by the state. In Hungary around half thought that, and in Slovakia and the Czech Republic closer to one-third.

Newspapers and television programmes were important in terms of the free flow of information to citizens as well as in purely industrial terms. Again attitudes towards the two were hardly distinguishable. And this time, even more people favoured state control – over three quarters in the FSU, over half in Slovakia as well as in Hungary, though close to a third in the Czech Republic.

Farming has always raised peculiar issues that vary very much with the nature of the land and the traditions of the area. In the FSU, there was far less support for state control of farming than of any other industry.[6] Overall, just over half in the FSU and ECE felt farming should be run mainly by the state, but attitudes varied from country to country, and in an unusual way: support for state control of farming was lowest in Ukraine, especially in west Ukraine but also in the rest of Ukraine, even lower than in ECE. Under the Tsars, a relatively low proportion of peasants in southern and eastern Ukraine – the Crimea and the provinces of Voronezh, Kharkov, Ekaterinoslav, Kherson especially – were serfs[7] and these areas overlapped with those that most fiercely resisted Stalin's collectivisation in the late 1920s and early 1930s.[8] Additionally, our 'west Ukraine', the inter-war Polish ruled oblasts, did not experienced communist collectivisation until after 1945. Further analysis of our data shows that, within Ukraine as well as elsewhere, farmers themselves were *more* favourable than others towards state control of farming (though farmers were also more favourable than others to state control generally).[9] But whatever farmers themselves might think about collectivisation or state run farming, the issue of state control of the land was deeply entwined with the historic grievances and national feelings that affected most people who lived in Ukraine.

More personally, we asked each respondent what kind of enterprise they themselves would prefer to work for 'if you had a choice'. We listed 'state enterprises, cooperatives, private companies, foreign or joint venture companies, and self-employment' and we noted those few who replied that they would prefer not to work at all.

Remarkably few people anywhere wished to work for a private company – only 13 per cent, on average, both in ECE and the FSU. Another 20 per cent – again in both the FSU and ECE – wished to work for a foreign firm or joint venture, though the attraction of that was almost certainly its 'foreignness' implying high standards and high wages, rather than its 'privateness'. And very few wished to work for a cooperative.

Table 6.2:   State control of industry

| | These should be run mainly by the state, rather than mainly by private businesses: | | | | |
	Farming	*Car factories*	*Computer manufacturers*	*Newspapers*	*Television programming*
	%	%	%	%	%
Russia	60	79	68	79	83
Ukraine	43	73	71	72	75
East Uk	48	76	72	72	73
Mid Uk	45	71	71	72	76
West Uk	27	70	72	71	79
Czech Rep	53	39	27	34	38
Slovakia	72	44	32	57	53
Hungary	44	55	55	46	57
AVERAGE:					
FSU	52	76	69	76	79
ECE	56	46	38	46	49

Note: 'Don't Knows', 'Can't decide' etc. excluded from calculation of percentages.

Most people wished to work either for the state or for themselves. The option of self-employment was about 10 per cent more popular in ECE and west Ukraine than in the rest of the FSU; while the option of state employment was especially popular in Russia (52 per cent) less so in Ukraine, Slovakia and Hungary, and least popular in the Czech Republic (30 per cent). Nonetheless, the option of state employment was the single most popular option everywhere, with only the partial exception of the Czech Republic where it tied for top place with self employment.

For whatever reason – positive ideology, timidity or insecurity – there was widespread support for the concept of public enterprise, as a prescription both for the economy and for personal employment.

THE ROLE OF THE STATE IN MANAGING SOCIAL WELFARE

Even those who do not accept a role for the state in the ownership and management of particular industries may accept a role for the state in managing the economy as a whole or in providing a safety net of welfare services.

Over 90 per cent everywhere, except in the Czech Republic and west Ukraine, said the provision of health care should be 'done mainly by the government' rather than 'left mainly to private business and the market economy'; and even in those two exceptional places, over 80 per cent took that view. Similarly an average of over 80 per cent said the provision of housing should be left mainly to government rather than to private businesses and the market economy – a figure that rose to 90 per cent in Ukraine[10] (including west Ukraine) and dropped only to 69 per cent in the Czech Republic. Fully 81 per cent in ECE and 91 per cent in the FSU said that 'the prices of basic goods and services' should be set mainly by government rather than by the market economy; and that figure sank no lower than 73 per cent even in the Czech Republic.

Table 6.3:   Preferred employers

	state	cooperative	private	foreign	self
		If had the choice, would prefer to work for …			
	%	%	%	%	%
Russia	52	4	11	17	17
Ukraine	40	4	15	23	19
East Uk	41	4	15	23	17
Mid Uk	39	3	17	25	16
West Uk	38	6	9	15	32
Czech Rep	30	5	15	20	30
Slovakia	38	6	12	24	21
Hungary	35	7	12	14	33
AVERAGE:					
FSU	46	4	13	20	18
ECE	34	6	13	19	28

Note: 'Don't Knows', 'Can't decide' etc. excluded from calculation of percentages.

There was more variation in attitudes to job creation however. Fully 89 per cent in the FSU said the provision of jobs should be the responsibility of government rather than being left mainly to private business, as did 84 per cent in Hungary and 77 per cent in Slovakia. But this figure sank right down to 56 per cent in the Czech Republic – though that is still a majority of those with an opinion on the issue. But the overall pattern of these results suggests that there was even more support, and even more widespread support, for a government role in managing general welfare than in managing particular industries, factories or businesses.

STATE RESPONSIBILITY FOR CULTURE

We also asked about the proper role of government in the cultural sphere: 'should the government use state funds to support each of the following?:

- opera and ballet companies
- the Orthodox church/Catholic church [in FSU/ECE respectively]
- other Christian churches
- non-Christian religions
- political parties.'

Opera was notoriously a favourite of the communist regime, especially Stalin, to the point where the opera house he had built in Tashkent is now boycotted by the Uzbek population as a symbol of Russian imperialism and communist dictatorship. But opera is heavily subsidised in the West also. Similarly, churches enjoy state subsidies, open or covert, in many western countries, as do political parties. And during the difficult transition to multi-party democracy there is an even better case than usual for the state to subsidise parties. On the other hand, one of the main faults of the old regime had been a failure to keep state and party separate.

Throughout our FSU countries (which did *not* include the Central Asian republics) 87 per cent of the public approved state subsidies for opera and ballet. This level of support extended right across the Ukraine and, indeed, beyond the FSU and into Hungary; but it dropped to less than half in Slovakia and the Czech Republic despite Prague's strong cultural links with opera. In Prague, unlike Tashkent, opera was indigenous and popular, yet support for state subsidies was low.

Table 6.4:   State responsibilities for social welfare

| | These should be mainly done by the state, rather than left mainly to private businesses and the market-economy: | | | |
	Health care	Jobs	Housing	Setting prices for basic goods and services
	%	%	%	%
Russia	93	89	75	93
Ukraine	88	89	90	88
East Uk	90	89	93	88
Mid Uk	90	90	89	88
West Uk	81	85	89	85
Czech Rep	81	56	69	73
Slovakia	97	77	85	91
Hungary	94	84	85	78
AVERAGE:				
FSU	91	89	82	91
ECE	91	72	80	81

Note: 'Don't Knows', 'Can't decide' etc. excluded from calculation of percentages.

Table 6.5: Should the government use state funds to support?

	Opera and ballet	The principal church (Orthodox in FSU; Catholic in ECE)	Other Christian churches	Non-Christian religions	Political parties
	%	%	%	%	%
Russia	87	64	50	35	19
Ukraine	87	49	40	21	13
East Uk	86	43	34	20	18
Mid Uk	88	51	43	25	10
West Uk	86	54	44	14	11
Czech Rep	49	20	18	11	22
Slovakia	48	39	35	19	22
Hungary	79	60	60	42	36
AVERAGE:					
FSU	87	57	45	28	16
ECE	59	40	38	24	27

Note: 'Don't Knows', 'Can't decide' etc. excluded from calculation of percentages.

Similarly with attitudes to state funding for the (unofficial) state churches, the Orthodox or Catholic (we asked about 'the Orthodox church' in the FSU and 'the Catholic church' in ECE): half or more of the public supported such church subsidies throughout the FSU and in Hungary, but only 39 per cent in Slovakia and a mere 20 per cent in the Czech Republic. Even the Hussite legacy could not explain that finding in purely religious terms: it was primarily opposition to state intervention in the cultural sphere. Indeed public support for state subsidies to other Christian churches followed the same pattern – relatively high in the FSU and Hungary, but down to a mere 18 per cent in the Czech Republic. Still less, only 11 per cent of the Czechs would agree to state subsidies for non-Christian religions.

However the pattern was partially reversed on attitudes to state subsidies for political parties. Whereas there was *more* support in the FSU than in ECE for state funding of opera, dominant churches, other Christian churches, and even non-Christian religions, there was substantially *less* support in the FSU than in ECE for state subsidies to political parties. One legacy of the 'party-state' was an allergy to the word 'party' and in a striking recognition of this fact many of the newly-established parties carefully avoided using that word in their official designations.

EQUALITY

Apart from its view about the proper role of the state, socialism is most closely connected to ideas of economic equality. We asked three relevant questions about that. In very general abstract terms we asked people to choose between:

- 'giving everyone the freedom to make as much money as they can'

and

- 'ensuring that the gap between rich and poor does not become too wide'.

For all its abstract nature, few respondents had any difficulty making their choice. The level of 'don't knows' was less than one per cent throughout ECE, 4 per cent in Ukraine and only 7 per cent in Russia. We shall as usual exclude these 'don't knows' and report the balance of opinion amongst the vast majority who stated their choice.

Very surprisingly perhaps, it was the people of ECE who showed the greatest commitment to equality. Perhaps they were less easily intoxicated by the idea of 'freedom', perhaps they were sufficiently comfortable to think about something other than the desperate struggle for survival, perhaps they had a greater sense of community, perhaps they had greater confidence in the fairness of their bureaucrats who would have to restrict people's 'freedom to make money' in order to moderate the gap between rich and poor. Whatever the reason, two thirds of people in ECE but only half in the FSU opted for equality.[11]

Other indicators also revealed widespread support for equality but did not suggest it was greater in ECE than in the FSU. We asked one question about 'the new rich' and another about the unemployed – who were included in, but by no means coextensive with, the new poor. What, we asked, were people's attitudes towards the 'new rich' – a term widely used in ECE and the FSU to describe those who had done well for themselves out of the chaos of transition. Did people:

- '*admire* them'
- 'feel *indifferent* towards them'
- '*dislike* them'
- 'feel they should be *jailed*'.

Few people had no view, and 44 per cent of those with a view said they disliked the new rich or would even go so far as to jail them. Such attitudes were just as common in ECE as in the FSU but no more so.[12]

As for unemployment we asked whether people felt it was:

- 'unacceptable'
- 'unavoidable, because loss-making factories must be closed'

or

– 'necessary to encourage people to work hard'.

Table 6.6: Attitudes to winners and losers (%)

	Restricting gap between rich and poor is more important than freedom to make money	Dislike 'new rich', or would even jail them	Unemployment is 'unacceptable'	Unemployment is 'necessary'
Russia	52	44	54	14
Ukraine	46	42	49	21
East Uk	50	43	52	17
Mid Uk	41	39	47	26
West Uk	57	51	50	17
Czech Rep	53	40	19	46
Slovakia	63	51	41	29
Hungary	74	41	47	8
AVERAGE:				
FSU	49	43	52	18
ECE	63	44	36	28

People in ECE might have been more committed to the principle of equality than those in the FSU, but their attitudes to unemployment varied in the opposite way. Around half the public in the FSU (including west Ukraine), and in Hungary, said that unemployment was simply 'unacceptable'; but only 41 per cent in Slovakia, and a mere 19 per cent in the Czech Republic. Conversely only 18 per cent in the FSU and a mere 8 per cent in Hungary said unemployment was 'necessary to encourage people to work hard'; but that extreme right-wing view was taken by 29 per cent in Slovakia and by a remarkable 46 per cent in the Czech Republic. The unemployed themselves did not agree with that, in the Czech Republic or anywhere else; but, in the Czech Republic, those who had a job were much more willing to accept unemployment – for other people – than those who lived in Slovakia or Hungary.[13]

COMPOSITE INDICATORS

We have discussed a wide range of questions that have a bearing on commitment to socialist values – indeed too wide a range. In later chapters we wish to investigate, for example, the relationships between socialist values and nationalism, socialist values and commitment to democracy, or the influences that support or inhibit commitment to socialist values. For those purposes we have far too many questions about socialist values. We must either select or combine our different questions about socialist values in order to get down to a more manageable set of indicators.

A preliminary factor analysis including most of the questions discussed in this chapter, plus some from the previous chapter and others, clearly suggests that answers to various groups of questions tend to hang together. Guided by that we can construct four composite measures of different aspects of socialist values.

First there are the five questions about whether government or private businesses should run key industries. For each question we give the answer 'mainly by the state' a value of 5; the answer 'mainly by private business' a value of 1; and all other answers ('both', 'don't know') a value of 3. If we then average a person's score across these five questions, we get an indicator of their general support for the public ownership and control of industries on a scale that runs from 1 (= low) to 5 (= high).

A factor analysis of these five questions alone shows that some slight distinction could be drawn between attitudes to three different groups of industries – (i) car and computer companies, (ii) press and television, and (iii) agriculture. Nonetheless it still makes sense to group these five together. A single factor can explain 48 per cent of their total variation and a second factor would only just meet conventional criteria for recognition with an eigenvalue of 1.02. Averaging scores across the five questions produces a composite indicator with a high reliability coefficient (alpha) of 0.72 which would not be improved by a more complex weighted average of the answers to the five questions. Of course, the high reliability coefficient means nothing more than that answers to the individual questions correlated well with each other, and that in turn partly reflects the fact that they were all asked in the same standard format and in quick succession to each other. Nonetheless this simple composite measure does indicate a general tendency to support state enterprise. It correlates at about 0.7 or above with all the separate questions about state enterprise except agriculture where the correlation is a little less. For brevity let us call it an indicator of support for *State Industry*.

Similarly, answers to the four questions about the state being mainly responsible for providing jobs, health care or housing and for fixing the prices of basic goods and services also hang together. A factor analysis reveals only one factor, accounting for 49 per cent of their variation; and a composite indicator formed by averaging answers to the four separate questions has a reliability coefficient of 0.65 which, again, would not be improved by a more complex combination. This composite indicator correlates at between 0.65 and 0.74 with each of the separate questions. Let us call it, for brevity, an indicator of support for *State Welfare*.

Answers to our five questions about state subsidies for opera, churches and parties also hang together. A factor analysis produces only one factor which explains 55 per cent of their variation; and a composite indicator formed by averaging answers to the five questions has a reliability coefficient of 0.78 which would not be improved by a more complex combination. This composite indicator correlates at over 0.8 with all three questions about subsidising religion but rather less well with the questions about subsidising opera and political parties. Let us call it, for brevity, an indicator of support for *State Culture*.

Finally let us group together the three questions that touch upon equality. These are clearly a much more disparate collection of indicators which vary sharply both in format and in content. Naturally they do not correlate so well with each other as do five questions taken from a repetitive battery. They are:

(1) the question that posed a choice between 'the freedom to make as much money as possible' versus 'ensuring that the gap between rich and poor does not become too wide' – coding the first as 1 and the second as 5;

(2) the question about the 'new rich' – coding 'admire them' as 1, 'feel indifferent' as 2, 'dislike' as 4, 'jail' as 5, and 'don't know' as 3;

(3) the question about unemployment – coding 'necessary' as 1, 'unacceptable' as 5, and anything else as 3.

Table 6.7: Correlations between composite indicators of socialist values and the questions on which they were based

	r x 100
State industry	55 farming
	71 car factories
	69 computer manufacturers
	76 newspapers
	73 television programmes
	alpha 72 (72)
State welfare	74 jobs
	65 health care
	73 housing
	68 setting prices for basic goods
	alpha 65 (65)
Equality	76 equality versus freedom to make money
	62 new rich
	62 unemployment
	alpha 38 (40)
State culture	55 opera and ballet
	85 Orthodox Church (in FSU) / Catholic (in ECE)
	87 other Christian churches
	80 non-Christian religions
	54 political parties
	alpha 78 (77)

Notes: r × 100 = (Pearson) correlation coefficient times 100 to remove the decimal point. All respondents are included in the construction of these composite indicators, by coding 'Don't Knows', 'Can't Decides' etc. at 3, the mid point on each variable, before averaging to get the composite score. Alpha figures in brackets are the maximum alpha values that could be obtained by using a more complex average. However, we have used a simple average for clarity.

A factor analysis of these three questions produced one factor explaining 46 per cent of their variation. A composite indicator formed by averaging answers to the three questions has a low reliability coefficient (alpha) of 0.38, but it could only be raised to 0.40 by a more complex combination. Clearly the reliability of this indicator is much less than of the others, but these are the only three questions which span the concept of equality, and that concept is far too important for us to ignore. The composite indicator, based as it is on only three questions, correlates at over 0.62 with each of them. Let us call this composite indicator, for brevity, *Equality*.

Three of our four composite indicators of socialist values correlate quite well with each other: *State Industry* and *State Welfare* correlate at 0.48; and both correlate at about 0.33 with *Equality*.

However the fourth does not correlate well with the others. State Culture correlates at only 0.14 with State Industry, 0.10 with State Welfare, and 0.05 with Equality. A factor analysis of the four indicators produces a single factor that correlates well with the first three indicators but hardly at all with State Culture. The propensity to subsidise cultural organisations seems to be something different from socialism. Indeed there must be some doubt as to whether we should retain State Culture within our concept of socialist values. So, as an overall measure of commitment to Socialist Values ('Socialism' for short) we shall average scores on State Industry, State Welfare, and Equality, but exclude State Culture from this overall average.

Table 6.8:   Correlations between socialist values

	S. Industry rx100	S. Welfare rx100	Equality rx100	S. Culture rx100
State Industry	100	48	32	14
State Welfare		100	34	10
Equality			100	.
State Culture				100

Note: Correlations less than 0.10 have been replaced by a full-stop.

CONCLUSION: THE PATTERN OF COMMITMENT TO SOCIALIST VALUES

We shall use these composite indicators directly and unmodified in computer driven multivariate calculations where they have considerable advantages in precision and discrimination. But scores on these indicators do not have enough intuitive 'feel' about them for ease of exposition. In comparing countries or social groups, for example, we shall find it more useful to present the percentage of people in each country or social group who score above the mid-point (3.0) on each composite measure. That figure is fairly easy to understand intuitively: it is the percentage of people who, on average, take the socialist side either in general or more specifically on the question of state ownership, or welfare, or equality, or who favour rather than reject state subsidies in the cultural sphere. By these criteria, we found that 74 per cent were committed to socialist values in general; 81 per cent were committed to socialist welfare values, but only just over half were committed to equality or state control of industry, and less than half to state intervention in the cultural sphere.

Table 6.9: Percentage scoring above the mid-point (3.0) on composite measures of socialist values

	Socialism	State Industry	State Welfare	Equality	State Culture
	%	%	%	%	%
All respondents	74	52	81	56	41
Russia	81	66	85	56	51
Ukraine	76	59	84	50	39
East Uk	75	58	83	56	36
Mid Uk	76	60	85	42	41
West Uk	81	60	82	63	42
Czech Rep	51	29	62	40	16
Slovakia	78	44	85	59	29
Hungary	79	45	84	73	56
AVERAGE:					
FSU	79	63	85	53	45
ECE	69	39	77	57	34

Notes: The composite indicator of Socialism is the average of Equality, State industry and State welfare – omitting State culture for the reasons given in the text. Each scale runs from 1 to 5 with 3 as the neutral point – thus over 3, means more pro-socialist than anti-socialist. Entries are the percentages who score (strictly) over 3, i.e. who are pro-socialist.

In every country except the Czech Republic, between 76 per cent and 81 per cent were committed to socialist values; but in the Czech Republic only 51 per cent. So on socialist values, there was no break point at the FSU/ECE border, and no break point between west Ukraine and the rest of the FSU. The break point was at the Czech border. Since support for the different aspects of socialist values varied within each country, that overall level of 51 per cent support in the

Czech Republic meant that there was majority support for socialist welfare values even in the Czech Republic, though a small majority in the Czech Republic opposed equality values, a larger majority opposed state control of industry and, of course, an overwhelming majority opposed state intervention in the cultural sphere.

SOCIALIST VALUES AND THE MARKET ECONOMY

We can also use our four composite indicators to investigate the meanings underlying people's declarations of attachment to such phrases as 'communist ideals' or the 'market economy' by correlating each of our four composite measures of socialist values with answers to relevant questions including whether respondents:

(1)   now believe in communist ideals
(2)   ever believed in communist ideals
(3)   were ever a member of the Communist Party
(4)   prefer Sweden to the USA as a model for their country
(5)   feel the creation of the market economy is right for their country
(6)   say the idea of a market economy is broadly satisfactory.

Some of our findings are easily stated. None of the answers to these questions correlated with *State Culture*, confirming our suspicion that this is indeed something quite separate from socialist values. The choice of Sweden rather than the USA as the 'best model' hardly correlated with any socialist values except, marginally, with *State Industry*, confirming our suspicion that this question reflected other things than the degree of socialism in those two countries.

Table 6.10:   Correlations between socialist values and attitudes to communism and markets

	Ever a Communist Party Member	*Believe now in communist ideals*	*Believed in the past in communist ideals*	*Market economy wrong for this country*	*Idea of market economy is unsatis-factory*	*Prefer Sweden to USA*
	r×100	*r×100*	*r×100*	*r×100*	*r×100*	*r×100*
Equality	.	21	17	32	23	.
S.Industry	.	16	19	35	17	10
S.Welfare	.	14	16	29	17	.
S.Culture	.	.	.	.	.	.

Note: Correlations less than 0.10 have been replaced by a full-stop.

More remarkably, declared membership (mainly in the past of course) of the Communist Party failed to correlate at all with any indicator of socialism. So we have to conclude that membership of the Communist Party under the old communist regime was only a career move and had nothing to do with genuine adherence to socialist values.[14] On the other hand, genuine commitment to socialist values did correlate somewhat with expressed 'belief in communist ideals' and more strongly with criticism of the market economy.

Multiple regression provides an even better way of interpreting the meaning of opposition to the market economy or belief in communist ideals. By using multiple regression we can see which aspect of socialist values was most closely linked to declarations of belief in communist ideals or opposition to the market economy. Opposition to the market economy was based in equal measure on support for the values of Equality and State Industry and, to a lesser extent, upon the value of State Welfare. Former belief in communist ideals was also based on support for State Industry and Equality. But *current* belief in communist ideals in the early 1990s was based exclusively upon support for the value of Equality, rather than on attitudes towards State Industry or even State Welfare.

Table 6.11: Multiple regressions predicting attitudes to communist ideals and the market economy from all four socialist values

	Now believe in communist ideals *multiple corr* $(\times 100) = 24$	*Market economy wrong for this country* *multiple corr* $(\times 100) = 43$
	beta $\times 100$	beta $\times 100$
Equality	17	21
State Industry	.	23
State Welfare	.	10
State Culture	.	.

Note: Entries are path coefficients (betas, standardised regression coefficients). Those less than 0.10 have been replaced by a full-stop.

7 External and Internal Nationalism

Nationalism is often portrayed as a slippery concept, difficult to define. But, in fact, the word (singular!) is more slippery, ambiguous and difficult to define, than the concepts (plural!) to which it is applied.[1]

It is essentially negative, both in style and in definition. Nationalism, in all its guises, is most easy to define in terms of what it is *not* rather than in terms of what it *is*. It is about the contrast and potential conflict between 'us' and 'them' but not, of course, about all of the 'us versus them' contrasts and conflicts: the word nationalism is used to denote conflicts between those of different blood, different religion, different territory, and different historical experience but not usually the conflict between different classes, genders or age cohorts. This categorisation of these conflicts is essentially arbitrary. The British Prime Minister, Benjamin Disraeli, famously used the phrase 'two nations' not to describe people of different race or religion but different wealth: 'an impassable gulf divided the Rich from the Poor ... the Privileged and the People formed Two Nations, governed by different laws, influenced by different manners, with no thoughts or sympathies in common.'[2] After a century and a half it remains a key phrase in the rhetoric of the 1990s, and Disraeli gets to the essence of nations and nationalism when he emphasises, albeit in an unusual context, differences that are deep, differences that are categorical not quantitative, differences that coincide and cumulate, and boundaries that are difficult or impossible to cross.

We shall look at three sets of issues, three sets of potential conflicts, which are different in kind but which are all labelled 'nationalist', and which are all matters of importance for contemporary politics in the FSU and ECE. First there is the question of asserting the *independence* of the state and casting resentful, aggressive and even acquisitive eyes beyond its immediate borders. We shall call that External Nationalism. Second there is the question of asserting the *integrity* of the state, the indivisibility of its territory, against those who would wish to secede – and even perhaps against those who would advocate more territorial autonomy for regions within the state. We shall call that Centralist Nationalism. Finally, there is the question of imposing cultural *conformity* within the boundaries of the state. Historically that usually meant religious conformity or, under the Soviets, irreligious conformity. We asked no questions about religious conformity, but we did ask questions about linguistic conformity which was a particularly acute issue in the contemporary politics of Ukraine and Slovakia. We shall describe calls for cultural conformity as Cultural Nationalism.

124

Nationalist conflicts were expected to fill the vacuum left after the collapse of communism. In 1990, 'now that the Soviet Union has resigned as the gendarme of eastern Europe',[3] Ascherson listed 46 potential flash points across the new Europe, mainly in the Caucasus or in the area of east Europe stretching from the Baltic to the Mediterranean and bounded by Germany in the west and the Soviet border lands in the east – including divisions within Ukraine and Slovakia, and Hungarian concerns for their kinfolk in neighbouring states. Despite its length, it was far from an exhaustive list: Ascherson failed to include the British/Spanish dispute over Gibraltar, problems with Tatarstan and the other ethnic minority areas in the Russian Federation, or even the potential break up of Czechoslovakia, for example. Given these well known problems of nationalism in eastern Europe, the subsequent peaceful dissolution of the Soviet Union, and later of Czechoslovakia, the continuing peace between the nationalities in Ukraine, and the absence of international war on any of Hungary's borders proved as much, if not more, of a surprise than the carnage in Yugoslavia and the Caucasus.

EXTERNAL NATIONALISM

In ECE and the FSU, external nationalism itself had two aspects. There was antagonism both towards near neighbours – the Times–Mirror surveys reported bluntly, 'the peoples of eastern Europe...do not like their neighbors'[4] – and also resentment of triumphalist western imperialism.

Table 7.1:   Asserting independence

	Referendum vote for Ukraine's independence	*It is a mistake to break up a large country just to give each national or ethnic group its own state*	*Recent changes are turning us into a colony of the West*
	%	%	%
Russia	na	81	62
Ukraine	83	76	46
East Uk	72	83	51
Mid Uk	86	74	47
West Uk	98	64	27
Czech Rep	na	73	53
Slovakia	na	62	61
Hungary	na	66	60
AVERAGE:			
FSU	na	79	54
ECE	na	67	58

Note: 'Don't Knows', 'Can't decide' etc. excluded from calculation of percentages.

We asked whether 'recent changes are turning us into a colony of the West?' That charge was levelled at market reformers everywhere and also, in non-Russian republics of the FSU, at those who had sought their republic's independence from the USSR. On average, throughout ECE and the FSU, just over half agreed that their country was being turned into a colony of the West. In Russia, Hungary and Slovakia the proportion was over 60 per cent, and in the Czech Republic and most of Ukraine about 50 per cent, only dropping to well under half in west Ukraine where fears of imperialism were focused more on the east than the west.

One question that, in theory, gets right to the heart of territorial nationalism was whether 'in general, it is a mistake to break up a large country just to give each national or ethnic group its own state.' Two-thirds agreed with that in ECE and four-fifths in the FSU. This sentiment was stronger in the Czech Republic than elsewhere in ECE, and stronger in east Ukraine and Russia than in the rest of Ukraine, which suggests a lingering regret for the break-up of Czechoslovakia and the Soviet Union, especially amongst the formerly dominant parts of those former multi-national states.

However the problem with this question – and it is a problem with the very concept of nationalism itself – is that there is no logical end to the process of division and sub-division. So a Ukrainian who agreed with our proposition might have been looking backwards with regret to the break-up of the Soviet Union, or forwards with apprehension to separatist tendencies in Krym (Crimea). Similarly a Slovak who agreed with our proposition might have been looking back with regret to the 'velvet divorce' from the Czech Republic or forward with apprehension to separatist tendencies along Slovakia's border with Hungary. Or, in either case, the sentiment might have encompassed both regret for the divisions of the past and apprehension about the potential divisions of the future. Nationalism itself is inherently ambiguous in its respect for state borders.

Within our survey at the end of 1993, 83 per cent in Ukraine recalled that they had voted for Ukraine's independence in the December 1991 referendum (if they recalled voting at all) – slightly, but only slightly less than the 90 per cent who actually did so. In our survey, the figure ranged up to 98 per cent in west Ukraine, yet down only to 72 per cent in east Ukraine – a very large majority in favour of Ukraine's independence everywhere despite some regional variation in the size of the majority.

Those who seek to explain away that uniformity point out that a vote for Ukraine's independence was not a vote for the excesses of ethnic nationalism, nor even a cultural rejection of Russianness; that to a large extent it merely expressed a wish to get out of the hands of the Moscow Kremlin's 'evil empire' – a wish that was shared by many, probably most, even within the boundaries of the Russian Federation itself: that it was a vote against the past, rather than a vote against another place. But that seems somewhat beside the point. The same could have been said with equal or greater truth of the American revolutionaries who rebelled against the Hanoverian government in London. They were culturally English: indeed, in many ways, far more English than those who held power in London at the time. So, there is no logical contradiction in the fact that a large majority in Ukraine voted for Ukraine's independence, yet almost as many said it was a mistake to break up a large country just to give ethnic groups their own states. There were far better reasons for detaching Ukraine from Moscow than that. The American Revolutionaries would have understood.

Two of our questions revealed the peculiar attitudes of the public in the old imperial powers of Russia and Hungary. First, we asked whether 'there are parts of neighbouring countries that really should belong to (Country)?' Within the FSU, 71 per cent in Russia but only 30 per cent in Ukraine agreed to that. Similarly in ECE, 60 per cent in Hungary but less than half that number in former Czechoslovakia agreed. Clearly, those who lived in Russia and Hungary still had imperial instincts. Significantly however, there was no evidence that the people of the Czech Republic took the same view about the former Czechoslovakia: indeed far less in the Czech Republic (only 18 per cent) than in Slovakia laid any claims to neighbouring territories. Within Ukraine, it was the west Ukrainians who expressed the greatest support for territorial expansion, despite the fact that some ethnographers would describe great tracts of southern Russia – far away from west Ukraine – as 'ethnically Ukrainian'.[5]

Table 7.2: Attitudes to the 'near abroad'

	There are parts of neighbouring countries that really should belong to (our country)	When ethnic conflicts affect the rights of (our country's) people living in neighbouring countries, our government should threaten military action if necessary
	%	%
Russia	71	26
Ukraine	30	5
East Uk	25	6
Mid Uk	27	3
West Uk	49	6
Czech Rep	18	2
Slovakia	32	3
Hungary	60	3
AVERAGE:		
FSU	51	16
ECE	37	3

Notes: 'Don't Knows', 'Can't decide' etc. excluded from calculation of percentages. The words in brackets were replaced by the appropriate names of states or state nationalities in each of the five countries in our survey.

But while the Russian and Hungarian publics were united in expressing territorial claims, only the Russian public was willing, in any significant degree, to advance those claims by force of arms. We asked: 'When ethnic conflicts occur where the rights of (country) people living in neighbouring countries are threatened, how should our government respond? Should it

- do nothing, stay neutral
- try to resolve the conflict but only by diplomatic or economic means
- threaten military action if necessary?'

Only a very small minority anywhere suggested their government should do nothing. But on the other hand, only in Russia was there much public support for military threats: 26 per cent in Russia compared to only 3 per cent in Hungary. Russia's neighbours were right to be nervous of its violently irredentist tendencies; but the other publics were remarkably free of that tendency despite, in most cases, good excuses for it.

CENTRALIST NATIONALISM

Throughout ECE and the FSU large majorities – two-thirds in the FSU, rising to 90 per cent in the Czech Republic – supported the concept of greater regional autonomy within an undivided state. They were for 'devolution' but against 'separatism'. Significantly, even in relatively nationalist west Ukraine there was 58 per cent support for 'giving greater powers of self-government to regions within Ukraine.'

But opposition to regional separatism was strong. We asked whether 'If a majority of people in a region want to separate from (country) that region should be allowed to do so.' Only around 38 per cent in the FSU and Hungary agreed; and far less, only half that number, in the former Czechoslovakia. Clearly the vast majority of Czechs and Slovaks thought that the repeated sub-division of their states had gone far enough. Indeed they were both very small in population and territory. But it did mean that those countries where people were *most* willing to tolerate further moves towards regional devolution were the same ones where people were *least* willing to tolerate moves towards regional separatism.[6]

Within Ukraine there was a sharp east–west variation in opinion: only 13 per cent in west Ukraine but 49 per cent in east Ukraine would permit a region to separate. Paradoxically, across the territory of Ukraine, the more the public felt it was a mistake to break up a large country to placate ethnic groups, the more they felt that regions should be allowed to separate from Ukraine if a local majority wished to do so. It is a paradox that is very easy to explain however: if any regions in east Ukraine were to separate from the Ukrainian state, it would only be to submerge themselves in an even larger state, in Russia or in a reconstructed Soviet Union. However, at the least, that underscores the ambiguous practical implications of our question about 'breaking up a large country' and shows that we cannot assign it unambiguously to either the category of 'internal' or 'external' nationalism. The methodological paradox is that this question which specifies *so clearly* the key element of principle in territorial nationalism, produces answers which reflect *so obscurely* the variety of its practical applications.

Table 7.3:   Attitudes to separatism and devolution

	It is a mistake to break up a large country just to give each national or ethnic group its own state	*If a majority of the people in a region want to separate from (Country) that region should be allowed to do so*	*Support giving greater powers of self-government to regions within (Country)*
	%	%	%
Russia	81	38	65
Ukraine	76	38	66
East Uk	83	49	65
Mid Uk	74	38	69
West Uk	64	13	58
Czech Rep	73	24	90
Slovakia	62	20	77
Hungary	66	40	70
AVERAGE:			
FSU	79	38	65
ECE	67	28	79

Note: 'Don't Knows', 'Can't decide' etc. excluded from calculation of percentages.

CULTURAL NATIONALISM

By cultural nationalism we mean, in this context, an insistence on conformity to the dominant culture throughout the state.

One important aspect of this is religious conformity. In postcommunist countries it is particularly relevant to ask how many conformed to the religious teaching of the old regime by denying religion. We found that a very high percentage in the Czech Republic (55 per cent) declared that they had no religion, rather less in Russia (44 per cent) and Ukraine (33 per cent) and relatively few in Hungary or Slovakia. Lack of religion was therefore the dominant element only in the Czech Republic, where old traditions of anti-Catholicism seem to have transformed into anti-religious sentiment itself. At the time of our surveys the Catholic church in the Czech Republic was mounting a strong effort to regain its former property from the state, which may have further stimulated traditional Czech anti-religious sentiment.

Table 7.4:   Religious conformity

	Russian Orthodox	Ukrainian Orthodox	Catholic (Latin or Greek rite)	Protestant & other Christian	Jewish, Muslim, other non-Christian	No religion
	%	%	%	%	%	%
Russia	48	0	0	6	2	44
Ukraine	21	25	4	14	3	33
East Uk	29	13	0	14	0	44
Mid Uk	18	27	1	18	4	32
West Uk	10	44	27	5	5	9
Czech Rep	0	0	32	8	2	59
Slovakia	0	0	70	8	3	19
Hungary	1	0	54	22	1	22
AVERAGE:						
FSU	35	13	2	10	2	39
ECE	0	0	52	13	2	33

Notes: 'Don't Knows', 'Can't decide' etc. excluded from calculation of percentages. Entries show answers to the question: 'Do you consider yourself as belonging to a particular religion? (If Yes) Which?'.

Insofar as it was religious at all, the Russian public was overwhelmingly Orthodox, and unquestioningly *Russian* Orthodox. Similarly, in the Czech Republic and even more so in Slovakia, the religious were overwhelmingly Catholic. But in Hungary, while a majority of the religious were Catholic, over a third were not. And in Ukraine as a whole we found more people who described themselves as Ukrainian Orthodox than Russian Orthodox. We appreciate that our religious categories were insufficient to model the full complexity of current religious schisms in Ukraine, but the subtleties of those schisms are too subtle even for most of the Ukrainian public. Within east Ukraine, Russian Orthodox identifications predominated, while in mid-Ukraine and even more in west Ukraine 'Ukrainian Orthodox' identifications predominated. In addition 27 per cent in west Ukraine, though very few elsewhere in Ukraine, described themselves as Catholic or Uniate ('Eastern' or 'Greek' rite Catholic). Most would probably have been Greek rite, conveniently distinguishing them from Latin rite Catholic Poles and from Orthodox Russians. Indeed one striking characteristic of west Ukraine was the very small number (a mere 9 per cent) who identified with no religion at all.

Both Ukraine as a whole and the broad regions within it, were characterised by a degree of religious pluralism that we found nowhere else. The principal or dominant religious category in Slovakia and Hungary was clearly Catholic, in the Czech Republic it was the irreligious, even in Russia it might just be possible to describe the Russian Orthodox Church as the national church on the basis of religious identification alone. But in Ukraine there was no sufficiently national church for anyone to talk of religious conformity, and the concept of diversity was much more applicable.

Table 7.5: Ethno-linguistic homogeneity

	Russian	Ukrainian	Czech	Slovak	Hungarian	Other
	%	%	%	%	%	%
Russia	**87/95/100**	3/1/0	0/0/0	0/0/0	0/0/0	10/5/0
Ukraine	26/49/62	**68/48/37**	0/0/0	0/0/0	0/0/0	6/3/1
East Uk	38/68/91	**57/31/9**	0/0/0	0/0/0	0/0/0	5/1/0
Mid Uk	23/46/56	**68/47/42**	0/0/0	0/0/0	0/0/0	9/6/2
West Uk	8/8/6	**91/92/94**	0/0/0	0/0/0	0/0/0	0/0/0
Czech Rep	0/0/0	0/0/0	**94/97/100**	2/0/0	0/0/0	3/2/0
Slovakia	0/0/0	0/0/0	1/0/0	**87/88/92**	11/11/8	1/1/0
Hungary	0/0/0	0/0/0	0/0/0	0/0/0	**97/100/100**	2/0/0

Note: 'Don't Knows', 'Can't decide' etc. excluded from calculation of percentages.

Happily, none of the postcommunist regimes in our areas of investigation (unlike some outside those areas) seemed bent on imposing or even encouraging religious conformity. The same could not be said of linguistic conformity however. 'Problems of power, status, politics and ideology and not of communication or even culture, lie at the heart of the nationalism of language.'[7] The ability to speak the language, or even a willingness to learn it, can be used as a test of loyalty to an immature and uncertain state. Ignoring the examples of Hapsburg Austria,[8] or modern Finland, Belgium, Switzerland and Luxembourg, as well as of other more distant countries, language laws were passed in all of the Soviet republics as the Soviet Union was disintegrating, adopting the language of the 'titular nationality' (after which the republic was named) as the single 'state language'.[9] These laws were particularly oppressive in the Baltic states, but less oppressive in Slovakia, and liberal, flexible, and frequently ignored in Russia and Ukraine. In Estonia they excluded non-Estonian speakers from citizenship rights, including voting.[10] But in Russia and Ukraine they were merely declarations of the language in which the state would do its business, not a test of citizenship. And even then, the state proved willing to adjust to local circumstances. Article 68 of the 1993 Constitution allowed republics within the Russian Federation to establish their own state language, to be used alongside Russian.[11]

From our surveys, we have three different pieces of information about ethnic nationality and language:

- self assigned 'nationality / ethnic background?'
- the language 'you primarily use within your household?'
- the language chosen for the interview.

Table 7.6:   Enforcing social conformity

	The unity and independence of (country) is more important than guaranteeing equal rights for all who live in it	Only people who speak (the state language) should be full citizens and have the right to vote in elections	All schools in (country) should teach all subjects in (the state language)
	%	%	%
Russia	45	19	45
Ukraine	20	8	25
East Uk	15	5	12
Mid Uk	15	6	24
West Uk	51	26	65
Czech Rep	39	34	58
Slovakia	39	29	65
Hungary	41	61	34
AVERAGE:			
FSU	33	14	35
ECE	40	41	52

Notes: 'Don't Knows', 'Can't decide' etc. excluded from calculation of percentages. '(Country)' and '(the state language)' replaced by the appropriate state or state language in each of the five countries.

In Ukraine and Slovakia, special efforts were made to interview respondents in the language of their choice – either Russian or Ukrainian (in Ukraine), and either Slovakian or Hungarian (in Slovakia). It is also very important to understand that people in the FSU and ECE distinguish between their 'nationality' and their 'citizenship' to a degree that is unusual in the West – though not unknown, for example in our home base of Scotland. The term 'passport nationality' was familiar to people in the old Soviet Union, but even the passport distinguished clearly between 'nationality' – essentially a personal characteristic, 'residence' – the permitted area of residence, and 'citizenship' – with all its myriad rights and duties: the passports were Soviet, even if the description of the person in them was Russian, Ukrainian, Jewish, Lithuanian or whatever. Moreover, as late as 1991, about half the public in Russia and Ukraine described their country as 'the Soviet Union', rather than Russia or Ukraine, while nonetheless describing their nationality as 'Russian' or 'Ukrainian' whether of not they lived in the republics of the same name.[12] The identification of state with nationality is simply an ideological ambition of ethnic nationalists, a fact which is obscured in countries where the vast majority of citizens voluntarily accept the state nationality.

In four of our countries there was a clear gradient which largely reflected respondents' own preferences: more people spoke the state language at home than claimed that nationality, and even more opted to use the state language for the interview. The exception was Ukraine where 68 per cent described their nationality as Ukrainian, but only 48 per cent said they spoke Ukrainian at home, and only 37 per cent chose to be interviewed in Ukrainian.[13] In west Ukraine over 90 per cent claimed Ukrainian nationality, spoke it at home, and chose to be interviewed in it; but in east Ukraine, 57 per cent claimed Ukrainian nationality, but only 31 per cent spoke Ukrainian at home, and a mere 9 per cent chose to be interviewed in Ukrainian.

We asked one general question about imposing cultural conformity (Table 7.6), posing the choice between communitarianism and individualism: 'Which should be more important at the moment?

– securing the independence and unity of (country)
– guaranteeing equal rights to everyone who lives in (country)'.

Close to 40 per cent in every country except Ukraine put the unity and independence of their country ahead of equal rights for their citizens; but in Ukraine as a whole, only 20 per cent did so. Ukraine was strong polarised between east and west on this as on so much else. In west Ukraine 51 per cent put the interest of the state before its citizens – a little more than in any other country, while in mid and east Ukraine only 15 per cent did so – a lot less than in any other country. So while east Ukraine put particular stress on the community and the collective in economic terms (see Chapter 6), it put particular stress on the individual in terms of equal rights.

More specifically, we also put two direct questions about language rights. 'Should only those people who speak (the state language) be full citizens and have the right to vote in (country) elections?'; and 'Should all schools in (country) teach all subjects in (the state language)?' The first question clearly measured support for restricting the rights of those who did not speak the state language. The second question did so only by implication. Conceivably all schools could teach all subjects in the state language and also, at the same time, teach them in other languages as well. That kind of permissive, inclusive interpretation might have been given to our question if we had asked about a minority language – Hungarian teaching in Slovakia for example. But we think the question would normally be interpreted in an exclusive, conformist, way when asked, as it was, about the state language: Slovak teaching of all subjects in all schools in Slovakia, for example, strongly implies a restriction or infringement of the Hungarian minority's rights or privileges.

134   *Values and Political Change in Postcommunist Europe*

In terms of language requirements for citizenship and voting the Hungarian public showed the greatest support, 61 per cent, for culturally conformist nationalism, but we should remember that a negligible percentage of Hungarian residents did not speak Hungarian at home. So the practical implications of this view were negligible in Hungary. Indeed our question may have seemed so far away from the practical issues of politics as to be irrelevant in Hungary. If that was so however, the liberalism of the public in the Czech Republic was all the more remarkable, since so few Czech residents were unable to speak Czech yet relatively few Czechs would make language a criterion for citizenship. Similarly, there were only a few more in Russia who could not speak Russian, yet the Russian public were also very unwilling to impose language restrictions on citizenship. Perhaps they were only too aware of the plight of Russian speakers outside Russia. Even against this background of fairly general reluctance to impose language requirements on citizens, the liberalism of the public in west Ukraine, reinforced by self-interest in east and central Ukraine, was striking: only 26 per cent in west Ukraine and a mere 5 per cent in east Ukraine would limit voting rights to those who could speak the state language.

On the other hand much larger numbers would insist that all schools teach all subjects in the state language.[14] A majority took that view in the Czech Republic, Slovakia, and west Ukraine; though only a minority in Russia and Hungary, and a mere 12 per cent in east Ukraine.

Table 7.7: A ban on ethnic parties?

	Ban Rukh	Ban parties representing Russians living in Ukraine	Ban parties representing Hungarians in Slovakia
	%	%	%
Russia	na	na	na
Ukraine	31	11	na
East Uk	43	8	na
Mid Uk	29	9	na
West Uk	11	25	na
Czech Rep	na	na	na
Slovakia	na	na	37
Hungary	na	na	na
AVERAGE:			
FSU	na	na	na
ECE	na	na	na

Notes: 'Don't Knows', 'Can't decide' etc. excluded from calculation of percentages. Support for a ban on Hungarian parties ran at 31 per cent in East Slovakia, 34 per cent in West Slovakia (including Bratislava), and 46 per cent in Mid Slovakia – where very few Hungarians actually lived. Most Hungarians lived in West Slovakia (though outside Bratislava) which is the most southerly part of the country, and very close to Budapest.

One issue perhaps combined fears of territorial separatism with demands for cultural conformity. We asked whether various parties, including separatist and ethnic based parties, were 'so dangerous that they should be banned.' In Slovakia 37 per cent of the entire public opted to ban parties representing the Hungarian minority, 'the Hungarian Christian Democratic Movement/Coexistence'. In Ukraine as a whole just 11 per cent would ban unspecified 'parties representing Russians living in Ukraine' though support for such a ban reached 25 per cent in west Ukraine. Conversely 31 per cent in Ukraine as a whole would ban the moderate (Ukrainian) nationalist Rukh, a figure that ranged from a mere 11 per cent in west Ukraine up to 43 per cent in east Ukraine.

COMPOSITE INDICATORS

As we did with the different aspects of socialist values, we can construct composite indicators of different aspects of nationalism.

Averaging answers to the questions about turning our country into a 'colony of the west' and whether 'parts of neighbouring countries really should belong to (our country)' gives a composite measure of *External Nationalism*. It seems inadvisable to include answers to the question about using force abroad – which may depend upon credibility (credible for Russia, not for Hungary) as much as on nationalism itself, or the question about the break-up of large countries – whose status as an indicator of external versus internal nationalism we have found to be ambiguous. Our two question composite indicator of external nationalism has a low reliability coefficient (alpha) of 0.25 which would not be improved by a more complex combination than a simple average – reflecting two widely different kinds of external nationalism. The composite measure correlates at over 0.75 with answers to each of the two individual (and rather disparate) questions however.

Similarly we can construct a composite measure of *Centralist Nationalism* by averaging attitudes towards regional autonomy and regional separatism. Again the reliability coefficient is low and would only be slightly improved by a more complex combination (from 0.21 to 0.23) reflecting two widely different kinds of centralism, but the composite measure correlates at 0.62 with attitudes to autonomy and 0.85 with attitudes to separatism.

We can construct a composite measure of *Cultural Nationalism* by averaging the answers to the question about national unity versus equal rights with the answers to the two questions about imposing the state language. This time the reliability is much higher, with an alpha of 0.38, which might be raised to 0.44 by a more complex combination, and could be raised to 0.61 by omitting the question of unity versus rights and retaining only the two language questions. However, this seems a particularly good example of a situation in which we could improve the technical reliability of an indicator by changing and restricting its focus – that is, essentially, by reducing its validity. We decline to do so. The composite based on all three questions correlates at over 0.65 with both language questions and at 0.71 with the unity versus rights question.

Just as we investigated the intercorrelations between the different aspects of socialist values, we can also investigate the interconnections between different aspects of nationalism. The intercorrelations are weak, perhaps in part because of the low reliability of our indicators, but probably more because of the disparate and heterogeneous nature of nationalist values. It is very important that we acknowledge that heterogeneity, but we can nonetheless construct an overall measure of commitment to nationalist values by averaging scores on the external, centralist, and cultural conformist aspects of nationalism. The highest scores on this composite measure go to those who were not only aggressive towards foreign countries but also demanded territorial and cultural unity within their state.

Table 7.8:   Correlations between aspects of nationalist values

	External nationalism	Centralist nationalism	Cultural nationalism
	r×100	r×100	r×100
External nationalism	100	6	14
Centralist nationalism		100	6
Cultural nationalism			100

CONCLUSION: THE PATTERN OF COMMITMENT TO NATIONALIST VALUES

As with socialist values, we shall use our composite indicators of nationalist values directly and unmodified in computer driven multivariate calculations where they have considerable advantages in precision and discrimination. But we shall find it useful to present the percentage of people in each country or social group who score above the mid-point (3.0) on each composite measure of nationalist values. It is the percentage of people who, on average, take the nationalist side either in general or more specifically on the external, centralist or conformist aspects of nationalism. By these criteria, only a minority – but a large minority – qualified as nationalists: 37 per cent were committed to nationalist values generally, 40 per cent were committed to external nationalist values, and 28 per cent to centralist or conformist nationalist values.

Overall nationalist values were weakest in the Czech Republic and in Ukraine as a whole. However they were stronger in west Ukraine than in any other country while, at the same time, they were weaker in the rest of Ukraine than in any other country.

External nationalism was strongest in Russia, followed by Hungary and Slovakia. It was weak in the Czech Republic and throughout the whole of Ukraine – east and west. *Centralist nationalism* was strongest in the FSU – about equally strong in Russia and Ukraine – and weakest in the Czech Republic. *Cultural nationalism*, with its conformist demands, was outstandingly strong in west Ukraine but outstandingly weak in the rest of Ukraine; and outside Ukraine's borders, it was noticeably stronger in ECE than in Russia.

Table 7.9:　Percentage scoring above the mid-point (3.0) on composite measures of nationalist values

	Overall nationalism	External nationalism	Centralist nationalism	Cultural nationalism
All respondents	37	40	28	28
Russia	44	53	34	26
Ukraine	22	27	34	13
East Uk	16	26	32	7
Mid Uk	18	27	32	9
West Uk	52	28	41	45
Czech Rep	26	25	11	34
Slovakia	43	34	25	39
Hungary	43	46	29	36
AVERAGE:				
FSU	33	40	34	20
ECE	37	35	22	36

Notes: The composite indicator of Overall Nationalism is the average of the scores on External, Centralist, and Cultural Conformist Nationalism. Each scale runs from 1 to 5 with 3 as the neutral point – thus over 3, means more pro-nationalist than anti-nationalist. Entries are the percentages who score (strictly) over 3, i.e. who are pro-nationalist.

So commitment to nationalist values did not break at the FSU/ECE border, nor divide ECE plus west Ukraine from the rest of the FSU. The greatest extremes were to be found within Ukraine itself. And while Russia was more nationalist than ECE in terms of external and especially centralist nationalism, it was less nationalist than ECE in terms of cultural conformist nationalism. These patterns of nationalist values are very easy to understand in terms of the history, culture, and size of each particular country, but they really do not lend themselves to the simple Huntington-style lines of division we discussed earlier and it would be perverse to pretend otherwise. The crude 'clash of civilisations' approach outlined by Huntington[15] grievously neglects the complexity of cultural divisions in eastern Europe. And complexity does not mean obscurity: the divisions are clear and very widely understood, but there is more than one important line of division and they do not coincide.

NATIONALIST VALUES IN PRACTICE

Our measures of different aspects of nationalist values are so weakly correlated that we hardly need to use multiple regression to analyse their relationship to other variables; simple correlations will suffice.

Not surprisingly we found that support for the use of military threats in the 'near abroad' (the FSU term for neighbouring countries, especially other former members of the Soviet Union) was related almost exclusively to external nationalism whether in our full cross-national data-set or within Russia (the only country where many were willing to support such threats) alone.

Less obviously, we can use our three indicators of aspects of nationalism to help interpret answers to our question about the break up of large countries. Taking interviews across all five countries we found that opposition to the break-up of large countries correlated modestly with external nationalism (r = 0.13), only marginally with centralist nationalism (r = 0.10) and negligibly with cultural nationalism (r = − 0.03).

Table 7.10:   Correlations between nationalist values and support for use of military threats against neighbours

	External nationalism	*Centralist nationalism*	*Cultural nationalism*
	r×100	r×100	r×100
Within the FSU and ECE	13	.	.
Within Russia alone	13	.	.

Notes: Correlations less than 0.10 have been replaced by a full-stop. All correlations within countries other than Russia were less than 0.10.

Within ECE countries all the correlations were negligible (i.e., less than 0.10). In Ukraine and Russia, answers to the 'break-up' question correlated more strongly with aspects of nationalism, but the pattern of correlations was markedly different in these two countries. In both, opposition to the break-up of large countries correlated fairly well with external nationalism (at 0.20 in Russia and 0.17 in Ukraine), but there the similarity ended. Within Russia, opposition to the break-up of large countries also correlated fairly well with centralist nationalism (r = 0.18) but not at all with cultural nationalism. Russian centralists opposed the break-up of large countries. But by contrast, within Ukraine, opposition to the break-up of large countries hardly correlated at all with centralist nationalism but correlated fairly strongly – and negatively – with cultural nationalism. Ukrainian cultural nationalists actually supported the break-up of large countries in order to establish more ethnically homogenous states.

Table 7.11: Correlations between nationalist values and opposition to the break-up of large countries just to create ethnic states

	External nationalism	*Centralist nationalism*	*Cultural nationalism*
	r×100	r×100	r×100
Within the FSU and ECE	13	10	.
Within Russia alone	20	18	.
Within Ukraine alone	17	.	−16

Notes: Correlations less than 0.10 have been replaced by a full-stop. All correlations within the countries of ECE were less than 0.10.

We can now see how our respondents reacted to the 'break-up' question. Within ECE it had little resonance. But within the whole of FSU it evoked reactions to the break-up of the Soviet Union which led Russian centralists to oppose the 'break-up of large countries' and led Ukrainian cultural nationalists to support it.

8 Liberal Values

T.H. Marshall's classic lecture on citizens' rights in Britain divided them into three categories: civil rights, political rights, and social rights.[1] To those, others might add a fourth category of community rights. In broad terms we dealt with what Marshall called social rights in our chapter on socialist values, and community rights in our chapter on nationalist values.

It might be tempting now to switch our focus simply to democratic values.[2] In his attempt to answer the question 'what is democracy' Sorensen lists three criteria:

1. *meaningful political competition*: 'meaningful and extensive competition among individuals and organised groups (especially political parties) for all effective positions of government power, at regular intervals and excluding the use of force'
2. *inclusive political participation*: 'a highly inclusive level of political participation in the selection of leaders and policies, at least through regular and fair elections, such that no major social group is excluded'
3. *civil and political liberties*: 'a level of civil and political liberties – freedom of expression, freedom of the press, freedom to form and join organisations – sufficient to ensure the integrity of political competition and participation.'[3]

But these criteria come into two kinds, roughly corresponding to Marshall's useful distinction between civil and political rights, or between the values of liberalism and popular control. Civil rights, which Marshall claimed had been established in Britain by the start of the nineteenth century, concern the rights of the citizen to fair and equal treatment before the law and corresponding limitations upon government's freedom of action. They focus upon the need to prevent arbitrary and capricious action by those in authority rather than on any measure of popular control over policy – 'a government of laws not of men' perhaps, but 'good government' rather than 'self-government'. This idea of limited law-bound government is a central tenet of liberalism. Then there are what Marshall called political rights, which concern the public's ability to influence or control government policy. He argued these had only been established in Britain towards the end of the nineteenth century and the start of the twentieth.[4]

Sorensen's own conception of democracy is based upon the fusion of *liberal values* with notions of *popular control* but, as he himself point out, others like 'Friedrich von Hayek make a sharp distinction between liberalism and democracy...the former a doctrine about what the law ought to be, and the latter a doctrine about the manner of determining the law. For Hayek democracy [i.e. 'popular control' in our terms] is of only secondary importance.'[5]

Of course it may be the case that, contrary to Hayek, liberalism and popular control are actually inseparable in practice, that governments which are not subject to the constraints of popular control naturally tend to behave in an illiberal manner. Logic may run in exactly the opposite direction to history – at least as interpreted by Marshall – and popular control may be a necessary precondition (though usually the historical consequence) of liberalism in practice, if not in theory. Nonetheless the two ideas are clearly separate and it is not absurd in principle, however misguided it may be in practice, to support the one but oppose the other. Certainly, under postcommunist regimes it was neither absurd nor unusual for people to welcome freedom from arbitrary government while lamenting the inadequacies of popularly elected governments. So particularly when we look at postcommunist societies, it makes sense to separate our discussion of these twin strands of democratic values. Accordingly, in this chapter we shall focus upon liberal values and leave our investigation of public attitudes to popular control until the next.[6]

While postcommunist constitutions did not make a complete break with the past, they devoted a great deal of space to articles associated with liberal values. The 1993 Russian constitution, for example, included articles that reflected socialist values – guaranteeing low cost housing for the poor, free health care and free legal aid; but it also reflected liberal values in articles guaranteeing privacy, property rights, free speech, freedom of association, freedom of religion, and the right to peaceful protest though, in line with western constitutional law, it also provided for states of emergency and limited freedom of speech by a specific ban on incitement to 'social, racial, national or religious hatred' or the advocacy of 'linguistic supremacy'.[7]

A great deal of external pressure has also been applied to postcommunist countries to improve their human rights record. Storey points out that 'in respect of membership of the Council of Europe itself, [postcommunist] countries have to jump more and higher hurdles than faced either the original members or the earlier joiners' and, for ECE countries, 'the Council of Europe features as the antechamber to the main room of the European home – the European Union.'[8]

In this chapter we shall gauge the extent to which the liberal values advocated by the Council of Europe and enshrined in the postcommunist constitutions were also a part of popular political culture in the FSU and ECE. To what extent were liberal values alien to the aspirations of FSU/ECE publics, or merely alien to their experience? We need to stress the phrase 'to what extent' however. Our objective is not to decide categorically whether public opinion in the FSU/ECE was democratic or not, but to see how much commitment there was to liberal and democratic values.

Writers such as Shlapentokh warn that people may subscribe to a 'politically correct' public morality without feeling they should abide by it in their personal lives.[9] In the postcommunist era, people may similarly support civil rights and liberal values in principle without supporting their practical implementation. We have already found that their overwhelming support for the idea of a 'market economy' did not mean that they rejected a major role for the state in welfare or the control of industry, and did not indicate any great desire to work for private companies other than well-paying foreign companies. So it is necessary to pose concrete questions about the application of liberal and democratic values in particular circumstances – questions about the right to strike even by workers in essential services rather than abstract questions about freedom of association; questions about which groups should be banned from holding public rallies rather than abstract questions about freedom of speech; questions about press intrusions into private lives or the government's right to dismiss the head of state television rather than abstract questions about censorship and freedom of information; and questions about which specific political parties should be banned rather than just abstract questions about support for the principle of pluralist competition.

PUBLIC DOUBTS ABOUT DEMOCRACY

Throughout ECE and the FSU the majority of the public were clearly unhappy with the way democracy functioned. Roughly four-fifths in every country (only

Table 8.1:   Doubts about democracy

	Politics is so complicated that I often cannot understand what's going on	(Country) is not yet ready for democracy
	%	%
Russia	83	70
Ukraine	83	76
East Uk	78	74
Mid Uk	85	77
West Uk	84	75
Czech Rep	72	53
Slovakia	78	64
Hungary	84	65
AVERAGE:		
FSU	83	73
ECE	78	61

Note: 'Don't Knows', 'Can't decide' etc. excluded from calculation of percentages.

slightly less in the Czech Republic) complained that 'politics is so complicated that I often cannot understand what's going on.' Such complaints are sometimes interpreted as indicating a lack of personal efficacy but, given the chaos of postcommunist politics, only the self-deluded could have claimed their country's politics were easily understood. Another question confirmed that the criticism was levelled at the political system rather than at the respondents themselves: 53 per cent in the Czech Republic, over 64 per cent in Slovakia and Hungary and 73 per cent in the FSU agreed that their country 'was not yet ready for democracy'.

But it was the concrete realities of postcommunist regimes, rather than the idea of democracy, that the public rejected.[10] Both in ECE and the FSU around 60 per cent said the 'idea of democracy' was 'broadly satisfactory' and over 80 per cent declared there was 'no real alternative' to it. At the same time only about a quarter said that their government was broadly satisfactory, and only a fifth that their government's policies were broadly satisfactory – except in the Czech Republic where 61 per cent were broadly satisfied with their government, and 51 per cent with its policies. So, with the sole exception of the Czechs, people found it easy enough to distinguish between the idea of democracy and their democratically elected government. Despite the claim that their country was not yet ready for democracy, and despite great dissatisfaction with elected governments, it was still possible to hold democratic values.

Table 8.2: Distinguishing democracy from the incumbents or their policies

	Broadly satisfactory			No real alternative to		
	-the idea of democracy	-the govern- ment	-govern- ment policies	-the idea of demo- cracy	-the govern- ment	-govern- ment policies
	%	%	%	%	%	%
Russia	63	36	31	84	59	52
Ukraine	61	13	9	86	54	45
East Uk	59	12	9	86	61	52
Mid Uk	66	11	8	87	46	36
West Uk	54	20	13	82	65	55
Czech Rep	67	61	51	88	80	73
Slovakia	47	25	18	73	51	38
Hungary	59	28	23	82	61	48
AVERAGE:						
FSU	62	25	20	85	56	49
ECE	58	38	31	81	64	53

Note: 'Don't Knows', 'Can't decide' etc. excluded from calculation of percentages.

FREEDOM OF INFORMATION

Gorbachev's first move towards dismantling the communist regime was to promote the idea of *glasnost* – a word which has now entered the English language, denoting openness, or freedom of information and debate. We asked four questions about freedom of information: the question whether secret police files from the old regime should now be made public which we discussed in Chapter 4, and three others: whether 'the government should be able to dismiss the head of state television if it does not like what he is doing?'; whether 'newspapers should be banned from publishing embarrassing details about the private lives of government ministers?'; and whether 'people should have a right to know about factories which are polluting the area where they live, even if this means some of the factories have to close?'

Apologists for government use conceptions of a right to privacy to argue that a ban on publishing details of ministers' private lives is not an illiberal act. However, we know from our British surveys that the public, at least in Britain, distinguish very clearly between invading the privacy of ordinary people and invading the privacy of senior politicians – by substantial majorities they disapprove the former but support the latter.[11] It is difficult to defend politicians on liberal grounds when they try to limit their embarrassment by suppressing the truth. Privacy for politicians is usually a conspiracy against the public, and frequently a successful one.

Table 8.3:   Issues of glasnost

	Right to know about factory pollution even if factories then have to close	Ban publication of embarrassing details about the private lives of government ministers	The government should be able to dismiss the head of state television if it does not like what he is doing
	%	%	%
Russia	98	36	21
Ukraine	99	36	17
East Uk	99	39	17
Mid Uk	99	35	14
West Uk	99	33	24
Czech Rep	99	56	55
Slovakia	97	56	43
Hungary	98	51	38
AVERAGE:			
FSU	98	36	19
ECE	98	54	45

Note: 'Don't Knows', 'Can't decide' etc. excluded from calculation of percentages.

Almost everyone, everywhere, demanded the right to know about factory pollution. As we saw in Chapter 4, about half the public, in all countries except Russia – and over a third in Russia – supported open publication of secret police files. Less than half in ECE, but two-thirds in the FSU, would allow publication of embarrassing details about government ministers. Half the public in ECE but four-fifths in the FSU opposed their government's right to arbitrarily dismiss the head of state television.[12] When viewed in the context of state control of different industries, we found, in Chapter 6, that FSU publics were much more favourable than ECE publics toward government control of television programming – as they were toward government control of most other industries.[13] But on balance, answers to our more specific questions about *glasnost* suggest much greater commitment to the liberal value of free information, unrestricted by the whims or convenience of government, in the FSU than in ECE. On this key aspect of liberal democratic values, the public in Ukraine proved the most liberal and the Czechs the least – and by very large margins that ranged up to 38 per cent on individual questions. The FSU publics' longer familiarity with draconian censorship seems to have bred nothing but deeper suspicion and contempt for it.

ORDER AND AUTHORITY

Variations in attitudes to order and authority were quite complex. It would be simplistic and misleading to interpret our evidence as indicating simply greater *deference to authority* in the FSU: more correct to see it as indicating greater *respect for order*. The difference will become clear from one key question that we asked about police behaviour.[14]

On two questions the public in the FSU, and especially in Russia, clearly gave much more support to authority than the public in Slovakia and the Czech Republic: questions that asked whether people 'should have more respect for authority' and whether 'the only alternative to strong government is disorder and chaos'. But the public in the FSU were only slightly more inclined to agree that 'even if a law is unjust, people should obey it until it is changed' and – significantly – the public in the FSU were very much *more* inclined than those in Slovakia or the Czech Republic to insist that 'the police themselves should never break the law, even though that means some criminals escape punishment.' In short, what distinguished FSU opinion was commitment to order, not support for arbitrary behaviour by the authorities – despite much journalistic commentary to the contrary.[15] Perhaps this pattern of attitudes reflected a greater lack of order in the FSU, combined with the bitter experience of officials whose track record suggested they could not be trusted to use discretion without abusing it to a greater degree than in ECE.[16]

Our findings for Hungary were somewhat surprising. On every one of the four indicators, the Hungarian public showed a remarkably strong commitment to order, more similar to that in the FSU than in the former Czechoslovakia.

Table 8.4:   Law and order

	(Country) people should have more respect for authority	*The only alternative to strong government is disorder and chaos*	*Even if a law is unjust, people should obey it until it is changed*	*The police themselves should never break the law, even though that means some criminals escape punishment*
	%	%	%	%
Russia	79	72	56	75
Ukraine	67	59	71	81
East Uk	63	67	68	77
Mid UK	63	59	74	81
West Uk	85	41	73	87
Czech Rep	56	20	64	36
Slovakia	53	21	54	44
Hungary	69	89	71	70
AVERAGE:				
FSU	73	66	63	78
ECE	59	43	63	50

Notes: 'Don't Knows', 'Can't decide' etc. excluded from calculation of percentages. '(Country)' replaced by the name of the appropriate state in each of the five countries.

TOLERANCE AND INTOLERANCE

This commitment to order was reflected in an intolerance of extremism. About 88 per cent in the FSU, and around 65 per cent in Hungary and Slovakia, but only 42 per cent in the Czech Republic would 'ban speeches by people with extreme views.' Similarly around three-quarters of the public both in ECE and the FSU agreed that 'if something deeply offends most (country)[17] people then it should be made illegal.' The figure rose to 91 per cent in Russia[18] but sank to only 63 per cent in Ukraine largely because the public in east Ukraine (not in the west) were unusually tolerant of deviance – perhaps as a defensive reaction by a potential ethnic 'minority'.

We asked in detail about whether people would tolerate free speech – 'the right to hold public meetings and rallies' – for 'fascists, communists, evangelical Christians, Jews, Muslims, gypsies and homosexuals.' On average only 27 per cent in both ECE and the FSU would tolerate this. Across the range of minority and extremist groups, tolerance was greatest for evangelical Christians and Jews, much less for gypsies and homosexuals, and almost non-existent for 'fascists'. Amongst the most striking variations by country: the Czechs were unusually tolerant of homosexuals, and the Russians were unusually tolerant of communists; while both the Hungarians and, even more so, the west Ukrainians were unusually intolerant of communists.

Table 8.5:   Toleration – in principle

	Ban public speeches by people with extreme views	If something deeply offends most (Country) people, then it should be made illegal
	%	%
Russia	87	91
Ukraine	89	63
East Uk	89	50
Mid Uk	92	64
West Uk	81	89
Czech Rep	42	74
Slovakia	63	75
Hungary	67	72
AVERAGE:		
FSU	88	77
ECE	57	74

Notes: 'Don't Knows', 'Can't decide' etc. excluded from calculation of percentages. '(Country)' replaced by the name of the appropriate state in each of the five countries.

Table 8.6:   Tolerating free speech for political and social minorities

	Support the right of each of the following to hold public meetings and rallies...							
	fasc-ists	commun-ists	evange-licals	Jews	Mus-lims	gypsies	homo-sexuals	AVER-AGE
	%	%	%	%	%	%	%	%
Russia	4	42	40	35	36	27	10	28
Ukraine	2	31	41	39	33	26	11	26
East Uk	1	35	34	29	28	16	9	22
Mid Uk	2	35	49	48	39	33	13	31
West Uk	2	9	34	33	28	30	7	20
Czech Rep	1	27	51	52	34	20	30	31
Slovakia	0	26	47	36	25	15	14	23
Hungary	3	19	50	44	37	30	16	28
AVERAGE:								
FSU	3	37	40	37	35	27	10	27
ECE	1	24	49	44	32	22	20	27

Note: 'Don't Knows', 'Can't decide' etc. excluded from calculation of percentages.

Table 8.7: Rights of opposition and protest

	Criticism from opposition politicians weakens national unity and causes disruption	All public workers, even those in essential public services like hospitals and electricity power stations should have the right to strike	If some citizens felt a law was very unjust or harmful, they should be allowed to				
			-hold protest meetings	-call nationwide strikes	-appeal through the courts	-hold protest marches and demonstrations which block traffic for a few hours	-occupy government buildings
	%	%	%	%	%	%	%
Russia	14	49	76	35	92	31	8
Ukraine	13	49	76	37	90	29	18
East Uk	19	45	72	36	89	29	16
Mid Uk	8	48	81	41	92	32	16
West Uk	16	59	72	28	83	17	27
Czech Rep	8	57	93	56	89	36	12
Slovakia	25	64	89	55	85	47	18
Hungary	16	60	79	56	89	36	7
AVERAGE:							
FSU	14	49	76	36	91	30	13
ECE	16	60	87	56	88	40	12

Note: 'Don't Knows', 'Can't decide' etc. excluded from calculation of percentages.

RIGHTS TO PROTEST

Western journalists sometimes claimed that to FSU/ECE publics 'loyal opposition is a sophisticated idea' and that they had a 'romantic yearning for national
unity in which opposition is still suspect.'[19] But although tolerance of minorities
and extremists was low, there was a great deal of support for the notion of
public criticism and protest. The right to hold peaceful protest rallies and
demonstrations was included in the 1936 and 1977 Soviet Constitutions[20] as
well as in postcommunist constitutions. Even though Stalin did not permit
people to exercise that right in practice, his constitution inevitably publicised
it as part of 'normal' political life, which Soviet citizens could contrast with the
abnormality of the 'really existing' communist regime under which they lived.
Hypocrisy can transmit a culture quite opposite to that of the hypocrite, and
one important function of constitutions – Soviet no less than American – is to
create political aspirations for the future rather than to describe current legal or
bureaucratic realities. The concept of public protest, like the concept of national
self-determination, was supported by the old communist regimes *in principle*,
though not of course in practice. These were not new or alien ideas in postcommunist countries.

We found that only about 15 per cent throughout ECE and the FSU agreed
that 'criticism from opposition politicians weakens national unity and causes
disruption' rather than being 'useful to prevent governments abusing power' –
though there was somewhat less tolerance of opposition criticism in Slovakia.
And, despite their severe economic problems, half the public in the FSU and 60
per cent in ECE agreed that 'all workers, even those in essential public services
like hospitals and electricity power stations, should have the right to strike.'

To test further the degree of public support for the idea of specifically
political protest, we asked whether: 'If some citizens felt a law was very unjust
or harmful should they be allowed to:

– hold protest meetings
– call nationwide strikes
– appeal through the courts
– hold protest marches and demonstrations which block traffic for a few hours
– occupy government buildings?'

There was little difference between the public in ECE and the FSU on
whether protesters should be allowed to appeal through the courts (about 90
per cent agreed in both) or occupy government buildings (only about 13 per
cent agreed in both). But support for the other forms of protest behaviour,
which received less universal support or criticism, was between 10 per cent and
20 per cent lower in the FSU than in ECE.

And irrespective of the method of protest, the public in the FSU expected it
to be less effective than did the public in ECE. We asked about the perceived

Table 8.8: Perceived effectiveness of protest methods

The following would have a 'very big' or 'quite big' effect in enabling citizens to get a law changed

	Working through state officials			Working through civil society			Protest action	
	Appeal through the courts	Letters or petitions to the PM (C,S,H) or Pres. (R,U)	Letters or petitions to MPs	Working through a political party	Working through a non-party organisation	Letters or petitions to the newspapers	Protest marches and demonstrations	Violent action
	%	%	%	%	%	%	%	%
Russia	29	24	19	22	16	14	22	8
Ukraine	24	16	13	20	15	14	21	12
East Uk	25	16	13	25	16	13	21	14
Mid Uk	24	13	11	16	15	13	18	11
West Uk	25	25	19	23	15	20	29	6
Czech Rep	51	26	18	40	26	18	34	7
Slovakia	53	30	27	41	31	26	43	17
Hungary	57	24	21	24	22	20	38	11
AVERAGE:								
FSU	26	20	16	21	16	14	22	10
ECE	54	27	22	35	30	21	38	12

Note: 'Don't Knows', 'Can't decide' etc. excluded from calculation of percentages.

effectiveness of eight kinds of protest activity, some of which involved working directly through state officials, some of which involved working through the autonomous institutions of civil society, and some of which were 'unconventional' or 'elite-challenging' modes of protest – marches, demonstrations and violence. In ECE 38 per cent thought demonstrations would have at least 'quite a big effect' but only 22 per cent in the FSU; 30 per cent in ECE but only 16 per cent in the FSU thought working through a non-party organisation would be effective; 22 per cent in ECE but only 16 per cent in the FSU thought a letter to an MP would be effective.

But the greatest divergence came on people's expectations of the courts: 54 per cent in ECE but only 26 per cent in the FSU thought an appeal through the courts would be effective. The public in the FSU were, in fact, slightly more committed than in ECE to the right of citizens to appeal through the courts against unjust or harmful laws, yet they were much less hopeful that it would do any good. Their own principles were the same as those of ECE publics in this particular matter but they felt their system would be less responsive.

Table 8.9   Should government be above the law?

	Allow the Constitutional Court to overrule the government	A strong leader who has the trust of the people should not be restricted by the law
	%	%
Russia	77	27
Ukraine	80	27
East Uk	79	29
Mid Uk	84	23
West Uk	70	39
Czech Rep	73	16
Slovakia	74	16
Hungary	81	34
AVERAGE:		
FSU	79	27
ECE	76	22

Note: 'Don't Knows', 'Can't decide' etc. excluded from calculation of percentages.

GOVERNMENT ABOVE THE LAW?

A government of laws means government under the law. During the last decade of communist rule there was increasing emphasis on the need for law-based, rather than arbitrary or discretionary government.[21] We asked two key questions about this principle. First: 'If the government wanted to take action but the constitutional court said it violated the constitution, who should have the final say?

– the government because it represents the people

or

– the court, because it is necessary to defend the constitution.'

It was a rather difficult choice, but a little less difficult in ECE where only about 7 per cent could not decide, than in the FSU where about 19 per cent were unable to decide. Excluding those who could not decide, around three-quarters of the public everywhere supported the idea of a constitutional court overruling their elected government.

We also put the proposition: 'A strong leader who has the trust of the people should *not* be restricted by the law.' Only 27 per cent in the FSU and 16 per cent in the former Czechoslovakia agreed. Support for this 'Fuhrer principle' was a little higher in Hungary (at 34 per cent) and west Ukraine (at 39 per cent) but remained very much in the minority.[22]

COMPOSITE INDICATORS

As in previous chapters we can simplify further analysis of public opinion by grouping answers to these questions about liberal values into a set of five composite indicators representing attitudes towards freedom of information (*Glasnost*), order (*Anti-order*), tolerance of minorities and extremists (*Tolerance*), support for rights of protest and criticism (*Protest*), and commitment to the idea that government should operate under the law (*Law-based Government*). In each case we averaged the answers to several relevant questions to produce a composite indicator. Our grouping of questions into composite indicators of more general principles was guided by preliminary factor analyses as well as by the content and meaning of the questions. All individual questions and composite indicators were measured on a scale from 1 to 5 with 3 indicating a neutral response. Scores above 3 always represented relatively liberal responses, and scores beneath 3 represented relatively authoritarian responses. Inelegant though it is, we shall use the term 'Anti-order' to emphasise that high scores on our measure of order represented relatively liberal, anti-authoritarian responses on this composite indicator as on all the others.

None achieved high levels of reliability, though none of the reliability coefficients (alphas) would have been much improved by more complex combinations. This reflected the disparate formats and contents of the different questions used to construct each composite indicator. Nonetheless we needed that range of questions to span each composite concept as adequately as possible.

Averaging answers to the questions about opening secret police files, banning publication of details about ministers' private lives, the government's right to arbitrarily dismiss the head of state television, and the right to know about factory pollution (each oriented in the direction of freedom of information) produced a composite measure of *Glasnost* with a reliability coefficient (alpha) of 0.32. The composite measure correlated at only 0.36 with attitudes towards factory pollution, which were almost unanimously on the side of freedom of information, but at over 0.61 with answers to each of the other three questions.

Averaging answers to the questions about the need for both the people and the police to obey the law, the need to respect authority, and support for strong government as a bulwark against chaos produced a composite measure of support for *Order* (which can be inverted to produce a measure of Anti-order) with a reliability coefficient of 0.43. We should emphasise the perhaps surprising but significant finding that those who were more inclined to say the *people should obey laws they did not like*, were also more inclined to insist that the *police should stay within the law*; so our composite measure reflected the degree of support for order – defined as strict legality – rather than submission to arbitrary and capricious authority. The correlation between requiring the people and the police to remain within the law was *plus* 0.32 overall, and within individual countries it was always strongly positive, though varying from around 0.25 in the former Czechoslovakia to over 0.35 in the FSU and Hungary. The composite measure of *Order* correlated at over 0.62 with demands that the people and the police both remain within the law; and at over 0.55 with answers to the other two questions.

Our composite measure of *Tolerance* was based upon support for the rights of seven specific minority or extremist groups to hold public meetings and rallies – averaged over the seven cases, and then averaged with the question of general support for the right of people with extreme views to make public speeches and the opinion that even something that deeply offended most people in the country should not automatically be made illegal. This two stage averaging process prevented the repetitive battery of questions about free speech for seven specific groups from dominating the composite measure. That reduced the technical reliability coefficient of course (it was only 0.29) but ensured that the composite measure was based on a broader spread of question formats. This composite measure correlated at over 0.62 with each of the three elements on which it was based.

Our composite measure of support for rights of *Protest* was formed by another, similar, two-stage averaging procedure. First we averaged answers to the five specific types of protest action discussed earlier, then averaged the result with attitudes to the principle of the right to strike and the value of criticism from opposition politicians. That composite also had a reliability coefficient (alpha) of only 0.29. Of course, we could spuriously inflate the reliability coefficient – at the expense of distorting our measure of attitudes to protest – by including the battery of repetitive format questions about protest action separately, but we have chosen not to do so. The composite measure correlated at over 0.63 with each of the three elements on which it was based.

Finally our composite measure of support for *Law-based* government was formed by averaging answers to the questions about the need for even a strong and trusted leader to be restricted by the law, and for a constitutional court to exercise supremacy over the government. Once again the reliability coefficient (alpha) was a low 0.29 though the composite measure correlated at over 0.67 with answers to both the questions on which it was based.

Just as we investigated the intercorrelations between the different aspects of socialist and nationalist values, we can also investigate the interconnections between different aspects of liberal values. *Order* and *Tolerance* correlated negatively at –0.24; and *Protest* correlated at 0.19 with both *Tolerance* and *Law-based government*; while other correlations between composite indicators of liberal values were lower.

We can construct an overall measure of commitment to liberal values by averaging scores on *Glasnost, Anti-order, Tolerance, Protest and Law-based Government*.

Table 8.10   Correlations between liberal values

	Glasnost	Anti-Order	Tolerance	Protest	Law-based Government
	r×100	r×100	r×100	r×100	r×100
Glasnost	100	.	.	16	13
Anti-Order		100	24	11	.
Tolerance			100	19	16
Protest				100	19
Law-based					100

Note: Correlations less than 0.10 have been replaced by a full-stop.

CONCLUSION: THE PATTERN OF COMMITMENT TO LIBERAL VALUES

As with socialist and nationalist values, we shall use our composite indicators of nationalist values directly and unmodified in computer driven multivariate calculations where they have considerable advantages in precision and discrimination. But we shall find it useful to present the percentage of people in each country or social group who score above the mid-point (3.0) on each composite measure of liberal values. It is the percentage of people who, on average, take the liberal rather than authoritarian side either in general or more specifically on Glasnost, Anti-order, Tolerance, Protest and Law-based Government. By these criteria, two thirds of the public had liberal values. They were most *liberal* on Glasnost, followed by Law-based Government, and citizens' rights of Protest. But they were *authoritarian* on questions of Order and Tolerance.

The people of the Czech and Slovak Republics were the most liberal, while the people of the FSU and Hungary were somewhat less so. Within Ukraine, those who lived in the west were the least liberal, not the most. On liberal principles west Ukraine showed no 'western' tendencies. People in the FSU were more liberal than those in ECE on Glasnost but on nothing else, and they were much more authoritarian than those in ECE especially on their commitment to Order and, to a lesser extent, on their tendency towards Intolerance.

Table 8.11 Percentage above the mid-point (3.0) on composite measures of liberal values

	Overall liberal values	Glasnost	Anti-Order	Tolerance	Protest	Law-based government
	%	%	%	%	%	%
All respondents	68	80	27	16	74	69
Russia	64	89	19	8	71	68
Ukraine	67	90	18	12	70	69
East Uk	65	88	19	14	63	68
Mid Uk	70	91	20	13	72	73
West Uk	59	89	13	7	76	58
Czech Rep	78	70	50	29	84	70
Slovakia	74	65	53	19	75	71
Hungary	62	71	14	21	75	70
AVERAGE:						
FSU	65	89	19	10	71	68
ECE	71	69	39	23	78	70

Notes: The composite indicator of Overall Liberalism is the average of the scores on Glasnost, Anti-order, Tolerance, Protest, and Law-based Government. Note that Order has been inverted to measure Anti-order (simply by subtracting its the Order score from 6). Each scale runs from 1 to 5 with 3 as the neutral point – thus over 3 means more liberal than authoritarian. Entries are the percentages who score (strictly) over 3, i.e. who have liberal values.

LIBERAL VALUES IN PRACTICE

We asked a battery of five questions about whether it would or would not be 'acceptable for the government to suspend citizens' usual rights and take emergency powers in each of the following situations:

- widespread corruption and mafia crime
- widespread public disorder
- widespread strikes in essential industries
- a campaign of slander against the government
- if parliament obstructed the government.'

Averaging across these five circumstances, there was somewhat more support for the use of emergency powers in the FSU than in ECE though support varied sharply within ECE.

There was also far more support for the use of emergency powers to combat crime and disorder than to combat a campaign of slander against the government or an obstructive parliament. In the FSU about 80 per cent backed the use of emergency powers in the first two situations, but only 40 per cent in the last two; in ECE, about 60 per cent in the first two situations, but under 30 per cent in the last two.

Table 8.12 Support for emergency powers which suspend citizens' rights

	It would be acceptable for the government to suspend citizens' usual rights and take emergency powers if confronted by:					
	wide spread corruption and mafia crime	*wide spread public disorder*	*widespread strikes in essential industries*	*a campaign of slander against the government*	*a parliament which obstructed the government*	*AVER-AGE*
	%	%	%	%	%	%
Russia	79	79	52	40	30	56
Ukraine	80	82	60	40	38	60
East Uk	81	83	61	41	42	62
Mid Uk	79	79	61	38	32	58
West Uk	85	86	54	50	44	64
Czech Rep	79	63	41	29	37	50
Slovakia	47	47	25	21	24	33
Hungary	68	68	46	31	26	48
AVERAGE:						
FSU	79	80	56	40	39	59
ECE	65	59	37	27	29	43

Note: 'Don't Knows', 'Can't decide' etc. excluded from calculation of percentages.

Opposition to the use of emergency powers in general correlated about equally well with the principles of Anti-Order, Tolerance, Protest and Law-based Government. But the pattern of correlations with different liberal democratic principles varied according to the purposes for which emergency powers were to be used. Hardly surprisingly, opposition to the use of emergency powers to combat strikes correlated best with the principle of Protest; less obviously but more significantly, opposition to the use of emergency powers to combat slander and obstruction correlated best with the principle of legally constrained, Law-based Government; and opposition to the use of emergency powers to combat crime or disorder correlated best with the principle of Anti-Order (equivalently and more elegantly: *support* for emergency powers to combat crime or disorder correlated best with the principle of Order).

Table 8.13 Correlations between liberal values and opposition to the government's use of emergency powers that suspend citizens' rights

	Glasnost	Anti-Order	Toler-ance	Protest	Law-based Government
Circumstances:	r×100	r×100	r×100	r×100	r×100
Generally	·	12	14	11	12
Corruption and crime	·	·	·	·	·
Public disorder	·	14	10	·	·
Strikes in essential industries	·	11	11	13	10
Slander against the government	·	·	14	11	16
An obstructive parliament	·	·	·	·	16

Note: Correlations less than 0.10 have been replaced by a full-stop.

Table 8.14 Yeltsin was right to suspend the Russian parliament in September 1993

	%
Russia	53
Ukraine	59
East Uk	53
Mid Uk	59
West Uk	70
Czech Rep	73
Slovakia	69
Hungary	68
AVERAGE:	
FSU	56
ECE	70

Note: 'Don't Knows', 'Can't decide' etc. excluded from calculation of percentages.

Finally, we asked people – in every country – whether Yeltsin had been right or wrong to suspend the Russian parliament on 21 September 1993, which even

Yeltsin acknowledged was a violation of the constitution. We did not ask whether he had been right or wrong to go on to use tanks against it as he did in the first week in October, merely whether he had been right to suspend it. In ECE, 70 per cent of the public said he was right, but in the FSU only 56 per cent. So on this key issue of practice, it was FSU publics who took a more legal, constitutional view. They were, of course, nearer to the tanks.

Table 8.15 Correlations between liberal values and the view that Yeltsin was wrong to suspend the Russian parliament

	Glasnost	Anti-Order	Tolerance	Protest	Law-based government
	rx100	rx100	rx100	rx100	rx100
In Russia alone	·	·	10	·	23
In Ukraine alone	·	·	·	·	12
In the FSU	·	·	·	·	20
In ECE	−11	·	·	·	·

Note: Correlations less than 0.10 have been replaced by a full-stop.

In the FSU, and especially in Russia, criticism of Yeltsin's suspension of parliament correlated strongly (at 0.23 in Russia) with commitment to the principle of Law-based government – even if commitment to such liberal constitutional principles failed to stimulate criticism of Yeltsin's action in Western capitals.

9 Popular Control: Direct or Representative Democracy?

In the previous chapter we looked at the liberal dimension of democracy, focused upon limited, law-based government and on the rights and freedoms of citizens. Now we turn to the second main element in the concept of liberal democracy: popular control, the extent to which citizens can impose their will upon government. Under the despotism – sometimes enlightened, more often not – of the Tsars and their communist successors political control operated in the reverse direction: the government controlled the people.[1] Indeed both Tsarist and Communist governments saw it as their duty not just to provide the conditions for citizens to live their own lives free from foreign invaders or domestic criminals, but to mould and 'improve' the religion, ethics and morals of citizens themselves. To a degree, of course, all governments do that, but the long sequence of Soviet 'campaigns' to reform their citizens – of which the last was Gorbachev's campaign against alcohol[2] – expressed a uniquely paternalistic contempt for public opinion.

In the most general terms, popular control concerns the extent to which citizens can influence government, with or without the formal mechanical mechanisms of electoral democracy. This is important not just in places where there are no elections, or in places where electoral mechanisms are defective, but also in places where electoral mechanisms are beyond reproach. Even in mature democracies, elections are usually infrequent occurrences while government is continuous, and citizens influence government in many other ways as well as through the mechanism of elections. Responsive government is not an occasional event, nor a matter of a crude choice between two or three alternatives. So in one respect, the concept of popular control goes much wider than competitive elections, even though elections may be one important mechanism for establishing and maintaining that control.

But in another respect, the concept of competitive elections with its implications of competing parties, of organised and continuous opposition may be wider than that of popular control. Biryukov and Sergeyev have pointed out that the Russian empire's tradition of democratic institutions, slight though it was, centred on the sixteenth and seventeeth century 'Zemskii Sobor' – a secular assembly modelled on the church's ecclesiastical councils.[3] And like those ecclesiastical assemblies, or a modern scientific conference, the purpose of a Sobor was not to reach a balanced opinion or negotiate a compromise or tolerate factions and opposition, but to seek the 'right' decision, the 'correct' decision, the 'true' decision, or perhaps 'ultimate truth' itself.[4]

159

That is very different from the value-free concept of pluralist democracy, which Birch describes as 'an American intellectual export'.[5] On the other hand it is remarkably similar to some British and European ideas of democracy. Lindsay, following Mill, claimed that democracy 'does not mean that what everyone has to say is of equal value. It assumes that if the discussion is good enough the proper value of each contribution will be brought out in the discussion.'[6] According to Birch, British and European notions of democracy give more weight to the goal of consensus, or a 'general will' than do American theorists: in Laski's words, 'the underlying thesis of parliamentary government is that discussion forms the popular mind and . . . the legislature translates into statute the will arrived at by that mind.'[7] Sometimes this idea is advocated under the banner of 'deliberative democracy.'[8] Commitment to popular control need not imply commitment to unlimited and undifferentiated pluralism – either in west or east Europe.

POPULISM

Going right to the heart of this matter we asked: 'Which comes closer to your view? Governments should

– ignore public opinion if they think it is wrong for the country
– *not* ignore public opinion even if they think it is wrong.'

British prime ministers have certainly taken the view, as they did over entry into the EEC (now EU) or over the sweeping privatisation of national assets at discount prices, that they should get the policy right first, and then wait for public opinion to come round later.

But overwhelmingly, the people of ECE and the FSU took a more populist view: only around 15 per cent said governments should ignore public opinion 'even when they [the government] think it is wrong for the country.' And a large majority, 72 per cent in ECE though only 65 per cent in the FSU, also said that 'the most important and difficult issues facing the country should be decided by the people in a referendum' rather than by even 'elected' politicians.

Referenda had been 'instrumental in accelerating the collapse of communist rule and confirming the break up of the federal Soviet Union.'[9] They had also been used to ensure that postcommunist Russia would be a presidential rather than a parliamentary regime.[10] In principle, but not in practice they were a traditional mechanism of the Soviet state. Provision for popular referenda had been included in Stalin's 1936 constitution though the first Soviet Referendum did not take place until 17 March 1991, when Gorbachev attempted to hold a referendum on 'a renewed federation of equal sovereign republics.' It was not a complete success: six republics refused to take part and others modified the question to suit their own purposes. In Ukraine, it was accompanied by a second question seeking support for Ukraine's declaration of sovereignty; and in Russia, by a second question, on whether there should be a Russian president directly elected by the people, rather than simply a parliamentary chairman elected by parliament. On 1 December that same year, Ukraine held a referendum on outright independence. Altogether there were eight referenda in eastern Europe between 1987 and 1993, and nine in Russia or Ukraine (25 in the FSU as a whole). Initially, this wave of referenda achieved high turnouts – 80 per cent in the Soviet Union referendum of March 1991, and 84 per cent in the Ukrainian independence referendum in December that year. But later turnout fell to a claimed 55 per cent in the Russian Constitutional referendum in December 1993, and even that figure is not now generally believed – in reality it may have been under 50 per cent.[11] Brady and Kaplan ended their analysis with the conclusion that they were more likely to encourage the 'weed of nationalism' than the 'flower of reform'.[12] Given that sour experience especially in the FSU, it is perhaps remarkable that so many as 65 per cent still backed them as the best mechanism for deciding important issues.

Table 9.1: Populism

	Governments should ignore public opinion if they think it is wrong for the country	The most important issues should be decided in a referendum	The government should be allowed to overrule parliament	It is better if governments lose elections reasonably often, to stop them getting too powerful or corrupt
	%	%	%	%
Russia	12	65	*39	60
Ukraine	17	66	36	65
East Uk	20	66	34	62
Mid Uk	11	67	38	71
West Uk	30	63	35	49
Czech Rep	17	71	46	35
Slovakia	26	76	22	42
Hungary	8	69	14	62
AVERAGE:				
FSU	14	65	38	62
ECE	17	72	27	46

Notes: 'Don't Knows', 'Can't decide' etc. excluded from calculation of percentages.
* refers to 'the new parliament, elected on 12th December 1993'.

Although it would not usually be classified as 'populism', the fact that 62 per cent in the FSU and much more in Slovakia and Hungary (though rather less in the Czech Republic) would back their elected parliament against their government, if the two were locked in dispute, still reflected consistent support for the principle of 'bottom-up' control and influence.[13] Since the government was appointed by the president in Russia and Ukraine,[14] that indicated a fundamental rejection of the principle of presidentialism in the FSU. Indeed our question mirrored that proposed in December 1992 by Yeltsin for a referendum in January 1993 which, in the event, was never held: 'To whom do you entrust the task of extricating the country from economic and political crisis and serving the Russian Federation: the Congress of the Supreme Soviet as now constituted [i.e. the existing parliament] or the President of Russia?'[15] It might be said that Russians did not show much practical support for that principle when Yeltsin sent the tanks in to shell the Russian parliament but we should note that our question, in Russia, referred to whether they would back the 'new parliament to be elected in December 1993' against the president, not the old parliament that had been tagged with the 'Soviet communist' label and dispersed under gunfire.

The ultimate democratic mechanism of popular control is defeat of the government at an election however. We measured support for the concept of democratic alternation of governments by asking: 'Which comes closer to your view? It is better if governments
– stay in power for a long time, to give their policies time to work

or

– lose elections reasonably often, to stop them getting too powerful or corrupt.'

Over 60 per cent throughout the FSU and Hungary opted for the regular defeat of governments, though only 42 per cent in Slovakia and 35 per cent in the Czech Republic. It seems that the popularity of the incumbent government, especially in the Czech Republic, sharply reduced support for the principle of regular government defeats.

COMPETITIVE ELECTIONS

On the other hand there was widespread support for the principle of elections as such – without prejudice to their outcome.[16] Over 93 per cent in every country said local councils should be 'elected by people who live in the area' rather than 'appointed by national government' even if appointment were designed 'to prevent endless political quarrelling.' That was not such an obvious finding as it might appear. Presidential representatives were appointed to oversee local affairs in both Russia and Ukraine. In ECE postcommunist local government reforms were characterised as a move 'from democratic centralism to local democracy'[17] but in Russia the 'replacement in a growing number of Russian regions and cities of elected bodies of self-government with officials appointed from above' constituted 'a profound threat to the development of democratic values'[18] and Russia 'provide[d] an example of decentralisation on a large scale coinciding with the marginalisation of the local democratic process.'[19]

At the national level, large majorities in all countries agreed that 'parliamentary elections offer a clear choice between different directions for our country', though they were less willing to agree that their elections were likely to be 'free and fair' and still less that their elections would make politicians conform to the wishes of public opinion. Outside Russia we asked whether 'the next parliamentary elections' (inside Russia we asked about the election that took place in the midst of our interviewing, adjusting the wording as appropriate before and after election day) would be 'free and fair'. All but a few per cent had a view about that in the former Czechoslovakia, but around a fifth were undecided elsewhere. Amongst those who did have a view however, an overwhelming majority of between 74 per cent and 84 per cent in the former Czechoslovakia said that their parliamentary elections would be free and fair; and just over half in Hungary, though only a third in Ukraine agreed. In Russia the figure was 55 per cent in the three weeks before the election of 12 December 1993, but rose to 77 per cent in the week or two after it.[20]

Table 9.2:   Support for the idea of competitive elections

	Local councils should be elected, not appointed	Parliamentary elections offer a clear choice between different directions for our country	The next parliamentary elections will be 'free and fair' (R: the 'December elections will be/were...')	Regular elections have 'very much' or 'some' effect in making politicians do what ordinary people want	The multi-party system is better than a one-party or no-party system
	%	%	%	%	%
Russia	94	83	66	40	70
Ukraine	93	82	36	47	63
East Uk	89	79	32	43	61
Mid Uk	96	83	33	43	63
West Uk	96	88	55	67	66
Czech Rep	97	82	84	68	94
Slovakia	95	70	74	53	86
Hungary	95	65	54	39	81
AVERAGE:					
FSU	94	83	51	43	67
ECE	96	72	71	53	87

Note: 'Don't Knows', 'Can't decide' etc. excluded from calculation of percentages.

We asked whether people thought 'having regular elections makes politicians do what ordinary people want. Do you think elections have very much effect, some, not much, or none at all?' Over two thirds in the Czech Republic, though only about half in Hungary and 40 per cent in Russia thought regular elections would have at least 'some' effect in making politicians responsive.

Throughout most of Ukraine public opinion mirrored that in Russia, but opinion in west Ukraine was unusually enthusiastic about elections by FSU standards: 55 per cent in west Ukraine compared to only 32 per cent in east Ukraine thought that their parliamentary elections would be free and fair; 88 per cent in the west compared to 79 per cent in east Ukraine thought they offered a clear choice of direction, and 67 per cent in the west compared to only 43 per cent in east Ukraine thought they would make politicians responsive to the wishes of ordinary people.

There always had been elections, of course, even under the old regime. So it was worth enquiring specifically about support for competitive elections based upon a *multi-party* system. We asked: 'Which of these would be best for (country) today

- a one-party system
- the multi-party system as it is now
- a multi-party system with fewer parties than now
- no parties at all?'

Although framed in terms of parties, this was by implication a question about competitive elections as well as about parties themselves. In Chapter 6 we saw that there was overwhelming public opposition to the idea of providing state subsidies to help political parties establish themselves. Parties, as parties, were unpopular. But the multi-party system was much more popular than parties themselves. Given the choice, 87 per cent in ECE – though only 67 per cent in the FSU – supported the multi-party system of competitive elections against either a single party or a no-party system.[21]

In the initial transition from communism, electoral systems were designed to be inclusive in order to maximise support for the new democratic system amongst political actors.[22] They did so at the expense of permitting, even encouraging, fragmentation. Later, electoral laws were changed in order to encourage the development of a limited number of significant parties and thereby give more structure and meaning to the choice on offer to the voters.[23] By 1993 it was clear that the public throughout ECE and the FSU, while welcoming multi-party democracy, did not want a multitude of parties. In every country, the most popular option was 'a multi-party system with fewer parties than now', though 'the multi-party system as it is now' came close behind in the Czech Republic.[24]

Support for the principle of multi-party competition did not prevent large numbers of people expressing the wish to ban at least some particular parties in

Table 9.3: Acceptance of a multi-party electoral system – in practice

	Would not ban any of the named parties	% of 'government supporters' who would ban the communist party or its successor party	% of 'government opponents' who would ban the main pro-government party	% of titular ethnic group who would ban parties representing the second most numerous ethnic group	% of the second most numerous ethnic group who would ban the main pro-government party	% who would ban a named party of which their view was neutral/ unfavourable/very unfavourable
	%	%	%	%	%	%
Russia	43–59	30	25	na	na	13/30/59
Ukraine	33–55	35	35	13	40	10/33/62
East Uk	37–58	15	48	9	40	na
Mid Uk	33–57	34	32	10	39	na
West Uk	20–40	59	12	26	47	na
Czech Rep	56–59	28	8	na	na	2/6/18
Slovakia	51–55	8	15	40	28	2/11/39
Hungary	64–72	6	14	na	na	3/11/19
AVERAGE:						
FSU	38–57	32	30	13	40	12/31/60
ECE	57–62	14	12	40	28	2/9/25

Notes: 1. Two figures are shown for those who would not ban any of the named parties. The lower figure – *un*ambiguous support for unrestricted party competition – is the percentage of all respondents who answered 'no' to each question about banning a party. The higher figure – ambiguous support for unrestricted party competition – is the percentage who never answered 'yes'. The difference – very small within the Czech Republic, but large within Ukraine – reflects the numbers who answered 'don't know' to one or more of the questions.
2. For this table, the 'communist party or successor' is the Socialist Party in Hungary, and the Democratic Left in Slovakia and the Czech Republic.
3. For this table the 'main pro-government' parties are Russia's Choice, Rukh, HDF, MDS, and Civic Democratic Party in Russia, Ukraine, Hungary, Slovakia and the Czech Republic respectively.
4. The 'ethnic groups' in Ukraine are Ukrainians and Russians, and in Slovakia they are Slovaks and Hungarians. The analysis shown in this table is by self-assigned 'nationality', though the results are very similar if the analysis is repeated by 'home language'.

their country however. We asked about eight parties in Russia, eight in Ukraine, ten in Hungary, ten in Slovakia and eleven in the Czech Republic. For each party we asked people whether they were favourable or unfavourable to it (on a five point scale from 'very favourable' to 'very unfavourable') and later, whether they thought it was 'so dangerous that it should be banned?'

Naturally people who felt favourable to a party seldom felt it was so dangerous that it should be banned. On the other hand 60 per cent in the FSU though only 25 per cent in ECE would ban parties towards which they felt '*very* unfavourable'.[25] Indeed 31 per cent in the FSU though only 9 per cent in ECE would ban parties towards which they felt merely 'unfavourable'; and 12 per cent in the FSU, though only 2 per cent in ECE, would even ban parties towards which they felt 'neither favourable nor unfavourable'. This instinct to ban opponents, or even any party other than one they positively favoured, was particularly pervasive in the FSU. Only 38 per cent in the FSU, compared with 57 per cent in ECE, consistently refused to ban any of the parties that we named.

In each country we included right-wing nationalist, communist, and ethnic parties wherever possible. In 1993 the swing back to the left was only just beginning and all governments in our five countries could be described as anti-communist at that time. For people who described themselves as 'government supporters' therefore, a test of their commitment to fully competitive elections was whether or not they would ban the Communist Party or its principal successor. Very few would do so in Slovakia or Hungary, but around 30 per cent in the FSU[26] and the Czech Republic – an unusual but, in this case, understandable combination: the FSU public were inclined to ban any party they disliked, and though the Czech public was more liberal in many respects it was also the most anti-communist and the most intent upon revenge (see Chapter 4). Conversely we assessed the commitment to fully competitive elections of those who described themselves as 'government opponents' by noting whether they would choose to ban the main pro-government party. Once again about 30 per cent in the FSU but, this time, only 8 per cent in the Czech Republic would do so. This underlines the distinction between the vengeful anti-communist mood in the Czech Republic which targeted the party of the old regime, and the general instinct of all sides to ban their opponents in the FSU.

Ethnic minority parties were particularly significant in Ukraine and Slovakia. Once again we looked at the issue of full and free competition from both sides. First we noted the percentage of the titular ethnic group (Ukrainians and Slovaks) who would ban parties representing the principal minority (Russians in Ukraine, Hungarians in Slovakia). The figure was 13 per cent in Ukraine as a whole, but varied from 9 per cent in the east to 26 per cent in the west. However that degree of political intolerance was far exceeded in Slovakia where the figure rose to 40 per cent.[27] Conversely we noted whether members of the principal minority would ban the main pro-government party (Rukh in Ukraine, the MDS in Slovakia) even though these were not the most virulently nationalist parties in Ukraine and Slovakia. In Slovakia, 28 per cent of Hungarian ethnic identifiers would ban the MDS; in Ukraine, 40 per cent of Russian ethnic identifiers would ban Rukh and, interestingly, Russian identifiers who lived in the relatively non-Russian west were even more inclined than the average Russian identifier in Ukraine to ban Rukh.[28]

PARTIES

Questions about multi-party competition or banning opponents were as much about the nature of competitive elections as about parties themselves. But we also asked a range of questions about commitment to parties as such. Without such commitments it is difficult to see how a large scale democracy could function well. For all their faults and inadequacies, parties provide the most effective means yet devised for linking civil society and the state in large-scale democracies. The decay of parties in the USA reinforces rather than undermines this conclusion. It has produced gridlock between Congress and President, an inability to grapple with pressing problems such as the budget deficit, and a degree of personalisation in elective politics which exposes the *naïveté* of the American voter and the personal inadequacies of American politicians most cruelly. For the former communist countries personality-based American-style politics represents close to a worst-case scenario.

But the 'distinctive feature of the politics of transition from communism was the role played by very loosely structured groups' – movements, citizens action groups and popular fronts rather than organised parties, and parties remained notoriously weak in postcommunist countries: 'underdevelopment of parties and party systems was one of the major problem areas' in the new democratic systems.[29] In Russia the 'democratic movement [was] united only by their hatred for the bankrupt CPSU regime' and the 'unstructured party system was unable to assert its role against other potential political actors like the military, industrial interest groups, and the [presidential] government itself.'[30] When a party-list system of election was devised for the 1993 Russian parliamentary election, only 5 of the 13 competing groups – technically 'electoral alliances' – actually called themselves 'parties'.

But parties of some kind did exist.[31] Given the legacy of the communist regime and the postcommunist impediments to constructing a new party system it was 'surprising just how much was achieved by the nascent party-political system' even in the FSU.[32] In Ukraine, where parties were least visible, and only 11 per cent of candidates at the 1994 parliamentary election had a party affiliation, 44 per cent of the winners had party affiliations and 56 per cent had at least 'close ties' to parties.[33] Within the FSU countries especially, the role of communist successor parties should not be ignored: in Russia and Ukraine, a communist successor party had by far the largest membership, the best organisation and, the greatest electoral success.[34] Moreover, they provided a reference point for the whole of the rest of the party system in our FSU countries, unmatched by a clear and consistent alternative party. In Hungary, a very different, and greatly reformed, communist successor party, renamed as the Hungarian Socialist Party, also won the 1994 election, though communist successor parties did less well in Slovakia and the Czech Republic. Other parties developed much more successfully in ECE than in the FSU and went some way towards providing the electorate in ECE with a structured choice.

Table 9.4:   Alternatives to parties

	Total who either support or oppose the government	Total who would vote in parliamentary elections for candidates who supported or opposed the President	Total who believe that the personality of a party leader is more important than its policies
	%	%	%
Russia	65	73	33
Ukraine	77	82	39
East Uk	78	87	43
Mid Uk	77	80	35
West Uk	77	77	40
Czech Rep	75	na	22
Slovakia	69	na	24
Hungary	61	na	20
AVERAGE:			
FSU	71	77	36
ECE	68	na	22

Note: 'Don't Knows', 'Can't decide' etc. excluded from calculation of percentages.

What were the alternatives to *parties*? If voters' political choices were not structured adequately by their long-term acquaintance with parties, they could be structured – however capriciously – by their short-term acquaintance with *government* or with *personalities* – especially presidential personalities. We asked about both these alternatives. First we asked: 'Generally speaking, do you think of yourself as a *supporter* of the present government and what it is trying to do, or as an *opponent*?' We did not offer the option of 'neither supporter nor opponent' but recorded the substantial numbers who volunteered that response. Overall, just under a third refused to take sides, rather less in Ukraine where the government was outstandingly unpopular and in the Czech Republic where it was outstandingly popular. Conversely, of course, that means over two-thirds of people could use their support or opposition to government as the basis for their political thinking and voting choices. Both countries of the FSU had adopted a presidential system with government focused upon the person of the president rather than on the parties in parliament. So, for the public in these two countries, it made sense to ask whether people would vote in parliamentary elections, on the basis of whether *parliamentary candidates supported or opposed the president*. Again we did not offer a 'neither' option but noted any respondents who volunteered the view that 'the parliamentary candidates' support or opposition to the president would not affect my choice.' In the event, three quarters of the Russian public and four fifths in Ukraine said the candidates' attitude to the president would indeed affect their parliamentary voting choice. So in the presidential democracies of the FSU at least, personality was a particularly significant alternative to parties as a basis for political choice.

Some of the 'parties', especially in the FSU, consisted of little more than a handful of elite politicians. In some extreme cases even the party names such as 'Yabloko' (made up of letters taken from the names of its original leaders, Yavlinsky, Boldyrev and Lukin) reflected this. So we asked whether 'the most important thing about a political party is its policies or the personality of its leader?' Although only a minority openly expressed the view that what mattered most was the leader's personality, it was a substantially larger minority in the FSU (36 per cent) than in ECE (22 per cent).

Yet another way of measuring the significance of parties in politics was to note the percentages who had any view, whether favourable or unfavourable, about each of the specific parties we asked about in the different countries.[35] We might label this the 'visibility' of the parties. By this standard, parties were much more visible in ECE than in the FSU and, within the FSU, more visible in Russia than in Ukraine. The average visibility of named parties was 53 per cent in ECE but only 37 per cent in Ukraine, and the maximum visibility of any party averaged 74 per cent in ECE countries but only 58 per cent in Ukraine.

Table 9.5:   Party visibility

	Average visibility of named parties	*Maximum visibility of any party named*	
Russia	42	LDP	61
Ukraine	37	Rukh	58
East Uk	42	Rukh	63
Mid Uk	32	Rukh	54
West Uk	41	Comm	64
Czech Rep	56	Republicans	79
Slovakia	54	Hungarian	78
Hungary	50	Fidesz	65
AVERAGE:			
FSU	40		60
ECE	53		74

Notes: Party visibility = % of all respondents who feel either favourable or unfavourable towards named party. 'Don't Knows' and 'Can't Decides' are not excluded from this table: they make up the difference between the tabulated percentages and 100 per cent.

Positive feelings about parties were, by definition, less than the sum of positive and negative feelings. So support for parties was inevitably less than their visibility. On the other hand, with parties – as with newspapers – diverse specific commitments by different people can reasonably be cumulated. Earlier, in Chapter 5, we found that only 45 per cent in Russia trusted 'newspapers in general' yet 70 per cent trusted 'the newspaper you read most often.' Similarly, to be tied into party-based politics it is sufficient for each individual to be committed to one, and only one, party. People may say they dislike and distrust 'parties', but if each person likes and trusts just one specific party, there is a firm basis for party politics. Indeed strong positive feelings towards one party may combine quite well with negative feelings towards others to produce a strong commitment to party politics. So if we want to measure the degree of identification with political parties in postcommunist regimes it is proper to cumulate disparate party commitments across different sections of the public.

Table 9.6:   Party identification

	'Very favourable' to one or more of the named parties	*At least 'favourable'* to one or more of the named parties	*Generally speaking do you think of yourself as a supporter of any political party?*	*None of the existing parties represents the interests and views of people like me*
	%	%	%	%
Russia	22	73	26	60
Ukraine	18	59	13	71
East Uk	17	60	12	73
Mid Uk	19	57	10	71
West Uk	17	66	29	66
Czech Rep	31	88	37	35
Slovakia	29	87	33	54
Hungary	35	83	28	66
AVERAGE:				
FSU	20	66	20	65
ECE	32	86	33	52

Note: 'Don't Knows', 'Can't decide' etc. excluded from calculation of percentages in the last two columns.

Across the range of specific parties we named in our questions, we found 20 per cent in the FSU and 32 per cent in ECE were 'very favourable' towards at least one party; while 66 per cent in the FSU and 86 per cent in ECE were at least 'favourable' to at least one party. Connections, perhaps weak but nonetheless detectable, between parties and voters were therefore quite widespread. Intense loyalties were not, however. Only 33 per cent in ECE, fewer in Russia, and a mere 13 per cent in Ukraine said that 'generally speaking they thought of themselves as a supporter of any political party.' And conversely, over 60 per cent in Hungary and the FSU complained that '*none* of the existing parties represents the interests and views of people like me'; over half said the same in Slovakia, though only 35 per cent in the Czech Republic.

And finally, as we saw in the previous chapter (Table 8.8) people throughout ECE and the FSU regarded 'working though a political party' as one of the more effective ways of reacting to an 'unfair or unjust law' – about as effective as protest rallies and demonstrations and in the FSU, though not in ECE, as effective as an appeal through the courts.[36]

THE DIMENSIONS OF PARTY SYMPATHY

There is a more complex sense in which parties may be said to structure political choice: namely, if the whole constellation of parties available to the voter constitutes a widely recognised menu of choice. If there is general agreement about the relationship between the different parties, perhaps that some are more left-wing than others, or some more nationalist than others, then there is at least a 'common menu' available to all the voters. On the other hand, if each voter has their own view of the menu, it will be impossible to interpret the collective decisions of the voters as anything more than a random cumulation of idiosyncratic judgements.

We took the answers to the questions about whether people felt favourable or unfavourable towards each of our set of named parties – ranging from eight in Russia to eleven in the Czech Republic – and then subjected them to a factor analysis within each country. In every country there was clearly a strong dimensional structure to the patterns of feelings about the parties. Certainly the explanatory power of the general factors shows that, to a considerable degree, the voters in any one country were remarkably united in recognising a clear common menu of party choices.

Surprising perhaps, we found a slightly stronger structure in the pattern of feelings towards parties in the FSU than in ECE – but that just means a simpler structure in the FSU countries. A single factor solution could explain 35 per cent of the variation in feelings towards FSU parties, and 27 per cent of the variation in feelings towards ECE parties; and a two factor solution could explain 50 per cent of the variation in feelings towards FSU parties, and 41 per cent of the variation in feelings towards ECE parties. In terms of formal membership and organisation, parties may have had only a shadowy existence, especially in the FSU, but as objects of the public's political imagination they provided the salient features in a common mental map of political choice.[37]

In Russia a single factor solution polarised the choice between Gaidar's 'Russia's Choice', Shakhrai's 'Russian Unity and Consent' and Yavlinsky's 'Yabloko' at one end of the spectrum, and Zyuganov's Communists, Rutskoi's 'Free Russia' and Zhirinovsky's LDP at the other. In Ukraine a single factor

Table 9.7: The structure of party sympathies (%)

% explained by first factor/and by addition of second	Loadings on single factor		% explained by first factor/and by addition of second	Loadings on single factor
Russia 36/+14	A RED–BROWN ALLIANCE		**Czech Rep** 31/+14	LEFT versus RIGHT?
	Gaidar's 'Russia's Choice'	+77		Klaus's 'Civic Democratic Party' +78
	Shakhrai's 'Unity and Consent'	+76		'Christian Democratic Party' +64
	Yavlinsky's 'Yabloko'	+61		'Civic Democratic Alliance' +64
	Volsky's 'Civic Union'	+13		'Christian Democratic Union' +56
	'National Salvation Front'	-44		'Entrepreneurs Party' +27
	Zhirinovsky's 'LDP'	-58		'Civic Movement' +16
	Rutskoi's 'Free Russia'	-60		'Liberal and Social Union' -42
	Zyuganov's 'Communist Party'	-63		'Movt for a Self-Governing Democ' -48
				'Assembly for the Republic' -58
				'Social Democratic Party' -59
				'Communist/Democratic Left' -72
Ukraine 33/+16	A RIGHT–BROWN ALLIANCE		**Slovakia** 27/+15	A RED–BROWN ALLIANCE
	'Rukh'	+65		'Hungarian CDM/Coexistence' +64
	'Conservative Republican'	+49		'Conservative Democratic Party' +60
	'Cong. of Nat. Democratic Forces'	+49		'Christian Democratic Movement' +59
	'Greens'	+38		'Alliance of Democrats' +45
	'New Ukraine'	+34		'Democratic Party' +34
	'Parties representing Russians'	-31		'Green Party' -12
	'Socialist Party'	-82		'Social Democratic Party' -21
	'Communist Party'	-85		'Democratic Left' -48
				'Slovak National Party' -70
				'Meciar's 'MDS'' -71

Hungary	23/+14	A RIGHT–BROWN ALLIANCE	
		Antall's 'HDF'	+63
		Czurka's 'Hungarian Justice Party'	+53
		'Smallholders'	+49
		'Christian Democrat PP'	+44
		'Workers Party'	0
		Poszgay's 'Nat'l Democ. Assoc.'	-11
		'Republican Party'	-34
		'Young Democrats (Fidesz)'	-48
		Horn's 'Socialist Party'	-56
		'Free Democrats'	-70
		AVERAGE: ECE	27/+14

AVERAGE: FSU 35/+15

Notes: This factor analysis is based on 'relative favourabilities'. For each respondent we calculated the average of their favourabilities to all the parties in their country. We calculated the respondent's 'relative favourability' to each party by subtracting this average. Our intention was to discount favourable (or unfavourable) ratings by people who were just generally favourable (or unfavourable) to most parties.

The eigenvalues for the second factors, excluded from the single-factor solutions, were 1.1, 1.3, 1.5, 1.5, and 1.4 in Russia, Ukraine, the Czech Republic, Slovakia and Hungary respectively.

put Rukh at one end of the spectrum and the Communists and Socialists at the other. In Hungary the governing HDF and extreme nationalist Justice Party at one end faced the Free Democrats, Socialists and Young Democrats at the other. In Slovakia the governing MDS and the nationalist SNP were at one end of the spectrum followed by the ex-communist Democratic Left while the minority Hungarian Christian Democrats plus the rest of the Christian Democrats were at the other. In the Czech Republic, Klaus's governing Civic Democratic Party at one end of the spectrum was balanced by the ex-communist Democratic Left at the other.

So, in terms of party sympathies, the notorious 'red–brown alliance' of sympathies for communist and nationalist parties existed only in Russia and Slovakia;[38] in Ukraine and Hungary there was a 'right-brown alliance' of sympathies for right-wing and nationalist parties; and in the Czech Republic something close to a western style 'left versus right' polarisation of party sympathy.[39]

COMPOSITE INDICATORS

Not all the questions discussed in this chapter are suitable for use in constructing composite indicators of values associated with popular control. Our discussion has ranged a little wider than that. However we can construct composite indicators of Populism, support for Electoral Competition, and Party Commitment.

For a measure of *Populism*, we averaged answers to the questions about ignoring public opinion, referenda, parliamentary supremacy over the government, and the desirability of frequent government defeats (all oriented in the appropriate, populist, direction). That provides a measure with a low reliability coefficient (alpha) of 0.29 but which correlates at over 0.49 with answers to each of the constituent questions.

For a measure of support for *Electoral Competition* we averaged answers to the questions about whether elections offered a clear choice, whether they were free and fair, and whether they had much effect in making politicians conform to the wishes of public opinion, together with the explicit question about support for a multi-party system. That provided a composite measure with a rather better reliability coefficient of 0.40 which correlated at 0.46 with the question about 'a clear choice' and at over 0.61 with each of the other three questions.

Finally, for a composite measure of *Party Commitment* we have averaged answers to the questions about being a 'party supporter' and whether 'any party represents the interests and views of people like me.' That provided a composite measure with a reliability coefficient (alpha) of 0.42 which correlated at over 0.69 with both the questions on which it was based.

The composite measures of Party Commitment and support for Electoral Competition correlated strongly at 0.32 with each other, but both correlated negligibly (even very slightly negatively) with Populism. For that reason we shall not attempt to combine our indicators of Populism and Electoral Competition into an overall indicator of Popular Control values: they are to some extent opposites rather than aspects of the same underlying concept, two very different and essentially antagonistic interpretations of the meaning of Popular Control. We shall keep them separate.

Table 9.8: Percentage who score above the mid-point (3.0) on composite measures of populist, electoral and party values

	Populist values	*Electoral values*	*Party values*
	%	%	%
All respondents	64	63	25
Russia	65	58	25
Ukraine	64	47	12
East Uk	61	42	12
Mid Uk	69	44	9
West Uk	53	65	26
Czech Rep	51	86	35
Slovakia	60	73	30
Hungary	79	59	25
AVERAGE:			
FSU	65	53	19
ECE	63	73	30

Notes: Each scale runs from 1 to 5 with 3 as the neutral point – thus over 3, means more pro-than anti-populist, electoral or party values. Entries are the percentages who score (strictly) over 3, i.e. who are pro- the value.

CONCLUSION: THE PATTERN OF COMMITMENT TO POPULAR CONTROL

As with socialist, nationalist and liberal values, we shall use our composite indicators of popular control values directly and unmodified in computer driven multivariate calculations where they have considerable advantages in precision and discrimination. But we shall find it useful to present the percentage of people in each country or social group who score above the mid-point (3.0) on each composite measure of popular control values. It is the percentage of people who, on average, support rather than oppose the values of populism, electoral control, or party-based politics.

By these criteria, two-thirds of the public were committed to Populist values, and two-thirds to Electoral values, but only a quarter to Party values. Hungary was the most populist, and the Czech Republic the least, with Slovakia and the FSU in between. Conversely, the Czechs were the most committed to elections and parties, while the countries of the FSU closely followed by Hungary were the least. This pattern reinforces our decision to keep our measures of populist and electoral values separate.

Within the FSU there was not much difference between Russia and Ukraine as a whole but, within Ukraine itself, west Ukraine was somewhat less populist yet somewhat more committed to parties, and very much more committed to elections than the rest of Ukraine.

It is revealing to see how the three aspects of popular control values, plus the five aspects of liberal values discussed in Chapter 8, correlated with answers to questions about whether 'the idea of democracy', 'the government', and 'governing policies' were 'broadly satisfactory' (see Chapter 8). Satisfaction with the idea of democracy, with the government and with government policies all correlated moderately well with a commitment to Electoral Competition – support for the idea of democracy at 0.19 and satisfaction with the government or its policies at about 0.24. None of the other aspects of democratic principle correlated well with the idea of democracy: the public clearly associated the phrase with competitive elections and not with liberal values, populist values or commitments to parties. On the other hand Populism, along with Glasnost, Protest, and Law-based Government correlated with dissatisfaction about the government and its policies: Populism at about 0.22, Glasnost, Protest, and Law-based Government at about 0.12. So these principles of citizens' rights and limited government seem to be associated in the public mind more with negative attitudes towards the incumbent government and its policies than they are with positive attitudes towards 'the idea of democracy'.

Having completed our review of the political values of FSU/ECE publics we move on, in the next two chapters, to look at the political values of those they elected to represent them. How far were the values of the public represented in postcommunist parliaments? And in what ways did the political values of members of postcommunist parliaments differ from those of the people that elected them?

10 Entrepreneurial MPs

Public opinion exists on many levels. Indeed it forms a complex web of influence and representation. We were interested not just in the opinions of the mass public but in the opinions of their democratically elected representatives. So at the end of 1994, a year after our surveys of the opinions and values of the general public, we went back to interview a sample of members of parliament in Russia, Ukraine, Hungary and the Czech Republic.[1] The questionnaire consisted of most, though not quite all, of the questions that we had already put to the general public in these countries. So we can compare the attitudes of people and their elected politicians in these four countries.[2]

Our sample of each parliament were quite large – 128 in Russia (all from the Duma, the lower house), 132 in Ukraine, 110 in Hungary and 134 in the Czech Republic. In each country, the MPs selected for interview were approximately representative of the balance of parties, or parliamentary factions, in parliament as a whole; and they were then weighted to make them *exactly* representative of the current balance of parliamentary factions. There can be no doubt that our interviews therefore represent the expressed views of the then current members of parliament in the four countries.

However, there was a twelve month gap between our interviews with the public and with their elected politicians, and that difference of timing is important. It might be thought that the only proper way to compare the views of people and their parliamentary representatives would be to interview them both at the same time. In fact that is wrong. As Rousseau pointed out two centuries ago, we can only expect an elected parliament to be representative on the very day of its election: thereafter electors and representatives drift apart. Typically, in the middle of a parliamentary term, the views of people and parliaments – especially on transient issues of the day – diverge greatly, before coming closer together again as the next election approaches.

But consider the situation where an unpopular parliament that has failed to achieve a sufficient 'swing-back' of support is replaced by a very different parliament at a general election. In that case, comparisons of the views of people and parliament one week before the election will necessarily differ from a similar comparison one week after the election. This is not a contrived example, since our survey of the general public in Russia was carried out over the three weeks before the 1993 election and the fortnight after it. During the period of interviewing no Russian parliament actually existed; and it makes good sense to compare the views of the electorate with the views of the parliament which they elected at that time – the new parliament rather than the old – even if we did not interview its members until approximately eleven months after their election.

In fact there is no perfect time, or combination of times, at which to compare the views of peoples and parliaments. What is important is that we take account of the political situation at the time – or times – when their opinions were sought. Most of our survey focused upon fairly fundamental aspects of political values which should change relatively slowly and for which the precise timing of interviews would not be too critical. However, for a very few of our questions such as, for example, those about levels of trust in the prime minister or government, timing is critical: the 'prime minister' referred to in the question might well have changed between the times of our interviews with the public and their MPs, and that certainly changes the meaning of question even though the same words were used on the two occasions.

In Russia, the 'government' was President Yeltsin's government, and the 'prime minister' was Viktor Chernomyrdin at both times. In addition, during our 1993 interviews with the Russian public our questions explicitly specified whether they were about the old parliament dissolved (technically suspended) in September and later shelled into submission, or the new one being elected during the survey. In Russia no confusion could arise: the focus of questions put to the public and their MPs did not change – though, of course, levels of trust could change over the period of almost a year.

In the Czech Republic, there were no elections between our 1993 and 1994 surveys. So its figurehead president Havel, its government and its forceful right-wing prime minister Klaus remained in office. Klaus would probably have won an election in 1994 if there had been one. He retained the office of prime minister after the 1996 election, despite a swing of support against his party which cost him his parliamentary majority.

But in Ukraine both a new parliament and a new president were elected in mid 1994, between our public and parliamentary surveys. President Kuchma replaced Kravchuk, and the prime minister also changed. And in Hungary, while the figurehead president remained in office, the 1994 parliamentary elections brought victory for the former communists of the Socialist Party, and a new socialist prime minister, Gyula Horn. (In fact the Hungarian Democratic Forum's prime minister at the time of our 1993 survey, Antall, died and was replaced by a HDF colleague shortly before the 1994 election – though that has no implications for our survey comparisons.)

So, in all four countries, we compare the opinions of the general public at the end of 1993, with those of the MPs that they elected at that time, or shortly afterwards or, in the Czech Republic, that they would probably have re-elected in large measure if given the chance. By happy chance, more than by design, these are the most interesting and appropriate comparisons to make, since these are the parliaments that flowed from the electorates as we observed them at the end of 1993, rather than the old parliaments (in Russia, Ukraine and Hungary) that existed in 1993 but had by then clearly lost touch with their electorates.

However the interval between our surveys of publics and their MPs does mean that we have to take note that questions about governments, parliaments, and prime ministers in Ukraine and Hungary, and also about presidents in Ukraine, refer to different personalities in 1993 and 1994 – though these do not, in fact, provide the most interesting points of comparison between public and parliamentary opinion anyway.

OLD APPARATCHIKI WITHOUT COMMUNIST IDEALS

Three-quarters of Russian and Ukrainian MPs together with half the Hungarian MPs, though only a quarter of Czech MPs, admitted that they had been members of the Communist Party at one time or another. There was a high degree of personal continuity in political control, therefore, in every country except the Czech Republic. Moreover, on average, the levels of former Communist Party membership were 42 per cent greater amongst MPs than amongst their publics. Indeed, that difference reached 64 per cent in the FSU.

Table 10.1:   MPs' belief and practice of communism

	Do you believe in communist ideals now?	Did you ever believe in communist ideals?	Were you ever a member of the Communist Party?
	%	%	%
Russia	31 (+12)	64 (+4)	71 (+59)
Ukraine	38 (+21)	72 (+20)	79 (+68)
Czech Rep	9 (−6)	22 (−7)	25 (+4)
Hungary	3 (−18)	32 (+3)	49 (+37)
Average difference	(+2)	(+5)	(+42)

Notes: 'Don't Knows', 'Can't decide' etc. excluded from calculation of percentages. Figures outside parentheses are percentages of MPs; figures inside parentheses are the difference between the percentages of MPs and of their publics. Thus in Russia, 31 per cent of MPs said they believed in communist ideals at the time of the interview, and that was 12 per cent more than the 19 per cent of the Russian public who did so.

But in striking contrast to those claims – or admissions – about Communist Party membership, MPs, on average, claimed scarcely any more belief, past or present, in communist ideals than did their publics. True, MPs in the FSU claimed more belief in communist ideals than their publics, while MPs in ECE claimed less than theirs, but it was really only in Ukraine that MPs claimed very much more belief in communist ideals than did their public. Like their publics, a majority of MPs in the FSU said they used to believe, but by the end of 1994 their current level of belief had fallen to half what it had been previously.

On average MPs were almost as willing as their publics to punish those responsible for the injustices of the communist regime – a little less so in the FSU, but a little more so in ECE. However, they displayed much more sophistication – or perhaps enlightened self-interest – in the way they would go about it. MPs were 26 per cent less willing than their publics to dismiss factory managers merely on the grounds that they had been (like so many MPs) members of the Communist Party. And MPs were 18 per cent more inclined than the public to restrict the opening of secret police files to those who were named in them, rather than either making them public, or destroying them.

Table 10.2:   MPs' attitudes to revenge

		Secret police files		Do more to punish those responsible for the injustices of the communist regime	Dismiss factory managers who were members of the Communist Party
	make public	open only to those named	keep secret or destroy		
	%	%	%	%	%
Russia	23 (−14)	65 (+15)	12 (−1)	35 (−20)	7 (−24)
Ukraine	45 (−4)	47 (+8)	8 (−4)	44 (−10)	5 (−23)
Czech Rep	43 (−9)	46 (+28)	11 (−19)	93 (+12)	23 (−19)
Hungary	36 (−11)	36 (+21)	28 (−10)	78 (+4)	5 (−37)
Av. difference	(−10)	(+18)	(−8)	(−4)	(−26)

Note: 'Don't Knows', 'Can't decide' etc. excluded from calculation of percentages.

OPTIMISTIC MPS

Although MPs in the FSU and Hungary were about 13 per cent more likely than their publics to pick the Gorbachev/Reform Communist period when asked what was the 'best time' this century for their country, they were even more biased towards the present: about 25 per cent more MPs than members of the public described the present as the best time for their country. Perhaps, as incumbents, they felt a special responsibility to speak well of the present. Conversely MPs in these three countries were 34 per cent less likely than their publics to choose the Brezhnev/Kadar era of stagnation.

MPs were also more inclined than their publics to look back on pre–1918 empires with favour: 25 per cent of Russian MPs and a remarkable 32 per cent of Hungarian MPs opted for those days of imperial glory.

The Czechs were very different: they had a wider range of good times to look back on, and their MPs did not focus so strongly on the present – good though they no doubt felt it was. Instead, 41 per cent of Czech MPs chose the inter-war republic of Masaryk – far more than the 26 per cent who chose the present, far more than even a combination of the present with the united democratic Czechoslovakia of 1989–92 for which, unlike their public, they had few regrets.

Table 10.3:   MPs' views on the best time this century for (country)

	Pre–1914 Empires	Between wars	Prague spring 1968	Brezhnev time	Gorbachev time	Democratic Czechoslovakia	Since 1992 (1989 in Hungary)
	%	%	%	%	%	%	%
	Tsar	Stalin	na	Brezhnev	Gorbachev	na	Since 1992
Russia	25 (+8)	5 (−5)	na	28 (−31)	12 (+7)	na	30 (+20)
Ukraine	3 (−5)	0 (−4)	na	49 (−28)	11 (+8)	na	37 (+29)
	Empire	Masaryk	Spring '68	Husak	na	1989–92	Since 1992
Czech R	15 (+12)	41 (+9)	12 (−5)	0 (−7)	na	6 (−13)	26 (+5)
	Monarchy	Horthy	na	Kadar	Reform Comms	na	Since 1989
Hungary	32 (+20)	4 (−4)	na	9 (−42)	15 (−1)	na	40 (+26)
Av. diff.	(+9)	(−1)	na	(−27)	(+5)	na	(+20)

Notes: 'Don't Knows', 'Can't decide' etc. excluded from calculation of percentages.

However, the overall impression conveyed by this selection of 'best times' is simply one of much greater confidence and optimism amongst MPs than amongst their publics. This was also reflected in MPs' perceptions of their economy's recent performance and, still more, in their expectations for its future development. The year 1994 was not an easy one for the economy either in ECE or in the FSU; so other things being equal, we might have expected less economic optimism when MPs were interviewed at the end of 1994 than when the public were interviewed at the end of 1993. But that is *not* what we found.

On average, MPs were 12 per cent less critical of their economy's recent performance and 27 per cent more optimistic about its immediate future, than were their publics. This relative (not absolute, of course!) optimism amongst MPs was greatest in Ukraine where the public were by far the most pessimistic but a large majority of MPs had evidently concluded – rightly or wrongly – that things could only improve in the future.

Table 10.4:   MPs' economic experiences and perceptions

	(Country's) economy has got worse over the last two years	(Country's) economy will get worse over the next two years	Government action can improve or damage the economy – 'a great deal' or 'quite a lot'
	%	%	%
Russia	80 (−14)	47 (−17)	54 (+9)
Ukraine	95 (−5)	29 (−51)	66 (+35)
Czech Rep	36 (−21)	21 (−10)	86 (+10)
Hungary	90 (−6)	42 (−29)	50 (+4)
Av. difference	(−12)	(−27)	(+15)

Notes: 'Don't Knows', 'Can't decide' etc. excluded from calculation of percentages. Also, as in previous chapters, the figures for perceptions and expectations of economic trends have been calculated as percentages of those who said 'better' or 'worse', excluding 'no change'.

Table 10.5:   Statements which MPs said were more true now than they were of the communist regime

	Political leaders have too many privileges now	The poor are well cared for now	The economy is well run now	(Country) is properly defended now	Human rights are respected by the government now
	%	%	%	%	%
Russia	60 (+6)	6 (−14)	35 (+26)	9 (−2)	65 (+16)
Ukraine	24 (−34)	14 (0)	16 (+10)	39 (+17)	60 (+10)
Czech Rep	11 (−27)	48 (+16)	83 (+3)	52 (+6)	93 (−1)
Hungary	2 (−55)	20 (+3)	87 (+69)	61 (+18)	100 (+22)
Av. difference	(−28)	(+1)	(+27)	(+10)	(+12)

Notes: 'Don't Knows', 'Can't decide' etc. excluded from calculation of percentages. As in the preceding table, the figures in this table have been calculated as percentages of those who said 'more true now' or 'more true of the communist regime'; they exclude very high numbers of people who said 'no difference'; so they highlight the direction of change very well, but perhaps overstate the degree of change.

MPs were also 27 per cent more likely than their publics to say that the economy – despite its difficulties – was better run by the new regime than under the communist regime. And they also took a much more favourable view than their publics about other consequences of the transition from communism. Relative to their publics, they were 28 per cent less likely to criticise their new political leaders privileges; 12 per cent more likely to praise the effect of the new regime on human rights; even 10 per cent more likely to praise the effect of the new regime on the handling of their country's defence; though they agreed closely with their publics about the decline in provision for the poor.

Political changes during 1994, especially in Hungary, may help to explain the difference between MPs and their publics on the performance of postcommunist regimes, but even in the Czech Republic where no such change took place, MPs took a more favourable view than their public of the effects of the transition from communism.

NOT MUCH MORE CONFIDENCE THAN THE PUBLIC IN POSTCOMMUNIST INSTITUTIONS OR OFFICIALS

MPs had far more confidence in elected parliaments than did their publics, 51 per cent more. But then they would, wouldn't they? Perhaps it is worth noting that the difference between the MPs' and the public's confidence in parliament seemed largest in Ukraine and Hungary but in those two countries – and only those two – the parliament in question was not the same one in 1994 as in 1993. Nonetheless MPs everywhere clearly had much more confidence in parliament than did their publics.

Table 10.6:   MPs' trust in elected authorities

	President	*Prime Minister*	*The government*	*Parliament*
	%	%	%	%
Russia	28 (−11)	29 (−8)	21 (−15)	86 (+38)
Ukraine	76 (+55)	52 (+36)	38 (+21)	75 (+54)
Czech Rep	70 (−7)	68 (−4)	61 (−2)	80 (+51)
Hungary	85 (+14)	67 (+32)	74 (+50)	90 (+61)
Av. difference	(+13)	(+14)	(+14)	(+51)

Notes: 'Don't Knows', 'Can't decide' etc. excluded from calculation of percentages. Between our interviews with the public and with MPs, the prime minister and government changed in Hungary and Ukraine; and the president also changed in Ukraine. So, in these countries , the table does not compare like with like.

On the other hand, the much greater degree of confidence in their government, prime minister, and president, which was expressed by Hungarian and Ukrainian MPs than by their publics probably reflected the consequences of the intervening elections (which changed all the incumbents except the Hungarian figurehead President) more than a real difference between MPs and their publics. In Russia and the Czech Republic, where the same incumbents were in office in 1993 and 1994, MPs proved to have *less* confidence than their publics in all three – president, prime minister and government.

Overall therefore, and discounting their understandable degree of confidence in themselves, MPs did *not* seem to have more confidence in elected institutions than did their publics.

Nor was there any evidence that MPs had more confidence than their publics in most institutions of civil society. They had very slightly more confidence than their publics in churches and in the 'newspaper they read most often', but slightly less confidence than their publics in trade unions and the radio, and considerably less in television or the press in general. On average, despite exceptions in particular countries, MPs had roughly the same level of confidence as their publics in the army, the security forces and the police. However, MPs had around 20 per cent more confidence than their publics in two things: 'judges and courts' on the one hand, and 'most ordinary people that you meet in everyday life' on the other. It was a very short list.

Table 10.7:   MPs' trust in civil society

	Most ordinary people	The news paper you read most often	Radio	Chur-ches	Tele-vision	News-papers in general	Trade unions
	%	%	%	%	%	%	%
Russia	98 (+19)	82 (+12)	40 (−21)	74 (−3)	34 (−26)	28 (−16)	20 (−18)
Ukraine	90 (+14)	77 (+18)	59 (+3)	68 (−3)	52 (−8)	42 (+1)	40 (+8)
Czech Rep	96 (+17)	74 (−12)	72 (−7)	42 (+12)	36 (−39)	28 (−32)	20 (−21)
Hungary	96 (+24)	89 (+15)	72 (+8)	69 (+8)	50 (−4)	42 (−10)	45 (+7)
Av. difference	(+19)	(+8)	(−4)	(+4)	(−19)	(−14)	(−6)

Notes: 'Don't Knows', 'Can't decide' etc. excluded from calculation of percentages. Entries are the percentage who trust.

Table 10.8: MPs' trust in the organs of power (%)

	Army	Security services	Police	Judges and courts
	%	%	%	%
Russia	76 (+4)	42 (−14)	29 (−11)	59 (+17)
Ukraine	73 (+6)	79 (+30)	50 (+12)	54 (+16)
Czech Rep	33 (−22)	30 (0)	51 (+3)	81 (+34)
Hungary	86 (+10)	69 (−1)	83 (+11)	92 (+17)
Av. difference	(−1)	(+4)	(+4)	(+21)

Notes: 'Don't Knows', 'Can't decide' etc. excluded from calculation of percentages. Entries are the per cent who trust.

FSU MPs had remarkably little confidence in junior officials either. In Chapter 5 we found that only 14 per cent of the public in the FSU, though 53 per cent in ECE, would expect 'fair treatment' if they 'took a problem to a government office – for example, a problem about tax or housing.' On average, 6 per cent more MPs than members of the public in the FSU would expect fair treatment in those circumstances, and about 25 per cent more in ECE – which left MPs' levels of expectation of fair treatment a dismally low 20 per cent in the FSU, though a relatively healthy 79 per cent in ECE. We find the similarity between the expectations of people and politicians in the FSU far more remarkable than the difference between the expectations of people and politicians in ECE. Membership of parliament clearly carried much less clout in the presidential democracies of the FSU than in the parliamentary democracies of ECE.

Table 10.9:   Did MPs expect fair treatment by officials, for example in a tax or housing office?

	No	*Only by using connections or bribes*	*Yes*
	%	%	%
Russia	73 (+7)	8 (−10)	19 (+3)
Ukraine	74 (+4)	5 (−13)	21 (+9)
Czech Rep	16 (−15)	5 (0)	79 (+15)
Hungary	17 (−33)	4 (−3)	79 (+36)
Av. difference	(−9)	(−7)	(+16)

Note: 'Don't Knows', 'Can't decide' etc. excluded from calculation of percentages.

ANTI-SOCIALIST FORMER COMMUNISTS

MPs were not much more favourable than their publics towards postcommunist institutions or officials; but they were far more favourable than their publics toward postcommunist values.

At the start of this chapter we found that, on their own admission, MPs were very much more likely than their publics to have been members of the Communist Party at one time – usually in the past. And in the FSU, though not in ECE, MPs claimed higher levels of continuing 'belief in communist ideals' than their publics. But judged by their answers to our questions about socialist values, MPs in the FSU as well as in ECE were in fact much less committed to socialist values, and much more committed to market principles, than their publics – despite their record of Communist Party membership and even their claimed belief in communist ideals. Like the Vicar of Bray, they retained their old vanguard role as they moved off in a new direction.

Amongst the public, support for the undefined principle of 'a market economy' was high; amongst MPs it was near total, except in Ukraine – and even there it reached 81 per cent. So on average MPs gave 23 per cent more support than their publics, to the principle of a market economy.

Indeed that understates their relative enthusiasm, because since 88 per cent of the Czech public favoured that principle, their MPs simply could not be more than 12 per cent more favourable to it. In the other countries, MPs were between 18 per cent and 33 per cent more favourable than their publics to the market principle.

Table 10.10:   MPs' support for a market economy

	The creation of a market economy is right for (country)	Attitude to the idea of market/economy:			Best model for country is Sweden rather than USA
		it is broadly satisfactory	there is no real alternative	there is a better alternative	
	%	%	%	%	%
Russia	97 (+32)	56 (+8)	25 (+3)	19 (−12)	69 (+9)
Ukraine	81 (+18)	48 (+9)	26 (−7)	26 (−2)	86 (+28)
Czech Rep	97 (+9)	75 (+17)	17 (−4)	8 (−14)	61 (−13)
Hungary	97 (+33)	66 (+26)	30 (+3)	4 (−29)	79 (+9)
Av. difference	(+23)	(+15)	(−1)	(−14)	(+4)

Notes: 'Don't Knows', 'Can't decide' etc. excluded from calculation of percentages. On the 'best model' question 48 per cent of Russian MPs and 31 per cent of the Russian public rejected both Sweden and the USA as models; rejection of both was much lower elsewhere, but always higher amongst MPs.

We noted before than many who supported the move to a market economy did so, not because they found 'the idea broadly satisfactory', but only because 'there was no alternative'. On average, only 45 per cent of the public (in the four counties) found the 'idea of a market economy broadly satisfactory'; but 61 per cent of their MPs did so. Thus while a majority of the public refused to endorse the idea of a market economy as positively satisfactory, a substantial majority of MPs did so.

More practical questions confirm these patterns of principle. When we asked whether various enterprises should be 'run mainly by the state' or 'mainly by private businesses' we found MPs gave 38 per cent less support than their publics to state control of computer manufacture, 32 per cent less to state control of car manufacture, 22 per cent less to state farming, and 42 per cent less to state control of the press – though only 16 per cent less to state control of television programmes.

We asked four questions related to state responsibility for social welfare. MPs did not differ from their publics on the question of health care: both were almost unanimous that it should be mainly a state responsibility – except in the Czech Republic where only 81 per cent of the public and 70 per cent of MPs thought so. But MPs gave on average between 28 and 38 per cent less support than their publics to the view that the state should be responsible for jobs, housing or setting the prices of basic goods and services. Hungarian MPs, despite the recent success of the Socialist Party at the 1994 election and the consequently high number of Socialist MPs in the Hungarian parliament, differed from their public by especially large margins.

Table 10.11:   MPs' attitudes to state control of industry

| | *These should be run mainly by the state, rather than mainly by private businesses:* | | | | |
	Television programming	*Car factories*	*Newspapers*	*Farming*	*Computer manufacturers*
	%	%	%	%	%
Russia	65 (−18)	42 (−37)	27 (−52)	40 (−20)	28 (−40)
Ukraine	51 (−24)	51 (−22)	29 (−43)	42 (−1)	37 (−34)
Czech Rep	18 (−20)	14 (−25)	5 (−29)	27 (−26)	1 (−26)
Hungary	54 (−3)	11 (−44)	4 (−42)	3 (−41)	4 (−51)
Av. difference	(−16)	(−32)	(−42)	(−22)	(−38)

Notes: 'Don't Knows', 'Can't decide' etc. excluded from calculation of percentages. Particularly high numbers in the FSU and, in all countries when asked about television, responded that both private business and the state should be involved equally. And within the FSU, MPs were even more inclined to that response than their publics: so around half the FSU MPs gave the 'both equally' response when asked about the press or television. Entries in the table however show, as usual, the balance of opinion amongst those who would take sides.

Table 10.12:   MPs' attitudes to state responsibilities for social welfare

| | *These should be mainly done by the state, rather than left mainly to private businesses and the market-economy:* | | | |
	Health care	*Jobs*	*Housing*	*Setting prices for basic goods and services*
	%	%	%	%
Russia	96 (+3)	65 (−24)	59 (−16)	62 (−31)
Ukraine	94 (+6)	82 (−7)	65 (−25)	65 (−23)
Czech Rep	70 (−11)	39 (−17)	30 (−39)	32 (−41)
Hungary	92 (−2)	20 (−64)	49 (−36)	22 (−56)
Av. difference	(−1)	(−28)	(−29)	(−38)

Notes: 'Don't Knows', 'Can't decide' etc. excluded from calculation of percentages. Entries show, as usual, the balance of opinion amongst those who would take sides.

Although we did not offer respondents the option explicitly, our interviewers were primed to record any answers that approximated 'equally by both state and private businesses.' One striking feature of MPs' replies was the very high number of them who spontaneously gave this very reasonable, but relatively sophisticated, response when asked about the press or television. MPs were scarcely any more inclined than their publics to fudge their answers to questions about state control of farms, car or computer factories; but they were 21 per cent more inclined than the public to advocate mixed responsibility for the television. Over half the MPs in the FSU and over a third in ECE advocated mixed responsibility for television. And whereas with farms, cars, computers and even the press, MPs gave much less support to state control and much more support to private business than did their publics, with television programmes their reduced support for state control was balanced by increased support for mixed control, rather than for private business control. Television was special: even amongst news media, it was special.

On social welfare also, MPs were much more inclined than their publics to volunteer the (unprompted and uninvited) response that jobs, health and especially housing should be a joint responsibility of state and market, though few MPs (and few amongst the public) suggested that setting basic prices could be a joint responsibility. On basic prices a very large majority of the public assigned responsibility to the state while a plurality of MPs assigned it to the market.

Table 10.13:   MPs' tendencies to opt for a mixed economy

	Car/computer factories	Farms	Press	Television programmes
	%	%	%	%
State	18 (−31)	20 (−20)	9 (−36)	24 (−24)
Both	18 (+3)	22 (+2)	30 (+8)	46 (+21)
Market	65 (+29)	58 (+18)	61 (+15)	30 (+3)
	Health	Jobs	Housing	Prices
	%	%	%	%
State	57 (−19)	33 (−30)	27 (−43)	39 (−36)
Both	35 (+20)	35 (+14)	43 (+26)	14 (+4)
Market	8 (−1)	33 (+16)	30 (+17)	47 (+32)

Notes: Only 'Don't Knows' excluded from calculation of percentages. Entries are the percentages who spontaneously said 'both state and private, about equally'. Figures are the averages across all four countries.

But MPs took the opposite view on state responsibilities for culture. On the question of subsidising the (unofficial) state church or other Christian churches, the public and MPs hardly differed on average – though ECE MPs were more favourable than their publics to such subsidies, while MPs in the FSU were less favourable than their publics. However on subsidies to opera and ballet, MPs everywhere were more favourable than their publics especially, but not exclusively in ECE. And on subsidies to political parties, while MPs in Ukraine were roughly as favourable as their public (which was to say, *not* very favourable), MPs in Russia were 22 per cent more favourable than their public, and MPs in ECE about 54 per cent more favourable than their public. State intervention to help political parties, high culture –and, in ECE, religious organisations also – was more popular with MPs than with their publics even though state intervention to control industry or provide social welfare was not.

Table 10.14: MPs' attitudes to state responsibilities for culture

| | *Percentage who support state subsidies for* | | | | |
	opera and ballet	*the principal church (Orthodox in FSU; Catholic in ECE)*	*other Christian churches*	*non-Christian religions*	*political parties*
	%	%	%	%	%
Russia	96 (+9)	44 (−20)	35 (−15)	31 (−4)	41 (+22)
Ukraine	95 (+8)	25 (−24)	20 (−20)	17 (−4)	12 (−1)
Czech Rep	72 (+23)	31 (+11)	31 (+13)	24 (+13)	78 (+56)
Hungary	95 (+16)	86 (+26)	86 (+26)	84 (+42)	87 (+51)
Av. difference	(+14)	(−2)	(+1)	(+12)	(+32)

Note: 'Don't Knows', 'Can't decide' etc. excluded from calculation of percentages.

MPs were a little less inclined than their publics to restrict 'the gap between rich and poor' or to express dislike or antagonism towards 'the new rich'. They were on average 26 per cent less willing to describe unemployment as 'unacceptable', 18 per cent more willing to regard it as 'unavoidable', and even 8 per cent more inclined to view it as a necessary spur to encourage the workers to work.

Table 10.15: MPs' attitudes to equality

	Restricting gap between rich and poor is more important than freedom to make money	*Dislike 'new rich' or would even jail them*	*Unemployment is 'unacceptable'*	*Unemployment is 'necessary'*
	%	%	%	%
Russia	57 (+5)	31 (−13)	20 (−34)	23 (+9)
Ukraine	32 (−14)	44 (+2)	26 (−23)	36 (+15)
Czech Rep	40 (−13)	38 (−2)	10 (−9)	55 (+9)
Hungary	62 (−12)	30 (−11)	11 (−36)	6 (−2)
Av. difference	(−9)	(−6)	(−26)	(+8)

Note: 'Don't Knows', 'Can't decide' etc. excluded from calculation of percentages.

CONCLUSION: THE PATTERN OF SOCIALIST VALUES AMONGST MPS

Judged by their scores on the composite indicators of support for equality and state intervention in industry, welfare and culture that we constructed in Chapter 6, MPs were over 30 per cent less committed than their publics to state intervention in industry and welfare, but only 11 per cent less committed than their public to equality, and actually 5 per cent more committed than their publics to state subsidies in the cultural sphere.

By our overall measure of socialist values (which excludes questions about state intervention in culture) MPs – well over half of whom admitted to being members of the Communist Party at one time or another – were clearly much less committed to socialist values, and much more committed to the market, than were their publics.[3] Many of them no doubt hoped to benefit personally from the switch to a market economy.

In the next chapter we shall see whether MPs' greater levels of support for reform extended to support for liberal and democratic values as well as commitment to the market and rejection of socialist values.

Table 10.16: Percentage of MPs scoring above the mid-point (3.0) on composite measures of socialist values

	Socialism	Equality	S.industry	S.welfare	S.culture
Russia	51 (−30)	46 (−10)	36 (−30)	55 (−30)	43 (−8)
Ukraine	49 (−27)	34 (−16)	35 (−24)	58 (−26)	23 (−17)
Czech Rep	28 (−23)	31 (−9)	5 (−24)	35 (−28)	32 (+16)
Hungary	24 (−55)	63 (−9)	3 (−42)	32 (−52)	86 (+30)
Av. difference	(−34)	(−11)	(−30)	(−34)	(+5)

Notes: Composite indicators of Equality, State industry, State welfare and State culture defined as in Chapter 6. The composite indicator of Socialism is the average of Equality, S.industry and S.welfare – omitting S.culture for the reasons given in Chapter 6. Each scale runs from 1 to 5 with 3 as the neutral point – thus over 3, means more pro-socialist than anti-socialist. Entries outside parentheses are the percentage of MPs who score (strictly) over 3, i.e. who are pro-socialist; entries in parentheses show the difference between the percentages of MPs and of the public who are pro-socialist.

11 The Nationalist, Liberal and Democratic Values of MPs

As we saw in the last chapter, members of postcommunist parliaments had remarkably pro-market values for people with such a communist past. But the communist regime had not only supported socialist values, it had also rejected the values of nationalism and liberal democracy. Did those elected to postcommunist parliaments now reject all the principles of the old regime by accepting nationalist, liberal and democratic values as well as rejecting socialist ones?

In western democracies elected politicians tend to differ from the general public in two important ways. Elected politicians tend to be more tolerant of diversity and more tolerant of citizen protests against authority, than are the citizens themselves. But this tolerance has clear limits. Even elected western politicians have a 'governing perspective'. When they perceive a serious threat to the state itself they suddenly become even more ruthlessly authoritarian than the public, at least in the means they are prepared to use to combat that threat. So for example, British politicians are more willing than the public to tolerate public demonstrations and protests, yet at the same time more insistent than the public that the law should be obeyed, more willing than the public to accept the declaration of a state of emergency and, in less extreme circumstances, more willing to support the use of telephone tapping and monitoring of bank accounts by the security services.[1] British politicians are also more willing than their public to accept – at least in principle – the devolution of powers from central government to regional and local councils, yet very much opposed to Welsh or Scottish separatism. Moderate reform, moderate protest, moderate decentralisation wins more support from British politicians than from the public, yet these same politicians show at least as much, and usually more, determination than the public to combat serious threats to state authority. As part of the state apparatus, even if their role is that of *opposition* politicians, elected British politicians feel an obligation to defend as well as to criticise and reform the state. It is not too difficult to understand their perspective. But it implies a degree of sophistication and maturity which may not apply to newly elected politicians in a new democracy. Let us see.

NATIONALIST VALUES

In Chapter 6 we looked at three aspects of nationalism – resentful and aggressive external nationalism, territorial centralism within the state, and support for cultural conformity within the state.

191

Moderate but firm external nationalism

Let us look at external nationalism first. MPs in the FSU were no more inclined than their publics to allege that 'recent changes are turning us into a colony of the west', and in ECE MPs were far less likely than their publics – between 27 per cent and 48 per cent less – to take this view. In every country MPs were also far less likely to support the irredentist claim that 'parts of neighbouring countries should belong to (our country)' – on average 21 per cent less.

But at the same time MPs were just as willing as their publics to support the threat of force in the 'near abroad' to defend the interests of their kith and kin. In Russia that meant 30 per cent of MPs compared to 26 per cent of the public were willing to use military threats to protect the interests of Russians living in neighbouring countries. Although Chechnya is officially part of the Russian Federation and not technically a 'neighbouring country', answers to this question might have been affected by Russian attitudes to the Chechen situation. So it is worth stressing that our interviews with members of the Russian Duma took place between 4th October and 8th December 1994 – just before the tragic bloodbath in Grozny later in that month. Our findings may help to explain the mood that led to that bloodshed, but they are not a consequence of it.

Table 11.1:   MPs' attitudes to the near and far abroad

	Recent changes are turning us into a colony of the west	There are parts of neighbouring countries that really should belong to (Our Country)	When ethnic conflicts affect the rights of (Our Country's) people living in neighbouring countries, our government should threaten military action if necessary	It is a mistake to break up a large country just to give each national or ethnic group its own state
	%	%	%	%
Russia	55 (−7)	47 (−24)	30 (+4)	89 (+8)
Ukraine	47 (+1)	11 (−19)	7 (+2)	51 (−25)
Czech Rep	26 (−27)	8 (−10)	4 (+2)	77 (+4)
Hungary	12 (−48)	28 (−32)	2 (−1)	60 (−6)
Av. difference	(−20)	(−21)	(+2)	(−5)

Note: 'Don't Knows', 'Can't decide' etc. excluded from calculation of percentages.

In the other three countries only a few per cent were willing to threaten military force in the near abroad.[2] Nonetheless, on average, one per cent more of their MPs than of their publics – 4 per cent against 3 per cent – were willing to do so. The difference is clearly not significant statistically. But that is our point: MPs everywhere were around 21 per cent less willing than their publics to support irredentist claims but no less willing to threaten military force in the near abroad.

More devolutionary yet less separatist

The Chechen situation, like that in Krym (Crimea), also highlights the relevance of our questions about centralist nationalism. Again these reveal a combination of moderation but firmness amongst MPs; more tolerance in the face of limited demands coupled with more resistance to extreme demands. In every country MPs were more willing than their publics to grant greater powers of self-government to regions within their country – on average 12 per cent more. But, at the same time, MPs in every country were less willing than their publics to allow a region to break away from their country – on average 19 per cent less.[3] In both Russia and Ukraine that meant 80 per cent of MPs supported moves towards greater regional autonomy but only 8 per cent would allow a region to break away from the state entirely. For MPs, regional autonomy was an alternative to separation, not a step towards it.

Table 11.2:   MPs' attitudes to devolution and separatism

	Support giving greater powers of self-government to regions within (Country)	*If a majority of the people in a region want to separate from (Country) that region should be allowed to do so*
	%	%
Russia	80 (+15)	8 (−30)
Ukraine	80 (+14)	8 (−30)
Czech Rep	96 (+6)	14 (−10)
Hungary	84 (+14)	36 (−4)
Av. difference	(+12)	(−19)

Note: 'Don't Knows', 'Can't decide' etc. excluded from calculation of percentages.

Less culturally conformist

MPs in our four postcommunist countries were on average 16 per cent less religious than their publics. Indeed, excluding the Czech Republic where even the public were remarkably irreligious, MPs were between 19 and 27 per cent less religious than their publics. That was mainly at the expense of the Orthodox Church in the FSU and of the Catholic Church in Hungary. So, amongst those who were religious, the sectarian balance amongst MPs was more favourable to religious minorities – Protestants, Jews, Muslims and others, plus Ukrainian (as distinct from Russian) Orthodox in Ukraine. On our figures the number of

Catholic MPs in Hungary, for example, was less than one and a half times the number of Protestant MPs; and in Ukraine twice as many MPs were Ukrainian Orthodox as Russian Orthodox. Given that the principle of atheistic conformity had been discredited along with the rest of the Soviet system, the pattern of religious divisions amongst MPs was more favourable to diversity and tolerance than that amongst the public.

Table 11.3:   MPs' religious affiliations (%)

	Russian Orthodox	Ukrainian Orthodox	Catholic	Protestant & other Christian	Jewish, Muslim, other non-Christian	No religion
Russia	29 (−19)	0 (0)	0 (0)	6 (0)	4 (+2)	63 (+19)
Ukraine	11 (−10)	21 (−4)	3 (−1)	9 (−5)	1 (−2)	56 (+23)
Czech Rep	1 (+1)	0 (0)	32 (0)	10 (+2)	4 (+2)	54 (−5)
Hungary	1 (0)	0 (0)	29 (−25)	20 (−2)	1 (0)	49 (+27)

Note: 'Don't Knows', 'Can't decide' etc. excluded from calculation of percentages.

Language and nationality were, however, the main bases for ideas of cultural conformity in the postcommunist world. On these, MPs were fairly closely representative of their publics. In Hungary they were almost exactly representative. In the Czech Republic, 10 per cent of MPs described themselves as Moravian rather than Czech which produced a distortion perhaps more apparent than real. In Russia similarly, MPs were 11 per cent less likely than the public to describe themselves as Russian, and more likely than the public to describe themselves as Soviet (3 per cent), Ukrainian (7 per cent), Jewish (4 per cent) or by another minority label. In Ukraine the diverse minor nationalities were neither under nor over represented in parliament; but Ukrainian MPs were 10 per cent more likely than their public to claim Ukrainian nationality and correspondingly less likely to claim Russian nationality, though – significantly – only 3 per cent more likely than their public to speak Ukrainian at home. So 78 per cent of Ukraine's MPs claimed that their 'nationality' was Ukrainian, although only 51 per cent used Ukrainian as their main language 'within their own household.'

There was very little difference between MPs and their publics in Russia and ECE on the principle of whether 'the unity and independence of (country) is more important than guaranteeing equal rights to all who live in it'; but there was a 37 per cent difference between Ukraine's MPs and its public. The public in Ukraine came down overwhelmingly on the side of equal rights, while a majority of Ukraine's MPs gave priority to national unity and independence.

Table 11.4:   MPs' self-assigned nationalities and home languages

| | Nationality/Language spoken at home | | | | |
	Russian	*Ukrainian*	*Czech*	*Hungarian*	*Other*
	%	%	%	%	%
in Russia	76(−11)/96(+1)	7(+4)/1(0)			17(+7)/4(−1)
in Ukraine	17(−9)/45 (−4)	78(+10)/			5(−1)/4(+1)
		51(+3)			
in Czech Rep			86(−8)/99(+2)		12(+9)/1(0)
in Hungary				97(0)/99(−1)	2(0)/0(0)

Note: In addition to the entries shown, one per cent of Hungarian MPs spoke Russian at home; and one per cent of Hungarian MPs and two per cent of Czech MPs claimed Slovak nationality.

Table 11.5:   MPs' attitudes to enforcing social conformity

	The unity and independence of (Country) is more important than guaranteeing equal rights for all who live in it	*Only people who speak (State Language) should be full citizens and have the right to vote in elections*	*All schools in (Country) should teach all subjects in (State Language)*
	%	%	%
Russia	47 (+2)	3 (−16)	38 (−7)
Ukraine	57 (+37)	4 (−4)	23 (−2)
Czech Rep	39 (0)	20 (−14)	37 (−21)
Hungary	44 (+3)	16 (−45)	3 (−31)
Av. difference	(+11)	(−20)	(−15)

Note: 'Don't Knows', 'Can't decide' etc. excluded from calculation of percentages.

But whatever Ukraine's MPs meant by that, it did not seem to imply cultural conformity. Possibly the MPs were thinking more in terms of regional separatism and their public more in terms of cultural diversity. In every country, including Ukraine, MPs were less inclined than their publics to insist on imposing the state language throughout the school system (on average 15 per cent less), or as a condition for full rights of citizenship (on average 20 per cent less).

Nor could Ukraine's MPs have been thinking in terms of political conformity, within the state political system, either. For within every country MPs were even more inclined than their publics to support 'opposition criticism' as a useful means of restraining governments' abuse of power rather than attacking it for 'weakening national unity' – on average 12 per cent more. Indeed the percentage of MPs who could not cope with the clamour of opposition criticism ranged only from zero in the Czech Republic to a maximum of 3 per cent in Ukraine. And in more practical terms too, MPs in Ukraine were less willing than their public to ban both the anti-Russian Rukh and 'parties representing Russians in Ukraine'.

So on cultural conformity there was no evidence of a 'governing perspective', no subtleties or paradoxes: MPs were unambiguously less nationalist and more tolerant than their publics. The state was not in danger and MPs could afford to be liberal.

Table 11.6:   MPs' attitudes to a ban on ethnic parties in Ukraine

	Ban Rukh	*Ban 'parties representing Russians living in Ukraine'*
	%	%
Ukraine	12 (−19)	10 (−1)

Note: 'Don't Knows', 'Can't decide' etc. excluded from calculation of percentages.

THE IDEA OF DEMOCRACY

With some variations from country to country, MPs were somewhat more satisfied than their publics with 'the idea of democracy'; yet at the same time they were less satisfied than their publics with their governments or with government policies. In short, MPs were better able to distinguish between the democratic system and those who temporarily held power.

In Russia, Ukraine and the Czech Republic, for example, MPs were 9 per cent *more* likely than their publics to say there was no real alternative to the idea of democracy, yet 16 per cent *less* likely than their publics to say there was no real alternative to the government and 18 per cent *less* likely to say there was no real alternative to government policies. Hungary provided an apparent exception, in that Hungarian MPs appeared more satisfied than their public with the government as well as with the idea of democracy, but there we have to remember that an election and a radical change of government intervened between our interviews with the Hungarian public and their MPs; so 'the government' that Hungarian MPs had in mind was the new one, while 'the government' their public had in mind was the old one.

A clearer indication of commitment to the new democratic system, unaffected by changes of government, was provided by two other questions. With relatively little variation, MPs in all four countries were 66 per cent less likely than their publics to agree that 'politics is so complicated that I often cannot understand what is going on' and 41 per cent less likely to agree that their country was 'not yet ready for democracy.' The first of these questions might be disregarded as a mere self-assessment, but the second could not. MPs were clearly much more willing to back the general idea of a democratic system. Whether MPs had values that were consistently more liberal and democratic than those of their publics, however, remains to be seen.

Table 11.7:   MPs' ability to distinguish between the idea of democracy and the incumbents or their policies

| | Broadly satisfactory: | | | Broadly satisfactory, or no real alternative: | | |
	the idea of democracy	the govern-ment	govern-ment policies	the idea of democr-acy	the govern-ment	govern-ment policies
	%	%	%	%	%	%
Russia	61 (−2)	9 (−27)	3 (−28)	93 (+9)	28 (−31)	16 (−36)
Ukraine	69 (+8)	11 (−2)	9 (0)	95 (+9)	42 (−12)	36 (−9)
Czech Rep	72 (+5)	53 (−8)	44 (−7)	97 (+9)	75 (−5)	63 (−10)
Hungary	82 (+23)	59* (+31)	46* (+23)	99 (+17)	83* (+22)	70* (+22)
Av. diff.	(+9)	(−2)*	(−3)*	(+11)	(−7)*	(−8)*

Note: * not fully comparable – see text. 'Don't Knows', 'Can't decide' etc. excluded from calculation of percentages.

Table 11.8:   MPs' doubts about democracy

	Politics is so complicated that I often cannot understand what's going on	(Country) is not yet ready for democracy
	%	%
Russia	8 (−75)	35 (−35)
Ukraine	18 (−65)	48 (−28)
Czech Rep	12 (−60)	9 (−44)
Hungary	20 (−64)	8 (−55)
Av. difference	(−66)	(−41)

Note: 'Don't Knows', 'Can't decide' etc. excluded from calculation of percentages.

LIBERAL VALUES

MPs had generally higher levels of commitment to liberal values than their publics. We compared MPs and their publics on five aspects of liberal values: attitudes towards freedom of information, order and legality, tolerance of minorities and extremists, support for rights to protest, and support for the notion that government should operate only within the confines of the law.

Freedom of information

On average 98 per cent of the public had agreed that they should have a right to know about factory pollution even if factories then had to close. MPs could hardly give that any more support, though it is significant that they gave it no less. We might doubt whether MPs would really be so open in practice but at least they professed support for the principle of openness. That was not a principle in which politicians of the old regime had believed prior to Gorbachev, let alone one that they had practised; and even Gorbachev himself had not lived up to his principle in the immediate aftermath of Chernobyl.

The difference between MPs and their publics on the question of opening up the old regimes' secret police files suggested that MPs might be more sophisticated rather than any more or less open than their publics: MPs were more inclined than their publics to open these files to those named in them, but less inclined either to allow fully open access, or to keep them completely secret.

Our other two questions about freedom of information, however, suggested that MPs in ECE were much more committed to freedom of information than their publics, while MPs in the FSU were rather less committed than theirs. MPs in ECE were about 21 per cent *less* inclined than their publics to ban publication of stories that would embarrass government ministers,[4] or to allow the government to sack the head of state television simply because it did not like what he was doing; but MPs in the FSU were about 8 per cent *more* willing than their publics to allow such restrictions on the free flow of information.

Table 11.9:   MPs' attitudes to freedom of information

	Right to know about factory pollution even if factories then have to close	Ban publication of embarrassing details about the private lives of government ministers	The government should be able to dismiss the head of state television if it does not like what he is doing
	%	%	%
Russia	99 (+1)	36 (0)	27 (+6)
Ukraine	97 (−2)	46 (+10)	31 (+14)
Czech Rep	98 (−1)	31 (−25)	38 (−17)
Hungary	100 (+2)	37 (−14)	12 (−26)
Av. difference	(0)	(−7)	(−6)

Note: 'Don't Knows', 'Can't decide' etc. excluded from calculation of percentages.

More insistent on obedience to the law

Similarly, MPs in the FSU were 6 per cent *more* inclined than their publics to agree that 'people should have more respect for authority'; while ECE MPs were 26 per cent *less* inclined to agree than were ECE publics.

On the other hand, MPs everywhere were more inclined than their publics to insist that the people should 'obey even unjust laws' (on average 30 per cent more) and that 'the police themselves should never step outside the law, even if that meant some criminals escaped punishment' (on average 23 per cent more). So MPs everywhere were much more committed to strict legality – whether applied to people or agents of the state – than were their publics.

MPs everywhere were *less* inclined than their publics to agree that 'the only alternative to strong government is disorder and chaos' (on average 14 per cent less) which was consistent, as we shall see later, with their special commitment to limited government. MPs really were committed to 'law and order' – in the literal meanings of those words – rather than to the abuse of power which is so often associated with those that mouth these words as a mere political slogan.

Table 11.10: MPs' attitudes to order and legality

	(Country) people should have more respect for authority	*Even if a law is unjust, people should obey it until it is changed*	*The police themselves should never break the law, even though that means some criminals escape punishment*	*The only alternative to strong government is disorder and chaos*
	%	%	%	%
Russia	79 (0)	95 (+39)	96 (+21)	39 (−33)
Ukraine	80 (+13)	96 (+25)	89 (+8)	54 (−5)
Czech Rep	42 (−14)	94 (+30)	72 (+36)	13 (−7)
Hungary	32 (−37)	97 (+26)	94 (+26)	77 (−12)
Av. difference	(−10)	(+30)	(+23)	(−14)

Note: 'Don't Knows', 'Can't decide' etc. excluded from calculation of percentages.

More tolerant

The public in the FSU were 31 per cent more willing than in ECE to 'ban speeches by people with extreme views'; but MPs in the FSU were 61 per cent more willing to do so than MPs in ECE. On top of the already large difference between publics in ECE and the FSU, MPs in ECE were 36 per cent more tolerant than even their relatively tolerant publics, while MPs in the FSU were only 5 per cent more tolerant than their relatively intolerant publics.

Similarly, when we asked whether something that 'deeply offends most people in (this country) should be made illegal' – a question with ethnic and social as well as political overtones – MPs in ECE proved 44 per cent more tolerant than their publics, while Russian MPs were only 7 per cent more tolerant than the Russian public, and Ukrainian MPs were actually 12 per cent *less* tolerant than the Ukrainian public.

Table 11.11:   MPs' attitudes to toleration – in principle

	Ban public speeches by people with extreme views	If something deeply offends most (Country) people, then it should be made illegal
	%	%
Russia	85 (−2)	84 (−7)
Ukraine	81 (−8)	75 (+12)
Czech Rep	17 (−25)	27 (−47)
Hungary	29 (−48)	33 (−39)
Av. difference	(−21)	(−20)

Note: 'Don't Knows', 'Can't decide' etc. excluded from calculation of percentages.

On the other hand, when we asked specifically about free speech for fascists, Communists, evangelical Christians, Jews, Muslims, gypsies and homosexuals, MPs in all four countries proved much more tolerant than their publics of these manifestations of free speech. In every country, and on the rights of every minority, MPs were more tolerant than their publics – on average by a massive 42 per cent. Even in Ukraine, where MPs tended not to be more tolerant than their public on other questions, they were 33 per cent more tolerant than their public on rights of free speech for these seven social and political minorities. Whatever their gut feelings about tolerance, they seemed to have accepted free speech as an important procedural value of the new democratic system to which they were so committed.[5]

We might ask why FSU MPs displayed so much relative tolerance to these seven specific minorities yet appeared so very much less tolerant than ECE MPs on our more general question about 'speeches by people with extreme views'. We can only surmise that the scale of extremism with which they were faced was longer and more deadly in the FSU than in ECE; that FSU 'extremists' were much more 'extreme' than ECE 'extremists'. Comparing like with like certainly showed much the same levels of support for free speech in the FSU as in ECE, both amongst their publics and (at a higher level) amongst their MPs.

Table 11.12:   MPs' toleration of free speech for political and social minorities

	Fascists	Comm-unists	Evang-elical Chris tians	Jews	Muslims	Gypsies	Homo-sexuals	AVE-RAGE
	Support the right of certain groups to hold public meetings and rallies							
Russia	12 (+8)	94 (+52)	85 (+45)	89 (+54)	91 (+55)	85 (+58)	52 (+42)	73 (+45)
Ukraine	6 (+4)	71 (+40)	77 (+36)	79 (+40)	80 (+47)	77 (+51)	20 (+9)	59 (+33)
Czech Rep	9 (+8)	51 (+24)	98 (+47)	97 (+45)	91 (+57)	91 (+71)	79 (+49)	74 (+43)
Hungary	5 (+2)	44 (+25)	98 (+48)	98 (+54)	97 (+60)	97 (+67)	77 (+61)	74 (+46)
Av. diff.	(+6)	(+35)	(+44)	(+48)	(+55)	(+62)	(+40)	(+42)

Note: 'Don't Knows', 'Can't decide' etc. excluded from calculation of percentages.

More support for rights to protest

Around 15 per cent of the public in ECE and the FSU had agreed that 'criticism from opposition politicians weakens national unity and causes disruption' rather than being a useful check on the abuse of government power. Amongst MPs, only 3 per cent in Ukraine, and elsewhere only one per cent or less, agreed with that. The concept of opposition criticism, a pluralist notion perhaps more fundamental even than competitive elections, was almost universally accepted by MPs – including those who supported their governments as well as those who opposed them.

MPs in all countries were more tolerant than their publics towards most peaceable forms of public protest. Compared to their publics, MPs were 9 per cent more willing to allow appeals through the courts (they could not be any more, since that made them over 98 per cent willing to allow such appeals). MPs were also 15 per cent more willing than their publics to allow protest meetings, 21 per cent more willing to allow demonstrations and protest marches even if they blocked traffic for a few hours, and 23 per cent more willing to allow protesters to call nationwide strikes.

But as we have noted before, there are limits beyond which MPs became less tolerant and more authoritarian than their publics rather than the reverse. MPs in all countries were *less* willing than their publics to allow protesters to occupy government buildings (on average 6 per cent *less*) or to allow 'workers in essential public services such as hospitals and electricity power stations' to strike (on average 10 per cent *less*).

More support for law-bound government

MPs were much less willing than their publics to accept the declaration of a state of emergency that would curtail citizens' rights – though the peculiar

Table 11.13: MPs' attitudes to opposition and protest behaviour

	Criticism from opposition politicians weakens national unity and causes disruption	All public workers, even those in essential public services like hospitals and electricity power stations should have the right to strike	If some citizens felt a law was very unjust or harmful, they should be allowed to				
			hold protest meetings	call nation-wide strikes	appeal through the courts	hold protest marches and demonstrations which block traffic for a few hours	occupy government buildings
	%	%	%	%	%	%	%
Russia	1 (−13)	39 (−10)	95 (+19)	77 (+42)	100 (+8)	53 (+22)	3 (−5)
Ukraine	3 (−10)	41 (−8)	94 (+18)	51 (+14)	98 (+8)	40 (+11)	9 (−9)
Czech Rep	0 (−8)	49 (−8)	96 (+3)	70 (+14)	99 (+10)	65 (+29)	8 (−4)
Hungary	1 (−15)	46 (−14)	98 (+19)	77 (+21)	97 (+8)	57 (+21)	1 (−6)
Av. difference	(−12)	(−10)	(+15)	(+23)	(+9)	(+21)	(−6)

Note: 'Don't Knows', 'Can't decide' etc. excluded from calculation of percentages.

combination of liberalism and authoritarianism that characterises the 'governing perspective' showed up in the way MPs were 28 per cent less willing than their publics to accept a state of emergency to combat 'a campaign of slander against the government' but only 7 per cent less willing to accept a state of emergency to combat 'widespread public disorder'.

Earlier we saw that MPs everywhere, and by an average of 23 per cent, were less willing than their publics to let the police step outside the law. They had the same attitude towards the government itself. MPs everywhere, and by an average of 21 per cent, were more willing than their publics, to let a constitutional court overrule their government even though the government could claim an electoral and representative mandate against the purely procedural legitimacy of the court. In fact, over 98 per cent of MPs everywhere backed the constitutional court. So the 21 per cent difference between them and their publics was just about as large as it could possibly be.

Table 11.14: MPs' support for emergency powers which suspend citizens' rights

	It would be acceptable for the government to suspend citizens' usual rights and take emergency powers if confronted by:					
	widespread corruption and mafia crime	widespread public disorder	widespread strikes in essential industries	a campaign of slander against the government	a parliament which obstructed the government	*AVERAGE*
	%	%	%	%	%	%
Russia	31 (−48)	58 (−21)	19 (−33)	0 (−40)	1 (−29)	22 (−34)
Ukraine	71 (−9)	87 (+5)	63 (+3)	14 (−26)	11 (−27)	49 (−11)
Czech Rep	68 (−11)	59 (−4)	13 (−28)	3 (−26)	15 (−22)	32 (−18)
Hungary	38 (−30)	59 (−9)	24 (−22)	10 (−21)	5 (−21)	27 (−21)
Av. diff.	(−25)	(−7)	(−20)	(−28)	(−25)	(−21)

Note: 'Don't Knows', 'Can't decide' etc. excluded from calculation of percentages.

Table 11.15: MPs' support for law-bound government

	Allow the Constitutional Court to overrule the government	A strong leader who has the trust of the people should not be restricted by the law
	%	%
Russia	99 (+22)	2 (−25)
Ukraine	99 (+19)	7 (−20)
Czech R	98 (+25)	1 (−15)
Hungary	98 (+17)	5 (−29)
Av. diff.	(+21)	(−22)

Note: 'Don't Knows', 'Can't decide' etc. excluded from calculation of percentages.

Similarly, MPs everywhere, and by an average of 22 per cent, were less willing than their publics to agree that 'a strong leader who has the trust of the people should not be restricted by the law.' And again, the difference could hardly have been any greater: on average under 4 per cent of MPs – rising to a maximum of 7 per cent in Ukraine – would let even a trusted leader disregard the law. Once again we can see that MPs' belief in 'law and order' extended to demands for law-abiding and orderly government, as much as for law-abiding and orderly citizens.

We asked two questions about conflicts between parliaments and governments. First a general point of principle: 'If the government wanted to take action but was opposed by parliament, who should have the final say – parliament or the government?' Second a question of practice: 'Do you think that President Yeltsin was right or wrong to suspend the Russian parliament in September 1993?' In every country, and on average by about 23 per cent, MPs were less inclined than their publics to agree that the government should be able to overrule an obstructive parliament and, by about the same margin, less inclined to accept that Yeltsin had been right to suspend the Russian parliament in September 1993. But there were sharp differences between MPs in the FSU and ECE. In the FSU only around a quarter of MPs either accepted the principle that the government should overrule parliament or approved Yeltsin's action. In ECE, on the other hand, although almost no MPs accepted the principle that government should be able to overrule parliament, well over half of them approved Yeltsin's action against the Russian parliament. Even in Kyiv, the shelling of the Moscow parliament must have seemed a bit too close for comfort – in terms of culture and precedent perhaps even more than geography. In Prague and Budapest, MPs felt able to dissociate Yeltsin's action from the general principle or from their own situation – though the question about Yeltsin's action came almost immediately after the question of principle in our interviews, separated from it only by the question about the constitutional court.

Table 11.16: MPs' attitudes to parliamentary supremacy – in principle and practice

	The government should be able to take action even if opposed by parliament	Yeltsin was right to suspend the Russian parliament
	%	%
Russia	17 (−22)	27 (−26)
Ukraine	25 (−11)	27 (−32)
Czech Rep	0 (−46)	57 (−16)
Hungary	1 (−13)	55 (−13)
Av. difference	(−23)	(−22)

Note: 'Don't Knows', 'Can't decide' etc. excluded from calculation of percentages.

POPULAR CONTROL VALUES

MPs proved less populist than their publics but more committed to the values and institutions of representative democracy. That was one reason why we found it so necessary to distinguish between these two aspects of popular control: they differ sharply not only in logic but in their patterns of support.

Less populist

No one would expect populist ideas to be particularly appealing to elected members of parliament anywhere. On average MPs were no more and no less inclined than their publics to feel that it would be 'better if governments lost elections reasonably often to stop them becoming too powerful or corrupt'. But MPs were 16 per cent more inclined than their publics to agree that 'governments should ignore public opinion if they think it is wrong for the country.' This anti-populist tendency was more pronounced amongst ECE MPs than amongst those in the FSU: MPs in the FSU were only 8 per cent more inclined to say governments should ignore public opinion than their publics, but MPs in ECE were 23 per cent more so. More strikingly, MPs everywhere, and on average by 27 per cent, were less inclined than their publics to allow important political issues to be decided by popular referendum.

Table 11.17: MPs' attitudes to populism

	Governments should ignore public opinion if they think it is wrong for the country	*The most important issues should be decided in a referendum*	*The government should be allowed to overrule parliament*	*It is better if governments lose elections reasonably often, to stop them getting too powerful or corrupt*
	%	%	%	%
Russia	16 (+4)	45 (−20)	17* (−22)	76 (+16)
Ukraine	30 (+13)	44 (−22)	25 (−11)	59 (−6)
Czech Rep	37 (+20)	48 (−23)	0 (−46)	29 (−6)
Hungary	34 (+26)	25 (−42)	1 (−13)	58 (−4)
Av. difference	(+16)	(−27)	(−23)	(0)

Notes: * refers to 'the new parliament, elected on 12th December 1993'. 'Don't Knows', 'Can't decide' etc. excluded from calculation of percentages.

More pro-elections

MPs did not differ from their publics on whether local government councils should be elected or appointed. But on three significant questions MPs were clearly much more favourable than their publics to the idea of competitive elections. MPs everywhere, and on average by 12 per cent, were more inclined than their publics to agree that 'parliamentary elections offer a clear choice between different directions for our country.' Although there were wide variations from country to country, on average MPs were 17 per cent more inclined than their publics to describe elections in their country as 'free and fair'. Indeed almost all the MPs in ECE, though only just over half in the FSU, agreed that their parliamentary elections were 'free and fair'. And in every country, by an average of 36 per cent, MPs were more willing than their publics to agree that 'regular elections' had at least 'some effect' in 'making politicians do what ordinary people want.'

Again, in every country, MPs were significantly more inclined than their publics to back the concept of competitive multi-party elections against the concept of 'one party' or 'no party' elections. About 96 per cent of MPs in the FSU and almost all in ECE preferred multi-party elections. Paradoxically that made MPs' attitudes more distinctive in the FSU than in ECE where so many of the public also preferred multi-party elections. Indeed, the difference between MPs and their publics on multi-party elections was greatest in Ukraine (31 per cent) and least in the Czech Republic (only 5 per cent).[6]

Table 11.18:   MPs' support for the idea of competitive electionso %

	Local councils should be elected, not appointed	Parliamentary elections offer a clear choice between different directions for our country	Parliamentary elections 'free and fair'	Regular elections have 'very much' or 'some' effect in making politicians do what ordinary people want	The multi-party system is better than a one-party or no-party system
Russia	99 (+5)	87 (+4)	62 (−4)	87 (+47)	97 (+27)
Ukraine	94 (+1)	87 (+5)	50 (+14)	81 (+34)	94 (+31)
Czech Rep	94 (−3)	92 (+10)	99 (+15)	91 (+23)	99 (+5)
Hungary	100 (+5)	93 (+28)	98 (+44)	79 (+40)	100 (+19)
Av. difference	(+2)	(+12)	(+17)	(+36)	(+21)

Notes: 'Don't Knows', 'Can't decide' etc. excluded from calculation of percentages. The 'free and fair' question referred to specific elections as follows: Russia – 12th December 1993 election; Czech Republic – the 'next' election; Ukraine and Hungary – in 1993 the public were asked about the 'next' election while in 1994 the MPs were asked about the election earlier in 1994, thus maintaining a constant focus.

Table 11.19:   MPs' attitudes to a multi-party electoral system – in practice

	Would not ban any of the named parties	Would ban a named party of which their view was neutral/ unfavourable/very unfavourable
	%	%
Russia	71(+28) – 76(+17)	0(−13)/4(−26)/17(−42)
Ukraine	58(+25) – 64(+9)	5(−5)/13(−20)/35(−27)
Czech Rep	84(+28) – 86(+27)	0(−2) / 0(−6) / 5(−13)
Hungary	87(+23) – 87(+15)	0(−3)/1(−10)/3(−16)
Av. difference	(+26) – (+17)	(−6) / (−16) / (−25)

Note: Two figures are shown for those who would not ban any of the named parties. The lower figure – *un*ambiguous support for unrestricted party competition – is the percentage of all respondents who answered 'no' to each question about banning a party. The higher figure – ambiguous support for unrestricted party competition – is the percentage who never answered 'yes'. The difference – very small within the Czech Republic, but large within Ukraine – reflects the numbers who answered 'don't know' to one or more of the questions.

Table 11.20:   Visibility of parties amongst MPs (%)

	Average visibility of named parties	Maximum visibility of any party named	Total who either support or oppose the government	The personality of a party leader is more important than its policies
Russia	68 (+26)	84 (+23)	72 (+7)	26 (−7)
Ukraine	61 (+24)	81 (+23)	26 (−51)	14 (−25)
Czech Rep	70 (+14)	93 (+14)	91 (+16)	8 (−14)
Hungary	71 (+21)	92 (+27)	99 (+38)	10 (−10)
Av. difference	(+21)	(+22)	(+3)	(−14)

Note: Party visibility = Percentage of all respondents who feel either favourable or unfavourable towards named party.

In practice too, MPs were more committed to the idea of a system of competition between parties. Compared to their publics, MPs were 25 per cent less willing to ban a party which they regarded very unfavourably, and 16 per cent less willing to ban a party they regarded merely unfavourably. Again MPs were most distinctive in the FSU where, although they were much more willing than ECE MPs to ban their opponents, they differed far more from the FSU publics than ECE MPs did from ECE publics. So FSU MPs were 35 per cent less willing than their publics to ban a party they regarded very unfavourably, but in ECE MPs differed from their publics by only 15 per cent.

More pro-party

Parties were much more visible to MPs than their publics – by an average of 22 per cent. And MPs stressed the importance of party policies rather than leaders somewhat more than their publics.

ECE MPs were strikingly more favourable to the idea of state subsidies for political parties – fully 54 per cent more so than their publics; while Russian MPs were only 22 per cent more favourable to party subsidies than their public; and Ukrainian MPs did not differ at all from their public who were over-whelmingly against state subsidies for parties.

We felt it would be too brutal to ask MPs – especially in ECE – whether they 'supported' a political party. Instead we got at the degree of commitment to parties more obliquely. In every country, and by an average of 41 per cent, we found MPs less willing than their publics to agree that 'none of the existing parties represents the interests and views of people like me.' That left only 5 per cent of MPs in ECE, but 29 per cent of MPs in the FSU, who felt no party exactly matched their interests and views.

But most MPs felt at least mildly favourable towards at least one of the specific parties that we asked them about, even in the FSU. On average 18 per cent more MPs than members of their publics felt at least 'favourable' towards at least one party, and there was a similar difference (17 per cent) between the percentages of MPs and their publics who felt 'very favourable' towards at least one party.

Table 11.21:   MPs' levels of party identification

	None of the existing parties represents the interests and views of people like me	*At least 'favourable' to one or more of the named parties*	*'Very favourable' to one or more of the named parties*
	%	%	%
Russia	29 (−31)	94 (+21)	35 (+13)
Ukraine	29 (−42)	85 (+26)	29 (+11)
Czech Rep	4 (−31)	95 (+7)	48 (+17)
Hungary	5 (−61)	99 (+16)	60 (+25)
Av. difference	(−41)	(+18)	(+17)

Note: 'Don't Knows', 'Can't decide' etc. excluded from calculation of percentages.

MPs also had more structured attitudes than their publics towards the whole range of parties that we asked about in their countries. Factor analyses of positive and negative attitudes towards parties revealed a similar (though not always identical) underlying structure to these attitudes amongst MPs and their publics; but this underlying structure was more powerfully predictive for MPs than for their publics. Basing our factor analyses on 'relative favourabilities', a single dimension could explain 35 per cent of the variation in the FSU publics' attitudes towards individual parties, and 27 per cent of the variation in ECE publics' attitudes. But a single dimension could explain 53 per cent of the variation in FSU MPs' attitudes towards individual parties, and 40 per cent of the variation in ECE MPs' attitudes. The weakness of parties as organisations should not blind us to the fact that they served as useful psychological reference points in the political imaginations of both publics and MPs, but particularly so for MPs.

Table 11.22: The structure of MPs' sympathies for parties
(factor analyses based on relative favourabilities) (%)

| | *Variation in attitudes to set of named parties which can be explained by* | |
	one factor	*two factors*
Russia	51 (+15)	67 (+17)
Ukraine	54 (+21)	66 (+17)
Czech Rep	39 (+8)	53 (+8)
Hungary	41 (+18)	58 (+21)
Av. difference	(+16)	(+16)

CONCLUSION: THE PATTERNS OF NATIONALIST, LIBERAL AND DEMOCRATIC VALUES AMONGST MPS

As with attitudes towards socialist values, we can usefully summarise the differences between MPs and their publics on nationalism, liberal values, and popular control by using the composite indicators constructed in earlier chapters (Chapters 7, 8 and 9). Judged by those standards, MPs were about 14 per cent less nationalist than their publics – about 17 per cent less committed to external nationalism than their respective publics, and 10 per cent less committed to centralist or culturally conformist nationalism. Differences between MPs and their publics on nationalist values were greater in ECE than in the FSU.

MPs were also on average about 27 per cent more committed to liberal values than their respective publics. MPs and their publics diverged most (38 per cent) on tolerance of minorities, and least (10 per cent) on Glasnost or 'freedom of information', but on everything except attitudes to Order, MPs were more liberal than their publics.[7] However on attitudes to Order, MPs were less liberal and more authoritarian than their publics in every country, by an average of 13 per cent – in keeping with their 'governing perspective'.

Table 11.23:   MPs scoring above the mid-point (3.0) on composite measures of nationalist values

	Overall nationalism	External nationalism	Centralist nationalism	Cultural nationalism
	%	%	%	%
Russia	39 (−6)	45 (−8)	22 (−12)	17 (−9)
Ukraine	17 (−5)	15 (−12)	20 (−13)	18 (+4)
Czech Rep	13 (−13)	10 (−15)	8 (−3)	23 (−11)
Hungary	11 (−32)	12 (−34)	15 (−14)	12 (−24)
Av. difference	(−14)	(−17)	(−11)	(−10)

Notes: Composite indicators of External, Centralist and Cultural Nationalism defined as in Chapter 7. Composite indicator Nationalism is the average of all three. Each scale runs from 1 to 5 with 3 as the neutral point – thus over 3, means more pro-nationalist than anti-nationalist. Entries outside parentheses are the percentages of MPs who score (strictly) over 3, i.e. who are pro-nationalist; entries in parentheses show the difference between the percentages of MPs and of the public who are pro-nationalist.

Table 11.24:   MPs scoring above the mid-point (3.0) on composite measures of liberal values

	Overall liberal values	Glasnost	Anti-Order	Tolerance	Protest	Law-based Government
	%	%	%	%	%	%
Russia	98 (+34)	93 (+4)	5 (−15)	37 (+29)	97 (+26)	98 (+30)
Ukraine	86 (+18)	91 (+1)	4 (−14)	25 (+12)	85 (+16)	97 (+28)
Czech Rep	99 (+20)	88 (+18)	31 (−19)	83 (+54)	92 (+8)	98 (+28)
Hungary	97 (+35)	90 (+18)	6 (−7)	77 (+56)	97 (+22)	97 (+27)
Av. difference	(+27)	(+10)	(−13)	(+38)	(+18)	(+28)

Notes: Composite indicators of Glasnost, Order (and Anti-Order), Tolerance, Protest, and Law-base Government are defined as in Chapter 8. The composite indicator Liberal Values is the average of these five. Each scale runs from 1 to 5 with 3 as the neutral point – thus over 3, means more pro-liberal than anti-liberal. Entries outside parentheses are the percentages of MPs who score (strictly) over 3, i.e. who are pro-liberal; entries in parentheses show the difference between the percentages of MPs and of the public who are pro-liberal.

MPs were about 10 per cent more committed than their publics to the general principle of popular control, but that obscured a striking difference between MPs and their publics over their preferred mechanisms for popular control: MPs were 9 per cent *less* committed to the populist principles of direct democracy, yet 33 per cent *more* committed to the electoral principles of representative democracy. It is not difficult to imagine why, but this chasm between the opinions of the public and their MPs – which has close parallels in western democracies – is nonetheless significant.

Table 11.25: MPs scoring above the mid-point (3.0) on composite measures of populist and electoral values

	Popular control	*Populist values*	*Electoral values*
	%	%	%
Russia	94 (+22)	72 (+7)	95 (+37)
Ukraine	83 (+13)	57 (−7)	91 (+45)
Czech Rep	98 (+11)	47 (−3)	99 (+13)
Hungary	88 (+4)	56 (−23)	94 (+35)
Av. difference	(+10)	(−7)	(+33)

Notes: Composite indicators Populist and Electoral Values defined as in Chapter 9. Composite indicator Popular Control is the average of these. Each scale runs from 1 to 5 with 3 as the neutral point – thus over 3, means more pro- than anti-popular control. Entries outside parentheses are the percentages of MPs who score (strictly) over 3, i.e. who are pro-popular control; entries in parentheses show the difference between the percentages of MPs and of the public who are pro-popular control.

12 A Red–Brown Alliance of Ideas?

In previous chapters we simplified our discussion of political values in post-communist societies by grouping answers to many specific questions under four broad headings: socialism, nationalism, liberal values, and popular control. Within these broad categories we grouped questions under 15 sub-headings ranging, for example, from 'state control of industry' to 'tolerance' and 'populism'. That hierarchy of headings and subheadings was intended to reflect both the perspectives of political theory and the debates in contemporary politics within postcommunist Europe.

In this chapter we submit that proposed hierarchy of values to more intensive analysis. We want to see how well that structure describes the patterns in public opinion. How far did people have consistent or coherent attitudes towards the various issues that we have labelled 'socialist', or 'nationalist', for example? Did members of parliament have more coherent attitudes than ordinary members of the public? How were the values of socialism, nationalism and liberal democracy interrelated? Was there, in particular, a 'red–brown' alliance of ideas? By that we mean: did socialist and nationalist ideas appeal to the same people? And did those with socialist and/or nationalist values reject the values of liberal democracy?

POLITICAL SOPHISTICATION: A PROBLEM OF INTERPRETATION

Usually, in surveys of opinion in western democracies, we find that answers to specific questions correlate more strongly amongst political elites than amongst the general public; and more strongly amongst the better educated and more politically involved sections of the general public than amongst the less educated or less politically involved. And usually that is interpreted as evidence that these elite or well educated groups have a clearer understanding of principle, that they are more politically alert, and more able to link specific issues to more general principles.[1] In addition, these groups tend to have simpler and more coherent ideologies connecting their principles together.

But we should beware of the assumption that greater political sophistication must necessarily, and in all circumstances, reveal itself in the form of stronger correlations between answers to specific questions, or between one broad principle and another. There are circumstances in which greater political sophistication may allow people to see the subtle differences between two apparently similar questions and therefore *lower rather than raise*, the correlation between answers to them.

Let us take one example from our FSU/ECE surveys. One battery of questions asked: 'For each of the following, please tell me whether you think it should be run mainly by the state or by private businesses: farming? car factories? computer manufacturers? newspapers? television programmes?' Now, it seems reasonable to us that those who were more inclined towards state control of car factories should logically be more inclined towards state control of computer manufacturers. Overall support might be different, since the two industries were not identical, but people with relatively socialist values should be more inclined than others to support state control in both industries. Across the five countries in our surveys, the correlation between support for state control of the car and computer industries was a high 0.59 amongst the public and an even higher 0.70 amongst MPs. Excluding those who refused to take sides between state and private enterprise, the correlations were even higher: 0.65 amongst the public and 0.73 amongst MPs. The conventional interpretation of the difference between these correlations seems acceptable enough: MPs were simply more consistent in their support for, or opposition to, state control when asked similar questions about different industries.

But we find a different pattern, and we are forced to a different conclusion, when we look at the correlation between attitudes towards state control of car factories and of television programmes. There the correlation was only 0.23 amongst the public and an even *lower* 0.15 amongst MPs. Excluding those who refused to take sides between the state and private business, the correlations were 0.35 amongst the public and a *lower* 0.23 amongst MPs. How are we to interpret that finding? Are we to say now that MPs were less politically sophisticated than the public, less able to see the general socialist principle underlying state control of these two industries? Or are we to hold on to the assumption that MPs are more politically sophisticated than the public – now with the analytical status of an assumption rather than an empirical finding – and conclude that they were better able to see that the production of television programmes was not just another industry in the same mould as car or computer manufacturing? That seems the more plausible interpretation.

So although we shall be interested to compare the coherence of opinions amongst the public with the coherence of opinions amongst MPs we shall not interpret that level of coherence as an automatic index of their levels of political sophistication. Instead we shall invert the usual logic of interpretation. We shall *assume* that MPs were more politically sophisticated, and then ask what effect that greater sophistication had upon their patterns of opinions and values.

THE COHERENCE OF ATTITUDES TOWARDS SOCIALIST, NATIONALIST AND LIBERAL VALUES

In Chapter 6 we developed four indicators of support for equality and state intervention in industry, welfare and culture. Three of these four correlated with each other fairly strongly while the fourth, attitudes to state intervention in the cultural sphere did not. Factor analyses confirm that state intervention in the cultural sphere is something very different from socialism as defined by the other three measures.

Across all countries, taken together, the correlation between attitudes towards state intervention in industry and in welfare was 0.48 amongst the public and 0.66 amongst MPs, while the correlations between attitudes towards equality and state intervention in either industry or welfare averaged 0.33 amongst the public and 0.43 amongst MPs. The three therefore intercorrelated rather well, and the higher correlations amongst MPs than amongst the public matched our assumption that MPs would display greater political sophistication and recognise, more easily, the interconnections between different but closely related principles.

However, the correlation between attitudes towards equality and state intervention in culture was a negligible 0.05 amongst the public and only 0.14 amongst MPs. Even more striking: the correlations between state intervention in culture and in either industry or welfare averaged 0.12 amongst the public, but a *negative* −0.15 amongst MPs: amongst MPs, it was those who were most opposed to state intervention in industry and welfare that gave most support to state intervention in the cultural sphere. MPs who opposed subsidies to car workers often approved of subsidies to opera and ballet companies, or to themselves in the guise of political parties. This further supports our decision to exclude attitudes to state intervention in the cultural sphere from our overall summary measure of socialist values. That summary measure correlated at between 0.74 and 0.87 with attitudes towards equality and state intervention in industry or welfare amongst MPs, and at between 0.72 and 0.80 amongst the public.

Table 12.1:   Correlations between potential indicators of socialism – amongst MPs and the public

	State welfare	*Equality*	*State culture*
	r×100	r×100	r×100
State industry	66 (+18)	40 (+8)	−19 (−33)
State welfare		46 (+12)	−11 (−21)
Equality			14 (+9)

Note: Figures outside brackets are the (Pearson) correlations (times 100 to remove decimal points) amongst MPs. Figures inside brackets are the difference between the correlations amongst MPs and the public. For brevity, in these analyses, we have merged our samples of MPs from all four countries, and our samples of publics from all five countries.

In Chapter 7 we developed three indicators of support for external, centralist and cultural nationalism. These three did not hang together nearly as well as our indicators of socialist values. Nonetheless support for the three varieties of nationalism correlated positively with each other both amongst the public and, to a greater extent, amongst MPs. The strongest correlation was between external and cultural nationalism which was 0.14 amongst the public and 0.26 amongst MPs. The other correlations averaged only 0.06 amongst the public and 0.14 amongst MPs however. So although MPs' attitudes to the different varieties of nationalism were more coherent than their publics', it was clear that they represented different varieties of nationalism that need not necessarily go together: a cultural nationalist need not have aggressive feelings towards the territories or peoples outside the state borders; and support for the territorial integrity of the state within its existing borders need not imply aggressive intent to enlarge it, nor even an insistence upon cultural conformity within it. Nonetheless, the top score on our overall summary measure of attitudes towards nationalist values would go to those who were, coincidentally, aggressive towards their neighbours and both territorially centralist and culturally conformist within their state, even if such coincidences were relatively infrequent.

Table 12.2: Correlations between potential indicators of nationalism – amongst MPs and the public

	Centralist nationalism	Cultural nationalism
	r×100	r×100
External nationalism	13 (+7)	26 (+12)
Centralist nationalism		14 (+8)

Note: Figures outside brackets are the (Pearson) correlations (times 100 to remove decimal points) amongst MPs. Figures inside brackets are the difference between the correlations amongst MPs and the public. For brevity, in these analyses, we have merged our samples of MPs from all four countries, and our samples of publics from all five countries.

We developed five indicators of liberal values in Chapter 8: glasnost, law-based government, protest, tolerance and order (or its negative inverse, 'anti-order'). Except for tolerance and respect for order which correlated (negatively, as we should expect) at −0.24 amongst the public, and −0.36 amongst MPs, these indicators correlated only modestly well with each other, much less well than attitudes towards different aspects of socialist values for example.[2] However, they did address clearly different values which, when taken together, constitute liberal ideology. An ideology that spans freedom of information, rights of association and protest, tolerance, suspicion of authority, and insistence upon limited government may simply be more inherently complex than the strict and narrow definition of socialist values we have used in this book. A negative ideology may be inherently more complex than a positive one. Or longer experience of communist than postcommunist rule may have made socialist ideology more explicit than liberal ideology. Whatever the reason, correlations between different aspects of liberal values averaged only 0.13 amongst the public and scarcely any more, 0.14, amongst MPs. However factor analysis provided no good grounds for subdividing this set of indicators (the eigenvalues of the second factors were only 1.06 amongst the public and 1.05 amongst MPs[3]) and so we averaged the five to provide a single overall measure of commitment to liberal values. That summary measure correlated with different aspects of liberal values at between 0.45 and 0.77 amongst MPs, and between 0.44 and 0.67 amongst the public.

Table 12.3:   Correlations between potential indicators of liberal values – amongst MPs and the public

	Law-based government	Protest	Tolerance	Anti-Order
	r×100	r×100	r×100	r×100
Glasnost	16 (+3)	8 (−8)	19 (+13)	5 (+2)
Law-based government		3 (−16)	18 (+2)	5 (0)
Protest			18 (−1)	10 (−1)
Tolerance				36 (+12)

Note: Figures outside brackets are the (Pearson) correlations (times 100 to remove decimal points) amongst MPs. Figures inside brackets are the difference between the correlations amongst MPs and the public. For brevity, in these analyses, we have merged our samples of MPs from all four countries, and our samples of publics from all five countries.

Larger correlations do not always mean greater sophistication, however. We have already argued that a greater ability to draw fine and meaningful distinctions may serve only to reduce correlations, to free thoughtful minds from the shackles of irrational 'belief constraint'. Interestingly, the correlations between attitudes to different aspects of liberal values were generally *greater amongst MPs* than amongst the public, yet they were significantly *lower amongst MPs* than amongst the public when they involved attitudes to protest. We have already shown that MPs' attitudes to protest were particularly complex, much more so than the public's, much more dependent upon the particular type of protest method involved (see Chapter 11). Since MPs attitudes to protest were so complex, and so far removed from the simple gut feelings that might produce 'belief constraint',[4] it is not entirely surprising to find that this was one aspect of liberal values which correlated less well amongst MPs than amongst the public with other aspects of liberal values.

A RED–BROWN ALLIANCE: THE ALLEGATION

In Russia especially, but also in other postcommunist countries such as Slovakia, socialists and communists have been accused of courting nationalism and rejecting liberal-democratic values. A 'red–brown alliance' is alleged to have emerged between socialists and nationalists to fight liberal democratic reformers. Ironically, socialism and nationalism had long been seen as intrinsically incompatible collectivist ideologies. As Norman Stone notes in his account of the origins of the First World War: 'Marxist contemporaries argued that, in Europe's march to war, a prime motive, in all countries, had been to defeat socialism by nationalism: in other words, national unity, and not class-war, was to be stressed ... German historians [called this] *Primat der Innenpolitik* – the primacy of internal politics.'[5] Just because they were both collectivist ideologies, socialism and nationalism had important values in common, but nonetheless they had others that were inevitably in conflict: the 1986 Programme of the CPSU stated that Soviet citizens must be patriotic, ready to defend the motherland, and proud of achieving the first socialist society, but at the same time they must show 'intolerance of any manifestations of nationalism, chauvinism, national narrow-mindedness or egoism.'[6]

The allegation of a red–brown alliance might imply that although the ideas of socialism and nationalism were inherently opposed to each other and could not be held by the same people at the same time, either (i) opportunist politicians had switched from a communist rhetoric to a nationalist rhetoric in order to hang on to their power and privileges – perhaps without ever really believing in either communist or nationalist ideas, or (ii) communists and nationalists – like Bosnian Muslims and Croats – had formed a limited tactical alliance against their mutual foes without accepting each other's values or ultimate ambitions.

The first of these variants is almost meaningless. Throughout the FSU the great majority of politicians and power holders were former members of the Communist Party. We found in Chapter 10 that three-quarters of all MPs in our two FSU parliaments claimed former membership of the Communist Party, along with half the MPs in the Hungarian parliament. So of course some nationalist politicians may have had a communist past; but then so did many of those who were now liberal and anti-nationalist politicians. Yeltsin and Chernomyrdin had both held more senior positions in the communist regime – and indeed within the CPSU – than Zyuganov, while Zhirinovsky had not even been a member of the CPSU at all. Whether true or false, it would be equally misleading to accuse nationalist politicians in Russia of having a communist past.

The second variant is worth more attention. In Chapter 9 we used factor analysis to investigate whether people who sympathised with communist parties (or their successors) also sympathised with nationalist parties and not with liberal parties; and in a later chapter (Chapter 16) we shall investigate the extent to which the voters and MPs of communist and nationalist parties shared each other's values. But in this chapter we ask an even more basic question: ignoring party labels, and even ideological slogans, was there a red–brown alliance *at the level of ideas*? By that we mean: did people – of whatever party or of none – who had *socialist values* also tend to have *nationalist values* and reject *liberal-democratic values*? That is quite different from the question of whether those who voted for the Russian Communist Party had nationalist values – since they might not even have had socialist values; or whether those who voted for the Russian Liberal Democratic Party had socialist as well as nationalist values – though they were alleged *not* to have liberal-democratic values, whatever other political values they may have had. Those questions are addressed in Chapter 16. But here we focus on the extent to which those people who, by *our* definitions rather than their party labels, really did have socialist values, also had nationalist or liberal–democratic values. Fundamentally we are asking whether these values were themselves compatible with each other.

To investigate the extent of a red–brown alliance of ideas, we look first for a positive correlation between socialist and nationalist values; and then for a negative correlation between both socialism and nationalism on the one hand, and liberal democratic values on the other.

A POSITIVE ALLIANCE BETWEEN SOCIALISM AND NATIONALISM?

There certainly was a strong correlation between our overall measures of commitment to socialist and nationalist ideas. Taking all our interviews together, the correlation was 0.22 amongst the public and 0.38 amongst MPs. And within each and every country the correlations were substantially higher amongst MPs than the public. They varied from country to country but hardly differed between the FSU and ECE since the correlations were greatest in Russia and least in Ukraine. In Russia, they rose to 0.24 amongst the public and 0.47 amongst MPs, while in Ukraine they fell to only 0.15 amongst the public and 0.22 amongst MPs. Russian MPs with socialist values tended very strongly to have nationalist values also, while in Ukraine this tendency was much weaker. Of course, the issues of nationalism were different in Russia and Ukraine, not least because being a nationalist in Ukraine had anti-Soviet overtones which inevitably damped down the correlation with socialist values.

It is illuminating to correlate commitment to socialist values with our three separate indicators of nationalism. Overall there was a very strong correlation between socialism and *external* nationalism: 0.33 amongst the public and 0.54 amongst MPs. But there was only a modest correlation between socialism and *centralist* nationalism, and a negligible correlation between socialism and *cultural* nationalism – at least in our combined multi-state samples. In some degree therefore, our statistical findings reflect the 1986 CPSU Programme's call for good communists to be patriotic and ready to defend the motherland while also, in their personal relationships, being 'intolerant of nationalism and chauvinism' though our findings perhaps distinguish the different aspects of nationalism even more clearly than the CPSU's Programme did.

Table 12.4: Correlations between socialism and nationalism

	Amongst MPs	Amongst the public
	r ×100	r ×100
Combined samples	+38	+22
Russia	+47	+24
Ukraine	+22	+15
Czech Rep	+31	+22
Slovakia	na	+23
Hungary	+30	+13

Note: Entries are Pearson correlations times 100.

Table 12.5: Correlations between socialism and three different aspects of nationalism

	Amongst MPs			Amongst the public		
	External	Centralist	Cultural	External	Centralist	Cultural
	r ×100	r ×100	r ×100	r ×100	r ×100	r ×100
Combined samples	54	13	.	33	14	.
Russia	56	.	32	32	15	.
Ukraine	57	.	−21	23	19	−11
Czech Rep	59	−22	14	33	.	11
Slovakia	na	na	na	28	.	11
Hungary	29	17	14	19	.	.

Note: Entries are Pearson correlations times 100. Correlations less than 0.10 have been replaced by full-stops for clarity.

This interpretation is strengthened if we break down our index of external nationalism into its two components – anti-Western nationalism and anti-neighbour nationalism.[7] Overall, in our combined sample, socialism correlated with anti-Western nationalism at 0.28 amongst the public and 0.63 amongst MPs; but with anti-neighbour nationalism at only 0.21 amongst the public and even less, 0.19, amongst MPs. So socialist values were linked to external nationalism more than internal nationalism, and to anti-Western nationalism more than anti-neighbour nationalism.

Separate analyses within each country confirmed that there was a strong correlation between socialism and external nationalism within each country, particularly when directed against the West rather than against neighbours. By contrast, there was a very variable relationship between socialist values and cultural nationalism. Amongst the public, this correlation was negligible in Russia and actually negative in Ukraine;[8] amongst MPs it was a large and positive 0.32 in Russia, but a large and negative −0.21 in Ukraine. Socialist-minded MPs in Russia supported cultural conformity while socialist-minded MPs in Ukraine opposed it. Of course, cultural conformity in Russia and opposition to cultural conformity in Ukraine both meant support for the Russian language, the language of 'inter-ethnic communication' as it was called in the old Soviet Union.

Table 12.6:   Correlations between socialism and different components of external nationalism

	Amongst MPs		Amongst the public	
	Anti-Western nationalism	*Anti-neighbour nationalism (irredentism)*	*Anti-Western nationalism*	*Anti-neighbour nationalism (irredentism)*
	r ×100	r ×100	r ×100	r ×100
Combined samples	63	19	28	21
Russia	58	36	35	14
Ukraine	68	.	21	13
Czech Rep	67	24	34	15
Slovakia	na	na	22	20
Hungary	37	10	23	.

Note: Entries are Pearson correlations times 100. Correlations less than 0.10 have been replaced by full stops for clarity.

Similarly, although generally weaker, the relationship between socialist values and centralist nationalism also varied – positive in most countries but negative in the Czech Republic, especially amongst MPs. Czech MPs with socialist values tended to oppose centralism while they supported it in Hungary and were more neutral in the FSU. By the end of 1994 when they were interviewed, the central government in the Czech Republic was headed by the anti-socialist Klaus and in Hungary by the socialist Horn.

And although the relationship between socialist values and the anti-Western component of external nationalism was consistently strong in all countries, the correlation between socialist values and the anti-neighbour component of external nationalism was not only lower but more variable. Amongst MPs, for example, it reached 0.36 in Russia but was negligible (actually 0.04) in Ukraine: socialists in the Russian parliament tended towards irredentism, while socialists in the Ukrainian parliament did not.

In sharp contrast to these variable correlations between socialist values and different aspects of nationalism, correlations between our summary measure of nationalism and each of our three composite indicators of socialism hardly differed one from another. That was because our three indicators of socialist values each reflected one relatively coherent concept of socialism while our indicators of nationalist values spanned very disparate aspects of the much less homogenous and coherent concept of nationalism, and because the nationalisms of neighbouring countries were often opposed to each other – 'similar in form, but opposed in content'.[9]

A NEGATIVE ALLIANCE: SOCIALISM AND NATIONALISM AGAINST LIBERAL VALUES?

Lenin regarded socialism and liberal democracy as incompatible. Conversely 'new right' theorists argue that 'the market constitutes a necessary condition for democracy' or even that 'the market is more democratic than the polity.'[10] Both would expect a negative correlation between ideas of socialism and liberal democracy. But many who are not on the far left or far right in western politics would deny the incompatibility of socialist and liberal democratic ideas. For two centuries since the French revolution, demands for 'liberty and equality' have regularly appeared side by side on the same banner. Our own surveys of political culture in Britain found a positive correlation between commitment to the principles of liberty and equality amongst politicians and the highly educated, and a negative correlation only amongst those with the least education.[11] The correlation between socialist and liberal values is certainly not 'necessarily negative'. On the other hand, decades of Leninist rule by authoritarians who professed to be socialists and at least in matters of state control of industry really were socialists, must have encouraged the peoples of ECE and the FSU to regard socialist and liberal values as alternatives. For decades socialism had been the ideology of government in the FSU/ECE but, more often than not, the ideology of opposition in the West and that must also have affected its relationship to liberal values.

The relationship between nationalism and liberalism is also ambivalent. When a minority nationalism seeks liberation from an oppressive empire, the ideas of nationalism and liberal democracy seem to fit together naturally. But when state nationalists demand cultural conformity within the state or launch aggressive wars against their neighbours, then nationalism and liberal democracy seem completely incompatible.

Did socialists and nationalists in the FSU/ECE oppose liberal values? Taking all our interviews together, there was clearly a moderately strong – and negative – correlation between liberal values on the one hand and either socialism or nationalism on the other. Both amongst the public and amongst MPs, this correlation reached – 0.20 or slightly more.[12] However the interconnections between socialist, nationalist and liberal values varied sharply from country to country.

Table 12.7:   Negative correlations between liberal values and socialist or nationalist values

| | Amongst MPs | | Amongst the public | |
	with socialist values	with nationalist values	with socialist values	with nationalist values
	r ×100	r ×100	r ×100	r ×100
Combined samples	−25	−21	−21	−20
Russia	.	−13	.	.
Ukraine	−12	.	−19	−31
Czech Rep	.	.	−25	−17
Slovakia	na	na	−26	−29
Hungary	−49	−47	−26	−18

Note: Entries are Pearson correlations (times 100) with liberal values. Correlations less than 0.10 have been replaced by full stops for clarity.

Amongst the public in ECE, and in Ukraine also, there was a strong, negative correlation between liberal values and either socialist or nationalist values. But in Russia, unlike all the other countries, commitment to socialist or nationalist values did very little to prevent people supporting liberal values or vice versa. To a greater extent than elsewhere, the red–brown alliance of ideas in Russia was based more upon a positive correlation between socialist and nationalist values than upon a rejection of liberal values.

Amongst MPs there was a very strong, negative correlation between liberal values and either socialist or nationalist values in Hungary, but not elsewhere – only modest negative correlations with socialist values in Ukraine and with nationalist values in Russia. As we showed in Chapter 11, most MPs, unlike their publics, were committed to liberal values, which restricts the tendency for liberal values to correlate well with other values amongst MPs, though the Hungarian example shows that this remains possible. But, in addition, it is worth noting that, amongst MPs, the very small correlations between liberal and socialist values, though not between liberal and nationalist values, were actually positive in Russia and the Czech Republic.

Both socialism and nationalism correlated negatively with most aspects of liberal values. Socialists and nationalists were less likely than others to be committed to glasnost and law-based government, and more likely to emphasise respect for order and authority, though these correlations were fairly weak. The negative correlation between tolerance of minorities and either socialism or nationalism was much higher however. Support for rights of protest provided a interesting exception: it correlated positively with both socialism and nationalism amongst MPs, though negatively amongst their publics.

Table 12.8: Correlations between socialism, nationalism and five different aspects of liberal values

	Glasnost	Law-based government	Protest	Tolerance	Anti-Order
	r×100	r×100	r×100	r×100	r×100
Corr. with socialism amongst:					
MPs	−19	.	10	−37	.
public	.	.	−12	−24	−16
Corr. with nationalism amongst:					
MPs	−14	−14	.	−26	.
public	.	−10	−10	−20	.

Note: Entries are Pearson correlations (times 100) with aspects of liberal values. Correlations less than 0.10 have been replaced by full stops for clarity. This table is based exclusively on combined samples.

Socialists and nationalists in both the Czech and the Russian parliaments were particularly inclined to support rights of protest – socialists even more so than nationalists. That explained why liberal values as a whole did not correlate strongly and negatively with socialist or nationalist values in those parliaments. But in the Hungarian parliament, those who were most committed to socialist and nationalist values tended to oppose rights of protest as well as displaying a uniquely strong commitment to order and a uniquely high level of intolerance of minorities. They had a socialist-led government, of course.

SOCIALIST, NATIONALIST AND LIBERAL ATTITUDES TO POPULAR CONTROL

In addition to indicators of socialist, nationalist and liberal values we also constructed three indicators of attitudes towards popular control – populism, support for multi-party elections, and identification with political parties (see Chapter 9).

Amongst the public, our composite indicators of identification with parties and support for multi-party elections correlated fairly strongly at 0.32; but both of these correlated negligibly (though negatively) with populism. Since we did not ask MPs the full range of questions about parties we cannot report the correlation between identification with parties and support for elections amongst MPs; but amongst MPs, there was also a negligible though negative correlation between support for elections and populism (−0.05 compared to −0.07 amongst the public). It made no sense therefore to combine populism and support for multi-party elections into a single measure of support for popular control: to a degree, these were seen as alternative ways of achieving popular control, exclusive and mutually incompatible alternatives. Most political theorists would agree. So we shall look at the correlations between socialist, nationalist and liberal values with each of our indicators of popular control separately.

Popular control and socialist values
Amongst MPs socialist values correlated strongly (at +0.40) with populism but negatively (at -0.14) with support for multi-party elections. Amongst the public the positive correlation between socialist values and populism was weaker (+0.11) but the negative correlation with support for multi-party elections was stronger (-0.27). And, amongst the public, socialist values also correlated negatively with support for parties. So amongst both MPs and the public those with socialist values clearly tended to support the ideals and mechanisms of direct democracy but oppose those of representative democracy.

Table 12.9: Correlations between socialism and three different aspects of popular control

| | Amongst MPs | | Amongst the public | | |
	Populism	Multi-party elections	Populism	Multi-party elections	Identification with parties
	r×100	r×100	r×100	r×100	r×100
Combined samples	40	−14	11	−27	−14
Russia	37	−14	14	−22	.
Ukraine	43	.	.	−13	−11
Czech Rep	65	−38	.	−25	−17
Slovakia	na	na	.	−19	−12
Hungary	13	.	.	−16	−13

Note: Entries are Pearson correlations times 100. Correlations less than 0.10 have been replaced by full stops for clarity. MPs were not asked all the questions necessary to construct our indicator of identification with parties.

Popular control and nationalist values
Nationalists also tended to support the mechanisms of direct democracy but oppose those of representative democracy, though the correlations were weaker with nationalist than with socialist values (Table 12.10).

Popular control and liberal values
By contrast liberal values correlated positively with support for elections and parties. These correlations were weak but at least they were positive, unlike the correlations with socialist and nationalist values. Amongst MPs there was a negligible correlation between populism and liberal values but amongst the public, populism correlated more strongly with liberal values than with socialist or nationalist values. Liberal members of the public, unlike liberal MPs, were

relatively favourable to popular control by both direct and indirect means (Table 12.11).

Table 12.10: Correlations between nationalism and three different aspects of popular control

| | Amongst MPs | | Amongst the public | | |
	Populism	Multi-party elections	Populism	Multi-party elections	Identification with parties
	r×100	r×100	r×100	r×100	r×100
Combined samples	20	−14	.	−11	.
Russia	22	−12	.	−15	.
Ukraine	13	−21	.	.	.
Czech Rep	31	−14	.	−17	−17
Slovakia	na	na	−19	.	.
Hungary	.	−19	.	−17	−11

Note: Entries are Pearson correlations times 100. Correlations less than 0.10 have been replaced by full stops for clarity. MPs were not asked all the questions necessary to construct our indicator of identification with parties.

Table 12.11: Correlations between liberal values and three different aspects of popular control (r×100)

| | Amongst MPs | | Amongst the public | | |
	Populism	Multi-party elections	Populism	Multi-party elections	Identification with parties
	r×100	r×100	r×100	r×100	r×100
Combined samples	.	.	20	.	12
Russia	.	−14	27	.	.
Ukraine	.	.	17	.	.
Czech Rep	.	.	21	12	18
Slovakia	na	na	34	.	10
Hungary	.	10	16	.	11

Note: Entries are Pearson correlations times 100. Correlations less than 0.10 have been replaced by full stops for clarity. MPs were not asked all the questions necessary to construct our indicator of identification with parties.

CONCLUSION

We can get a simple overview of the interrelationship between values, and between different aspects of values, by applying the factor analysis method to our whole set of 15 composite indicators. In fact, for comparability between our analyses of MPs and publics we shall exclude one of these, identification with parties, which was measured more comprehensively amongst the public than amongst MPs.

According to the conventional, but very lax, Kaiser criterion[13] there were five factors underlying the patterns of values amongst both MPs and the public. However, three of these in each case had very low eigenvalues of 1.3 or less – that is they explained only 1.3 or less times as much of the joint variation in the 14 indicators as would be explained by a single indicator that, pathologically, proved to be totally uncorrelated with any of the others. Both amongst MPs and the public these three factors explained respectively, only 9 per cent, 8 per cent and 7 per cent of the joint variance.

Table 12.12:   Factor analyses of 14 indicators of socialism, nationalism, liberalism and popular control

Amongst combined samples of MPs			*Amongst combined samples of publics*		
	F1	F2		F1	F2
Cumulative percent of variance explained:	22	34		18	29
Eigenvalues:	3.1	1.7		2.5	1.6
State welfare	77	.	State industry	72	.
External nationalism	75	.	State welfare	69	.
State industry	73	−33	Equality	63	.
Equality	72	.	External nationalism	56	.
Populism	63	.	Elections	−46	.
Elections	.	.	Order	33	.
Cultural nationalism	.	.	State culture	.	
			Centralist nationalism	.	.
Tolerance	−32	72	Protest	.	62
Order	.	−52	Populism	.	59
Protest	.	48	Law-based government	.	56
Centralist nationalism	.	−46	Glasnost	.	49
Glasnost	.	38	Tolerance	−40	41
Law-based government	.	37	Cultural nationalism	.	−35
State culture	.	32			

Notes:
1. Entries grouped by the factor with which they correlate best, and arranged in order of declining correlations with that factor. All correlations under 0.30 replaced by full-stops for clarity.
2. Factor analysis retaining factors with eigenvalues exceeding 1.5 (a somewhat more conservative criterion than the usual Kaiser criterion) followed by varimax rotation. The next highest eigenvalues were 1.3 amongst MPs and 1.2 amongst the publics.

Amongst both MPs and the public, just two factors had eigenvalues exceeding 1.5, the minimum criterion that we prefer. Together they explained 29 per cent of the variance of values amongst the public, and 34 per cent amongst MPs.[14] In each case, the less powerful of these two factors added 12 per cent to the variance explained; so a single factor could only explain under 18 per cent of the variance amongst the public and just 22 per cent amongst MPs. There is, therefore, some reason to use a two-factor explanation of the pattern of values amongst both MPs and the public.

Accepting a two-factor solution, and applying the usual varimax rotation produced similar findings for MPs and the public: a first factor focused upon socialist values and external nationalism; and a second factor focused upon liberal values. Amongst both MPs and the public, the four indicators with the highest loadings upon the first factor were the three socialist values of equality, state control of industry, and state welfare, plus external nationalism. The five indicators with the highest loadings upon the second factor amongst the public – and five of the six with the highest loadings on the second factor amongst MPs – were indicators of liberal values. Reflecting the different perspectives of MPs and the public towards liberal values, this second factor was centred on tolerance amongst MPs but on rights of citizen protest amongst the public

What does this two-factor solution tell us about the red–brown alliance of ideas? Two conclusions are obvious: a third somewhat less so. First, there *was* indeed a positive red–brown alliance of ideas: commitment to socialist and specifically *external* nationalist values tended to run together. Second, there was a coherent syndrome of liberal values: commitments to citizens' rights of protest, to tolerance for minorities, to glasnost or freedom of information, and to government limited and constrained by law also tended to run together. So there was a red-brown syndrome of values, and there was a coherent syndrome of liberal values. But there is a third, less obvious, conclusion that must be drawn from this two-factor solution. If the liberal and red–brown syndromes of values were clearly incompatible with each other they would not be uncorrelated, they would be correlated so strongly and negatively with each other that a single-factor solution would suffice to describe the pattern of values in post-communist societies. To the extent that there was a need for a two factor solution, the incompatibility (that is the negative correlation) between liberal and red–brown ideas was far from total.

Indeed, if we look back to our earlier tables in this chapter, we see that the positive correlation between socialist values and external nationalism was very strong indeed, but the negative correlations between liberal values and socialist or nationalist values were much more modest. The concept of a 'red–brown alliance of ideas' is therefore justified more by the positive association between socialist values and external nationalism, particularly anti-Western nationalism, than by the alleged theoretical incompatibility between liberal values and either socialism or nationalism.

IV Influences on Values

13 Winners and Losers

Revolutions, even peaceful revolutions, create millions of highly visible and self-conscious winners and losers. In this chapter we shall look at the political values of those individuals, classes, genders, and generations that felt they had lost most in the transition from communism. Did their conscious sense of loss make them more committed to socialism and nationalism, and less committed to liberal and democratic values, than those who felt they could cope with the economic changes, or could even profit from them?

INDIVIDUAL WINNERS AND LOSERS

We asked five questions relevant to this sense of economic loss or, much less frequently, gain. We discussed them at length in Chapter 5. They were:

(A) 'Has your family's standard of living got better or worse over the last two years?'
(B) 'Do you feel your family's standard of living will get better or worse over the next two years?'
(C) 'Has (country's) economy got better or worse over the last two years?'
(D) 'Do you feel (country's) economy will get better or worse over the next two years?'
(E) 'How adequate is your family's income?'

Answers to all these questions were recorded on five point scales, where the mid-point represented 'don't know' or 'the same'. In addition to the question (E) about the level of economic circumstances, different questions focused on past or future tends, on trends in family circumstances, and trends in the country's economy. By averaging answers from pairs of these questions we can construct indicators of feelings about trends in the past, the future, or family circumstances, and the progress of the country, as follows:

– past trends = average A and C
– future trends = average B and D
– family trends = average A and B
– country trends = average C and D.

Finally we can construct an overall indicator of general feelings about economic progress or decline by calculating the average of all four of A,B,C and D.

We correlated our measures of socialist, nationalist, liberal and democratic values, and the 15 more specific indicators on which they were based, with all these questions – and combinations of questions – about economic circum-stances and trends. Within our combined sample of publics, and within each of the five separate publics, political values always correlated best with answers to question E, or with one of the indicators formed by averaging two or more of A, B, C and D. So we can ignore the correlations with the individual questions A, B, C and D.

Table 13.1:   Correlations between economic loss and socialist, nationalist or liberal values

	Family income not enough to live on	Feel that things have got/will get worse				
		For family	For country	In past	In future	Generally
	r×100	r×100	r×100	r×100	r×100	r×100
Socialist values	31	32	29	34	25	34
Nationalist values	·	·	·	·	·	·
Liberal values	·	·	·	·	·	·

Note: Entries are Pearson correlations. For clarity, correlations less than 0.10 have been replaced by full-stops.

Within our combined sample of the five publics, feelings about economic change correlated strongly with socialist values, but *not* with nationalist or liberal values.[1] And socialist values correlated best of all with the overall average indicator of general feelings about economic trends in the past and the future, as they affected both the family and the country at large. Those who generally felt they were losers because of economic change were much more likely to support socialist values (r = 0.34) though only slightly more likely to support nationalist values (r = 0.09), and they hardly differed from others in their commitment to liberal values (r = 0.02).

Socialist values correlated more strongly with perceptions of *past* economic trends (r = 0.34) than with expectations about the *future* (r = 0.25); and slightly more with feelings about trends in *family* circumstances (r = 0.32) than with feelings about the *country*'s economy (r = 0.29). Socialist values also correlated with the *level* of the family's economic circumstances to much the same degree as with perceptions of economic *trends*.[2]

Breaking socialist, nationalist and liberal values down, by using the 12 more specific indicators in which they were based provides further insights. Feelings of economic loss correlated strongly with all three indicators of socialist values, but with commitment to equality (r = 0.32) more than support for state inter-vention in industry (r = 0.22) or welfare (r = 0.25) – and not at all with support for state intervention in culture (r = 0.01).

Feelings of loss correlated very weakly, if at all, with all aspects of liberal values. But although feelings about economic trends did not correlate well with nationalist values (r = 0.09) as a whole, they did correlate well with external nationalism (r = 0.22), though hardly at all with other aspects of nationalism (r = 0.05 with centralist nationalism, and negatively at r = −0.08 with cultural nationalism). Those who felt they were losing out through economic change tended to support external nationalism. With external nationalism, as with socialist values, the past (r = 0.21) was slightly more important than the future (r = 0.18); though for external nationalism, *unlike* socialism, the country (r = 0.22) was slightly more important than the family (r = 0.19).

Table 13.2: Correlations between economic loss and specific indicators of socialist, nationalist or liberal values

	Family income not enough to live on	Feel that things have got/will get worse				
		For family	For country	In past	In future	Generally
	r×100	r×100	r×100	r×100	r×100	r×100
State industry	24	19	19	23	14	22
State welfare	24	23	22	26	17	25
Equality	23	31	26	29	26	32
State culture	.	.	.	.	.	.
External nationalism	19	19	22	21	18	22
Centralist nationalism	.	.	.	.	.	.
Cultural nationalism	.	.	.	.	.	.
Tolerance	−11	.	.	−10	.	.
Glasnost	12	.	12	14	.	11
Protest	.	.	.	.	.	.
Law-based govt	.	.	.	.	.	.
Anti-Order	−12	.	.	−12	.	.

Note: Entries are Pearson correlations. For clarity, correlations less than 0.10 have been replaced by full-stops.

Feelings of loss correlated strongly, though in opposite directions, with the two alternative strategies of popular control: positively with support for populism (r = 0.22) and negatively with support for multi-party elections (r = −0.35). Those who felt the greatest sense of loss were the *most* inclined towards populist principles but the *least* favourable to representative democracy based upon competitive elections.[3]

Table 13.3: Correlations between economic loss and alternative principles of popular control

	Family income not enough to live on	Feel that things have got/will get worse				
		For family	For country	In past	In future	Generally
	r×100	r×100	r×100	r×100	r×100	r×100
Populism	·	17	22	20	18	22
Elections	−31	−30	−33	−32	−29	−35
Parties	−19	−15	−18	−17	−15	−19

Note: Entries are Pearson correlations. For clarity, correlations less than 0.10 have been replaced by full-stops.

All these patterns were broadly similar within each of the five countries though feelings about economic trends – as they affected both family and country – correlated most strongly with political values in the Czech Republic and least strongly with political values in Ukraine. As we saw in Chapter 5, almost everyone felt a loser – to a greater or lesser extent – in Ukraine; while the Czechs were the most evenly divided between those who felt themselves winners and losers.

Table 13.4: Correlations between economic loss and selected political values within countries

	Correlation between general feeling of loss and:				
	Socialist values	Equality	External nationalism	Populism	Support for elections
	r×100	r×100	r×100	r×100	r×100
Russia	34	37	33	19	−24
Ukraine	·	11	·	11	−20
Czech Rep	45	41	33	33	−36
Slovakia	22	31	13	17	−25
Hungary	18	21	19	14	−27

Note: Entries are Pearson correlations. For clarity, correlations less than 0.10 have been replaced by full-stops.

Correlation coefficients are a useful way of analysing the connection between our scales of values and such quantitative scales as attitudes to economic trends, but they are not so useful when we want to relate our scales of values to more categorical variables such as marital status, or occupational sector. They also perform badly as measures of curvilinear relationships and they are less

Table 13.5: Economic winners and losers

	SOCIALIST VALUES	NATIONALIST VALUES			LIBERAL VALUES	POPULAR CONTROL (DEMOCRATIC) VALUES		
	Socialist values	External nationalism	Centralist nationalism	Cultural nationalism	Overall liberal values	Populist values	Pro-election values	Pro-party values
	%	%	%	%	%	%	%	%
Losers	83	49	35	25	71	74	48	23
Intermediate	80	43	28	29	65	66	60	22
Winners	53	25	23	29	69	51	83	34
Diff: Losers—winners	+30	+24	+12	-4	+2	+23	-35	-11

Notes: Economic losers and winners are defined in terms of their scores on the composite index of general feelings about economic trends, the average of answers to economic trend questions A, B, C and D which are set out at the start of the chapter (trends in past and present, personal and country economic circumstances). The index ranges from 1='much worse', through 2='worse', 3='same' and 4='better' to 5='much better'.

Those who score less than 2 are designated 'losers'; those who score over 3 as 'winners'; and the rest as 'intermediate'. Our low threshold for designating people as 'winners' reflects the general decline in postcommunist economies.

intuitively easy to interpret than simple percentages and percentage differences. So we shall present our analysis mainly in terms of the percentage of people in each country or social group who score above the mid-point (3.0) on each composite measure of political values – the technique we have already used in chapters 6 to 11. By that measure, economic losers were 30 per cent more socialist than economic winners, 24 per cent more externally nationalist – but only 12 per cent more centralist and actually 4 per cent less culturally conformist, hardly any different from economic winners on liberal values, but at once 23 per cent more populist and 35 per cent less committed to multi-party electoral values than economic winners.

THE LOSING CLASSES

We had access to several different indicators of social class but one of the simplest and most illuminating was one with a long history in the FSU – the division between workers (the proletariat), farmers (or peasants), and intellectuals. We added two further categories: managers (the more senior of whom tended to be called 'red directors' in the FSU since they were managers of socialist enterprises), and private 'business persons' (or 'businessmen' in the sexist and inaccurate languages of the FSU). The vast majority of our respondents were willing to place themselves in one or other of these five categories.[4]

When asked whether they saw themselves as 'part of the work-force' or 'part of the management' over 91 per cent of the workers and managers unequivocally opted for the 'work-force' and the 'management' respectively. Less obviously the farmers divided 85 per cent for the work-force and only 9 per cent for the management; and intellectuals 74 per cent for the work-force and 21 per cent for the management. Only business persons had much difficulty with this concept: 51 per cent opted for the management, 32 per cent for the work-force, and 17 per cent for 'neither or both'. Perceptions of class conflict remained high despite seventy years in a classless society: between 60 per cent and 70 per cent in each class said that workers and managers 'would always have conflicting interests.'

Lack of belief in communist ideals distinguished business persons from all the others. Whether the question was asked about past or present belief, the percentages who said they believed in communist ideals did not vary much between workers, farmers, intellectuals and managers but was always at least twice as high as amongst business persons. Business persons were also the least willing to defend the old regime. Only about 8 per cent in each of the other classes, but 21 per cent of business persons said the communist regime had no redeeming features.

However business persons were not so unique when asked about the *faults* of the old regime: then the divide was more between workers and farmers on the one hand versus intellectuals, managers and business persons on the other. For example, 11 per cent of workers and 20 per cent of farmers said the old regime had no faults but only between 4 and 5 per cent of intellectuals, managers and business persons agreed. Conversely, only 21 per cent of farmers and 26 per cent of workers cited the oppression of human rights as its worst feature, but between 31 and 33 per cent of intellectuals, managers and business persons did so. And while only 9 per cent of workers and farmers cited economic stagnation, between 15 and 18 per cent of intellectuals, managers and business persons did so. Similarly, managers as well as business persons were particularly inclined to allege that they had been personally oppressed under the communist regime.

Table 13.6:   Class and communist oppression

	Felt personally oppressed by the communist regime
	%
Self-described:	
workers	16
farmers	17
intellectuals	20
managers	28
business-persons	27
Diff: workers–business persons	−11

Note: 'Don't Knows', 'Can't decide' etc. excluded from calculation of percentages.

Consistent with these perceptions of the old regime, business persons took the most favourable view of the new regime – uniquely so on the question of whether the economy was run better under the new regime, but not so uniquely on whether human rights were respected more under the new regime, where they were joined by intellectuals and managers. Farmers were nearly always the most critical of the new regime.

These different class perspectives were also reflected in answers to our questions about the 'best time for (country)' this century. In Russia, intellectuals and business persons were specially attracted to the Tsar's time; and there was a very sharp spectrum of disapproval for the present and nostalgia for Brezhnev's time that ran from farmers and workers to intellectuals, managers and business persons. Compared to farmers, business persons gave 30 per cent more approval to the present, and 41 per cent less to Brezhnev's time. In Ukraine by contrast, all classes opted overwhelmingly for the Brezhnev period, managers and business persons even more so than others, though intellectuals displayed an above average preference both for the Tsar's time and the present. In Hungary also, intellectuals were specially attracted to the days of empire – in their case under the Hapsburgs. But the main pattern in Hungary was a very simple dichotomy between farmers and workers who favoured the Kadar period, versus intellectuals, managers and business persons who favoured the post-Kadar reform-communists or the present. Even intellectuals displayed very little affection for the Hapsburg days in either Slovakia or the Czech Republic, however. Czech intellectuals hardly differed from the average Czech. But Slovak intellectuals were uniquely attached to the period 1989–92 when Czechoslovakia had been united, free and democratic. Business persons were specially attracted to the present in both countries, and to the Masaryk period in the Czech Republic. Farmers were uniquely attracted to the Husak period in both countries.

Table 13.7:   Class perspectives on their country's best time this century(%)

		Worker	Farmer	Intellectual	Manager	Business
Russia						
	Tsars	14	10	25	19	29
	Brezhnev	63	71	46	47	30
	Now	8	4	15	21	35
Ukraine						
	Brezhnev	78	82	68	87	93
Hungary						
	Monarchy	9	11	23	0	15
	Kadar	61	63	18	19	26
	Reform communist	14	9	23	50	31
	Now	10	6	25	18	19
Czech Rep						
	Masaryk	30	24	34	30	45
	Husak	8	20	4	5	3
	United democratic Czechoslovakia	22	13	17	17	11
	Now	20	21	24	23	32
Slovakia						
	Masaryk	3	9	3	0	0
	Husak	21	28	10	22	9
	United democratic Czechoslovakia	25	15	41	15	27
	Now	18	16	16	17	35

Note: 'Don't Knows', 'Can't decide' etc. excluded from calculation of percentages.

At one stage, the Russian deputy prime minister in charge of science and education, Boris Saltykov, complained that badly engineered economic reforms were not only producing rapidly rising income differentials, but ruining the 'middle class' of 'creative and scientific workers.'[5] But our data suggests other classes had fared even worse. By each of our five measures of economic trends – family, country, past, future, and combined – business persons had done best and farmers had done worst. Workers had done almost as badly as farmers, and intellectuals not much better, though managers' economic experiences were exactly intermediate between those of business persons and farmers. It should be noted that, in postcommunist countries, especially in the FSU, managers would mainly be former communist managers, managing enterprises that were still state enterprises, or were at most successors to state enterprises – 'socialist managers' rather than Harvard Business School alumni.

In terms of economic *trends* since the fall of the communist system – as distinct from their *level* of living standards – class differences were widest on perceptions of trends in family circumstances and much less on perceptions about the progress of the country's economy, on which there was more consensus. They were also slightly wider on perceptions of the past than on expectations for the future.

Table 13.8: Class and economic loss

	Family income only just enough to live on	Feel that things have got/will get worse:				
		For family	For country	In past	In future	Generally
	%	%	%	%	%	%
All respondents	75	69	71	81	47	76
Self-described:						
workers	79	72	72	82	47	78
farmers	85	77	80	86	52	84
intellectuals	69	67	71	81	47	76
managers	47	61	61	71	47	66
business-persons	47	36	51	57	30	48
Diff: workers–busines-persons	+32	+36	+21	+25	+17	+30

Notes: Entries are the percentage who score strictly above the mid-point on each scale, that is who said their family had got 'only just enough to survive on' (col. 1) or that things had got/would get 'worse' rather than 'better' (cols. 2–6). Those whose score averaged out exactly at the mid-point – corresponding to 'undecided', or 'no change' – were counted with the optimists. So our figures underestimate the sense of loss, if anything!

If we focus on that aspect of economic change on which class differences were widest – trends in family circumstances, class differences (between business persons and workers for example) were largest in the FSU, less in the former Czechoslovakia, and least in Hungary where even the businessmen were unhappy about postcommunist trends.

Of course the transition from communism involved non-economic gains and losses, as well as economic gains and losses, but simply on grounds of their reactions to economic decline under the postcommunist regime we might expect business persons to support the ideals and values of the new regime far more than workers or farmers. Indeed, if support for democratic values closely reflected economic experiences under the new regime, the spectrum of support should run from business persons through managers, intellectuals, and workers and finally to farmers – especially in the FSU.

Table 13.9:   Class and recent personal economic loss within countries

	Worker	*Farmer*	*Intellectual*	*Manager*	*Business*	*Difference: Worker – Business*
	%	%	%	%	%	%
Russia	71	78	65	70	27	44
Ukraine	90	89	89	86	44	46
Czech Rep	53	60	43	47	17	36
Slovakia	73	63	68	64	42	31
Hungary	74	70	63	59	70	4

Notes: Entries are the percentage who score strictly above the mid-point on the scale, that is who said that things had got/would get 'worse' rather than 'better' (cols. 2–6). Those whose score averaged out exactly at the mid-point – corresponding to 'undecided', or 'no change' – were counted with the optimists. So our figures underestimate the sense of loss, if anything!

Table 13.10:   Class and values

| | *Per cent whose values:* | | | | | |
	Socialist	*Nationalist*	*Liberal*	*Populist*	*Pro-elections*	*Pro-parties*
	%	%	%	%	%	%
All respondents	74	37	68	64	63	25
Self-described:						
workers	79	40	64	65	60	23
farmers	87	43	58	63	56	21
intellectuals	66	30	77	62	71	30
managers	60	29	81	63	80	42
business-persons	40	26	79	64	70	32
Diff: workers–business persons	+39	+14	–15	+1	–10	–9

Note: Entries are the percentage who score strictly above the mid-point on each value scale.

It was certainly true that support for socialist values followed the same class spectrum as economic loss: the classes that had lost most were the ones most committed to socialist values; and class differences on socialist values were large: workers differed from business persons by 39 per cent, and farmers by 47 per cent. Support for nationalist values also followed the class spectrum of economic loss exactly, but class differences were smaller: workers differed from business persons by only 14 per cent, and farmers by 17 per cent. Class differences were rather larger on external nationalism, somewhat less on centralist nationalism, and very small indeed on cultural nationalism.

Class differences on liberal values were also modest: workers differed from business persons by only 15 per cent. Class differences were even less on support for multi-party elections or identification with political parties, and non-existent on populism. So the classes that had lost or gained most from economic trends under the postcommunist regime differed very sharply on socialist values, only modestly on nationalist or liberal values, and even less on the specifically democratic values of popular control.

The reactions of the intellectual class were particularly interesting. Their sense of economic loss was not much less than that of workers, and they were much closer to workers than to business persons on socialist values, yet much closer to business persons than to workers on nationalist and liberal values, support for multi-party elections and identification with parties.

If we focus on the difference between support for socialist values amongst workers and business persons then, by that criterion, class differences were greater in the FSU (49 per cent in Russia, 45 per cent in Ukraine) than in ECE (26 per cent in the Czech Republic, 35 per cent in Slovakia, and 29 per cent in Hungary). That mirrored the pattern of class differences in terms of economic loss with only one partial exception: Hungarian business persons were very critical of economic trends under the postcommunist regime yet not very committed to socialist values – though more committed to socialist values than business persons in any other country.

LOST GENERATIONS

We divided respondents into three generations: those aged under 35, those aged 35 to 54, and those aged 55 or over. It is a crude categorisation but it leaves large and therefore reliable samples in each of the age categories. Such categories can be conceptualised in two very different ways: we can regard the young and old as people at different stages in their own life cycle; or we can regard them as political generations who have suffered different formative experiences whose imprints remain visible in their values and opinions, and may continue to do so throughout their lives.

People generally get more authoritarian as they get older. That is true in long-established democracies and we should expect to find that pattern – perhaps overlaid by others – in postcommunist countries as well. More instrumentally, the young and old have different interests and different planning horizons. The old have a greater interest in accessible health care and income support. And the promise of future economic gain, after a period of economic pain, makes more rational sense to the young than to the old. These are life-cycle influences upon opinions and values.

But in the peculiar circumstances of a change of regime we should expect to find some evidence of generational influences as well.[6] On the one hand the old had more direct experience of the worst communist oppression which might make them less favourable to the old regime. But the old were exposed to high levels of communist propaganda and they could take some pride in the defeat of fascist Germany. That might reasonably make them more socialist and more nationalist. Most of all, the older generations had contributed to the construction of a socialist society. Whether that was voluntary or involuntary does not matter. They had invested their lives in a system that gave them low living standards in return for the promise of relatively high levels of social security. The collapse of the communist system meant that they had endured all the privations of communism without any hope of retaining its meagre benefits. The collapse of communism wiped out their personal investments as surely as the Wall Street crash wiped out those of capitalist shareholders. So there was more reason than usual for generational as well as a life-cycle resentment of the young by the old.

When asked explicitly, the old declared more support for communist ideals than the young: 23 per cent versus 14 per cent for current belief, and 53 per cent versus 37 per cent for past belief. But the old complained more than the young about their own personal experience of oppression under the communist regime and their assessments of the strengths and weaknesses of the old and new regimes did not differ greatly.

Table 13.11:   Generations and communist oppression

	Felt personally oppressed by the communist regime
	%
Aged:	
18–34	15
35–54	19
55 and over	21
Difference: old–young	+6

Note: 'Don't Knows', 'Can't decide' etc. excluded from calculation of percentages.

There was a clear generational (as opposed to life-cycle) flavour to the perspectives of different age groups on answers to our questions about the

Table 13.12: Generational perspectives on the best time this century for our country

	Young 18–34	Middle 35–54	Old 55 and over
	%	%	%
Russia			
Tsars	24	18	8
Stalin	5	6	18
Brezhnev	51	62	65
Now	13	10	7
Ukraine			
Brezhnev	77	79	75
Now	6	8	10
Hungary			
Horthy	4	3	15
Reform communist	14	21	13
Now	19	12	11
Slovakia			
'Independence' 1939–45	8	6	17
United democratic Czechoslovakia	36	29	13
Now	21	18	17
Czech Rep			
Dubcek's Prague Spring	4	24	20
United democratic Czechoslovakia	21	20	17
Now	28	22	14

Note: 'Don't Knows', 'Can't decide' etc. excluded from calculation of percentages.

best time for their country this century. In Russia the young were specially attracted to romantic visions of the Tsar's time and, less so, to the present; while the old were unusually favourable to the Brezhnev era and – more surprisingly – to Stalin's time as well. In Ukraine too, the young were more attracted than the old to the days of the Tsar despite the fact that the Tsar had been Russian, not Ukrainian. However all age groups in Ukraine opted overwhelmingly for the Brezhnev period and there was no tendency at all for the young to be specially favourable to the present. In Hungary an unusually high 15 per cent of the old opted for Horthy's authoritarian inter-war regime, the middle-aged were specially attracted to the reform communist period, and the young to the present; and the young were also slightly more favourable than the old to the Hapsburgs. In Slovakia the old displayed unusual affection for the puppet state set up by the Nazis between 1939 and 1945 – paralleling the attraction of the Horthy regime for the old in Hungary. Conversely the young in Slovakia were three times as favourable as the old to the united democratic Czechoslovakia of 1989–92, and also slightly more favourable to the present. In the Czech Republic, the young were twice as favourable as the old to the present, and also slightly more favourable to the united democratic Czechoslovakia; but the young favoured the postcommunist period in the Czech Republic at the expense of Dubcek's Prague Spring of 1968 which was remembered with affection by the middle aged more even than the old.

The old certainly felt a greater sense of economic loss under the new regime. Everyone, young and old, was more optimistic about the future than the recent past, but the young were a little more optimistic about the future and a little less resentful of the first years of the postcommunist regime than their elders. Yet these differences, in purely economic terms, were remarkably small. At most, we found the young only 13 per cent more optimistic than the old about the impact of economic trends on their families. Differences between young and old on political values were actually greater than the differences in their sense of economic loss – so their political differences could not be attributed purely to their recent economic experiences or their hopes for the near future.

Table 13.13:   Generation and economic loss

	Family income only just enough to live on	Feel that things have got/will get worse:				
		For family	For country	In past	In future	Generally
	%	%	%	%	%	%
Aged:						
18–34	72	61	68	77	43	71
35–54	74	72	72	82	48	77
55 and over	79	74	72	84	49	80
Diff: old–young	+7	+13	+4	+7	+6	+9

Notes: Entries are the percentage who score strictly above the mid-point on each scale.

The old were 23 per cent more committed to socialist values than the young. Differences were rather less on state welfare to which the overwhelming majority in each age group were committed, but greater on equality which was supported by 71 per cent of the old but only 42 per cent of the young. Differences were less on nationalist values and very small on the democratic values of popular control. Indeed, although the old were 23 per cent more socialist and 10 per cent more nationalist than the young they were no less committed to multi-party elections and actually more committed to political parties than the young.[7]

Old and young differed by 18 per cent on liberal values. But paradoxically that substantial difference does not provide good evidence that a new, more liberal generation had appeared amongst the young in postcommunist countries because the young – for life-cycle reasons rather than generational – have been substantially more liberal than the old throughout western democracies for as long as survey evidence has been available.[8] That age pattern is a constant of nature, rather than a harbinger of a new age.

We have probably detected a real generational shift on socialist values, but very little difference on the democratic values of popular control, and a routine life-cycle tendency towards authoritarianism amongst the old.[9]

Within the different countries, generational differences on socialist values ranged from a low of 15 per cent in Hungary to 26 per cent in Russia and 30 per cent in the Czech Republic. In Russia the size of that gap reflected the very strong socialist values of the old (94 per cent), while in the Czech Republic it reflected the very weak socialist values of the young (only 41 per cent). Generational differences in nationalist values were largest in Russia (15 per cent) and negligible in Hungary. And generational differences on liberal values were particularly small in the former Czechoslovakia.

Table 13.14:   Generations and values

	Socialist	Nationalist	Liberal	Populist	Pro-elections	Pro-parties
	%	%	%	%	%	%
Aged:						
18–34	64	33	74	62	62	21
35–54	72	35	72	67	64	28
55 and over	87	43	56	63	62	26
Diff: old–young	+23	+10	−18	+1	0	+5

Note: Entries are the percentage who score strictly above the mid-point on each scale.

GENDER AND MARITAL STATUS

Gender differences in expressed belief in communist ideals were negligible. So were gender differences in perceptions of the best and worst features of communism or the benefits of the new postcommunist regime.

But women were somewhat less likely than men to complain that they had been personally oppressed by the communist regime. Women were 10 per cent more inclined to cite the Brezhnev period as the best for Russia, 15 per cent more inclined to cite the Kadar period as the best for Hungary, and also more inclined to cite the united democratic period in the former Czechoslovakia. In short, they displayed a slight preference for recent times against both the present and the distant past, but there was no consistent ideological tendency in their choice of time periods.

Table 13.15:   Gender and communist oppression

	Felt personally oppressed by the communist regime
	%
Gender:	
men	22
women	15
Diff: women–men	−7

Note: 'Don't Knows', 'Can't decide' etc. excluded from calculation of percentages.

The old communist regimes were intensely proud of their policy of treating men and women equally. Although, in practice, they failed to do so, the transition to a postcommunist regime may have increased still further the burdens upon women.[10] Despite that, we found very little difference between men and women in their assessment of how economic trends affected their country or their family, though we did not ask how they had been affected still more personally.

Table 13.16:   Gender, marital status and economic loss

	Family income only just enough to live on	Feel that things have got/will get worse:				
		For family	For country	In past	In future	Generally
	%	%	%	%	%	%
Gender:						
men	74	67	70	79	46	74
women	75	71	72	82	48	78
Diff: women–men	+1	+4	+2	+3	+2	+4
Marital status:						
single	71	62	67	77	45	73
married or living as	73	69	72	81	47	76
div. sep., widowed	84	75	71	82	47	79
Diff: div etc.–single	+13	+13	+4	+5	+2	+6

Notes: Entries are the percentage who score strictly above the mid-point on each scale.

However we found larger variations in the sense of economic loss by marital status. We divided respondents into three groups: first the single; second, those who were married or living as married; third, those who were divorced, separated or widowed. Obviously there was an age dimension to these different categories but that does not explain all of the difference in their perceptions of economic trends and the divorced, separated and widowed were 13 per cent more pessimistic than the single about how economic trends affected themselves and their families.

Women proved a little more socialist and less liberal than men, though no different on nationalist values; and they were 11 per cent less committed to political parties than men.[11] By contrast, the divorced, separated and widowed were 20 per cent more socialist than the single, 17 per cent less liberal, and 9 per cent more nationalist though they differed less on the democratic values of popular control.

Table 13.17:   Gender, marital status and values

	Socialist	Nationalist	Liberal	Populist	Pro-elections	Pro-parties
	%	%	%	%	%	%
Gender:						
men	70	37	71	65	66	31
women	78	36	65	64	60	20
Diff: women–men	+8	−1	−6	−1	−6	−11
Marital status:						
single	65	33	74	64	65	24
married or living as	73	36	69	65	64	26
div., sep., widowed	85	42	57	62	58	21
Diff: div. etc.–single	+20	+9	−17	−2	−7	−3

Note: Entries are the percentage who score strictly above the mid-point on each scale.

THE MILITARY–INDUSTRIAL COMPLEX

Communist regimes had a huge military-industrial complex of police, armed forces and state owned defence industries, as well as a huge state-owned civilian sector of administrators and productive industries, which were inevitably bequeathed to their successors. It would not be surprising if the military–industrial complex in particular had distinctive values arising both from its threatening past and its now threatened future. In fact, the big surprise is that it did not. Values differed sharply between the public and private sectors but not between the various branches of the public sector itself. To simplify our analysis we have put all employed people into one of four groups:

1. *The military sector*: state owned defence industries, plus the police and military
2. *The civil state sector*: other state employment: state owned civil industries, plus administrators, teachers etc.
3. *The cooperative sector*: cooperative workers

4. *The private sector*: self-employed, plus employees in private, joint-stock, joint-venture, and foreign companies.

Only 56 per cent in the private sector, but 71 or 72 per cent in each of the other sectors, felt that postcommunist economic trends were hurting their families. Between 17 and 21 per cent in each of the sectors claimed to have suffered personal oppression under the communist regime – lowest in the cooperative sector and highest in the private sector. So, insofar as the sectors differed at all, it was the private sector that stood out, and mainly because of its postcommunist experience.

When asked about the best time this century for their country it was again the private sector that stood out from the others – in Russia, Ukraine and Hungary, private sector workers were the most likely to cite the imperial days of Tsar or Hapsburg, but the military sector was no more likely to do so than the civil state sector, and none of the four sectors stood out consistently as the one most likely to opt for the postcommunist present.

The private sector was much less committed than the others to socialist values (it would have been very surprising if it had not been so), a little less nationalist, and a little more committed to liberal values and representative democracy. But there was scarcely any difference between the military and civil state sectors on anything, and it was the cooperative sector that was, marginally, the most socialist, the most nationalist, the least liberal and the least committed to democratic values.

In short, the military–industrial complex was in no respect unrepresentative of the norm in postcommunist societies. It was the private sector that was deviant.

Table 13.18:   Values by sector

	Socialist	Nationalist	Liberal	Populist	Pro-elections	Pro-parties
	%	%	%	%	%	%
Military	75	36	67	65	62	28
Civil state	78	38	67	65	62	24
Cooperative	81	41	62	61	62	22
Private	57	31	74	63	70	28

Note: Entries are the percentage who score strictly above the mid-point on each scale.

CONCLUSION

Amongst individuals, we have found a strong correlation between a pessimistic outlook on postcommunist economic trends – especially as they affected the family – and support for socialist values, especially the principle of equality. That pessimistic outlook also correlated with external (but not internal) nationalism, with populism, and with alienation from parties and multi-party elections – though not with antagonism to liberal values as distinct from support for the institutions of representative democracy.

We also found that there were very large class differences, smaller generational differences and negligible gender differences in feelings about economic trends under the postcommunist regime. These were reflected in large class differences, smaller generational differences and even smaller gender differences in support for socialist values, to a lesser degree in rejection of liberal values, and to an even lesser degree in support for nationalist values. But since there was little or no correlation between a personal sense of economic loss and rejection of liberal values, the class, generational and gender differences on liberal values probably owed more to other causes than their sense of economic loss under the new regime.

Table 13.19: Regressions predicting political values from class and economic loss

	Socialist values	Nationalist values	Liberal values
Multiple correlation:	47	30	27
	betas	betas	betas
Family sense of economic loss	24	·	·
Contrasted with workers:			
farmers	·	·	·
intellectuals	−17	−11	14
managers	·	·	·
business-persons	−14	·	·
Contrasted with Russia:			
Ukraine	−11	−26	·
Czech Rep	−27	−15	20
Slovakia	·	·	10
Hungary	·	·	·

Note: Entries are path coefficients (betas, standardised regression coefficients). Those less than 0.10 have been replaced by a full-stop.

We can use multiple regressions to assess the influence on political values of class and generation, above and beyond the effect of personal economic experience or country of residence. They show that, compared to the workers, intellectuals were biased against socialism and nationalism, and in favour of liberal values, while business persons were biased against socialism – quite independently of their reactions to economic trends. And the old were biased strongly in favour of socialism and against liberal values – again quite independently of their reactions to economic trends.

But the multiple regression coefficients also show that the impact of postcommunist economic trends on the family had an influence on individuals' values even within classes and generations. This personal sense of economic loss had a large, positive and independent effect upon socialist values, though relatively little on nationalist or liberal values. (Surprisingly perhaps, a sense of personal economic loss actually *increased* commitment to liberal values slightly once other factors such as class and generation had been taken into account.)

A set of dummy variables representing countries was included in these regressions primarily to remove the influence of country from our analysis of economic loss and social categories. But, in passing, it shows that after controlling both for personal economic loss and for social differences, people in the Czech Republic were still unusually sympathetic to liberal values, unsympathetic to nationalist values, and especially unsympathetic to socialist values; while people in Ukraine were somewhat less socialist and a lot *less* nationalist than might be predicted from their social background and dire economic experiences.

Table 13.20: Regressions predicting political values from generation and economic loss

	Socialist values	Nationalist values	Liberal values
Multiple correlation:	49	30	29
	betas	betas	betas
Family sense of economic loss	25	.	.
Age	28	11	−21
Contrasted with Russia:			
Ukraine	−12	−27	.
Czech Rep	−30	−15	22
Slovakia	.	.	10
Hungary	−10	.	.

Note: Entries are path coefficients (betas, standardised regression coefficients). Those less than 0.10 have been replaced by a full-stop.

This chapter has focused primarily upon reactions to postcommunist economic trends, and on those sections of society which did better or worse out of these trends – on class, generation, gender and marital status therefore. But there have been some hints that these different social groups were differentiated by intellectual flexibility and sophistication as well as by economic experiences. The intellectual class for example had suffered economically to much the same degree as the workers, but it showed much less affection than the working class for the Brezhnev era and much more for Tsarist, or Hapsburg times and for the various eras when Czechoslovakia was united and democratic; and intellectuals were markedly less socialist, less nationalist, more liberal and more committed to the mechanisms of representative democracy than were the workers.

One indicator of intellectual flexibility was provided by our question of whether 'women should stay at home and look after their families' rather than 'go to work and have careers of their own.' Significantly, the greatest divisions on this question were not between men and women, but between generations and classes. Although about 41 per cent said the decision should be left to women themselves, the 'stay at home' option was supported by 50 per cent of men and 41 per cent of women; by 37 per cent of the young but 53 per cent of the old, and by 35 per cent of intellectuals, managers and business persons but by 51 per cent of workers and farmers. Differences of opinion on this question owed more to age and class than to gender.

In the next chapter we shall pursue the question of intellectual flexibility further by focusing upon social groups which are still more clearly differentiated in such terms than classes, generations and genders: the most and least educated, the most and least religious, the inhabitants of cosmopolitan cities and rural villages.

14 Adaptable Minds

The previous chapter focused upon individuals who emerged as economic winners or losers in the immediate postcommunist years. We looked at class, generation and gender not just because they were intrinsically interesting but also because particular occupational classes, generations and genders were reputed to have lost more than others in the transition from communism, and their differential losses might have influenced their commitment to socialist, nationalist and liberal democratic values.

In this chapter we look at the influence of education, religiosity and rurality. Of course, they are not entirely unconnected with class, generation and gender, nor entirely uncorrelated with economic gains or losses but, in addition, they are the social variables which are usually most closely associated with mental flexibility and adaptability, with radicalism or conservatism.[1]

Some social groups are inherently more radical or more conservative than others – more or less willing to adapt to change – despite, rather than because of, their economic experiences. The class difference, between workers and businesspeople, was over twice as great on economic loss as on attitudes to whether women's place was in the home. By contrast, those with the highest and lowest levels of education differed by over twice as much on whether women's place was in the home as they did on their experience of economic loss; and although the most religious had done better than the least religious out of postcommunist economic change they took a far more conservative attitude towards women's role in society. Conservatism was not by any means simply the product of declining living standards.

The term 'cosmopolitan' had a special flavour under the communist regime where it was used to attack intellectuals with international connections – or simply to attack Jews. But the contrast between the educated and uneducated, between free-thinkers and the devout, or between people from rural villages and those from great cities is often the contrast between cosmopolitans and those with a narrow, rigid and parochial outlook. Irrespective of their material gains or losses, we should normally expect flexibly minded cosmopolitans to cope better psychologically with rapid change than those from more naturally conservative backgrounds.

The key indicator of adaptability is education, just as class was the key variable in the last chapter on winners and losers. But religiosity and rurality may also prove to have at least some influence. Age, conceptualised in terms of life cycle rather than generation, should also be considered an important indicator of intellectual rigidity: we usually get more set in our ways and more resistant to change as we get older. However, we included age in the previous chapter because, in the peculiar circumstances of the transition from commun-

252

ism, the old could be considered a disadvantaged generation that had borne the costs of socialism and were now to be deprived of its meagre, but real, benefits.

Flexibility need not always imply initiative. It is sometimes argued that intellectual flexibility is nothing more than an ability to accommodate oneself to the spirit of the times,[2] the ability to learn a new slogan fast rather than the ability to think new thoughts, the ability to seize new opportunities not the ability to create them. Thus the young are forever swept enthusiastically along with the tides of politics, convinced that they truly and independently believe in the latest political line drawn up by the old men in the Kremlin or the Forbidden City – whether it be Mao's cultural revolution, Gorbachev's perestroika, or Yeltsin's free market democracy. But it is not so easy to argue the same about the better educated. Our own experiments on manipulating public opinion suggest that the highly educated are significantly more difficult to manipulate than the least educated.[3]

There was a direct link between age and education. Using a crude six point scale of education, there was a correlation of 0.36 between youth and education. Amongst the young (up to age 34) 5 per cent told us they had no education beyond elementary school, and amongst the middle aged 12 per cent, but amongst the old (55 years and older) 54 per cent. Conversely only 7 per cent of the old claimed to have graduated from a university or equivalent compared to 13 per cent of the middle aged and 11 per cent of the young. If we added in those who had some experience of higher education but had not graduated these figures would rise to 8 per cent amongst the old and 15 per cent amongst both the middle aged and the young. Similarly, there was a strong link between education and class: 39 per cent of higher education graduates but only 4 per cent of those with an elementary education viewed themselves as part of the management rather than as part of the work-force. We shall need to separate out the impact on values of age and class from that of education later on (in Chapter 17), but here we begin by focusing upon education alone.

EDUCATION

It can be useful to distinguish between the 'intelligentsia' and the 'technocrats': they do have distinctive political values, even in the West.[4] And within the FSU, some claim to see 'a profound cleavage' between 'the intelligentsia, a creation of the process of modernisation initiated by Peter the Great' and those who 'live within the framework ... of Muscovite culture.'[5] But even without such subtle elaborations, it is clear that there was a strong relationship between education and political values or behaviour. Higher education graduates were 35 per cent more likely than those with only an elementary education to be at least 'quite' interested in politics, 27 per cent more likely to discuss politics at least 'quite' often, 29 per cent more likely to follow politics in the press and even 17 per cent more likely to follow politics on television. They were much more psychologically involved with politics therefore.

Table 14.1:   Psychological involvement with politics by education

	Very/quite interested in politics	Very/quite often discuss politics	Regularly follow politics in press	Regularly follow politics on TV
	%	%	%	%
Elementary	23	20	40	64
Secondary	34	31	48	66
Vocational	36	31	53	72
Higher	58	49	69	81
Diff: Higher–elem.	+35	+29	+29	+17

Notes: 'Don't Knows', 'Can't decide' etc. excluded from calculation of percentages. Those with 'incomplete secondary' or 'incomplete higher' education have been excluded for clarity.

Graduates were also more active in every sphere of social and political life except for religion: compared to those with only elementary education, graduates were 30 per cent more likely to participate in hobby, sports or cultural organisations, and 23 per cent more likely to participate actively in trade union or professional organisations – though 11 per cent *less* likely to participate in church organisations. Very few people at any educational level said they participated actively in party political organisations – but five times as many amongst graduates as amongst those with only an elementary education.

All of this involvement – both psychological and behavioural – partly reflected the wider interests of those with higher levels of education but should itself have reinforced and encouraged their intellectual flexibility and adaptability.

Table 14.2:   Social and political participation by education

	In hobby, sports, or cultural organisation	In church or religious organisation	In trade union or professional organisation	In party or political organisation
	%	%	%	%
Elementary	11	17	13	1
Secondary	31	7	29	3
Vocational	32	8	28	3
Higher	41	6	36	5
Diff: Higher–elem.	+30	−11	+23	+4

Notes: 'Don't Knows', 'Can't decide' etc. excluded from calculation of percentages. Those with 'incomplete secondary' or 'incomplete higher' education have been excluded for clarity.

In behaviour and opinions, those with secondary or vocational education tended to be intermediate between graduates and those with only elementary education. They were usually almost indistinguishable from each other and they were not consistently closer to graduates, or to those with only an elementary education.

Compared to those with only an elementary education, graduates were just 10 per cent less likely to have suffered from postcommunist economic trends, but they were 22 per cent less likely to say they disliked or would even jail the 'new rich' and also 22 per cent less likely to say that women's place was in the home.

Table 14.3: Economic loss and reactionary responses by education

	Family economic loss	Dislike/jail the new rich	Women's place is in the home
	%	%	%
Elementary	75	57	56
Secondary	66	38	43
Vocational	70	36	45
Higher	65	35	34
Diff: Higher–elem.	−10	−22	−22

Notes: 'Don't Knows', 'Can't decide' etc. excluded from calculation of percentages. Those with 'incomplete secondary' or 'incomplete higher' education have been excluded for clarity.

When asked to reflect upon the best times this century for their country, graduates were 26 per cent less likely than those with only an elementary education to cite Brezhnev's time in Russia, and 49 per cent less likely to cite Kadar's in Hungary, though the equivalent patterns were weaker in Ukraine and the former Czechoslovakia.

Those with only an elementary education were especially prone to cite Stalin's time in Russia (18 per cent) and Father Tiso's 1939–45 Nazi-puppet state in Slovakia (14 per cent) despite the brutality of those times. But graduates in the old imperial nations of Russia and Hungary were much more inclined than those with only an elementary education to cite the days of the Tsars or the Hapsburgs – exactly 23 per cent more in both Russia and Hungary (so that fully 28 per cent of graduates in Russia and 30 per cent in Hungary opted for the days of empire) – though there was no glimmer of this tendency in Slovakia and only a very slight one in Ukraine or the Czech Republic. In every country, graduates were between 8 per cent and 16 per cent more willing than those with only an elementary education to cite the present as the best time for their country – most so in the Czech Republic, least so in Ukraine.

Graduates were 13 per cent more likely to cite the post-Kadar reform-communist period in Hungary. But perhaps the saddest of all these patterns was the contrast between Czech and Slovak attitudes to postcommunism in a united Czechoslovakia. Only 8 per cent of Czech graduates, but 31 per cent of Slovak graduates, looked back on that brief interlude with particular regret: so graduates in Slovakia were 16 per cent *more* likely than their least educated compatriots to cite united democratic Czechoslovakia as best for Slovakia, while graduates in the Czech Republic were 13 per cent *less* likely than their least educated compatriots to do so.

More personally, higher education graduates were 7 per cent more likely than the least educated, to complain that they had personally felt oppressed under the communist regime.

Table 14.4:   Nostalgia by education

	Russia	Ukraine	Czech Rep	Slovakia	Hungary
	%	%	%	%	%
	Under the Tsars		Under the Hapsburg Monarchy		
Elementary	5	4	2	1	7
Higher	28	9	10	2	30
Diff: Higher–elem.	+23	+5	+8	+1	+23
	Under Stalin		Under Masaryk		Under Horthy
Elementary	18	8	38	5	8
Higher	6	2	37	2	10
Diff: Higher–elem.	−12	−6	−1	−3	+2
	Under Brezhnev		Under Husak		Under Kadar
Elementary	69	81	7	22	65
Higher	43	70	1	10	16
Diff: Higher–elem.	−26	−11	−6	−12	−49
	Under Gorbachev		In united democratic Czechoslovakia 1989–92		Under reform communists
Elementary	3	1	21	15	11
Higher	6	3	8	31	24
Diff: Higher–elem.	+3	+2	−13	+16	+13
	Since 1992		Since 1992 in the Czech Rep	Since 1992 in Slovakia	Since 1989
Elementary	5	7	16	20	9
Higher	17	15	32	25	21
Diff: Higher–elem.	+12	+8	+16	+5	+12

Notes: 'Don't Knows', 'Can't decide' etc. excluded from calculation of percentages. For brevity, only those with 'higher' education and those with no more than elementary education have been included in this table.

As for political values, graduates were 31 per cent less committed to socialist values than the least educated,[6] and 16 per cent less committed to nationalist values, but 28 per cent more committed to liberal values.[7] On all three sets of values, those with secondary and vocational qualifications were almost identical to each other and intermediate between the best and least educated, though a little closer to the best educated. Populism proved unrelated to education; but graduates were 17 per cent more committed to the mechanisms of representative democracy and 13 per cent more to political parties than the least educated.

Table 14.5:   Education and values

	Socialist	Nationalist	Liberal	Populist	Pro-elections	Pro-parties
	%	%	%	%	%	%
Elementary	89	44	52	65	56	20
Secondary	71	33	72	62	65	25
Vocational	70	37	71	66	61	24
Higher	58	28	80	66	73	33
Diff: Higher–elem.	−31	−16	+28	+1	+17	+13

Note: Entries are the percentage who score strictly above the mid-point on each scale.

The effect of education was sufficiently similar within each of our five countries for us to ignore the differences between countries. Of more interest is the variation in the effect of education across different indicators of socialism, nationalism and liberal values. Education had less effect upon attitudes towards welfare on which graduates were only 18 per cent less committed than the least educated, than attitudes towards equality on which graduates were 29 per cent less committed; and less upon attitudes towards centralist nationalism where graduates were only 6 per cent less committed, than on attitudes towards external nationalism where they were 17 per cent less committed. Graduates' support for order was much the same as amongst the least educated, but their support for law-bound government was 22 per cent higher.[8]

Table 14.6:   Education and selected value indicators

	Welfare	Equality	External nationalism	Centralist nationalism	Law-based government	Anti-Order
	(socialist values)		*(nationalist values)*		*(liberal values)*	
	%	%	%	%	%	%
Elementary	90	72	48	31	60	21
Secondary	79	52	36	29	72	30
Vocational	78	49	40	30	71	25
Higher	72	43	31	25	82	25
Diff: Higher–elem.	−18	−29	−17	−6	+22	+4

Note: Entries are the percentage who score strictly above the mid-point on each scale.

Education consists of more than formal qualifications however. Socialists have always admired those working class people who had few opportunities to gain a formal education but were nonetheless 'self-taught' and 'well read'. As a primitive measure of that voluntary and informal element of education we asked each respondent whether they had a 'personal book collection of over 200 books.' Books were cheap under communism; so this is more an indicator of disposition and less an indicator of affluence than it would be in the West. Just over a third of respondents claimed to have such a personal book collection (and less than one per cent could not tell us whether they did or not). Of course possession of such a book collection varied with education: 72 per cent amongst graduates, 40 per cent amongst those with secondary or vocational qualifications, and only 16 per cent amongst those with only an elementary education. Nonetheless, at all levels of formal education there were people who had collected books and others who had not.

Overall, those with a book collection were 15 per cent less socialist, 10 per cent more liberal and 12 per cent more committed to elections than those who did not have one. And the effect of a personal book collection did not disappear when we controlled for formal education; indeed, in some respects, it strengthened. Amongst people with only an elementary education, those with a book collection were 10 per cent less socialist, 7 per cent more liberal, 16 per cent more committed to elections and 20 per cent more committed to political parties. Both formal and informal education therefore had independent effects upon values, and effects that ran in the same direction. To some extent they reinforced each other, though the substitution effect is more significant: amongst those with the least formal education, a book collection had the greatest impact. Since it seems likely that most of these collections were built up during the communist regime, it is ironic, but not surprising, that books which circulated under a regime so devoted to censorship should prove so subversive of its values.

Table 14.7: Books and values

	Socialist	Nationalist	Liberal	Populist	Pro-elections	Pro-parties
	\multicolumn{6}{c}{*Difference between those who had a personal book collection of over 200 books, and those who did not:*}					
	%	%	%	%	%	%
Amongst all resps	−15	−3	+10	+1	+12	+8
Amongst those with						
elementary educ.	−10	−2	+7	+6	+16	+20
secondary & voc.	−10	0	+6	+1	+9	+6
higher educ.	−9	−3	0	−2	+5	+4

Finally, we can return to the question of whether the apparent influence of education merely reflected the much better formal education of the middle-aged and young as compared to the old. We can investigate this directly by calculating the effect of formal education on values within each generation. That confirms the independent effect of education. Because age also had an independent effect upon values, the effect of education within age cohorts was, of course, smaller than amongst the public generally, but it remained substantial.

Table 14.8:   Education and values within generations

	Socialist	Nationalist	Liberal	Populist	Pro-elections	Pro-parties
	%	%	%	%	%	%
Amongst all resps	−31	−16	+28	+1	+17	+13
Amongst:						
18–34 yr olds	−10	−14	+13	−7	+22	+2
35–54 yr olds	−27	−14	+25	−5	+26	+12
55 yrs and older	−16	−7	+24	+1	+10	+25

Difference between those most and least educated on:

RELIGIOSITY

We constructed a scale of religiosity by dividing people into those that attended a place of worship at least once a week, those that attended less often, those that claimed to be religious but admitted they never attended, and those who denied any religious commitment at all.

Unlike education, religiosity had very little effect – either positive or negative – on interest in politics, the amount of political discussion, or the tendency to follow politics in the press and on television. So it made little difference to psychological involvement with politics. But nonetheless, religiosity had some effect upon active participation. The religious were, of course, much more likely than the irreligious to take an active part in a religious organisation. Less obviously perhaps, they were a lot *less* likely to take an active part in a hobby, sports or cultural organisation. Sport and culture were, to some extent, alternatives to and substitutes for religion.

And although the differences were never large, we found that the highly religious were more active in political organisations (by only one per cent compared to the irreligious however); more likely to have signed a petition (by 3 per cent), or written to a newspaper (by 2 per cent), contacted an elected official (by 4 per cent) or been on a protest demonstration (by one per cent), though less likely to have been on strike (by 2 per cent). Obviously these are very small though consistent differences. The religious were not much more active than the irreligious but the important point is that they were clearly *not less* involved in political activity. So the levels of political interest, involvement and activity of the *most religious* clearly distinguished them from the *least educated*, though they had, as we shall see, some important values in common.

Table 14.9:   Social and political participation by religiosity

	In hobby, sports, or cultural organisation	In church or religious organisation	In trade union or professional organisation	In party or political organisation
	%	%	%	%
Religious and attend:				
at least weekly	18	34	22	4
less	25	16	24	3
never	25	4	30	3
Not religious	37	1	22	3
Diff: Most relig.–least	−19	+33	0	+1

Note: 'Don't Knows', 'Can't decide' etc. excluded from calculation of percentages.

It is also significant that the highly religious reported very slightly more than average satisfaction (albeit only by 2 per cent) with the way postcommunist economic trends had affected their families; but despite that, they took a more conservative line both on women's employment or the new rich: the most religious were 9 per cent more inclined than the irreligious to express dislike of the new rich or even say they should be jailed; and 12 per cent more inclined to say women's place was in the home.

When asked to choose the best time for their country this century the highly religious in Russia were 10 per cent more likely than the irreligious to cite Gorbachev's time, and less likely to cite the postcommunist period. In Ukraine however they were 19 per cent more likely than the irreligious to cite the postcommunist period, though also 40 per cent more likely to cite Gorbachev's period – for which they had some justification despite his extreme unpopularity for non-religious reasons in Ukraine, including his handling of the Chernobyl disaster.[9] In Hungary the highly religious were 9 per cent more likely than the irreligious to cite Horthy's regime; in Slovakia they were 11 per cent more likely than the irreligious to cite the present; though in the Czech Republic they were most distinguished by being 19 per cent more likely than the irreligious to cite Mazaryk's time despite the secularising tendencies of Masaryk's regime.

Although the highly religious were scarcely any less likely than the irreligious to claim a current belief in communist ideals, they were 26 per cent less likely to say they had 'ever believed' in communist ideals. Their attitudes to communism had remained more stable and consistent than other people's. Moreover the

highly religious were 17 per cent more likely to complain that they had personally experienced oppression by the communist regime. This was reflected in
their assessment of the best and worst features of the communist regime. The
highly religious were much more likely than the irreligious to praise the old
regime for job security, and much less likely to praise it for keeping the peace
between the nationalities. Conversely they were much more likely to criticise it
for the oppression of human rights and much less likely to criticise it for
bureaucracy.

Table 14.10: Religiosity and communist oppression

	Felt personally oppressed by the communist regime
	%
Religious and attend:	
at least weekly	30
less	20
never	17
Not religious	13
Diff: Most relig.–least	+17

Note: 'Don't Knows', 'Can't decide' etc. excluded from calculation of percentages.

Table 14.11: Best and worst features of the communist regime by religiosity

	Best features		Worst features	
	peace between nationalities	job security	bureaucracy	oppressed human rights
	%	%	%	%
Religious and attend:				
at least weekly	8	52	16	44
less	14	43	24	27
never	17	43	24	27
Not religious	20	35	31	22
Diff: Most relig.–least	−12	+17	−15	+22

Note: 'Don't Knows', 'Can't decide' etc. excluded from calculation of percentages.

In the West, highly religious people tend to be authoritarian and illiberal.
After all, they accept the authority of religion, and indeed they often seek to
impose it. Authority and religion sit well together. But the effect of religiosity is
not a simple inverse of the effect of education. The religious may combine their
authoritarianism with a tendency to be at least as caring as the irreligious, for
example. In terms of values, the highly religious in the FSU/ECE were 10 per
cent less liberal than the irreligious. They were also 14 per cent more nationalist

– which also fits the way in which religion had been used throughout the centuries to help define the nations, and even the states, of eastern Europe. But the highly religious were also slightly more committed to competitive elections and political parties – the mechanisms and institutions of representative democracy – despite being relatively authoritarian. And the highly religious were, if anything, *more* committed to socialist values than were the irreligious. That seems to contradict their explicit rejection of communist ideals (at least in the past, if not the present), and the accusations of general and personal oppression which they levelled at the old communist regime. However, we have taken great pains to separate actual commitment to socialist principles from support for the old regime or its slogans. And the combination of greater authoritarianism, without less commitment to caring, equality or socialist values is exactly the pattern we have found in our study of British political culture.[10] We suggest it is normal throughout Christendom, east or west.

Table 14.12:   Religiosity and values

	Socialist	Nationalist	Liberal	Populist	Pro-elections	Pro-parties
	%	%	%	%	%	%
Religious and attend:						
at least weekly	78	45	61	57	67	28
less	76	40	62	64	61	25
never	71	36	71	66	63	24
Not religious	75	31	71	63	62	25
Diff: Most relig.–least	+3	+14	−10	−6	+5	+3

Note: Entries are the percentage who score strictly above the mid-point on each scale.

Table 14.13:   Religiosity and selected value indicators

	Equality (socialist values)	Cultural subsidies (socialist values)	External nationalism (nationalist values)	Cultural nationalism (nationalist values)	Rights of protest (liberal values)	Glasnost (liberal values)
	%	%	%	%	%	%
Religious and attend:						
at least weekly	55	48	37	39	66	68
less	54	50	42	30	72	79
never	49	37	40	28	77	81
Not religious	48	37	39	23	76	85
Diff: Most relig.–least	+7	+11	−2	+16	−10	−17

Note: Entries are the percentage who score strictly above the mid-point on each scale.

Amongst the different indicators of socialist values, the highly religious were 7 per cent *more* committed than the irreligious to equality, and just as committed to welfare, but 6 per cent *less* committed to state control of industry. It really was the caring rather than the controlling aspect of socialism that attracted the religious.

Although we excluded our indicator of support for state subsidies in the cultural sphere from our general measure of socialism, it is worth noting that the highly religious were particularly favourable to that aspect of state intervention, not least because churches as well as ballet, opera and political parties might benefit from such subsidies.

The highly religious were not specially attracted to external nationalism but they were 16 per cent more likely to support nationalist notions of cultural conformity within the state – something that is at once nationalist and authoritarian. Amongst the liberal values, the highly religious were particularly unwilling to support glasnost or rights of protest.

COSMOPOLITAN VALUES

People who were brought up, or who now live, in great cities are usually more receptive to change than those with a small town, village or rural background; and those who live in a capital city are likely to be the most receptive of all. Indeed they are usually, though not always, the vanguard of the revolution. In Russia, we put the last Tsarist capital, St Petersburg, as well as the communist capital of Moscow into our most cosmopolitan category of living environments.

We found that people brought up in large towns and cities complained more about their personal experience of oppression under the communist regime – and residents of the capital cities even more than others. Conversely we found that those who lived in capital cities had suffered less than others from post-communist economic trends. Not surprisingly therefore, they were less antagonistic towards the 'new rich' than those who lived in the villages and on the farms.

Residents of capital cities were not just more exposed to new ideas and arguments however, they were also affected – afflicted perhaps – by sentiments of grandeur and nationalism. This was reflected in their choice of the best times this century for their country. In every country, those who lived in the capital were somewhat more favourable than others to the postcommunist present. But in Russia, and to a lesser extent in Hungary and Ukraine, residents of the capital cities were particularly attracted to the days of the Tsars or the Hapsburgs: 37 per cent of those who lived in Moscow or St Petersburg – and more remarkably, even 18 per cent in Kyiv – opted for the days of the Tsars; in Budapest 22 per cent chose the days of the Hapsburgs. Those days of imperial grandeur were a lot less popular in the villages – 27 per cent less in Russia, 13 per cent less in Hungary and 11 per cent less in Ukraine. Only Prague and Bratislava were immune to the appeal of the Hapsburgs. The residents of these capitals showed a particular affection for the days of Masaryk (39 per cent in Prague) or the Slovak Dubcek (40 per cent in Bratislava) however (Table 14.15).

Table 14.14:   Communist oppression, postcommunist loss, and reactionary attitudes by cosmopolitan background

	Felt personally oppressed by the communist regime	Family economic loss	Dislike/jail the new rich	Women's place is in the home
	%	%	%	%
Grew up in:				
rural area	17	72	49	48
small town	18	67	39	41
big town or city	20	66	35	44
Diff: city–rural	+3	−6	−14	−4
Now live in:				
village or rural area	18	72	46	45
town	17	69	43	45
capital city	26	59	34	43
Diff: capital–rural	+8	−13	−12	2

Notes: 'Don't Knows', 'Can't decide' etc. excluded from calculation of percentages. In Russia both Moscow and St Petersburg are counted as 'capital cities' – which, in mind-set, they are!

As for political values, those who were brought up in the cities, or who now lived in the capitals were 17 per cent less committed to socialist values than people from the villages and countryside; to a lesser extent, they were also more committed to liberal and democratic values. On nationalist values, however, we found that while those who had been brought up in large towns or cities were 10 per cent less nationalist than the villagers, those who now lived in capital cities were as nationalist as those who lived in the villages. People who lived in towns other than the capital were slightly less nationalist than either villagers or those who lived in capital cities. Clearly the influence of city-dwelling towards toler-ance and cosmopolitanism was offset by the influence of capitals – as capitals – towards nationalism.

CONCLUSION

We have looked at three aspects of social background that usually affect the extent to which people are receptive to change: education, religiosity and a cosmopolitan versus rural milieu. Of these, education had the greatest influence, increasing support for liberal values by 28 per cent and reducing support for socialist values by 31 per cent, as well as reducing support for nationalism and increasing support for representative democracy by around 17 per cent. Religiosity and a rural versus cosmopolitan milieu had much less effect. Nonetheless religiosity reduced support for liberal values by 10 per cent and increased support for nationalism by 14 per cent though it had little or no effect upon socialist values. A rural background increased support for nationalist values by 10 per cent and for socialist values by 17 per cent – though residence in a capital city completely offset the urban tendency to be less nationalist.

Table 14.15: Nostalgia by cosmopolitan background

	Russia	Ukraine	Czech Rep	Slovakia	Hungary
	%	%	%	%	%
	Under the Tsars		Under the Hapsburg Monarchy		
Now live in:					
village or rural	10	7	2	2	9
town	17	7	5	0	9
capital city	37	18	4	0	22
Diff: capital–rural	+27	+11	+2	−2	+13
	Under Brezhnev		Under Husak		Under Kadar
Now live in:					
village or rural	76	76	7	24	63
town	56	78	7	16	51
capital city	28	64	2	2	29
Diff: capital–rural	−48	−12	−5	−22	−34
	Since 1992		Since 1992 in the Czech Rep	Since 1992 in Slovakia	Since 1989
Now live in:					
village or rural	3	10	20	18	9
town	11	7	21	18	14
capital city	19	13	32	23	22
Diff: capital–rural	+16	+3	+12	+5	+13

Notes: 'Don't Knows', 'Can't decide' etc. excluded from calculation of percentages.
In Budapest 13 per cent cited Horthy's time, but only 5 per cent in rural Hungary.
In Bratislava 40 per cent cited Dubcek's time, but only 21 per cent in rural Slovakia.
In Prague only 9 per cent cited Dubcek's time, but 20 per cent in rural parts of the Czech Republic.
Analysis by rural/town/city upbringing showed variations of opinion similar to those in this table, though usually less sharp.

Table 14.16:   Values by cosmopolitan background

	Socialist	Nationalist	Liberal	Populist	Pro-elections	Pro-parties
	%	%	%	%	%	%
Grew up in:						
rural area	81	40	65	65	60	25
small town	69	36	69	63	67	27
big town or city	64	30	72	64	65	24
Diff: city–rural	−17	−10	+7	−1	+5	−1
Now live in:						
village or rural	80	39	66	64	61	24
town	73	35	68	65	63	26
capital city	63	38	70	63	71	26
Diff: capital–rural	−17	−1	+4	−1	+10	+2

Notes: Entries are the percentage who score strictly above the mid-point on each scale. Note the difference between living in the capital and being brought up in a city is large in only two columns: on support for elections and more especially on nationalism. Residents of capitals were more nationalist than those brought up in cities on all three aspects of nationalism – external, centralist, and cultural conformist.

These effects of education, religiosity and metropolitan residence could not be ascribed to differential experience of postcommunist economic trends alone, nor to personal experience of oppression under the communist regime. The highly educated had suffered from postcommunist economic trends only 10 per cent less than those with only elementary education; yet they were around 30 per cent less socialist and more liberal than the least educated. Similarly, the most religious had survived postcommunist economic trends as well as anyone else and they complained far more than others about their experience of personal oppression under the communist regime, yet their values were, if anything, slightly *more* socialist than those of the less religious. And the relatively small differences in postcommunist economic experience between those who lived in capital cities and rural areas could not explain their larger differences in terms of socialist values.

The educated were distinguished far more by their interest in politics than by their economic experiences; the religious far more by complaints about communist oppression of human rights, and of course by their religious activity, than by their economic experiences; and residents of capital cities far more by their rejection of the Brezhnev, Husak and Kadar regimes and their nostalgia for the Tsars and the Hapsburgs than by their recent economic experiences.

In this chapter we have looked at religiosity but carefully avoided the question of divisions between those who adhered to different religions. In the next chapter we turn to questions of ethnic, linguistic and religious divisions and their influence on values. Similarly, in this chapter we have looked at the difference between values in capital cities and the villages, but in the next we turn to questions of regional divisions which cross-cut the urban/rural division but correlate with religious and ethnic divisions.

15 Land, Language, Culture and Nationality

Stalin defined a nation as a group of people united with each other and divided from their neighbours by land, language, culture and a common economic life.[1] It was one of his earlier writings. Characteristically the future dictator concluded, dogmatically, that 'it is only when all these characteristics are present together that we have a nation' and that intellectual dogmatism caused him peculiar problems in understanding the Jews because they had no 'land'. We shall take a less dogmatic and more empirical view. Indeed we are not concerned to arrive at any particular definition of a nation and it would be of no practical use to us here even if we could invent one. Instead, we are interested in that collection of attributes which Stalin – and many others – have associated with the idea of a nation, and in their impact upon political values. We shall investigate how political values varied with land, language, culture and self-conscious nationality within each of the five states under study. In more prosaic terms that means we shall look at how political values varied according to region, the language our respondents used in their own homes, the religious sect with which they identified, and their own self-image of national identity.

Like Stalin we shall, of course, be interested in the coincidence of land, language, culture, and national identity but, unlike him, we shall be interested in the impact of these variables whether or not they happen to coincide.

STATES AND NATIONS IN THE FSU/ECE

It is often said that 'current national borders ... seldom coincide with ethnic and religious boundaries' in eastern Europe.[2] Not so. It is crucially important to recognise that while, in ECE, these variables generally did not coincide at the beginning of this century, they do so very much more now.[3] Before the First World War, ECE was divided between three multi-national empires – the German, the Russian and the Austro-Hungarian; and within the Austro-Hungarian empire, Hungary itself included present day Slovakia as well as much of present day Croatia, Serbia and Romania.[4] Indeed Bratislava – now capital of Slovakia – was capital of Hungary for several centuries, and remained the Hungarian coronation city until 1835.

After the First World War however, Hungary lost two-thirds of its former territory to the new Czechoslovakia, Austria, Yugoslavia, and Romania – and with it nearly all of its non-Hungarian (Magyar) population, leaving it 92 per cent Magyar.[5] However, inter-war Poland was only 69 per cent Polish, and inter-war Czechoslovakia only 51 per cent Czech.[6]

But during the decade from 1939 – continuing after the war as well as during it – 62 million people in ECE were killed or displaced, and state boundaries were changed throughout the region. With the murder of the Jews, the expulsion of the Germans, and the post-war rearrangement of ECE state boundaries by Stalin, states in ECE became much more 'ethnic'. So, when the communist system began to collapse in 1989, Poland was by then 97 per cent Polish, Hungary over 99 per cent Hungarian (Magyar), and Czechoslovakia 95 per cent Czech, Moravian or Slovak.[7] The 'velvet divorce' between the Czech and Slovak Republics completed the alignment of states and nations in ECE, leaving the Czech Republic about 94 per cent Czech, and the Slovak Republic about 87 per cent Slovak.[8] Similarly the collapse of the Soviet Union also left the new Russian state, unlike both its Soviet and Tsarist predecessors, 87 per cent Russian.[9] So while there remained significant ethnic minorities in Russia and Slovakia, all the countries in our study, except for Ukraine, at least came near to approximating mono-ethnic states by the mid 1990s.

Mono-ethnic states were not, of course, nation-states. Most inhabitants of Russia in the 1990s were Russian, but many Russians now lived outside the state, particularly in neighbouring states known, in Russia, as 'the near abroad'. And while nearly all the inhabitants of Hungary were now Hungarians, two-thirds of historic Hungarian territory lay outside the state. Although only around one quarter of ethnic Hungarians now lived in Hungary's own 'near abroad', that was higher than the proportion of Russians who lived in Russia's 'near abroad'.[10]

We have usually tried to avoid a country by country analysis. But, to do justice to the peculiar problems of land, language, culture and nationality as they affect each country in different ways, we shall, in this chapter, look at each country separately, before attempting a more general and comparative overview.

RUSSIA

Both to outside observers and to its inhabitants, one of the most striking features of Russia has long been its sheer size. Although the Tsarist and Stalinist empires were even larger, Yeltsin's Russian Federation remains enormous. Conventionally, its territory has usually been divided into populous 'European Russia' – west of the Ural mountains, and largely empty 'Asiatic Russia' or more loosely 'Siberia' – to the east of the Urals. There is even a monument on the Moscow–Vladivostok railway purporting to mark the boundary between Europe and Asia.

But in truth, the Urals are very old geologically, and therefore low and unimpressive mountains. They do not constitute a physical barrier like the

Alps or the Pyrenees and there is no reason why they should represent a cultural or political frontier any more than a physical one. The Tsarist empire emphasised uniformity throughout the Tsar's dominions and the communists continued that tradition though they hid it behind the slogan 'national in form, socialist in content' – by which they meant that local variations in folk-dancing styles were permitted but political deviations were not.[11] These attempts to impose uniformity met with considerable resistance in, for example, the heavily populated Caucasus or Central Asia, but much less in the thinly populated Asiatic lands of the Russian Federation itself. So while we shall pose the question whether political values in European Russia differ in any significant way from those in Asiatic Russia we may well find that the Europe/Asia distinction is insignificant in terms of the political values of the local inhabitants however significant it may be in geographic, climatic, economic or high policy terms.

There is another regional division within the Russian Federation, potentially more important for political values than that of Europe versus Asia: the division between Russian areas and non-Russian autonomous areas within the Federation.[12] In terms of land area these lie mainly to the east of the Urals but, paradoxically, the most populous autonomous areas lie mainly within European Russia, pointing like a dagger towards Moscow: including the Bashkortostan, Chuvash, Mordovian, and Tatarstan Republics. Our sample of the Russian Federation included interviews in some but not all of the autonomous areas and even in some of the autonomous areas an overwhelming majority of our respondents claimed Russian nationality. We have separated out the 218 respondents interviewed in the Bashkortostan, Mordovian, Tatarstan and Komi Republics – all to the west of the Urals, and therefore technically in 'European' Russia – because between 44 and 74 per cent of our respondents in these areas claimed a non-Russian nationality.[13] In every other area where we carried out interviews the percentage who claimed a non-Russian nationality was less than half that, peaking at 19 per cent in Rostov-on-Don.

So we now have a regional division with three categories:

(1) Asiatic Russia;
(2) the non-Russian autonomous areas (comprising the four listed above) within European Russia; and
(3) the rest of European Russia which, for brevity only, we shall somewhat inaccurately call 'European Russia'.

In the Russian Federation as a whole, 14 per cent of our sample claimed a non-Russian nationality: 8 per cent in European Russia (as we have defined it), 12 per cent in Asiatic Russia, and 53 per cent in our four autonomous ethnically-named areas. More people spoke Russian at home than claimed Russian nationality, however: only 2 per cent in European or in Asiatic Russia spoke a non-Russian language at home, though 33 per cent in the autonomous areas.

Within the Russian Federation most people either identified with the Orthodox Church (48 per cent) or with no religion (44 per cent). Another 6 per cent said they were just 'Christian' and just 2 per cent that they were Muslim. However there were sharp regional variations on religion also: Asiatic Russia was notably irreligious – 69 per cent compared to 36 per cent in European Russia; and our four autonomous areas had a larger minority of Muslim identifiers, 13 per cent, than either European or Asiatic Russia which both had only one per cent – enough for them sometimes to be characterised as 'Muslim Republics' though only a small minority of their populations actually claimed to be religious Muslims.

Land in Russia

Those who lived in Asia and Europe hardly differed at all from each other on the question of the best time for Russia this century, but those who lived in the autonomous areas were 13 per cent less likely to opt for Tsarist times and 17 per cent more likely to opt for the Brezhnev era.

Similarly, those who lived in Asiatic Russia were 11 per cent more committed to liberal values than those who lived in Europe but otherwise hardly differed from them on any aspect of political values. Our main finding must be that the Europe/Asia distinction was almost totally irrelevant in terms of political values.

Table 15.1: Russia – values by region

	Socialist	Nationalist	Liberal	Populist	Pro-elections	Pro-parties
	%	%	%	%	%	%
Region:						
Europe	80	24	59	66	60	25
Minority republics	89	18	75	61	48	21
Asia	81	22	71	63	56	25

Notes: See text for definition of regions. Entries are the percentage who score strictly above the mid-point on each scale.

Somewhat by contrast, those who lived in our four autonomous areas – all west of the Urals – were 9 per cent more socialist than those who lived in the rest of European Russia, 6 per cent less (Russian) nationalist, 15 per cent more liberal, and 12 per cent less favourable to multi-party elections – a combination of relatively liberal but anti-democratic tendencies that is a natural response of any minority fearful of being dominated by the majority. None of these differences were very large however.[14] Such as they were, these differences might reflect the fact that ethnic minorities had different political values or alternatively, that people – of whatever nationality – who lived in a less Russian and more multi-national region had different values from those who lived in a homogeneously Russian environment. We shall see.

Nationality and language in Russia

Minority nationalities – as distinct from people who lived in minority auto-nomous regions – were slightly less likely than Russians to choose the Tsarist era as the best time for Russia and slightly more likely to opt for the Brezhnev or Stalin eras, but none of these differences exceeded 8 per cent.

Minority nationalities also differed only slightly if at all on socialism and populism, support for multi-party elections, liberal values and – most surprising of all – (Russian) nationalist values. This last finding is so counter-intuitive that it merits more detailed investigation. In fact, minority nationalities were just 2 per cent less nationalist than Russians with respect to the outside world, and just 3 per cent less territorially centralist, but were 8 per cent less likely to support (Russian) cultural nationalism despite the psychological and other pressures to assimilate to what the Tsarist and communist empires regarded – sometimes openly, at other times more covertly – as a 'higher' form of civilisation. Minority nationalities were only 5 per cent more willing to support greater autonomy for regions within Russia and only 6 per cent more willing to accept the right of regions to secede from Russia; though 7 per cent more opposed to making Russian-speaking a requirement for voting rights and 13 per cent more opposed to the imposition of Russian language teaching in all schools.

Table 15.2:   Russia – values by national identity and language

	Socialist	Nationalist	Liberal	Populist	Pro-elections	Pro-parties
	%	%	%	%	%	%
National identity:						
Russian	80	23	64	65	58	25
Other	85	23	64	61	58	23
Language:						
Russian	80	23	64	64	59	25
Other	87	29	63	69	51	25

Note: Entries are the percentage who score strictly above the mid-point on each scale.

Relatively few people in our survey – only 116, or 5 per cent in all – spoke a minority language. That was far fewer than the numbers who identified with a minority nationality. Those who did speak a minority language at home were 10 per cent less likely to choose the Tsarist era as the best for Russia and 12 per cent more likely to opt for the Brezhnev era. In general they differed little from Russian speakers on socialist, nationalist, populist or electoral values, though they were 13 per cent more committed to equality, and were very slightly more nationalist in terms of external nationalism or centralism but 10 per cent *less* nationalist in terms of (Russian) cultural conformity.

Non-Russian speakers were 14 per cent *more* likely than Russian speakers to agree that recent changes were reducing Russia to being a colony of the West. But they were 5 per cent *less* likely to claim parts of the near abroad for Russia, and 7 per cent more likely to say their government should do nothing at all to protect the rights of Russians living in the near abroad. Even their external nationalism therefore, was directed more against the West and less against the near abroad, than that of Russia speakers. Non-Russian speakers were only 5 per cent more opposed than Russian speakers to the idea of making Russian-speaking a condition for voting rights – largely because the overwhelming majority of Russian speakers also opposed such an illiberal policy, but also because such a restriction would have had very little practical effect since the pressures of everyday life had traditionally encouraged linguistic minorities within Russia to be bilingual anyway, unlike the Russian speaking minorities in FSU republics like Estonia or Uzbekistan for example. That did not prevent a wider division on other aspects of language rights: non-Russian speakers were 17 per cent more opposed to the imposition of the Russian language in schools. Half the Russian speakers, but only a third of the non-Russian speakers would accept that.

Table 15.3: Russia – nationalist values by national identity and language

	External (Russian) nationalist	*Centralist (Russian) nationalist*	*Cultural (Russian) nationalist*
	%	%	%
National identity:			
Russian	34	31	20
Other	31	28	13
Language:			
Russian	33	30	20
Other	34	32	10
Combinations:			
Russian national identity and language	34	31	20
Minority identity but Russian language	29	26	14
Minority national identity and language	35	31	10

Notes: 'Don't Knows', 'Can't decide' etc. excluded from calculation of percentages. Only one person combined a Russian national identity with speaking another language at home.

The interaction of land and nationality in Russia

Although our sample sizes are barely adequate we can make some attempt to investigate the interaction of land and nationality in their effects upon attitudes towards the various aspects of nationalism by comparing the values of Russians and non-Russians in the autonomous areas with each other, and with the values of Russians and non-Russians in European Russia. Of these four groups we interviewed over 1,300 Russians living in European Russia, and over 100 in each of the other three groups.

Within both regions, minority nationalities were even more opposed to Russian cultural nationalism than were Russians (the vast majority of whom *also* opposed Russian cultural nationalism, however). But there were also regional differences within each nationality and the effects cumulated: 22 per cent of Russians living in European Russia were cultural nationalists; 17 per cent of the minority nationalities living in European Russia or Russians living in the autonomous areas also supported Russian cultural nationalism; but only 5 per cent of the minority nationalities living in the autonomous areas did so.

Table 15.4:   Russia – cultural nationalist values by region and national identity

| | *(Russian) cultural nationalist values* | |
	In European Russia	*In autonomous area*
	%	%
If national identity is:		
Russian	22	17
Other	17	5

Notes: 'Don't Knows', 'Can't decide' etc. excluded from calculation of percentages.

Thus both region and nationality had independent and cumulative effects. However the greatest effect clearly occurred when land and nationality coincided. In statistical parlance this is an interactive effect; in substantive terms it means that individual members of the minority nationalities were much more likely to oppose Russian cultural imperialism when they lived in an autonomous area and had the support of other members of a minority nationality locally. Living in an autonomous minority area reduced support for Russian cultural imperialism by 5 per cent even amongst Russians themselves, but by 12 per cent amongst members of the minority nationalities.

Religious sects in Russia

Most Russians claimed to be either Orthodox Christians or irreligious; a few claimed to be Christians of other kinds; and very few claimed to be anything else. In particular, only 45 people in our sample claimed to be Muslims – too small a number to provide a very reliable account of the political values of Muslims in Russia. Compared to Orthodox Christians however, those few Muslims that we did interview were 10 per cent less likely to choose the days of the Tsars as the best for Russia, 10 per cent more likely to choose the Brezhnev era, and they were even a little more favourable to Stalin. In terms of values they were somewhat more socialist but less (Russian) nationalist than Orthodox Christians. Our few Muslims were 11 per cent *more* likely to agree that recent changes were turning Russia into a colony of the West, but 8 per cent *less* likely to support Russian territorial claims on the near abroad, and 9 per cent *less* willing to threaten military force to protect the rights of Russians living in the near abroad. So while they were a little more anti-Western, they were less aggressive towards the near abroad than Orthodox Christians.

Table 15.5:   Russia – nationalist values by religion

	External (Russian) nationalist	Centralist (Russian) nationalist	Cultural (Russian) nationalist	Support right of regions to secede from Russia
	%	%	%	%
Religion:				
Orthodox Christian	34	35	22	33
Muslim	27	18	15	62

Notes: *Values*: Entries are the percentage who score strictly above the mid-point on each scale.
Right of secession: 'Don't Knows', 'Can't decide' etc. excluded from calculation of these percentages.
Sample size: We had very few Muslims in our sample and these results are subject to potentially large sampling errors, but the differences on centralist nationalism are large and consistent.

Muslims were 11 per cent less willing than the Orthodox to make knowledge of the Russia language a condition for voting and 23 per cent less willing to make it compulsory in schools. They were 21 per cent less likely than the Orthodox to agree that it was 'a mistake to break up a large country just to give each national or ethnic group its own state', 23 per cent more in favour of regional autonomy, and 29 per cent more willing to support the right of regions to secede from the Russian Federation. So even on our very small sample of Muslims these differences are sufficiently large and consistent as to justify the conclusion that although Muslims resented the increasing influence of the West, they were particularly opposed to Russian nationalism when directed against the near abroad, against minority languages, or against minority regions within the Federation.

Russia: conclusions

Land, language, religion and national identity had only modest impacts on political values within the Russian Federation. Differences were detectable, and plausible in direction though usually quite small. Where the differences were larger they applied to very small groups such as those members of minority nationalities who lived in autonomous areas, or who were religious Muslims.

Differences between European and Asiatic Russia, by contrast, were slight. We have found a remarkable uniformity of political values despite the vast territory of the Russian Federation. That monument beside the railway tracks in the Urals has no significance in terms of political culture despite the fact that it marks the division between two continents.

Of course, differences of interest and identity can lead to political conflict even between people whose political values are very similar. The American War of Independence was not prompted by a conflict of values, but by a conflict of interest and identity. And even very small groups of people – like the Chechens – can, through extreme violence, have an impact upon the political life of a country which is out of all proportion to their size. We have been investigating the uniformity or diversity of political values, not the prospects for civil peace. The two are quite different.

UKRAINE

Geographically, Ukraine is much smaller than the Russian Federation – yet far more divided by land, language, culture and nationality. Its present borders date only from 1954, its capital city only from 1934.

The Crimea was acquired in 1954 from the Russian Federation. Only a little earlier, in 1945, Ukraine acquired six Western oblasts[15] from inter-war Poland, one from inter-war Czechoslovakia, two from inter-war Romania and the existing Odessa Oblast was expanded to take in part of inter-war Moldova. Paradoxically, most people in these recently acquired western oblasts claimed Ukrainian nationality while a large minority in the older established eastern oblasts claimed Russian nationality, and an actual majority in several densely populated eastern oblasts – and in the capital city of Kyiv – preferred to speak Russian rather than Ukrainian when they were at home.

Ukraine's frontiers have never been stable for long, and its state boundaries do not coincide with the extent of Ukrainian national identity, the use of the Ukrainian language, or affiliation with the Ukrainian Orthodox Church. Large numbers of people who claim Ukrainian nationality and/or speak the Ukrainian language live across the state borders in southern Belorussia and western Russia, at least as far as Rostov-on-Don and Krasnodar[16] – or even, according to some Ukrainian nationalists, as far as Stavropol, Mozdok and the gates of

Volgograd.[17] Conversely very large numbers of people who live within Ukraine, and are citizens of that state, claim Russian nationality and speak the Russian language. In addition there are small but locally numerous concentrations of Crimean Tatars in Krym (Crimea) and of Moldovans in Chernivtsy.

While most religious people in Ukraine are Orthodox Christians of one sort or another, there is a local concentration of Catholics in the former Polish oblasts, especially around Lviv. Before the Nazi conquest, Jews were numerous in western and mid Ukraine, though less so in the eastern oblasts, but now they are very few in number and scattered across Ukraine.

Bearing in mind that we have a total sample of only one thousand interviews we divided them into those living to the east and west of Kyiv, allocating the Kyiv oblast to the west and Kyiv city to the east. This division provides sufficiently large samples in each region to permit further sub-division where appropriate – just under 400 interviews in the west and just over 600 in the east. Using this definition of east and west Ukraine we found that only 10 per cent in the west, but 36 per cent in the east, claimed Russian nationality; while only 18 per cent in the west, but 68 per cent in the east, spoke Russian as their principal language at home. As for religion, 42 per cent in the west, but only 11 per cent in the east, identified with the Ukrainian Orthodox Church; while conversely, only 13 per cent in the west, but 24 per cent in the east, identified with the Russian Orthodox Church. Equally striking: only 16 per cent in the west, but 43 per cent in the east, claimed to be irreligious. About 11 per cent in the west were Catholic (including both the Latin and Greek rite Catholics together), but almost none in the east. In fact, 54 per cent of those interviewed in the Lviv oblast were Catholics but very few elsewhere, even in other parts of western Ukraine. We also found 16 per cent were Muslim in Krym (Crimea) but none elsewhere.

One obvious feature of these different levels of Ukrainian identification – through nationality, language and religion – is that many people claimed Ukrainian nationality while speaking the Russian language at home. Very few did the reverse. Almost half (but not quite) the Ukrainian population both claimed Ukrainian nationality and spoke the Ukrainian language at home; about a quarter claimed Russian nationality and spoke the Russian language at home; and about a quarter claimed Ukrainian nationality but spoke Russian at home. So in terms of language, Ukraine was split almost equally between Russian and Ukrainian speakers; but in terms of freely-chosen self-conscious national identification, Ukraine was about two-thirds Ukrainian and only a quarter Russian.

Outsiders such as the Polish-American Brzezinski warned that disaffection amongst the Russian minority in Ukraine might 'tempt the Kremlin to apply pressure to Ukraine, first to obtain for this minority a special status and then perhaps even to exploit its grievances as the leverage for destabilising Ukrainian statehood.'[18] Certainly nationalism and separatism can be stimulated from outside. Superpowers can destabilise their neighbours, as Brzezinski would know only too well. But Russians and Ukrainians got on remarkably well in newly independent Ukraine. The existence of a large number of Russian speakers who claimed Ukrainian nationality helped to bridge the Russian–Ukrainian divide.[19] Times–Mirror surveys in 1991 showed that over 90 per cent of people in Ukraine viewed Russians favourably, in sharp contrast to their attitudes towards Armenians, Azerbaijanis, Georgians, and even Jews.[20] Conversely, Golovakha, Panina and Churilov showed that, in 1992, Russian identifiers living in Ukraine were as ready to accept a close family relationship through marriage with Ukrainians as with Russians; Ukrainian identifiers in Ukraine did not reciprocate to the same degree – they were much less willing to accept a family connection with Russians than with Ukrainians, but nonetheless much more willing to accept Russians than they were to accept Poles, Americans, or even Ukrainians living abroad.[21] Churilov and Koshechkina's focus groups suggested that despite well articulated Ukrainian resentments, 'the idea of violent civil conflict inside Ukraine seemed unnatural' in the early 1990s, and 'most people also found violence between Ukraine and Russia as states hard to image.'[22]

Churilov and Koshechkina also asked rhetorically: 'who was the minority in Ukraine' in the early 1990s? Statistically, Ukrainian identifiers formed the majority, but roughly as many in Ukraine spoke Russian as Ukrainian when at home, and Churilov and Koshechkina's focus group studies suggested that 'from an emotional viewpoint many *Ukrainians* feel that *their* position is really the "minority" position in society': the Russian language predominated in the cities, 'for generations, everyone in Ukraine has believed that to be a "well-educated person" meant to speak fluent Russian . . . [and in the early 1990s] three-quarters of the Ukrainian population regularly watched the main television channel of Russia, called Ostankino . . . several leading Russian [i.e. published in Russia, not just in the Russian language] newspapers were amongst the most widely read newspapers in Ukraine . . . [so that] Ukrainians were presented on a daily basis with the Russian point of view on events.'[23]

A 1989 Ukrainian language law called for the 'sole use of Ukrainian as the language of administration in all regions of Ukraine by the mid–1990s' but 'in practice [it was] not implemented [and] a July 1992 law on national minorities allowed for the official use of non-Ukrainian languages . . . where a certain national minority constitutes the majority of the population.'[24] Language problems were further eased by the fact that bilingualism meant that four out of five Russians in Ukraine claimed to be able to converse in Ukrainian, though only half that number claimed to be fluent in it.[25]

We shall be particularly interested to see how land, language and nationality combined and interacted to affect political values. Did the Russian speaking people with Ukrainian nationality side with those who were ethno-linguistic Ukrainians or with those who were ethno-linguistic Russians? Russian speaking

Ukrainian-identifiers held the balance of numbers and, in a democratic system, that should mean they held the balance of power.

Land in Ukraine

Compared to those who lived to the east of Kyiv, those who lived to the west were 13 per cent more likely to cite the present as the best time for Ukraine – mainly at the expense of the Brezhnev era but also at the expense of Stalin's time.

In terms of values, the west was 9 per cent more (Ukrainian) nationalist but hardly differed from the east on liberal or populist values, or attitudes towards elections and parties. Surprisingly perhaps, the west was also 8 per cent more committed to socialist values than the east.

Table 15.6: Ukraine – values by region

	Socialist	Nationalist	Liberal	Populist	Pro-elections	Pro-parties
	%	%	%	%	%	%
Region:						
west of Kyiv	81	15	64	64	50	14
east of Kyiv	73	6	68	64	45	11

Notes: Entries are the percentage who score strictly above the mid-point on each scale. In this chapter, unlike earlier chapters, we have divided Ukraine into just two parts. Interviews were conducted in the following oblasts:
West of Kyiv – Lviv, Volynia, Rivne, Chernivitsy, Vinnystsia, and Kyiv oblasts – the *maximum* percentage claiming Russian nationality in these areas was 15 per cent in Kyiv oblast.
East of Kyiv – Kharkiv, Donetsk, Dnipropetrovsk, Zaporizhzhia, Kherson, and Kirovohrad oblasts, Krym (Crimea), and Kyiv city – the *minimum* percentage claiming Russian nationality was 20 per cent in Kirovohrad.

Nationality and language in Ukraine

Judged by their self-assigned nationality,[26] Ukrainian identifiers were 7 per cent more socialist than Russian identifiers, 5 per cent more nationalist and 12 per cent less liberal. But judged by the language they used at home, Ukrainian speakers were 16 per cent more socialist than Russian speakers, 11 per cent more nationalist, and 17 per cent less liberal.

The differences all ran in the same directions whether people were categorised by nationality or language, but language clearly made more difference than nationality. Significantly, the differences were larger on liberal values than on nationalist values.

Table 15.7:   Ukraine – values by national identity and language

	Socialist	Nationalist	Liberal	Populist	Pro-elections	Pro-parties
	%	%	%	%	%	%
National identity:						
Ukrainian	78	11	63	64	47	13
Russian	71	6	75	65	45	12
Language:						
Ukrainian	84	15	58	63	47	13
Russian	68	4	75	66	46	12

Notes: Entries are the percentage who score strictly above the mid-point on each scale.

We can usefully divide most people who lived in Ukraine into three groups: ethno-linguistic Ukrainians, ethno-linguistic Russians, and Russian speaking ethnic Ukrainians.[27] Using this classification, ethno-linguistic Russians and Ukrainians differed by 27 per cent on whether to put the 'unity and independence of Ukraine' above 'equal rights for all who live in Ukraine'; by 23 per cent on respect for authority and by a huge 46 per cent on whether 'whatever offends the majority should be made illegal', with the Russians consistently the more liberal. On each of these issues the attitudes of Russian speaking Ukrainians were about half way between those of the ethno-linguistic Ukrainians and Russians.[28]

If we focus upon the three separate aspects of Ukrainian nationalist values – external nationalism, centralism, and (Ukrainian) cultural conformity – then it is clear that Ukrainians differed most from Russians on cultural conformity and least on external nationalism. And on all three aspects of Ukrainian nationalist values, language made more difference than national identity. Within Ukraine, those who combined Ukrainian nationality and language were 9 per cent more externally nationalist than those who combined Russian nationality and language, 13 per cent more centralist, and 19 per cent more insistent on cultural conformity. Ethno-linguistic Ukrainians and Russians differed by 17 per cent on whether speaking the state language should be a condition for voting rights, and by a massive 47 per cent on whether all schools should teach all subjects in Ukrainian.[29] On both aspects of internal nationalism (but not on external nationalism), those who spoke Russian but claimed Ukrainian nationality sided far more with the ethno-linguistic Russians than with the ethno-linguistic Ukrainians.

Sometimes intellectuals are described as 'keepers of the culture'; thus, although intellectuals may generally be more liberal, cosmopolitan and less nationalist than the rest of the population, at times of nationalist ferment, intellectuals may perhaps be the most nationalist of all. Amongst the people of Ukraine as a whole, university graduates were less nationalist than the least educated on nationalist values and, indeed, on each aspect of nationalist values. But Russian speakers were over twice as likely as Ukrainian speakers to be university graduates. If we look at the ethno-linguistic Russians and Ukrainians separately we can see whether, for example, the liberal cosmopolitanism of Russian graduates simply overwhelmed the nationalism of Ukrainian graduates.

Amongst both the ethno-linguistic Russians and the ethno-linguistic Ukrainians, graduates were about 13 per cent less centralist, but only 3 per cent less externally nationalist, and actually 5 per cent *more* culturally conformist. The striking thing is that education not only made Ukrainian graduates a little more inclined than the least educated Ukrainians to impose the state language, it also made Russian graduates a little more willing than the least educated Russians to accept it. But because so many graduates were Russian, graduates as a whole were slightly less inclined to impose the state language, even though graduates within both the Russian and Ukrainian ethno-linguistic groups were more willing to do so. The patterns were weak and complex. But their significance is that they were *not* strong and simple: it was *not* the case that education polarised the people of Ukraine even on questions of cultural nationalism.

Table 15.8: Ukraine – nationalist values by national identity and language

	External (Ukrainian) nationalist	Centralist (Ukrainian) nationalist	Cultural (Ukrainian) nationalist
	%	%	%
National identity:			
Ukrainian	13	34	14
Russian	7	24	2
Language:			
Ukrainian	15	37	19
Russian	9	24	2
Combinations:			
Ukrainian national identity and language	15	37	20
Ukrainian identity but Russian language	10	25	4
Russian national identity and language	6	23	1

Notes: Entries are the percentage who score strictly above the mid-point on each scale. Only 19 people, 2 per cent, combined a Russian national identity with speaking the Ukrainian language at home.

The interaction of land and language in Ukraine

Both to the west and to the east of Kyiv, Russian speakers were less nationalist than Ukrainian speakers, but the polarisation of opinion on nationalist values between them varied across the regions.[30]

Russian speakers were almost completely opposed to Ukrainian cultural nationalism (discrimination against the Russian language) no matter where they lived. By contrast, only 11 per cent of Ukrainian speakers who lived to the east of Kyiv, but 24 per cent of those who lived to the west were cultural nationalists.[31] Conversely, the division between Russian and Ukrainian speakers on centralist nationalism (resistance to regional autonomy or separation) was far greater in east Ukraine than in the west, as much because Russian speakers in east Ukraine were particularly favourable to regional autonomy as because Ukrainian speakers in east Ukraine were particularly opposed to it. So ethno-linguistic polarisation was greater in the west on cultural issues, but greater in the east on centralist issues. Being surrounded by fellow ethnics amplified the tendency of Ukrainians towards cultural nationalism in the west, and of Russians towards secessionist tendencies in the east.

Table 15.9:   Ukraine – internal nationalist values by region and language

| | *(Ukrainian) values* *centralist nationalist* | | *(Ukrainian) values* *cultural nationalist* | |
	West of Kyiv	*East of Kyiv*	*West of Kyiv*	*East of Kyiv*
	%	%	%	%
Language:				
Ukrainian	35	41	24	11
Russian	30	23	2	2
Difference:	+5	+18	+22	+9

Note: Entries are the percentage who score strictly above the mid-point on each scale.

Religious sects in Ukraine

Sect, language and nationality correlated strongly in Ukraine. Most religious people were Orthodox, of one kind or another, but they were divided between Russian and Ukrainian Orthodox. There were no real differences of doctrine or liturgy between the various strands of Orthodoxy in Ukraine: the differences were almost entirely about their degree of autonomy or independence from the Moscow Patriarch. For centuries, in the lands of Orthodox Christianity, state independence – originally from the Byzantine Empire – had been asserted by declaring a local patriarch to be the equal of the ecumenical patriarch of Constantinople, and ultimately obtaining recognition from the ecumenical patriarch himself.[32] Conversely, the subordination of one patriarch to another had been closely tied to the subordination of one state to another. In the aftermath of state independence in 1991, there were acrimonious disputes between rival Ukrainian patriarchs, one owing allegiance to the Moscow patri-arch, another backed by the state President Kravchuk, and a third residing in

America – complete with tabloid style allegations of sexual misbehaviour.[33] Not surprisingly, our interviewers reported that when people were asked whether they were Russian or Ukrainian Orthodox some replied that although they were certain that they themselves were Orthodox, they were unsure whether their parish was Russian or Ukrainian Orthodox. In fact, the Orthodox divided sharply along linguistic lines in their self-assigned religious identities: 73 per cent of the Ukrainian Orthodox spoke Ukrainian at home, while 60 per cent of the Russian Orthodox spoke Russian at home though two-thirds of them claimed Ukrainian nationality. Even the very small religious sects were distinguished by language: 97 per cent of the Catholics in our survey spoke Ukrainian and 90 per cent of the Muslims spoke Tatar.

Table 15.10:   Ukraine – nationalist values by religion

	External (*Ukrainian*) *nationalist*	*Centralist* (*Ukrainian*) *nationalist*	*Cultural* (*Ukrainian*) *nationalist*
	%	%	%
Religion:			
Catholic (including Uniate)	15	51	56
Ukrainian Orthodox	15	36	14
Russian Orthodox	9	26	5
Other Christian	4	26	5

Notes: Entries are the percentage who score strictly above the mid-point on each scale. We had very few Catholics in our sample and these results are subject to potentially large sampling errors, but the differences on cultural and centralist nationalism are large and consistent.

On all three aspects of nationalist values, but particularly on internal nationalist values, the Ukrainian Orthodox were more nationalist than the Russian Orthodox. However the nationalism of the Ukrainian Orthodox paled by comparison with that of the very few Catholics (Latin or Greek rite) that we encountered in Ukraine. Few though they were, they resembled the Muslims within the Russian Federation in their political extremism. So just as even a very small sample was sufficient to show that Muslims in Russia were quite unusually *opposed* to state centralism, a very small sample of Catholics in Ukraine was sufficient to reveal their unusual *support* for state centralism. Compared to the Russian Orthodox, Catholics in Ukraine were 25 per cent more centralist, and 51 per cent more intent on imposing conformity to the state language. Ukrainian Catholics were, in fact, far more nationalist than even the Ukrainian Orthodox. No one would suggest that their nationalism derived directly from their faith, but Catholics had always been harassed by the Tsars or their communist successors in Moscow,[34] and Ukrainian nationalism was directed against Russia and all things Russian. The Russian Orthodox Church came into existence as an imperial church of the Muscovite Tsars, to the great dismay of the ecumenical patriarch in Constantinople, and those who stayed outside it were always natural opponents of Moscow.

Support for independence, secession and irredentism in Ukraine

After centuries of rule by Russian Tsars and Soviet Communists, the independence of Ukraine was at least debatable, and was debated. Churilov and Koshechkina found that fear of a Russian 'Anschluss' rose after Zhirinovsky's success in the December 1993 Russian elections, and 'rose again after the Russian attack on Chechnya, beginning in December 1994.'[35] Melvin notes that 'at the end of 1993 the question of whether Ukraine could survive as an independent state was being asked more and more frequently' though he felt that 'by mid–1995, despite continuing chronic problems, especially economic, Ukraine seemed unlikely to disintegrate and the prospect of ethnic conflict had receded.'[36] There were clearly waves of concern and troughs of complacency.

Moreover, since, irrespective of its degree of independence or autonomy, Ukraine's borders have seldom remained fixed for long, the question of whether a region should be allowed to secede from Ukraine was also an important and live issue. The present borders now extend almost as far westwards as even the most nationalist could claim as 'ethnically Ukrainian' but not nearly as far eastwards, not by hundreds of miles. Churilov and Koshechkina's focus groups indicated that while 'people were well aware that Russia, Poland and Romania could make claims on Ukrainian territory' they were also 'keenly aware that Ukraine could make claims on some land presently held by Russia and land held by neighbours to the west.'[37] That is not a practical issue at present. Ukraine has enough problems with Russia without claiming huge tracts of ethnically Ukrainian territory from it. Nonetheless, some Ukrainians – like most Hungarians – might feel that some territory in their near abroad should belong to their state, even if they were unwilling to do anything about it, and were certainly opposed to the use of military threats. So it makes sense to look at these three issues – of independence, secession and irredentism – together because they all reflect opinions about state sovereignty and integrity, whether the state should exist at all, and whether it should be larger or smaller.

Attitudes to independence in Ukraine were very different from those in the Baltic states. In 1990, before the collapse of the Soviet Union a survey of Russia, Ukraine and Lithuania by Hesli and Barkan found that 'non-titular groups (Russians living in Ukraine, and Ukrainians living in the RSFSR) were even more supportive of independence than their indigenous counterparts.'[38] That was certainly not true in their Lithuanian survey. Similarly, while Wilson feared that 'militant separatism, with a Ukrainian army becoming a real threat to stability is too awesome to contemplate', what he actually observed in Kyiv on the eve of the December 1991 Referendum on independence from the USSR was that 'the contrast with popular feeling before Baltic independence is staggering. There are no flags; no slogans on the walls... following the Soviet demise a "yes" vote is taken for granted.'[39]

We asked people to tell us how they had voted in that December 1991 referendum on Ukraine's independence from the USSR. Then 90 per cent had voted for independence, a percentage that varied remarkably little across different areas of Ukraine prompting Fukuyama to conclude that 'the issue for most people was not mindless nationalism but a desire to get away from the old hated communist centre – in other words, political freedom [in its widest sense, not just national freedom] as much as ethnicity.'[40] Of course, people might have changed their minds in the two years that elapsed between that vote and our interviews at the end of 1993. Churilov and Koshechkina point out that 'the level of nationalist feelings, and of national consciousness' can vary: they were probably 'at their height around the time, late in 1991, that Ukraine became independent, and have since declined... [though] a fresh wave of nationalist feelings could be triggered off by certain dramatic events.'[41] Usually, people tend to adjust their memories somewhat, in order to bring them closer to their current opinions. For our present purpose, that would be no bad thing. Our purpose was not so much to analyse the 1991 referendum itself as to use answers to our question about it to see which groups within Ukraine were more or less favourable to their state's independence.

Of those who remembered their vote, 83 per cent said they had voted for Ukraine's independence – a little less than the 90 per cent who had actually done so, but perhaps a better indicator of relative support for independence in 1993 than their actual votes in 1991. The difference between 1993 memories and actual 1991 votes is illuminating. The 95 per cent in west Ukraine who, in 1993, remembered voting 'yes' reflected the actual figures in 1991; but the 74 per cent in east Ukraine who, in 1993, remembered voting 'yes' was about 10 per cent lower than the numbers who actually did so in 1991. All of the 'memory adjustments' seem to have taken place in the east.[42]

In our survey, those who lived to the west of Kyiv were 21 per cent more favourable to independence than those who lived to the east: the percentages in favour ran from 53 per cent in Krym (Crimea) and 62 per cent in Donetsk to 100 per cent in Lviv. There was a difference of 27 per cent between those who claimed Russian nationality and spoke Russian on the one hand, and those who claimed Ukrainian nationality and spoke Ukrainian on the other. Unusually, the Russian-speaking Ukrainian-identifiers were midway between the ethno-linguistic Russians and ethno-linguistic Ukrainians, instead of siding with the Russians as they did on cultural issues. But as usual, Catholics proved the most solidly nationalist, 100 per cent for independence while the difference between the Russian and Ukrainian Orthodox was only 13 per cent.

Table 15.11:   Ukraine – independence, secession, and irredentism

	Independence: Remember voting favour of in independence at the Dec 1991 referendum	Secession: Accept the right of regions to secede from Ukraine	Irredentism: Claim parts of neighbours for Ukraine
	%	%	%
Ukraine average:	83	38	30
Region:			
West of Kyiv	95	22	34
East of Kyiv	74	48	27
Oblasts:			
Crimea	53	82	19
Kharkiv	68	77	23
Donetsk	62	70	26
Chernivtsi	93	28	42
Lviv	100	3	67
National identity and language:			
Ukrainian id and lang.	93	23	41
Uk id. but Russian lang.	79	49	21
Russian id. and lang.	66	53	15
Language alone:			
Ukrainian	93	23	42
Russian	72	51	19
Religion:			
Catholic & Uniate	100	0	67
Ukrainian Orthodox	92	21	37
Russian Orthodox	79	51	24
Other Christian	75	41	21

Notes: 'Don't Knows', 'Can't decide' etc. excluded from calculation of these percentage. Sample sizes in individual oblasts, and of Catholics, are very small and random sampling errors potentially large.

At 48 per cent, support for the right of a region to secede from Ukraine was twice as high in east Ukraine as in the west. It ranged from 82 per cent in Krym (Crimea) and 77 per cent in Kharkiv right down to a mere 3 per cent in Lviv. Those who were both Russian identifiers and Russian speakers were 30 per cent more likely than ethno-linguistic Ukrainians to support the right of secession; and Russian-speaking Ukrainian-identifiers were almost indistinguishable from the ethno-linguistic Russians. Over half the Russian Orthodox, but not one of the Catholics we interviewed, and only 21 per cent of the Ukrainian Orthodox, supported the right of a region to secede.

Conversely, irredentist claims on neighbouring territory ran from a low of 19 per cent in Krym (Crimea) right up to 67 per cent in Lviv. They were almost three times as high amongst the ethno-linguistic Ukrainians as amongst the ethno-linguistic Russians. Once again the Russian-speaking Ukrainian-identifiers sided with other Russian speakers. Irredentist claims were also supported by 67 per cent of Catholics, but by only 37 per cent of the Ukrainian Orthodox, and by only 24 per cent of the Russian Orthodox. And although the bulk of ethnically Ukrainian territory outside Ukraine lay across its eastern border, irredentist support was higher in the west than in the east.

Ukraine: conclusions

Although a continuing belief in communist ideals was expressed by 13 per cent more in the east than in the west, by 8 per cent more Russian identifiers than Ukrainian identifiers, by 7 per cent more Russian speakers than Ukrainian speakers, and by 5 per cent more Russian Orthodox than Ukrainian Orthodox, these patterns seemed to reflect attitudes to nationalist rather than socialist values in Ukraine.

Indeed, we found that while 90 per cent of Catholics in Ukraine said they had never believed in communist ideals, 76 per cent of them scored above the mid-point on our scale of socialist values: it was clearly other aspects of communism that offended them most. When asked what was the worst feature of communism 72 per cent of these Catholics cited the oppression of human rights (compared to just 18 per cent amongst the Russian Orthodox). Less dramatically, Russian speakers were 17 per cent more likely than Ukrainian speakers to cite bureaucracy or corruption as the worst feature of communism, and 6 per cent less likely to cite oppression of human rights. And on the positive side Russian speakers were 11 per cent more likely than Ukrainian speakers to cite 'peace between nationalities' as the best feature of communism and 16 per cent less likely to cite a stable economy or job security.

Land, language, culture and nationality – but especially language – had a large and important impact on nationalist values in Ukraine. On almost every aspect of nationalist values, language had much more influence than nationality – so much so that Russian-speaking Ukrainian-identifiers usually differed only marginally from other Russian speakers. Language, rather than nationality, defined whether religious people would classify themselves as Russian Orthodox or Ukrainian Orthodox. Russian speakers were 21 per cent less likely than Ukrainian speakers to have voted for Ukraine's independence, 28 per cent more likely to support rights of regional secession, and 23 per cent less likely to support Ukrainian irredentist claims on neighbouring territories.

The overriding significance of language meant that there was no majority in Ukraine. The numbers of Russian and Ukrainian speakers were approximately equal and each comprised just under half the population. The notion of a Ukrainian majority and a Russian minority – based upon nationality or religion – is misleading. In terms of the social characteristic that had the greatest impact upon political values, Ukraine was divided between two equal groups, both of which fell just short of a majority. And the 'state language' currently being imposed by law was – albeit by a small margin – just one of two minority languages.

Ethnic nationalism could not provide as secure a basis for the Ukrainian state as it could for the Czech, Hungarian or even Russian states – and to their credit Ukraine's political leaders did not attempt to base citizenship on either language or ethnicityg.[43] Ethnic nationality, which had appeared in old Soviet passports, was conspicuous by its absence from the new Ukraine passport. But civic nationalism, based on citizenship, or simple fear of Moscow centre's tendency towards dictatorship, imperialism, oppression and violence might provide a sufficient basis for an independent but heterogeneous Ukrainian state.

HUNGARY

Looking for ethnic divisions in contemporary Hungary is a bit like trying to split the atom. Hungary is more united than divided by land, by language, by culture and by nationality – a country where irredentist claims on its neighbours were far more significant than the notion of regional secession.

Geographically, Hungary is usually divided into the 'Great Plain' to the east of the Danube and Transdanubia to the west. Socially and politically it makes sense to abstract a third region, centred on the capital Budapest, and straddling the Danube, for post-imperial Hungary is a country unusually dominated by the capital city and its immediate environs.

In total contrast to Russia and Ukraine there are no statistically significant divisions of language or nationality. In our survey we found 97 or 98 per cent in each of our three regions (east, west, and centre) claimed Hungarian nationality. Gypsy was the second largest nationality, though only one per cent in our survey even if something of an underestimate.[44] Over 99 per cent in each region spoke Hungarian. So the only bases left for internal nationalist divisions were religion and region itself.

Overall, we found just over half claimed to be Catholic, about one-fifth claimed to be Protestant and another fifth were irreligious. At start of the century a quarter of Budapest's population were Jews, and the restored Synagogue remains one of the largest and most impressive buildings in the city, but there are few Jews left there now. Catholics were 14 per cent more numerous in the west than in the east, and Protestants were 10 per cent more numerous in the east – where, historically, they had been sheltered from Catholic oppression by the Ottomans. Protestants were particularly numerous around the Debrecen area within east Hungary.

Land and culture in Hungary

In the event, political values did not vary much across regions or religious sects. Indeed, there was a visibly greater difference between the central region around

Budapest on the one hand, and the east and west on the other, than between east and west themselves. That is more of a metropolitan effect than a regional one and we have already dealt with such effects in previous chapters. Similarly on religion, sectarian antagonisms have declined and there was more difference between the political values of the religious and irreligious than between those of Protestants and Catholics.

Table 15.12: Hungary – values by region and religion

	Socialist	Nationalist	Liberal	Populist	Pro-elections	Pro-parties
	%	%	%	%	%	%
Region:						
central	72	17	66	78	67	29
east (Great Plain)	84	11	56	81	56	24
west (Transdanubia)	80	16	67	78	55	23
Religion:						
none	74	10	74	84	66	28
Catholic	81	14	58	78	56	22
Protestant	81	19	60	79	55	27

Notes: Entries are the percentage who score strictly above the mid-point on each scale.

Table 15.13: Hungary – church subsidies by region and religion

		Support state subsidies for:		
	Catholic church	Protestant churches	opera and ballet	parties
	%	%	%	%
Region:				
central	59	57	84	44
east (Great Plain)	61	63	76	41
west (Transdanubia)	58	58	79	41
Religion:				
none	40	37	82	38
Catholic	67	66	79	37
Protestant	63	69	77	31

Notes: 'Don't Knows', 'Can't decide' etc. excluded from calculation of these percentages.

Even when we investigated support for state subsidies to Catholic and Protestant churches we found very little difference between Catholics and Protestants: Catholics were 4 per cent more willing than Protestants to subsidise Catholic Churches, and 3 per cent less willing than Protestants to subsidise Protestant Churches. These differences are reassuringly plausible in their direction but politically insignificant. By contrast the irreligious were 25 to 30 per cent less

willing than the religious to subsidise either Catholic or Protestant churches –
though very slightly *more* willing to subsidise opera, ballet or political parties.

The most striking feature of Hungarian nationalism was the very high percentage of Hungarians who supported the irredentist view that parts of neighbouring countries should really belong to Hungary. It was certainly true that
Hungary had been roughly three times larger than at present in the days of the
Hapsburgs. In Chapter 7 we noted that 60 per cent in Hungary – like 71 per cent
in Russia but no more than 32 per cent elsewhere – took the irredentist line.
That view clearly expressed Hungarian nationalism but it was not confined to
any particular group within Hungary. Support for irredentism was almost the
same in east and west and amongst Catholics and Protestants, though about 15
per cent less amongst the irreligious than the religious.

Table 15.14:   Hungary – irredentism by region and religion

	Hungary should own parts of neighbours
	%
Region:	
central	61
east (Great Plain)	61
west (Transdanubia)	57
Religion:	
none	50
Catholic	62
Protestant	67

Notes: 'Don't Knows', 'Can't decide' etc. excluded from calculation of these percentages.

Hungary: conclusions

Land, language, and nationality were clearly important for Hungarians in one
sense: the cut-down, reduced extent of their country's territory, and their
homogeneity in terms of language and national identity, encouraged a majority
of them to express at least a moral claim to neighbouring territory. These
factors united Hungarians and divided them from their neighbours, but they
did not divide the people of Hungary from one another. Hungary, unlike
Ukraine, was an ethnic state in the 1990s.

SLOVAKIA

Though linked together from 1918 to 1992 (except for an interlude under Nazi
domination during the Second World War) the Czech and Slovak lands had a

very different historical experience for centuries before 1918. The Slovaks were ruled by Magyars from the tenth to the twentieth century. For two centuries the Hungarian capital was located in what is now the capital of Slovakia, Bratislava. Later, in the nineteenth century, Slovakia was ruled from Budapest while the Czech and Moravian lands were ruled from Vienna, and any pressure on the Czechs to adopt German culture against their will was far exceeded by the pressure on Slovaks to accept Magyar culture. According to Schlesinger 'the Slovaks, like all the non-Magyar nationalities of Hungary proper, [were] left as illiterate as possible, and denied an intelligentsia of their own, apart from the lower clergy...so, while the Czechs, in struggling to overcome the Hapsburgs, remembered their Hussite past, any Slovak national feeling was connected with the [Catholic] Church, which was the only place outside the home where Slovak could be spoken, and the only substitute for the educational facilities denied by the Magyar State. ...The Slovaks...had no middle class, and almost no political life of their own.'[45] After 1992, the Czechs celebrated an annual national holiday in honour of Hus and the Slovaks an annual national holiday in honour of Saints Cyril and Methodius, while the Catholic Church tried, with some success, to claim these Orthodox and Protestant luminaries as its own. More specifically, Slovakia's distinctive historical experience under the Hungarians left a visible imprint on their political attitudes in the 1990s, which were focused on religion, language and national identity as much as Czech attitudes were focused on repudiation of communism and support for economic reform.

Between the wars Slovakia was joined to the former Austrian provinces of Bohemia and Moravia to constitute the new Czechoslovakia. Under German threats the eastmost province of Slovakia was given autonomy as Carpatho-Ukraine in September 1938 but the southern part of Slovakia – including the south of Carpatho-Ukraine was transferred to Hungary the next month. Five months later Hungary took the rest of Carpatho-Ukraine. Under German occupation the parts of Slovakia that had not been seized by Hungary were separated from the Bohemian and Moravian lands and formed into the supposedly independent state of Slovakia headed by a Catholic priest, Father Tiso. After the war, Hungary lost all her recent acquisitions, Carpatho-Ukraine went to Ukraine, and the rest of interwar Slovakia – including those parts taken by Hungary in 1938 – were once more joined with the Bohemian and Moravian lands in a new, slightly smaller Czechoslovakia.

At the end of 1992 the 'velvet divorce', which suited the pride of the Slovaks and the pockets of the Czechs, transformed Slovakia into a genuinely independent state for the first time. It had few claims against the new Czech Republic but it had lost territory to Ukraine and it had a significant minority of Hungarians living in the south. On the first day of independence, Slovak Prime Minister Meciar declared that 'differences between people must never be placed above the interests of the whole...[and] Hungary should first look towards how it treats its Slovak minority before criticising other countries.'[46] There were some Baltic tendencies in the new Slovak Republic. More generally, Eyal claimed that 'Hungary's neighbours quickly realised that taunting their Hungarian minorities is not only electorally profitable but also fairly safe'[47] – at least in the short term, though he worried about how long Hungary's patience would last.

We have retained the conventional division of Slovakia into four parts: the capital Bratislava, which is located right on the western border of the state, plus west, mid, and east Slovakia. The term 'west Slovakia' is slightly misleading: because of Slovakia's shape, west Slovakia is the most southerly region, and the one closest to Budapest. Almost two-thirds of the Hungarian minority live in this region.

In our survey, 11 per cent in Slovakia claimed Hungarian nationality and 11 per cent said they spoke the Hungarian language as their main language at home. And unlike the situation in Ukraine, the correlation between nationality and language was not only extremely high but also symmetric: 88 per cent of those who claimed Hungarian nationality spoke that language at home; and 85 per cent of those who spoke the Hungarian language at home, claimed that nationality. Our sample in Slovakia was small – only 665 interviews. On such a small sample, though probably on a large one too, we cannot usefully distinguish between language and nationality for the Hungarian minority within Slovakia: they were simply Hungarian. Within the different regions, Hungarian speakers made up 23 per cent in west Slovakia, 10 per cent in east Slovakia and 4 per cent in both mid Slovakia and Bratislava.

Although, on our figures, 14 or 15 per cent of the Hungarians (however defined) were Protestants compared to only 5 per cent of those who either claimed Slovak nationality or spoke the Slovak language, both Hungarians and Slovaks were overwhelmingly Catholic: Slovaks were 70 per cent Catholic, those who claimed Hungarian nationality were 68 per cent Catholic, and those whose main language was Hungarian were 65 per cent Catholic. Protestants made up over 7 per cent of both West and East Slovakia though only one per cent in Bratislava. But the most obvious pattern linking religion and region was the monotonic increase in the percentage irreligious from 14 per cent in the east, through 16 in mid Slovakia to 21 in the west and 25 per cent in Bratislava on the western border.

Land in Slovakia

Differences between east and west Slovakia never exceeded 6 per cent on any of our composite scales of political values and were typically about 4 per cent. Those who lived in Bratislava differed more: they were the least socialist, the most nationalist, the most liberal, and the most favourable to elections and parties – but all of that hints more at metropolitan influence than purely regional influence.

Table 15.15:   Slovakia – values by region

	Socialist	Nationalist	Liberal	Populist	Pro-elections	Pro-parties
	%	%	%	%	%	%
Region:						
Bratislava	62	21	86	58	85	39
west	74	17	78	62	72	31
mid	84	24	69	55	68	25
east	80	21	73	64	76	34

Note: Entries are the percentage who score strictly above the mid-point on each scale.

Nationality and language in Slovakia

Hungarians, however defined, were about 18 per cent less (Slovakian) nationalist compared to ethnic Slovaks, 17 per cent more liberal, 15 per cent more populist, but slightly less favourable to elections, though more favourable to parties. This is the combination of tendencies typical of a fearful minority – emphasising liberal rights but fearing the majority's weight in elections – except that the minority in Slovakia, unlike the minorities in Russia for example, had a party that existed exclusively to represent them.

Table 15.16:   Slovakia – values by national identity, language and religion

	Socialist	Nationalist	Liberal	Populist	Pro-elections	Pro-parties
	%	%	%	%	%	%
National identity:						
Slovak	79	23	72	57	74	30
Hungarian	71	5	90	76	69	33
Language:						
Slovak	79	23	73	59	74	30
Hungarian	72	6	86	70	66	34
Religion:						
Catholic	79	21	71	58	74	30
Protestant	80	18	80	63	75	39

Note: Entries are the percentage who score strictly above the mid-point on each scale.

Ethnic Hungarians differed from ethnic Slovaks by about 14 per cent on external nationalism and centralism – slightly more if categorised by national identity than if categorised by language. But they differed by about 37 per cent on cultural conformity – this time very slightly more if categorised by language than if categorised by national identity.

Table 15.17:   Slovakia – nationalist values by national identity and language

	External (Slovak) nationalist	Centralist (Slovak) nationalist	Cultural (Slovak) nationalist
	%	%	%
National identity:			
Slovak	20	25	39
Hungarian	4	9	3
Language:			
Slovak	19	25	39
Hungarian	7	13	1

Note: Entries are the percentage who score strictly above the mid-point on each scale.

On some individual questions about nationalist issues, the differences were even greater. Hungarian identifiers gave 29 per cent more support than Slovaks to the right of secession, and 29 per cent less to irredentist claims on neighbouring countries; they were 29 per cent more opposed to making the Slovak language a condition for voting, and 71 per cent more opposed to its imposition in all schools. These were live issues in Slovakia. So there was also a 28 per cent difference between ethnic Slovaks and ethnic Hungarians in their perceptions of whether human rights in Slovakia were respected more by the present government than by the communist regime though, on balance, ethnic Hungarians still favoured the new regime over the old even on human rights issues.

Table 15.18:   Slovakia – nationalist issues by national identity and language

	Support right of regions to secede	Slovakia should own parts of neighbours	Only Slovak speakers to have votes	All schools to teach all subjects in Slovak language	Human rights are respected more now than under the communist regime
	%	%	%	%	%
National identity:					
Slovak	17	35	33	74	86
Hungarian	46	6	4	3	58
Language:					
Slovak	16	35	33	74	85
Hungarian	44	9	3	4	67

Notes: 'Don't Knows', 'Can't decide' etc. excluded from calculation of these percentages.

Religious sects in Slovakia

Within the former Czechoslovakia there were significant religious differences between the free-thinking Bohemians and the overwhelmingly Catholic Slovaks, but the 'velvet divorce' transformed that into a division between states. The puppet state of Slovakia during the war was known as a Catholic state and was headed by a priest. And even the new Slovakia was so overwhelmingly Catholic that there was little potential for sectarian differences. That also meant we had so few Protestants in our sample (only 40 people) that they cannot provide very statistically reliable information on Protestant opinion in Slovakia.

Nonetheless, Catholics and Protestants in our sample had strikingly similar political values. They differed more on state subsidies to their respective churches than Catholics and Protestants in Hungary: in Slovakia, Catholics were 19 per cent more favourable than Protestants to state subsidies for the Catholic church, and 9 per cent less favourable than Protestants to state sub-sidies to Protestant churches. But, as in Hungary, the main difference on church subsidies lay between the religious and the irreligious who were 16 per cent less favourable even than Protestants towards Catholic subsidies, and 29 per cent less favourable even than Catholics towards Protestant subsidies.

Table 15.19:   Slovakia – church subsidies by religion

| | *Support state subsidies for:* | | | |
	Catholic church	*Protestant churches*	*opera and ballet*	*parties*
	%	%	%	%
Religion:				
none	14	12	45	18
Catholic	49	41	49	23
Protestant	30	50	50	31

Notes: 'Don't Knows', 'Can't decide' etc. excluded from calculation of these percentages.

Slovakia: conclusions

The only significant ethnic or nationalist division in Slovakia was between the small Hungarian minority and the rest. But the differences between ethnic Hungarians and Slovaks on nationalist values were very large. The Hungarian minority was 29 per cent more willing to support the right of regions to secede from the Slovak state, 29 per cent less willing to support Slovakia's irredentist claims, and up to 71 per cent less willing to accept enforced conformity to Slovakian as a state language.[48] As a typically fearful minority, ethnic

Hungarians also gave above average support to liberal and populist values but not to elections. It was a small but intense minority, with very strong feelings against cultural conformity.

THE CZECH REPUBLIC

By January 1993 the Czech Republic had almost become, like Hungary, an ethnic state – almost, but not quite perhaps, because there had always been a distinction between Bohemia and the rest of the republic. Historically, Bohemia, Moravia, and Silesia were known as the 'lands of the Bohemian Crown'. At the start of this century all three were provinces of Hapsburg Austria. Under the Hapsburgs the educated classes spoke German at least as a second language, and a large minority of all classes considered themselves to be German. According to A.J.P. Taylor's reading of the 1910 census: 'Bohemia had 62 per cent Czechs...Moravia had 70 per cent Czechs [and] Silesia was predominantly German, with a large Polish population.'[49]
After the collapse of the Hapsburg Empire, Czech nationalists succeeded in creating the new state of Czechoslovakia which included not only the Austrian provinces of Bohemia, Moravia and Silesia, but also the Hungarian province of Slovakia. Masaryk's tract advocating and justifying this new state was published in London under a title, *The New Europe*, which has became as popular in the aftermath of the communist collapse as it was in the aftermath of the Hapsburg collapse.[50] Europe, it seems, is ever new – and never new.

On any consistent logic, Czechoslovakia was either unnecessary or undesirable. Czechoslovakia, as Masaryk admitted in *The New Europe*, was itself a miniature version of the Hapsburg Empire – a multi-national rather than an ethnic state, but one whose existence was justified, unlike the Hapsburg Empire's, on ethnic grounds. Masaryk was reduced to asking what would be fairer – 9 million Czechs and Slovaks under German rule, or 3 million Germans under Czechoslovak rule?[51] If ethnic states were unnecessary then there was no need to rearrange the Hapsburg lands along ethnic lines; and, if ethnic states *were* necessary, the new Czechoslovakia with its large German minority, its smaller Hungarian, Ukrainian, Polish and Jewish minorities, and its doubtful combination of Czechs and Slovaks was clearly undesirable.

But tragically, the Czech Republic is now an ethnic state. During the Second World War the German occupying forces murdered most of the Jews. Immediately after the war, the new Czechoslovak government took revenge upon its German minority by expelling them in what are now accepted as conditions of great hardship resulting in many deaths; and the Ukrainian lands were absorbed by the USSR and added to Ukraine. Finally, at the end of 1992, the link with Slovakia was broken.

After that there remained only Bohemia, Moravia and Austrian Silesia – now classified as part of northern Moravia – minus their former German and Jewish minorities. The citizens of the new republic now appeared almost as ethnically homogeneous as in Hungary. So by 1993 we found that 94 per cent of those remaining claimed Czech nationality and 97 per cent spoke Czech at home. About two and a half per cent claimed Slovak nationality and the same number Moravian nationality, though over 11 per cent in southern (i.e. historic) Moravia claimed 'Moravian' nationality and a party called the Society for Moravia and Silesia which advocated autonomous government for the territories of Moravia-Silesia won 22 of the 200 seats in the Czech parliament at the 1990 election, and 14 in 1992.

The great ethnic paradox of inter-war Czechoslovakia had been eliminated by 1993. Another paradox remained, however. The heroic myth of the Czechs centres upon the martyrdom of Jan Hus who challenged the religious authority of Rome and the (much later) defeat of Protestant Czechs by the Catholic Hapsburgs at the Battle of the White Mountain in 1620. In the three decades after that battle 'Bohemia's population fell by 50 per cent... Moravia's by 30 per cent'[52] as the Hapsburgs imposed a reign of Catholic reaction and terror that far exceeded the later horrors of communist rule. Paradoxically, twentieth century Czechs have sought – successfully – to overturn the secular consequences of that Battle, but not its religious consequences. By 1993 the Hapsburg empire had been destroyed and Czechs expressed no regrets or nostalgia for it; yet insofar as they were religious at all they remained overwhelmingly Catholic. One explanation for this paradox lies in the very high percentage of Czechs who rejected religion altogether: 59 per cent in the Czech Republic compared to just 43 per cent even in Russia, 33 per cent in Ukraine, 22 per cent in Hungary and a mere 19 per cent in Slovakia. Czechs were uniquely irreligious and suspicious of 'the church' (see Chapter 5). Although the religious minority in the Czech Republic was overwhelmingly Catholic it was a small minority: only 32 per cent of people in the Czech Republic actually claimed to be Catholic, compared to 70 per cent in Slovakia and 54 per cent in Hungary.

Bohemia and Moravia

In the Czech Republic the only potentially significant nationalist division that remained was focused upon the lands of Bohemia and Moravia, especially South Moravia. But Moravia, even South Moravia, was little different from Bohemia on any of our composite indicators of values except socialism. Socialist values won just over 10 per cent more support in Moravia than in Bohemia. That reflected a greater sense of economic loss in the immediate postcommunist years: 42 per cent in Bohemia, 57 per cent in northern Moravia and 62 per cent in southern Moravia complained that postcommunist economic trends were hurting their families.

Table 15.20:   The Czech Republic – values by region

	Socialist	Nationalist	Liberal	Populist	Pro-elections	Pro-parties
	%	%	%	%	%	%
Region:						
Bohemia	47	13	79	50	86	37
Moravia	57	15	76	52	87	32
South Moravia	59	11	79	56	88	34

Note: Entries are the percentage who score strictly above the mid-point on each scale.

On more specific questions we also found that those who lived in South Moravia were 10 per cent more willing than those who lived in Bohemia to accept the right of regions to secede from the republic, though support for regional autonomy (as distinct from secession) was uniformly high throughout the republic. Understandably, Moravians were also 10 per cent less willing than Bohemians to support state subsidies for opera.

Table 15.21:   The Czech Republic – autonomy, secession and opera by region

	Support greater self-government for regions	Support right of regions to secede from the Republic	Support state subsidies for opera and ballet
	%	%	%
Region:			
Bohemia	90	22	53
Moravia	90	27	43
South Moravia	90	32	43

Note: 'Don't Knows', 'Can't decide' etc. excluded from calculation of these percentages.

Finally, compared to Catholics, the irreligious in the Czech Republic were slightly *more* willing to subsidise opera and 10 per cent *more* willing to subsidise political parties but 20 per cent *less* willing to subsidise the Catholic church – though also 15 per cent *less* willing to subsidise Protestant churches. Given the number of irreligious Czechs, divisions between the religious and irreligious were unusually important in the Czech Republic, but they are not usually considered aspects of ethnicity and nationalism in the same way as sectarian differences. Perhaps they should be.

The Czech Republic: conclusions

Compared to interwar Czechoslovakia, the Czech Republic was so reduced by loss of territory and, additionally, by loss of minority populations, that the only remaining potential for internally divisive nationalism was Moravian resentment against Prague government. But that potential remained unfulfilled. The vast majority of people in Moravia claimed Czech rather than specifically Moravian nationality and their political values remained very close to those of the people in Bohemia. So, in terms of internal divisions, the Czech Republic appeared fairly similar to Hungary.

Table 15.22: The Czech Republic – cultural subsidies by religion

| | Support state subsidies for: | | | |
	Catholic church	Protestant churches	opera and ballet	parties
	%	%	%	%
Religion:				
none	14	13	49	26
Catholic	34	28	47	16

Note: 'Don't Knows', 'Can't decide' etc. excluded from calculation of these percentages.

But with respect to the near abroad, the peoples of Hungary and the Czech Republic were very different. As the Hungarian state was reduced in size it left many ethnic Hungarians beyond its borders. That did not happen with the Czech Republic. For that, or for more imperialist reasons, we found that 60 per cent of people in Hungary took the irredentist view that parts of their neighbours' territory should belong to Hungary; but only 18 per cent in the Czech Republic made similar claims. In that sense, the Czech Republic was a more perfect ethnic state even than Hungary, more perfectly coextensive with its national group, neither larger nor smaller. That made the Czech Republic totally different from Masaryk's state.

LAND, LANGUAGE, CULTURE AND NATIONALITY: COMPARATIVE CONCLUSIONS

Land, that is to say region, was not by itself an important influence upon political values. Self-conscious nationality or language had more influence. But spatial concentrations of national or linguistic groups had an influence that went beyond their numbers: minority nationalities in Russia, and Russian-speaking autonomists or Ukrainian nationalists in Ukraine, adopted unusually strong views when they lived in the supportive environment of a local concentration of their own kind. In that respect, and through that mechanism, land proved an important catalyst in the formation and strengthening of nationalist values.

In the countries we studied, language proved the decisive variable. It had more influence than religion. Many people were irreligious and those that were religious were overwhelmingly Orthodox in Russia and Ukraine, and Catholic in Slovakia and the Czech Republic. Religious Hungarians were divided between Catholics and Protestants but they supported state subsidies for each other's churches and differed little on political values. The Orthodox in Ukraine were split into Russian and Ukrainian Orthodox and their political values differed from each other, but the split itself reflected the places where they lived and the languages they spoke. Divisions between the Orthodox in Ukraine were a reflection rather than a cause of other differences and these other differences would have existed without the religious split. The cultural issues of the 1990s in the countries we studied were about the language to be used in schools, not about the religious doctrine to be taught in them: the medium mattered more than the message.[53]

In Ukraine, where differences of language and nationality were sufficiently extensive and sufficiently uncorrelated to allow us to test their relative influence, we found that language was also a more important source of division than self-conscious nationality. Those who spoke Russian, but claimed Ukrainian nationality, generally sided with those who were Russian on both counts rather than with those who were Ukrainian on both counts. Crucially that meant there was no majority in the nationalist politics of Ukraine since the two language groups were equal in size and both of them were just short of a majority. It also meant that the state language adopted by Ukraine was *not* the language of the majority: no such language existed. Within Slovakia the Hungarian minority was so small, and the correlation between speaking Hungarian and feeling Hungarian was so high that we could hardly distinguish between the two. However, self-conscious nationality seemed to have very slightly more influence than language upon political values – and certainly no less. In Russia also, minority nationalities who spoke Russian did not clearly take sides on political values either with those who were Russian on both counts or with those who were Russian on neither. Our Ukrainian findings on language versus nationality should not be taken as universal.

Land, language, religion and nationality divided Ukraine and cut off small minorities from the great majority in Slovakia and Russia. But Hungary and the Czech Republic had lost so much population and territory that land, language, religion and nationality could no longer cause any significant divisions within these countries.

In addition, the Czechs had no significant diaspora in neighbouring countries. So for them language and nationality could not enflame irredentist sentiment. But there were significant Russian and Hungarian diaspora in neighbouring countries. So although language and nationality did not cause large scale divisions within these countries, they did encourage irredentist claims on their neighbours.

Finally we need to reiterate the fact that our focus has been on political values and, in this chapter, on the possibility that people in different parts of the state, or in different ethno-linguistic groups within the state, might have different political values. Our focus has *not* been on inter-ethnic tensions as such. It is perfectly possible for two ethnic groups to descend into open warfare while holding the same political values: differences of identity and of interest are sufficient for that, value differences are not necessary. And conversely, it is perfectly possible for two ethnic groups to differ greatly in terms of certain political values – commitment to socialism for example – without inflaming inter-ethnic tensions; though that may not be so true when the political value in question concerns the imposition of cultural conformity. Nonetheless it is important not to confuse an analysis of value differences with an analysis of inter-ethnic tensions.

In the next chapter we turn from the influence on political values of national and ethno-linguistic divisions – so different in different countries, to the more uniform influences of their common experience of communism up to the 1980s, and their common experience of reformist governments in the early 1990s.

16 Political Identifications

Previous chapters have looked at the connections between political values and various aspects of social structure – including class, generation, gender, education, religiosity, a cosmopolitan milieu, and ethnicity. In this chapter we look at the connection between political values and what, by analogy, might be called the 'political structure'.

Just as people may identify with particular classes or religions, they may also identify with political organisations such as parties, governments, or oppositions. As we shall see, these are certainly important for an understanding of the patterns of political values in postcommunist societies. Of much less real importance, but of some related interest, is the way that people in these societies use the ideological labels 'left' and 'right' which are conventional in west European politics. Both in east and west Europe we have reservations about the significance of those labels but there is at least a case to be made that, in some circumstances, they indicate identification with a particular ideological camp and in that sense they are similar to identification with parties or governments. We shall see.

IDENTIFICATION WITH GOVERNMENT AND OPPOSITION

Traditionally, the study of political identification has been interpreted as the study of *party* identification, at least since the classic studies of *The American Voter* by the team at Michigan University in the 1950s.[1] However, even the Michigan team did not regard identification as being exclusively *party* identification: they put forward the concept of party identification quite explicitly on the analogy with religious identification: 'The term "identification" is used quite intentionally to express the assumption that the relationship often involves an extension of ego...an important part of the individual's self-identity...Religious identification is thus generically similar to the concept of political party identification.'[2] And even within the purely political sphere we suggest that there is one important rival focus for identification: government, or in its inverse form, opposition. Indeed, we suggest that government provides a more fundamental basis for political identification even than party. Where parties are weak – as in the United States and in the FSU in the 1990s, for not entirely dissimilar reasons – then the significance of government identification relative to party identification may be correspondingly strong. The fundamental question in such places is not whether party A is preferable to party B, but 'do we want this government to continue, or do we want to throw it out of office.'

Naturally, the answer to that question must take account of the alternatives, but to a lesser extent than the government itself. Even in Britain where there is a long established concept of a well-defined 'loyal opposition', with a leader paid directly by the state for organising opposition, the usual view of political change is that 'oppositions do not win elections, governments lose them.' In the FSU, where the concept of a coherent, well-organised and well-respected 'loyal opposition' has had less time to develop, the government itself is likely to provide a stronger focus for identification and the opposition – if 'the' opposition can be defined at all – is likely to provide less. People may easily reject identification with the government without automatically identifying with 'the opposition'.

Nonetheless, a large majority of people – around 70 per cent across our five countries – were willing to declare themselves as 'supporters' or 'opponents' of 'the present government and what it is trying to do'; and large numbers in both Russia and Ukraine even said that their vote for candidates in the territorial parliamentary constituencies would be influenced by whether the candidate supported or opposed their country's executive president, the actual if not titular head of government.

At the time of our interviews with the general public (December 1993), each country's government could be considered its first postcommunist government – even in Slovakia and the Czech Republic, the governments were still led by those who had taken power in Czechoslovakia after the collapse of communism – with claims to represent the new reformist ideals of democracy and the market economy. Their actions sometimes belied their words however, and it is reasonable for us to ask whether these governments' supporters were measurably more democratic, as well as more market oriented, than their opponents.

Table 16.1:   Economic loss by government support

| | Jail 'new rich' | Family experience economic loss | Family experience economic loss in: | | | | |
			Russia	Ukraine	Czech Rep	Slovakia	Hungary
	%	%	%	%	%	%	%
Govt supporters	10	49	53	74	34	53	48
Neither	11	72	72	87	57	68	73
Govt opponents	21	84	82	91	79	78	82
Diff: Supp–Opp	−11	−35	−29	−17	−45	−25	−34

Notes: 'Don't Knows', 'Can't decide' etc. excluded from calculation of percentages.
Family experience and expectation of economic loss defined as index 'AB' in Chapter 13.

It was certainly true that government supporters generally felt much better than government opponents about their personal experience of economic trends under the postcommunist regime. Government opponents were 35 per cent more likely to claim that the changes were hurting their families and twice as willing to jail the 'new rich'. Government supporters seemed to be surviving economic change much better than government opponents within each and every country, though most so in the Czech Republic and least so in Ukraine.

When asked about the best time for their country, government supporters everywhere except in Ukraine were around 20 per cent more likely than government opponents to choose the postcommunist present. In Russia, government supporters were also 16 per cent more likely than government opponents to choose the days of the Tsars, as well as 20 per cent more likely to choose the present – both at the expense of the Brezhnev era, which they were 34 per cent less likely to choose. In Hungary also, though to a very limited extent, government supporters were more likely to choose the days of the Hapsburgs as well as the present – at the expense of both the Kadar period and the post-Kadar period of reform communism. In the Czech Republic government supporters opted more for the Masaryk period and the present – at the expense of both the Dubcek and Husak periods. In Slovakia, although government supporters were also more inclined than opponents to opt for the present, they did so entirely at the expense of the 1989–92 period of democracy in a united Czechoslovakia.

Table 16.2: Best time for country by government support

| | Difference between percentage of government supporters and opponents who choose time in: | | | | |
	Russia	Ukraine	Czech Rep	Slovakia	Hungary
	%	%	%	%	%
Tsars or Hapsburgs	+16	−3	0	−2	+4
Interwar: Stalin/Masaryk/ Horthy	−6	−3	+8	−1	+3
Independent Slovak state 1939–45	na	na	na	+7	na
Dubcek	na	na	−20	−2	na
Mature communist: Brezhnev/ Husak/Kadar	−34	−3	−17	0	−16
Reform Communist: Gorbachev/ Hungarian	+4	+3	na	na	−12
United democratic Czechoslovakia 1989–92	na	na	+5	−22	na
Present democratic regime since 1992: (since 1989 in Hungary)	+20	+5	+24	+20	+20

Notes: 'Don't Knows', 'Can't decide' etc. excluded from calculation of percentages. 'na' = not applicable.

Ukraine was unique: identification with the government or opposition in Ukraine had relatively little influence on the choice of 'best times for Ukraine' – just as it had relatively little correlation with family experiences of postcom-

Table 16.3: Values by government support

	Socialist	External nationalist	Centralist nationalist	Cultural nationalist	Liberal	Populist	Pro-elections	Pro-parties
Public:	%	%	%	%	%	%	%	%
Govt supporters	63	30	24	32	61	46	84	35
Govt opponents	80	46	31	25	75	77	50	26
Diff: Supp-Opp	-17	-16	-7	+7	-14	-31	+34	+9
MPs:	%	%	%	%	%	%	%	
Govt supporters	19	4	14	12	97	47	98	
Govt opponents	54	48	19	20	97	76	91	
Diff: Supp-Opp	-35	-44	-5	-8	0	-29	+7	

Notes: Entries are the percentage who score strictly above the mid-point on each scale. In comparing MPs with the public, account should be taken of the change in governments in Hungary and Ukraine between the dates of our surveys of public and parliamentary opinion.

munist economic trends. We are left with the impression that the concept of government and opposition were particularly unclear in Ukraine.

Taking our five countries together, government supporters were 17 per cent less committed than government opponents to socialist values, and 16 per cent less committed to external nationalism, though slightly more committed to cultural conformity. Surprisingly perhaps, government supporters' rejection of socialism was definitely *not* combined with greater support for liberal values: government supporters were 14 per cent *less* liberal as well as 17 per cent less socialist.

Government supporters were also 9 per cent more committed to political parties. But the most dramatic differences between government supporters and their opponents were on attitudes towards populism and representative democracy: government supporters were 31 per cent *less* populist than their opponents, but 34 per cent *more* committed to the core institutions of representative democracy, multi-party elections. Almost by definition, government supporters had reason to be satisfied with election results and, by association, with the principle of elections.

Amongst MPs, government supporters and opponents differed by even larger margins on socialist and nationalist values, but hardly differed at all on liberal values or support for representative democracy.

Table 16.4:   Values by government support within countries

	Difference between percentage of government and opposition supporters whose values are:					
	Socialist	Nationalist	Liberal	Populist	Pro-elections	Pro-parties
	%	%	%	%	%	%
Russia	−22	−18	−21	−30	+34	−3
Ukraine	+6	+8	−29	−25	+18	0
Czech Rep	−35	−9	0	−35	+37	+11
Slovakia	+1	+12	−18	−36	+19	+12
Hungary	+4	−6	−24	−19	+20	+8

Note: Entries are the differences in the percentages who score strictly above the mid-point on each scale.

Naturally there was considerable variation across the five countries, if only because the governments in question were different. But in every country there was evidence of a strong link between government support and commitment to multi-party elections, coupled with an equally strong link between populism and being a government opponent. In every country except the Czech Republic there was also a strong link between liberal values and being *opposed* to the government. However, the link between socialist values and opposition was only really visible in Russia and the Czech Republic where, in both countries, it was strong. And the link between nationalist values and government support actually varied in sign as well as in strength from country to country: in the Czech Republic, Hungary and especially in Russia, government *opponents* were the most nationalist; but in Ukraine and especially in Slovakia – where ethnic and regional problems were greatest, government *supporters* were the most nationalist.

IDENTIFICATION WITH LEFT/RIGHT IDEOLOGY

The question: 'In political matters, people often talk of the *left* and the *right*. Would you place yourself on the left, in the centre, or on the right?' provides a crude measure of ideological self-images. Despite its simplicity it proves a very discriminating measure in western Europe – both between and, more significantly, within political parties. In Britain those who describe themselves as being on the left are notably committed to both liberty and equality, while those who place themselves on the right tend to be both authoritarian and inegalitarian.[3] It is important to note that the terms, as used by western publics, are not linked exclusively to socialist values but also to liberal values, in the sense in which we have defined them – that is, the opposite of authoritarian values.

No one suggests that people derive their values from these ideological self-images, but they do indicate a degree of coherence in people's values. In western Europe, people who place themselves firmly on the left or on the right do not approach each political issue in isolation: they have, and maintain, coherent sets of principles which they and others can easily recognise as being 'left-wing' or 'right-wing'. Of course, in ECE or the FSU people might well adopt coherent sets of principles without finding a simple word or phrase to describe them or, if they did, that word might not be 'left' or 'right'. Researchers who came equipped with the American ideological terminology of 'liberal versus conservative' instead of 'left versus right' might well be met with incomprehension on the streets of western Europe, and west European terminology may not apply in east Europe. So, in seeking to discover whether the phrases 'on the left' and 'on the right' (literally translated, for example into 'k levym/k pravym' in Russian or 'do livikh/do pravikh' in Ukrainian) are linked to values in postcommunist countries we are investigating their people's recognition of this terminology rather than the coherence of their values – which we have already investigated by other, more direct, methods in Chapter 12.

There should be nothing very foreign about the political meanings of the words left and right in ECE or the FSU: they derive from the seating arrangements in the French revolutionary assemblies, and all the countries in our sample were invaded by French revolutionary armies. 1812, if not 1789, made a deep and lasting impression on the Tsarist empire. On the other hand, in postcommunist countries any simple left-right ideological distinction was 'blurred and distorted' because 'virtually all parties were overtly committed to dismantling state socialism'; because of the 'urban-rural cultural divide'; and because of 'the importance of nationalism in east European culture' coupled with the fact that 'committed nationalists often identified themselves as "right" and anti-communist, but on economic policy they were often strongly statist and their basic philosophy was collectivist rather than individualist and thus they had more in common with the left.'[4]

In fact, over half the public in the FSU felt they could not answer the question whether they were on the left or on the right; and while very few FSU MPs felt they could not answer the question, many plumped for the option of placing themselves 'in the centre'. So in the FSU, only around 15 per cent of the public and 42 per cent of MPs could or would place themselves firmly on the left or on the right.[5] By contrast, 25 per cent of the public and 61 per cent of MPs in Hungary, and 42 per cent of the public and 74 per cent of MPs in the Czech Republic put themselves firmly on the left or the right. Clearly, the familiarity and acceptability of these ideological labels rose from a low in the FSU to a high in the Czech Republic both amongst the public and MPs.[6] Nonetheless, our figures show that MPs in the FSU used these labels as freely as did ordinary citizens in the Czech Republic.

Table 16.5: Recognition of 'left' and 'right'

	'don't know'		left or right	
	Public	MPs	Public	MPs
	%	%	%	%
Russia	61	3	13	38
Ukraine	53	1	17	46
Czech Republic	4	1	42	74
Slovakia	8	na	30	na
Hungary	21	1	25	61

Note: In this table, percentages are percentages of all respondents, including 'don't knows etc.'. Many respondents placed themselves 'in the centre'.

But what meaning did these labels have for those who used them? Overall, those on the left were 10 per cent more willing to jail the new rich and 28 per cent more likely to complain that postcommunist economic trends were hurting their families. But there were sharp differences between countries: left and right differed by 43 per cent in their complaints about postcommunist economic trends in the Czech Republic but by only a negligible 3 per cent in Russia.

Table 16.6:   Economic loss by self-assigned 'left/right'

| | Jail 'new rich' | Family experience economic loss | Family experience economic loss in: | | | | |
			Russia	Ukraine	Czech Rep	Slovakia	Hungary
	%	%	%	%	%	%	%
Left	20	76	62	94	72	75	82
Centre	12	65	61	86	53	67	69
Right	10	48	59	77	29	62	63
Diff: Left–right	+10	+28	+3	+17	+43	+13	+19

Notes: 'Don't Knows', 'Can't decide' etc. excluded from calculation of percentages.

Table 16.7:   Best time for country by self-assigned 'left/right'

| | Difference between percentage of self-assigned 'left' and 'right' who choose time in: | | | | |
	Russia	Ukraine	Czech Rep	Slovakia	Hungary
	%	%	%	%	%
Tsars or Hapsburgs	−1	−3	0	−4	0
Interwar: Stalin/Masaryk/ Horthy	−2	+4	−11	0	−9
Independent Slovak state 1939–45	na	na	na	−11	na
Dubcek	na	na	+22	+17	na
Mature communist: Brezhnev/Husak/Kadar	+3	+26	+22	+30	+21
Reform Communist: Gorbachev/Hungarian	0	+2	na	na	+10
United democratic Czechoslovakia 1989–92	na	na	−2	−15	na
Present democratic regime since 1992: (since 1989 in Hungary)	0	−28	−31	−17	−21

Notes: 'Don't Knows', 'Can't decide' etc. excluded from calculation of percentages. 'na' = not applicable.

Similarly, while left and right did not differ in their choice of the best time for Russia, in the Czech Republic the left were 28 per cent *less* likely to opt for the present, and 44 per cent more likely to opt for the Dubcek or Husak eras. In Hungary the left were 21 per cent less likely to opt for the present and 21 per cent more likely to opt for the Kadar era. Surprisingly perhaps, left and right differed sharply in Ukraine as well, where the left were 17 per cent more likely to complain about the effect of postcommunist economic trends, 28 per cent less likely to opt for the postcommunist present, and 26 per cent more likely to opt for the Brezhnev era. So in every country west of Russia itself, those who did accept the labels left and right had perspectives on the present and the recent past that differed in ways that are consistent with west European understanding of those terms.

Amongst the public in all five countries taken together, the left proved 27 per cent more committed to socialist values – again consistent with west European meanings of left and right, and 22 per cent more populist, though 14 per cent *less* committed to multi-party elections.

Table 16.8:   Values by self-assigned 'left/right'

	Socialist	Nationalist	Liberal	Populist	Pro-elections	Pro-parties
	%	%	%	%	%	%
Left	75	37	74	73	69	37
Centre	72	35	70	62	69	24
Right	48	33	71	51	83	47
Diff: Left–right	+27	+4	+3	+22	−14	−10

Note: Entries are the percentage who score strictly above the mid-point on each scale.

Table 16.9:   Values of MPs by self-assigned 'left/right'

	Socialist	Nationalist	Liberal	Populist	Pro-elections
	%	%	%	%	%
Left	58	18	94	72	97
Centre	41	23	94	63	91
Right	14	24	97	35	96
Diff: Left–right	+44	−6	−3	+37	+1

Notes: Entries are the percentage who score strictly above the mid-point on each scale. MPs commitments to parties were not measured as extensively as those of the public.

MPs were not just much more willing than their publics to accept and use these labels, they also invested them with more meaning. On socialist values, left and right differed by 44 per cent amongst MPs, compared to 27 per cent amongst the public; and on populist values, left and right differed by 37 per cent amongst MPs, compared to 22 per cent amongst the public.

Overall, left and right differed little on nationalist or liberal values either amongst the public or amongst MPs. Indeed, since almost all MPs were relatively liberal and in favour of multi-party elections, it was not possible for left and right to differ much on these values. We classified people as being relatively liberal if they scored above 3 (the mid point) on our scale of liberal values, which ran from 1 to 5. Now while almost all MPs scored above that threshold, it could be the case that left wing and right wing MPs could differ from each other on liberal values even though both groups scored above 3. But in fact that was not so: our presentation of the findings about MPs' values in percentage form – to provide comparability with our analysis of the public – does not mislead. The mean scores on our five point scale of liberal values were 3.6 both for MPs on the left and for MPs on the right. Neither group was extremely committed to liberal values but almost every MP in both groups was moderately committed to them.

Amongst the public in the Czech Republic, the left was 52 per cent more socialist, 35 per cent more populist and 19 per cent less committed to multi-party elections. But it was really only in Slovakia and the Czech Republic that left and right differed greatly on socialist values.[7] In Russia left and right differed most on liberal values – though it was the left, not the right, that were most committed to liberal values there as elsewhere. However left and right were not consistent in their attitudes towards nationalism across different countries: the left was less nationalist than the right in Ukraine, but more nationalist than the right in Slovakia. In Ukraine, left and right differed substantially only on nationalist values though, in the context of Ukraine's politics, the left's rejection of nationalist values was itself a commitment to one kind of liberal value.

Table 16.10: Values by self-assigned 'left/right' within countries

	Socialist	Nationalist	Liberal	Populist	Pro-elections	Pro-parties
	Difference between percentage of self-assigned 'left' and 'right' whose values are:					
	%	%	%	%	%	%
Russia	−1	+5	+20	+11	+1	+4
Ukraine	0	−17	+5	0	−1	−2
Czech Rep	+52	+2	+2	+35	−19	−9
Slovakia	+30	+10	+5	+9	−11	−19
Hungary	+8	−17	−1	+7	−6	−11

Note: Entries are the percentage who score strictly above the mid-point on each scale.

In Russia, Ukraine and the Czech Republic, left wing and right wing MPs differed by over 70 per cent in their commitments to socialism. But although our evidence does not permit a comparison of left and right wing MPs in Hungary (we only interviewed 9 MPs who described themselves as 'on the right' in Hungary in 1994[8]) it does show, without question, that self-designated left-wing MPs in Hungary were remarkably uncommitted to socialist values as we have defined them: only 27 per cent scored above the mid-point on our scale of socialist values. That was above average for Hungarian MPs however, and it also reflected their complete disillusionment with state control of industry, rather than their failure to support other socialist values. We interviewed 56 Hungarian MPs who placed themselves firmly 'on the left'. Of these only 2 per cent were committed to state control of industry, but 34 per cent to state welfare, and 72 per cent to equality. Compared to left-wing MPs in other countries – a comparison that numbers do allow us to make – left-wing Hungarian MPs were far less committed to state control of industry, and far less committed to state welfare, but at the same time they were fairly typical in their commitment to equality.

Overall we found little difference between left and right-wing MPs on nationalist values. But in the Russian parliament the left was 35 per cent *more* nationalist than the right, while in Ukraine it was 21 per cent *less* nationalist than the right, reflecting – in exaggerated form – a contrast that we had already found between the Russian and Ukrainian publics.

Table 16.11: Values of MPs by self-assigned 'left/right' within countries

	Difference between percentage of self-assigned 'left' and 'right' whose values are:				
	Socialist	Nationalist	Liberal	Populist	Pro-elections
	%	%	%	%	%
Russia	+70	+35	+3	+35	−3
Ukraine	+78	−21	−13	+47	+1
Czech Republic	+76	+8	+2	+75	−4

Notes: MPs' commitments to parties were not measured as extensively as those of the public. There was no survey of MPs in Slovakia. In Hungary, although many of the 110 MPs we interviewed placed themselves 'in the centre', only 9 placed themselves 'on the right'; so we regard left/right comparisons in the Hungarian parliament as unreliable. Nonetheless it is clear that even left-wing MPs in Hungary were unusually opposed to state control of industry, though committed egalitarians. On our overall measure of socialist values, only 27 per cent of Hungarian MPs 'on the left' scored above the mid-point, though even that was above the average for Hungarian MPs.

IDENTIFICATION WITH COMMUNISM

Almost everyone could be divided into those who had always (and continued) to believe in communist ideals, those who had never believed in them, and those who had once believed but had now lost their faith. Less than two per cent of the public said they had recently acquired a belief in communist ideals, but 55 per cent said they had never believed, 26 per cent that they had formerly (but no longer) believed, and 17 per cent continued to believe as they had in the past. Amongst MPs the corresponding figures were zero, 49, 29 and 22 respectively.

Compared to those who had never believed, those who continued to believe in communist ideals were 20 per cent more likely to complain about the effect of postcommunist economic trends on their families (the difference was greater in the Czech Republic; less in Ukraine) and 12 per cent more willing to jail the 'new rich'.

Table 16.12:   Economic loss by belief in communist ideals

| | Jail 'new rich' | Family experience economic loss | Family experience economic loss in... | | | | |
			Russia	Ukraine	Czech Rep	Slovakia	Hungary
	%	%	%	%	%	%	%
Believed							
always	24	82	80	94	79	77	82
formerly	13	72	70	89	53	64	79
never	12	62	61	85	41	65	68
Diff: always–never	+12	+20	+19	+9	+38	+12	+14

Notes: 'Don't Knows', 'Can't decide' etc. excluded from calculation of percentages.

Table 16.13:   Best time for country by belief in communist ideals

| | Difference between percentage of those who always and never believed who choose time in: | | | | |
	Russia	Ukraine	Czech Rep	Slovakia	Hungary
	%	%	%	%	%
Tsars or Hapsburgs	−18	−11	−3	0	−8
Interwar: Stalin/Masaryk/ Horthy	+11	+6	−20	+1	−4
Independent Slovak state 1939–45	na	na	na	−4	na
Dubcek	na	na	+12	−2	na
Mature communist: Brezhnev/Husak/Kadar	+23	+21	+32	+33	+25
Reform Communist: Gorbachev/Hungarian	0	−1	na	na	−1
United democratic Czechoslovakia 1989–92	na	na	+1	−13	na
Present democratic regime since 1992 (since 1989 in Hungary)	−15	−15	−22	−15	−13

Notes: 'Don't Knows', 'Can't decide' etc. excluded from calculation of percentages. 'na' = not applicable.

In every country these continuing believers were around 15 per cent less likely to choose the postcommunist present as the best time for their country, and between 21 and 33 per cent more likely to choose the days of Brezhnev, Kadar or Husak. In the FSU and Hungary they were less likely to choose the imperial days of Tsars and Hapsburgs and, in the Czech Republic, 20 per cent less likely to choose the days of Masaryk.

Continuing believers were 22 per cent more committed to socialist values, 11 per cent more committed to populism and 8 per cent *less* committed to multi-party elections than those who had never believed. Unusually, their rejection of multi-party elections did not prevent them being 6 per cent more committed to parties – though that is quite reasonable in this case.

Table 16.14:   Values by belief in communist ideals

	Socialist	Nationalist	Liberal	Populist	Pro-elections	Pro-parties
	%	%	%	%	%	%
Believed						
always	89	43	69	72	59	32
formerly	75	35	68	63	63	23
never	67	35	68	61	67	26
Diff: always – never	+22	+8	+1	+11	−8	+6

Note: Entries are the percentage who score strictly above the mid-point on each scale.

Table 16.15:   Values by belief in communist ideals within countries

	Difference between percentage of those who always and never believed whose values are:					
	Socialist	Nationalist	Liberal	Populist	Pro-elections	Pro-parties
	%	%	%	%	%	%
Russia	+23	+16	+7	+14	−6	+12
Ukraine	+12	−5	−4	−3	+7	+7
Czech Rep	+36	+3	−7	+17	−17	0
Slovakia	+14	+13	0	+12	−12	+5
Hungary	+10	0	+7	+7	−7	+4

Note: Entries are the percentage who score strictly above the mid-point on each scale.

These same general patterns occurred within each country though to differing degrees: in Russia and the Czech Republic continuing believers were between 23 and 36 per cent more committed to socialist values than those who had never believed, but in other countries the difference was less.

Those who had lost their faith had values that were intermediate between those of the continuing believers and those who had never believed. It is significant however, that on every aspect of values, these former believers were closer to the 'never believed' than to the continuing believers. Thus, current belief was more important than past belief in structuring current values.

Communist identification through behaviour

This distinction between past and present links to communism can usefully be applied in terms of behaviour as well as in terms of belief – specifically in terms of past membership of the Communist Party, and present intentions to vote for its successor parties. The Communist Party under the old regime had a membership large enough to be roughly comparable to the size of the small vote for its successor parties under the new regime.

Table 16.16: Communist Party membership and belief

| | If **had** been a member of the Communist Party | | If had **never** been a member of the Communist Party | |
	Public	MPs	Public	MPs
	%	%	%	%
Always believed	34	35	14	2
New convert to belief	1	1	2	0
Formerly believed	39	43	24	9
Never believed	25	22	60	89
	100	100	100	100

Notes: 'Don't Knows', 'Can't decide' etc. excluded from calculation of percentages.

Under the old regime, membership of the Communist Party had been a career necessity rather than a reflection of political ideals. Amongst those who had never been a member of the Communist Party, 60 per cent of the public and 89 per cent of MPs had never believed in communist ideals. Much more significantly, *even amongst those who had been members* of the Communist Party, 25 per cent of the public and 22 per cent of MPs said they had never believed in its ideals, and a majority of those who had believed no longer did so. By their own accounts, while there was some correlation between former party membership and belief it had never been total at any time – though for varying reasons. At one time, many outside the party had believed in its ideals though a minority within the party did not; now, although very few who had never been members continued to believe, a majority of former members no longer believed either. The correlation was greater amongst MPs than amongst the public however, not so much because MPs who had been members had a different pattern of past or present belief from others who had been members, but because so many of the current MPs who had never been members had always been so very opposed to communist ideals. Probably it had been their lack of belief rather than their lack of personal eligibility which had kept them out of the party. Unlike ordinary people who had not been Communist Party members, the kind of people who could make their way into parliament were the kind who would have been invited or even pressured to become members of the Communist Party: formally or informally they had probably resisted that pressure.

On average former members of the party were only 6 per cent more likely than other people to complain about postcommunist economic trends; but in sharp contrast, those who currently intended to vote for the communists were on average, 23 per cent more likely to complain. The figures were higher in the Czech Republic and lower elsewhere but, in every country, economic complaints were more strongly related to current voting intentions than to past membership.

Table 16.17:   Economic loss by former Communist Party membership and current voting preferences for communist parties

| | Jail 'new rich' | Family experience economic loss | Family experience economic loss in | | | | |
			Russia	Ukraine	Czech Rep	Slovakia	Hungary
	%	%	%	%	%	%	%
Under former regime:							
CP member	21	74	69	88	71	73	78
Not	13	68	69	88	42	67	70
Diff: member – not	+8	+6	0	0	+29	+6	+8
Current vote pref:							
'communist'	26	85	88	92	84	75	86
other party	13	62	66	86	42	64	68
Diff: comm-other	+13	+23	+22	+6	+42	+11	+18

Note: In this table, current voting preference for 'communist' parties includes preferences for the Hungarian Socialist Party and for the Democratic Left in Slovakia.

Former Communist Party members had different perspectives upon the past in Slovakia and the Czech Republic – where they were about 25 per cent more likely than others to choose the Dubcek or Husak periods – but they were not much different from others anywhere else.

Again, in very sharp contrast, those with currently voting preferences for communist parties had very different perspectives on the past from those who preferred other parties. They were up to 34 per cent more likely to choose the Brezhnev/Kadar/Husak eras as the best time for their country, and up to 22 per cent less likely choose the present. In the Czech Republic they were also 21 per cent less likely to choose the Masaryk period, and 20 per cent more likely to opt for Dubcek's Prague Spring. And in Russia they were also 11 per cent more likely to opt for Stalin, and 19 per cent less likely to opt for the Tsar.

Table 16.18: Best time for country by former Communist Party membership and current voting preferences for communist parties

	Difference between percentage of former CP members and non-members who choose time				
	Russia	*Ukraine*	*Czech Rep*	*Slovakia*	*Hungary*
	%	%	%	%	%
Tsars or Hapsburgs	−3	−3	0	+1	+3
Interwar: Stalin/Masaryk/Horthy	+10	+4	−12	−2	−4
Independent Slovak state 1939–45	na	na	na	−4	na
Dubcek	na	na	+19	+12	na
Mature communist: Brezhnev/Husak/ Kadar	−6	0	+8	+12	0
Reform Communist: Gorbachev/ Hungarian	0	0	na	na	+9
United democratic Czechoslovakia 1989–92	na	na	−5	−11	na
Present democratic regime since 1992: (since 1989 in Hungary)	−1	−1	−10	−7	−9
	Difference between percentage of CP 'supporters' and those other parties' voters who choose time				
	Russia	*Ukraine*	*Czech Rep*	*Slovakia*	*Hungary*
	%	%	%	%	%
Tsars or Hapsburgs	−19	−11	−2	−1	−2
Interwar: Stalin/Masaryk/Horthy	+11	+2	−21	0	−1
Independent Slovak state 1939–45	na	na	na	−5	na
Dubcek	na	na	+20	+3	na
Mature communist: Brezhnev/Husak/ Kadar	+22	+26	+34	+17	+12
Reform Communist: Gorbachev/ Hungarian	−1	−1	na	+6	na
United democratic Czechoslovakia 1989–92	na	na	−9	−4	na
Present democratic regime since 1992: (since 1989 in Hungary)	−13	−16	−22	−10	−14

Notes: 'Don't Knows', 'Can't decide' etc. excluded from calculation of percentages.

In terms of values, former Communist Party members were only 3 per cent more socialist than others, but those with current voting preferences for communist parties were 21 per cent more committed than others to socialist values.[9]

Both nationalist and populist values were also much more related to current communist voting preferences than to past Communist Party membership. But conversely, support for political parties was slightly more strongly linked to past Communist Party membership than to current communist voting preferences. The pattern of attitudes to democratic elections was specially interesting: those with current communist voting preferences were 17 per cent *less* favourable to democratic elections than those with other voting preferences; but former Communist Party members were actually 6 per cent *more* favourable towards democratic elections than those who had never been CP members.

Table 16.19:   Values by former Communist Party membership and current voting
preferences for communist parties

	Socialist	Nationalist	Liberal	Populist	Pro-elections	Pro-parties
	%	%	%	%	%	%
Under former regime:						
CP member	77	36	74	68	68	36
Not	74	37	67	64	62	23
Diff: member – not	+3	−1	+7	+4	+6	+13
Current vote pref:						
'communist'	90	45	74	78	59	44
Other party	69	35	68	60	76	35
Diff: comm–other	+21	+10	+6	+18	−17	+9

Note: Entries are the percentage who score strictly above the mid-point on each scale.

Table 16.20:   MPs values by former Communist Party membership

	Socialist	Nationalist	Liberal	Populist	Pro-elections
	%	%	%	%	%
Under former regime:					
CP member	52	21	94	66	94
Not	23	23	95	51	95
Diff: member–not	+29	−2	−1	+15	−1

Note: Entries are the per cent who score strictly above the mid-point on each scale.

Within individual countries former members of the Communist Party seemed very little more (or less) socialist than non-members except in the Czech Republic.[10] The only consistent relationship of any size was the almost tautological one between former Communist Party membership and identification with parties. By contrast, current voting preferences for the communists rather than for other parties went with much greater support for socialist and populist values and much less support for multi-party elections in every country except Hungary (where the effects were more modest).

Amongst MPs, unlike the public however, former members of the Communist Party were 29 per cent more committed to socialist values than those who had never been members, and 15 per cent more populist. Amongst the new political elite former membership of the Communist Party – *and more especially non-membership* – did correlate with political values, even though former membership did not correlate with current political values amongst the public.

IDENTIFICATION WITH PARTIES IN THE POSTCOMMUNIST REGIME

The end of communist regimes and the advent of multi-party elections brought a flood of new parties onto the scene, some with deep historical roots, some with clear ideologies, some with at least the vestige of a structure and organisation, and many with none of these.

We asked people whether they 'supported' a party and, if so, which? We also asked which party they would prefer to vote for in a parliamentary election. Very few were 'supporters' of any one party – too few for reliable analysis, though many more expressed voting preferences. So we can at least compare the political values of those who would vote for at least the more popular parties. We are reluctant to extend that investigation to some of the less popular parties – interesting though they may be in terms of their leadership, their policies, or their contribution to public debate – simply because their unpopularity makes our samples of their voters too small for statistically reliable analysis.

Amongst the public 32 per cent of Communist voters in Russia said they had been former members of the Communist Party, as did 24 per cent of Communist voters in Ukraine, 34 per cent in Slovakia, 35 per cent in Hungary and a huge 73 per cent in the Czech Republic – where the small vote for the Communist Party in this postcommunist republic was overwhelmingly drawn from old party comrades.

Party voters in Russia
In Russia sample sizes allow us to say something about the values of those who preferred to vote for the Agrarians, the LDP,[11] Russia's Choice and Yabloko as well as the Communists. The first four groups were less committed to socialist values than those who preferred the Communists, but to varying degrees: those with Agrarian or LDP preferences were not much less socialist than Communists, while those who preferred Yabloko or Russia's Choice were both about 35 per cent less socialist than those who preferred the Communist Party.

LDP and Communist voters were the most nationalist – almost 30 per cent more so than Yabloko or Russia's Choice voters – while Agrarian voters were closer to Communist voters but still 10 per cent less nationalist than them.

On liberal values, Russia's Choice voters were ranged against all the other parties: it was a simple government versus opposition parties split, with the governing Russia's Choice voters between 12 and 18 per cent *less* liberal than the others – despite the liberal pretensions of its leaders. On our strict definition of liberal values (as the opposite of authoritarian values, disentangled from market values or democratic values), Russia's Choice voters were not only less liberal than those of all the other parties, they were actually more committed to socialist values than to liberal values (64 per cent socialist, 53 per cent liberal).

Similarly on populism, Russia's Choice voters were between 20 and 38 per cent less populist than any other party's voters, though there was a considerable difference between Communist voters (the most populist) and Yabloko voters (half-way between Communist and Russia's Choice voters). Communist voters were at once the most sympathetic to parties and the least sympathetic to multi-party elections, while Yabloko or Russia's Choice voters were at the opposite extreme.

Russia's Choice voters were on balance socialists, albeit less so than other parties' voters; they were outstandingly illiberal; they were outstandingly opposed to populist values; but they were also outstandingly committed to multi-party competitive elections. In that sense, but *only* in that sense, they were good democrats.

Party voters in Ukraine
Party preferences were so scarce and so fractionised in Ukraine that we can only sensibly look at Communist and Rukh voters. There were too few with any other preference for reliable analysis. Compared to Communist voters, those who preferred Rukh were 32 per cent less socialist, and 15 per cent less populist, but 27 per cent more committed to multi-party elections – though neither much more nationalist nor liberal.

Party voters in the Czech Republic
Plenty of people had party preferences in the Czech Republic but so many of them preferred Klaus's Civic Democratic Party (ODS) that we shall focus just on the ODS and the Communists. Compared to Communist voters, ODS voters were 58 per cent less socialist, and 43 per cent less populist but 24 per cent more committed to multi-party elections; they were also 12 per cent *less* liberal and no different from the Communists on nationalist values.

Party voters in Slovakia
In very sharp contrast to the situation in the Czech Republic, Communist voters in Slovakia were scarcely any more socialist than those who preferred the governing MDS (Movement for a Democratic Slovakia). Compared to the Communists, MDS voters were, however, 8 per cent more nationalist, 16 per cent less liberal, 35 per cent less populist and 17 per cent more committed to elections – typical of a governing party's voters.

Party voters in Hungary

Socialist Party voters provide the reference point in Hungary. They were *not*, however, much more socialist in terms of values than those who preferred other parties. Those who preferred the opposition Free Democrats were very similar to Socialist Party voters on everything except nationalism, where the Free Democrats were 20 per cent less nationalist. Free Democrats had a long cosmopolitan tradition. Those who preferred the then-governing HDF (Hungarian Democratic Forum) were fairly similar to Socialist Party voters on socialism and nationalism but 18 per cent *less* liberal, 25 per cent less populist, and 27 per cent more committed to multi-party elections – again, typical of a governing party's voters in a postcommunist regime.

Table 16.21: Values by selected party preferences within countries

Former Communist Party Member	Socialist	Nationalist	Liberal	Populist	Pro-elections	Pro-parties
%	%	%	%	%	%	%
(12) *Russia:*						
32 Communist	100	58	71	82	46	66
15 Agrarian	93	48	65	75	71	33
10 LDP	88	59	68	73	66	40
16 Yabloko	67	33	67	64	73	29
13 Russia's Choice	64	29	53	44	83	37
(11) *Ukraine:*						
24 Communist	92	25	69	76	46	48
8 Rukh	60	27	73	61	73	40
(21) *Czech Rep:*						
73 Communist	95	25	89	80	75	60
11 Civic Dem Party	37	24	77	37	99	47
(16) *Slovakia:*						
34 Democratic Left	89	46	75	67	68	34
14 MDS	86	54	59	32	85	43
(12) *Hungary:*						
35 Socialists	82	49	72	82	60	30
6 Young Democrats	72	34	65	78	64	37
10 Free Democrats	76	29	77	90	61	39
7 Smallholders	82	57	39	78	64	46
8 HDF	73	42	54	57	87	48

Note: Entries are the percentage who score strictly above the mid-point on each scale.

MPS' IDENTIFICATION WITH PARLIAMENTARY FACTIONS

Much higher proportions of MPs than of the public were former Communist Party members in all countries – except in the Czech Republic where only 25 per cent of MPs compared to 21 per cent of the public claimed, or admitted, to being former Communist Party members. And differences between parliamentary factions in their levels of former Communist Party membership were also greater in every parliament than amongst their voters. All the Communist MPs in Russia, Ukraine and the Czech Republic and 87 per cent of the Socialist Party MPs in Hungary were former Communist Party members. By contrast, former CP members comprised only 50 per cent of Russia's Choice MPs, 33 per cent of Rukh's MPs, 8 per cent of the HDF MPs, and a mere 4 per cent of Civic Democratic Party MPs in the Czech Republic. MPs from different parties clearly had, or claimed, *very* different pasts; and their values differed accordingly.

Table 16.22:   Values of MPs by selected parliamentary faction

Former Communist Party Member	Socialist	Nationalist	Liberal	Populist	Pro-elections
%	%	%	%	%	%
(71) *Russia*:					
100 Communist	92	67	100	83	100
88 Agrarian	81	69	94	94	75
47 LDP	82	88	94	88	100
50 Russia's Choice	0	18	100	36	100
(79) *Ukraine*:					
100 Communist	93	17	83	69	97
100 Agrarian	65	12	94	71	94
33 Rukh	0	33	100	25	100
(25) *Czech Republic*:					
100 Communist	89	11	100	89	100
4 Civic Dem Party	0	4	100	8	100
(49) *Hungary*:					
87 Socialists	30	7	98	61	98
5 Free democrats	0	5	100	45	95
8 HDF	8	17	100	33	83

Note: Entries are the percentage who score strictly above the mid-point on each scale.

Indeed the value differences between MPs in different parliamentary factions differed so much in some – but not all – ways as to appear like something from an overdrawn caricature of party politics. *In Russia*, Russia's Choice MPs were 92 per cent less socialist than Communist MPs, and 47 per cent less populist; while LDP MPs were 70 per cent more nationalist than those in the Russia's Choice faction. *In Ukraine*, Rukh MPs were 93 per cent less Socialist, 26 per cent more nationalist and 74 per cent less populist than Communist MPs. *In the Czech Republic*, MPs from the governing ODS were 89 per cent less socialist and 81 per cent less populist than the Communists. Even *in Hungary*, MPs from the governing HDF were 22 per cent less socialist, 10 per cent more nationalist, and 28 per cent less populist than the Socialist Party MPs even though Hungarian Socialist Party MPs – like their voters – were remarkably uncommitted to socialist values. These value differences between MPs from different parliamentary factions are enormous, not just in relation to the scale of value differences between their voters, but in absolute terms.

However, it was striking that MPs were overwhelmingly committed to liberal values and to multi-party elections – in all the major parliamentary factions in all the countries. What united MPs of all party factions was therefore as significant as what divided them so deeply. And it is worth stressing that what united MPs of all party factions did *not* unite their voters. It was not surprising to find that almost all the MPs of Russia's Choice, Rukh, ODS and the HDF favoured multi-party elections – as did an overwhelming majority of their voters. But it was much more interesting and very much more politically significant that almost all the Communist MPs in every country favoured multi-party elections although only 75 per cent of their voters in the Czech Republic, 60 per cent in Hungary, and 46 per cent in the FSU did so.

CONCLUSION

Our broad conclusion must be that identification with government, ideology and party did make a surprisingly large difference to political values, particularly amongst MPs but also amongst members of the general public – surprising because western commentators had written so much about the weakness and irrelevance of parties in these postcommunist countries. Clearly, weak organisation does not prevent party being a useful psychological reference point.

Amongst the public, those who identified themselves as government supporters were 17 per cent *less* socialist, 14 per cent *less* liberal and 31 per cent *less* populist, but 34 per cent *more* favourable to multi-party elections than government opponents. Those who placed themselves 'on the left' were 27 per cent more socialist, 22 per cent more populist and 14 per cent *less* committed to multi-party elections than those who placed themselves 'on the right' – though these effects were much stronger in ECE than in the FSU. Former membership of the Communist Party made little difference to people's values (except in the Czech Republic) but current belief in communist ideals or a preference for voting communist had much more effect. Those who preferred to vote communist were 21 per cent more socialist, 10 per cent more nationalist, 18 per cent more populist and 17 per cent less committed to multi-party elections than those who preferred other parties.

Amongst MPs, those who placed themselves on the left were 44 per cent more socialist and 37 per cent more populist than those who placed themselves on the right and these differences, especially on socialist values, were even larger in the

FSU than in ECE chiefly because the Hungarian left had lost its faith in public enterprise. Former membership of the Communist Party made a difference to the values of MPs if not to the values of the general public. MPs who had been members of the Communist Party were 29 per cent more socialist than those who had not been. That, of course, may have reflected the fact that some still were members of the Communist Party, but most former Communist Party members who had been elected to postcommunist parliaments now represented other parties: their CP membership really *was* 'former'. In fact the value differences between MPs reflected the long term and extreme antagonism to socialist ideals of those MPs who had never been members of the Communist Party. Amongst MPs there were also huge differences between rival parliamentary factions on socialism, populism and, in Russia, on nationalism. However MPs were united in their support for liberal values and the democratic procedures of multi-party elections even though their voters were not.

Some of these patterns were universal, others had been limited in the past to western democracies. Being in opposition is likely, anywhere and everywhere, to encourage support for liberal values – the rights of the citizen against government, and to encourage support for populism – the demand that government should pay attention to the people. The concepts of left and right, however, are relatively new to postcommunist countries. A large percentage of postcommunist publics, though not of their MPs, were still unwilling to use them in the early 1990s. Amongst those who did, the terms left and right correlated with socialist values as they do in the west, but they did not correlate with liberal values as they do in the west. On the other hand, we found no evidence for the sometimes-mooted theory that the left in postcommunist countries might be authoritarian and anti-liberal as well as pro-socialist. All we found was that the left in our five postcommunist countries was not so especially anti-authoritarian and pro-liberal as in the West.

17 A Multivariate Model

Previous chapters have had a relatively narrow focus, which has allowed considerable attention to nuance and detail. In this chapter we broaden the focus in three ways: first, to look at the relationship between different kinds of values – a topic which we began to explore in Chapter 12; second, to look at how all these values were influenced by a combination of social, economic and cultural factors; third, to see how these values combined to affect attitudes to political parties. Our aim is to develop a relatively simple model that nonetheless encompasses all our main findings with as little distortion as possible. Inevitably these aims of simplicity, comprehensiveness and minimum distortion will have to be weighed against each other.

THE CONTENT AND STRUCTURE OF OUR MODEL

We have seen how values varied with social factors that included class, age, gender and occupational sector; with economic experience and perceptions; and with such socio-cultural factors as education, religion, metropolitanism, language, nationality and state. One of our objectives in this chapter will be to investigate the relative importance of these different social, economic and cultural factors on political values. But our model also needs to say something about the inter-relationship between different kinds of political values; and, as Chapter 16 showed, it needs to take account of one very special kind of political experience, the experience of opposition.

We suggest that there is a hierarchy or sequence of values. Values differ not just in substantive content but in terms of the degree to which they are associated with substance rather than with process. Substantive values are about the ends of politics, procedural values are about the means which may reasonably be employed to attain these ends. Socialist and nationalist values are the ones most closely associated with substance, with policies, with the outputs of government. Liberal values are more closely associated with the political process, with the way in which the political system operates, rather than with the policies and outputs of government as such. For that reason liberal values are sometimes called 'procedural values' though that term is often reserved, more strictly, for values associated with such concrete mechanisms of decision making as trial-by-jury or competitive multi-party electoral systems. We would certainly recognise what we have termed populist, electoral and party values as being even more closely associated with process, and even less associated with substance, than what we have termed liberal values. That gives us a three stage hierarchy of values ranging from the most substantive to the most procedural:

1) substantive: socialist and nationalist values
2) intermediate: liberal values
3) procedural: populist, electoral and party values.

For purposes of analysis, we shall assume that all six of these sets of values may be influenced by social, economic and cultural factors. But, in addition, we suggest that the more substantive values may influence the more procedural values yet *not* be influenced by them. That is to say, we suggest that adherence to socialist or nationalist values (which concern ends) may influence support for liberal values, and for populist, electoral and party values (which concern means) but not vice versa. We accept that philosophers such as Hayek may start from a commitment to liberal procedural values and reason back to argue that socialist values should be rejected as incompatible with this prior commitment to liberal values. But we suggest such people are in a small minority. Of course in extreme situations the usual direction of influence may be reversed for many less intellectual than Hayek. No doubt for most people a commitment to liberal values would influence them to reject the excesses of the Stalinist dictatorship. Yet liberal values (defined strictly as the opposite of authoritarian values) are unlikely to be the deciding factor when considering questions of a national health service or other aspects of the welfare state which form the basis of our measure of socialist values.

In Chapter 16 we found an important and complex relationship between being in opposition and commitments to liberal and electoral values. The experience of opposition was clearly a good teacher of support for liberal values of dissent, though not of deference towards electoral majorities. And conversely, the experience of government – or more strictly of being a supporter of the incumbent government – taught respect for electoral mechanisms but not for the values of minority dissent. We cannot exclude this key variable from our model. The question is where to place it. It must be influenced by the substantive values of socialism and nationalism, since socialists and nationalists will naturally support a socialist or nationalist government and oppose governments of the opposite hue. At the same time, it should be prior to liberal values. Those who oppose the government are likely to support the rights of opposition, but most people are not so likely to oppose the government simply because they accept the legitimacy of dissent. Again, we can accept that a few exceptional individuals may be so committed to upholding the right of dissent that they are moved to oppose any and every government because they have fallen into the habit of opposition, or because they fear that the right to oppose will wither if it is not frequently exercised. But we suggest such individuals are exceptional.

So, within our proposed model, we suggest that opposition sentiment may be influenced by social, economic and cultural background, and by socialist and nationalist values; and that opposition sentiment may then influence liberal, populist, electoral and party values.

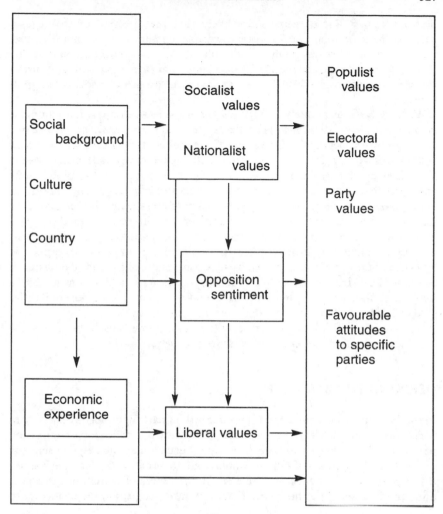

Figure 17.1 Schematic diagram of the multivariate model

Finally, we have included sympathy for specific political parties within our model. We suggest that this may be influenced by social, economic and cultural background; by socialist, nationalist and even by liberal values; and perhaps also by opposition sentiment; but not by populist, electoral and party values. Populist, electoral and party values are so purely procedural that we do not see them as a basis for partisan preferences. Of course there are correlations: people who sympathise with a party that has done well in an election tend to support electoral values. But it seems more likely that the direction of that causal influence runs from electoral success towards commitment to electoral values, rather than the other way round, and insofar as we wish to take account of this effect, we can do so adequately by focusing upon the impact of opposition sentiment on electoral values. The structure of our proposed model is shown in Figure 17.1.

We have been deliberately ambiguous about the role of opposition sentiment in influencing sympathy towards particular political parties however – hence our use of the word 'perhaps'. The essence of the ambiguity is this: it seems almost tautologous to suggest that support for the government influences people towards sympathy for the principal governing party; but it is not so tautologous to suggest that sympathy for one of the other parties is influenced by opposition to the government. In particular, it makes sense to investigate whether sympathy for one of the parties outside the government comes more from those who broadly support or oppose the government (not all parties outside government are 'opposition' parties), and whether – if it is an opposition party – its support is influenced more by ideologies such as socialism, nationalism and liberalism, or by economic distress, or by simple blanket opposition to the government. As we shall see, different opposition parties have ideological bases of support that differ in kind as well as in degree. We shall return to this later.

But, having defined the structure of our model, we must now define the variables to be used in quantifying it more precisely.

DEFINING THE VARIABLES

Inevitably, our results and conclusions depend, in part, upon the precise way in which we define such variables as 'class'. We trust our definitions are not too perverse and our analysis techniques fairly robust; so that an analysis using any reasonable alternative definitions would lead to broadly similar conclusions. But it is as well to be specific. Quite small differences of definition can sometimes produce small but theoretically important differences in the results.

Social factors
As a measure of *working class self-image* we contrasted these who described themselves as 'workers' or 'farmers' (coded +1), with those who described themselves as 'intellectuals', 'managers', or 'businesspeople' (coded –1). As a measure of *age* we contrasted those aged under 35 (coded –1) with those aged between 35 and 55 (coded 0) and those aged 55 or more (coded +1). As a measure of *gender* we contrasted women (coded +1) with men (coded –1). And as a measure of occupational *sector* we contrasted those who worked for private or foreign companies or were self-employed (coded +1) with everyone else (coded 0).

Socio-cultural factors

As a measure of *education* we contrasted those with only elementary schooling (coded −1), and those with higher education (coded +1), with everyone else (coded 0). As a measure of *religiosity* we used a scale running from zero for those who were not religious, through +1 for those who claimed to be religious but said they never attended any religious function, through to +6 for those who attended more than once a week (with intermediate scale points for intermediate frequencies of attendance). As a measure of metropolitanism we contrasted those who were brought up in rural areas (coded −1), with those brought up in small towns (coded 0), and large towns or cities (coded +1). As a measure of ethno-linguistic identity we contrasted those whose main language at home was the *state language* (coded +1) with those who spoke another language at home (coded 0). For this purpose the 'state language' was defined as Russian, Ukrainian, Hungarian, Slovak and Czech in Russia, Ukraine, Hungary, Slovakia and the Czech Republic respectively. A categorisation of individuals by state identity would have been very similar, except in Ukraine where so many Russian speakers claimed Ukrainian identity.

Finally we defined five 'country' or *state of residence* variables, Russia, Ukraine, Hungary, Slovakia and the Czech Republic, coded +1 if the respondent lived in the state in question, and zero otherwise. Logically, one of these variables is redundant, since the values of any four determine the value of the fifth. So while it is possible to calculate simple bivariate correlations between political values and each one of these state of residence variables – essentially contrasting those who live in that state with everyone else, when we move on to a multivariate analysis, using multiple regression, we can only use four of the five state of residence variables – essentially contrasting those who live in each of these four countries with a reference group consisting of those who live in the fifth. We take Russia as the reference group.

Economic experience

We shall focus most attention upon very general attitudes towards economic trends. But we shall also consider more briefly the differential impact of perceptions about trends in personal economic circumstances or the country's economy, and about past or future trends – and, in addition, the impact of perceptions about the level, rather than the trend, of personal economic circumstances. To measure the *level of personal economic circumstances* we have a scale running from 'not enough to survive on' (coded 1) to 'enough for a good standard of living' (coded 4). To measure trends we have a set of four scales running from 'very much worse' (coded 1) to 'very much better' (coded 5). The individual trend scales refer to the 'family's standard of living' and the 'country's economy' over the 'last two years' or the 'next two years'. Averaging responses to all four provides a measure of perceptions about *general economic trends* which we shall simply label *economic optimism*. Averaging the two questions about the family, the two about the country, the two about the past, or the two about the future, provides measures of *family trends, country trends, past trends* and *future trends.*

Political variables

We shall use our standard measures of political values – socialist, nationalist, liberal, populist, electoral and party values as defined in earlier chapters. However, for our multivariate model calculations we shall use the full continuous scales running from 1 to 5 and not dichotomise them at the mid-points (code 3) as we usually did for simplicity of exposition in earlier chapters. So we shall take account of the degree of commitment for example, to socialist values and not just focus upon whether, on balance, people were more pro- or anti-socialist.

In addition, as a measure of *opposition sentiment* we shall contrast those who said they 'thought of themselves as a supporter of the present government and what it is trying to do' (coded −1) with those who thought of themselves as an 'opponent' (coded +1) and those who could not or would not take sides (coded 0).

Although our measure of pro-party values concerns parties, it makes no distinction between one party and another. It is concerned with the concept of a party-structured political life, not with attitudes towards different parties. Since we also wish to assess the impact of values (and of socio-economic and cultural background) on *attitudes towards particular parties* we need some appropriate measures of such attitudes. One obvious possibility is voting choice. But that is a good deal less satisfactory than it seems. Of course, an election study would naturally focus upon voting choice as the 'bottom line', the ultimate dependent variable. But this is not an election study. We are primarily concerned with political values and only concerned with political parties insofar as their support is based upon political values. For our purposes, a much better measure of attitudes towards parties is provided by our five point scales of party sympathy contrasting those who said they felt 'very *un*favourable' towards a party (coded −2) through to those who said they felt 'very favourable' towards it (coded +2).

Voters can only vote for one party although they may sympathise almost equally with several. Many do not vote at all, although they have attitudes – often negative – towards parties. Those who vote for party A may feel almost equally favourable to party B, or alternatively, they may utterly detest party B – but the mere fact of their voting choice gives us no clue to their attitude. People may vote for a party because they see it as the best of several good alternatives or the least bad of several bad alternatives. And voters are swayed by campaign publicity, charismatic leadership, and the credibility of a party (i.e. the party's chances of success) as well as by their generally favourable attitude towards it. People may vote for a party that is not the one they view most favourably, simply because they feel – with regret perhaps – that their favourite party has no real chance of success (however defined) in the election. For all these reasons, votes are always a poor guide to party sympathy and, happily, we are able to measure party sympathy directly.

PATTERNS OF ECONOMIC PERCEPTIONS

Although we focus mainly on our overall measure of perceived economic trends we will also find it useful to distinguish between the six economic measures defined above: the level and trends in personal economic circumstances, perceptions of trends in the country's economy, perceptions of past and future trends, as well as our overall measure of trends which combines personal and national, past and future, trends. These experiences and perceptions varied across countries and social groups in somewhat different ways.

Table 17.1: Correlations between socio-cultural variables and different aspects of economic perceptions

Economic perceptions:	Personal level	Personal trend	Country trend	Past trend	Future trend	General optimism
	r×100	r×100	r×100	r×100	r×100	r×100
(Working) Class	−20	−12	.	−12	.	−10
(Old) Age	.	−13	.	−10	.	.
(Female) Gender	.	.	.	.	.	.
(Private) Sector	18	15	12	16	10	15
(High) Education	11	.	.	.	.	.
(High) Religiosity	.	.	.	.	.	.
City upbringing	.	.	.	.	.	.
Speak state language	18	17	18	19	15	19
Live in:						
Russia	−21	.	.	.	.	.
Ukraine	−29	−25	−26	−32	−17	−28
Hungary	.	.	.	.	.	.
Slovakia	14	.	.	.	.	.
Czech Republic	39	23	39	39	21	34

Notes: Correlations less than 0.10 have been replaced by full-stops for clarity.
Personal level = How adequate is your family income: not enough to survive on, just enough to survive on, enough for a fair standard of living, enough for a good standard of living (coded 1,2,3,4 respectively).
Perceptions of economic trends are based on questions about trends in:
A) family's standard of living over the last two years
B) family's standard of living over the next two years
C) country's economy over the last two years
B) country's economy over the next two years
coded from 1 (very much worse) through 5 (very much better).
Personal trend = average of A and B; Country trend = average of C and D;
Past trend = average of A and C; Future trend = average of B and D;
General economic optimism = average of A,B,C and D.

The *level of personal economic experiences* (the perceived adequacy of family income) correlated fairly strongly with class, occupational sector, speaking the state language, and country. But once we took account of other factors in a multiple regression it was clear that only class and country had important effects. The working class and people who lived in the FSU, especially in Ukraine, complained most about their living standards while those who lived in ECE, especially the Czech Republic, complained least. Multiple regressions within countries showed that only class had an important and consistent influence across countries, supplemented by education in Hungary and Slovakia where the highly educated were relatively satisfied with their living standards.

Table 17.2:   Influence of socio-cultural variables on different aspects of economic perceptions (path coefficients, standardised regression coefficients, or betas)

Economic perceptions:	Personal level	Personal trend	Country trend	Past trend	Future trend	General optimism
Mult R =	53	37	44	49	29	44
(RSQ) =	(28)	(13)	(19)	(24)	(8)	(19)
	beta ×100	beta ×100	beta ×100	beta ×100	beta ×100	beta ×100
(Working) Class	−14	−10	.	.	.	.
(old) Age	.	−10				
(Female) Gender						
(Private) Sector	.	.	.	.	.	.
(High) Education	.	.	.	.	.	.
(High) Religiosity	.	.	.	.	.	.
City upbringing	.	.	.	.	.	.
Speak state language	18	.	.	.	.	.
Live in:						
Russia	*	*	*	*	*	*
Ukraine	−11	−19	−17	−24	−13	−20
Hungary	15	.			.	
Slovakia	21	.	.	.	.	.
Czech Republic	41	16	33	34	14	28

Notes: Multiple regressions calculated by the 'forward inclusion' option in SPSS-PC regression. For clarity, full-stops indicate variables not chosen by SPSS for inclusion, or with betas less than 0.10.
* 'Country of residence' effects in the multiple regressions are measured relative to living in Russia.

Class and country had rather less influence on perceptions of *personal economic trends*, though the people of Ukraine were strongly pessimistic, the Czechs strongly optimistic, and both the working class and the old somewhat pessimistic.

When it came to perceptions of the *trends in their country's economy*, none of the social variables had an important effect, though the people of Ukraine were strongly pessimistic and the Czechs strongly optimistic – views that probably match the relative success of their real economies. Even when account is taken of the uniquely large sector of Ukraine's economy which was unofficial (about half of Ukraine's GDP at the time of our survey according to necessarily imprecise IMF estimates) the people of Ukraine had good reason to be pessimistic.

Similarly our *overall measure of economic trends* was influenced strongly by country – negatively in Ukraine, positively in the Czech Republic – but only very weakly affected by social variables. That remained true within each country, except the Czech Republic, where the old and the working class were notably pessimistic, and the religious as well as the private sector workers were notably optimistic.

So, levels of economic deprivation were very strongly linked to country, and consistently linked to class; while economic trends, especially for the country, but also for individuals as well as country, over the past and – in expectation – the future, were only weakly related to class and less strongly linked to country also.

Moreover, while the level of economic deprivation distinguished the FSU from the ECE, the trends distinguished Ukraine and the Czech Republic (in opposite directions of course) from the other three countries.

INFLUENCES ON SOCIALIST VALUES

In terms of simple bivariate correlations, socialist values correlated well (at over 0.20) with class, age, sector, education, metropolitanism, economic perceptions and country of residence. The old, the working class and those who lived in Russia tended towards socialist values, while those who worked in the private sector, the highly educated, those brought up in the cities, the economically optimistic and the Czechs all tended against socialist values.

The strongest correlation was with general economic optimism about trends. Our five detailed measures of economic perceptions show that socialist values correlated about equally well with the level and the trend of economic circumstances; very slightly more strongly with perceptions of trends in personal economic circumstances than with trends in the country's; and substantially more with perceptions of the past than with hopes or fears for the future.

Multiple regression reveals the independent impact of these different influences net of each other. Once other factors were taken into account, education and sector proved unimportant and the influence of metropolitanism and even class was reduced, but the old still tended strongly towards socialist values, while the economic optimists and the Czechs still tended strongly against.

The Czechs were, as we know, much more economically optimistic than those who lived in other countries, but the multiple regression shows that their opposition to socialist values went well beyond anything that could be explained merely on the basis of that economic optimism – which is ironic, given the relatively large support for socialism and communism in Czechoslovakia, including the Czech part of that state, before the communist coup of 1948.

Table 17.3: Influence of economic and socio-cultural variables on socialist values (path coefficients, standardised regression coefficients, or betas)

		All respondents	Russia	Ukraine	Hungary	Slovakia	Czech Rep
Mult R =		55	56	44	42	36	55
(RSQ) =		(30)	(31)	(20)	(18)	(13)	(31)
	r×100	beta ×100	beta ×100	beta ×100	beta ×100	beta ×100	beta ×100
Economic optimism	−34	−23	−27	.	−13	−19	−37
(Working) Class	25	13	12	18	12	15	.
(Old) Age	29	19	25	22	.	17	18
(Female) Gender	10	.	12	.	11	.	.
(Private) Sector	−22	.	.	−10	−15	.	.
(High) Education	−26	.	.	−11	−13	.	−12
(High) Religiosity	.	.	.	.	.	.	.
City upbringing	−20	−11	−15	.	−11	.	.
Speak state language	.	.	.	13	.	.	.
Live in:							
Russia	19	*					
Ukraine	.	−10					
Hungary	.						
Slovakia	.	.					
Czech Republic	−29	−24					

Notes: Multiple regressions calculated by the 'forward inclusion' option in SPSS-PC regression. For clarity, full-stops indicate variables not chosen by SPSS for inclusion, or with betas less than 0.10.
* 'Country of residence' effects in the multiple regressions are measured relative to living in Russia.

Within-country analyses generally confirmed the importance of age and economic optimism, though their impact varied somewhat from country to country. Age had least effect in Hungary where sector and education had more effect. And economic optimism had by far the most effect within the Czech Republic, and the least effect in Ukraine where people were so universally pessimistic about their economy.

INFLUENCES ON NATIONALIST VALUES

Nationalist values correlated strongly only with speaking the state language, living in Ukraine and, to a lesser extent, with living in Russia: those who spoke the state language or lived in Russia were more nationalist than those who did not; while those who lived in Ukraine were much *less* nationalist than those who lived elsewhere. Multiple regression confirmed the strong and independent effects of these factors. The overall weakness of economic pessimism as an influence towards nationalism is striking and reassuring.

Table 17.4: Influence of economic and socio-cultural variables on nationalist values (path coefficients, standardised regression coefficients, or betas)

	All respondents	Russia	Ukraine	Hungary	Slovakia	Czech Rep
Mult R =		37	30	43	19	41	23
(RSQ) =		(14)	(9)	(18)	(3)	(17)	(5)
	r×100	beta×100	beta×100	beta×100	beta×100	beta×100
Economic optimism	·	−12	−22	+7	·	·	−14
(Working) Class	13	·	·	·	12	10
(Old) Age	11	·	13	·	·	10
(Female) Gender	·	·	·	·	·	·
(Private) Sector	·	·	·	·	·	·
(High) Education	−12	·	·	−17	·	·
(High) Religiosity	·	·	11	·	·	·
City upbringing	−11	·	·	·	·	·
Speak state language	27	22	·	35	·	40
Live in:						
Russia	16	*				
Ukraine	−21	−17				
Hungary	·	·				
Slovakia	·	·				
Czech Republic	−11	−13				

Note: We have departed from our usual convention by displaying the small, but positive, influence from economic optimism on nationalism in Ukraine, because its influence was negative in other countries.

Within individual countries the pattern of influences varied sharply, reflecting the particular ethnic divisions and imperial aspirations within different countries. In Hungary alone, where both ethnic divisions and imperial aspirations had been reduced by downsizing, the highly educated tended strongly against nationalism. The influence of speaking the state language was extremely strong in Ukraine and Slovakia – reflecting their large Russian speaking and Hungarian speaking communities respectively, but almost non-existent elsewhere.

Economic perceptions had a large effect on nationalist values in Russia where economic pessimists tended strongly towards nationalism – in sharp contrast to Ukraine where economic perceptions had relatively little effect on nationalist values at all but, insofar as they had an effect, it was the economic *optimists* in Ukraine who were most inclined towards nationalism. Russian and Ukrainian nationalism were not merely opposed to each other, their patterns of support also reflected the difference between Russian fears and Ukrainian hopes.

INFLUENCES ON OPPOSITION SENTIMENT

Economic perceptions dominated opposition sentiments even more than they influenced socialist values. And whereas *personal* economic level, and *personal* economic trends correlated more strongly than perceptions of the country's economy with socialist values, the reverse was true for opposition sentiment. Opposition sentiment correlated at 0.43 with pessimism *about the country*, at 0.36 with pessimism about personal economic trends and at only 0.25 with pessimism about the level of personal economic circumstances. As with socialist values however, opposition correlated more strongly with perceptions about the past than expectations about the future.

Apart from economic pessimism, opposition correlated strongly (at over 0.20) only with speaking the state language, with socialist values, and with country of residence: those who spoke the state language at home were less likely to oppose the government; those who held socialist values were more likely to oppose it; and while Czechs were the least likely to oppose their government, those who lived in Ukraine were the most likely to do so.

But using multiple regression to take account of other factors – principally economic optimism or pessimism – eliminated the apparent influence of speaking the state language, of socialist values, and even of living in the Czech Republic: the Czechs were so unusually supportive of their government only because they were so happy about economic trends in their country, though Ukrainians' economic pessimism was not, by itself, enough to explain their opposition to their government.

Within every country, opposition sentiment was dominated by economic pessimism. Amongst the weaker influences there was a general tendency across countries for the old to be *less* opposed to their government (once their relatively poor economic circumstances had been taken into account). Since governments varied from country to country, it would have been surprising if the pattern of opposition sentiment had not varied to some degree across countries, reflecting the political complexion of the government. And so it did. Above and beyond the reaction against poor economic performance, there was a tendency for socialists in Russia to oppose their government;

for the religious in Hungary to support theirs; for Czech socialists to oppose their government and religious Czechs to support it; and for nationalists to oppose the government in Russia, but to support the government in Slovakia – all very plausible reactions to the nature of their governments but nonetheless all fairly weak effects.

Table 17.5: Influence of socialist and nationalist values and other factors on opposition sentiment (path coefficients, standardised regression coefficients, or betas)

	r×100	*All respondents*	*Russia*	*Ukraine*	*Hungary*	*Slovakia*	*Czech Rep*
Mult R =		49	41	29	41	39	55
(RSQ) =		(24)	(17)	(8)	(17)	(15)	(30)
		beta ×100	beta ×100	beta ×100	beta ×100	beta ×100	beta ×100
Socialist values	19	.	17	.	.	.	13
Nationalist values	.	.	10	.	.	−13	.
Economic optimism	−44	−35	−27	−24	−34	−36	−44
(Working) Class	.	.	.	.	.	.	.
(Old) Age	.	.	−12	−10	−11	.	.
(Female) Gender	.	.	.	.	.	.	.
(Private) Sector	.	.	.	.	.	.	.
(High) Education	.	.	.	.	.	.	.
(High) Religiosity	.	.	.	.	−18	.	−13
City upbringing	.	.	.	.	.	.	.
Speak state language	−18	.	.	.	.	.	.
Live in:							
Russia	.	*					
Ukraine	25	17					
Hungary	.	13					
Slovakia	.	.					
Czech Republic	−24	.					

INFLUENCES ON LIBERAL AND AUTHORITARIAN VALUES

Our measure of liberal values was essentially the inverse of a measure of authoritarian values; so we can describe the patterns in either terminology.

Economic optimism or pessimism had very little impact but, insofar as it had any at all, we found a difference between the impact of economic levels and trends. Those with a high *level* of personal economic circumstances tended towards liberal values. But at the same time, those who felt relatively comfortable about economic *trends* were in fact no more liberal, and even slightly more authoritarian than the economic pessimists – especially in Ukraine and the former Czechoslovakia.

Correlations with class, age, education, country, socialism, nationalism and opposition sentiment were larger: authoritarian values were stronger amongst the working class, the old, socialists, nationalists and the people of Russia; liberal values were stronger amongst the highly educated, the Czechs, and those who opposed their government.

Taking account of other influences through multiple regression eliminated all social, economic and cultural influences except living in the Czech Republic, reduced the apparent importance of socialist and nationalist values, and increased the apparent importance of opposition sentiment – which the multiple regression revealed as the most important influence of all.

Table 17.6:   Influence of socialist and nationalist values, opposition sentiment and other factors on liberal values (path coefficients, standardised regression coefficients, or betas)

	All respondents	Russia	Ukraine	Hungary	Slovakia	Czech Rep
Mult R =		42	34	46	47	48	38
(RSQ) =		(18)	(12)	(21)	(22)	(23)	(15)
	r×100	beta ×100	beta ×100	beta ×100	beta ×100	beta ×100	beta ×100
Socialist values	−21	−12	.	−10	−14	−21	−22
Nationalist values	−20	−15	.	−23	−11	−20	−13
Opposition sentiment	15	19	25	14	22	20	.
Economic optimism	.	.	.	−17	.	−10	−16
(Working) Class	−17	.	.	−11	.	−11	.
(Old) Age	−18	.	−10	−13	−15	.	.
(Female) Gender	.	.	.	.	.	.	−15
(Private) Sector	10	.	.	.	.	.	.
(High) Education	20	.	.	.	19	.	10
(High) Religiosity	.	.	.	.	.	−12	.
City upbringing	.	.	.	.	.	.	.
Speak state language	.	.	.	.	.	.	.
Live in:							
Russia	−12	*					
Ukraine	.	.					
Hungary	.	.					
Slovakia	.	.					
Czech Republic	17	19					

Regressions within countries confirmed the importance of opposition sentiment as an influence towards liberal values in every country except the Czech Republic; and the importance of socialist and nationalist values on authoritarian values in every country except possibly Russia – though even in Russia there was some evidence that nationalist values slightly increased support for authoritarianism. In Hungary alone, education had a large influence towards liberal values – consistent with our earlier finding that education had a large influence in reducing nationalist values in Hungary alone. Amongst the weaker influences, age and (working) class had a consistent influence towards authoritarian values in all countries – but seldom a large influence. Religion had most influence towards authoritarianism in Slovakia – though that too was not large.

INFLUENCES ON POPULAR CONTROL VALUES

Influence on populist values
Populist values correlated most strongly with opposition sentiment, economic pessimism and liberal values – all of which influenced people towards populist values. But populism correlated much more strongly with perceptions of economic *trends* than with the *level* of personal economic circumstances and in multiple regressions the apparent influence of economic factors was much reduced or eliminated altogether, except in the Czech Republic. In every country, however, the impact of opposition sentiment and liberal values was substantial. These two factors dominated populist values. (See table 17.7).

Influences on electoral values
Support for the principle of competitive elections correlated strongly and positively with economic optimism and with living in the Czech Republic; and strongly, but negatively, with socialism and opposition sentiment. Once account had been taken of other influences, multiple regression showed that only opposition sentiment and, to a somewhat lesser degree, economic optimism had a strong impact. In all countries economic optimists tended to support electoral values and those who opposed their government tended to oppose competitive elections. These effects were especially strong in the Czech Republic. Amongst the weaker effects, age and education tended to increase support for electoral values, and commitment to socialist values tended to reduce support for electoral values – but all these effects were relatively weak. (See table 17.8).

Influences on pro-party values
There were no very large or consistent (across countries) influences towards support for the idea of political parties. However, there were modest but fairly consistent tendencies for the old, the well educated and liberals to support party values, and for the working class and women to reject them. (See table 17.9).

INFLUENCES ON ATTITUDES TOWARDS SPECIFIC PARTIES

The collapse of communist regimes allowed entry to numerous political parties, mostly with few members, little organisation, vague ideologies and little experience. We asked about public attitudes towards 47 of these parties but we shall focus upon a more limited selection here. In each country we shall look at public attitudes towards the communist party or its principal successor, and at attitudes towards the principal government party. In addition we shall look at attitudes towards selected nationalist or ethnic parties, some self-styled liberal parties, and at socialist rivals to the communists.

Table 17.7: Influence of socialist, nationalist and liberal values, and other factors on populist values (path coefficients, standardised regression coefficients, or betas)

	All respondents		Russia	Ukraine	Hungary	Slovakia	Czech Rep
Mult R =		39	38	26	30	44	45
(RSQ) =		(15)	(14)	(7)	(9)	(19)	(20)
	r×100	beta×100	beta×100	beta×100	beta×100	beta×100	beta×100
Socialist values	11	·	·	·	13	11	·
Nationalist values	·	·	·	·	·	−10	·
Opposition sentiment	29	19	17	15	15	25	24
Liberal values	20	20	23	15	15	27	19
Economic optimism	−22	−10	·	·	·	·	−22
(Working) Class	·	·	·	·	·	·	·
(Old) Age	·	·	·	·	·	·	·
(Female) Gender	·	·	·	·	·	10	·
(Private) Sector	·	·	·	·	·	·	·
(High) Education	·	·	·	·	·	·	·
(High) Religiosity	·	·	·	·	·	·	·
City upbringing	·	·	·	·	·	·	·
Speak state language	·	·	·	·	·	·	·
Live in:							
Russia	·	*					
Ukraine	·	·					
Hungary	16	14					
Slovakia	·	·					
Czech Republic	−12	·					

Attitudes towards parties in Russia

In Russia we focus on the Communist Party of the Russian Federation led by Gennadii Zyuganov, Russia's Choice led by Yegor Gaidar and implicitly – but not explicitly – backed by President Yeltsin, Vladimir Zhirinovsky's Liberal Democratic Party (a nationalist, not a liberal party, despite the name) and Grigorii Yavlinsky's Yabloko which could lay more genuine claim to liberal credentials.

Table 17.8: Influence of socialist, nationalist and liberal values, and other factors on electoral values (path coefficients, standardised regression coefficients, or betas)

		All respondents	Russia	Ukraine	Hungary	Slovakia	Czech Rep
Mult R =		49	38	29	36	37	54
(RSQ) =		(24)	(14)	(9)	(13)	(13)	(29)
	r×100	beta ×100	beta ×100	beta ×100	beta ×100	beta ×100	beta ×100
Socialist values	−27	.	−10	.	−10	−11	.
Nationalist values	−11	.	.	.	−12	.	.
Opposition sentiment	−33	−19	−21	−12	−11	−21	−37
Liberal values	.	.	.	.	.	.	11
Economic optimism	35	16	12	16	20	16	18
(Working) Class	−13	.	.	.	.	−11	.
(Old) Age	.	.	10	.	10	.	14
(Female) Gender	.	.	−10	−10	.	.	.
(Private) Sector	.	.	.	.	.	.	.
(High) Education	11	.	.	.	13	.	12
(High) Religiosity	.	.	.	.	.	.	.
City upbringing	.	.	.	.	.	.	.
Speak state language	12	.	.	.	.	.	.
Live in:							
Russia	.	*					
Ukraine	−18	.					
Hungary	.	.					
Slovakia	.	10					
Czech Republic	30	15					

Attitudes towards the Communist Party correlated with various social, economic and cultural variables but all of these correlations were eliminated once we took account of the impact of values. Multiple regression showed that favourable attitudes towards the Communist Party were influenced mainly by socialist values, and to a lesser extent by opposition sentiment and liberal values. This last is very significant: it was liberal values, *not* authoritarian values that went with favourable attitudes towards the Communist Party – despite the deluge of ill-informed journalistic commentary to the contrary. And once these values had been taken into account, the apparent influence of nationalism, metropolitanism, economic pessimism and other factors such as age and education so often mentioned by journalists also proved relatively unimportant – either because they had little impact on anyone, or because they applied to only a small minority of the public, or a combination of both.

Attitudes towards the main pro-government party[1] Russia's Choice were not at all the inverse of attitudes towards the Communist Party. The principal determinant of favourable attitudes towards Russia's Choice was support for the government. If that seems too tautologous – and in the Russian situation where government was in the hands of the President who refused to join any party the tautology is less real than apparent – then let us exclude opposition sentiment from the multiple regression. If we do that, the principal determinant of favourable attitudes towards Russia's Choice becomes economic optimism (especially perceptions about the country's economy rather than personal circumstances), though there are smaller influences from socialist, nationalist and liberal values – all negative. Here at least is one inverse of the influences on attitudes towards the Communist Party: while liberal values inclined people towards the Communist Party, it was *authoritarian* values that inclined people towards Russia's Choice.[2] In the west, Russia's Choice may have been described – reluctantly and inaccurately perhaps – as a 'liberal' party; within Russia it was known as 'the party of power' or in plain English, 'the authorities'.

Table 17.9: Influence of socialist, nationalist and liberal values, and other factors on party values (path coefficients, standardised regression coefficients, or betas)

	All respondents	Russia	Ukraine	Hungary	Slovakia	Czech Rep
Mult R =	32	25	25	23	26	41
(RSQ) =	(11)	(6)	(6)	(5)	(7)	(17)
	r×100	beta×100	beta×100	beta×100	beta×100	beta×100
		beta×100				
Socialist values	−14	·	·	−12	·	·
Nationalist values	·	·	·	10	·	·
Opposition sentiment	−13	·	·	·	−17	−10
Liberal values	12	·	·	·	12	14
Economic optimism	19	10	·	10	·	16
(Working) Class	−14	·	·	·	−13	−15
(old) Age	·	12	15	·	·	17
(Female) Gender	−13	−12	−13	−17	−13	−12
(Private) Sector	·	·	·	·	·	·
(High) Education	11	·	16	17	·	·
(High) Religiosity	·	·	·	·	·	·
City upbringing	·	·	·	·	·	·
Speak state language	·	·	·	·	·	·
Live in:						
Russia	·	*				
Ukraine	−15	−10				
Hungary	·	·				
Slovakia	·	·				
Czech Republic	16					

Zhirinovsky's Liberal Democratic Party was an alternative opposition party for those who wished to oppose the government without voting communist. There is a suspicion that it was promoted by the authorities in 1993, as Alexander Lebed was admittedly promoted in the 1996 presidential election, as a means of dividing the opposition and preventing a surge of popular support towards the more dangerous and better organised Communist Party. Favourable attitudes towards the LDP did not correlate well with economic pessimism: they correlated more strongly with class, metropolitanism, political values and, above all, opposition sentiment. Nationalist values had no more impact than socialist values, and clearly less than opposition sentiment. But compared to the pattern of attitudes towards the Communist Party, attitudes towards the LDP were very much less dependent upon socialist values and a little more dependent upon nationalism and opposition sentiment.

Attitudes towards Yabloko were also influenced most by opposition sentiment – though also, to a lesser extent, by socialist values, education and age. Not surprisingly the influence of socialist values was against Yabloko and the influence of education towards Yabloko. There was also a metropolitan influence towards Yabloko but that was almost eliminated once other factors were taken into account. But there are two surprises concerning the pattern of favourable attitudes towards Yabloko. First, although Yavlinsky was not part of the government his party was regarded more favourably by supporters than by opponents of the government. That is not a great surprise however, because although Yavlinsky was outside the government he was clearly willing to join it on his own terms, and occasionally held discussions on that point. His position could be described as that of a moderately sympathetic critic of the government rather than that of an opponent. Our finding here is not controversial. But the second surprise is more significant: commitment to liberal values had almost no effect upon attitudes towards the self-styled 'liberal' Yabloko. Liberal values went with favourable attitudes towards the Communists and the LDP, and unfavourable attitudes towards Russia's Choice, but with neither favourable nor unfavourable attitudes towards Yabloko.

How can we explain the paradox that liberal values had no effect upon attitudes toward the party which was most self-consciously attached to western liberal values? Part of the explanation is that liberal values were not just, or even mainly, an influence upon attitudes towards parties but, in fact, a reflection of party support: those who favoured opposition parties became more favourable towards the rights and liberties of opposition and less favourable towards the authorities. We can take account of that reverse causation by including opposition sentiment along with liberal values as an influence upon attitudes to parties. That reduces the apparent effect of liberal values and suggests that, once we take account of opposition sentiment, commitment to liberal values was *not* an important influence on favourable attitudes towards the LDP or unfavourable attitudes to Russia's Choice, and only a marginally important influence on favourable attitudes towards the Communist Party; and it also suggests a positive influence of liberal values on favourable attitudes towards Yabloko, though only a very small one.

Table 17.10: Influence of socialist, nationalist and liberal values, and other factors on favourable attitudes to parties in Russia (path coefficients, standardised regression coefficients, or betas)

	Communist Party			LDP			Russia's Choice			Yabloko		
Mult R =		43	41		33	29		52	40		25	20
	r	beta	beta	r	beta	beta	r	beta	beta	r	beta	beta
Socialist values	34	24	26	17	10	14	−23	−11	−14	−16	−12	−14
Nationalist values	18	·	·	16	10	12	−22	·	−15	·	·	·
Opposition	29	16	ex	25	18	ex	−47	−37	ex	−18	−17	ex
Liberal values	13	12	15	·	·	10	−17	·	−17	·	·	·
Economic optimism	−23	·	·	−12	·	·	30	11	21	·	·	·
(Working) Class	14	·	·	15	10	11	·	·	·	·	·	·
(Old) Age	12	·	·	·	·	−10	·	·	·	·	·	10
(Female) Gender	·	·	·	·	·	·	·	·	·	·	·	·
(Private) Sector	·	·	·	·	·	·	·	·	·	·	·	·
(High) Education	−10	·	·	·	·	·	·	·	·	11	11	10
(High) Religiosity	·	·	·	·	·	·	·	·	·	10	·	·
City upbringing	−17	·	·	−14	·	·	·	·	·	·	·	·
Speak state language	·	·	·	·	·	·	·	·	·	·	·	·

Note: 'ex' means opposition sentiment was excluded from consideration as an influence upon attitudes towards the party in this regression.

Another part of the explanation is that support for Yavlinsky was based on economic liberalism (equivalent to opposing socialist values as we have strictly defined them) rather than on political liberalism (liberal values as we have strictly defined them). But there is yet another explanation. Recent focus group studies suggest that one of the main characteristics of Yavlinsky in Russian voters' eyes was his intellectual pride rather than his liberal values.[3] Interestingly, our analysis of Yabloko support back in 1993 shows that the influence of education was at least twice as great as the influence of liberal values on favourable attitudes towards his party: Yabloko appealed to intellectual snobs.

Attitudes towards parties in Ukraine

In Ukraine we focus upon three parties: the Communist Party and the Socialist Party, both of which had some claims to be the successor party to the CPSU, and Rukh, which formally changed in 1992 from being a broad national democratic movement into a moderate nationalist party or, as Kuzio and Wilson classified it, a party of 'national democrats'.[4] In sharp contrast to Russia, attitudes towards all of these parties was largely unaffected by economic perceptions or even by opposition sentiments – not least perhaps because government in Ukraine was even less party-based than in Russia.

The patterns of attitudes towards the Communist and Socialist parties were strikingly similar, dominated in both cases by socialist values and influenced, to a lesser extent in both cases, by religiosity, gender and nationalist values or speaking the state language. Favourable attitudes towards both parties were increased by a commitment to socialist values or by being female, and reduced by being religious, speaking the state language at home, or being committed to nationalist values. The main difference was that socialist values had an even stronger influence on attitudes towards the Communist Party than on attitudes towards the Socialist Party.

Attitudes towards Rukh were dominated by a combination of nationalist values and speaking the state language both of which had a strong effect on favourable attitudes towards Rukh. At the same time socialist values had a strong effect on *un*favourable attitudes towards Rukh.

Other social, economic and cultural factors correlated with attitudes towards these parties but their influences were eliminated once account was taken of the impact of socialist and nationalist values (or language) and, for the Communist and Socialist parties, of religiosity. Thus the apparent effects of age and education on Communist and Socialist party support were eliminated in the multiple regressions, as were the apparent effects of economic optimism, religiosity and metropolitanism on support for Rukh.

Table 17.11: Influence of socialist, nationalist and liberal values, and other factors on favourable attitudes to parties in Ukraine (path coefficients, standardised regression coefficients, or betas)

	Communist Party			Socialist Party			Rukh		
Mult R =		40	41		34	31		37	37
	r	beta	beta	r	beta	beta	r	beta	beta
Socialist values	36	37	36	24	26	25	−13	−19	−19
Nationalist values	.	.	.	.	.	−10	25	19	19
Opposition	.	.	ex	.	−11	ex	.	.	ex
Liberal values	−11	.	.	.	.	.	.	.	.
Economic optimism	.	.	.	.	.	.	14	.	.
(Working) Class	.	.	.	.	.	.	10	.	.
(Old) Age	13	.	.	.	.	.	.	.	.
(Female) Gender	.	.	.	.	.	10	.	.	.
(Private) Sector	−10	.	.	.	.	.	.	.	.
(High) Education	−13	.	.	−10	.	.	.	.	.
(High) Religiosity	−10	−10	−11	−13	−12	−14	16	.	.
City upbringing	.	.	.	.	.	.	−12	.	.
Speak state language	.	.	−12	.	.	.	25	18	18

Note: 'ex' means opposition sentiment was excluded from consideration as an influence upon attitudes towards the party in this regression.

Attitudes to parties in Hungary

In Hungary we focus on five parties. First the Socialist Party, which was the organic successor to the Communist Party but a Communist Party that had spent two decades gradually rejecting both the style and content of a communist system. So despite the historical continuity of its personnel and organisation, its practice and ideology had long ceased to be communist. By the time of our survey it had 'an authentically social democratic orientation' according to Racz.[5] Then we focus on the major governing party, the Hungarian Democratic Forum founded in 1987 as a dissident but patriotic party, and its minor ally, the Smallholders' Party, which could claim to be the leading 'historic' party – the Smallholders had obtained 57 per cent of the vote in the 1945 election, but in the 1990s they became obsessive about the single issue of land restitution and had relatively little support; and finally, the two self-styled liberal opposition parties, the Free Democrats and the Young Democrats, both founded by dissidents in 1988 (see Chapter 2).

Not only did the pattern of attitudes towards the Hungarian Socialist Party look quite unlike the pattern of attitudes towards a communist party, they scarcely resembled the pattern we might expect of attitudes towards a social democratic party. By far the strongest correlation was with opposition sentiment, followed by fairly weak correlations with economic optimism, religiosity and then socialist values. Economic optimism and religiosity worked against support for the Socialist Party; socialist values worked in its favour, but very weakly. Indeed liberal values had almost as much effect on favourable attitudes towards the Hungarian Socialist Party as did socialist values. That lack of a sharp profile of support probably helped the Socialist Party towards its election victory six months after our survey.

The increasingly unpopular Hungarian Democratic Forum had the sharpest profile of support. It correlated most with opposition sentiment followed by economic optimism, liberal values and religiosity. It did best amongst the economic optimists and the religious, worst (not surprisingly) amongst those who opposed the government and (more dishearteningly) amongst those committed to liberal values. If we include opposition sentiment in the multiple regression, it totally dominates the pattern of attitudes to the HDF; if we exclude it, the main influences are economic pessimism and liberal values which both influenced people against the HDF.

Although the Smallholders' Party was a junior partner in government, the pattern of attitudes towards it was quite different from the HDF's. The strongest correlations were with education, opposition sentiment, class, the level (*not* the trend) in personal economic circumstances, and nationalism. As was usual with governing parties, though unusually clearly in Hungary, favourable attitudes towards the HDF correlated much more with perceptions of favourable perceptions of economic trends rather than with the level of personal economic circumstances. But favourable attitudes towards the Smallholders did *not* correlate at all with economic trends, and correlated *negatively* with the level of personal economic circumstances. The Smallholders' Party also did best amongst the working class (which, in our definition, included farmers), the least educated, the most nationalist, and government supporters. Excluding opposition sentiment, multiple regression suggested only two important influences on Smallholders support: a lack of education followed, far behind, by nationalist values.

The patterns of attitudes towards the Free Democrats and the Young Democrats were fairly similar to each other.[6] Both were favoured most by the young, and least by nationalists. Not surprisingly, given their name, youth correlated even more strongly with support for the Young Democrats than for the Free Democrats. Economic optimism and socialist values had no effect upon attitudes to either party. But opposition sentiment and liberal values seemed to have a slight influence on favourable attitudes towards the Free Democrats, yet none on attitudes to the Young Democrats.

Attitudes towards parties in Slovakia

In Slovakia we focus on the Democratic Left – the successor to the Communist Party; on the governing Movement for a Democratic Slovakia which was led,

Table 17.12: Influence of socialist, nationalist and liberal values, and other factors on favourable attitudes to parties in Hungary (path coefficients, standardised regression coefficients, or betas)

	Socialist Party			Young Democrats			Free Democrats			HDF			Smallholders		
	r	beta	beta	r	beta	beta	r	beta	beta	r	beta	beta	r	beta	beta
Mult R =	10	28	21	·	32	32	·	28	26	·	57	39	·	29	25
Socialist values	·	11	11	·	·	·	·	·	·	-55	-48	·	·	·	·
Nationalist values	·	·	·	-15	-13	-13	-14	-13	-12	-22	·	-20	14	10	10
Opposition	25	24	ex	·	·	ex	15	11	ex	·	·	ex	-17	-15	ex
Liberal values	·	·	10	·	·	·	16	·	11	·	·	·	-13	·	·
Econ optimism	-14	·	-11	·	·	·	·	·	·	30	14	28	·	·	·
(Working) Class	·	·	·	·	·	·	·	·	·	·	·	·	17	·	·
(Old) Age	·	·	·	-27	-26	-26	-19	-17	-18	·	·	·	·	·	·
(Female) Gender	·	·	·	·	10	10	·	·	·	·	·	·	·	·	·
(Private) Sector	·	·	·	·	·	·	·	·	·	·	·	·	·	·	·
(High) Education	·	·	·	·	·	·	·	·	·	·	·	·	-23	-20	-21
(High) Religiosity	-12	·	-11	·	·	·	·	·	·	17	·	13	·	·	·
City upbringing	·	·	·	·	·	·	·	·	·	·	·	·	·	·	·
Speak state language	·	·	·	·	·	·	·	·	·	·	·	·	·	·	·

Note: 'ex' means opposition sentiment was excluded from consideration as an influence upon attitudes towards the party in this regression.

Table 17.13: Influence of socialist, nationalist and liberal values, and other factors on favourable attitudes to parties in Slovakia (path coefficients, standardised regression coefficients, or betas)

	Democratic Left			MDS			SNP			Hungarian Minority Parties		
	r	beta	beta	r	beta	beta	r	beta	beta	r	beta	beta
Mult R =		26	26		67	53		50	47		57	56
Socialist values	13	15	15	13			29	16	17			
Nationalist values				26			−31	−18		−41	−25	−25
Opposition			ex	−58	−45	ex			ex	18	10	ex
Liberal values				−41	−22	−31	−23		−12	18		
Economic optimism				28	11	25	27	17	23			
(Working) Class				11								
(Old) Age												
(Female) Gender												
(Private) Sector												
(High) Education										−12	−10	
(High) Religiosity										12	17	17
City upbringing	−22	−22										
Speak state language				25	17	17	33	22	23	−46	−35	−36

Note: 'ex' means opposition sentiment was excluded from consideration as an influence upon attitudes towards the party in this regression.

however, by Meciar who had a communist past and continuing communist style; the Slovak National Party, which claimed to be a successor to the party that had governed the Nazi puppet state of Slovakia between 1939 and 1945[7]; and the minority Hungarian parties – the Hungarian Christian Democratic Movement/Coexistence.[8]

The Democratic Left had the least well defined profile of support. Only two influences were important: religiosity, followed by socialist values, and religiosity had more impact on reducing support for the Democratic Left than socialist values had on increasing it. Opposition sentiment and economic optimism had no influence on support for the Democratic Left.

Attitudes towards the governing MDS correlated most strongly with opposition sentiment, followed by liberal values, economic optimism, speaking the state language, and nationalism. These last two reinforced or substituted for each other. The MDS did best amongst those who supported the government (naturally), but also amongst authoritarians, economic optimists, Slovak speakers and nationalists. Excluding opposition sentiment, the multiple regression showed strong influences towards MDS support from authoritarianism, followed by economic optimism and speaking the state language. Including opposition sentiment on the other hand, still left strong influences from authoritarianism and speaking the state language.

The pattern of attitudes towards the SNP (Slovak Nationalist Party) was more nationalist, but less authoritarian and pro-government than that which underpinned MDS support. Excluding opposition sentiment, the multiple regression showed strong influences towards SNP support both from speaking the state language and, in addition, from commitment to nationalist values, as well as from economic optimism and, to a much lesser extent, from authoritarianism. Including opposition sentiment merely reduced each of these effects slightly.

Favourable attitudes towards minority Hungarian parties were based overwhelmingly on language, nationalism and religiosity in that order of importance. Their support was greatly increased by speaking Hungarian, greatly reduced by a commitment to Slovak nationalist values, and substantially increased by religiosity. Economic optimism and socialist values had no effect, and liberal values only a little.[9]

Attitudes towards parties in the Czech Republic

In the Czech Republic we focus on the Communist Democratic Left, the Social Democratic Party and the governing Civic Democratic Party of Prime Minister Klaus. As in Ukraine, the patterns of attitudes towards the Communists and Socialist parties were broadly similar though, again, the pattern of attitudes towards the Communists was better defined. But in the Czech Republic, the pattern of attitudes towards the governing Civic Democratic Party was also the same – though inverse, of course – as for the Communists and Socialists, and even better defined than that for the Communist Party. It was a peculiarly simple structure of party sympathies.

If we *exclude* opposition sentiment, the key influences on party support were economic optimism, followed by socialist values and religiosity. Socialist values increased support for the Communist and Socialist Parties and decreased support for the Civic Democratic Party, while religiosity and economic optimism did the opposite. Of these three influences, religiosity was always the weakest. But the balance of importance between socialist values and economic optimism varied: for the Socialist Party socialist values were slightly more important; for the Communist Party economic pessimism was slightly more important; but by contrast Civic Democratic Party support depended *very much* more upon good economic performance than on ideological opposition to socialist values. For all three parties, economic trends mattered much more than the level of personal economic circumstances, and – especially for the Civic Democratic Party – national economic trends mattered much more than even the trends in personal economic fortunes.

If, on the other hand, we *include* opposition sentiment, the apparent influence of economic optimism is reduced, though still strong. Opposition sentiment itself then rivals socialist values and economic optimism as an influence on attitudes to the Communist Party, and becomes by far the strongest influence upon attitudes towards the Civic Democratic Party. While there is an element of tautology in saying that support for the government is by far the main influence upon favourable attitudes towards the governing party – and government in the Czech Republic was party based government to a greater degree than anywhere else in our survey – it is worth noting that this was true even when we took explicit account of economic optimism and the rejection of socialist values. That seems to indicate that government support in the Czech Republic had a basis that was independent in some degree of both ideology and economic performance – perhaps just a pervasive ethos of competence.

Finally let us draw attention to the absence of an influence that we have detected everywhere else except Ukraine. In Russia, Hungary and especially in nearby Slovakia there was clear evidence that authoritarian values correlated strongly with support for the governing party. Even when we controlled for inverse causation, by taking account of opposition sentiment, some such effect remained, and it was particularly strong in Slovakia. By contrast, in the Czech Republic, no analysis – bivariate or multivariate, with or without controls for opposition sentiment – could link Civic Democratic Party support to authoritarianism. That is a very important finding, but it should not be overstated: it would be totally wrong to go further and claim evidence of a link between Civic Democratic Party support and liberal values. What we have found is the absence of such a link, negative or positive.

Table 17.14:   Influence of socialist, nationalist and liberal values, and other factors on favourable attitudes to parties in the Czech Republic (path coefficients, standardised regression coefficients, or betas)

	Communist/ Democratic Left			Social Democrats			Civic Democratic Party		
Mult R =		51	47		34	34		71	59
	r	beta	beta	r	beta	beta	r	beta	beta
Socialist values	36	20	23	29	21	21	−35	−12	−19
Nationalist values	12	.	.	.	.	.	−15	.	.
Opposition	40	23	ex	22	.	ex	−65	−49	ex
Liberal values	.	.	.	.	.	.	.	.	.
Economic optimism	−41	−19	−29	−28	−18	−18	55	−27	47
(Working) Class	.	.	.	.	.	.	−10	.	.
(Old) Age	11	.	.	11	.	.	.	.	11
(Female) Gender	.	.	.	.	.	.	.	.	.
(Private) Sector	.	.	.	.	.	.	.	.	.
(High) Education	.	.	.	.	.	.	.	.	.
(High) Religiosity	−14	.	−12	.	.	.	18	.	13
City upbringing	−11	.	.	.	.	.	.	.	.
Speak state language	.	.	.	.	.	.	.	.	.

Note: 'ex' means opposition sentiment was excluded from consideration as an influence upon attitudes towards the party in this regression.

CONCLUSION

Amongst social, economic and cultural variables three stand out as having special significance. First *economic pessimism*, understood as focused on perceptions of national economic trends rather than personal economic trends, still less on the level of personal economic circumstances: that increased opposition sentiment and support for socialist values (though this latter also reflected the level of personal economic circumstances). Second, *language*: where ethnolinguistic divisions existed, as in Ukraine and Slovakia, speaking the state language at home had a strong influence on nationalist values. Third, *country*: even when all other factors were taken into account, the people of the Czech Republic had notably anti-socialist and pro-liberal values and the people of Ukraine were, as a whole, remarkably opposed to the extremes of nationalist sentiment.

Although there were crude correlations between liberal/authoritarian values and age, class and education, these values depended more directly upon *opposition sentiment* and attitudes to socialism and nationalism. Socialist and nationalist values inclined people towards authoritarianism but their influence was offset by the experience of opposition which taught liberal values.

Of the more exclusively procedural values, populism was influenced by opposition sentiment and liberal values, while electoral values were influenced most by economic performance and opposition sentiment. Although opposition sentiment increased support for liberal versus authoritarian values, and for populism, it decreased support for the principal mechanism of representative government: elections. It seems therefore, that the effect of opposition sentiment is largely instrumental and self-interested: it makes the opposition more favourable to rights of protest but less favourable to the system of elections that produced their opposition status in the first place. Support for the idea of political parties was only weakly related to anything but was a little higher amongst men, the educated, the old, and those who were more optimistic about economic trends.

Favourable attitudes towards the *Communist Party* or its successors were influenced most by socialist values in Russia, Ukraine and the Czech Republic; but socialist values were just one of several weak and competing influences in Hungary, and religiosity had more influence than socialist values in Slovakia. Almost tautologously the main influence upon attitudes towards *governing parties* was opposition sentiment rather than ideology of any kind. If, however, that explanation is excluded, the main influences appear to be economic optimism and authoritarian values in Russia, Hungary and Slovakia; and economic optimism plus anti-socialist values in the Czech Republic. The link between authoritarian sentiments and favourable attitudes to non-communist governing parties is striking, however it is explained. Of the *nationalist or ethnic parties* whose support we analysed, support for the LDP in Russia was clearly more dependent upon opposition sentiment than nationalism; but attitudes to Rukh in Ukraine and the SNP in Slovakia were primarily based on language and nationalism, as were to an even greater extent, attitudes towards the minority Hungarian parties in Slovakia. Language or nationalist values were also a significant element in support for the MDS in Slovakia, and for the Free Democrats/Young Democrats in Hungary – though the MDS attracted nationalists while the FD/YD repelled them.

Finally, what can be said about *the pattern of party politics* in each country? Was it driven more by values and ideology or more by economic interests and performance? In Russia only attitudes (positive and negative of course) towards the Communist Party were primarily ideological; attitudes towards the other parties were driven more by economic pessimism and general opposition sentiment. Values and ideology were relatively unimportant influences on attitudes to parties in Hungary with the possible exception of the link between authoritarian values and the governing HDF. Social variables such as age, education or religion were more important in Hungary. Socialist and nationalist values were the basis of attitudes to parties in Ukraine however. Socialist values, along with economic performance, were important across the board in the Czech Republic. And nationalist values, along with economic performance, were particularly important in Slovakia.

Certainly, attitudes to political parties were fairly strongly structured – that is to say, fairly predictable – despite the short life of most of the parties and the electorate's short experience of postcommunist politics. Whatever else may be said, attitudes towards parties were neither random nor inexplicable.[10] Even if we exclude from consideration those regressions that use opposition sentiment on the grounds of tautology, the multiple correlations for predictions of attitudes towards *Communist Parties* or their successors were 0.41 in Russia, 0.41 in Ukraine, and 0.47 in the Czech Republic, though only 0.21 in Hungary and 0.26 in Slovakia; for non-communist *governing parties* they were 0.40 in Russia, 0.39 in Hungary, 0.53 in Slovakia and 0.59 in the Czech Republic; and for *nationalist or ethnic parties*, 0.37 for Rukh in Ukraine, 0.47 for the SNP in Slovakia and 0.56 for the Hungarian Parties in Slovakia. Including opposition sentiment would increase these correlations further. Less than two years after the collapse of the Soviet system there was clearly a degree of order amidst the chaos of the new politics.

Perhaps the novelty of the new party politics has been overemphasised. Many of the parties in ECE – though not in the FSU – were deliberate, self-conscious revivals or imitations of parties that existed before the imposition of communism. But in fact that was *not* the basis of the structure we have uncovered in this chapter, because so many of those revivals attracted little support.[11] There were three other and more important roots for the party systems of ECE and the FSU in the early 1990s: (i) communism versus its opponents; (ii) incumbent governments versus their opponents; and (iii) nationalism. Of the non-communist parties with enough support to be worth analysing in this chapter, only the Hungarian Smallholders, the Slovak Nationalist Party, and the Czech Social Democrats could be classified as revivals or imitations of pre-communist parties. The three main parties in Russia were based on the destruction of the communist regime, resistance to that destruction, and opposition to both the new and the old regime. These were historic tendencies if not, apart from the communists, historic parties. In Ukraine the main parties were based on the different but not entirely unrelated themes of communism and Ukrainian nationalism – again historic themes if not, apart from the communists, historic parties. In Hungary the revived Smallholders were less significant than the four parties that had emerged out of the struggle to dismantle the communist regime – a struggle that had been going on for over three decades. In Slovakia continuity was provided by the communist successor, the Democratic Left and the historic tensions between ethnic Slovaks and Hungarians in which the revived SNP was only one element. And in the Czech Republic, as in Russia, the parties whose support we have analysed were based upon the destruction of the communist regime, resistance to that destruction, and opposition to both the new and the old regime.

By the early 1990s the old communist regimes had been replaced by new postcommunist regimes, but the old issues, the old value conflicts remained. The *party* politics of the 1990s was recognisably the *value* politics of the 1970s and 1980s but now given an expression through contending parties which had previous been unnaturally denied by the heavy but weakening hand of the communist dictatorship. That, and not the reinvention of old pre-communist parties, was the real reason why the party politics of the 1990s was neither new nor unstructured – either in ECE or the FSU.

V Stability and Change

18 Intra-election Trends: Value Stability During a Crisis Election

It used to be said that no one would ever write the history of a communist regime in terms of its elections. They were not the most important events in the political life of the country. Certainly they were not political crises in any sense. But in postcommunist countries, as in other democracies, elections are political crises with far reaching effects. This chapter looks at the effect, if any, of the 1993 Russian election campaign on political attitudes and values.

Not all elections are equally important. For very good reasons, local government elections usually command less attention than national elections – amongst voters as well as historians. Sometimes it is argued that only the 'first-order' or 'peak' elections have a life and significance of their own – parliamentary elections in Britain or Germany, presidential elections in France or the United States. And Yeltsin's suspension of the Russian parliament in September 1993, followed by the tank assault on the parliament building – more than the constitution published and approved so hastily thereafter – seemed to suggest that Russia had become a purely presidential democracy in which only presidential elections mattered.

However, it is worth recalling that the parliamentary election in December 1993 was certainly the first post-Soviet, and arguably the first postcommunist election in Russia. There had never been an election for the presidency of an independent Russia. Yeltsin had been elected to a very different and much less powerful office in the very different political structure of a Soviet republic back in 1991. So had the members of the now dispersed Russian parliament who were elected in 1990 as the first and last Congress of People's Deputies of the Russian Federation within the USSR, and had themselves elected Yeltsin to preside over them, before they amended the law to allow his direct election by the people in 1991.

Even in a presidential system, the election of a parliament may be a key mechanism, ritual, and crisis point in democratic politics. That was particularly true for Russia in 1993 however much the president might succeed in dictating policy at the point of a gun. It was certainly an election with some classic second-order features. In particular it was more about representation than responsibility: it could influence the government but not overthrow it, for example. But if it was a second-order election it was an unusually important one, with much of the character of a first-order election. It involved all the main national political leaders except Yeltsin himself. And it was not reduced to purely second-order status by a simultaneous election for the presidency – as had at one stage seemed likely.

By a fortunate coincidence we were in the midst of planning our 1993 survey of political values when Yeltsin suspended the Russian parliament, ordered the tanks in to shell the parliament building, tore up the existing constitution and set December 12th as the date for a referendum on a new, hastily drawn up constitution and, simultaneously, for the first parliamentary election to be held under that constitution. We were planning a 2000 respondent survey of Russian political values for December 1993 but, in response to these events, we were able to change our plans and conduct two separate surveys, one before the election of 12 December, the second immediately after it.

Interviewing for the *pre-election survey* ran from 25 November to 9 December. Interviewing for the *post-election survey* began just after the close of poll on 12 December and ran to 13 January 1994. We used the same questionnaire in both surveys, with only a few minor changes of tense – for example, from 'will you vote?' to 'did you vote?'. Equally important, we used the same sample points and the same team of interviewers, though different respondents, in the two surveys. Thus they did not constitute a panel survey, which would have involved reinterviewing the same people before and after the election and would probably have generated a spuriously high level of consistency at a time of potentially rapid change – even if the same people would have been willing to answer a whole hour of identical questions immediately before and after the election. At the same time the two surveys were not a pair of completely independent samples, but a pair of separate though closely matched samples. Indeed, apart from the short time interval between them, the two samples could be viewed as a classic 'split half' design. In the conditions of December 1993 we felt that was the best design for precise measurement of change.

The post election survey was carried out as rapidly as possible in order to maximise the accuracy of recalled vote: 87 per cent of the 1046 interviews were carried out within one week of the election and 95 per cent within ten days. However the 1095 interviews in the pre-election survey were spread more evenly over the 15 days from 25 November to 9 December, with the median interview exactly ten days before the election. So a comparison of the findings in our pre- and post-election surveys will reveal the changes, if any, between opinion ten days before the election and immediately after it. And by dividing the pre-election survey at the median interview for example, we can investigate – on smaller samples, of course – any change in opinion between the earlier and later stages of the election campaign.

REGULAR TRENDS: INCREASING PARTY IDENTIFICATION BUT VALUE STABILITY

In a mature democracy, we have fairly clear expectations about the effect of a parliamentary election upon public opinion. First there are a set of contingent changes: changes that depend upon the particular events and debates of the campaign. The popularity of different parties and politicians can change quite rapidly. The electoral credibility of parties – that is their perceived chances of doing well in the election – can change even more rapidly and affect the tactical decisions of potential voters who are likely to switch away from a party that they think has little chance of success, even if they still like its leaders and policies. An appearance of disunity amongst the leaders of a party can affect both its credibility and its basic popularity. Or the glare of election-time publicity may expose the inadequacies of leaders or policies. There is no reason to expect Russia to differ from other democracies in this respect.

Conversely, there are other aspects of public opinion where change is either regular and predictable, or unlikely to occur at all. The most obvious example of regular change is the increasing strength of party identification and enthusiasm as the election battle hots up.[1] Other aspects of public opinion should usually be unaffected by an election. Insofar as they truly merit the title 'values', basic political values should be so deeply rooted that they do not change easily or quickly in response to an election campaign.[2] Indeed parties and politicians usually try to succeed in an election by appealing to firmly established values rather than by trying, in the short term at least, to change them. Again, there is no reason to expect Russia to differ from other democracies in this respect either.

On the other hand, the circumstances surrounding the 1993 Russian election were very different from those of a normal election in a mature democracy. First, the 1993 election was the first parliamentary election since the creation of an independent Russia and, more significantly, the first explicitly multi-party election. Yeltsin's new (though as yet unapproved) constitution provided radically new arrangements designed in part to encourage multi-party thinking. Instead of the former system of strictly majoritarian elections in single-member territorial constituencies, half the Duma (the lower house of the new bicameral parliament) were to be elected on the British first-past-the-post system in territorial constituencies, while the other half were to be elected on a party-list system of proportional representation. Formally, the 13 labels that appeared on the list were 'electoral alliances' rather than 'parties', but several claimed to be parties and the system was designed to encourage the development of party thinking. Although partisanship – commitment, identification or support for parties in general – usually tends to rise at election time in mature democracies anyway, these constitutional changes might be expected to increase partisan commitment more than would a normal election in a mature democracy, albeit from a very low level in Russia however.

Second, the 'democratic crisis' of an election had been precipitated and overshadowed by the less metaphorical crisis of military power which had included the shelling of the former Russian parliament by Yeltsin's troops. After that, an election could only be something of an anti-climax. While public interest in politics usually tends to rise at election time we could hardly expect any increase in public interest in politics during such a period of anti-climax.

Finally, this was in every respect an illegal election. It marked not only a break with the communist past, but one that had been imposed by force of arms. There was no other basis for the new electoral law. Yeltsin held a constitutional conference but the draft constitution largely bypassed it. There was no 'round table' of consensual support from all parts of the political spectrum as had happened in various ECE countries, no elected constituent assembly – indeed the only body that could have claimed such a status was the parliament that had been shelled by Yeltsin's tanks, and no popular referendum, except for that which took place simultaneously with the election itself and which is widely reputed to have failed to meet its own imposed conditions.[3] So this was an election during which the electoral system and, by association, the very idea of competitive elections was on trial, and although the conduct of the election might not affect basic political values in general, it might still be expected to affect those values which were explicitly tied to support for competitive elections.

CONTINGENT TRENDS: POPULARITY AND CREDIBILITY

A myth has grown up around the 1993 Russian election: that all the Russian pollsters 'got it wrong', and so very wrong and that the result was a shock.[4] It is a myth with some basis in fact.[5] With hindsight, it is clear even from the press reports of the campaign that Yeltsin's favoured party, Russia's Choice, was failing to maintain its early lead over Zhirinovsky's nationalist Liberal Democratic Party, but at the time, those same press reports read differently. As the date of the election approached Yeltsin's own team drew public attention to the rapid rise in support for Zhirinovsky's LDP, but overly sceptical journalists – and readers – were inclined to interpret this as a scaremongering attempt to boost support for Yeltsin's favoured candidates. The day before the election Jonathan Steele reported in *The Guardian*: 'The pro-Yeltsin forces are putting out the word that Vladimir Zhirinovsky, the extreme rightwing nationalist, is rapidly gaining ground *but this looks like a device to scare the majority into voting.*' [emphasis added][6] In Russia, the first television reports of the result announced that Russia's Choice was in the lead, followed by Yabloko – before the programme was abruptly suspended amidst fears that the authorities would either disregard the true results or just make up a fictitious set. So there was indeed a genuine sense of surprise at the result.

But that surprise owed as much to the failure of pundits as of pollsters. The law prohibited any publication of opinion polls in the last ten days of the campaign (though that did not prevent some 'illegal' publications) and our own surveys show a clear trend towards Zhirinovsky's LDP during that period, which would have justified and explained the messages Jonathan Steele was reporting – but discounting – from the Yeltsin camp. Comparing voting intentions and reported votes for the party list element of the Duma in our pre- and post-election surveys, the LDP gained 14 per cent in the last ten days of the campaign, Russia's Choice lost one per cent, the Communists and their Agrarian allies gained 4 per cent, and the collection of minor parties (plus the 'against all' option which was available to Russian voters) lost 17 per cent – a sharp trend towards Zhirinovsky's LDP mainly at the expense of the minor parties.

Table 18.1:   Trends in voting intentions and party sympathies

	Pre-election	Post-election	Change	Early pre-election	Late pre-election	Post-election	Change
Vote/intention for Duma list:	%	%	%	%	%	%	%
LDP	13	27	+14	11	16	27	+16
RC	18	17	−1	20	17	17	−3
C&A	13	17	+4	12	14	17	+5
Other	56	39	−17	57	53	39	−18
Favourable to:							
LDP	38	45	+7	35	41	45	+10
RC	52	48	−4	50	54	48	−2
Communist Party	42	54	+12	40	45	54	+14
Vote intention for presidential:							
Yeltsin	38	30	−8	40	36	30	−10
Zhirinovsky	14	22	+8	14	15	22	+8
Vote/intention in territorial seats at Duma election:							
Pro-Y cand	46	38	−8	48	43	38	−10
Anti-Y cand	30	31	+1	32	28	31	−1
Y irrelevant	24	31	+7	20	29	31	+11

Notes: 'Don't Knows', 'Can't decide' etc. excluded from calculation of percentages. Percentage 'favourable' is as a percentage of those who were favourable or unfavourable i.e. excluding those who said 'neither' as well as 'don't know'.
LDP = Liberal Democratic Party; RC = Russia's Choice; C&A = Communist plus Agrarian.
Pro-Y cand = vote for a candidate who supports president Yeltsin; Anti-Y cand = vote for a candidate who opposes president Yeltsin.

Moreover that trend towards the LDP is visible *within* our pre-election survey when that is broken down by the date of interview. In the first half of our pre-election survey the LDP were 9 per cent behind Russia's Choice, in the second half of our pre-election survey only one per cent behind, and in our post election survey 10 per cent ahead – though most of that change was due to the rise in voting intentions (and eventual votes) for the LDP rather than a decline in voting intentions for Russia's Choice. There can be little doubt that this was a real change rather than a sampling accident since the change is visible within our pre-election survey as well as between our pre and post-election surveys. Elsewhere we have subjected our pre-election survey to more intensive analysis which shows a trend towards the LDP not just between the first and second halves of that survey but continuously throughout the three or four weeks leading up to the election.[7]

Similarly there were trends towards the Communists and the LDP on the less exclusive question of whether people felt favourable or unfavourable towards each of the parties, though the Communists gained even more than the LDP on that score. From roughly equal starting points the LDP ran well ahead of the Communists in terms of voting intentions (and actual votes) but, in a portent for the future, the Communists ran well ahead in terms of broad public sympathy. Because votes are exclusive but sympathy is not, a party can do very well in a multi-party contest despite relatively restricted public sympathy for it. Sympathy for Russia's Choice remained fairly stable: the Communist and LDP gains were not balanced by a corresponding decline in sympathy for Russia's Choice.

Yeltsin himself lost ground in the campaign although, of course, he was not a candidate and he formally refused to support any of the parties, preferring to remain as a president 'above party politics'. During the campaign his lead over Zhirinovsky in terms of voting intentions for a future presidential election declined by 16 per cent. And when asked about their votes or voting intentions for candidates in the territorial constituencies of the Duma, there was a 10 per cent decline in the numbers who said they would vote for 'a candidate who supported Yeltsin', matched however by an 11 per cent rise in the percentage who said the candidates' support or opposition to Yeltsin was 'irrelevant to their choice' rather than by a rise in the per cent who intended to vote for anti-Yeltsin candidates.

Several pieces of evidence suggest that the LDP gains in the 'party-list' vote came largely from a tactical squeeze on the minor centrist and opposition parties as they lost electoral credibility. Between our pre- and post-election surveys, these parties collectively lost 17 per cent while the LDP gained 14 per cent. Moreover the LDP gains and the minor parties' losses were twice as great amongst those who described themselves as 'opponents' of the government, as amongst those who described themselves as its 'supporters'. The number of government opponents hardly increased in total during the campaign but they increasingly deserted the minor parties and switched their voting intentions to the LDP.

Table 18.2: Trends in voting intentions and party sympathies amongst supporters and opponents of the government

	Amongst government supporters			Amongst government opponents		
	Pre-election	Post-election	Change	Pre-election	Post-election	Change
	%	%	%	%	%	%
Vote/intention for Duma list:						
LDP	6	15	+9	24	44	+20
RC	40	37	−3	3	2	−1
C&A	4	9	+5	25	24	−1
Other	50	39	−11	48	29	−19
Favourable to:						
LDP	28	22	−6	47	70	+23
RC	83	83	0	9	11	+2
Communist Party	20	30	+10	66	75	+9

Notes: 'Don't Knows', 'Can't decide' etc. excluded from calculation of percentages. Percentage favourable is as a percentage of those who were favourable or unfavourable i.e. excluding those who said 'neither' as well as 'don't know'.
LDP = Liberal Democratic Party; RC = Russia's Choice; C&A = Communist plus Agrarian.

Government supporters were always very much more favourable to Russia's Choice and unfavourable to the Communist Party. Comparing our pre- and post-election surveys, the attitudes of government supporters and opponents towards Russia's Choice hardly changed, while both became about 10 per cent more favourable towards the Communist Party. However the gap between government supporters' and opponents' attitudes towards the LDP widened sharply: already unfavourable towards the LDP before the election, government supporters became 6 per cent even less favourable to it after the election; while government opponents – who were fairly evenly divided in their attitudes towards the LDP before the election – became 23 per cent more favourable towards it after the election. This confirms our view that the election campaign polarised attitudes towards the LDP but not towards the Communists who gained in sympathy across the board.

Additional evidence that the LDP gains came from a squeeze on minor parties is provided by the patterns of partisan commitment. In our pre-election survey, intending Communist voters were the most strongly committed partisans, and those who intended to vote for the minor parties the least: 78 per cent of intending Communist voters described themselves as party 'supporters', compared to 41 per cent amongst intending LDP voters, 39 per cent amongst intending Agrarian voters, 30 per cent amongst intending Russia's Choice voters, and a mere 22 per cent amongst the large number who at that stage intended to vote for one or other of the minor parties. That indicates pre-election vote intentions for the Communists were especially 'firm' (though small in number) and pre-election vote intentions for minor parties were especially 'soft' (though, collectively, large in number).

So the pattern of partisan commitment in our pre-election survey is consistent with the trends within it, and both pointed to a likely collapse of minor party vote intentions and a surge in the Communist or LDP vote by election day. Our pollsters did not fail and, in retrospect, the result should not have been a surprise.

But we are not primarily concerned here to explain the result of the 1993 Russian election, interesting though that may be. Our prime purpose is to explain the impact that the election had – or did not have – upon political values. For our present purpose, the details of these changes in voting intentions during the campaign hardly matter. What is important is that our surveys show there were substantial, interpretable, plausible and genuine changes in voting intentions and sympathy towards particular parties as the election campaign progressed – and not a simple discrepancy between pre- and post-election polls attributable to the vagaries of sampling or the insincerity of Russian voters. If our measures of fundamental political values prove to be stable, their stability will be all the more remarkable when judged against our own evidence of the scale and speed of changes in voting intentions; and if some of our measures of fundamental political values do show evidence of change, then our surveys' ability to provide plausible explanations of the detailed changes in voting intentions will give us some confidence that we are dealing with something more significant than random sampling discrepancies between pre- and post-election surveys.

POLITICAL INTEREST AND DISCUSSION

Elections in mature democracies constitute a regular and predictable form of political crisis which usually increases public interest in politics, increases the public's psychological sense of commitment to parties, and increases support for the incumbent government. These changes may occur over a period of months rather than days before the election however, and since the median interview in our pre-election survey took place only ten days before the election we can detect only fairly late changes in these factors.

We found hardly any increase in political interest or discussion as the election approached. The percentage who declared themselves 'very' or 'quite' interested in politics rose by only 3 per cent between our pre- and post-election surveys, as did the percentage who said they discussed politics 'very' or 'quite' often. Within our pre-election survey there was even evidence of a slight drop in interest and discussion as the election approached, followed by a recovery of interest and discussion in the immediate aftermath of the result. Since only one third or less ever said they were even 'quite' interested in politics or discussed politics even 'quite' often, the level of interest and discussion was not only stable but low. The election clearly did *not* stimulate great interest in politics and what interest there was seemed more that of spectators viewing the game rather than of participants concerned about their own role and decisions within the electoral process. Since they had behaved almost exclusively as spectators through the much more dramatic crisis of the suspension of the old parliament in September and the tank attacks on it in October, it was not so surprising that they continued in that mood through the election in December.

Roughly one third, both before and after the election, declared themselves to be supporters of the government, slightly less to be opponents, and slightly more to be 'neither'. There was hardly any change – a mere 2 per cent increase in the number of opponents – and certainly no evidence of any swing-back towards the government – at least during the last ten days of the campaign.

SOCIALIST, NATIONALIST AND LIBERAL VALUES

Given some of the press coverage at the time, it may come as a surprise to find that there was very little change in commitment to socialist, populist, liberal or even nationalist values. After all, the big winner in the campaign was Zhirinovsky's ultra-nationalist LDP, while the parties of self-proclaimed liberals like Yavlinsky (Yabloko) and Gaidar (Russia's Choice) did badly. Yet the percentages who scored above the mid-points on each of our composite scales of these four values never changed by more than 7 per cent between our pre- and post election surveys; and on all four the slight trends within our pre-election survey ran in the opposite direction to the difference between the pre- and post-election surveys, revealing more of a slight 'wobble' rather than any kind of trend.

Indeed even the very small changes on these composite indicators of values owed as much to changes in the coherence of answers to the individual questions on which they were based (i.e. the correlations between them) as to significant trends in opinion. For example, on socialist values, explicit support for a market economy ran at 67 per cent before the election and 63 per cent after it; on populist values, support for the principle of using popular referenda to decide important issues ran at 66 per cent before the election and 64 per cent after it; and on liberal values, the numbers who agreed that 'the only alternative to strong government is disorder and chaos' remained unchanged at 72 per cent. Based upon a comparison between two clustered random samples of just over a thousand respondents any percentage differences of up to 5 per cent or less would usually be judged statistically insignificant.

Most surprisingly, despite the huge swing to Zhirinovsky's nationalist LDP, the numbers who said parts of neighbouring countries should belong to Russia remained unchanged at 71 per cent; and the numbers willing to threaten military force in the near abroad remained unchanged at 26 per cent. This is so surprising that it is worth a little further investigation.

Table 18.3:	Trends in political values

	Pre-election	Post-election	Change	Early pre-election	Late pre-election	Post-election	Change
	%	%	%	%	%	%	%
Socialism	79	83	+4	80	78	83	+3
Nationalism	41	48	+7	42	41	48	+6
Liberalism	67	60	−7	64	70	60	−4
Populism	65	64	−1	67	63	64	−3
Pro-elections	52	64	+12	48	57	64	+16
Pro-parties	20	30	+10	20	20	30	+10

Note: Entries are the percentage who score strictly above the mid-point on each scale.

How could a nationalist gain so many new voters without persuading Russians to become more nationalist? First, as these figures remind us, Russians were far more aggressively nationalist – in the irredentist sense – than the people of any of the other countries we surveyed, and Zhirinovsky's LDP only went up from 13 to 27 per cent between our two surveys. So the LDP could have gained in voting intentions (and ultimately votes) by taking a larger share of nationalists, expanding its share to include all of those who were prepared to threaten military force in the near-abroad, or to include just over a third of those many people who had irredentist claims on the near-abroad, without any need to expand the total number of nationalists in Russia.

In fact that did *not* happen. The LDP increased its share of voting intentions (and ultimately votes) by squeezing the minor parties and winning over a larger share of government opponents, as we have already shown. But, between our pre- and post-election surveys, it did *not* increase its vote exclusively or even mainly amongst the more nationalist voters. Quite the opposite. The LDP did not even expand its vote equally amongst the more and less nationalist sectors of the Russian electorate: it won more new ground amongst less nationalist Russians and, in consequence, its vote became less nationalist as it became larger.[8] It expanded beyond its originally ultra-nationalist core. In our pre-election survey the LDP had the voting intentions of 20 per cent of the ultra-nationalist minority who would threaten force in the near abroad, and only 9 per cent of the majority who would not. According to our post-election survey, the LDP won the actual votes of 30 per cent of the ultra-nationalist minority (a gain of 10 per cent amongst them) and 24 per cent of the less nationalist majority (a gain if 15 per cent). It made greater gains – proportionately, and therefore even more in the absolute –

amongst the relatively less nationalist majority than amongst the ultra-nationalist minority.

Paradoxically, the strong swing to the ultra-nationalist LDP during the campaign was not built on a swing towards nationalist values.

PARTY AND ELECTORAL VALUES

By contrast we found some evidence of growing support for values associated with parties, party competition and elections. Between the earlier half of our pre-election survey and our post-election survey, the percentages who scored above the mid-point on our composite indicator of party values rose by 10 per cent and on our composite indicator of electoral values by 16 per cent.

The percentage who described themselves as party 'supporters' rose from 21 per cent before the election to 31 per cent afterwards. There was also an increase, though a smaller one of only 6 per cent, in the numbers who felt that at least one party 'represents the interests and views of people like me'.

But the largest changes concerned attitudes to the electoral process itself. Our composite measure of support for democratic electoral values was based upon four questions – whether people explicitly supported a multi-party system, whether they felt that having regular elections make politicians do what ordinary people want, whether they felt parliamentary elections offered a clear choice between different directions for their country, and whether the elections on December 12th would be, or had been, 'free and fair'.

Table 18.4: Trends in attitudes to parties and elections

	Pre-election	Post-election	Change	Early pre-election	Late pre-election	Post-election	Change
	%	%	%	%	%	%	%
Party supporter	21	31	+10	21	21	31	+10
Party represents	37	43	+6	33	42	43	+10
Elections:							
effective	38	42	+4	34	42	42	+8
offer choice	80	86	+6	76	83	86	+10
free and fair	55	77	+22	52	58	77	+25
For multi-pty syst	71	70	−1	68	74	70	+2

Notes: 'Don't Knows', 'Can't decide' etc. excluded from calculation of percentages.

Explicit support for a multi-party system remained high both before and after the election, at about 70 per cent, but it did not increase. The percentage who thought that elections had at least 'some' effect on making politicians do what ordinary people want was low, but it increased slightly from just under 40 per cent to just over 40 per cent. The percentage who thought parliamentary elections offered a clear choice of direction was very high and also increased slightly. These changes were not large, though they were progressive – so that elections were rated 8 per cent better on effectiveness and 10 per cent better on choice after the election than they had been in the earlier half of our pre-election survey.

But there was a large increase, of 22 per cent, between the pre- and post-election surveys, in the numbers who described the December elections as 'free and fair'. Within the pre-election survey itself there was a small increase in the numbers describing it as 'free and fair', from 52 per cent to 58 per cent, but then a sharp increase to 77 per cent immediately after the election – cumulating to produce a 25 per cent increase in the 'freedom and fairness' rating between the earlier part of the campaign and the post-election week.

The election had been called illegally and unfairly in the wake of Yeltsin's tank assault on the previous parliament. He had tried to ban all communist successor parties from taking part in the election. Ironically he had introduced the new national party-list system of election for half the Duma just because his supporters, unlike the communists, had no grassroots organisation or network and relatively few prominent personalities outside national politics who could organise or motivate local support across the vast territory of Russia. He also tried to prevent national television being used as a platform for his opponents. But in the end he failed. Despite the obvious attempts to rig the election, a combination of internal and external pressures led to Zyuganov's Communist Party being allowed onto the ballot and to a degree of opposition access to television which was exploited, in particular, by Zhirinovsky. As David Hearst wrote in the *Guardian*: 'the real election campaign started on 22 November when Russian viewers had their first taste of uncensored party political broadcasts.'[9] Even after that, the conduct of the election remained unfair. Right at the end, on the eve of the vote, the main television channel screened a special profile of Zhirinovsky 'in violation of the election rules' that began with his photo captioned 'I am the almighty. I am a tyrant. I will follow in Hitler's footsteps.'[10] Though it may well have had the opposite effect, it was designed to frighten viewers back into the pro-Yeltsin camp.

Yet despite the clumsy attempts to make the election unfree and unfair, there was a sense amongst western journalists that the election was escaping from those who would manipulate it. That sense was reflected in our pre-election survey where there was a small pre-election increase – but, despite the visible evidence to the contrary, an *increase* nonetheless – in the numbers who described the election as free and fair.

But it was the result – not the conduct – of the election which convinced so many that it had, in retrospect, been free and fair. The result was a major rebuff for Yeltsin and his government. As the first trickle of results filtered through, the overnight television results programme was hastily closed down and replaced by music videos, raising fears that the authorities would falsify or reject the result. When the flow of results resumed the next day however, the scale of the government defeat was confirmed and not inexplicably reversed. The fact that the authorities accepted such a resounding election defeat, albeit after some hesitation, no doubt convinced many that the election had been free and fair after all. The irony is that the authorities were able to accept the election defeat because their tenure of office did not depend upon the election to an emasculated Duma and, in that sense at least, the election remained unfree and unfair.

Table 18.5: Free and fair?

	Pre-election	Post-election	Change
	%	%	%
Amongst all respondents	55	77	+22
Amongst intending voters/voters for:			
Communist party	19	66	+47
Agrarian party	52	82	+30
LDP	52	82	+30
RC	84	92	+8
Others	58	81	+23
Amongst:			
government supporters	78	89	+11
government opponents	35	69	+34
neither	49	70	+21

Notes: 'Don't Knows', 'Can't decide' etc. excluded from calculation of percentages.

The post-election increase in perceptions that the election had been free and fair was very large but it was far from evenly spread. Amongst government opponents the increase ran at 34 per cent, but amongst government supporters at only 11 per cent (they had always claimed the election was free and fair), and amongst those who neither supported nor opposed the government at 21 per cent.

Differences between parties were even greater: amongst Communist voters there was a 47 per cent increase in perceptions that the election had been free and fair, and amongst LDP voters 30 per cent, but amongst Russia's Choice voters only 8 per cent. Of course, the vast majority of Russia's Choice voters had always maintained that the election was free and fair anyway, but it is still significant that amongst Communist voters (or intending voters) the number who accepted the election as free and fair more than tripled from 19 per cent before the election to 66 per cent after it.

International organisations are very keen to assess whether an election has been free and fair and, other things being equal, public agreement that an election has been free and fair must help to consolidate support for the democratic process within the country. So while the 1993 election may have been a defeat for the self-proclaimed democrats it was in one respect a victory for the principle of democracy since it changed the communist and nationalist opposition's view of the electoral process. The authorities' acceptance of an adverse result outweighed all their crude attempts before the election to make it unfair and unfree, and won much wider respect for the electoral process than before.

The significance of that widening respect should not be overestimated however. Although Russian public opinion about the freedom and fairness of the election increased very sharply after the election, support for the principle of multi-party elections did not change, and perceptions of the effectiveness of elections as a means of controlling politicians or choosing between alternative paths for the country improved only slightly. And, although it does not seem to have greatly damaged public assessments of whether the election was free and fair, few if any outside observers now believe the official claim that the turnout level was high enough to validate the new constitution, which had a self-imposed requirement of majority support on a turnout of over 50 per cent. It is doubtful whether a constitution put forward unilaterally by a president who had shown so little respect for constitutional restraint in September and October could, or should, be taken seriously in December.

STATE TELEVISION

In all our surveys we asked whether 'the government should be able to dismiss the head of state television if it does not like what he is doing.' Before the election 16 per cent of Russians agreed; after the election, 26 per cent. It was one of the largest changes in opinion between our two surveys and, paradoxically it appeared to suggest growing support for the government. But that appearance was deceptive.

Before the election, government supporters were 12 per cent more willing than government opponents to accept the arbitrary sacking of the head of state television – for all that the government claimed to represent democrats and reformers. It was the usual illiberal tendency of government supporters, no matter what their government's proclaimed values. After the election the gap between government supporters and opponents widened to 18 per cent. The gap between Russia's Choice and LDP voters widened still more: support for the arbitrary dismissal of the head of state television rose from 18 to 40 per cent amongst Russia's Choice voters but from 11 to only 19 per cent amongst LDP voters. The trend owed more to the increasing irritation of government supporters than to the increasing submissiveness of government opponents.

Shortly before the election, Yeltsin had installed Vyacheslav Bragin as head of Ostankino, the main Russia-wide television channel. During the campaign Ostankino became notorious for its clumsy and overtly biased attempts to help the government, including that critical and illegal eve of poll profile on Zhirinovsky. It seems that Zhirinovsky's LDP voters forgave Bragin's attempts to influence the election in the government's favour more easily than Russia's Choice voters – or Yeltsin – forgave him for his lack of success. Soon after the election, Yeltsin sacked him.

Table 18.6: Government should have the right to dismiss arbitrarily the head of state television

	Pre-election	Post-election	Change
	%	%	%
Amongst all respondents	16	26	+10
Amongst intending voters/voters for:			
Communist party	10	28	+18
Agrarian party	9	34	+25
LDP	11	19	+8
RC	18	40	+22
Others	20	27	+7
Amongst:			
government supporters	22	37	+15
government opponents	10	19	+9
neither	15	21	+6

Notes: 'Don't Knows', 'Can't decide' etc. excluded from calculation of percentages.

CONCLUSION

Comparison of our pre- and post-election surveys has shown that there were large, rapid and progressive changes of voting intentions during the 1993 Russian election campaign. Sympathy for different political parties also changed sharply during the campaign. Yet the campaign had remarkably little effect upon political values. Amongst the public, changes in voting intentions reflected the campaigning skills of politicians, the crude, over-obvious and self-defeating bias in the state controlled media, and the tactical decisions by voters who were only weakly attached to political parties in the first place. But they did *not* reflect any net change in fundamental political values.

During the campaign there was little or no change in overall commitment to socialist, populist or liberal values and, despite rapidly increasing voting intentions for Zhirinovsky's ultra-nationalist LDP, there was little or no change in nationalist values either. In particular there was no increase at all in aggressive irredentist nationalism. As the potential LDP vote increased it became much *less* nationalist, because it gained most new coverts amongst less nationalist Russians, expanding its original support beyond its ultra-nationalist base. Of course, that does not mean that the LDP or Zhirinovsky himself became any the less nationalist as the campaign developed,[11] but it does mean that those voters who wished to oppose the government increasingly opted for the LDP as a vehicle of protest even if they themselves were not, in Russian terms, especially nationalist.

After the excitements of the conflict, ultimately armed conflict, between the president and parliament earlier in the autumn, interest in politics and discussion of political issues did not rise as the election campaign neared its close. However, the level of identification with parties did rise, though from a very low base.

In most respects, electoral values did not change during the campaign: support for a multi-party system and for parliamentary elections as offering a clear choice of direction remained stable and high, while the feeling that elections had at least some effect on making politicians responsive to public opinion remained stable and low. But there was a very large increase after the election, of 22 per cent overall and of 47 per cent amongst communist voters, in the numbers who felt the election was free and fair. And in contrast to the changes in voting intentions which were spread throughout the campaign, this huge increase in the numbers describing the election as free and fair occurred mainly after the results were announced. It was a public reaction to the authorities' acceptance of an unwelcome result rather than a response to their conduct of the campaign itself, and it occurred despite continuing controversy amongst politicians and expert commentators about the statistical accuracy of the results.

At a more general level, these findings remind us of the distinction that must always be drawn between votes and perceptions on the one hand, and principles and values on the other. Rising support for a nationalist politician need not imply rising support for nationalist values; and conversely a collapse of support for a nationalist politician need not imply any decline in nationalist values amongst the public. Russian nationalism is endemic, part of the fabric of Russian politics, not the short term creation of a politician in an election campaign.

Less obviously, and less reassuringly, they also suggest that commitment to the principle of multi-party competition may not be affected by perceptions of whether a particular election, even such a critical one as the first multi-party election since the days of the Tsars, is free and fair. People do want freedom and fairness; but they want more than that. In the FSU their answers to our other questions showed that they also wanted orderly and effective government, respect for the law and economic competence. Freedom and fairness are valuable in themselves, but not – for Russians – an adequate substitute for these other goals.

19 Inter-election Trends 1993–96

Since our first surveys at the end of 1993 there has been a swing to the left in elections throughout most of ECE and the FSU. Indeed it began in Poland and Lithuania shortly before our surveys, but continued in the Bulgarian and Hungarian parliamentary elections of 1994, the Ukrainian parliamentary and presidential elections of 1994, Polish presidential election of 1995, the Russian parliamentary election of 1995, the Russian presidential election of 1996, and even the Czech parliamentary elections of 1996.

Within the area of our surveys in particular, the Socialist Party won the 1994 Hungarian parliamentary election,[1] the leftist Prime Minister of Slovakia was confirmed in power at the 1994 election, and even the highly successful right-wing Prime Minister Klaus lost ground to the socialists in the Czech Republic's parliamentary election in 1996. In Ukraine, the results of the 1994 parliamentary elections were mixed but President Kravchuk was replaced by Kuchma who – at the time of his election, if not later – was regarded as the representative of Russian speaking heavy industrial workers.[2] In Russia the Communist Party vote increased to 22 per cent in the parliamentary election of December 1995 and rose further to 41 per cent in the second round of the presidential election of 1996. Although the communist candidate, Gennadii Zyuganov, was narrowly beaten, a Communist Party minister entered the government shortly afterwards.

But values, and value change cannot be inferred from election results. While values form the background against which elections are fought, and perhaps determine the range of possibilities within which election results must fall, too many short term factors have a major influence upon election results for them to be a simple, direct, or precise reflection of values. Our year long study of British political culture, from the six months before the 1992 General Election to six months after, showed no change at all in basic commitments to the values of liberty and equality, while the Conservative Party's lead in voting preferences changed by 14 per cent and the balance of economic optimism first increased by 22 per cent and then dropped by 46 per cent.[3] Similarly, over the much shorter period of a month, from just before to just after the 1993 Russian parliamentary election, Chapter 18 showed a 14 per cent rise in voting preferences for the LDP without any significant change in nationalist values. No doubt it would have been more difficult for the LDP to gain so much so quickly if Russian voters had not already been fairly sympathetic to nationalist values and even more to nationalist rhetoric. But throughout ECE and the FSU socialist values were already so strong in 1993 that they were by no means incompatible with some degree of leftward movement in elections. The subsequent swings to the left

375

in elections do not, by themselves, provide evidence of any leftward shift in values.

Firm proof of value change since our 1993–94 surveys would require a full scale and exact replication of those surveys. We have not yet done that, but we were able to repeat some of our 1993–94 questions in a survey of the Russian electorate in January 1996, and that provides some indication of what was changing – and what was not – in the largest and most powerful of our five countries, and one where election results seemed to provide particularly clear evidence of the supposed 'swing back to the communists'.

In January 1996, shortly after the second Duma election (held in December 1995), we interviewed a representative sample of 1581 Russian adults and repeated 13 of the questions from our 1993–94 surveys of public and parliamentary opinion. The format and wording of the questions was the same as before, and the survey was again carried out for us by ROMIR. The timing, particularly with respect to the electoral cycle, was similar to that of our post-election survey in 1993, though about one month later – late January instead of late December. So a comparison of this 1996 survey with our 1993 post-election survey really does compare like with like. Any differences – for example in the strength of public identification with parties – cannot be attributed to a change of questions or to a different stage in the electoral cycle. And on sample sizes of 1581 in 1996 and 2141 in 1993, sampling variations are not likely to account for differences of more than a few per cent. Changes of any substantial magnitude between our 1993 and 1996 surveys are likely to reflect real change in Russian attitudes and values. Even more certainly however, any *lack of change* between our 1993 and 1996 surveys provides very strong evidence of real stability in Russian opinion.

SOCIALIST AND NATIONALIST VALUES

We found almost no change in support for the market economy,[4] or in support for the right of regions to secede from Russia, or in willingness to make military threats if Russians living outside Russia, in the 'near abroad', got caught up in ethnic conflicts.[5] Despite Russia's economic troubles, and the conflict in Chechnya, Russians remained – as they had been in 1993 – about two-thirds in favour of the market economy, two-fifths in favour of a right of secession for regions, and one quarter willing to make military threats against the near abroad when necessary – this last a relatively belligerent attitude compared to public opinion in every other FSU/ECE country we surveyed, but no different at all from Russian public opinion in 1993. In terms of these questions at least, the socialist, internal nationalist, and external nationalist values of Russians remained remarkably stable: only a minority, but a substantial minority, continued to take the socialist or nationalist view on these questions.

Table 19.1:   Socialist and nationalist values in Russia, 1993–96

	Dec 1993	Jan 1996	Change
	%	%	%
The creation of a market economy is wrong for Russia	35	37	+2
Accept right of regions to secede from Russia	38	41	+3
Threaten military force in near abroad if necessary	26	26	0

Note: Percentages of those with opinions: 'don't knows' etc. excluded.

LIBERAL AND DEMOCRATIC VALUES

The percentage who described themselves as 'supporters, rather than opponents of the government and what it is trying to do' went down sharply between 1993 and 1996. Excluding the 36 per cent who would not take sides on either occasion, the number of 'government supporters' fell from 52 per cent to 31 per cent.

Table 19.2:   Government support in Russia, 1993–96

	Dec 1993	Jan 1996	Change
	%	%	%
Generally speaking, think of self as			
a government supporter	33	20	−13
a government opponent	31	44	+13
neither	36	36	0
Government supporters:			
as a percentage of supporters plus opponents	52	31	−21

Note: Percentages of those with opinions: 'don't knows' etc. excluded.

Support for the liberal values of limited government and parliamentary supremacy also declined between December 1993 and January 1996. The numbers who backed parliament when asked: 'If the government wanted to take action but was opposed by parliament, who should have the final say?' declined from 61 per cent in 1993 to 52 per cent in 1996 – despite the increasing unpopularity of the government. In fast moving political situations the timing of surveys and the precise wording of questions is all-important, however.[6] When we carried out our survey in December 1993 it was impossible to ask questions about the Russian parliament without specifying whether the question referred to the old communist-era parliament which Yeltsin had suspended before the election (and dispersed under gunfire), or to the new postcommunist parliament elected in the midst of our survey on 12 December. Necessarily, the logic of that situation forced us to specify 'the *new* parliament elected/to be elected in December', and that parliament – which was elected, but did not meet, before the close of our survey – was undoubtedly much more popular, untested as it was, than the old parliament. For example, of those with a view, 48 per cent said they trusted the new parliament, but only 24 per cent the old parliament in 1993. So our 1993 question about parliamentary supremacy was asked at the peak of the new parliament's post-election honeymoon.

Indeed, our 1993 and 1996 questions strictly compared like with like: each asked about an unambiguously postcommunist parliament, and each asked about a newly elected parliament at the very beginning of its term. The decline from 61 per cent to 52 per cent in the numbers committed to parliamentary supremacy is therefore likely to be real: the second postcommunist parliament began its term in 1996 with slightly less authority than the first in 1994, though with rather more authority than the old communist-era parliament at the end of its term in 1993.

Table 19.3:   Support for parliamentary supremacy in Russia, 1993–96

	Dec 1993	Dec 1993	Jan 1996	Change
	%	%	%	%
Yeltsin wrong to suspend old communist-era parliament	47			
Newly elected parliament should be able to over-rule the government		61	52	−9

Notes: Percentages of those with opinions: 'don't knows' etc. excluded. The 1993 question referred explicitly to 'the *new* parliament elected in December 1993' in the post-election wave. In the pre-election wave the wording was 'the *new* parliament to be elected in December 1993'.

We have defined both commitment to the electoral process and commitment to parties as aspects of democratic values since they are generally regarded as necessary for a stable and successful democracy. There was almost no change in the numbers who felt that regular elections had at least 'some effect in making politicians do what ordinary people want': it rose only one per cent from 40 per cent in 1993 to 41 per cent in 1996. And there was no perceived improvement in the treatment of citizens by state officials. In 1993, only a dismal 16 per cent said they would expect fair treatment if they took a tax or housing problem to a government official; and by 1996 the figure also rose by only one per cent to 17 per cent. So there was no sense of improving responsiveness either in high or low politics, no improvement either in what *The Civic Culture* termed 'citizen competence', or in what it termed 'subject competence' – the twin foundations of a democratic culture according to authors of *The Civic Culture*.[7]

Table 19.4:   No improvement in democratic responsiveness in Russia, 1993–96

	Dec 1993	Jan 1996	Change
	%	%	%
Regular elections have at least some effect in making politicians do what ordinary people want	40	41	+1
Would you expect fair treatment on, for example, a tax or housing problem, by officials in a government office?			
yes	16	17	+1
no	66	66	0
only by using connections or bribes	18	17	−1

Note: Percentages of those with opinions: 'don't knows' etc. excluded.

But increasing numbers described parliamentary elections, in themselves, as 'free and fair'. When the authorities accepted the unwelcome election result in 1993, Russian faith in the 'freedom and fairness' of their electoral process increased: the percentage who described the election as 'free and fair' rose from 55 per cent before the 1993 election to 77 per cent after it. In 1996, that percentage rose still higher, to 84 per cent. These were generous percentages in both years, evidence of gratitude for small mercies perhaps, though there are good reasons for regarding the 1995 parliamentary election as more free and fair than the 1993: in 1995 no parties were banned from the contest, no prominent opposition leader was arrested, and media coverage was more carefully balanced (which could not be said of the later presidential election however).

Table 19.5:   Evaluation of elections and support for parties in Russia, 1993–96

	Dec 1993 (pre-election)	Dec 1993 (post-election)	Jan 1996	Change 1993 (Pre) to 1996
	%	%	%	%
Elections to the Russian parliament were 'free and fair'	55	77	84	+29
Feel some party 'represents the interests and views of people like me'	37	43	45	+8
Generally speaking, think of self as a party supporter	19	29	46	+27
Included in the above: Communist Party supporters	3	5	20	+17

Note: Percentages of those with opinions: 'don't knows' etc. excluded.

As the 1993 election campaign progressed, we also found that Russians became more committed to political parties. The numbers who felt that any party 'represents the interests and views of people like me' rose from 37 per cent before the 1993 election to 43 per cent after it. In 1996, this number increased slightly more to 45 per cent. Similarly, and more dramatically, the numbers who described themselves as 'party supporters' also continued to rise. In 1993 the percentage of Russians who regarded themselves as 'party supporters' increased from 19 per cent before the election to 29 per cent after it. In 1996 this number increased sharply to 46 per cent.[8]

By 1996, these figures for attitudes to the electoral process and for commitment to parties had reached the levels that we found for the Czech Republic in 1993: Russians in 1996 were still a little less sure than the Czechs in 1993 that their parliamentary elections were free and fair, but they were a little more committed to political parties (compare Chapter 9). Indeed the level of identification with parties in Russia had, by 1996, reached a level typical of that for Britain in a non-election year – though party commitment rises higher than 46 per cent when an election is held in Britain. By either standard of comparison – with the Czech Republic, or with Britain – the Russian electorate of 1996 seemed to have become much more 'Western' in their commitment to parties.

COMMUNIST IDEALS

But there was a great irony in all this: the huge increase in commitment to the Communist Party – from 5 per cent just after the 1993 election to 20 per cent just after the 1995 election was, by itself, enough to account for nearly all of the overall increase in the level of 'party supporters' – from 29 per cent to 46 per cent.

Consistent with that, the percentage who said they now 'believed in the *ideals* of communism, even if, in practice it was not perfect' rose from 19 per cent in 1993 to 30 per cent in 1996 – still very much a minority, and far less than the 60 per cent in Russia who told us, in 1993, that they had formerly believed in communist ideals (see Chapter 4) – but a marked resurgence compared to the low point of belief in 1993 itself. Clearly 'communism' had become a much more acceptable word as Yeltsin's government had got less popular – a fact that was not lost on Yeltsin himself as he planned his bitter and unscrupulous re-election campaign.

Table 19.6:   Support for communist ideals in Russia, 1993–96

	Dec 1993	Jan 1996	Change
	%	%	%
Formerly believed in the ideals of communism	60	na	na
Now believe in the ideals of communism	19	30	+11

Note: Percentages of those with opinions: 'don't knows' etc. excluded.

Moreover, Russian support for the multiparty system declined sharply between 1993 and 1996.[9] The number who said that a one-party system would be best for Russia doubled from 17 per cent in 1993 to 35 per cent in 1996, while support for the 'multi-party system as it is now' dropped from 19 per cent in 1993 to only 6 per cent in 1996 – though the most popular choice, 'a multi-party system with fewer parties', maintained its support almost unchanged at 50 per cent.

So although commitment to socialist and nationalist values remained fairly stable between 1993 and 1996, and the new electoral system was seen increasingly as 'free and fair', the postcommunist multi-party system in Russia was a failure and early enthusiasm for it continued to decline. And the growth of party commitment in Russia between 1993 and 1996 reflected a resurgence of communist ideals, or at least a sharply increased willingness to declare support for them, rather than a growth of support for a competitive postcommunist system.

Table 19.7: Support for the multi-party system in Russia, 1993–96

	Dec 1993	*Jan 1996*	*Change*
	%	%	%
Best system for Russia today?:			
multi-party system as it is now	19	6	−13
multi-party system with fewer parties	52	50	−2
a one-party system	17	35	+18
no parties at all	13	9	−4

Note: Percentages of those with opinions: 'don't knows' etc. excluded.

A GROWING GENERATION GAP

The old were always more likely to believe in communist ideals than the young. But by 1996, the gap had doubled from 15 per cent to 29 per cent. Belief in communist ideals scarcely increased at all amongst the young (it rose by a mere 3 per cent), but it increased by 17 per cent amongst the old. Similarly, support for a 'one-party system' was always stronger amongst the old, but it also increased more amongst the old, and the gap widened from 9 per cent in 1993 to 17 per cent in 1996. In 1993 it looked almost as if support for the Communist Party might die away in time: only one per cent of the young described themselves as Communist Party 'supporters'. By 1996 support was rising amongst both young and old, but much faster amongst the old: so the generation gap rose from 7 per cent in 1993 to 21 per cent in 1996.

Table 19.8:   Communist connections by age in Russia, 1993–96

	Dec 1993	Jan 1996	Change
	%	%	%
Now believe in the ideals of communism			
amongst young (under 35)	12	15	+3
amongst old (over 55)	27	44	+17
Say that a one-party system is best for Russia			
amongst young (under 35)	13	26	+13
amongst old (over 55)	22	43	+21
Generally speaking, think of self as a Communist Party 'supporter'			
amongst young (under 35)	1	9	+8
amongst old (over 55)	8	30	+22

Notes: Percentages of those with opinions: 'don't knows' etc. excluded.

By 1996 there was obviously a general swing of opinion back towards communist ideals, towards the communist one-party system, and towards the Communist Party. But it was much stronger amongst the old than the young.[10] Perhaps it is appropriate that a counter-revolution should be led by the old rather than the young.

SOCIALISM, NATIONALISM AND COMMUNIST IDEALS

Amongst government supporters, belief in communist ideals rose from only 12 per cent to 19 per cent between 1993 and 1996; amongst government opponents it rose twice as much, from 30 per cent to 44 per cent. Opponents of the government not only increased in numbers, they became more willing to declare a belief in communist ideals.

However, we found that there had been little or no change in our indicators of socialist and nationalist values – that is, in support for the market economy, regional secession or the use of military threats against the near-abroad. But there was a substantial increase in willingness to declare a belief in communist ideals. So was this trend towards communist ideals evenly spread, or did it run more strongly in some of these stable value categories than in others? A breakdown of trends towards belief in communist ideals within socialist and nationalist value categories shows that the trend was no different amongst the more and the less nationalist, but three times as strong amongst the minority who opposed the market economy as amongst the majority who supported it. The link between expressed belief in communist ideals and socialist values – already quite strong – strengthened still further, while the link with nationalist values – already very weak – did not strengthen and, judged by one indicator of nationalism (willingness to use force in the near abroad), it disappeared altogether.

Table 19.9: Support for communist ideals in Russia by socialist and nationalist values, 1993–96

	Now believe in the ideals of communism		
	Dec 1993	Jan 1996	Change
	%	%	%
Amongst those who:			
support government	12	19	+7
neither	14	21	+7
oppose government	30	44	+14
support market economy	11	17	+6
oppose market economy	31	50	+19
accept regions' right of secession	16	23	+7
do not accept regions' right of secession	21	33	+8
support military threats to near-abroad	20	28	+8
do not support military threats to near-abroad	18	29	+11

Note: Percentages of those with opinions: 'don't knows' etc. excluded.

LIBERAL DEMOCRATIC VALUES AND COMMUNIST IDEALS

In 1993, in the aftermath of Yeltsin's tank attack on the Russian parliament, those who expressed belief in communist ideals were overwhelmingly in favour of parliament having the power to veto government action, but their support for parliamentary supremacy declined; so that by 1996 they were only 15 per cent more favourable to it than other people.

Before the 1993 election, those who expressed belief in communist ideals were also exceedingly suspicious that the election would not be 'free and fair' – much more suspicious even than the rest of a generally suspicious Russian public. Once the authorities accepted the unwelcome (to them) result however, communist sympathisers became much less suspicious, scarcely any more suspicious than the rest of the electorate. The numbers of communist believers who thought the election 'free and fair' rose from 42 per cent to 75 per cent almost overnight. By 1996, in the aftermath of an even greater electoral success for the Communist Party, 90 per cent of communist believers said the election had been 'free and fair' – which now made them 9 per cent *less* suspicious of elections than the rest of the public. Continuing electoral success made them praise at least one aspect of the new democratic system. And the percentage of communist believers who said that having regular elections had at least 'some' effect in making politicians responsive also gradually increased from 5 per cent less than other people to 3 per cent more.

Table 19.10:   Liberal and democratic values in Russia by belief in communist ideals, 1993–96

	1993 (pre-election)	1993 (post-election)	1996 (Jan)	Change 1993(Pre) to 1996
	%	%	%	%
Would back parliament against the government:				
those who believe in communist ideals	80	72	63	−17
those who do not	54	58	48	−6
Agree that Duma elections will be/were 'free and fair':				
those who believe in communist ideals	42	75	90	+48
those who do not	59	78	81	+22
Say elections have at least some effect on politicians:				
those who believe in communist ideals	35	41	43	+8
those who do not	40	44	40	0
Say that a one-party system is best for Russia:				
those who believe in communist ideals	28	29	53	+25
those who do not	11	15	26	+15
Say some party represents my views and interests:				
those who believe in communist ideals	46	49	57	+11
those who do not	38	41	41	+3
Generally speaking, think of self as a party 'supporter':				
those who believe in communist ideals	30	42	66	+36
those who do not	19	29	42	+23
Think of self as a Communist Party 'supporter':				
those who believe in communist ideals	15	16	45	+30
those who do not	1	2	9	+8

But amongst those who said they believed in communist ideals, support for a 'one-party system' doubled between 1993 and 1996, from 28 per cent to 53 per cent. So the gap between the level of support for a 'one-party system' amongst those who did and did not believe in communist ideals widened, even though both groups became more favourable to such a system as time has passed.

Communist believers were always *more* likely than others to agree that at least some party 'represents the views and interests of people like me', but the gap between them and others on this doubled from 8 per cent to 16 per cent. So did the gap between the numbers of communist believers and other people who described themselves as 'party supporters': in 1993 only 30 per cent of communist believers described themselves as party supporters, and only half of those that did (15 per cent of all communist believers) supported Zyuganov's Communist Party rather than, for example, the Agrarians or the LDP. But by 1996, 66 per cent of communist believers declared themselves 'party supporters', and two thirds of them (45 per cent of all communist believers) supported Zyuganov's Communist Party. So there was a sharp increase in the correlation between believing in communist ideals on the one hand, and being a self-conscious 'supporter' of the Communist Party on the other.

In some respects the turn of the year 1995–96 was a high point for the communists. They had done very well in the parliamentary election in December, and their candidate for the presidency was running well ahead of Yeltsin in the opinion polls. In terms of votes, the communists did even better in the 1996 presidential election that they lost than the December 1995 parliamentary election that they were perceived to have 'won'. But they might have expected to do better. That they did not, could be attributed in part to Yeltsin's complete domination of the press and television, and his use of those media to establish an equation in the public mind between the latter day Communist Party of 1996 and the unforgivable abuse of human rights under Stalin.[11] Our surveys made it clear that most Russians rated Brezhnev's era of stagnation, but not Stalin's era of repression, as better than the present. Identifying Zyuganov with Stalin was exactly equivalent, in propaganda terms, to identifying the Pope of the 1990s (John Paul II) with the 15th century Hapsburg Inquisition – though easier to do, since more recent, but equally inaccurate, equally unscrupulous and equally offensive to liberal democratic values of fair and balanced media coverage of an election, yet equally effective.

CONCLUSION

Since our first surveys at the end of 1993 there has been a swing to the left in elections throughout most of ECE and the FSU, but value change cannot be inferred from election results. The electoral swings were consistent with the pattern of political values that already existed in 1993.

Investigating value change directly, we found no evidence of a change in socialist or nationalist values; there was almost no change in support for the market economy, or in support for the right of regions to secede from Russia, or in willingness to make military threats if Russians living outside Russia, in the 'near abroad', got caught up in ethnic conflicts. Despite Russia's economic troubles, and the conflict in Chechnya, Russians remained – as they had been in 1993 – about two-thirds in favour of the market economy, two-fifths in favour of a right of secession for regions, and one quarter willing to make military threats against the near abroad when necessary

On democratic values, we found almost no change in the numbers who felt that regular elections helped to make politicians responsive, an increase in the numbers who described their elections as 'free and fair', and a particularly sharp increase in identification with political parties. By 1996, our figures for attitudes to the electoral process and for commitment to parties in Russia had reached the levels that we had found for the Czech Republic in 1993. But the great irony was that nearly all of the overall increase in party commitment could be attributed to an increase in commitment to the Communist Party.

Consistent with that, the numbers who said they believed in the ideals of communism rose by half and support for the multi-party system declined sharply. Indeed support for a one-party system doubled from 17 per cent in 1993 to 35 per cent in 1996. The trend towards declared support for communist ideals was no different amongst the more and the less nationalist, but three times as strong amongst the minority who opposed the market economy as amongst the majority who supported it. So the link between expressed belief in communist ideals and actual socialist values, which was already quite strong, strengthened still further. And so too did the correlation between expressed belief in communist ideals and support for a one-party system. Even in 1996, only a minority were willing to declare their belief in communist ideals but it was a growing minority, and one which had increasingly distinctive and coherent views. It did not presage a return to the old regime but, paradoxically, open support for communist ideals – now freed from the chains of communist practice – did represent an increasingly important, coherent and self-confident element in the new 'postcommunist' politics.

VI   Values in Perspective

20 Postcommunist Values in a Western Perspective

Throughout this book we have focused our attention on the values held by those who live in postcommunist countries. We have looked at the variations in those values between those who lived in different postcommunist countries, between their publics and their politicians, and between different social and political groups within countries. Now we want to see how those values differ from those in a 'typical' western democracy.[1] We are interested in the extent to which the people and politicians in postcommunist countries are more or less socialist than their western counterparts, or more or less nationalist. But still more, we are interested in the extent to which they are more or less committed to liberal and democratic values.

Our study of postcommunist values was prompted in part by Glasgow University's earlier study of political culture within Britain which was carried out just two years before our study of opinion in postcommunist countries.[2] In turn that study drew on earlier American[3] and Canadian[4] research. Although there are differences in the detail of question wording, many similar questions were put to the public and politicians in Britain and the FSU/ECE and the two-level design allows us to view the values of both the FSU/ECE publics and of their politicians in a comparative perspective.

Britain is a particularly good point of comparison because it can claim a long and uninterrupted democratic tradition and, at the same time, it is as European as Russia, if not quite so European as the Czech Republic. In Almond and Verba's classic, *The Civic Culture*, Britain was held to be the best example of a democratic culture, certainly better than Germany or the United States whose democratic cultures were, according to Almond and Verba, deficient in different ways. And even those who have reservations about whether Britain is still the best example of a democratic culture could hardly deny that it remains a good one. So, in this chapter, we shall compare postcommunist values wherever possible with those in contemporary Britain. But let us begin with a comparison that is neither British nor contemporary.

NOSTALGIA

In his critique of *The Civic Culture* study, Conradt drew attention to the steady decline through the 1950s and 1960s in nostalgia for previous regimes in Germany.[5] Germans were asked: 'When in this century do you think Germany has been best off?' It is not a perfect question because it could have been

389

interpreted in purely economic terms. But nonetheless, it is revealing. In 1951, 45 per cent opted for the Kaiser's pre-1914 Empire and 42 per cent for Hitler's pre-1939 Third Reich; only 2 per cent chose the post-war democracy of the Federal Republic. Thereafter support for both the Kaiser and Hitler regimes declined and support for the Federal Republic rose to 42 per cent by the end of the 1950s and to 81 per cent by the end of the 1960s.

Table 20.1:   Best time for country is a democratic period

	Germany (Fed Rep)				Russia	Ukraine	Hungary	Slovakia	Czech Republic
	1951	1959	1963	1970					
	%	%	%	%	%	%	%	%	%
Politi cians	na	na	na	na	30	37	40	na	73
People	9	46	67	83	10	8	14	48	73

Note: The figures for Germany[6] are for the post-war Federal Republic and the inter-war Weimar Republic. However they include only 7, 4, 5, and 2 per cent for the Weimar Republic in the four successive surveys. For Russia, Ukraine and Hungary they include only the postcommunist period. For Slovakia and the Czech Republic they include the pre-war democratic regime of Masaryk, as well as the postcommunist period. Only 3 per cent in Slovakia chose the Masaryk period, but 32 per cent of the Czech public, and 41 per cent of Czech politicians chose it.

We can compare those findings with answers to our rather more carefully worded 'Taking *everything* into account, which of the times shown on this card do you feel was best for (country)?' Perhaps because time has moved on by forty years, support for the pre-1914 empires was much less in our FSU/ECE surveys. But because there was the option of supporting a post-Stalin communism, nostalgia for the communist regime in the FSU/ECE was even greater than that for the Hitler regime in 1951 Germany. And while nostalgia for the inter-war democracy of the Weimar Republic never reached more than 7 per cent in the German surveys, nostalgia for the inter-war democracy of Masaryk ran at 32 per cent amongst the Czech public and 41 per cent amongst Czech politicians – though at only 3 per cent in Slovakia.

We can usefully calibrate the degree of non-democratic nostalgia amongst postcommunist publics and politicians by noting the date at which there was a similar degree of non-democratic nostalgia in post-war Germany. By that criterion, Czech commitment to the democratic period (helped by their reverence for Masaryk) ran at the level of Germany in the mid 1960s; and Slovak commitment (unaffected by Masaryk) at the level of Germany at the end of the 1950s. But the Russian and Ukrainian publics look very much like the sullen and demoralised Germans of 1951, and the Hungarians not much better – though politicians in those three countries look more like Germans in the mid-1950s.

SOCIALIST VALUES

In Britain we asked: 'Here are a number of things which many people think are very desirable goals but, at the same time, many people feel that it is *not* the responsibility of government to provide them. Do *you* think each of the following should, or should not, be the *government's* responsibility?' The list that followed included:

- health care: 'good medical care for everyone'
- jobs: 'that everyone who wants a job can have one'
- housing: 'adequate housing for everyone'
- equal wealth: 'evening out differences in wealth between people'.

In the FSU/ECE we asked whether 'providing health care, jobs, and housing should be done mainly by the government or left mainly to private businesses and the market economy?' While these are not exact equivalents of the British questions they come close to the same ideas. True, there is a difference in logic between government 'being responsible for' and actually 'mainly providing', but given the differences in the economic order of Britain and the FSU/ECE countries that difference in wording tends more towards functional equivalence than the reverse.

In the FSU/ECE we also posed what might be considered an unreal, Hayekian choice[7] between freedom and equality: 'which should be more important at the moment – to ensure that the gap between rich and poor does not become too wide, or to give everyone the freedom to make as much money as they can?' While we did not ask that question in our British surveys, Times–Mirror surveys asked some very similar questions throughout east and west Europe – in Russia and Ukraine, posing the choice between freedom from government interference and equality and elsewhere, between individual freedom and a state guarantee that nobody would be left in poverty.

In terms of government responsibility for health care, British values were generally at least as socialist as those in the FSU/ECE; politicians in Britain were considerably more socialist than those in ECE, and even slightly more than those in the FSU. In terms of government responsibility for full employment, British values were rather more socialist than those in ECE but less than those in the FSU. And although we have no direct equivalent in Britain, it is worth recalling that 52 per cent of the public in the FSU but only 36 per cent in ECE, along with 23 per cent of politicians in the FSU but only 11 in ECE described unemployment as simply 'unacceptable' – which also shows more sensitivity to unemployment in the FSU than in ECE.

In terms of government responsibility for adequate housing, British values were more socialist than those in the FSU and much more than those in ECE. In terms of government responsibility for equalising wealth, British values were much the same as in the FSU and ECE; if anything, the people and politicians of the FSU were the most inclined to give free rein to the new rich. And when pressed to choose between freedom and equality or social welfare, it was the FSU countries, not ECE or west European countries, that were slightly less inclined to choose equality – both on our own figures and on Times–Mirror figures.

Table 20.2: Socialist values: social welfare

	Britain	FSU	ECE
	%	%	%
Govt responsible for health care:			
Politicians	99	95	81
People	98	91	91
Govt responsible for full employment:			
Politicians	65	74	30
People	78	89	72
Govt responsible for adequate housing:			
Politicians	90	62	40
People	91	82	80
Govt responsible for equalising wealth:			
Politicians	52	45	51
People	51	49	63
Equality or welfare more important than			
freedom:	64	49	63
People			

Notes: Because we carried out surveys of MPs in only four of the five countries, the figures for politicians in ECE are the average of the figures for Czech and Hungarian MPs; but the figures for the public in ECE are the average of the figures for publics in the Czech Republic, Hungary and Slovakia. Chapters 10 and 11 provide the best means of comparing politicians with their own publics. In this chapter however, we are concerned to compare FSU/ECE publics with the British public, and FSU/ECE politicians with British politicians – so the slight inconsistency between calculations for politicians and publics in ECE is not relevant.

Equality/welfare versus freedom: We asked this question in our FSU/ECE surveys but not in our British surveys. So we have taken the British figure (and only the British figure) for the equality/welfare versus freedom question from the 1991 Times–Mirror surveys; corresponding Times–Mirror figures for other countries were Russia 38 per cent, Ukraine 41 per cent, Czechoslovakia 45 per cent, Hungary 70 per cent.[9] Our own figures for the FSU/ECE countries were remarkably similar to these. Other west European countries in the Times–Mirror surveys had figures similar to those for Britain and Hungary.

In short, neither the public nor the politicians in the FSU and ECE looked very much more socialist than the British on the social welfare aspect of socialist values – not because they lacked any commitment to socialist values but because their commitment was, on average, no greater than in Britain.[8]

In our British survey we asked no questions comparable to those on the state ownership and control of industry in our FSU/ECE surveys: 'Should each of the following be run mainly by the state or mainly by private businesses? – farming, car factories, computer manufacturers, newspapers, television programmes.' But comparable questions were asked in nine surveys in the British election study series begun by Butler and Stokes: 'Are you generally in favour of more nationalisation of companies by government, more privatisation of companies by government, or should things be left as they are now?'[10] Given the British starting point of a mixed economy, this question about the direction of policy in Britain was very broadly comparable to the FSU/ECE question about the final resting place of policy, though the correspondence is clearly not exact.

In 1992, both the public and politicians in Britain were fairly evenly divided between those who wanted more nationalisation and those who wanted more privatisation.[11] So were the public in five surveys between 1963 and 1974 (average 56 per cent for more nationalisation), but not in three surveys between 1979 and 1987 (average only 31 per cent for more nationalisation).[12] Those trends showed reactions against the extent and performance of nationalised industries under the 1974–79 Labour government and, after a decade of privatisation under 1979–90 Thatcher governments, a counter-reaction against privatisation.

The extent of public enterprise was also declining rapidly in ECE and the FSU at the time of our surveys. Even in Russia – often depicted as dragging its heels on privatisation – the percentage of the labour force employed at state or municipal enterprises declined from 83 per cent in 1990 to 53 per cent in 1993 and 45 per cent in 1994.[13] At the end of 1993 the FSU public were evenly divided on whether the state should run farms, but 73 per cent in favour of the state running car and computer factories, while FSU politicians were around 60 per cent against both. In ECE the public were on balance marginally favourable to the state running farms but marginally against it running car and computer factories, while ECE politicians were overwhelmingly against the state running either. Compared to Britain therefore, the striking features of FSU/ECE opinion were the high level of support amongst FSU (but not ECE) publics for the state running car and computer factories (but not farming); and the overwhelming commitment of ECE politicians (though less amongst FSU politicians) to privatisation.

Perhaps it comes as a surprise to be reminded just how many of the public and politicians in Britain, on balance, favoured more rather than less state control of industry when they were asked that question. That puts FSU/ECE answers in context, and highlights ECE politicians' naive enthusiasm for privatisation as much as the FSU public's conservative attachment to public enterprise. Both were extreme by British standards.

Table 20.3:   Socialist values: state ownership of industry

	Britain	FSU	ECE
	%	%	%
BRITAIN: More nationalisation rather than more privatisation			
Politicians	47		
People	50		
FSU/ECE: Car and computer factories should be run mainly by the state rather than mainly by private businesses			
Politicians		40	8
People		73	42
FSU/ECE: Farms should be run mainly by the state rather than mainly by private businesses			
Politicians		41	15
People		52	56

Note: 'No change' and 'Both Equally' as well as 'Don't Knows', 'Can't decide' etc. excluded from calculation of percentages.

NATIONALIST VALUES

The main issue of practical concern for regional autonomy within Britain was the possibility of creating a 'devolved' (i.e. subordinate) Scottish Assembly or Parliament. There was clear evidence of a much stronger popular support for local autonomy for Scotland than for other parts of Britain. Throughout Britain (not just in the particular areas specified in the questions) we asked: 'Would you support or oppose giving greater powers of self government to Scotland? ...London?...and regions of England such as the north-west or south-east?' In the FSU/ECE we asked less specifically: 'Would you support or oppose giving greater powers of self-government to regions within (country)?'

Politicians in the FSU/ECE were somewhat more willing to support moves towards greater regional autonomy in their countries than British politicians were willing to accept the creation of a Scottish Assembly. But amongst the publics, the pattern was reversed: the public throughout Britain were somewhat more willing to accept a Scottish Assembly than FSU/ECE publics were willing to accept moves towards greater regional autonomy in their countries. Overall, ECE attitudes were a little more favourable to regional autonomy than the British, and FSU attitudes a little less favourable than the British – but the differences were not great. Support for more regional autonomy within England itself was relatively weak.

As every Scottish politician knows however, devolution is not separatism. Our FSU/ECE surveys showed opposition to separatism was almost as great as support for devolution and, in contrast to the pattern on regional autonomy, it was *greater* amongst FSU/ECE politicians than amongst their publics. We have no direct indicator of British attitudes to separatism but we suspect they would also be extremely negative and more so amongst politicians than the public.

Table 20.4: Self-government

	Support giving more powers of self-government to:				
	Scotland	London	English regions	Regions within (country)	Regions within (country)
	Britain	Britain	Britain	FSU	ECE
	%	%	%	%	%
Politicians	75	51	55	80	90
People	81	40	41	66	79

Note: All three British questions were asked throughout Britain, not just in the areas whose greater self-government was at issue.

Table 20.5: Cultural conformity: opposition to minority schooling

	Oppose Welsh language schools Britain	Oppose Muslim Schools Britain	All schools should teach all subjects in the state language	
			FSU	ECE
	%	%	%	%
Politicians	12	47	31	20
People	8	40	35	52

British support for cultural conformity in schools depended very much on whether the question was framed in terms of Welsh language schools, or Muslim schools. Inevitably Welsh language schools would be confined to Wales and would not be within the direct experience of over 90 per cent of the British. They could afford to be indulgent. But Muslim schools might be more visible and divisive – as the division between Catholic and Protestant (formally 'non-sectarian') schools had been. The British were even less willing to support Muslim schools than people in the FSU or ECE were willing to support teaching in languages other than the state language. And although we had no direct equivalent question in the FSU/ECE surveys, it is worth noting that 66 per cent of the British public and 49 per cent of their politicians agreed with the proposition that 'immigrants to Britain should try harder to be more like other British people'. The impulse towards cultural conformity was as strong in Britain as in the FSU/ ECE although its implications for civil peace varied greatly with the variety of objective conditions. Very strong support for cultural conformity in the Czech Republic, for example, had only limited practical consequences because there were no large visible minorities left in the Czech Republic. Conversely, if the proportion of Muslims in Britain had been as high as the proportion of Russian speakers in Ukraine, British support for cultural conformity would have much more serious practical consequences than it has at present.

Although we asked no questions about irredentism in our British survey, Times–Mirror surveys did ask such questions throughout east and west Europe in 1991. Like us, they found that a large majority in Hungary laid claim to parts of neighbouring countries. Opinion in Poland was very similar. Like us, they also found irredentist sentiment was much less in Czechoslovakia and weak in Ukraine – more like that in Greece and Italy, and significantly less than in Spain, though greater than in Britain – though some may be surprised that as many as a quarter of the British also laid claim to some neighbouring territory. Since they were not asked to specify the territory in question we can only speculate that the British had some part of Ireland in mind; it is a long time since the British crown laid claim to parts of France. Nonetheless, irredentist sentiment in the FSU and ECE was clearly greater than in Britain.

But comparison of the Times–Mirror surveys with our own also reveals sharp changes in public opinion in Russia during the early 1990s. In 1991, when there was still a Soviet Union, only 31 per cent in Russia laid claim to neighbouring territory; in 1993, after the collapse of the Soviet Union, 71 per cent did so. Irredentist sentiment in Russia suddenly rose from a Ukrainian level to match that in Hungary. But the break up of Czechoslovakia also seems to have had the opposite effect, reducing irredentist sentiment overall as well as differentiating between Czech and Slovak claims.

Table 20.6:   Parts of neighbouring countries really should belong to (our country):

	1991		*1991*	*1993*
	%		%	%
Britain (UK)	24	Russia	31	71
		Ukraine	35	30
Italy	37	Hungary	75	60
Greece	43	Czechoslovakia	53	
Spain	62	Czech Republic		18
Poland	73	Slovak Republic		32

Notes: 1991 figures calculated from Times–Mirror Surveys.[14] To maintain comparability with our own figures for 1993, we have excluded 'don't knows' etc. and recalculated Times–Mirror survey percentages. The Times–Mirror question referred to parts of neighbouring countries that really belonging ' to us' rather than 'to (our country)', which means, in particular that the 'us' was somewhat ambiguous for Soviet populations in 1991.

In Ukraine and throughout ECE, even in Hungary, we found very little support for military action when 'the rights of (country people) living in neighbouring countries are threatened' but, in such circumstances, 26 per cent of the Russian public and 30 per cent of their MPs were willing to threaten force outside the borders of the Russian Federation in the 'near abroad'. We asked no similar question in our British survey, but only a decade earlier the explosion of public and especially parliamentary support for military action in the Falklands suggested that British attitudes were at least as aggressive as Russian. Similarly, the report on the Times–Mirror surveys in 1991 concluded that 'Russian and Ukrainian peoples [are] far less enamoured of force as an instrument of policy than is the American population.'[15]

FREEDOM, TOLERANCE AND RIGHTS TO PROTEST

Overall our review of nationalist values in the FSU/ECE, like our review of socialist values, has suggested more points of similarity than difference between Britain and the FSU/ECE. The most important question remains: were FSU/ECE attitudes towards liberal and democratic values also similar to those in Britain?

Under the heading of liberal values we considered questions of freedom, order, authority, tolerance, rights of protest, and government constrained by law. Especially when we came to contrast the values of citizens and politicians, we found it useful to divide liberal values into those more concerned with freedom and tolerance – values that are primarily concerned with the rights of citizens – and those related but subtly different values which are more concerned with the restriction and constraint of rulers' discretion and prerogatives. But first, let us compare the degree of interpersonal and political trust in Britain and the FSU/ECE.

In the FSU/ECE we asked how much people trusted 'most ordinary people that you meet in everyday life.' In Britain we asked: 'Generally speaking would you say that most people you come into contact with are trustworthy or untrustworthy?' Only three-quarters of FSU/ECE publics felt they could trust most (not all, of course) people they met in everyday life, compared to 90 per cent in Britain. Politicians everywhere expressed higher levels of interpersonal trust. Our evidence suggests that interpersonal trust was lower in the FSU/ECE than in Britain but it was nonetheless high in absolute terms – and particularly high relative to the level of trust in politicians.[16]

In Britain we asked whether people thought 'most politicians can be trusted to do what they think is best for the country?' In the FSU/ECE we asked people to rate their degree of trust in 'the government, the president, the prime minister, and parliament' on the same scale as their degree of trust in ordinary people. We have averaged the results to get a single measure of trust in politicians. Some caution is necessary in interpreting these figures, though the conclusions are clear enough. Obviously they relate to the level of trust in governments and parlia-

ments at a particular time – and thus refer to the old (1993) parliaments in
Ukraine and Hungary, not the new (1994). In Russia, we took figures for trust
in the new parliament elected in December 1993. Levels of trust in different
politicians varied sharply in ECE, where the non-executive presidents scored
very high on trust and parliaments very low, but not so much in the FSU.

Table 20.7:   Trust ordinary people and politicians

		Britain	FSU	ECE
		%	%	%
Trust ordinary people:				
	Politicians	97	94	96
	People	90	78	76
Trust politicians:				
	Politicians	58	51	75
	People	33	30	47

Both in Britain and the FSU only a third of the public, and just over half the
politicians themselves, expressed trust in politicians. Levels of trust were much
higher in ECE partly because their non-executive presidents were so trusted, but
also because the Czech government and prime minister (but not their parliament) were so trusted. But whatever the reason, it is interesting that the highest
levels of trust were not in the old democracy of Britain, but in the new
democracies of ECE.

Table 20.8:   Expect fair treatment by officials in a tax or housing office

1959–61			1993
%			%
Britain (UK)	83	Russia	16
USA	83	Ukraine	12
Germany	65	Czech Republic	64
Italy	53	Slovak Republic	53
Mexico	42	Hungary	43

Note: The 1959–61 figures come from *The Civic Culture*.[17]

On the other hand the expectations of fair treatment by public officials in a
tax or housing office were low. In the FSU they were very much lower than in
any country where the question was originally asked for Almond and Verba's
1963 *Civic Culture* study. In ECE expectations of fair treatment by officials
almost exactly reflected the level of expectations reported by Almond and Verba

in Germany, Italy and Mexico – though that was far lower than in Britain or the USA at that time.

Citizens' respect for authority is central to the relationship between governors and governed. In the FSU/ECE we asked respondents whether they agreed or disagreed with the proposition that: '(country people) should have more respect for authority'. Within Russia we replaced '(country people)' with 'Russians'; in Ukraine with 'Ukrainians'; and so on. In Britain we asked a similar question but in a different format: we asked British respondents to give us a 'mark out of ten' to indicate 'how important to you is respect for authority'.

Table 20.9:   Respect for authority

	Britain marks out of ten	FSU %	ECE %
Politicians	7.5	80	37
People	8.2	73	59

There was clearly much more emphasis on the need to respect authority in the FSU than in ECE, and FSU politicians – unlike those in Britain or ECE – stressed authority more than their own public. The difference in question formats prevents a clear conclusion on whether the emphasis on authority in the FSU was higher or lower than in Britain, but it cannot obscure the fact that the British also gave great emphasis to the need to respect authority. Another question provides an exact comparison. Both in Britain and the FSU/ECE we asked whether people agreed or disagreed with the proposition that: 'the only alternative to strong government is disorder and chaos'. If we take agreement with this proposition as a measure of support for 'strong government', both the public and their politicians in Hungary and the FSU were more committed to strong government than their counterparts in Britain, but the public in Slovakia, and both the public and politicians in the Czech Republic were less committed to strong government than their counterparts in Britain.

Table 20.10:   The only alternative to strong government is disorder and chaos

	Britain	FSU	ECE
	%	%	%
Politicians	27	47	45
People	38	66	43

Turning to citizens' rights of protest and dissent, we asked in the FSU/ECE: 'If some citizens felt a law was very unjust or harmful do you think they should be allowed to hold protest marches and demonstrations which block traffic for a few hours?' This question combined the sentiments of two different questions we had used in our British surveys:

(1) 'If people wish to protest against a law they feel is really unjust or harmful they should have the right to hold protest marches and demonstrations. (Agree/disagree etc.?)'
(2) 'Should a political protest group be allowed to hold a parade that blocks town centre traffic for two hours?'

Overwhelming majorities of the British supported the abstract right to protest put forward in the first question, but not the practical implementation of that right if it caused disruption to traffic. Both in Britain and the FSU around half the politicians and 70 per cent of the public were unwilling to pay the price, in terms of traffic dislocation, of such rights of protest. But in ECE, both the public and their politicians were somewhat more liberal than their counterparts in Britain.

On freedom of speech we asked, in the FSU/ECE, whether 'public speeches by people with extreme views should be banned.' In Britain we again asked two different questions that get at the same idea:

(1) 'Free speech is just not worth it if it means we have to put up with the danger to society from extremist views. (Agree/disagree etc.?)'
(2) 'Political organisations with extreme views should be banned. (Agree/disagree etc.?)'

The first of these British questions might be considered a slightly milder version of the FSU/ECE question, the second slightly more repressive. In the event it does not matter which we use: by any standard, ECE politicians and publics were somewhat more willing than their British counterparts to ban speeches by extremists, and FSU politicians and public much more. There were other differences in the pattern of support for free speech however. In Britain and ECE politicians were much more willing to defend free speech than their own publics, but not in the FSU.

We also tried to pose questions about free speech in a more concrete way that might therefore be more meaningful to our interviewees. In the FSU/ECE we asked whether people would 'support or oppose the right of each of the following to hold public meetings and rallies – fascists, communists, evangelical Christians, Jews, Muslims, gypsies, and homosexuals?' In Britain, where we employed computer assisted telephone interviewing (CATI) we asked people to tell us how much they liked or disliked eleven different groups – 'gays and lesbians, environmental campaigners like Greenpeace, animal rights activists, communists, feminists, National Front supporters, Muslim activists, Militant Tendency[18] supporters, IRA sympathisers, people who sympathise with Protestant terrorists in Northern Ireland, and black activists.' The computer then identified which of these the interviewee liked least, which we can call the LLG (least liked group) for that particular interviewee. Then we asked whether respondents felt that their the LLG 'should not be allowed to make public speeches in my locality.'

In Britain 44 per cent of the public but only 29 per cent of politicians would ban their least liked group from making speeches. In the FSU/ECE we cannot identify which was the respondent's least liked group but that hardly proves necessary. Averaging over all seven groups, between a quarter and a third of FSU/ECE politicians would ban public meetings by these groups – similar to the British figure for banning speeches by their least liked group; but three quarters of the FSU/ECE publics would ban public meetings by these groups – almost twice the British figure. And given that this focuses upon the average of all groups in the FSU/ECE questions, rather than the individual's least liked group as in Britain, we can conclude that FSU/ECE publics were far more willing than the British to ban speeches by specific, named extremist or minority groups. At the same time we should note that the difference between the relatively liberal attitudes of politicians and the relatively repressive attitude of their publics towards the exercise of free speech by named extremist or minority groups was much greater in the FSU/ECE than in Britain: FSU/ECE politicians were fairly close to their British counterparts on this, but their publics were not.

Table 20.11: Opposition to citizens' rights of protest and dissent

	Britain	FSU	ECE
	%	%	%
Ban protest demonstrations that block traffic:			
Politicians	48	53	39
People	71	70	60
Britain: Free speech is not worth it (ban extreme organisations)			
FSU/ECE: Ban speeches by people with extreme views			
Politicians	12 (17)	83	23
People	36 (40)	88	58
Ban public meetings by specified minority groups:			
Politicians	29	34	26
People	44	73	73
The offensive (or morally wrong) should be made illegal:			
Politicians	25	80	30
People	57	77	74

Tolerance extends to issues beyond the overtly political. And toleration can, on the surface, appear to have both a moral and a legal (or coercive) dimension.

In fact, it is important to distinguish between tolerance and approval. The concept of tolerance requires *condemnation without coercion* if it is to have any meaning at all. So in East Europe we asked whether people would agree that 'If something deeply offends most (country) people, then it should be made illegal.' And in Britain we put a similar proposition: 'If something is morally wrong then it should be made illegal (Agree/disagree etc.?)'. ECE politicians were only slightly less tolerant than the British; but FSU/ECE publics were somewhat less tolerant than the British; and FSU *politicians* were quite outstandingly intolerant when compared to other politicians, though representative of their own publics.

Overall therefore, we have found that, on balance, there was more emphasis on the need for strong government, more fear of disorder, and less tolerance of extremist or offensive minorities in the FSU/ECE than in Britain. But the differences between Britain, ECE and the FSU were less clear-cut, less sharp, and more complex than might have been expected.[19]

THE PREROGATIVES OF GOVERNMENT

We have distinguished attitudes to the rights of citizens from attitudes towards the prerogatives of government because they are not – as might first appear – opposite sides of the same coin. In particular, politicians in Britain and the FSU/ECE have a 'governing perspective'. They have more trust and confidence in government than do their peoples; they may be more willing to tolerate citizens' protests than their peoples, but they are less willing than their peoples to tolerate anything that smacks of rebellion.

One key issue is obedience to the law, even when it appears unjust. The FSU/ECE have been afflicted by rapidly increasing crime rates since the fall of the communist regimes. Before that they had the even greater problem of governments that were themselves effectively unconstrained by law, but which inflicted harsh and irrational laws on their people. One of the most evocative reform slogans was the need to construct a 'law-based state' – what the American revolutionaries described as 'a government of laws, not men'. Although necessity forced people to evade the law both under the rigidities of communism and the chaos of transition, the principle of a 'normal', well-ordered, law-bound and law-abiding state remained an attractive, if perhaps unattainable goal in postcommunist countries. In Britain we asked: 'Suppose parliament passed a law you considered unjust, immoral or cruel. Would you still be morally bound to obey it?' In the FSU/ECE we put the proposition: 'Even if a law is unjust, people should obey it until it is changed. (Agree/disagree? etc.).' Support for obedience – at least in principle – to even unjust laws was about 13 per cent higher amongst the public in the FSU/ECE than in Britain, and 30 per cent higher amongst FSU/ECE politicians than British. And within every country, clear evidence of a governing perspective was provided by the fact that politicians insisted on obedience to unjust laws far more than their publics.

Table 20.12: Citizens should obey even unjust laws

	Britain	FSU	ECE
	%	%	%
Politicians	66	96	96
People	51	64	63

Table 20.13: Law-constrained government

	Britain	FSU	ECE
	%	%	%
BRITAIN: reject phone taps etc. FSU/ECE: trusted leader should still be restricted by law			
Politicians	46	95	97
People	52	73	78
BRITAIN: European (British) Courts to have final say FSU/ECE: Constitutional Court to have final say			
Politicians	59 (36)	99	98
People	55 (48)	79	76
BRITAIN: reject conviction-on-confession FSU/ECE: police must stay within the law			
Politicians	83	92	83
People	79	77	50

It would appear that the public, and more especially the politicians, in the FSU/ECE were simply more authoritarian than in Britain on the issue of obedience to the law. But that is not the case, or at least not if the word 'authoritarian' is restricted to its familiar 'top-down' meaning. The public, and more especially the politicians, in the FSU/ECE were also more insistent on law-constrained government than the British. In the FSU/ECE we put the proposition that: 'a strong leader who has the trust of the people should not be restricted by the law (Agree/disagree etc.?).' In Britain, we asked a question that was at least tangentially relevant: 'In order to combat [crime/terrorism/dangerous and undemocratic ideas] should the police or security services ever be allowed to [tap phones/inspect bank accounts]?'[20] Surveillance activities in Britain, as elsewhere, hover uneasily on the borders of illegality. Only half the British rejected the use of these surveillance measures, rising to only 60 per cent even when they were aimed at subversive ideas rather than at crime or terrorism.

By contrast three-quarters of the FSU/ECE public, and almost all their politicians rejected the proposition that a trusted leader should be unconstrained by law. Of course the questions are not perfect equivalents, but the comparison still shows relatively strong support for legal constraints in the FSU/ECE.

One mechanism for ensuring a law-based government is a strong, well-respected constitutional court – of which the best example is the United States Supreme Court. But even in Britain, courts restrain the government. British courts refuse to rule on the constitutionality of British law, but they do rule on whether government ministers are acting within the laws passed by parliament. In the early 1990s, decisions by the Home Secretary, Michael Howard, were repeatedly overturned by the courts. In addition, Britain's membership of the European Union and its adherence to the European Convention on Human Rights have made even the constitutionality of its laws subject to rulings by the European Court of Justice, and the European Court of Human Rights which have forced numerous changes to British law. Those courts play much of the role of a supreme court in British affairs, though they are both located outside Britain.

Throughout the FSU/ECE we asked: 'If the government wanted to take action but the Constitutional Court said it violated the constitution, who should have the final say?' That balanced the courts against the government. In Britain our question balanced the courts against parliament but, given the fusion of the legislative and executive arms in Britain, that does not prevent cross-national comparison. We asked two questions: one about the internal constitution Britain has *not* got, and one about the external constitution which it is gradually acquiring through its membership of European bodies. First we asked: 'Suppose we had a constitutional Bill of Rights as some other countries do. If parliament passed a law but the courts said it was unconstitutional, who should have the final say?' Second we asked: 'Suppose someone in Britain objects to a law passed by parliament and takes the case to the European Court of Human Rights. Who should have the final say?' Throughout the FSU/ECE, three-quarters of the public and almost all of the politicians paid at least lip-service to the supremacy of the courts. But in Britain, less than half would accept the supremacy of a British court, and only just over half would accept the supremacy of a European courts. The difference between Britain on the one hand, and the FSU/ECE on the other, on these questions of judicial supremacy echoes the difference between them on attitudes towards the government stepping outside the law.

Descending from high politics to low, in the FSU/ECE, we put the proposition: 'The police themselves should never break the law even though that means some criminals escape punishment (Agree/disagree etc.?)'. The head of the London police, Sir Paul Condon, was recently quoted as saying: 'because street cops see villains escape time and again, you risk 'noble cause' corruption [*i.e.* police officers bending evidence to convict people they are certain are guilty].'[21]

When senior police officers link the words 'noble' and 'corruption', even without advocating such behaviour, it is clear which answer many British police might be tempted to give to our FSU/ECE question. A series of notorious scandals in Britain had exposed illegal police activity connected with conviction-by-confession. The chief of the London police had been talking about the past as much as about the future. Reflecting that, we put the proposition: 'Courts should *not* convict people purely on the basis of a confession. (Agree/disagree etc.?)'. About 80 per cent in Britain rejected the idea of conviction-on-confession (higher still when we advanced explicit arguments against it). A similar percentage of the public in the FSU, and an even higher percentage of FSU politicians, were opposed to the police stepping outside the law to secure convictions. But not in ECE, where the Czechs took a particularly relaxed view of the need to constrain their police within the law. In ECE the public, if not politicians, were much more willing than the British to let the police drift outside the law in order to crack down on crime.

Support for law-constrained government in the FSU/ECE did not preclude support for the suspension of citizens' rights in an emergency or to protect essential public services however. In Britain, we used our CATI techniques to pose two related but different questions to random halves of our samples.

(1) 'Should workers who do *not* work in essential public services have the right to strike?'
(2) 'Should all workers, *even those in essential public services* like the Ambulance Service or the Fire Brigade, have the right to strike?'

In the FSU/ECE we asked a slightly amended version of the second question: 'All workers, even those in essential public services like hospitals and electricity power stations, should have the right to strike. (Agree /disagree etc.?).'

In Britain there was overwhelming support for the right of those who did not work in essential public services to strike, but once workers in essential public services were included, support dropped to around two-thirds. In the FSU/ECE, where our question always included essential public services, support for the right to strike was down to around a half. It was about 10 per cent lower in the FSU than in ECE, and about 10 per cent lower again amongst FSU/ECE politicians than amongst their publics.

In the FSU/ECE we asked whether 'it would be acceptable, or not acceptable, for the government to suspend citizens' usual rights and take emergency powers' in each of five situations that included 'widespread strikes in essential industries' and 'widespread public disorder'. In Britain we asked 'if there is a genuine national emergency, is it alright to suspend some of our usual civil rights?' and, if we received a positive reply, we then went on to ask whether each of four situations that included 'an economic crisis caused by strikes in important industries' and 'widespread public disorder' 'would be sufficient to justify suspending some of our usual civil rights?' The questions in Britain and the

FSU/ECE were very similar, at least with respect to these two scenarios of strikes and public disorder. Under both scenarios, there was somewhat greater support for emergency powers amongst the public and politicians in the FSU than amongst their counterparts in Britain; but no more support, perhaps slightly less even, amongst the public and politicians in ECE than in Britain.

Table 20.14:   Citizens' rights in emergency situations

		Britain	FSU	ECE
		%	%	%
Oppose right of essential public service workers to strike				
	Politicians	35	60	52
	People	32	51	40
Support state of emergency to combat widespread strikes				
	Politicians	29	41	19
	People	35	56	37
Support state of emergency to combat widespread disorder				
	Politicians	59	73	59
	People	58	80	59

Table 20.15:   Control and censorship of the mass media

		Britain	FSU	ECE
		%	%	%
Support direct government control of television				
	Politicians	15	29	25
	People	27	19	45
Ban media intrusions into the private lives of government ministers				
	Politicians	34	41	34
	People	43	36	54

Finally we asked two questions about the control or censorship of mass communications. First, in the FSU/ECE, we asked whether 'the government should be able to dismiss the head of state television if it does not like what he is doing' and in Britain we asked whether 'there should be more government control of television and the Press?' These questions were relevant because the heads of state television in Russia, Hungary – and Britain – had been summarily dismissed in recent years. Second, in the FSU/ECE we asked whether: 'Newspapers should be banned from publishing embarrassing details about the private lives of government ministers' and, in Britain, whether television or the press should be banned from publishing 'stories that intrude into [ordinary people's/ leading politicians'] private lives.'

Public support for direct government control of television was particularly strong in ECE and particularly weak in the FSU; British public attitudes were intermediate. But in sharp contrast, it was FSU politicians who backed government control of television most strongly. On this issue, politicians were more liberal than their publics in Britain and ECE but less liberal than their publics in the FSU. Amongst both the public and politicians in Britain there a majority in favour of a ban on media intrusions into the lives of ordinary people, but a majority against a ban on media intrusions into the lives of 'leading politicians'. And to their credit, British politicians were even less favourable than the public to a ban on the media prying into politicians' private lives. The same was true in ECE, but the opposite in the FSU. So on both questions about the control or censorship of the mass media, FSU politicians displayed a self-interested 'governing perspective', while politicians in Britain and ECE did not.

Overall, however, the differences between attitudes towards the media in Britain and the FSU/ECE were not large. On states of emergency British and ECE attitudes were similar, but FSU attitudes noticeably more authoritarian. But the greatest differences between Britain and the FSU/ECE lay in their attitudes to the role of the law. FSU/ECE politicians in particular clung to a rigid belief in the need for both a law-abiding society and a law-based government with all the passion of a drowning man clutching at a straw. It certainly did not reflect where they had come from, or where they were, but rather where they hoped to go.

THE PROCEDURAL VALUES OF DEMOCRACY

We have placed attitudes towards populism, elections and parties under the heading of procedural values. We investigated support for the populists' favourite mechanism, the referendum. In the FSU/ECE we asked: 'Which comes closest to your view? The most important and difficult issues facing the country should be decided: (i) by elected politicians; or (ii) by the people in a referendum?' In Britain we used the facilities of CATI to put the question in opposite ways to randomly selected half-samples which we have combined for this analysis (reversing the direction of the answers in one half-sample). The two propositions used in the British survey were:

(1) 'It would be better to let the people decide important political issues by everyone voting in a referendum rather than by leaving them to parliament as at present. (Agree/disagree?)'

(2) 'Important political issues are too complex to be decided by everyone voting in a referendum and should be left to parliament to decide. (Agree/disagree?)'

Overall, approximately two-thirds of the public supported referenda, and two-thirds of politicians opposed it. Differences between Britain and the FSU/ECE were not great. Parliamentary politicians in the FSU were unusually populist, but parliaments were unusually powerless in the FSU compared to presidents and governments, which probably explains their populism.

Table 20.16:   Support use of referenda on important issues

	Britain	*FSU*	*ECE*
	%	%	%
Politicians	33	45	37
People	64	66	72

Representation through competitive elections is the principal mechanism of modern democracy. For local governance however, direct local elections are no more than one option amongst many. Even in a national democracy there are other ways of organising and controlling local governance than through elections – as we know only too well in contemporary Britain! In our 1985 and 1986 surveys of attitudes towards local governance, we asked the British public whether local governance should be through elected councils or by means of appointed officials – and 87 per cent opted for elected councils.[22] In East Europe we repeated this question, but in a balanced form designed to allow people to admit anti-democratic tendencies. Our question was: 'Which comes closer to your view? Local councils should be: (i) elected by the people who live in the area; or (ii) appointed by the national government to prevent endless political quarrelling?' Despite being encouraged towards an anti-democratic response by the wording of the question, 95 per cent of the public and 97 per cent of politicians in the FSU/ECE opted for *elected* councils – even higher levels than in Britain.

To measure support for elections as a means of encouraging politicians to be responsive, we asked in the FSU/ECE: 'How much do you think having regular elections makes politicians do what ordinary people want? Do you think elections have very much effect, some, not much, or none at all?' Throughout the 1960s, Butler and Stokes asked a similar question in Britain: 'How much do you think having elections makes government pay attention to what people think – a good deal, some, not much?'[23] On average, over four surveys at different times they found 80 per cent of the British public said 'a good deal' or 'some'. That was far more than the percentage of the FSU/ECE public who said 'very much effect' or 'some effect', but about the same as the percentage of FSU/ECE politicians who said so.

We measured feelings about the organisation and conduct of elections by asking, in the FSU/ECE, whether elections were 'free and fair'. Just over half in the FSU, but three quarters of the public and almost all the politicians in ECE, said their elections were 'free and fair'. Lest we assume too readily that British elections get universal praise, we should note that when we asked, in our 1987 British election survey: 'Considering the number of votes each party got last week, did the voting system produce a fair or unfair result in terms of seats for each party in parliament?', only 45 per cent said it was 'fair'.[24] Obviously that reflected specific criticism of the system of electoral arithmetic in Britain, but other questions in that survey revealed strong criticism of the media bias that pervaded, and probably influenced, the whole election campaign. So the high figures for the freedom and fairness of ECE elections are more remarkable than the lower figures for FSU elections.

Table 20.17:   Support for competitive elections

		Britain	FSU	ECE
		%	%	%
Local government councils should be elected				
	Politicians	na	97	97
	People	87	94	96
Elections make politicians responsive				
	Politicians	na	84	85
	People	80	44	53
Elections are free and fair				
	Politicians	na	56	99
	People	47	51	71
Support alternation in power through govts losing elections				
	Politicians	na	68	44
	People	63	63	46

We sought to measure commitment to the alternation of governments through elections by asking, in the FSU/ECE: 'Which comes closer to your view? It is better if governments: (i) stay in power for a long time, to give their policies time to work, or (ii) lose elections reasonably often, to stop them getting too powerful or corrupt.' Again that reflected a question asked by Butler and Stokes in five British surveys during the 1960s : 'Over the years do you think that control of government should pass from one party to another every so often, or do you think its all right for one party to have control for a long time?'[25] In the FSU, as in Britain during the 1960s, just under two-thirds supported the alternation of governments, though both the public and politicians in ECE were much less committed to alternation.

Using surveys at the 1993 Russian and 1994 Ukrainian elections, Pammett and DeBardeleben have compared public attitudes towards the possible meanings and functions of elections in the FSU with findings from our 1987 British election survey.[26] The British question was: 'Here are some things that elections mean to different people. As I read each one, please tell me whether it has a lot, something, or not much to do with what elections mean to you.' The question format was the same in Russia and similar but not quite the same in Ukraine. People in Ukraine had perspectives on elections that were remarkably similar to those in Britain: elections for them were primarily about choice, accountability and an opportunity for the people to comment on the state of the country. People in Russia also put these functions at the top of their list, but they found them much less applicable – which implies that they saw elections as having a less important role in the politics of Russia, less influence on events, less impact.

Table 20.18:   Perceived functions of elections

	Britain	Russia	Ukraine
The meaning of elections has at least 'something' to do with:	%	%	%
Choosing among particular policies	86	53	88
Choosing among leaders' personalities	na	58	85
Holding governments accountable for their past actions	77	47	79
Commenting on the state of the country	68	53	79
Advancing the interests of a social class	59	40	67
Keeping politicians honest	54	42	65
Gaining particular things for myself and my family	69	36	56
Advancing the interests of an ethnic, national or religious group	na	26	53
Deceiving people	na	53	52

Notes: Figures calculated from Pammett and DeBardeleben, excluding 'don't knows'.

INTEREST IN POLITICS AND SUPPORT FOR PARTIES

Both in Britain and the FSU/ECE we measured interest in politics on a four point scale – 'a great deal, quite a lot, some, none' in Britain, and 'very, quite, only a little, not at all' in the FSU/ECE. Let us take the top two levels together as an indicator of interest in politics. By that criterion, interest in politics was the same in Britain as in ECE, but slightly lower in the FSU.

There are various ways of measuring the strength or weakness of commitment to existing parties. We put a variant of one standard party identification question: 'Generally speaking, do you think of yourself as a supporter of any political party?' to the public in the FSU/ECE and in Britain, though to politicians only in Britain. However, since we put the proposition that 'None of the existing parties represents the interests and views of people like me (Agree/disagree etc.?)' to both publics and politicians in the FSU/ECE we can use that to interpolate the likely level of party support amongst FSU/ECE politicians. Commitment to parties amongst the public was clearly much stronger in Britain than in the FSU/ECE, and particularly weak in the FSU.[27] It was also very much stronger amongst politicians than their publics. Amongst politicians it was probably strongest in the ECE parliaments, weakest in the FSU parliaments, and intermediate in the British local government councils that provided our sample of British politicians.

Table 20.19: Interest in politics and support for parties

		Britain	FSU	ECE
		%	%	%
Interested in politics				
	Politicians	93	na	na
	People	40	32	40
Party supporter				
	Politicians	85	na	na
	People	53	20	33
Some party represents my views and interests				
	Politicians	na	71	96
	People	na	35	48
Would not ban even parties which respondent regards very unfavourably (FSU/ECE) / as extremist (BRITAIN)				
	Politicians	83	74	96
	People	60	40	75

But commitment to one party is not the same as a real commitment to a competitive multiparty system. Just as tolerance itself requires a combination of 'condemnation without coercion', support for a competitive party system requires tolerance of opponents, tolerance of the habits and practice of opposition, and a reluctance to use coercion even against parties that we hate. So for each of 8 parties or political groups in Russia, 8 in Ukraine, 10 in Hungary and 11 in the Czech Republic, we asked people to describe their feelings on a five point scale ranging from 'very favourable' to 'very unfavourable'. Then we asked whether each of these 'parties or blocs are so dangerous that they should be banned?' The interesting figures are those that show the level of support for a ban on a party *amongst those who have already declared themselves 'very unfavourable' towards it*. Support for such a ban was much stronger in the FSU than in ECE, both amongst politicians and the public. Although it is not an exactly comparable question, in our British surveys we put the proposition: 'Political organisations with extreme views should be banned. (Agree/disagree?).' Judged by answers to that question, politicians and the public in Britain were more liberal than those in the FSU but less liberal than those in ECE.

CONCLUSION

By British standards, we have found that neither the public nor politicians in the FSU and ECE looked unusually socialist – not because they lacked any commitment to socialist values but because their commitment was no higher than in Britain. And although it is inherently difficult to compare levels of nationalism when the content of nationalism varies so much from country to country, we found more points of similarity than difference between Britain and the FSU/ECE.

But on balance, there was more emphasis on the need for strong government, more fear of disorder, and less tolerance of extremist or offensive minorities in the FSU/ECE than in Britain, though the differences were less clear-cut than might have been expected. On states of emergency British and ECE attitudes were similar, but FSU attitudes noticeably more authoritarian. Some of the greatest differences between Britain and the FSU/ECE lay in their attitudes to the role of law. FSU/ECE politicians in particular clung to a rigid belief in the need for a law-abiding society and a law-based government. The oxymoron, 'authoritarian liberalism', describes this combination of values rather well.[28] We have to remember that citizens in postcommunist countries faced particular problems of contemporary governance which would encourage anyone, whatever their personal inclinations, and whatever their cultural tradition, to give more stress both to social order and to legal constraints on government than they would do in more settled conditions.

Differences between Britain and the FSU/ECE on populism were not great. But a far higher percentage of the British than of the FSU/ECE public thought elections kept politicians responsive. Commitment to parties was also much stronger in Britain than in the FSU/ECE, and particularly weak in the FSU. But elections in ECE won unusually high marks for being 'free and fair' and support for governments alternating in power was as strong in the FSU as in Britain.

Notes

POLITICAL VALUES IN POSTCOMMUNIST EUROPE

1   See chapter 18.

2   Jan W. van Deth and Elinor Scarbrough, 'The concept of values' in Jan W. van Deth and Elinor Scarbrough (eds) *The Impact of Values* (Oxford: Oxford University Press, 1995) pp. 21–47 at p. 22. They also complain that 'the influence of values on political behaviour is relatively poorly researched – perhaps due to the behavioural orientations of political science, or even a certain calculated indifference due to worries that explaining behaviour in terms of values may not explain anything very much.' (p. 21) But see William L. Miller, Annis May Timpson and Michael Lessnoff, *Political Culture in Contemporary Britain: People and Politicians, Principles and Practice* (Oxford: Oxford University Press, 1996) which focuses on political principles and the relationship between principles and practice.

3   Mao Tse-Tung, 'Problems of War and Strategy' in his *Selected Works* (Beijing: Foreign Languages Press, 1965) vol.2 p. 224.

4   Quoted by Harry S. Truman in a speech reprinted in the *New York Times*, 14 September 1948, p. 24.

5   Gabriel A. Almond and Sidney Verba, *The Civic Culture: Political Attitudes and Democracy in Five Countries* (Princeton, NJ: Princeton University Press 1963; London: Sage, 1989) p. 3.

6   Guiseppe di Palma, *To Craft Democracy: An Essay on Democratic Transition* (Berkeley, CA: University of California Press, 1990) p. 138.

7   Robert A. Dahl, *Democracy and its Critics* (New Haven: Yale University Press, 1989) p. 314.

8   Hahn reaches that conclusion after reviewing: Robert Putnam, *Making Democracy Work* (Princeton, NJ: Princeton University Press, 1993); Larry Diamond (ed.) *Political Culture and Democracy in Developing Countries* (Boulder, CO: Lynne Rienner, 1993); Allan Kornberg and Harold D. Clarke, *Citizens and Community* (New York, NY: Cambridge University Press, 1992); and William Mishler and Richard Rose, 'Public support for legislatures and regimes in eastern and central Europe' A paper to the Conference on the Role of Legislatures and Parliaments in Democratising and Newly Democratic Regimes, Paris, May 1993. See Jeffrey W. Hahn, 'Changes in contemporary Russian political culture' in Vladimir Tismaneau (ed.) *Political Culture and Civil Society in Russia and the New States of Eurasia* (Armonk, NY: M.E. Sharpe, 1995) pp. 112–136 at p. 113.

9   Stephen White, Graeme Gill and Darrell Slider, *The Politics of Transition: Shaping a Post-Soviet Future* (Cambridge: Cambridge University Press, 1993) p. 229.

10   Georg Sorensen *Democracy and Democratization* (Boulder, CO: Westview, 1993) p. 46.

11   Larry Diamond (ed.) *Political Culture and Democracy in Developing Countries* (Boulder, CO: Lynne Rienner, 1993) p. 13.

12   Sorensen (1993) p. 46.

13   White, Gill and Slider (1993) p. 229.

14   Defined fully in Chapters 6, 7, 8 and 9 respectively.

15   We use 'right-wing' here in the conventional western sense of 'anti-socialist'. Sympathies for the Hungarian Democratic Forum and the Hungarian Justice Party were linked, as were those for Rukh and the Conservative Republicans in Ukraine.

16   Ralf Dahrendorf, *Reflections on the Revolution in Europe* (London: Chatto and Windus, 1990) p. 110. He was clear that the Baltic States would be part of Europe if, and only if, they left the Soviet Union, while Azerbaijan would not be European even if it did leave the Soviet Union. But would withdrawal from the Soviet Union affect Ukraine's claim to be European? Dahrendorf claims 'Europe is almost coextensive with the Zone of Central European Time.' He notes that this time-zone criterion excludes Britain, but ignores the fact that Bulgaria, Ukraine and the Baltics are in the same time zone, while Poland, Hungary and the former Czecho-slovakia are in another.

17   George Schopflin, 'Definitions of central Europe' in George Schopflin and Nancy Wood, *In Search of Central Europe* (Totowa, NJ: Barnes and Noble, 1989) p. 17.

18   Many Europeans seem to believe, privately, that not only Europe and European civilisation, but civilisation itself, ends at the eastern border of their country though they will seldom articulate it quite so crudely when sober. Perhaps this reflects a vague perception drawn from half remembered school history lessons that for a millennium after the decline of the Roman Empire, Europe was subject to successive waves of destructive invasion from the east.

19   Richard Sakwa, 'The development of the Russian party system: Did the elections change anything?' in Peter Lentini (ed.) *Elections and Political Order in Russia* (Budapest: Central European University Press, 1995) pp. 169–201 at p. 170.

20   William M. Reisinger, Arthur H. Miller, Vicki L. Hesli and Kristen Hill Maher, 'Political values in Russia, Ukraine and Lithuania: sources and implications for democracy', *British Journal of Political Science*, vol.24 no.2 (1994) pp. 183–224 at p. 220.

21   Though we have evidence that expressed belief in communist ideals (if not commitment to socialist values) increased in Russia in the mid-1990s. See Chapter 19.

22   See Chapter 9 for details of public support for the principle and practice of multiparty competition.

23   Samuel P. Huntington, 'The clash of civilizations?' *Foreign Affairs*, vol.72 no.3 (1993) pp. 22–49 at p. 30. A Russian translation with accompanying discussion appeared in *Politicheskie issledovaniya* no.1 (1994) pp. 33–57. A fuller statement of Huntington's thesis is available in his *The Clash of Civilizations and the Remaking of World Order* (New York, NY Simon and Schuster: 1996). For another attempt to map cultural 'fault lines', see Dennis P. Hupchick, *Culture and History in Eastern Europe* (New York, NY St. Martin's Press, 1994).

24   Krishan Kumar, 'The 1989 revolutions and the idea of Europe', *Political Studies*, vol.40. (1992) pp. 439–461 at p. 455.

25   Los Angeles Times–Mirror, *The Pulse of Europe: a Survey of Political and Social Values and Attitudes* (Los Angeles, CA Times–Mirror, 1991) p. 184–5.

26   Georg Sorensen, *Democracy and Democratization* (Boulder, CO: Westview, 1993) p. 26.

27   Ibid. pp. 26–27.

28   See Chapter 7 for clear evidence on this point.

29   Timothy Garton Ash, 'Does central Europe exist?' in George Schopflin and Nancy Wood (eds) *In Search of Central Europe* (Totowa, NJ: Barnes and Noble, 1989) pp. 195 and 196 respectively.

30   See Chapter 14 for more evidence of the effect on values of living in a former imperial capital.

31   MPs were 55 per cent more tolerant than even their relatively tolerant publics in ECE; but only 21 per cent more tolerant than their relatively intolerant publics in the FSU. See Chapter 11 for details.

32   On a composite scale of attitudes to different aspects of economic trends. For details see Chapter 13.

33   In 1868, Count Muenster described the Tsarist constitution as 'absolutism moderated by assassination.' Ernst Graf zu Muenster, *Political Sketches of the State of Europe* (Edinburgh: Edmonston and Douglas, 1868). An earlier version was 'absolutism tempered by assassination.' But for a picture of arbitrary government moderated by corruption rather than by assassination see Wayne DiFranceisco and Zvi Gitelman, 'Soviet political culture and covert participation in policy implementation', *American Political Science Review*, vol.78 no.3 (1984) pp. 603–21.

34   In Chapters 18 and 19 we document a very sharp increase in the percentage of opposition supporters who declared Russian elections 'free and fair' once their own candidates had done well in them.

35   On the importance of this precedent for the development of democracy in Ukraine see Taras Kuzio, 'Kravchuk to Kuchma: The Ukrainian presidential elections of 1994', *Journal of Communist Studies and Transition Politics*, vol.12 no.2 (1996) pp. 117–44 at pp. 137–8.

36   Wladyslaw Gomulka warned – reasonably enough, given the prospect of a Soviet clampdown – that the Polish election was not a test of the government, but a test of the electorate. See Martin Harrop and William L. Miller, *Elections and Voters: a Comparative Introduction* (London: Macmillan, 1987) p. 23.

1   STANDING ON THE RUINS OF EMPIRE

1   The texts of these and other communist constitutions appear in William B. Simons (ed.) *The Constitutions of the Communist World* (Alphen aan den Rijn/Germantown, MD: Sijthoff & Noordhoff, 1980).

2   The Czech party rules appeared as a supplement to *Rude pravo*, 1 June 1971.

3   *Ustav Kommunisticheskoi partii Sovetskogo Soyuza, utverzhden XXVII sezdom KPSS* (Moscow: Politizdat, 1986), p. 4. The texts of these and other party rules are available in William B. Simons and Stephen White (eds) *The Party Statutes of the Communist World* (The Hague and Boston: Martinus Nijhoff, 1984).

4   See *Czarna ksiega cenzury PRL*, 2 vols (London: Aneks, 1977–78).

5   *Kommunisticheskaya partiya Sovetskogo Soyuza v rezolyutsiyakh i resheniyakh sezdov, konferentsii i plenumov TsK*, 9th ed., 15 vols (Moscow: Politizdat, 1983–89), vol. 10, pp. 200–1.

6   Ibid., pp. 168–9.

7   See respectively Alfred G. Meyer in Donald W. Treadgold (ed.) *The Development of the USSR* (Seattle, WA: University of Washington Press, 1964), p. 24; and Samuel P. Huntington in Fred I. Greenstein and Nelson W. Polsby (eds) *Handbook of Political Science*, vol. 3 (Reading, MA: Addison-Wesley, 1975), p. 31.

8   *Sovetskaya istoricheskaya entsiklopediya*, vol. 13 (Moscow: Sovetskaya entsiklopediya, 1971), cols. 192–205.

9   S. G. Strumilin, *Byudzhet vremeni russkogo rabochego i krestyanina* (Moscow–Leningrad: Voprosy truda, 1924), pp. 24–6; G. E. Zborovsky and G. P. Orlov, *Dosug: deistvitelnost i illyuzii* (Sverdlovsk: Sredne-uralskoe knizhnoe izdatelstvo, 1970), p. 220.

10   *KPSS v rezolyutsiyakh*, vol. 12, p. 193.

11   L.A. Onikov and N. V. Shishlin (eds) *Kratkii politicheskii slovar*, 6th ed. (Moscow: Politizdat, 1989), pp. 526–7.

12   *Kommunist*, 1977, no. 4, p. 33.

13 See for instance Linda J. Cook, *The Soviet Social Contract and Why it Failed* (Cambridge, MA: Harvard University Press, 1993).
14 Ray Taras, *Poland: Socialist State, Rebellious Nation* (Boulder, CO: Westview, 1986), p. 144.
15 Patrick Brogan, *Eastern Europe 1939–1989: The Fifty Years War* (London: Bloomsbury, 1990) p. 121.
16 Ibid. p. 19.
17 Francois Fejto, *A History of the People's Democracies* (Harmondsworth: Penguin, 1974), pp. 35–7.
18 Paul G. Lewis, *Central Europe since 1945* (London: Longmans, 1994), pp. 160–1.
19 The text of the Action Programme was issued as a supplement to *Rude pravo*, 5 April 1968.
20 Leonid I. Brezhnev, *Leninskim kursom*, vol. 2 (Moscow: Politizdat, 1970), p. 329.
21 Neil Ascherson, *The Polish August* (Harmondsworth: Penguin, 1971), pp. 113–14.
22 Stephen White, *Political Culture and Soviet Politics* (London: Macmillan, 1979), p. 1.
23 Archie Brown and Jack Gray (eds) *Political Culture and Political Change in Communist States*, 2nd ed. (London: Macmillan, 1979), p. 1.
24 See Kendall L. Baker, Russell J. Dalton and Kai Hildebrant, *Germany Transformed: Political culture and the new politics* (Cambridge, MA: Harvard University Press, 1981).
25 Robert D. Putnam, *Making Democracy Work: Civic traditions in modern Italy* (Princeton, NJ: Princeton University Press, 1993), pp. 121, 162.
26 Seymour Martin Lipset, 'The social requisites of democracy revisited', *American Sociological Review*, vol. 59, no. 1 (1994), pp. 1–22, at p. 5. More general discussions of a political cultural approach include Archie Brown (ed.) *Political Culture and Communist Studies* (London: Macmillan, 1984); Stephen Welch, *The Concept of Political Culture* (London: Macmillan, 1993); and Frederic J. Fleron, 'Post-Soviet political culture in Russia: an assessment of recent empirical investigations', *Europe-Asia Studies*, vol. 48, no. 2 (March 1996), pp. 225–60.
27 Alexis de Tocqueville, *Democracy in America*, (ed.) Phillips Bradley (London: Everyman, 1994), p. 434.
28 For these developments see Olga Crisp and Linda Edmondson (eds) *Civil Rights in Imperial Russia* (Oxford: Clarendon Press, 1989).
29 Richard Pipes, *Russia under the Old Regime* (London: Weidenfeld and Nicolson, 1974), pp. 293–4.
30 Karl Baedeker, *Baedeker's Russia 1914* (London: George Allen & Unwin, 1914), pp. xix–xx, xviii.
31 Marquis de Custine, *Lettres de Russie* (Paris: Gallimard, 1975), p. 377.
32 Brown and Gray (eds) *Political Culture*, p. 161.
33 H. Gordon Skilling, *Czechoslovakia's Interrupted Revolution* (Princeton, NJ: Princeton University Press, 1976), p. 6.
34 George Schopflin, 'Hungary: an uneasy stability', in Brown and Gray, (eds) *Political Culture*, pp. 131–58, esp. pp. 132–6.

2 COMMUNISM AND AFTER

1 *XXVI Sezd Kommunisticheskoi partii Sovetskogo Soyuza 23 fevralya–3 marta 1981 goda. Stenograficheskii otchet*, 3 vols (Moscow: Izdatelstvo politicheskoi literatury, 1981), vol.1, p. 21.

2   M. S. Gorbachev, *Izbrannye rechi i stati*, 7 vols (Moscow: Izdatelstvo politicheskoi literatury, 1987–90), vol. 2, p. 178.

3   M. S. Gorbachev, *Perestroika i novoe myshlenie dlya nashei strany i dlya vsego mira* (Moscow: Izdatelstvo politicheskoi literatury, 1987), p. 169.

4   Samuel P. Huntington, 'Will more countries become democratic?', *Political Science Quarterly*, vol. 99 no. 2 (Summer 1984), pp. 193–218, at p. 217.

5   Jerry F. Hough, 'Understanding Gorbachev: the importance of politics', *Soviet Economy*, vol. 7 no. 2 (April–June 1991), pp. 89–109, at p. 106.

6   *Novayi i noveishaya istoriya*, 1996, no. 1, p. 113.

7   For general accounts of the transition see J. F. Brown, *Surge to Freedom: The end of communist rule in Eastern Europe* (Durham: Duke University Press, 1991); Stephen White, Judy Batt and Paul Lewis (eds) *Developments in East European Politics* (London: Macmillan, 1993); Gale Stokes, *The Walls Came Tumbling Down: The collapse of communism in Eastern Europe* (New York, NY: Oxford University Press, 1993); and Roger East and Jolyon Pontin, *Revolution and Change in Central and Eastern Europe*, 2nd ed. (London: Pinter, 1996). For a readable account of the years of communist domination in ECE preceding 1989, see Patrick Brogan, *Eastern Europe 1939–1989: The Fifty Years War* (London: Bloomsbury, 1990).

8   Adam Michnik, 'Does socialism have any future in Eastern Europe?', *Studium Papers*, vol. 13, no. 4 (October 1989), p. 184. On the Polish transition see for instance Bartolomiej Kaminski, *The Collapse of State Socialism: the case of Poland* (Princeton NJ: Princeton University Press, 1991) and Frances Millard, *Anatomy of the New Poland: Post-Communist Politics in its First Phase* (Aldershot: Elgar, 1994).

9   The line of 'socialist renewal' was approved at the PUWP's 9th Congress in 1981; the Party Programme that was adopted at the 10th Congress in 1986 made a more specific commitment to a 'socialism under Polish conditions' that would seek to 'extend the framework of national agreement and enrich the forms of public dialogue' (*X Zjazd Polskiej Zjednoczonej Partii Robotniczej 29 czerwca – 3 lipca 1986 g. Podstawowe dokumenty i materialy* (Warsaw: Ksiazka i Wiedza, 1986), pp. 140–1, 150).

10   *Gazeta wyborcza*, 7 April 1989, p. 1.

11   *Pravda*, 25 August 1989, p. 1.

12   This point is made in Mark R. Thompson, 'No exit: "nation-stateness" and democratization in the German Democratic Republic', *Political Studies*, vol. 44, no. 2 (June 1996), pp. 267–86. For a full account, see Karl-Dieter Opp, Peter Voss, and Christiane Gern, *Die volkseigene Revolution* (Stuttgart: Klett-Cotta, 1993) and Christian Joppke, *East German Dissidents and the Revolution of 1989: Social movement in a Leninist regime* (London: Macmillan, 1994).

13   See for instance Tom Gallagher, 'A feeble embrace: Romania's engagement with democracy, 1989–94', *Journal of Communist Studies and Transition Politics*, vol. 12, no. 2 (June 1996), pp. 145–72. There are several popular accounts of the overthrow of the Ceausescus including Edward Behr, *Kiss the Hand you Cannot Bite: The rise and fall of the Ceausescus* (London: Hamish Hamilton, 1991); John Sweeney, *The Life and Evil Times of Nicolae Ceausescu* (London: Hutchinson, 1991); and Mark Almond, *The Rise and Fall of Nicolae and Elena Ceausescu* (London: Chapman, 1992).

14   See Dennis Deletant, *Ceausescu and the Securitate: Coercion and dissent in Romania, 1965–1989* (London: Hurst, 1995).

15   See especially Bernard Wheaton and Zdenek Kavan, *The Velvet Revolution: Czechoslovakia, 1988–1991* (Boulder, CO: Westview, 1992); and J. F. N. Bradley,

Czechoslovakia's Velvet Revolution: A political analysis (Boulder, CO: East European Monographs, 1992). On the period after 1968 see Vladimir Kusin, *From Dubcek to Charter 77: a study of 'normalization' in Czechoslovakia, 1968–1978* (Edinburgh: Q Press, 1978).

16 *XIV. Sjezd Komunisticke strany Ceskoslovenska 25. kvetna – 29. kvetna 1971* (Prague: Svoboda, 1971), p. 20. The key resolution, adopted at a Central Committee plenum in December 1970, had defined the Prague Spring as an 'attempted counterrevolutionary coup': see *Dokumenty plenarniho zasedani Ustredniho vyboru Komunisticke strany Ceskoslovenska 10.–11. prosince 1970* (Prague: Svoboda, 1971).

17 Vaclav Havel, *Moc bezmocnych* (London: Edice Londynskych listu, 1979), p. 3. The classic account of 'adaptation' during this period is Milan Simecka, *Obnoveni poradku* (Cologne: Index, 1979).

18 *Charta 77 1977–1989: Od moralni k demokraticke revoluci. Dokumentace*, (ed.) Vilem Precan (Bratislava: Archa, 1990), p. 12 (there were 242 signatories in the first instance, p. 383). For a fuller account see H. Gordon Skilling, *Charter 77 and Human Rights in Czechoslovakia* (London: George Allen & Unwin, 1981).

19 Husak's remarks were made in an interview for Radio Prague on 15 February 1986. Gorbachev referred to his reception in *Izbrannye rechi i stati*, vol. 4, pp. 472–3. Husak himself spoke of the CPSU's 27th Congress of February 1986 as an 'inspiration' in his speech to the 17th Congress of the Communist Party of Czechoslovakia a month later in *XVII. Sjezd Komunisticke strany Ceskoslovenska, 24.–28. brezna 1986* (Prague: Svoboda, 1986), p. 14.

20 Wheaton and Kavan, *Velvet Revolution*, p. 28.

21 For a full documentation of the November revolution see *Deset prezskych dnu (17.–27. listopad 1989). Dokumentace* (Prague: Academia, 1990) and two photo-chronicles, Jiri Vsetecka *et al., Rok na namestnich: Ceskoslovensko 1989* (Prague: Academia, 1990) and *Listopad '89* (Prague: Odeon, 1990).

22 *Deset prezskych dnu*, pp. 503–6, at p. 503 (the statement, 'What we want', was adopted on 26 November 1989).

23 T. Zhivkov, *Osnovni polozheniya na kontseptsiyata za no-natatshnoto izgrazhdane na sotsialisma v NR Blgariya* (Sofia: Partizdat, 1988).

24 See *Za preustroistvoto na dukhovnata sfera* (Sofia: Partizdat, 1988).

25 Brown, *Surge to Freedom*, p. 189.

26 *Za sstoyanieto na stranata, partiyata i nepostredstevenite zadachi 11–13 dekembri 1989 godina* (Sofia: Partizdat, 1989), p. 26.

27 For the Programme see *XIV izvnreden Kongres na Blgarskata komunisticheska partiya 30 yanuari – 2 fevruari 1990 g.* (Sofia: Izdatelstvo na VKP, 1990), pp. 57–76, at pp. 68–9, 75–5.

28 As Kadar told the National Council of the Patriotic People's Front on 8 December 1961, 'the Rakosi group used to say, "Those who are not with us are against us"; and now this Kadar bunch says, "Those who are not against us are with us"' (*Nepszabadsag*, 10 December 1961, p. 2). The speech, he noted at a party congress a year later, had 'caused a considerable stir': *A Magyar Szocialista Munkaspart VIII. Kongresszusanak Jegyzokonve, 1962 november 20–24* (Budapest: Kossuth, 1963), p. 399. More detailed discussions of the Hungarian transition include Nigel Swain, *Hungary: The rise and fall of feasible socialism* (London: Verso, 1992); Andras Bozoki, Andras Korosenyi and George Schopflin, (eds.) *Post-Communist Transition: emerging pluralism in Hungary* (London: Pinter, 1992); Bela Kiraly and Andras Bosoki, (eds) *Lawful Revolution in Hungary, 1989–94* (Boulder, CO: East European Monographs, 1995); and Rudi Tokes, *Hungary's Negotiated Revolution: economic reform, social change and political succession* (Cambridge: Cambridge University Press, 1996).

29   *Turnabout and Reform* was published in *Medvetanc*, 1987, no. 2, pp. 5–46; the
      'New social contract' appeared in *Beszelo*, no. 20, January 1987, and in translation
      in Gale Stokes, ed., *From Stalinism to Pluralism* (New York, NY: Oxford Uni-
      versity Press, 1991), pp. 244–7.
30   The proceedings were published in *A Magyar Szocialista Munkaspart orszagos
      Ertekezletenek Jegyzokonyve, 1988 majus 20–22* (Budapest: Kossuth, 1988).
31   *Nepszabadsag*, 19 September 1987, p. 6; *Le Monde*, 10 November 1988, p. 8. On
      'reform circles' see Patrick H. O'Neil, 'Revolution from within: institutional ana-
      lysis, transitions from authoritarianism, and the case of Hungary', *World Politics*,
      vol. 48, no. 4 (July 1996), pp. 579–604.
32   Pozsgay's remarks were reported in *Le Monde*, 31 January 1989, p. 3.
33   *Nepszabadsag*, 23 February 1989, p. 1.
34   Ibid., 9 May 1989, pp. 1, 5.
35   For the text of the agreement see ibid., 19 September 1989, p. 5; a translation is
      provided in Tokes, *Hungary's Negotiated Revolution*, pp. 357–60.
36   For the proceedings see *Kongresszus '89: Rovidett, szerkesztett jegyzokonyv az
      1989, oktober 6–9. kozott tarbott kongresszus anyagobol* (Budapest: Kossuth, 1990).
37   For a fuller discussion of the development of the Hungarian party system see
      Adam Bozoki, 'Party formation and constitutional change in Hungary', in Terry
      Cox and Andy Furlong (eds), *Hungary: The Politics of Transition* (London: Cass,
      1995), pp. 35–55; and Laszlo Keri and Adam Levendel, 'The first three years of a
      multi-party system in Hungary', in Gordon Wightman, (ed.) *Party Formation in
      East-Central Europe* (Aldershot: Edward Elgar, 1995), pp. 134–53.
38   Swain, *Hungary*, p. 28.
39   See Barnabas Racz, 'Political pluralisation in Hungary: the 1990 elections', *Soviet
      Studies*, 1991, no. 1, pp. 107–36; and John R. Hibbing and Samuel C. Patterson, 'A
      democratic legislature in the making: the historic Hungarian elections of 1990',
      Comparative Political Studies, vol. 24, no. 4 (January 1992), pp. 430–54.
40   See Laszlo Bruszt, '1989: the negotiated revolution in Hungary', *Social Research*,
      vol. 57, no. 2 (Summer 1990), pp. 365–87.
41   See George Schopflin, *Politics in Eastern Europe* (Oxford: Blackwell, 1992), pp.
      233–6.
42   Gorbachev, *Perestroika*, p. 168.
43   Raisa Gorbacheva, *Ya nadeyus* (Moscow: Novosti, 1991), p. 14.
44   Tsentr khraneniya sovremennoi dokumentatsii, Moscow, *fond* 89, *opis* 36, *dok*. 16,
      11 March 1985.
45   For the Gorbachev reforms more generally see Richard Sakwa, *Gorbachev and his
      Reforms, 1985–1990* (London: Philip Allan, 1990); Stephen White, *After Gorba-
      chev*, 4th ed. (Cambridge: Cambridge University Press, 1994); and Archie Brown,
      The Gorbachev Factor (Oxford: Oxford University Press, 1996).
46   Gorbachev, *Izbrannye rechi i stati*, vol. 2, p. 131.
47   *XIX Vsesoyuznaya konferentsiya Kommunisticheskoi partii Sovetskogo Soyuza 28
      iyunya – 1 iyulya 1988 goda. Stenograficheskii otchet*, 2 vols (Moscow: Izdatelstvo
      politicheskoi literatury, 1988), vol. 1, pp. 46–8.
48   Ibid., vol. 2, pp. 135–44, 172–4.
49   Gorbachev, *Izbrannye rechi i stati*, vol. 6, p. 77.
50   *Ekonomika i zhizn*, 1992, no. 6, pp. 13–16.
51   *Pravda*, 27 April 1989, p. 3, and 11 July 1989, p. 2.
52   *Izvestiya*, 20 August 1991, p. 1.
53   See Stephanie Lawson, 'Conceptual issues in the comparative study of regime
      change and democratisation', *Comparative Politics*, vol. 25 no. 2 (January 1993),
      pp. 183–205; Sarah Meiklejohn Terry, 'Thinking about post-communist

transitions: how different are they?', *Slavic Review*, vol. 53, no. 1 (Summer 1993),pp. 333–37; Philippe Schmitter and Terry Lynn Karl, 'The conceptual travels of transitologists and consolidologists: how far to the East should they attempt to go?', *Slavic Review*, vol. 53, no. 1 (Spring 1994), pp. 173–85.

54   Examples include Dankwart Rustow, 'Transitions to democracy: toward a dynamic model', *Comparative Politics*, vol. 2, no. 3 (January 1970), pp. 337–63; Leonardo Morlino, 'Democratic establishments: a dimensional analysis', in Enrique Baloyra (ed.), *Comparing New Democracies: Transition and Consolidation in Mediterranean Europe and the Southern Cone* (Boulder, CO: Westview, 1987); Alfred Stepan, 'Paths toward redemocratization: theoretical and comparative considerations', in Guillermo O'Donnell, Philippe C. Schmitter and Laurence Whitehead (eds), *Transitions from Authoritarian Rule* (Baltimore: Johns Hopkins University Press, 1986); Samuel Huntington, 'How countries democratize', *Political Science Quarterly*, vol. 106, no. 4 (Winter 1991–92), pp. 579–616.

55   See Arend Lijphart (ed.), *Parliamentary Versus Presidential Government* (Oxford: Oxford University Press, 1992); Jon Elster and Rune Slagstad (eds), *Constitutionalism and Democracy* (Cambridge: Cambridge University Press, 1988); Jon Elster, 'Constitution-making in Eastern Europe: rebuilding the boat in the open sea', *Public Administration*, vol. 71 no. 1/2 (Spring/Summer 1993), pp. 169–217; Alfred Stepan and Cindy Skach, 'Constitutional frameworks and democratic consolidation', *World Politics*, vol. 46 no. 1 (October 1993), pp. 1–22; John Higley and Richard Gunther (eds), *Elites and Democratic Consolidation in Latin America and Southern Europe* (Cambridge: Cambridge University Press, 1992); Geoffrey Pridham (ed.), *Securing Democracy. Political Parties and Democratic Consolidation in Southern Europe* (London: Routledge, 1990); Geoffrey Pridham and Tatu Vanhanen (eds), *Democratization in Eastern Europe* (London: Routledge, 1994); Geoffrey Pridham and Paul Lewis (eds), *Stabilising Fragile Democracies. Comparing New Party Systems in Southern and Eastern Europe* (London: Routledge, 1996).

56   Giuseppe Di Palma, *To Craft Democracies* (Berkeley: University of California Press, 1990), p. 185; Kenneth Maxwell, 'Spain's transition to democracy: a model for Eastern Europe?', in Nils H. Wessell (ed.), *The New Europe: Revolution in East–West Relations* (New York: Proceedings of The Academy of Political Science, vol. 38, 1991); Huntington, 'How countries democratize', p. 592; Scott Mainwaring, Guillermo O'Donnell, and J. Samuel Valenzuela (eds), *Issues in Democratic Consolidation* (Helen Kellogg Institute for International Studies, Notre Dame: University of Notre Dame Press, 1992), p. 5; José M. Cuenca Toribio, 'La transición española, modelo universal', *Nueva Revista de Política, Cultura y Arte*, vol. 37 (December 1994), pp. 39–53.

57   Barrington Moore, *Social Origins of Dictatorship and Democracy* (Boston: Beacon Press, 1966).

58   Giuseppe Di Palma, 'Parliaments, consolidation, institutionalization: a minimalist view', in Ulrike Liebert and Maurizio Cotta (eds), *Parliament and Democratic Consolidation in Southern Europe: Greece, Italy, Portugal, Spain and Turkey* (London: Pinter Publishers, 1990), pp. 31–51.

59   See G. Bingham Powell, 'Social progress and liberal democracy', in Gabriel Almond *et al.*, *Progress and its Discontents* (Berkeley: University of California Press, 1982); S. M. Lipset, K.R. Seong and J. C. Torres, 'A comparative analysis of the social requisites of democracy', *International Social Science Journal*, vol. 45, no. 2 (May 1993), pp. 155–75; Mancur Olson, 'Dictatorship, democracy and development', *American Political Science Review*, vol. 87, no. 3 (September 1993), pp. 567–76; D. Rueschemeyer, E. Stephens and J. Stephens, *Capitalist Development and Democracy* (Cambridge: Polity, 1992).

60 Tatu Vanhanen, 'Social constraints of democratization', in Vanhanen (ed.), *Strategies of Democratization* (Washington, DC: Crane Russak, 1992), pp. 19–35.

61 To quote the title of M. Steven Fish's *Democracy from Scratch: Opposition and regime in the new Russian revolution* (Princeton, NJ: Princeton University Press, 1995).

62 A point that is made in Samuel P. Huntington's *The Third Wave: Democratization in the late twentieth century* (Norman: University of Oklahoma Press, 1991).

63 See for instance Valerie Bunce, 'Should transitologists be grounded?', *Slavic Review*, vol. 54, no. 1 (Spring 1995), pp. 111–27; and Terry, 'Thinking about post-communist transitions'. 'One need not go to Chile or Spain', as Rudi Tokes has commented, 'to explain what happened in Eastern Europe' (*Hungary's Negotiated Revolution*, p. 438).

64 Lucan A. Way, 'Apples and kangaroos? Comparing transitions in East Europe and Latin America', *Khronika of the Berkeley Program in Soviet and Post-Soviet Studies*, Spring 1996, pp. 8–9, at p. 9.

3 METHODOLOGY AND CONTEXT

1 Only lack of funds prevented us extending our parliamentary opinion surveys to include Slovakia.

2 For example, those in the widely quoted study by Arthur H. Miller, William M. Reisinger and Vicki L. Hesli (eds) *Public Opinion and Regime Change: The New Politics of Post-Soviet Societies* (Boulder, CO: Westview, 1993); or Jon H. Pammett and Joan DeBardeleben, 'The meaning of elections in transitional democracies: evidence from Russia and Ukraine', *Electoral Studies,* vol.15 no.3 (1996), pp. 363–81.

3 A full, 447 page technical report, including translated questionnaires, is available for consultation through the ESRC (Economic and Social Research Council, London) and the British Library.

4 Paul Robert Magocsi, *Ukraine: A Historical Atlas* (Toronto: University of Toronto Press, 1992) Commentary on Map 22. Maps 22 and 24 are specially relevant here.

5 Library of Congress transliteration of Ukrainian language names.

6 Samuel P. Huntington, 'The clash of civilisations?', *Foreign Affairs*, vol.72 no.3 (1993) pp. 22–49 at p. 30.

7 For these developments see Stephen White, Richard Rose and Ian McAllister, *How Russia Votes* (Chatham, NJ: Chatham, House, 1997), Chapter 5.

8 We have discussed the 1993 election results in Matthew Wyman, Stephen White, Bill Miller and Paul Heywood, 'Public opinion, parties and voters in the December 1993 Russian elections', *Europe-Asia Studies*, vol. 47 no. 4 (June 1995), pp. 591–614. See also Peter Lentini (ed.) *Elections and Political Order in Russia* (Budapest: Central European University Press, 1995); Richard Sakwa, 'The Russian elections of December 1993', *Europe-Asia Studies*, vol. 47 no. 2 (March 1995), pp. 195–227; and White, Rose and McAllister, *How Russia Votes*, Chapters 6–7. For indications that the turnout may have been less than 50 per cent of the electorate see for instance *Konstitutsionnyi vestnik*, 1994, no. 17, p. 32, and *Moskovskii komsomolets*, 11 January 1994, p. 1.

9 For a full report of the results see *Vybory deputatov Gosudarstvennoi Dumy 1995: elektoralnaya statistika* (Moscow: Ves mir, 1996); for a discussion see White, Rose and McAllister, *How Russia Votes*, Chapters 10 and 11.

10   Marco Bojcun, 'The Ukrainian parliamentary elections in March–April 1994'
        Europe-Asia Studies, vol. 47 no. 2 (1995), pp. 229–49; Taras Kuzio, 'The 1994
        parliamentary elections in Ukraine' *Journal of Communist Studies and Transition
        Politics*, vol. 11 no. 4 (1995), pp. 335–61; and Sarah Birch, 'The Ukrainian
        parliamentary and presidential elections of 1994' *Electoral Studies*, vol. 14 no. 1
        (1995), pp. 93–9, 115.

11   For a discussion of the presidential election see Andrew Wilson, 'Parties and
        presidents in Ukraine and Crimea, 1994' *Journal of Communist Studies and Transi-
        tion Politics*, vol. 11 no. 4 (1995), pp. 362–71; and Birch, 'Ukrainian parliamentary
        and presidential elections'.

12   See Gordon Wightman, 'The 1992 parliamentary elections in Czechoslovakia'
        Journal of Communist Studies, vol. 8 no. 4 (1992), pp. 293–301.

13   Gordon Wightman, 'The 1994 Slovak parliamentary elections' *Journal of
        Communist Studies and Transition Politics*, vol. 11 no. 4 (1995), pp. 384–92.

14   See Szonja Szelenyi, Ivan Szelenyi and Winifred R. Poster, 'Interests and symbols
        in post-communist political culture: the case of Hungary' *American Sociological
        Review*, vol. 61 no. 3 (1996), pp. 466–77.

15   See Barnabas Racz and Istvan Kukorelli, 'The "second-generation" post-
        communist elections in Hungary in 1994' *Europe-Asia Studies*, vol. 47 no. 2
        (1995) pp. 251–79.

4   A FOND FAREWELL?

1   The figures for 1976 were 6 per cent in the USSR, 7 per cent in Hungary, and 9 per
        cent in Czechoslovakia. See Paul Shoup (ed.) *The East European and Soviet Data
        Handbook* (New York, NY: Columbia University Press, 1981), Table B–1.

2   At much the same time, in 1992, a survey conducted on the anniversary of the 1938
        'Kristallnacht' attack on German Jews found that only 'one in three Germans
        thinks Nazi era had good points.' *Scotsman* 7 November 1992, p. 9. No doubt the
        92 per cent in the FSU/ECE who could find something good to say about the
        communist regime would have fallen to that level, or less, if they had focused only
        on Stalin's regime and not on its more tolerable successors.

3   White and Kryshtanovskaya reported that only 2 per cent had personal experience
        of the KGB though 28 per cent said members of their family had been affected. See
        Stephen White and Olga Kryshtanovskaya, 'Public attitudes to the KGB: a
        research note', *Europe-Asia Studies*, vol.45 no.1 (1993) pp. 169–75 at p. 173.

4   In 1995 VTsIOM reported that Russians were on balance unfavourable to the
        present, to the Stalin period and to the revolutionary period before that; con-
        versely, they were, on balance, favourable to the Brezhnev and Khrushchev
        periods. See *Ekonomicheskie i sotsialnye peremeny: monitoring obshchestvennogo
        mneniya* (1995) no.1 (January–February) p. 10. When asked to choose between the
        past, present and future in a succession of surveys between 1993 and 1995, people
        in Russia always put the past top, the future second, and the present third. But
        between 1993 and 1995 nostalgia for the past increased and support for the present
        decreased. See Richard Rose, 'Russia as an hour-glass society: a constitution
        without citizens', *East European Constitutional Review*, vol.4 no.3 (1995) pp. 34–
        53 at p. 39.

5   Welsh uses the term 'lustration' for acts of revenge, mistakenly describing it as a
        'translation from the Czech term.' It is, of course a normal word in English (see the
        Concise Oxford Dictionary, 1934 edition, for example) but the political association

of the word with the Czech Republic is definitely not a mistake. As Welsh notes: 'In general, communist party officials and members are only included in lustration or legal procedures if they had collaborated with state security agencies or if they had been involved in criminal activities. *The major exception to this rule is the former Czechoslovakia.*' [emphasis added] However, Welsh also notes that the Hungarian parliament passed a law in 1994 to require screening of officials for collaboration with the secret service or participation in the suppression of the 1956 uprising. See Helga A. Welsh, 'Dealing with the communist past: central and east European experiences after 1990', *Europe–Asia Studies*, vol.48 no.3 (1996) pp. 413–28 at p. 415.

6   Susan Greenberg, 'Czechoslovak parliament makes promoting communism an offence,' *Guardian*, 13 December 1991, p. 9.
7   John Miller, 'Scapegoats sought to square the accounts', *Glasgow Herald*, 21 January 1992, p. 11. The emphasis on liberals in the text has been added. For an insider's account of the right wing attack on even liberals in the Hungarian media see Elemer Hankiss, 'Witness: A media war of independence', in William L. Miller (ed.) *Alternatives to Freedom: Arguments and Opinions* (London: Longman, 1995) pp. 105–23.
8   Helga A. Welsh, 'Dealing with the communist past: central and east European experiences after 1990', *Europe–Asia Studies*, vol.48 no.3 (1996) pp. 413–28 at p. 424.
9   Though not strictly comparable, it is interesting to note that a survey in *Moskovskie novosti* no.33 (1993) p. 11A, reported that only 29 per cent quoted 'never a member of the Communist Party' as a characteristic of their 'ideal Russian President'. Yeltsin, of course, had been a member for over 30 years. Respondents rated education, decisiveness and Russian nationality – not the lack of a communist past – as their top three requirements. A recent study of the postcommunist political elite in Russia suggests that only 10 per cent had entered the elite under Yeltsin, though another 40 per cent had entered under Gorbachev. See Olga Kryshtanovskaya and Stephen White, 'From Soviet nomenklatura to Russian elite', *Europe–Asia Studies*, vol.48 no.5 (1996) pp. 711–33 at p. 728.
10   Nostalgia should not be interpreted as a simple wish to re-establish a former regime however. Rose and Haerpfer found that in Russia as well as in ECE, a large majority disagreed with the propositions that 'it would be better to restore the former communist system', or let the army rule, or restore the monarchy, though they found much more support for a 'strong leader', especially in Russia, and a majority in all postcommunist countries who would let 'experts' take decisions about the economy. Richard Rose and Christian Haerpfer 'New Russia Barometer III: the Results.' *Studies in Public Policy* no.228 (Glasgow: Centre for the Study of Public Policy, 1994).

5   A BRAVE NEW WORLD?

1   Willerton and Sigelman have reported overwhelming pessimism about the economy but less about personal finances at an earlier stage in the postcommunist experience. See John P. Willerton and Lee Sigelman 'Perestroika and the public: citizens' views of the fruits of economic reform' in Arthur H. Miller, William M. Reisinger and Vicki L. Hesli (eds) *Public Opinion and Regime Change: The New Politics of Post-Soviet Societies* (Boulder, CO: Westview, 1993) pp. 205–23 at pp. 210–11.

2 Earlier, Rose had reported much higher levels who said they did not get enough income 'from their regular job.' See Richard Rose, 'New democracies between state and market: a baseline report', *Studies in Public Policy*, no. 204 (Glasgow: Strathclyde University Centre for the Study of Public Policy, 1992) p. 15. But of course, in desperate and chaotic times a significant portion of income – often the major part of income – comes from sources other than 'regular jobs'. Indeed badly paid 'regular jobs' are often maintained primarily to provide the status and 'contacts' which are so essential for success in the black (or grey) economy.

3 The EU's Eurobarometer surveys also show that, compared to publics in our ECE countries, FSU publics are much more critical of their countries' inadequate respect for human rights in the postcommunist era. Since the Eurobarometer questions differ from ours, their findings are not strictly comparable to ours however. See *Central and Eastern Eurobarometer 6* (Brussels: European Union, 1996) Annex figure 7. For other evidence of mixed views about the new regime in Russia compared to the old see Richard Rose and Christian Haerpfer, *New Russia Barometer III: The Results* (Glasgow: Strathclyde University Centre for the Study of Public Policy, 1994) pp. 27–9.

4 Except for signing petitions, Reisinger, Miller and Hesli found similar figures to ours in Russia and Ukraine, when they asked a question with a limited time-window. They got higher figures when they asked 'have you *ever*.' Their higher figure for petitions may have reflected their use of a different Russian word. See William M. Reisinger, Arthur H. Miller and Vicki L. Hesli, 'Political behaviour among post-Soviet publics', Paper to AAASS (American Association for the Advancement of Slavic Studies) 27th National Convention, Washington, October 1995.

5 Fritz Plasser and Peter A. Ulram, 'Of time and democratic stabilisation.' Paper to WAPOR (World Association for Public Opinion Research) Seminar, Tallinn, June 1993, p. 3.

6 According to Rose, 'civil society integrates individuals and the state...through intermediary social institutions that are independent of the state'; though, in a civil society, 'individuals are not required to participate in politics', participation is voluntary. See Richard Rose, 'Russia as an hour-glass society: a constitution without citizens', *East European Constitutional Review*, vol.4 no.3 (1995) pp. 34–53 at p. 34.

7 VTsIOM annual surveys from 1988 to 1992 show the percentage claiming to take an active part in political life peaking at 13 per cent in 1989 but dropping steadily to just 3 per cent in 1992. Over the same period the percentage who said politics did not interest them doubled from 12 per cent to 25 per cent. See *Ekonomicheskie i sotsialnye peremeny: monitoring obshchestvennogo mneniya* (1993) no.3 (July) p. 5.

8 Troy McGrath, 'The legacy of Leninist enforced de-participation' in Peter Lentini (ed.) *Elections and Political Order in Russia* (Budapest: Central European University, 1995) pp. 226–45 at p. 228.

9 Nicholas Lampert, 'Patterns of participation' in Stephen White, Alex Pravda and Zvi Gitelman (eds) *Developments in Soviet Politics* (London: Macmillan, 1990) pp. 120–36 at p. 121 and p. 122 respectively; and Vladimir Shlapentokh, 'The destruction of civil society in Russia 1917–53', in Chandran Kukathas, David W. Lovell and William Maley (eds) *The Transition from Socialism: State and Civil Society in the USSR* (Melbourne: Longman Cheshire, 1991) pp. 82–106. But for contrary views see Chris Hann, 'Civil society at the grass roots: a reactionary view' in Paul Lewis (ed.) *Democracy and Civil Society in East Europe* (London: Macmillan, 1992) pp. 152–65; and Guiseppe Di Palma, 'Legitimation. from the top to civil society: politico-cultural change in eastern Europe' in Nancy Bermeo (ed.) *Liberal-*

ization and Democratization: Change in the Soviet Union and Eastern Europe (Baltimore, MD: Johns Hopkins University Press, 1992) pp. 49–80 at p. 63 where he notes that communist regimes failed to suppress the re-emergence of civil society even before 1989. For a wide ranging symposium on participation under communism see Donald E. Schulz and Jan S. Adams (eds) *Political Participation in Communist Systems* (New York, NY: Pergamon, 1981).

10   Cynthia S. Kaplan 'New forms of political participation' in Arthur H. Miller, William M. Reisinger and Vicki L. Hesli (eds) *Public Opinion and Regime Change: The New Politics of Post-Soviet Societies* (Boulder, CO: Westview, 1993) pp. 153–67 at p. 154. She was quoting Wayne DiFranceisco and Zvi Gitelman, 'Soviet political culture and covert participation in policy implementation', *American Political Science Review*, vol.78 (1984) pp. 603–21 at p. 611.

11   Remington quotes survey evidence of a 'strikingly low level of [interpersonal] trust, perhaps half that of the US level' in FSU countries. See Thomas F Remington, 'Agendas – researching the emerging political cultures' in Arthur H Miller, William M Reisinger and Vicki Hesli (eds) *Public Opinion and Regime Change* (Boulder, CO: Westview, 1993) pp. 197–202 at p. 199. Our figures for general interpersonal trust in the FSU/ECE are somewhat lower than in Britain (see Chapter 20) but not 'strikingly' lower. McIntosh and MacIver report that interpersonal trust in ECE is 'lower than in the US [but] higher than one might expect.' Mary E. McIntosh and Martha Abele MacIver, 'Coping with freedom and uncertainty: public opinion in Hungary, Poland and Czechoslovakia, 1989–92' *International Journal of Public Opinion Research*, vol.4 no.4 (1992) pp. 375–91 at pp. 379–80. Figures from the World Values Survey reported by Ester, Halman and Rukavishnikov suggests that interpersonal trust was relatively low in ECE but actually higher in Russia than in western Europe or north America. See Peter Ester, Loek Halman and Vladimir Rukavishnikov, 'The western world values pattern viewed cross-nationally: a comparison of findings of the European and North American value study with recent Russian data.' A paper to the symposium 'Values and Work – a Comparative perspective' Tilburg University, November 1994, p. 9. Times–Mirror surveys in 1991 found the levels of interpersonal trust in Russia and Ukraine slightly higher than in Britain, in Czechoslovakia much the same as in Britain, and in Hungary much lower. See Los Angeles Times–Mirror *The Pulse of Europe: a Survey of Political and Social Values and Attitudes* (Los Angeles, CA: Times–Mirror, 1991) Question Q113h.

12   Rose claims interpersonal, 'informal trust abounds' and reports very high expectations of what Russians expect their friend would do for them in time of need. He views Russia as an 'hour glass society' where 'there is a rich social life at the base, consisting of strong informal networks relying on trust between friends, relatives and other face to face groups . . . [and] at the top there is a rich political and social life as elites compete for power . . . [but] the links between top and bottom are very limited.' Richard Rose, 'Russia as an hour-glass society: a constitution without citizens', *East European Constitutional Review*, vol.4 no.3 (1995) pp. 34–53 at pp. 35–8 especially. Shlapentokh also notes that 'the notion of friend in the Soviet Union is different than in the United States' – superficial in the USA, intense in the USSR – and 'friends of friends' also had a significance under communism that far exceeded American notions of networks. See Vladimir Shlapentokh, *The Public and Private Life of the Soviet People* (Oxford: Oxford University Press, 1989) p. 170 and p. 176 especially. Hesli and Mills' focus groups showed that Russian women had more assistance from extended families and neighbours than in the USA. See Vicki L. Hesli and Margaret H. Mills, 'Reforms, restructuring and representation: addressing women's roles through group interviews', Paper to

AAASS (American Association for the Advancement of Slavic Studies) 27th National Convention, Washington, October 1995.

13 McIntosh and MacIver report a rapid decline between 1989 and 1992 in ECE publics' confidence in their governments which they characterise as 'from jubilation to disillusionment.' Mary E. McIntosh and Martha Abele MacIver, 'Coping with freedom and uncertainty: public opinion in Hungary, Poland and Czechoslovakia 1989–92', *International Journal of Public Opinion Research*, vol.4 no.4 (1992) pp. 375–91 at p. 375.

14 Elected originally as the Supreme Soviet of the Russian Federation within the USSR.

15 Though the Slovak constitution 'juxtaposed strong government with a strong presidency' and 'unlike the Hungarian and Czech constitutions, the Slovak constitution does not distinguish clearly' between the powers of the president and the government. See Spencer Zifcak, 'The battle over presidential power in Slovakia', *East European Constitutional Review*, vol.4 no.3 (1995) pp. 61–5 at p. 64 and p. 61 respectively.

16 Plasser and Ulram also found that, in terms of public trust, presidents in these parliamentary systems profit from being 'placed above everyday political life.' See Fritz Plasser and Peter A. Ulram, 'Monitoring democratic consolidation: political trust and system support in East Central Europe.' Paper to IPSA (International Political Science Association) 16th World Congress, Berlin, August 1994, p. 12.

17 Times–Mirror surveys confirm our finding that public attitudes towards the church (or churches) were much more favourable in the FSU than in ECE. They also tend to support our interpretation that institutions were more trusted if they stayed out of, or 'above', day to day politics. Within ECE the church was most notoriously involved in the politics of Poland; and it was precisely in Poland that the church was most distrusted and resented. In the Times–Mirror surveys, 70 per cent in Poland said the church played 'too great a role' in politics, compared to 31 per cent in Czechoslovakia and 27 per cent in Hungary, but only 6 per cent in Russia and 5 per cent in Ukraine. Conversely only 4 per cent in Russia and 6 per cent in Ukraine said the church had a 'bad' influence, compared to 13 per cent in Hungary, and 15 per cent in Czechoslovakia, but 39 per cent in Poland. See questions Q48 and Q69A in Los Angeles Times–Mirror *The Pulse of Europe: a Survey of Political and Social Values and Attitudes* (Los Angeles, CA: Times–Mirror, 1991).

18 Fritz Plasser and Peter A. Ulram, 'Monitoring democratic consolidation: political trust and system support in East Central Europe.' Paper to IPSA (International Political Science Association) 16th World Congress, Berlin, August 1994, pp. 17–18. They make similar points in Fritz Plasser and Peter A. Ulram, 'Of time and democratic stabilisation.' Paper to WAPOR (World Association for Public Opinion Research) Seminar, Tallinn, June 1993. For other studies of institutional trust within the FSU/ECE see Richard Rose and Christian Haerpfer, *New Russia Barometer III: The Results* (Glasgow: Strathclyde University Centre for the Study of Public Policy, 1994) pp. 31–3; and Richard Rose and Christian Haerpfer, *New Democracies Barometer III: Learning from What is Happening* (Glasgow: Strathclyde University Centre for the Study of Public Policy, 1994) Questions 48–62.

19 Mark Rhodes, 'Political attitudes in Russia', *Radio Liberty Research Report*, 15 January 1993 pp. 43–5 at p. 42.

20 Anthony King, 'Nation's morale approaching a crisis', *Daily Telegraph*, 22 February 1993, p. 4.

21 Thomas R. Dye, 'Elite autonomy and mass disaffection: can elite competition undermine regime legitimacy?'. Paper to IPSA (International Political Science

Association) 16th World Congress, Berlin, August 1994, at p7 and p. 13 respectively.

22 Others do not: Kaase and Newton conclude that 'claims about the legitimacy crisis in late capitalist societies were largely mythical.' See Max Kaase and Kenneth Newton, *Beliefs in Government* (Oxford: Oxford University Press, 1995) Chapter 7 entitled 'A crisis of democracy?' at p. 168. Whoever is right about the West, the comparative point remains: trust in elected politicians was low in both East and West, and if that did not pose a problem of legitimacy in the West, it should not cause great alarm in the East either.

23 The distinction between these two aspects of politics was made by Almond and Verba in their classic study of democratisation in western Europe after the war. See Gabriel A. Almond and Sidney Verba, *The Civic Culture: Political Attitudes and Democracy in Five Nations* (Princeton, NJ: Princeton University Press, 1963; New paperback edition, London: Sage, 1989) Chapter 3. For the distinction in a study of Soviet politics see Seweryn Bialer, *Stalin's Successors: Leadership, Stability and Change in the Soviet Union* (New York, NY: Cambridge University Press, 1980) pp. 166–7.

24 In one part of the FSU, Russia, Rose found that, on balance, people expected fair treatment from a doctor, and in a post office, bank, or grocer's shop, but not from the police or in a social security office or municipal office. See Richard Rose, 'Russia as an hour-glass society: a constitution without citizens', *East European Constitutional Review*, vol.4 no.3 (1995) pp. 34–53 at p. 39. But he found higher expectations of fair treatment in the Baltic States. See Richard Rose, *New Baltic Barometer II* (Glasgow: Strathclyde University Centre for the Study of Public Policy, 1995). Technically the Baltic States are part of the FSU, but a very small and atypical part. Culturally they have more in common with ECE.

25 See for example Vladimir Shlapentokh, *The Public and Private Life of the Soviet People: Changing Values in Post-Stalin Russia* (Oxford: Oxford University Press, 1989) Chapter 9 entitled 'Illegal life inside the state.'

26 See Olga Kryshtanovskaya and Stephen White, 'From Soviet nomenklatura to Russian elite', *Europe–Asia Studies*, vol.48 no.5 (1996) pp. 711–33.; Thomas A. Baylis, 'Plus Ca change? Transformation and continuity amongst East European elites', *Communist and Post-Communist Studies*, vol.27 no.3 (1994) pp. 315–28; John Higley and Jan Pakulski, 'Elite transformation in Central and Eastern Europe', *Australian Journal of Political Science*, vol.30 no.3 (1995) pp. 415–35; John Higley, Judith Kullberg and Jan Pakulski, 'The persistence of postcommunist elites', *Journal of Democracy*, vol.7 no.2 (1996) pp. 133–47): or the special issue of *Theory and Society*, vol. 24 no.5 (1995) entitled 'Circulation vs reproduction of elites during the postcommunist transformation of Eastern Europe.'

6 SOCIALISM AFTER COMMUNISM

1 This case is made for example in William L Miller, Annis May Timpson and Michael Lessnoff, *Political Culture in Contemporary Britain: People and Politicians, Principles and Practice* (Oxford: Oxford University Press, 1996) pp. 303–5.

2 The EU's Eurobarometer surveys defined the 'market economy' somewhat prejudicially as 'largely free from state control'. Their surveys are not directly comparable with ours, and tend to show more negative attitudes to the market economy. Our own focus group studies in small towns and villages of Ukraine suggest that ordinary people in the FSU/ECE are aware that west European

market economies are closely regulated by the state, and that a market 'free from state control' is a caricature of nineteenth century Dodge City at its worst. Respondents to the EU question probably felt, with some justification, that a market 'largely free of state control' would provide more freedom for a criminal and violent mafia than for anyone else.

3   Long term memories of voting behaviour are notoriously inaccurate and tend to come into line with current political preferences. Our interviews took place at the end of December. The actual result in the spring 1993 referendum was only 53 per cent 'yes'.

4   The Times–Mirror surveys also found that every public in eastern Europe preferred the Swedish model to the American. Los Angeles Times–Mirror, *The Pulse of Europe: a Survey of Political and Social Values and Attitudes* (Los Angeles, CA: Times–Mirror, 1991) p. 165. Ironically, Scandinavians themselves were beginning to have doubts: see Jan-Erik Lane, 'The twilight of the Scandinavian model', *Political Studies*, vol.41 no.2 (1993) pp. 315–24. A 1995 survey for the USIA posed the question in a non-comparative form, asking simply whether the USA provided a suitable model for Russia. By 48 per cent to 43 per cent, Russians said it did not. Anatole Shub, 'What Russians know and think about America' (Washington, DC: USIA Office of Research and Media Reaction, November 1995) p. 21.

5   A term for Russia that is associated with the establishment of an independent 'autocephalous' Orthodox Church in Russia between 1448 when it claimed independence and 1589 when that independence was recognised by the ecumenical patriarch in Constantinople. Constantinople was, of course, the 'new Rome' or 'second Rome'.

6   Similarly, the Times–Mirror survey reported that in Russia and Ukraine, there was a 'clear preference for privatisation in only one out of 13 areas – farming.' Los Angeles Times–Mirror, *The Pulse of Europe: a Survey of Political and Social Values and Attitudes* (Los Angeles, CA: Times–Mirror, 1991) p. 244.

7   Martin Gilbert, *The Dent Atlas of Russian History*, 2nd edition (London: Dent, 1993) p. 58

8   Gilbert (1993), pp. 113–4.

9   Similarly the Times–Mirror surveys found that 'those in the rural areas are markedly less enthusiastic about the prospect [of farm privatisation] than those who live in the cities.' Los Angeles Times–Mirror, *The Pulse of Europe: a Survey of Political and Social Values and Attitudes* (Los Angeles, CA: Times–Mirror, 1991) p. 249.

10   Despite that view, in 1961, 55 per cent of houses built in Ukraine were built privately or for cooperatives, but in 1991, only 10 per cent, because private house building had declined while state house building had maintained its previous level. Sitting tenants also had a 'right to buy' under the communist regime and, in 1991, 140,000 state flats were sold to sitting tenants in Ukraine. State rents were so low that ownership was not an asset except, for example, where the house or flat could be sold to a business or a westerner. See James Meek, 'Ukrainians pay price of government housing handout.' *Scotsman*, 19 October 1992, p. 6.

11   Our counter-intuitive findings are corroborated by other surveys however. Using a very similar question, but balancing freedom against state provided welfare rather than against equality, Times–Mirror surveys in 1991 also found that only a small minority chose freedom in Hungary, while Ukraine showed the highest commitment to freedom, followed by Russia and then Czechoslovakia – reproducing exactly the spectrum of opinion found in our own survey. See Los Angeles Times–Mirror, *The Pulse of Europe: a Survey of Political and Social Values and Attitudes* (Los Angeles, CA: Times–Mirror, 1991), question Q300; and Janos

Simon, 'What does democracy mean for Hungarians?' *Coexistence*, vol.32 no.4 (1995) pp. 325–40 who provides a useful discussion of the Times–Mirror findings, though he gives figures that differ from the Times–Mirror original. Interestingly, the public in several of the west European countries that were included in the Times–Mirror surveys took the same socialist view as the Hungarians.

12   They were strongly related to income however. See Matthew Wyman, Stephen White, Bill Miller and Paul Heywood, 'A culture in transition? Attitudes to inequality in post-communist Russia.' A paper to the conference on 'Russia in transition: elites, classes and inequalities' at Emmanuel College, Cambridge, December 1994.

13   See Bill Miller, Stephen White, Paul Heywood and Matthew Wyman, 'Essex man found alive and well and living in Prague', ESRC/Glasgow University Press Release, 2 February 1994, p. 4.

14   The 'career move' interpretation of Communist Party membership is supported by other evidence. See Aryeh L. Unger, 'Images of the CPSU: the views of Jewish emigrants', *Survey*, vol.23 no.4 (1977) pp. 23–34; and Aryeh L. Unger, 'Political participation in the USSR: YCL and CPSU', *Soviet Studies*, vol.33 no.1 (1981) pp. 107–24. The usual caveats about the credibility of *émigrés*' tales apply, but their tales are at least consistent with our analysis of those who did not emigrate.

7   EXTERNAL AND INTERNAL NATIONALISM

1   For a general introduction to issues of political nationalism see James G. Kellas, *The Politics of Nationalism and Ethnicity* (London: Macmillan, 1991); John Hutchinson and Anthony D. Smith (eds) *Nationalism* (Oxford: Oxford University Press, 1994); and John Breuilly, *Nationalism and the State*, 2nd Edition (Manchester: Manchester University Press, 1993). In his first edition (1982) Breuilly asserted that a rise of nationalist politics in eastern Europe was 'highly unlikely' (quoted at p. 340 in the second edition). Undaunted, in his second edition, he describes post-communist politics as 'the politics of inheritance' and argues that nationalism played no significant part in the collapse of the communist empire. Instead, he argues, 'it required the prior breakdown of Soviet state power before . . . a sense of nationality could be turned into political form.' (p. 348). His argument may seem somewhat similar to that between doctors about whether pneumonia or prior weakness caused the death, through pneumonia, of an already weakened patient, though perhaps the analogy of worms devouring an already dead corpse comes nearer to Breuilly's perspective. Either way, it seems to underestimate the destructive force of nationalism.

2   Benjamin Disraeli, *Sybil, or The Two Nations* (originally published 1845) Book 2, Chapter 5.

3   Neal Ascherson, 'Old Conflicts in the New Europe', *Independent on Sunday*, 18 February 1990, pp. 3–5.

4   Los Angeles Times–Mirror, *The Pulse of Europe: a Survey of Political and Social Values and Attitudes* (Los Angeles, CA: Times–Mirror, 1991) p. 140.

5   For a modest statement see Paul Robert Magocsi, *Ukraine: A Historical Atlas* (Toronto: University of Toronto Press, 1992) Map 2; for more extreme claims see Martin Gilbert, *The Dent Atlas of Russian History* 2nd edition (London: Dent, 1993) pp. 97–8.

6   We shall meet that combination of tendencies again, in Chapter 11, when we compare the attitudes of MPs with the attitudes of their publics.

7   Eric Hobsbawm, 'The rise of ethno-linguistic nationalisms' in John Hutchinson and Anthony D. Smith (eds) *Nationalism* (Oxford: Oxford University Press, 1994) pp. 177–84 at p. 184.

8   Which 'did not know the legal concept of a "state language"' though German was widely used as such. In the Vienna parliament deputies were allowed to speak in their own preferred tongue, but only German language speeches were recorded. See J.W.Bruegel, *Czechoslovakia before Munich* (Cambridge: Cambridge University Press, 1973) pp. 2–3.

9   Emil Payin, 'The disintegration of the empire and the fate of the 'imperial minority' in Vladimir Shlapentokh, Munir Sendich and Emil Payin (eds) *The New Russian Diaspora: Russian Minorities in the Former Soviet Republics* (Armonk, NY: Sharpe, 1994) pp. 21–36 at p. 26.

10 Mark Trevelyan, 'Doubts voiced on Estonian election', *Independent*, 21 September 1992 p. 9. An alleged 42 per cent of the population were excluded from the previous day's election because those considered to be non-Estonian residents had to 'prove two years' residence, *and at least a basic knowledge of Estonian*, as well as pledge loyalty to the [Estonian] republic.'

11 *Konstitutsiya Rossiiskoi Federatsii. Prinyataya vsenarodnym golosovaniem 12 dekabrya 1993 g.* (Moscow: Yuridicheskaya literatura, 1993).

12 Times–Mirror surveys in 1991 showed that when people in Russia, Ukraine and Lithuania were asked explicitly whether they 'thought of their country as Russia/Ukraine/Lithuania or as the Soviet Union', 42 per cent in Russia and 35 per cent in Ukraine (only 10 per cent in west Ukraine, but 42 per cent in the rest of Ukraine) chose the Soviet Union, and another 13 per cent in Russia and 19 per cent in Ukraine volunteered that they thought of their country as both Russia/Ukraine and as the Soviet Union. Yet when asked the more personal question 'what is your nationality' they did not describe themselves as Soviet. Lithuanians, like west Ukrainians, were unwilling even to describe their 'country' as the Soviet Union. See questions Q34 and Q103 respectively in Los Angeles Times–Mirror, *The Pulse of Europe: a Survey of Political and Social Values and Attitudes* (Los Angeles, CA: Times–Mirror, 1991). A 1995 Democratic Initiatives poll in Ukraine asked people whether they identified with Ukraine as a whole, or with their region, or with the FSU, or with Europe, or with Russia. With that prompting, 75 per cent in Lviv, 64 per cent in Kyiv but only 29 per cent in Donetz chose to identify with Ukraine. In Donetz, 33 per cent chose the FSU, 20 per cent the Donetz region, and only 2 per cent Russia. Identifying with Russian nationality was thus very different from identifying with Russia or the Russian state. Berglund, Aarebrot and Koralewicz use World Values Study surveys from 1990 to show that ethnic Russians in the Baltics tended to identify with the larger concept of the 'Soviet Union' as ethnic Balts identified with the larger concept of 'Europe', though more strongly. See Sten Berglund and Frank Aarebrot with Jadwiga Koralewicz, 'The view from central and eastern Europe' in Oskar Niedermayer and Richard Sinnott (eds) *Public Opinion and Internationalized Governance* (Oxford: Oxford University Press, 1995) pp. 368–401 at p. 383. The peculiar identity problems of ethnic Russians living outside Russia or Ukraine, in the less hospitable territory of Baltic or Central Asian republics are covered more extensively in Vladimir Shlapentokh, Munir Sendich and Emil Payin (eds) *The New Russian Diaspora: Russian Minorities in the Former Soviet Republics* (Armonk, NY: Sharpe, 1994). In our own survey we found only half a per cent in Russia and none in Ukraine who volunteered the self-description 'Soviet' in answer to the question: 'What is your nationality?'. So, in our survey, the bulk of the large number in Ukraine who did not claim Ukrainian nationality, claimed Russian nationality.

13 Meek quotes a survey in 1992 showing that, of those who claimed Ukrainian as their 'mother tongue', only 86 per cent would speak it to their parents, 68 per cent to their spouse, and 55 per cent to their doctor. In addition, only 33 per cent preferred to watch Ukrainian language rather than Russian language television. James Meek, 'Officially speaking, Russian is on the way out', *Scotsman*, 15 June 1992.

14 The right of all citizens to education in their native language was contained in both the 1936 and 1977 Soviet Constitutions, in articles 121 and 45 respectively.

15 Samuel P. Huntington, 'The clash of civilisations?', *Foreign Affairs*, vol.72 no.3 (1993) pp. 22–49.

8 LIBERAL VALUES

1 See T.H. Marshall and Tom Bottomore, *Citizenship and Social Class* (London: Pluto Press, 1992) for a reprint and discussion of Marshall's lecture.

2 For an earlier study of democratic values based on a survey of opinions in 1990 see James L. Gibson and Raymond M. Duch, 'Emerging democratic values in Soviet political culture', in Arthur H. Miller, William M. Reisinger and Vicki L. Hesli, *Public Opinion and Regime Change: The New Politics of Post Soviet Societies* (Boulder, CO: Westview, 1993) pp. 69–94. It is limited to European Russia, and in some respects even to Moscow, however. For a wider geographic coverage, based on a 1991 survey, see Los Angeles Times–Mirror, *The Pulse of Europe: a Survey of Political and Social Values and Attitudes* (Los Angeles, CA: Times–Mirror, 1991).

3 Georg Sorensen, *Democracy and Democratization* (Boulder, CO: Westview, 1993) p. 13. Sorensen based his criteria on a review of, amongst others, David Held, *Models of Democracy* (Cambridge: Polity Press, 1987; Oxford: Blackwell, 1992) and Robert A. Dahl, *Polyarchy: Participation and Opposition* (New Haven, CT: Yale University Press, 1971). See also Robert A. Dahl, *Democracy and its Critics* (New Haven: Yale University Press, 1989). For an alternative account of democratic principles, which rejects American notions of pluralism, see Anthony H. Birch, *The Concepts and Theories of Modern Democracy* (London: Routledge, 1993). The most lavishly illustrated account is Patrick Watson and Benjamin Barber, *The Struggle for Democracy* (London: W.H. Allen, 1990). For the extent to which the old communist regimes failed to meet Sorenson's criteria, and Gorbachev's belated attempts to do so, see Stephen White, John Gardiner, George Schopflin and Tony Saich, *Communist and Post-Communist Political Systems* (London: Macmillan, 1990) especially Chapters 7 and 8; and Stephen White, *After Gorbachev* (Cambridge: Cambridge University Press, 1993) especially Chapter 2.

4 Arguably, Marshall's time sequence, in which the establishment of civil rights (liberal values) is followed by the establishment of political rights (popular control) occurred in ECE and the FSU but on a time-scale of decades rather than centuries. See Nancy Bermeo (ed.) *Liberalization and Democratization: Change in the Soviet Union and Eastern Europe* (Baltimore, MD: Johns Hopkins University Press, 1992).

5 Georg Sorensen, *Democracy and Democratization* (Boulder, CO: Westview, 1993) p. 6. See Friedrich von Hayek, *The Constitution of Liberty* (London: Routledge and Kegan Paul, 1960) p. 103. Others also accept Hayek's distinction without necessarily accepting his priorities: Ranney and Kendall define democracy in terms of four principles – popular sovereignty, political equality, popular consultation,

and majority rule limited only by self-restraint – which focus on popular control almost to the exclusion of liberal values. See Austin Ranney and Willmoore Kendall, *Democracy and the American Party System* (New York, NY: Harcourt, Brace and World, 1956) pp. 23–37.

6   A 1992 survey by Miller, Hesli and Reisinger suggests that FSU publics associated the word 'democracy' primarily with freedom, while FSU elites associated it primarily with the rule of law. In our terms both freedom and the rule of law are 'liberal values' rather than 'popular control' values. See Arthur H. Miller, Vicki L. Hesli and William M. Reisinger, 'Understanding democracy: a comparison of mass and elite in post-Soviet Russia and Ukraine', *Studies in Public Policy*, no.247 (Glasgow: Strathclyde University Centre for the Study of Public Policy, 1995) p. 15. Outside observers would probably agree that 'really existing democracy' in the FSU during the early 1990s provided more opportunities for personal freedom than for public control of government. The rule of law was less evident.

7   *Konstitutsiya Rossiiskoi Federatsii. Prinyataya vsenarodnym golosovaniem 12 dekabrya 1993 g.* (Moscow: Yuridicheskaya literatura, 1993), Article 29.

8   Hugo Storey, 'Human rights and the new Europe: experience and experiment.' *Political Studies*, vol. 43 (1995) *Special Issue on Politics and Human Rights*, pp. 131–51 at p. 142 and p. 146 respectively.

9   Vladimir Shlapentokh, *The Public and Private Life of the Soviet People* (Oxford: Oxford University Press, 1989)

10   For an analysis of the distinction, in the eyes of western publics, between the abstract idea of democracy and its actual performance see Dieter Fuchs, Giovanna Guidorossi and Palle Svensson, 'Support for the democratic system' in Hans-Dieter Klingemann and Dieter Fuchs (eds) *Citizens and the State* (Oxford: Oxford University Press, 1995) pp. 323–353 at pp. 345–350. Toka analyses east European satisfaction with the functioning of democracy – but not support for the abstract idea of democracy – in Gabor Toka, 'Political support in east-central Europe' in Klingemann and Fuchs (eds) (1995) pp. 354–382.

11   William L Miller, Annis May Timpson and Michael Lessnoff, *Political, Culture in Contemporary Britain: People and Politicians, Principles and Practice* (Oxford: Oxford University Press, 1996) pp. 145–50.

12   Yeltsin dismissed one head of television, Yegor Yakovlev, after television screened the arguments of both sides in the Ossetian crisis ('TV boss sacked for Ossetian coverage', *Scotsman*, 25 November 1992 p. 8); and another, Vyacheslav Bragin, after the unwelcome result of the 1993 parliamentary election (and yet another after the 1995 election). His crackdown on the press immediately after his suspension of the Russian parliament in 1993 is described in Jamey Gambrell, 'Moscow: storm over the press', *The New York Review*, 16th December 1993 pp. 69–74. For the Hungarian government's attempts, ultimately successful, to dismiss their independent minded head of state television see Elemer Hankiss, 'Witness: A media war of independence' in William L. Miller (ed.) *Alternatives to Freedom: Arguments and Opinions* (London: Longman, 1995) pp. 105–23.

13   Others have also found a majority of Russians supported government control of the media, See Mark Rhodes, 'How Russians view their media', *Radio Liberty Research Report*, 31 July 1992.

14   Reisinger, Miller, Hesli and Maher make a somewhat similar point when they distinguish between 'the desire for strong leadership' and 'preference for order in society' though they regard both simply as 'two dimensions of authoritarianism'. (p. 191) They find no significant difference between Russians and Lithuanians in terms of their desire for strong leadership, but a significant difference in terms of desire for order – in 1991 but, inexplicably, not in 1992. (pp. 192–3) However their

measure of desire for order includes acceptance – not rejection – of illegal action by the police. (p. 221) See William M. Reisinger, Arthur H. Miller, Vicki L. Hesli and Kristen Hill Mather, 'Political values in Russia, Ukraine and Lithuania: Sources and implications for democracy.' *British Journal of Political Science*, vol.24 no.2 (1994) pp. 183–224. By contrast we have found a strong attachment in Russia and Ukraine to order, defined – very differently – as strict legality, a low politics version of that 'law-based state' which was the goal of the Gorbachev years.

15   McIntosh *et al.* found that when Hungarian, Polish, Romanian and Bulgarian publics were asked whether various features were 'essential for a society to be called a democracy', they found that the most essential feature was not multi-party competition or the freedom to criticise the government but equality under the law: 'a system of justice that treats everyone equally.' See Mary E. McIntosh, Martha Abele MacIver, Daniel G. Abele and Dina Mseltz, 'Publics meet market democracy in central and east Europe 1991–93', *Slavic Review*, vol.53 no.2 (1994) pp. 483–512, at p. 497.

16   See Chapter 5 on citizens' experience of unfair and corrupt officials.

17   As usual, '(Country)' was replaced by the adjective derived from the name of the appropriate state in each of the five countries – 'Russian' in Russia, through to 'Czech' in the Czech Republic.

18   VTsIOM surveys in 1989 and again in 1994 reported remarkable though generally declining levels of intolerance of deviance in Russia: 31 per cent wished to 'liquidate (likvidirovat)' homosexuals in 1989, and 22 per cent in 1994; and attitudes to prostitutes and drug users were not much different. See *Ekonomicheskie i sotsialnye peremeny: monitoring obshchestvennogo mneniya* (1995) no.1 (January–February) p. 12.

19   Peter McGrath, 'Eastern Europe: daydreams of democracy', *Newsweek*, 21 May 1990, p. 13.

20   In articles 125 and 50 respectively.

21   See William E. Butler, 'The rule of law and the legal system' in Stephen White, Alex Pravda and Zvi Gitelman (eds) *Developments in Soviet Politics* (London: Macmillan, 1990) pp. 104–19.

22   However a differently worded question found a narrow majority in Russia, though not in ECE for the 'need for' a strong leader rather than parliaments and elections. See Richard Rose and Christian Haerpfer, 'New Russia Barometer III: the Results', *Studies in Public Policy*, no.228 (Glasgow: Centre for the Study of Public Policy, 1994).

9   POPULAR CONTROL: DIRECT OR REPRESENTATIVE DEMOCRACY?

1   A point emphasised by Bertolt Brecht in his poem 'The Solution'. Commenting on the statement that 'the people had forfeited the government's confidence' by taking part in the 17 June 1953 Berlin uprising, he suggested 'Wouldn't it be simpler in that case if the government dissolved the people and elected another?' See Bertolt Brecht, 'The Solution' in Alan Bold (ed.) *The Penguin Book of Socialist Verse* (Harmondsworth: Penguin, 1980) p. 240.

2   For a full account of Gorbachev's campaign against alcohol, viewed as Soviet paternalism's last fling, see Stephen White, *Russia Goes Dry: Alcohol, State and Society* (Cambridge: Cambridge University Press, 1996).

3   Indeed 'Sobor' can be translated as 'cathedral', just as well as 'council', 'synod' or
     'assembly'. It was, for example, the eleventh century *Sofisky Sobor* in Kyiv that
     became the focus of public disorder in 1995 when Patriarch Volodimir was buried
     under the pavement outside its boundary walls – after the authorities, and rival
     religious groups, had forcibly prevented his burial within the Sobor or its precincts.

4   Nikolai Biryukov and Victor Sergeyev, 'The idea of democracy in the West and in
     the East' in David Beetham (ed.) *Defining and Measuring Democracy* (London:
     Sage, 1994) pp. 182–98 at p. 189. For a more extended discussion see Nikolai
     Biryukov and Victor Sergeyev, *Russia's Road to Democracy: Parliament, Commun-
     ism and Traditional Culture* (Aldershot: Edward Elgar, 1993)

5   Anthony H. Birch, *The Concepts and Theories of Modern Democracy* (London:
     Routledge, 1993) p. 160.

6   A.D. Lindsay, *The Essentials of Democracy* (Oxford: Oxford University Press,
     1935) pp. 40–1 – quoted by Birch.

7   Harold J. Laski, *The Development of the Representative System in our Times*
     (Geneva: Interparliamentary Union, 1928) p. 13 – quoted by Birch.

8   On deliberative democracy see David Miller, 'Citizenship and pluralism', *Political
     Studies*, vol.43 no.3 (1995) pp. 432–50 at p. 445; and David Miller, 'Deliberative
     democracy and social choice' in David Held (ed.) *Prospects for Democracy* special
     issue of *Political Studies*, vol.40 (1992) pp. 54–67 later published by Polity Press
     (1993).

9   Stephen White and Ronald J. Hill, 'Russia, the Former Soviet Union and Eastern
     Europe: the referendum as a flexible political instrument' in Michael Gallagher
     and Pier Vincenzo Uleri (eds) *The Referendum Experience in Europe* (London:
     Macmillan, 1996) p. 167. See also Stephen White, Graeme Gill and Darrell Slider,
     The Politics of Transition: Shaping a Post-Soviet Future (Cambridge: Cambridge
     University Press, 1993) pp. 88–92 especially.

10   The dominating influence of the president is set out in the Russian Constitution of
     1993. See *Konstitutsiya Rossiiskoi Federatsii. Prinyataya vsenarodnym golosovaniem
     12 dekabrya 1993 g.* (Moscow: Yuridicheskaya literatura, 1993), Articles 80–93.

11   For indications that the turnout may have been less than 50 per cent of the
     electorate see for instance *Konstitutsionnyi vestnik*, 1994, no. 17, p. 32, and *Mos-
     kovskii komsomolets*, 11 January 1994, p. 1. More accessibly, see also Wendy Slater
     'Russia's plebiscite on a new constitution' *Radio Liberty Research Report* 21
     January 1994; and Vera Tolz and Julia Wishnevsky 'Election queries make Rus-
     sians doubt democratic process' *Radio Liberty Research Report* 1 April 1994. For
     an analysis of the voting patterns in that referendum, especially the correlation
     between support for presidential supremacy and a 'yes' vote on the new constitu-
     tion see Matthew Wyman, Bill Miller, Stephen White and Paul Heywood,
     'The Russian elections of December 1993', *Electoral Studies*, vol.13 no.3 (1994)
     pp. 254–71 at p. 267.

12   Henry E. Brady and Cynthia S. Kaplan, 'Eastern Europe and the former Soviet
     Union' in David Butler and Austin Ranney (eds) *Referendums Around the World:
     The Growing Use of Direct Democracy* (London: Macmillan, 1994) pp. 174–217 at
     p. 216.

13   Other Russian surveys in the summer of 1993, before the dramatic events of the
     autumn, found the Russian public evenly divided between those who would back
     the parliament and those who would back the government. See Ronald J. Hill and
     Stephen White, 'The referendum in communist and postcommunist Europe', *Stu-
     dies in Public Policy*, no.243 (Glasgow: Strathclyde University, 1995) p. 17. How-
     ever those surveys weighed support for the president against support for the old,
     allegedly 'communist' parliament elected as the Supreme Soviet in 1989. Our

question weighed support for the government against support for the new, post-Soviet parliament being elected at the time of our survey in December 1993.

14 Technically presidential appointments were subject to parliamentary approval, but in practice this restriction could be circumvented by having an 'acting' prime-minister (such as Gaidar in Russia in 1992) or ministers who had not been approved by parliament. For the development of presidentialism in Russia see Stephen White, 'The presidency and political leadership in postcommunist Russia', in Peter Lentini (ed.) *Elections and Political Order in Russia* (Budapest: Central European University Press, 1995) pp. 202–25.

15 Taken from a speech of Yeltsin's on 10 December 1992, reported in full on the front page of that day's *Izvestiya*. A shortened translation was reported in the *Guardian*, 11 December 1992, p. 10 under the headline 'Yeltsin asks the people to decide.' He did hold a referendum in December 1993 on the new constitution which formally conferred decisive powers on the president, but only after his leading role had been established by force. On the arguments for and against presidentialism, see for example Arend Lijphart (ed.) *Parliamentary versus Presidential Government* (Oxford: Oxford University Press, 1994).

16 See Christian Lucky, 'Table of twelve electoral laws', *East European Constitutional Review*, vol.3 no.2 (Spring 1994) pp. 65–77 for a comparative table that includes the electoral laws in all of our countries except Ukraine.

17 Andrew Coulson, 'From democratic centralism to local democracy' in Andrew Coulson (ed.) *Local Government in Eastern Europe: Establishing Democracy at the Grassroots* (Aldershot: Edward Elgar, 1995) pp. 1–19. See also Francesco Kjellberg, Jana Reschova, Geog Sootla and John Taylor, 'The role of local autonomy in democratic and democratising societies: the new local government acts in the Czech Republic, Estonia and Norway'. Paper to IPSA (International Political Science Association) 16th World Congress, Berlin, August 1994.

18 Julia Wishnevsky, 'Problems of Russian regional leadership', *Radio Liberty Research Report*, 13 May 1994.

19 Adrian Campbell, 'Regional power in the Russian Federation' in Andrew Coulson (ed.) *Local Government in Eastern Europe: Establishing Democracy at the Grassroots* (Aldershot: Edward Elgar, 1995) pp. 145–67 at p. 166. There were similar moves in Britain at this time, with the replacement, for many purposes, of elected local councils by government appointed 'quangos'.

20 See Chapter 18 for further details of the impact of the 1993 Russian election on public attitudes.

21 The Times–Mirror surveys reported that, in 1991, 'a quarter of the Russian public explicitly disapproved of the effort to establish a multiparty system.' Conversely however, that means a large majority approved. See Los Angeles Times–Mirror, *The Pulse of Europe: a Survey of Political and Social Values and Attitudes* (Los Angeles, CA: Times–Mirror, 1991) p. 232. Our own surveys suggest steadily declining support for the multi-party system in Russia.

22 Marian T. Grzybowski, 'Parliamentary elections in the Czech and Slovak Republics and in Poland 1991–93: The search for an adequate electoral system'. A paper for the 16th World Congress of IPSA (International Political Science Association) Berlin, August 1994, pp. 38–9.

23 By introducing a party list element into the 1993 Russian election, and by increasing the thresholds required for election in various ECE party list systems. These changes failed to prevent a high degree of fragmentation in the 1993 Russian election but were more successful in 1995. See Robert G. Moser, 'The impact of the electoral system on postcommunist party development: The case of the 1993 Russian parliamentary elections', *Electoral Studies*, vol.14 no.4 (1995) pp. 377–98.

24   For details see Matthew Wyman, Stephen White, Bill Miller and Paul Heywood, 'The place of "party" in postcommunist Europe', *Party Politics*, vol.1 no.4 (1995) pp. 535–48 at p. 543.

25   Similarly, the Times–Mirror surveys reported that '54 per cent of Russians and 47 per cent of Ukrainians believe that even in a democracy certain political parties should be outlawed.' Los Angeles Times–Mirror, *The Pulse of Europe: a Survey of Political and Social Values and Attitudes* (Los Angeles, CA: Times–Mirror, 1991) p. 241.

26   Yeltsin banned the Communist Party in Russia after the 1991 coup, but the Constitutional Court legalised it at the end of 1992. There were further attempts to ban it after the violence following the 1993 suspension of parliament. The Communist Party was also banned in Ukraine following the 1991 Moscow coup, but a successor party was legalised in October 1993.

27   Indeed 52 per cent of ethnic Slovaks who backed Meciar's ruling Movement for a Democratic Slovakia were willing to ban Hungarian minority parties in Slovakia. See Bill Miller, Stephen White, Paul Heywood and Matthew Wyman, 'Ethnic divisions and democracy in Slovakia', ESRC/Glasgow University Press Release, 26 January 1994, p. 2.

28   Conversely about 40 per cent of Ukrainian speakers would ban the Communist Party, but only 25 per cent of Russian speaking ethnic Ukrainians, and a mere 16 per cent of ethnic Russians living in Ukraine would ban it. See Bill Miller, Stephen White, Paul Heywood and Matthew Wyman, 'Language versus nationality in the politics of Ukraine' ESRC/Glasgow University Press Release, 9 February 1994, p. 3.

29   Jan Ake Dellenbrant, 'Parties and party systems in Eastern Europe' in Stephen White, Judy Batt and Paul G. Lewis (eds) *Developments in East European Politics* (London: Macmillan, 1993) pp. 147–62 at p. 149 and p. 162 respectively. However Fitzmaurice points out that Hungary 'unlike her neighbours...skipped the umbrella movement stage and went straight to a viable party system which reflected some earlier elements of Hungarian political culture.' John Fitzmaurice 'The Hungarian election of May 1994', *Electoral Studies*, vol.14 no.1 (1995) pp. 77–80 at p. 77.

30   Richard Sakwa, 'The development of the Russian party system: Did the elections change anything?' in Peter Lentini (ed.) *Elections and Political Order in Russia* (Budapest: Central European University Press, 1995) pp. 169–201 at p. 173 and p. 169 respectively.

31   See for example the special issue of the journal, *Party Politics*, vol.1 no.4 (1995) pp. 443–621, edited by Michael Waller, *Party Politics in Eastern Europe*.

32   Sakwa (1995) in Peter Lentini (ed.) pp. 169–201 at p. 169. See also Paul Lewis, 'Civil society and the development of political parties in east central Europe', *Journal of Communist Studies*, vol.9 no.4 (1993) pp. 5–20; and Andrew Wilson and Artur Bilous, 'Political parties in Ukraine', *Europe–Asia Studies*, vol.45 no.4 (1993) pp. 693–704; Gordon Wightman (ed.) *Party Formation in East Central Europe* (Aldershot: Edward Elgar, 1995); Sten Berglund and Jan Ake Dellenbrant (eds) *The New Democracies in Eastern Europe: Party Systems and Political Cleavages*, 2nd Edition (Aldershot: Edward Elgar, 1994).

33   James I. Clem, 'The new party activists: survey results from Ukraine.' Paper to AAASS (American Association for the Advancement of Slavic Studies) 27th National Convention, Washington, October 1995, p. 9.

34   Certainly at the parliamentary elections of 1994 in Ukraine and 1995 in Russia. Arguably the Communists, with their Agrarian Party allies, were also the most successful at the 1993 Russian parliamentary election since together they won more seats in the Duma (lower house) than any other party, though their success was

overshadowed by the performance of Zhirinovsky's Liberal Democratic Party in the 'party-list' section (but only that section) of the 1993 election.

35   This approach was used, for example, in Stephen White, Matthew Wyman and Olga Kryshtanovskaya, 'Parties and politics in postcommunist Russia', *Communist and Postcommunist Studies*, vol.28 no.2 (1995) pp. 183–202.

36   This point is also made in Matthew Wyman, Stephen White, Bill Miller and Paul Heywood, 'The place of "party" in postcommunist Europe', *Party Politics*, vol.1 no.4 (1995) pp. 535–48 at p. 541–2.

37   For a good introduction to the mysteries of factor analysis and details of the factor analysis programmes used see Marija J. Norusis, IL *SPSS/PC+Statistics 4.0* (Chicago, IL: SPSS, 1990).

38   We discuss the 'red–brown alliance' in terms of principles, values and ideas in Chapter 12.

39   A similar factor analysis of Russian party sympathies in 1992, using a different set of 20 parties however, also revealed that the structure of party sympathy in Russia was dominated by a single factor. The first factor explained 40 per cent of the variance and the second only 14 per cent. See Ian McAllister and Stephen White, 'Democracy, political parties and party formation in postcommunist Russia', *Party Politics*, vol.1 no.1 (1995) pp. 49–72 at p. 61. McAllister and White use raw party sympathies, rather than the relative party sympathies, adjusted for average party sympathy, which we use here.

10   ENTREPRENEURIAL MPS

1   Purely for lack of funds, we omitted the Slovak parliament.

2   For an earlier comparison of mass and elite attitudes in the FSU see Arthur H. Miller, Vicki L. Hesli and William M. Reisinger, 'Comparing citizen and elite belief systems in post–Soviet Russia and Ukraine', *Public Opinion Quarterly*, vol.59 no.1 (1995) pp. 1–40; or Arthur H. Miller, Vicki L. Hesli and William M. Reisinger, 'Understanding democracy: a comparison of mass and elite in post-Soviet Russia and Ukraine', *Studies in Public Policy*, no.247 (Glasgow: Strathclyde University Centre for the Study of Public Policy, 1995). It was based upon June–July 1992 interviews with the public, and April 1992 interviews with a total of 138 respondents drawn from the old Russian and Ukrainian parliaments – technically the Supreme Soviets – that had been elected under Gorbachev. These differ from our own surveys of parliamentary opinion in that they include only half as many Russian and Ukrainian deputies; they exclude ECE; they are drawn from Soviet era Supreme Soviets; and the opinions of these elected deputies are merged with those of 39 appointed administrators.

3   Miller, Hesli and Reisinger also found that 'both the Russian and Ukrainian elite as of mid-1992 were definitely more favourable towards . . . the market than was the general population.' Arthur H. Miller, Vicki L. Hesli and William M. Reisinger, 'Comparing citizen and elite belief systems in post-Soviet Russia and Ukraine', *Public Opinion Quarterly*, vol.59 no.1 (1995) pp. 1–40 at p. 14. We have found that the post-Soviet MPs differed more from their publics than the deputies who Miller, Hesli and Reisinger interviewed after the fall of the Soviet Union, but who had all been elected as Soviet deputies when the Soviet Union was still in existence.

11   THE NATIONALIST, LIBERAL AND DEMOCRATIC VLAUES OF MP'S

1   William L. Miller, Annis May Timpson and Michael Lessnoff, *Political Culture in Contemporary Britain: People and Politicians, Principles and Practice* (Oxford: Oxford University Press, 1996) pp. 158–62.

2   Strictly speaking the term 'near abroad' is only a Russian term, but it is generally useful as a term for neighbouring countries whose borders and sovereignty may not, for historical or ethnic reasons, be totally unquestioned.

3   As we saw in Chapter 7, the countries where support for devolution was highest were also the ones where opposition to separatism was greatest.

4   British politicians were also more willing than their public to allow press intrusions into politicians' lives, though not by such a margin. See Miller, Timpson and Lessnoff (1996) p. 147.

5   British politicians were also much more tolerant of deviants and extremists than were their public – in political affairs, though not in everyday personal life. See Miller, Timpson and Lessnoff (1996) p. 125. The tolerance questions used in our FSU/ECE and more especially in our British surveys owe some inspiration to John L. Sullivan, James Pierson and George E. Marcus, *Political Tolerance and American Democracy* (Chicago, IL: University of Chicago, 1982), though they are not quite the same, and we would interpret them differently. See also their more recent George E. Marcus, John L. Sullivan, Elizabeth Theiss-Morse and Sandra L. Wood, *With Malice Towards Some: How People make Civil Liberties Judgements* (Cambridge: Cambridge University Press, 1995). For American findings that contrast the tolerance of elites and masses see the classic, Herbert McClosky and Alida Brill, *Dimensions of Tolerance: What Americans Believe about Civil Liberties* (New York, NY: Russell Sage, 1983). McClosky and Brill contrast the mass public with various elite groups, but not elected politicians as such.

6   Reisinger *et al.* also found MPs and executive officials in the FSU were about 31 per cent more favourable than their publics to a multi-party system both in 1992 and 1995 (30 per cent in Russia, 33 per cent in Ukraine). See Arthur H. Miller, William M. Reisinger and Vicki L. Hesli, 'Change in support for democracy and marketization among post-Soviet mass and elite, 1992–995', Paper to AAASS (American Association for the Advancement of Slavic Studies) 27th National Convention, Washington, DC, October 1995, Tables 1 and 2.

7   Miller, Hesli and Reisinger also found that 'both the Russian and Ukrainian elite as of mid-1992 were definitely more favourable towards ... democratic principles ... than was the general population ... but there was less distinction between the two [i.e. elites and publics] when nationality and ethnic interests are considered.' Arthur H. Miller, Vicki L. Hesli and William M. Reisinger, 'Comparing citizen and elite belief systems in post-Soviet Russia and Ukraine', *Public Opinion Quarterly*, vol.59 no.1 (1995) pp. 1–40 at p. 14. We have found that the post-Soviet MPs differed more on liberal values from their publics than the deputies who Miller, Hesli and Reisinger interviewed after the fall of the Soviet Union but who had all been elected when the Soviet Union was still in existence. And we have also found that members of the new Russian parliament elected in 1993 were less nationalist than their public, if only by a small amount. On their small sample, Miller, Hesli and Reisinger found that their quasi-Soviet Russian elites were slightly more nationalist than their public, not less.

12 A RED–BROWN ALLIANCE OF IDEAS?

1   Miller, Hesli and Reisinger adopt such an interpretation. See Arthur H. Miller, Vicki L. Hesli and William M. Reisinger, 'Comparing citizen and elite belief systems in post-Soviet Russia and Ukraine', *Public Opinion Quarterly*, vol.59 no.1 (1995) pp. 1–40 at p. 18. For a similar interpretation in our analysis of political culture in Britain, see William L. Miller, Annis May Timpson and Michael Lessnoff, *Political Culture in Contemporary Britain: People and Politicians, Principles and Practice* (Oxford: Oxford University Press, 1996) pp. 96–103.

2   Miller, Hesli and Reisinger also found that there 'was less constraint among attitudes regarding democracy than attitudes towards a market economy.' See Arthur H. Miller, Vicki L. Hesli and William M. Reisinger, 'Understanding democracy: a comparison of mass and elite in post-Soviet Russia and Ukraine', *Studies in Public Policy*, no.247 (Glasgow: Strathclyde University Centre for the Study of Public Policy, 1995) p. 30.

3   For the definition and interpretation of eigenvalues see Marija J. Norusis, *SPSS/PC+ Statistics 4.0* (Chicago, IL: SPSS, 1990).

4   In the political science literature, the concept of 'belief constraint' as an empirical equivalent of 'ideology' can be traced back to Philip E. Converse, 'The nature of belief systems in mass publics' in David E. Apter (ed.) *Ideology and Discontent* (Glencoe, IL: Free Press, 1964) pp. 206–61.

5   Norman Stone, *Europe Transformed* (Glasgow: Fontana, 1984) p. 147.

6   *Programma Kommunisticheskoi partii Sovetskogo Soyuza* (Moscow: Politizdat, 1986), p. 54. For a discussion on this point see Vladimir Shlapentokh, *The Public and Private Life of the Soviet People* (Oxford: Oxford University Press, 1989) p. 19.

7   Corresponding to agreement with the propositions that 'recent changes are turning us into a colony of the West'; and 'there are parts of neighbouring countries that really should belong to (our country).'

8   Sharp-eyed readers will detect an apparent – but not real – inconsistency in our findings here. It merits some attention. Here we find a *negative* correlation between socialist and cultural nationalist values in Ukraine. But in Chapter 6 we found west Ukrainians were more socialist than others; and in Chapter 7 we found that they were also more committed to cultural nationalism. That would suggest a *positive* correlation between socialist and cultural nationalist values in Ukraine. Looking ahead to Chapter 15, we will show that Ukrainian speakers were more committed (than Russian speakers in Ukraine) both to socialist values and to cultural nationalist values. Again that suggests a *positive* correlation between these values. Have we made a simple computing error? The answer is no. These suggestions are misleading. They are an interesting example of the 'ecological fallacy' long familiar to statisticians and first highlighted in the social sciences by W.S.Robinson, 'Ecological correlation and the behaviour of individuals' *American Sociological Review*, vol.15 (1950) pp. 351–71. For a recent non-technical account see William L. Miller, 'Quantitative methods' in David Marsh and Gerry Stoker (eds) *Theory and Methods in Political Science* (London: Macmillan, 1995) pp. 154–72 at pp. 155–6. In essence, correlations between aggregates – such as regions or language groups – frequently mislead. In this instance, there was indeed a strong *negative* correlation (−0.22) between socialism and cultural nationalism amongst Ukrainian speakers, and a similarly strong *negative* correlation (−0.20) amongst Russian speaking Ukrainians. Amongst Ukrainians as a whole the size of that negative correlation was halved (to −0.11), though not obliterated, because Ukrainian speakers were at once more socialist (correlation +0.18) and much more

culturally nationalist (correlation +0.43) than Russian speakers. So the difference between Ukrainian and Russian speakers partially, but only partially, obscured the strong negative relationship between socialism and cultural nationalism in Ukraine.

9   Ironically, communist doctrine towards politics in different national territories was expressed in the slogan 'national in form, socialist in content' which meant 'varied in form, but similar in content'.

10   These are two of the four theorems discussed by David Beetham in 'Four theorems about the market and democracy', *European Journal of Political Research*, vol.23, *Special issue on Capitalism, Socialism and Democracy Revisited* (1993) pp. 187–201, at p. 189 and p. 195 respectively.

11   See Miller, Timpson and Lessnoff (1996) pp. 100–101 and pp. 257–9 respectively.

12   Earlier, Times–Mirror surveys in 1991 had shown 'in every country in eastern Europe, a clear link between feelings about democracy and feelings about efforts to establish a market economy.' Los Angeles Times–Mirror *The Pulse of Europe: a Survey of Political and Social Values and Attitudes* (Los Angeles, CA: Times–Mirror, 1991) p. 7. Analysing 1994 surveys across nine countries in the FSU/ECE, Jerschina found correlations of 0.23 between 'nationalism' and 'economic statism', and correlations of 0.21 and 0.34 respectively between 'authoritarianism' on the one hand and 'nationalism' and 'economic statism' on the other. His 'authoritarianism' was not quite the inverse of our liberal values, nor were his 'nationalism' and 'economic statism' quite the equivalent of our nationalist and socialist values. Nonetheless, in general terms, his findings corroborate ours. See Jan Jerschina, 'Nationalism in nine central and east European countries' Paper to the ESRC (Economic and Social Research Council) Conference on 'Mass Response to the Transformation of Postcommunist Societies' St Antony's College, Oxford, March 1995, p. 30. Gibson found that 'attitudes towards the market and toward democracy are moderately correlated... but the interrelationship is not overwhelmingly strong.' James L. Gibson, 'Political and economic markets: connecting attitudes toward political democracy and a market economy within the mass culture of Russia and Ukraine' (*Journal of Politics*, forthcoming). In fact he found a rather stronger negative correlation than us between socialist and liberal values. Using two-stage least square estimates he also concluded that the correlation was due primarily to 'the primacy of political, not economic attitudes', that is, support for democracy had a greater influence upon support for market reforms than vice versa. Miller, Hesli and Reisinger found correlations between attitudes to democracy and the market economy that were similar in size to ours among FSU publics, but almost zero amongst FSU elites. However their 'elites' included bureaucrats as well as politicians and among the more politically minded sections of their elites they found correlations similar to ours. See Arthur H. Miller, Vicki L. Hesli and William M. Reisinger, 'Understanding democracy: a comparison of mass and elite in post-Soviet Russia and Ukraine', *Studies in Public Policy*, no.247 (Glasgow: Strathclyde University Centre for the Study of Public Policy, 1995) p. 27.

13   According to the conventional Kaiser criterion we should accept any factor with an eigenvalue of 1.0, that is one which explains as much common variance as a single variable which, pathologically, happens to be totally uncorrelated with all others in the analysis. That really is 'scraping the barrel' in the search for common factors.

14   Miller, Hesli and Reisinger state that their 'most surprising finding from [their] attitude consistency data... is the relatively low level of [belief] constraint among the elite compared to the most involved citizens.' See Arthur H. Miller, Vicki L. Hesli and William M. Reisinger, 'Comparing citizen and elite belief systems in

post-Soviet Russia and Ukraine', *Public Opinion Quarterly*, vol.59 no.1 (1995) pp. 1–40 at p. 22. Our factor analyses also suggest a surprising similarity between the levels of belief constraint amongst postcommunist MPs and their publics. But, particularly in the context of postcommunist politics across the FSU and ECE we are not entirely convinced that the level of belief constraint is a valid measure of political sophistication or capable of bearing quite the weight of theory placed upon it in the Western literature.

13 WINNERS AND LOSERS

1   This finding is corroborated by Gibson: 'democratic attitudes seem impervious – at least in the short term – to the failures of the Russian and Ukrainian economies.' James L. Gibson, 'A mile high but an inch deep: the structure of democratic commitments in the former USSR', *American Journal of Political Science*, vol.40 no.2 (1996) pp. 396–420 at p. 409. It is also corroborated by Evans and Whitefield who conclude 'there is very little link from economic experience to support for democracy.' See Geoffrey Evans and Stephen Whitefield, 'The politics of democratic commitment: support for democracy in transition societies', *British Journal of Political Science*, vol.25 no.4 (1995) pp. 485–514 at p. 485. Hahn found an erosion of support for democratic values in Yaroslavl between 1990 and 1993 but 'not much support for the argument that this erosion is a result of declining economic performance.' He interpreted the erosion as 'not a withering of support for democracy but a sign that the political euphoria of 1990 is wearing off.' See Jeffrey W. Hahn, 'Changes in contemporary Russian political culture' in Vladimir Tismaneau (ed.) *Political Culture and Civil Society in Russia and the New States of Eurasia* (Armonk, NY: M.E. Sharpe, 1995) pp. 112–36. But we have distinguished between the values of liberalism and popular control and, as we shall see later in this chapter, feelings about economic change did correlate with attitudes towards parties and elections. Only certain aspects of democracy were insulated from economic experience.

2   The Times–Mirror surveys claimed that 'how many rubles one earns says less about one's view of life than do income differences for Americans.' Los Angeles Times–Mirror, *The Pulse of Europe: a Survey of Political and Social Values and Attitudes* (Los Angeles, CA: Times–Mirror, 1991) p17. Our survey suggests that is true for liberal values, but not for socialist values, probably because the connection between education (which predisposes people towards liberal values) and income was stronger in the USA than in postcommunist countries, especially during the chaos of transition to a market economy.

3   On the basis of earlier surveys, Gibson concluded that support for democratic institutions and processes appears not to be contingent upon satisfaction with the performance of the economy in any simple way. See James L. Gibson, 'Political and economic markets: connecting attitudes toward political democracy and a market economy within the mass culture of Russia and Ukraine', *Journal of Politics* vol. 58 no.4 (1996) pp. 954–84 at p. 973. Our own findings are more complex: they suggest that while dissatisfaction with economic trends did not correlate strongly with liberal values, and correlated positively with populist values, it correlated negatively with commitment to elections and parties.

4   The communist regime had historically divided society into workers, peasants and intellectuals (or 'intelligentsia'). The same class schema as ours, with the same two additions of managers and businesspersons ('entrepreneurs') was used in Anthony

Heath, Geoffrey Evans and Ion Marginean, 'Social class and politics in eastern Europe' A paper to the Annual Conference of the PSA (Political Studies Association) Swansea, March 1994.

5   Jonathan Steele, 'Reform splitting Russian society', *Guardian*, 26 November 1992, p. 8; and Jonathan Steele, 'A market bereft of bargains', *Guardian*, 3 December 1992, p. 21.

6   See Richard Rose and Ellen Carnaghan, 'Generational effects on attitudes to communist regimes: a comparative analysis', *Post-Soviet Affairs*, vol.11 no.1 (1995) pp. 28–56.

7   Others have also noted the combination of political apathy and openness to the West (the opposite of one aspect of external nationalism at least) amongst the young. See Seamus Martin, 'Youth reacts to democracy with cynicism and apathy', *Herald*, 27 July 1992, p. 11; and Albert Motivans, 'Openness to the West', *Radio Liberty Research Report*, 27 November 1992. Commitment to parties usually does increase with age in established western democracies, which is usually attributed to the strengthening of party bonds over time. For an elegant analysis of this effect, using a long term panel survey, see David Butler and Donald Stokes, *Political Change in Britain: The Evolution of Electoral Choice* Second edition (London: Macmillan, 1974), Chapter 3 entitled 'The political life cycle', especially at p. 58. Although most parties in postcommunist countries were so new that the old could not have had much longer connections with them than the young, some, especially the communist successor parties, were not.

8   For an early statement of this thesis linking age and conservatism see Seymour Martin Lipset, *Political Man: The Social Bases of Politics*, Expanded edition (London: Heinemann, 1983) pp. 282–6, originally published in 1959. For a recent analysis see William L. Miller, Annis May Timpson and Michael Lessnoff, *Political Culture in Contemporary Britain: People and Politicians, Principles and Practice* (Oxford: Oxford University Press, 1996) pp. 240–4.

9   Similarly, after the transition from autocracy in Spain, Gunter found 'much to our surprise' that there was 'no significant cohort effect in which older Spaniards held less democratic attitudes than younger Spaniards.' Richard Gunter, 'The nature and consequences of democracy in the new southern Europe.' Paper to the ESRC (Economic and Social Research Council) Conference on 'Mass Response to the Transformation of Postcommunist Societies' St Antony's College, Oxford, March 1995, p. 5.

10 According to Hesli and Miller, women were 'desperately seeking to maintain the few advances they see themselves as having made within the structure of the Soviet state and they are realistically assessing the possibility of future deterioration in their economic, social and political position.' Vicki L. Hesli and Arthur H. Miller, 'The gender base of institutional support in Lithuania, Ukraine and Russia', *Europe-Asia Studies* vol.45 no.3 (1993) pp. 505–32 at p. 526. See also Chris Corrin, (ed.) *Superwomen and the Double Burden: Women's Experience of Change in Central and Eastern Europe and the Former Soviet Union* (London: Scarlet Press, 1992); Sue Bridger, Kathryn Pinnick and Rebecca Kay, *No More Heroines? Russia, Women and the Market* (London: Routledge, 1994); Nanette Funk and Magda Mueller (eds) *Gender, Politics and Post-Communism* (London: Routledge, 1993); Marilyn Rueschmeyer (ed.) *Women in the Politics of Postcommunist Eastern Europe* (Armonk, NY: M.E.Sharpe, 1994).

11 Times–Mirror surveys in 1991 reported a 'profound gender gap in attitudes to democracy and...a market economy...in every former communist country... women express more socialist values and less support for political freedom.' Los Angeles Times–Mirror *The Pulse of Europe: a Survey of Political and Social Values and Attitudes* (Los Angeles, CA: Times–Mirror, 1991) p. 13–14 . Our findings point

in the same direction on both counts, but the gender gap in our surveys was small, not 'profound'. Hesli and Miller also find 'women in general were more supportive of established political and social institutions and thus more opposed to current reforms' in Russia and Ukraine, but not in Lithuania. However the gender differences they found were seldom statistically significant and were sometimes inconsistent – operating in different directions in Russia and Ukraine. See Vicki L. Hesli and Arthur H. Miller, 'The gender base of institutional support in Lithuania, Ukraine and Russia' *Europe-Asia Studies*, vol.45 no.3 (1993) pp. 505–32 at p. 526. Their results are closer to our own.

14 ADAPTABLE MINDS

1   The Times–Mirror surveys also explicitly linked democratic values to intellectual flexibility: 'the young, better educated and those who lived in major cities express more approval of change and appear much more able to adjust to the new requirements.' Los Angeles Times–Mirror, *The Pulse of Europe: a Survey of Political and Social Values and Attitudes* (Los Angeles, CA: Times–Mirror, 1991) p. 9.

2   Reisinger, Miller, Hesli and Maher note that 'one cannot rule out the possibility that [the better educated and younger] show higher levels of pro-democratic values because they have reacted more strongly to the dominant intellectual current of their time.' William M. Reisinger, Arthur H. Miller, Vicki L. Hesli and Kristen Hill Maher, 'Political values in Russia, Ukraine and Lithuania: sources and implications for democracy', *British Journal of Political Science*, vol.24. no.2 (1994) pp. 183–223 at p. 221.

3   William L. Miller, Annis May Timpson and Michael Lessnoff, *Political Culture in Contemporary Britain: People and Politicians, Principles and Practice* (Oxford: Oxford University Press, 1996) pp. 215–16.

4   See Miller, Timpson and Lessnoff (1996) pp. 255–7.

5   Marc Raeff, 'The people, the intelligentsia, and Russian political culture', *Political Studies* vol.41 *Special Issue on 'The end of 'isms'?'* (1993) pp. 93–106 at p. 106.

6   There has been a lively debate between Finifter and Miller, Reisinger and Hesli in the *American Political Science Review* on the relationship between education and (in our terminology) socialist values. Finifter claims that the correlation between education and socialist values varied from country to country and from time to time; and, in particular, that it was positive in the USSR of 1989. Miller, Reisinger and Hesli claim that it was certainly negative in Russia, Ukraine and Lithuania throughout the period 1991 to 1995, and likely to have been so in 1989 as well. See Ada W. Finifter, 'Attitudes toward individual responsibility and political reform in the former Soviet Union', *American Political Science Review*, vol.90 no.1 (1996) pp. 138–52; and Arthur H. Miller, William M. Reisinger and Vicki L. Hesli, 'Understanding political change in post-Soviet societies: a further commentary on Finifter and Mickiewicz', *American Political Science Review*, vol.90 no.1 (1996) pp. 153–66. Our own findings in this chapter appear to support Miller, Reisinger and Hesli. Graduates were indeed less committed to socialist values than those with the least education. But we should warn that our multivariate analysis in Chapter 17 suggests that education had relatively little effect once age, class, sector and economic optimism were controlled. Brym's reanalysis of Finifter's and of Reisinger's data and of his own additional data confirms the conclusion that the effect of education was small once other influences were taken into account. See

Robert J. Brym, 'Re-evaluating mass support for political and economic change in Russia', *Europe-Asia Studies*, vol.48 no.5 (1996) pp. 751–66, Like Finifter we do not believe there is an inevitable conflict between education and socialist values, but we do believe that, for a variety of reasons, graduates in the FSU/ECE were more confident and better able to cope with fast moving change in the early 1990s.

7   This appears to contradict the finding of Times–Mirror surveys that '[although] in many societies, those who are better educated are more tolerant, that pattern does not hold in Russia or Ukraine.' Los Angeles Times–Mirror, *The Pulse of Europe: a Survey of Political and Social Values and Attitudes* (Los Angeles, CA: Times–Mirror, 1991) p. 228. Liberal values include much more than tolerance, however.

8   Interestingly, Gibson and Duch, in a Soviet study conducted in 1990, found that education contributed to general democratic values but not directly to political tolerance. See James L. Gibson and Raymond M. Duch, 'Political intolerance in the USSR: the etiology of mass opinion', *Comparative Political Studies*, vol.26 no.3 (1993) pp. 286–329.

9   Gorbachev himself had been baptised in the 1930s. More important, in April 1988 Gorbachev met with the Russian Orthodox Patriarch in the Kremlin. Under Gorbachev clergymen began to appear on television, they took their seats as deputies in the Soviets, and the millennium of the Russian Orthodox Church was widely celebrated – which produced somewhat bitter-sweet feelings amongst Ukrainians who regarded the church of 988 as Kyivan, not Muscovite. However, tolerance was at last extended to the Ukrainian 'Greek Catholic' (Uniate) Church. By any objective standard, Gorbachev was unquestionably good for believers in the FSU generally, and for those in Ukraine especially. See John Anderson, *Religion, State and Politics in the Soviet Union and Successor States* (Cambridge: Cambridge University Press, 1994)

10   For survey evidence see Miller, Timpson and Lessnoff (1996) pp. 244–51, especially at p. 246. The existence of so many specifically social charities organised by Christian religious groups is further evidence for this combination.

15 LAND, LANGUAGE, CULTURES AND NATIONALITY

1   For Stalin's answer to the question 'What is a nation?' see Iosif V. Stalin, *Sochineniya*, vol.2 (Moscow: Gosudarstvennoe izdatelstvo politicheskoi literatury, 1946) pp. 292–6; or more accessibly for English language readers, in Bruce Franklin (ed.) *The Essential Stalin: Major Theoretical Writings 1905–52* (London: Croom Helm, 1973) pp. 57–61.

2   Los Angeles Times–Mirror, *The Pulse of Europe: a Survey of Political and Social Values and Attitudes* (Los Angeles, CA: Times–Mirror, 1991) p. 140.

3   For an historical account of this century's great waves of 'nationalizing states' in east Europe see Rogers Brubaker, *Nationalism Reframed: Nationhood and the National Question in the New Europe* (Cambridge: Cambridge University Press, 1996).

4   Paul Robert Magocsi, *Historical Atlas of East Central Europe* (Seattle, WA: University of Washington Press, 1995) pp. 118–9.

5   Ibid. pp. 134–5.

6   Interwar Czechoslovakia was 22 per cent German, 16 per cent Slovak, 5 per cent Hungarian (Magyar), and 4 per cent Ukrainian, Russian or Rusyn. See Magocsi, *Historical Atlas of East Central Europe* (1995) pp. 130–3. One reason why the new state needed Slovakia was to dilute the German element by including more Slavs.

Without Slovakia, almost a third of the remaining population would have been German. There were other reasons: Masaryk, like Dubcek and Husak much later, but unlike Havel, was a Slovak.

7   Ibid. pp. 131,133, 135.

8   On our survey figures for freely chosen self-assigned 'nationality/ethnic group'. On language spoken at home, the figures would be slightly higher.

9   Again on our survey figures for freely chosen self- assigned 'nationality/ethnic group'. On language spoken at home, the figures would be slightly higher while, according to the official census of 1989, they would be slightly lower (82 per cent).

10   There are of course far more English speakers, or even English ethnics, outside England than inside it. But very few live in England's 'near abroad'. Despite the breadth of the Atlantic however, English attitudes to their cousins in America prior to the American War of Independence were somewhat similar to present day Russian attitudes towards their 'near abroad'.

11   For a discussion of nationalities policies under the old Soviet communist regime, see Zvi Gitelman, 'The nationalities' in Stephen White, Alex Pravda and Zvi Gitelman (eds) *Developments in Soviet Politics* (London: Macmillan, 1990) pp. 137–58.

12   For a review of disputes between Moscow and the various more or less autonomous 'subjects of the Russian Federation' – sometimes described as 'centre-periphery' disputes – see Leokadia Drobizheva, 'Processes of disintegration in the Russian Federation and the problems of Russians' in Vladimir Shlapentokh, Munir Sendich and Emil Payin (eds) *The New Russian Diaspora: Russian Minorities in the Former Soviet Republics* (Armonk, NY: Sharpe, 1994) pp. 45–55; David Triesman, 'The politics of intergovernmental transfers in post-Soviet Russia', *British Journal of Political Science*, vol.26 no.3 (1996) pp. 299–336; and Andrea Chandler, 'Center-periphery relations and the politics of taxation in Russia and Ukraine', Paper to AAASS (American Association for the Advancement of Slavic Studies) 27th National Convention, Washington, October 1995.

13   Official 1989 census figures reported the percentages with non-Russian nationality were 61 per cent in the Bashkortostan Republic, 39 per cent in the Mordovian, 57 per cent in the Tatarstan and 42 per cent in the Komi Republics.

14   Interestingly, voting patterns in these autonomous areas at the 1993 Duma election varied greatly from one area to another but, on average, did not differ greatly from the overall voting pattern in Russia as a whole. The most notable difference was greater than average support in these autonomous areas for the Communists and their Agrarian allies which is at least consistent with above average attachment to socialist values but probably reflected other influences as well.

15   Oblasts are political and administrative areas somewhere between a small English region and a large county in size. Since 1959, Ukraine, with a population about the same as Britain, has been divided into 25 Oblasts, subdivided in turn into 475 Rayons (Districts).

16   See Paul Robert, *Magocsi Ukraine: a Historical Atlas* (Toronto: University of Toronto Press, 1985) map 2.

17   Martin Gilbert, *The Dent Atlas of Russian History* 2nd edition (London: Dent, 1993) pp. 97–8.

18   Zbigniew Brzezinski, *Out of Control* (Oxford: Maxwell Macmillan, 1993) p. 158.

19   For a history of the concept of 'multiple identity' in Ukraine see Paul Robert Magocsi, 'The Ukrainian national revival: a new analytic framework', *Canadian Review of Studies in Nationalism*, vol.16 no.1–2 (1989) pp. 45–62 especially at pp. 57–8. The concept of simultaneously held multiple identities is, of course, very familiar in Scotland.

20 See question Q64I in Los Angeles Times–Mirror, *The Pulse of Europe: a Survey of Political and Social Values and Attitudes* (Los Angeles, CA: Times–Mirror, 1991).

21 Evgenii Golovakha, Natalia Panina and Nikolai Churilov 'Russians in Ukraine' in Vladimir Shlapentokh, Munir Sendich and Emil Payin (eds) *The New Russian Diaspora: Russian Minorities in the Former Soviet Republics* (Armonk, NY: Sharpe, 1994) pp. 59–71 at p. 69.

22 Nikolay Churilov and Tatyana Koshechkina, 'Public attitudes in Ukraine' in Richard Smoke (ed.) *Perceptions of Security: Public Opinion and Expert Assessments in Europe's New Democracies* (Manchester: Manchester University Press, 1996) pp. 189–208 at p. 195.

23 Churilov and Koshechkina (1996) pp. 189–208 at p. 194.

24 Vicki L. Hesli, 'Public support for devolution of power in Ukraine: regional patterns', *Europe-Asia Studies*, vol.47 no.1 (1995) pp. 91–121 at p. 95 and p. 113 respectively. On the question of imposing the Ukrainian language see also Paul Kolstoe, *Russians in the Former Soviet Republics* (London: Hurst, 1995) pp. 180–4.

25 Emil Payin, 'The disintegration of the empire and the fate of the "imperial minority"' in Vladimir Shlapentokh, Munir Sendich and Emil Payin (eds) *The New Russian Diaspora: Russian Minorities in the Former Soviet Republics* (Armonk, NY: Sharpe, 1994) pp. 21–36 at p. 24.

26 In Ukraine, both our Ukrainian and Russian language questionnaires used the word 'natsionalnosti'.

27 The class and educational profile of these three groups is interesting. In our survey, 25 per cent of ethno-linguistic Russians and 22 per cent of Russian speaking Ukrainians, but only 10 per cent of ethno-linguistic Ukrainians had received higher education. The parents of 28 per cent of Russians and 21 per cent of Russian speaking Ukrainians, but only 9 per cent of Ukrainians had been intellectuals or managers. Conversely the parents of only 22 per cent of Russians and 15 per cent of Russian speaking Ukrainians, but fully 52 per cent of Ukrainians had been farm workers or village people. See Bill Miller, Stephen White, Paul Heywood and Matthew Wyman, 'Language versus nationality in the politics of Ukraine' ESRC/Glasgow University Press Release, 9th February 1994, p. 2.

28 Miller, White, Heywood and Wyman, 'Language versus nationality in the politics of Ukraine', p. 3.

29 Ibid., p. 4.

30 For a survey specifically designed to study the interaction of land with ethno-linguistic divisions, i.e., the varying polarisation between ethnic Russians and Ukrainians in different parts of Ukraine see Ian Bremmer, 'The politics of ethnicity: Russians in the new Ukraine', *Europe-Asia Studies*, vol.46 no.2 (1994) pp. 261–83. That study interviewed people in just three locations: 800 in Kyiv, 800 in Lviv, and 500 in Simferopol. Bremmer's main finding is that 'regional differences matter' with 'low ethnic schism' between Ukrainians and Russians in Kyiv, more in Lviv and much more in Simferopol. (p. 281) Since there were no interviews in east Ukraine where most ethnic Russians are concentrated, Bremmer is unable to contrast the situation in east and west Ukraine.

31 Bremmer also found division over language issues greater in the west (Lviv) than elsewhere. See Bremmer (1994) p. 277.

32 Notably Bulgaria in 917, Serbia in 1217, and Russia in 1448 (asserted) or 1589 (recognised). See Paul Robert Magocsi, *Historical Atlas of East Central Europe* (Seattle, CA: University of Washington Press, 1995) pp. 44–5.

33 Seamus Martin, 'Unchristian struggle for hearts and souls of the faithful', *Herald*, 12 October 1992 p. 11.

34   Catholics were grudgingly tolerated in the Tsar's western Polish lands. But the Tsars discouraged Latin-rite Catholics in Ukraine and suppressed the Uniates ('Greek-rite' Catholics). The Uniate metropolitanate of Kyiv was abolished in 1796, and the last Uniate eparchy in the Russian Empire was abolished in 1875. See Paul Robert Magocsi, *Historical Atlas of East Central Europe* (Seattle, WA: University of Washington Press, 1995) p. 113. Stalin was not very sympathetic to any religion, but more to the Russian orthodox than to the Uniates or Catholics.

35   Nikolay Churilov and Tatyana Koshechkina, 'Public attitudes in Ukraine', in Richard Smoke (ed.) *Perceptions of Security: Public Opinion and Expert Assessments in Europe's New Democracies* (Manchester: Manchester University Press, 1996) pp. 189–208 at p,193.

36   Neil Martin, *Russians Beyond Russia: The Politics of National Identity* (London: Royal Institute of International Affairs, 1995) Chapter 5 entitled 'Russians, regionalism and ethnicity in Ukraine' pp. 78–99 at p. 99. By the time of the quinquennial independence celebrations in August 1996 the independence of Ukraine looked even more assured, but five years is not a long time in history.

37   Churilov and Koshechkina (1996) pp. 189–208 at p. 201. For a discussion of the internal and external challenges to Ukraine's territorial integrity see Roman Solchanyk, 'The politics of state building: centre-periphery relations in post-Soviet Ukraine', *Europe-Asia Studies*, vol.46 no.1 (1994) pp. 47–68; and Stephen R. Burant, 'International relations in a regional context: Poland and its eastern neighbours – Lithuania, Belarus and Ukraine', *Europe-Asia Studies*, vol.45 no.3 (1995) pp. 395–418.

38   Vicki L. Hesli and Joel D. Barkan, 'The centre-periphery debate: pressures for devolution within the republics' in Arthur H. Miller, William M. Reisinger and Vicki L. Hesli, *Public Opinion and Regime Change: The New Politics of Post Soviet Societies* (Boulder, CO: Westview, 1993) pp. 124–52 at p. 133.

39   Andrew Wilson, 'Ukrainians sleepwalk towards a chaotic independence' *Scotsman*, 25 November 1991, p. 6. The referendum on independence took place on 1 December 1991. However that referendum simply ratified the declaration of 24 August 1991, supported by an overwhelming vote of the Ukrainian Supreme Soviet in the aftermath of the Moscow coup, declaring Ukraine independent as well as sovereign and no longer subject to Soviet law. In 1996, Ukraine celebrated its first five years of independence on 24th August, not in December. Ironically, Poland 'the first nation to recognise Ukraine's independence [did so] one day after the referendum of December 1st 1991.' See Roman Szporluk, 'After empire: what?' *Daedalus: Journal of the American Academy of Arts and Sciences*, vol.123 no.3 (1994) pp. 21–39 at p. 33. For an account of the events surrounding Ukraine's seizure of independence in 1991 see Taras Kuzio and Andrew Wilson (eds) *Ukraine: Perestroika to Independence* (London: Macmillan, 1994).

40   Francis Fukuyama, 'States can break up, democracies can grow up', *International Herald Tribune*, 10 February 1992. It is also consistent with the earlier findings of Hesli and Barkan that, in 1990, support for republican independence in both Russia and eastern Ukraine was motivated primarily by 'alienation from the centre', in this case the CPSU Central Committee more than anything else. This same motivation was also important in west Ukraine, but so also was nationalist sentiment in that area. Vicki L. Hesli and Joel D. Barkan, 'The centre-periphery debate: pressures for devolution within the republics' in Arthur H. Miller, William M. Reisinger and Vicki L. Hesli, *Public Opinion and Regime Change: The New Politics of Post Soviet Societies* (Boulder, CO: Westview, 1993) pp. 124–52 at p. 141. Breuilly speculates – inevitably without survey evidence – that fifty years

earlier, in the 1940s, it was 'negative hatred for [the centralised Stalinist] system rather than well developed national feeling' that prompted Ukrainians to take up arms against the USSR. See John Breuilly, *Nationalism and the State*, 2nd edition (Manchester: Manchester University Press, 1993) p. 348. Breuilly is, of course, notoriously reluctant to accept a nationalist interpretation of events.

41 Churilov and Koshechkina (1996) pp. 189–208 at p,195.
42 For the actual levels of support in the Ukraine referendums on the Union (17 March 1991), on Sovereignty (also 17 March 1991) and on Independence (1 December 1991), within different regions of Ukraine, see Henry E. Brady and Cynthia S. Kaplan, 'Eastern Europe and the former Soviet Union' in David Butler and Austin Ranney (eds) *Referendums Around the World: The Growing Use of Direct Democracy* (London: Macmillan, 1994) pp. 174–217 at p. 200.
43 A point made in 1992 by Fukuyama (1992), and still true at the time of writing.
44 Informed estimates usually put gypsies at 5 per cent in Hungary. See Paul Robert Magocsi, *Historical Atlas of East Central Europe* (Seattle, WA: University of Washington Press, 1995) p. 135. There are problems in sampling gypsies and, in addition, a tendency for some people who appear, to interviewers, to be gypsies, to describe themselves simply as Hungarian. We use self descriptions, not interviewer ascriptions.
45 Rudolf Schlesinger, *Federalism in Central and Eastern Europe* (London: Kegan Paul, Trench and Trubner, 1945) at p. 299.
46 Jan Kremar, 'Leader demands oath of loyalty to new Slovakia', *Herald*, 2 January 1993, p. 5.
47 Jonathan Eyal, 'Hungarians abroad fear their hosts' long- term wrath', *Guardian*, 13 June 1992, p. 10.
48 Our findings on the cultural nationalism of the majority Slovak population are hardly consistent with the claim of Whitefield and Evans that 'Slovaks are not more nationalist or ethnically illiberal than Czechs.' Stephen Whitefield and Geoffrey Evans, 'Explaining the breakup of Czechoslovakia: the role of mass ideology and elite strategy.' Paper to the ESRC (Economic and Social Research Council) Conference on 'Mass Response to the Transformation of Postcommunist Societies' St Antony's College, Oxford, March 1995 (*Political Studies*, forthcoming) p. 1. Only the extreme opposition of the minority Hungarians to cultural uniformity brings our overall figures (in Chapter 7) for culturally conformist nationalism in Slovakia down close to those for the Czech Republic.
49 A.J.P. Taylor, *The Hapsburg Monarchy 1809–1918* (London: Penguin 1964) p. 288.
50 T.G. Masaryk, *The New Europe* (London, 1918).
51 Masaryk (1918) p. 53, quoted in J.W.Bruegel, *Czechoslovakia before Munich* (Cambridge: Cambridge University Press, 1973) p. 17.
52 Geoffrey Parker, *Europe in Crisis 1598–1648* (Glasgow: Fontana, 1984) p. 177.
53 The same could not be said for Bosnia in ECE nor for Northern Ireland in western Europe.

16 POLITICAL IDENTIFICATIONS

1 The classic studies by the Michigan University team are Warren E. Miller, Angus Campbell and Gerald Gurin, *The Voter Decides* (Evanston, IL: Row, Paterson, 1954); Angus Campbell, Philip E. Converse, Warren E. Miller and Donald E. Stokes, *The American Voter* (New York, NY: Wiley, 1960); and Angus Campbell,

Philip E. Converse, Warren E. Miller and Donald E. Stokes, *Elections and the Political Order* (New York, NY: Wiley, 1966).

2 Warren E. Miller, 'The cross-national use of party identification as a stimulus to political inquiry' in Ian Budge, Ivor Crewe and Dennis Farlie (eds) *Party Identification and Beyond* (London: Wiley, 1976) pp. 21–31 at p. 22.

3 See William L. Miller, Annis May Timpson and Michael Lessnoff, *Political Culture in Contemporary Britain: People and Politicians, Principles and Practice* (Oxford: Oxford University Press, 1996) pp. 295–320.

4 Jan Ake Dellenbrant, 'Parties and party systems in Eastern Europe' in Stephen White, Judy Batt and Paul G. Lewis (eds) *Developments in East European Politics* (London: Macmillan, 1993) pp. 147–162 at pp. 151–2.

5 Ester, Halman and Rukavishnikov also found remarkably large numbers in Russia who hesitated to place themselves on a left right scale, though the problem was less severe in ECE. See Peter Ester, Loek Halman and Vladimir Rukavishnikov, 'The western world values pattern viewed cross-nationally: a comparison of findings of the European and North American value study with recent Russian data.' A paper to the symposium 'Values and Work – a Comparative perspective' Tilburg University, November 1994, p. 22.

6 Our findings on ECE/FSU differences in the familiarity and acceptability of the terms 'left' and 'right' amongst the general public are also consistent with those of Hofrichter and Weller. See Jurgen Hofrichter and Inge Weller, 'On the application of the left-right schema in central and eastern Eurobarometer surveys'. Report to the Eurobarometer Unit, DG 10, European Community April 1993, p. 5. Eurobarometer surveys do not cover MPs however.

7 Hofrichter and Weller found that the correlation between left/right self placement and opposition to a free market economy in 1992 was 0.34 in Czechoslovakia but only 0.16 in Russia and not significantly different from zero in either Ukraine or Hungary – which, although based on a single question rather than on an index of socialist values, is nonetheless remarkably consistent with our own findings. See Hofrichter and Weller (1993) p. 19.

8 There was clearly an unusually strong trend against acceptance of a right-wing ideological label in Hungary. Hofrichter and Weller found that, amongst the general public, 33 per cent of Hungarians described themselves as on the right in 1990, but only 13 per cent in 1991 and 7 per cent in 1992. Amongst those intending to vote for the governing Hungarian Democratic Forum, 58 per cent placed themselves on the right in 1990, but only 25 per cent in 1991 and 18 per cent in 1992. See Hofrichter and Weller (1993) p. 11 and p. 16 respectively.

9 An earlier survey, restricted to Russia, also found that CPSU 'party members were a cross-section of their society in the late communist period' though current members were more distinctive. See Stephen White and Ian McAllister, 'The CPSU and its members: between communism and postcommunism', *British Journal of Political Science*, vol.26 no.1 (1996) pp. 105–22 at p. 122.

10 For another study of former Communist Party members see Richard Rose, 'Ex-Communists in postcommunist societies', *Political Quarterly*, vol.67 no.1 (1996) pp. 14–25.

11 LDP stands for the 'Liberal Democratic Party', but the name is misleading and best not used. The views expressed by its leader, Vladimir Zhirinovsky were neither liberal nor democratic in tone; and it had so few members that its claim to be a 'party' was also suspect.

17 A MULTIVARIATE MODEL

1   At the time of our survey, its leader Yegor Gaidar had already been replaced as prime minister by technocrat Viktor Chernomyrdin and Gaidar was no longer in the government. Later, but not in 1993, Gaidar and his party became stern critics of Yeltsin's government.

2   See also Robert D. Grey, William L. Miller, Stephen White and Paul Heywood, 'The structure of Russian political opinion', *Coexistence*, vol.32 no.3 (1995) pp. 183–215 at p. 200.

3   See Richard B. Dobson, *Russian Public Opinion and the 1996 Presidential Election: Views from Four Russian Towns* (Washington, DC: United States Information Agency, April 1996) pp. 15–16; and Richard B. Dobson, *Russians Choose a President: Results of Focus Group Discussions* (Washington, DC: United States Information Agency, June 1996) pp. 17–18.

4   For a review of the development of parties in Ukraine see Andrew Wilson and Artur Bilous, 'Political parties in Ukraine', *Europe-Asia Studies*, vol.45 no.4 (1993) pp. 693–704; Taras Kuzio, 'The 1994 parliamentary elections in Ukraine', *Journal of Communist Studies and Transition Politics*, vol.11 no.4 (1995) pp. 335–61; and Andrew Wilson, 'Parties and presidents in Ukraine and Crimea, 1994', *Journal of Communist Studies and Transition Politics*, vol.11 no.4 (1995) pp. 362–71. After the Communist Party in Ukraine was banned following the 1991 Moscow coup, communist sympathisers formed the Socialist Party, but some left when the Communist Party was legalised again on 5 October 1993. Technically the old communist party was not re-legalised in 1993 but permission was granted for communist sympathisers to found a new communist party. It promptly began numbering its congresses in sequence from the last congress of the old Communist Party of Ukraine. Nothing, of course, could be quite the same after 1991, however permissive the law.

5   Barnabas Racz, 'The socialist-left opposition in post-communist Hungary', *Europe–Asia Studies*, vol.45 no.4 (1993) pp. 647–70 at p. 660.

6   Evans and Whitefield have also noted 'the absence of ideological distinctions between the supporters of the two liberal parties [the Free Democrats and Young Democrats]' and 'a similar absence of social bases except for a very strong age effect in that, not surprisingly, Young Democrats attract younger supporters.' See Geoffrey Evans and Stephen Whitefield, 'Social and ideological cleavage formation in postcommunist Hungary', *Europe–Asia Studies*, vol.47 no.7 (1995) pp. 1177–204 at p. 1192.

7   Jan Ake Dellenbrant, 'Parties and party systems in Eastern Europe' in Stephen White, Judy Batt and Paul G. Lewis (eds) *Developments in East European Politics* (London: Macmillan, 1993) pp. 147–62 at p. 156.

8   Coexistence was the largest of the Hungarian minority parties. It had originally aimed to unite the Hungarian, Polish and Ukrainian minorities in Slovakia. See Dellenbrant (1993) pp. 147–62 at p. 157.

9   Our findings are broadly consistent with those of Whitefield and Evans who claim that Slovak politics is based on attitudes to human rights, especially Hungarian minority rights; while Czech politics is based on issues of economic distribution. See Stephen Whitefield and Geoffrey Evans, 'Explaining the breakup of Czechoslovakia: the role of mass ideology and elite strategy.' Paper to the ESRC (Economic and Social Research Council) Conference on 'Mass Response to the Transformation of Postcommunist Societies' St Antony's College, Oxford, March 1995 (*Political Studies*, forthcoming).

10   Evans and Whitefield's analysis of the purely social bases of party support, neglecting the influence of political values, also concluded that 'levels of cleavage structuration are surprisingly high.' See Geoffrey Evans and Stephen Whitefield, 'The social bases of electoral competition in eastern Europe'. A paper to the European Science Foundation Conference on 'Transition and political power', Cambridge, April 1996, p. 2.

11   Korosenyi discusses the 'revival' thesis in detail, as applied to Hungary. See Andeas Korosenyi, 'Revival of the past or a new beginning? The nature of postcommunist politics' in Andreas Bozoki, Andras Korosenyi and George Schopflin (eds) *Post-communist Transition: Emerging Pluralism in Hungary* (London: Pinter, 1992) pp. 111–31 especially at pp. 121–7. There are clearly some interesting correlations between voting patterns in the 1990s and the 1940s, though not all of them involve self-conscious 'revival' parties: for example, Korosenyi draws attention to the correlation between support for the Alliance of Free Democrats in 1990 and the Social Democratic Party in 1947. (p. 125) He also notes 'the first striking feature of the electoral results was the dominance of the *new parties*' [his emphasis] (p. 115), not the self-conscious 'revival' parties which together gained only 22 per cent (p. 121). But like us, he also emphasised the element of continuity provided by communist successor parties, and especially 'the signs of historical continuity on the *issue and ideological* levels.' [his emphasis] (p. 122). Evans and Whitefield quote Szelenyi and Szelenyi's claim that after an interruption of 'forty' [sic!] years, the old political divisions in Hungary had simply resurfaced. But they too had to found the claim of continuity more on 'long-standing Hungarian issues' rather than revived pre-communist parties, and they provided no evidence to suggest that value conflicts, as distinct from party conflicts, were interrupted for 'forty' – or fifty – years. See Geoffrey Evans and Stephen Whitefield, 'Social and ideological cleavage formation in postcommunist Hungary', *Europe–Asia Studies*, vol.47 no.7 (1995) pp. 1177–204 at pp. 1179–80. Similarly, in his study of continuity and change in the new Czech Republic, Klima divided parties into the 'traditional – prohibited during socialism', 'traditional – allowed during socialism', and the 'new'. See Michal Klima, 'The emergence of the Czech party system'. Paper to the conference 'Party Politics in the Year 2000', Manchester, January 1995. Again, he notes 'in terms of [voting] percentages, the new political parties are by far the most significant' (p. 6) while in terms of party membership the Communist Party predominated. He found interesting correlations between the location of Catholic party (KDU-CSL) support in the 1990s and the 1930s but its share of votes in the 1990s was minimal, though its share of party members was more substantial.

18   INTRA-ELECTION TRENDS: VALUE STABILITY DURING A CRISIS ELECTION

1   For evidence of this in a western democracy see William L. Miller, Harold D. Clarke, Martin Harrop, Lawrence LeDuc and Paul F. Whiteley, *How Voters Change: The 1987 British Election Campaign in Perspective* (Oxford: Oxford University Press, 1990) p. 274.

2   For a very clear example of the stability of political values coupled with the instability of economic perceptions and party preferences during an election year see William L. Miller, Annis May Timpson and Michael Lessnoff, *Political Culture in Contemporary Britain: People and Politicians, Principles and Practice* (Oxford: Oxford University Press, 1996) pp. 113–17.

3   For indications that the turnout may have been less than the 50 per cent of the electorate necessary to validate the constitution see for instance *Konstitutsionnyi vestnik*, 1994, no. 17, p. 32, and *Moskovskii komsomolets*, 11 January 1994, p. 1. More accessibly, see also Wendy Slater, 'Russia's plebiscite on a new constitution', *Radio Liberty Research Report*, 21 January 1994; and Vera Tolz and Julia Wishnevsky, 'Election queries make Russians doubt democratic process', *Radio Liberty Research Report*, 1 April 1994.

4   Powerfully and elegantly stated by Vladimir Shlapentokh, 'The 1993 Russian election polls', *Public Opinion Quarterly*, vol.58 no.4 (1994) pp. 579–602; but rebutted in our own paper, William L. Miller, Stephen White and Paul Heywood, 'Measuring and interpreting the trends in public opinion during the 1993 Russian election campaign', *Public Opinion Quarterly*, vol.60 no.1 (1996) pp. 106–27, which also contains an expanded version of some of the analysis and interpretation presented in this chapter. See also Matthew Wyman, Bill Miller, Stephen White and Paul Heywood, 'The Russian elections of December 1993', *Electoral Studies*, vol.13 no.3 (1994) pp. 254–71; Matthew Wyman, Stephen White, Bill Miller and Paul Heywood, 'Public opinion, parties and voters in the December 1993 Russian election', *Europe–Asia Studies*, vol.47 no.4 (1995) pp. 591–614; and Bill Miller, Stephen White, Paul Heywood and Matthew Wyman, 'Zhirinovsky's voters', ESRC/Glasgow University Press Release, 16 February 1994.

5   A detailed account of Russian elections from 1922 to 1996 is given in Stephen White, Richard Rose and Ian McAllister, *How Russia Votes* (Chatham, NJ: Chatham House, 1997). At pp. 119–20 it lists some of the more inaccurate polls that appeared in the Russian press in the weeks before the 1993 election. For other lists of polling inaccuracies see Stephen White, 'Public opinion and political science in postcommunist Russia', *European Journal of Political Research*, vol.27 no.4 (1995) pp. 507–26; and A.V.Dmitriev and Zh.T.Toshchenko, 'Sotsiologicheskii opros i politika', *Sotsiologicheskie issledovaniya*, no.5 (1994) pp. 42–51.

6   Jonathan Steele, 'The election will be just the start of a series of battles.' *The Guardian*, 11 December 1993, p. 14.

7   See William L. Miller, Stephen White and Paul Heywood, 'Measuring and interpreting the trends in public opinion during the 1993 Russian election campaign', *Public Opinion Quarterly*, vol.60 no.1 (1996) pp. 106–27.

8   An opinion poll in *Nezavisimaya gazeta* (18 December 1993) of LDP members suggested that 60 per cent of them would be willing to use force in the near abroad 'if need be.' But members of the party constituted an infinitesimal fraction of its vote in the election. See Vera Tolz, 'Russia's parliamentary elections: what happened and why', *Radio Liberty Research Report*, 14 January 1994, p. 7. Similarly, our own survey of the LDP MPs elected at the 1993 election showed that 53 per cent were willing to threaten to use force in the near abroad if the interests of the Russian diaspora were endangered. But their voters were not nearly so aggressively nationalist.

9   David Hearst, 'TV played key role for Yeltsin', *The Guardian*, 8 December 1993, p11.

10   Jonathan Steele and David Hearst, 'Yeltsin snatches victory', *The Guardian*, 13 December 1993, p. 1.

11   We showed in Chapter 16 that the LDP MPs elected in 1993 were 70 per cent more nationalist than Russia's Choice MPs, although the LDP voters who elected them were only 30 per cent more nationalist than Russia's Choice voters.

19   INTER-ELECTION TRENDS 1993-96

1   Our own survey at the end of 1993 was one of the first to predict the victory of the Hungarian Socialist Party which had sunk to fourth place with only 11 per cent of the vote at the 1990 election. It not only put the HSP in top place but noted the general acceptability of the HSP and concluded there was 'no basis in public opinion for a grand coalition designed specifically to exclude the Socialists from government after the forthcoming election.' See Bill Miller, Stephen White, Paul Heywood and Matthew Wyman, 'Ex-communists may win Hungarian election', ESRC/Glasgow University Press Release, 15 January 1994, p. 3. For discussions of the actual result see Barnabas Racz and Istvan Kukorelli, 'The "second generation" postcommunist elections in Hungary in 1994', *Europe–Asia Studies*, vol.47 no.2 (1995) pp. 251–80; Erzsebet Soltesz, 'Democracies in eastern Europe: Hungary, Poland and Slovakia'. A paper for the 16th World Congress of IPSA (International Political Science Association) Berlin, August 1994.

2   Though both Kuchma and Kravchuk had been Communist Party officials, and it was Kravchuk who had been in the central party apparatus. See Taras Kuzio, 'Kravchuk to Kuchma: The Ukrainian presidential elections of 1994', *Journal of Communist Studies and Transition Politics*, vol.12 no.2 (1996) pp. 117–44; and Taras Kuzio, 'The 1994 parliamentary elections in Ukraine', *Journal of Communist Studies and Transition Politics*, vol.11 no.4 (1995) pp. 335–61; Taras Kuzio, 'The 1994 parliamentary elections in Ukraine', *Journal of Communist Studies and Transition Politics*, vol.11 no.4 (1995) pp. 335–61; Marko Bojcun, 'The Ukrainian parliamentary elections in March–April 1994', *Europe–Asia Studies*, vol.47 no.2 (1995) pp. 229–50; Andrew Wilson, 'Parties and presidents in Ukraine and Crimea, 1994', *Journal of Communist Studies and Transition Politics*, vol.11 no.4 (1995) pp. 362–71; Sarah Birch, 'The Ukrainian repeat elections of 1995', *Electoral Studies*, vol.15 (1996) pp. 281–2.

3   See William L. Miller, Annis May Timpson and Michael Lessnoff, *Political Culture in Contemporary Britain: People and Politicians, Principles and Practice* (Oxford: Oxford University Press, 1996) p. 115.

4   Using a different question about the 'market economy', defined prejudicially as 'largely free from state control', the EU's Eurobarometer surveys found much more opposition to a market economy in Russia. They also found a somewhat greater trend against the market economy than we do in 1993–95, though they show the sharpest swing against the market economy took place before 1993, in 1990–93, rather than after 1993. Paradoxically they also show that, on balance, Russians criticised the pace of economic reform for being too slow, not too fast. See *Central and Eastern Eurobarometer 6* (Brussels: European Union, 1996) Text figure 15, and Annex figures 4 and 5.

5   Based on a slightly different question, Rose reports similar findings to ours on attitudes to the use of military force in the near abroad. See Richard Rose, 'New Russia Barometer V: Between two elections.' *Studies in Public Policy*, no.260 (Glasgow: Centre for the Study of Public Policy, 1996).

6   Our finding appears to conflict with the trends in VTsIOM surveys reported by Rose and Tikhomirov. They found a 14 per cent increase in the numbers supporting parliament's right to exercise a veto over Presidential action, though only a 3 per cent increase in the numbers who opposed the President's right to suspend parliament and rule by decree. Richard Rose and Evgeny Tikhomirov, 'Trends in the New Russia Barometer, 1992–1995.' *Studies in Public Policy*, no.256 (Glasgow: Centre for the Study of Public Policy, 1995) p. 23. But Rose and

Tikhomirov compared VTsIOM surveys in June/July 1993 – before the suspension of the old parliament – with others in March/April 1995. Their 1993 survey inevitably referred to the old parliament, technically the Congress of People's Deputies of the Russian Republic elected in 1990 under the old communist regime, which was very unpopular by the summer of 1993. Given the nature of their comparison – between a particularly fractious and obstructive communist-era parliament and a postcommunist one, the reported increase in support for parliamentary veto powers is surprisingly small. Our own questions focused on the new and, initially, much more popular parliament elected in December 1993.

7 See Gabriel A. Almond and Sidney Verba, *The Civic Culture: Political Attitudes and Democracy in Five Nations* (Princeton, NJ: Princeton University Press, 1963; London: Sage, 1989) Chapter 7 entitled 'Citizen competence and subject competence.'

8 Comparing Russian surveys in the summers of 1993 and 1995, rather than at election times, Whitefield and Evans also found a very sharp increase in the numbers who considered themselves 'supporters' of a political party. Since their surveys took place in the 'mid-term' rather than at election time, the numbers of party supporters in both their surveys were much lower than in our December 1993 and January 1996 surveys, but the trend was similar. See Stephen Whitefield and Geoffrey Evans, 'Support for democracy and political opposition in Russia, 1993 and 1995'. A paper to the Annual Conference of the PSA (Political Studies Association) Glasgow, April 1996.

9 Similar drops in support for multi-party competition between 1992 and early 1995 were reported by Arthur H. Miller, William M. Reisinger and Vicki L. Hesli, 'Change in support for democracy and marketisation among post-Soviet mass and elite 1992–95'. Paper to AAASS (American Association for the Advancement of Slavic Studies) 27th National Convention, Washington, DC, October 1995; and between mid-1993 and mid-1995 in Whitefield and Evans (1996). In 1995 VTsIOM reported that Russians felt that freedom of speech, freedom to emigrate, free enterprise and closer ties with the West had, on balance, done more good than harm; but that the collapse of the Soviet Union, the right to strike – and multi-party elections – had, on balance, done more harm than good! See *Ekonomicheskie i sotsialnye peremeny: monitoring obshchestvennogo mneniya* (1995) no.1 (January–February) p. 10.

10 With only three broad age bands and an elapse of only two years between the two parliamentary elections, our age bands are effectively age cohorts.

11 According to Shub, Yeltsin's comeback was 'helped by Kremlin control of the state TV networks, substantial campaign expenditures, and support from the West and from Russia's neighbors in the Commonwealth of Independent States.' See Anatole Shub, 'Political continuities overshadow Yeltsin comeback in Russian election', USIA (United States Information Agency) Opinion Analysis, 19 July 1996, p. 1. More forthrightly, Eyal claimed 'Yeltsin systematically broke every law governing the conduct of the elections . . . . often employing tricks reminiscent of old Soviet times.' See Jonathan Eyal, 'Confident Yeltsin looks to new term', *Scotsman*, 5 August 1996, p. 9.

20   POSTCOMMUNIST VALUES IN A WESTERN PERPECTIVE

1 For an ambitious attempt to compare values in east and west at an earlier stage in the transition from communism see the Los Angeles Times–Mirror, *The Pulse of*

Europe: a Survey of Political and Social Values and Attitudes (Los Angeles, CA: Times–Mirror, 1991) and the 17 September 1991 Special Edition of the Times–Mirror. Other, similar cross-national studies include the 1991–92 World Values Survey reported in Paul R. Abramson and Ronald Inglehart, 'The structure of values on five continents'. Paper to IPSA (International Political Science Association) 16th World Congress, Berlin, August 1994. All of these stem from an intellectual tradition founded by Almond and Verba in Gabriel A. Almond and Sidney Verba, *The Civic Culture: Political Attitudes and Democracy in Five Countries*, (Princeton NJ: Princeton University Press 1963; New paperback edition, London: Sage, 1989).

2   The British study interviewed 2060 members of the public and 1244 senior politicians – leaders of party groups on local government councils throughout Britain. See William L. Miller, Annis May Timpson and Michael Lessnoff, *Political Culture in Contemporary Britain: People and Politicians, Principles and Practice* (Oxford: Oxford University Press, 1996) for a full description of these surveys. A more introductory and thematic account of these surveys is given in William L. Miller (ed.) *Alternatives to Freedom: Arguments and Opinions* (London: Longman, 1995).

3   See Herbert McClosky and Alida Brill, *Dimensions of Tolerance: What Americans Believe about Civil Liberties* (New York, NY: Russell Sage Foundation, 1983); or, much earlier, Herbert McClosky, 'Consensus and Ideology in American Politics', *American Political Science Review*, vol.58 no.2 (1964) pp. 361–82.

4   For a recent account of the 1987 Canadian Charter Study Survey see Paul M. Sniderman, Joseph F. Fletcher, Peter H. Russell and Philip E. Tetlock, *The Clash of Rights: Liberty, Equality and Legitimacy in Pluralist Democracy* (New Haven, CT: Yale University Press, 1996).

5   See David P. Conradt, 'Changing German Political Culture' in Gabriel A. Almond and Sidney Verba (eds) *The Civic Culture Revisited* (Boston, MA: Little, Brown, 1980) pp. 212–72 at p. 226; and G. Robert Boynton and Gerhard Loewenberg, 'The decay of support for monarchy and the Hitler regime in the Federal Republic of Germany', *British Journal of Political Science*, 4 (1974) p. 465. See also David P. Conradt, *The German Polity* (New York, NY: Longman, 1978) p. 49; and Kendall L. Baker, Russell J. Dalton and Kai Hildebrant, *Germany Transformed: Political culture and the new politics* (Cambridge, MA: Harvard University Press, 1981). For a similar discussion of democratic development in Italy see Giacomo Sani, 'The political culture of Italy: continuity and change' in Gabriel A. Almond and Sidney Verba (eds) *The Civic Culture Revisited* (Boston, MA: Little Brown, 1980) pp. 273–324; or, more recently, Robert D. Putnam with Robert Leonardi and Raffaella Y. Nanetti, *Making Democracy Work: Civic Traditions in Modern Italy* (Princeton, NJ: Princeton University Press).

6   Calculated from David P. Conradt, 'Changing German Political Culture' in Gabriel A. Almond and Sidney Verba (eds) *The Civic Culture Revisited* (Boston, MA: Little, Brown, 1980) pp. 212–72 at p. 226.

7   The argument of Friedrich von Hayek, *The Road to Serfdom* (London: Routledge, 1976; originally published, 1944) is that freedom and equality are necessarily incompatible. It is disputed in Roy Hattersley, 'Argument: Through equality to liberty' in William L. Miller (ed.) *Alternatives to Freedom: Arguments and Opinions* (London: Longman, 1995) pp. 133–50. Support for liberty is positively correlated with support for equality amongst British politicians, and amongst the more highly educated sections of the British public. They are negatively correlated only amongst the least educated and the least politically involved. See Miller, Timpson and Lessnoff (1996) pp. 100–101 and pp. 257–9.

8   The report on the Times–Mirror surveys in 1991 concluded that, 'the great
     divide on attitudes towards the welfare state is not between eastern Europe and
     western Europe [but] between the United States and Europe'; and on social
     welfare 'publics in western Europe appear nearly as socialist as the publics of
     former communist nations.' Los Angeles Times–Mirror, *The Pulse of Europe: a
     Survey of Political and Social Values and Attitudes* (Los Angeles, CA: Times–
     Mirror, 1991) p. 15 and p. 28 respectively. Other studies based on the World
     Values Survey have identified a somewhat different cleavage – between egalitarian
     and state-paternalist societies including Russia, Hungary, France, Italy, Spain
     and Portugal and other less paternalist societies including Britain, Germany, and
     the Scandinavian countries as well as the USA and Canada. See Peter Ester,
     Loek Halman and Vladimir Rukavishnikov, 'The western world values pattern
     viewed cross-nationally: a comparison of findings of the European and
     North American value study with recent Russian data' (Tilburg: Tilburg Univer-
     sity, 1994, mimeo) pp. 34–5. Most of the Russian data in the Tilburg study came
     from a self-completion mail survey. A related study found Russian opinion the
     most left-oriented and the most inclined of all countries to agree that equality was
     more important than freedom. See Vladimir O. Rukavishnikov *et al.*, 'Rossiya
     mezhdu proshlym i budushchim', *Sotsiologicheskie issledovaniya*, no.5 (1995) pp.
     75–90 at p. 81 and p. 84. Our own data are more consistent with the Times–Mirror
     findings.
9   Los Angeles Times–Mirror, *The Pulse of Europe: a Survey of Political and Social
     Values and Attitudes* (Los Angeles, CA: Times–Mirror, 1991), question Q89.
10   That is the wording used in 1992. See Pippa Norris, 'Labour Party factionalism
     and extremism' in Anthony Heath, Roger Jowell and John Curtice with Bridget
     Taylor (eds) *Labour's Last Chance? The 1992 Election and Beyond* (Aldershot:
     Dartmouth, 1994) pp. 173–90 at p. 177.
11   Figures for the general public and for parliamentary candidates at the 1992 British
     General Election taken from Norris (1994) p. 177. Despite the title of her chapter,
     she presents comprehensive figures for voters and politicians of all parties, not just
     Labour.
12   We have calculated our figures from Ivor Crewe, Neil Day and Anthony Fox, *The
     British Electorate 1963–87: A Compendium of Data from the British Election
     Studies* (Cambridge: Cambridge University Press, 1991) p. 311. The question
     wording varied slightly over the years between 1963 and 1992.
13   *Rossiiskii statisticheskii ezhegodnik: Statisticheskii sbornik* (Moscow: Goskomstat
     Rossii, 1995) p. 57.
14   Los Angeles Times–Mirror *The Pulse of Europe: a Survey of Political and Social
     Values and Attitudes* (Los Angeles, CA: Times–Mirror, 1991) question Q112X.
     This data was also reported in Martin Linton, 'Fearful State of Mind', *The
     Guardian*, 4 October 1991, p. 21.
15   Los Angeles Times–Mirror, *The Pulse of Europe: a Survey of Political and Social
     Values and Attitudes* (Los Angeles, CA: Times–Mirror, 1991) p. 229. Russians
     themselves seem to agree. When asked what they associated with the USA, 'high
     living standards' came top at 83 per cent, but 'military power' very close behind at
     81 per cent; and 'political democracy' far behind at 58 per cent. See Anatole Shub,
     'What Russians know and think about America' (Washington, DC: USIA Office
     of Research and Media Reaction, November 1995) p. 19.
16   Times–Mirror surveys reported that 'trustworthiness is a value that divided Eur-
     ope's north from south, more than west from east.' Los Angeles Times–Mirror,
     The Pulse of Europe: a Survey of Political and Social Values and Attitudes (Los
     Angeles, CA: Times–Mirror, 1991) p. 202.

17   Gabriel A. Almond and Sidney Verba, *The Civic Culture: Political Attitudes and Democracy in Five Countries* (Princeton, NJ: Princeton University Press 1963; London: Sage, 1989) p. 70.
18   Often described as a 'Trotskyist' group.
19   Times–Mirror surveys concluded that publics in ECE were less supportive of 'personal freedoms' than in western Europe, but equally as supportive of 'political freedoms' as in western Europe. Los Angeles Times–Mirror, *The Pulse of Europe: a Survey of Political and Social Values and Attitudes* (Los Angeles, CA: Times–Mirror, 1991) p. 27. That conclusion about 'personal freedoms' depended, however, upon giving more weight to tolerance of homosexuality (lower in ECE than in the USA) than to tolerance of abortion (lower in the USA than in ECE). We have found postcommunist publics relatively intolerant of political extremism as well as social deviance, but there is an echo of the Times–Mirror conclusion in our findings, later in this chapter, about the procedural values of democracy.
20   Our CATI (Computer Assisted Telephone Interviewing) technique in Britain allowed us to randomly vary question wordings. We have used square brackets and slashes [/] to indicate alternative wordings which were available. If there are two alternatives, each was used in a randomly chosen half of the interviews; if three alternatives, each was used in a randomly chosen third of the interviews; and so on.
21   Duncan Campbell, 'Corruption fear as police lose faith in justice system', *The Guardian*, 11 March 1995, p. 1.
22   See William L. Miller, *Irrelevant Elections? The Quality of Local Democracy in Britain* (Oxford: Oxford University Press, 1988) pp. 34–6.
23   David Butler and Donald Stokes, *Political Change in Britain: The Evolution of Electoral Choice*, Second edition (London: Macmillan, 1974) p. 467.
24   William L. Miller, Harold D. Clarke, Martin Harrop, Lawrence LeDuc and Paul F. Whiteley, *How Voters Change: The 1987 British Election Campaign in Perspective* (Oxford: Oxford University Press, 1990) p. 286.
25   Butler and Stokes (1974) p. 467.
26   See Jon H. Pammett and Joan DeBardeleben, 'The meaning of elections in transitional democracies: evidence from Russia and Ukraine', *Electoral Studies*, vol.15 no.3 (1996) pp. 363–81 at p. 371; and Miller, Clarke, Harrop, LeDuc and Whiteley (1990) p. 269.
27   Plasser and Ulram found levels of party identification in the FSU and ECE similar to ours. They also noted that, at the same time, levels in Austria were only slightly above those in the Czech Republic though levels in West Germany (but not East Germany) were somewhat rather higher than our figure for Britain. See Fritz Plasser and Peter A. Ulram, 'Monitoring democratic consolidation: political trust and system support in East Central Europe.' Paper to IPSA (International Political Science Association) 16th World Congress, Berlin, August 1994, p. 16.
28   Twelve VTsIOM surveys between 1992 and 1995 asked Russians to choose between 'order or democracy.' There was very little evidence of trend. The numbers choosing 'order' always exceeded 75 per cent and the numbers choosing 'democracy' never exceeded 12 per cent. See Yuri Levada, 'Democratic disorder and Russian public opinion trends in VCIOM surveys, 1991–95'. *Studies in Public Policy*, no.255 (Glasgow: Centre for the Study of Public Policy, 1995). Question P.10. It will be obvious from our discussion in the text that we think this question poses a false choice. FSU/ECE attitudes to order were distinctive but subtle, not to be confused with simple authoritarianism or intolerance, not necessarily undemocratic, and perhaps not even illiberal.

Index